P9-DDZ-026

MACROECONOMICS

CANADA IN THE GLOBAL ENVIRONMENT NINTH EDITION

MyEconLab® Provides the Power of Practice

Optimize your study time with **MyEconLab**, the online assessment and tutorial system. When you take a sample test online, **MyEconLab** gives you targeted feedback and a personalized Study Plan to identify the topics you need to review.

Study Plan

The Study Plan shows you the sections you should study next, gives easy access to practice problems, and provides you with an automatically generated quiz to prove mastery of the course material.

Unlimited Practice

As you work each exercise, instant feedback helps you understand and apply the concepts. Many Study Plan exercises contain algorithmically generated values to ensure that you get as much practice as you need.

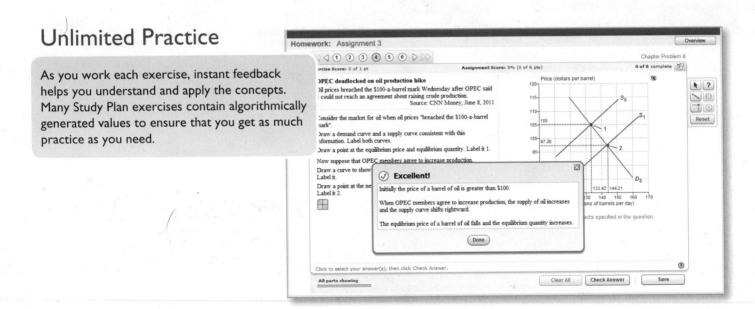

Learning Resources

Study Plan problems link to learning resources that further reinforce concepts you need to master.

- **Help Me Solve This** learning aids help you break down a problem much the same way as an instructor would do during office hours. Help Me Solve This is available for select problems.

- **eText links** are specific to the problem at hand so that related concepts are easy to review just when they are needed.

- A **graphing tool** enables you to build and manipulate graphs to better understand how concepts, numbers, and graphs connect.

Find out more at www.myeconlab.com

Real-Time Data Analysis Exercises

Up-to-date macro data is a great way to engage in and understand the usefulness of macro variables and their impact on the economy. Real-Time Data Analysis exercises communicate directly with the Federal Reserve Bank of St. Louis's FRED site, so every time FRED posts new data, students see new data.

End-of-chapter exercises accompanied by the Real-Time Data Analysis icon ⊕ include Real-Time Data versions in **MyEconLab**.

Select in-text figures labelled **MyEconLab** Real-Time Data update in the electronic version of the text using FRED data.

Current News Exercises

Posted weekly, we find the latest microeconomic and macroeconomic news stories, post them, and write auto-graded multi-part exercises that illustrate the economic way of thinking about the news.

Interactive Homework Exercises

Participate in a fun and engaging activity that helps promote active learning and mastery of important economic concepts.

Pearson's experiments program is flexible and easy for instructors and students to use. For a complete list of available experiments, visit *www.myeconlab.com*.

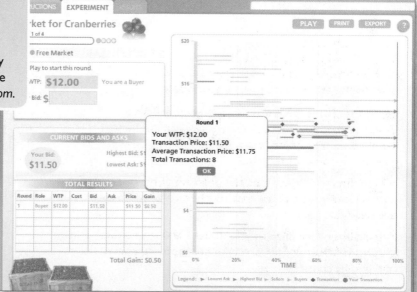

MACROECONOMICS

CANADA IN THE GLOBAL ENVIRONMENT NINTH EDITION

MICHAEL PARKIN **ROBIN BADE**

PEARSON

Toronto

Vice-President, CMPS:	Gary Bennett
Editorial Director:	Claudine O'Donnell
Marketing Manager:	Loula March
Developmental Editor:	Leanne Rancourt
Manager, Project Management:	Avinash Chandra
Manufacturing Manager:	Susan Johnson
Production Editor:	Leanne Rancourt
Copy Editor:	Susan Bindernagel
Proofreader:	Leanne Rancourt
Compositor:	Cenveo® Publisher Services
Technical Illustrator:	Richard Parkin
Project Manager, Permissions:	Joanne Tang
Text Permissions:	iEnergizerAptara®, Inc., Phyllis Padula
Photo Permissions:	iEnergizerAptara®, Inc., Lokesh Bisht
Digital Strategist:	Victoria Naik and Kristina Joie
Cover and Interior Designer:	Anthony Leung
Cover Image:	Fotolia

Credits and acknowledgments of material borrowed from other sources and reproduced, with permission, in this textbook appear on the appropriate page within the text and on p. C-1.

Statistics Canada information is used with the permission of the Minister of Industry, as Minister responsible for Statistics Canada. Information on the availability of the wide range of data from Statistics Canada can be obtained from Statistics Canada's Regional Offices, its World Wide Web site at www.statcan.gc.ca, and its toll-free access number 1-800-263-1136.

If you purchased this book outside the United States or Canada, you should be aware that it has been imported without the approval of the publisher or the author.

Copyright © 2016, 2013, 2010, 2006, 2003, 1997, 1994, 1991 Pearson Canada Inc., Toronto, Ontario. All rights reserved. Manufactured in the United States of America. This publication is protected by copyright and permission should be obtained from the publisher prior to any prohibited reproduction, storage in a retrieval system, or transmission in any form or by any means, electronic, mechanical, photocopying, recording, or likewise. To obtain permission(s) to use material from this work, please submit a written request to Pearson Canada Inc., Permissions Department, 26 Prince Andrew Place, Toronto, Ontario, M3C 2T8, or fax your request to 416-447-3126, or submit a request to Permissions Requests at **www.pearsoncanada.ca.**

10 9 8 7 6 5 4 3 2 1 [CKV]

Library and Archives Canada Cataloguing in Publication

Parkin, Michael, 1939-, author
      Macroeconomics : Canada in the global environment
/ Michael Parkin, Robin Bade. — Ninth edition.

Includes index.
ISBN 978-0-321-93120-7 (pbk.)

      1. Macroeconomics—Textbooks. 2. Canada—Economic conditions—1991- —Textbooks. I. Bade, Robin, author II. Title.

HB172.5.P363 2015   339   C2014-905296-0

ISBN 978-0-321-93120-7

TO OUR STUDENTS

Michael Parkin received his training as an economist at the Universities of Leicester and Essex in England. He is Professor Emeritus in the Department of Economics at the University of Western Ontario, Canada. Professor Parkin has held faculty appointments at Brown University, the University of Manchester, the University of Essex, and Bond University. He is a past president of the Canadian Economics Association and has served on the editorial boards of the *American Economic Review* and the *Journal of Monetary Economics* and as managing editor of the *Canadian Journal of Economics*. Professor Parkin's research on macroeconomics, monetary economics, and international economics has resulted in over 160 publications in journals and edited volumes, including the *American Economic Review*, the *Journal of Political Economy*, the *Review of Economic Studies*, the *Journal of Monetary Economics*, and the *Journal of Money, Credit and Banking*. He became most visible to the public with his work on inflation that discredited the use of wage and price controls. Michael Parkin also spearheaded the movement towards European monetary union.

Robin Bade earned degrees in mathematics and economics at the University of Queensland and her Ph.D. at the Australian National University. She has held faculty appointments at the University of Edinburgh in Scotland, at Bond University in Australia, and at the Universities of Manitoba, Toronto, and Western Ontario in Canada. Her research on international capital flows appears in the *International Economic Review* and the *Economic Record*.

Professor Parkin and Dr. Bade are the joint authors of *Foundations of Economics* (Addison Wesley), *Modern Macroeconomics* (Pearson Education Canada), an intermediate text, and have collabrated on many research and textbook writing projects. They are both experienced and dedicated teachers of introductory economics.

The future is always uncertain. But at some times, and now is one such time, the range of possible futures is enormous. The major sources of this uncertainty are economic policy and global macroeconomic forces. There is uncertainty about the way in which international trade policy will evolve as bilateral deals reshape the competitive landscape. There is uncertainty about exchange rate policy as currency fluctuations bring changes in international relative prices. There is extraordinary uncertainty about monetary policy with the Bank of Canada holding interest rates at historical lows in an attempt to stimulate a flagging economy. And there is uncertainty about fiscal policy as provincial budget deficits interacting with an aging population are ever harder to control. In the global economy, there is uncertainty about when, or even whether, a stagnating European economy will start to show life. And there is uncertainty about how fast China, India, and other developing economies will grow.

Since the global financial crisis of August 2007 moved economics from the business report to the front page, a fall in confidence has gripped producers, consumers, financial institutions, and governments.

Even the idea that the market is an efficient allocation mechanism has come into question. Many thoughtful people worry about increasing income inequality, and some political leaders called for the end of capitalism and the dawn of a new economic order in which tighter regulation reined in unfettered greed.

Rarely do teachers of economics have such a rich feast on which to draw. And rarely are the principles of economics more surely needed to provide the solid foundation on which to think about economic events and navigate the turbulence of economic life.

Although thinking like an economist can bring a clearer perspective to and deeper understanding of today's events, students don't find the economic way of thinking easy or natural. *Macroeconomics* seeks to put clarity and understanding in the grasp of the student with a careful and vivid exploration of the tension between self-interest and the social interest, the role and power of incentives—of opportunity cost and marginal benefit—and demonstrating the possibility that markets supplemented by other mechanisms might allocate resources efficiently.

Parkin-Bade students begin to think about issues the way real economists do and learn how to explore policy problems and make better-informed decisions in their own economic lives.

◆ The Ninth Edition Revision

Thoroughly updated, intuitive rather than technical, grounded in data and empirical evidence, extensively illustrated with well-chosen examples and photographs, enlivened with applications that focus on issues at play in today's world, focused on learning by doing, and seamlessly integrated with MyEconLab: These are the hallmarks of this ninth edition of *Macroeconomics: Canada in the Global Environment*.

This revision builds on the foundation of the previous edition and retains a thorough and careful presentation of the principles of economics, an emphasis on real-world examples and applications, the development of critical thinking skills, diagrams renowned for clarity, and path-breaking technology.

Most chapters have been thoroughly reworked to achieve even greater clarity and to place greater emphasis on applications to current issues. Some sections of chapters have been removed and other sections added to cover new issues, particularly those that involve current policy problems.

Economics in the News, a weekly feature on MyEconLab, appears in the revised text in two ways. First, the Parkin-Bade hallmark chapter-closing *Reading Between the Lines* is rebranded as *Economics in the News*. Second, additional *Economics in the News* boxes appear at appropriate points within chapters.

The aim of the end-of-chapter news feature is to encourage students to apply the tools they have learned in the chapter by analyzing an article from a newspaper or an online news source. The news article connects with the questions first raised in the chapter opener, and the analysis is reinforced with a related end-of-chapter problem.

Shorter, within-chapter *Economics in the News* boxes present brief news clips, relevant data, questions, and worked solutions. These boxes immediately apply a tool just explained and provide hand-held practice and help in approaching an economic analysis of the news.

A second new feature, **At Issue,** shows two sides of a controversial issue and helps students apply the economic way of thinking to clarify and debate the issues.

A third new feature is a full-page end-of-chapter **Worked Problem**. As part of the chapter review, the student has an opportunity to work a multi-part problem that covers the core content of the chapter and consists of questions, solutions, and key figures. This new feature increases the incentive for the student to learn by doing and actively, rather than passively, review the chapter.

Highpoints of the Revision

In addition to the new features that we have just reviewed, we have built on the strengths of the previous edition by substantially revising the following four topics. They are:

- Economic growth and business cycle expansion
- Financial markets
- The exchange rate
- Cycles, inflation, and deflation

Economic Growth and Business Cycle Expansion
Chapter 22, Economic Growth, now opens by clarifying the distinction between economic growth and a business cycle expansion. We now introduce the topic of economic growth by explaining this distinction and illustrating it with the production possibilities frontier *PPF*: a business cycle expansion being a return to the *PPF* and economic growth being an outward shift of the *PPF*.

Financial Markets Chapter 23, Finance, Saving, and Investment, has an expanded section on the global financial crisis and its aftermath that describes the growth of household debt and house prices. The section on real and nominal interest rates is expanded and illustrated with data. The chapter now contains more on the magnitudes of the sources and uses of loanable funds. The section on loanable funds in the global economy is moved to the chapter on the exchange rate and balance of payments.

The Exchange Rate Chapter 25, The Exchange Rate and the Balance of Payments, contains a heavily revised section entitled Arbitrage, Speculation, and Market Fundamentals that explains the powerful forces that equilibrate the foreign exchange market in the short run and the long run. This section includes a discussion of the Big Mac index. An *Economics in the News* examines the forces at work leading to a strong dollar in the summer of 2014. The section on the global loanable funds market is now integrated into this chapter in the section on the balance of payments.

Cycles, Inflation, and Deflation Chapter 28, The Business Cycle, Inflation, and Deflation, is re-titled, reorganized, and amended. The business cycle material is moved to the beginning of the chapter and a new final section describes and explains the problem of deflation that has gripped Japan for most of the 1990s and the 2000s and is feared in Europe at the present time. Coverage of the Phillips curve is retained but condensed.

Many other chapters have been thoroughly reworked to achieve even greater clarity and to place greater emphasis on applications to current issues. And every chapter now contains a new opening vignette linked directly to an *Economics in the News*, an end-of-chapter problem, and online practice.

All the end-of-chapter *Economics in the News* articles have been updated, and the analysis of the news and the linked problems and applications have been appropriately revised.

 ## Features to Enhance Teaching and Learning

The changes that we have described are adjustments to an already powerful teaching and learning package. Here, we briefly review the features retained from the previous edition.

Economics in Action Boxes

This feature uses boxes within the chapter to provide data and information that links models to real-world economic activity.

Some of the issues covered in these boxes include the best affordable choice of recorded music, movies, and DVDs; the cost of selling a pair of shoes; how Apple doesn't make the iPhone; taxing carbon emissions; how long a spell of poverty lasts; structural unemployment in Canada; how loanable funds fuel a home price bubble; the Canadian business cycle; and the size of the fiscal stimulus multipliers.

Chapter Openers

Each chapter opens with a student-friendly vignette that raises questions to motivate the student and focus the chapter. This chapter-opening story is woven into the main body of the chapter and is explored in the *Economics in the News* feature that closes each chapter.

In-Text Review Quizzes

A review quiz at the end of each major section enables students to determine whether a topic needs further study before moving on. This feature includes a reference to the appropriate MyEconLab study plan and a new **key terms quiz** to help students further test their understanding.

Diagrams That Show the Action

Through the past eight editions, this book has set the standard of clarity in its diagrams; the ninth edition continues to uphold this tradition. Our goal is to show "where the economic action is." The diagrams in this book continue to generate an enormously positive response, which confirms our view that graphical analysis is the most powerful tool available for teaching and learning economics at the principles level.

Because many students find graphs hard to work with, we have developed the entire art program with the study and review needs of the student in mind.

The diagrams feature:

- Original curves consistently shown in blue
- Shifted curves, equilibrium points, and other important features highlighted in red
- Colour-blended arrows to suggest movement
- Graphs paired with data tables
- Diagrams labelled with boxed notes
- Extended captions that make each diagram and its caption a self-contained object for study and review

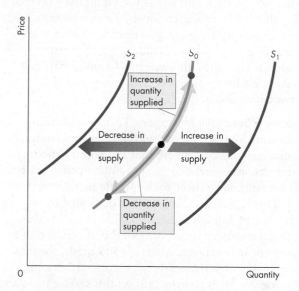

End-of-Chapter Study Material

Each chapter closes with a concise summary organized by major topics, a list of key terms with page references, a worked problem, and problems and applications. These learning tools provide students with a summary for review and exam preparation.

Interviews with Economists

Each part closes with an overview of the chapters and a teaser of an interview with a leading economist whose work correlates to what the student is learning. These interviews explore the education and research of these prominent economists and their advice for those who want to continue the study of economics. This edition has new interviews with Esther Duflo (MIT) and Raj Chetty (Harvard). The 65 past and present interviews we have conducted are available in full in MyEconLab.

▶ For the Instructor

This book enables you to focus on the economic way of thinking and choose your own course structure in your principles course.

Focus on the Economic Way of Thinking

As an instructor, you know how hard it is to encourage a student to think like an economist. But that is your goal. Consistent with this goal, the text focuses on and repeatedly uses the central ideas of choice; tradeoff; opportunity cost; the margin; incentives; the gains from voluntary exchange; the forces of demand, supply, and equilibrium; the pursuit of economic rent; the tension between self-interest and the social interest; and the scope and limitations of government actions.

Flexible Structure

You have preferences for how you want to teach your course, and we've organized this book to enable you to choose your teaching path. The chart on p. xxiii illustrate the book's flexibility. By following the arrows through the charts you can select the path that best fits your preference for course structure. Whether you want to teach a traditional course that blends theory and policy, or one that takes a fast-track through either theory or policy issues, *Macroeconomics: Canada in the Global Environment* gives you the choice.

Instructor's Supplemental Resources

The supplements for instructors are:

- Test Bank
- PowerPoint Resources
- Instructor's Manual
- Solutions Manual

Test Bank The ninth edition Test Bank (Test Item File), with more than 3,000 multiple-choice questions, has been prepared by Jeannie Gillmore of the University of Western Ontario. Jeannie has reviewed and edited all existing questions to ensure their clarity and consistency with the ninth edition and incorporated new questions. The new questions follow the style and format of the end-of-chapter text problems and provide the instructor with a whole new set of testing opportunities and/or homework assignments. Test Item File questions are available in MyEconLab for instructors to use in a test, quiz, or as homework.

Pearson's **Computerized Test Bank** allows instructors to filter and select questions to create quizzes, tests, or homework. Instructors can revise questions or add their own, and may be able to choose print or online options. These questions are also available in Microsoft Word® format.

PowerPoint Resources Our full-colour Microsoft PowerPoint® Presentations for each chapter contain:

- Lecture notes with all the textbook figures animated, tables from the textbook, and speaking notes from the Instructor's Manual
- Large-scale versions of all the textbook figures and tables, animated for instructors to incorporate into their own slide shows
- A set of lecture notes for students, which include animated versions of the textbook figures

The presentations can be used electronically in the classroom or printed to create hard-copy transparency masters. A student version of the lecture notes is also available on MyEconlab.

Instructor's Manual Our Instructor's Manual integrates the teaching and learning resources and serves as a guide to all the supplements. Each chapter contains an overview, a list of what's new in the ninth edition, and ready-to-use lecture notes.

A new user can walk into a classroom armed to deliver a polished lecture. The lecture notes provide an outline of the chapter; concise statements of key material; alternative tables and figures; key terms and definitions; boxes that highlight key concepts, provide an interesting anecdote, or suggest how to handle a difficult idea; and additional discussion questions. The PowerPoint® lecture notes incorporate the chapter outlines and teaching suggestions.

Solutions Manual Our comprehensive Solutions Manual provides instructors with solutions to the Review Quizzes and the end-of-chapter Problems and Applications.

Getting Your Instructor's Resources

Instructors can download supplements from a secure, instructor-only source via the Pearson Canada Higher Education Instructor Resource Centre Web page (www.pearsoncanada.ca/highered). Instructor resources are also available on a DVD.

Instructor's Resource Centre DVD (IRDVD) Fully compatible with Windows and Macintosh, this IRDVD contains Adobe PDF files of the Test Item File, the Solutions Manual, and the Instructor's Manual; PowerPoint resources; and the TestGen. Locate your local Pearson Canada sales representative at http://catalogue.pearsoned.ca/educator to request a copy of the IRDVD.

Other Instructor Aids

CourseSmart CourseSmart goes beyond traditional expectations—providing instant, online access to the textbooks and course materials you need at a lower cost for students. And even as students save money, you can save time and hassle with a digital eTextbook that allows you to search for the most relevant content at the very moment you need it. Whether it's evaluating textbooks or creating lecture notes to help students with difficult concepts, CourseSmart can make life a little easier. See how when you visit www.coursesmart.com/instructors.

Learning Solutions Managers Pearson's Learning Solutions Managers work with faculty and campus course designers to ensure that Pearson technology products, assessment tools, and online course materials are tailored to meet your specific needs.

This highly qualified team is dedicated to helping schools take full advantage of a wide range of educational resources by assisting in the integration of a variety of instructional materials and media formats. Your local Pearson Canada sales representative can provide you with more details on this service program.

Pearson Custom Library For enrollments of 25 students or more, you can create your own textbook by choosing the chapters of Parkin-Bade *Macroeconomics* that best suit your own course needs. To begin building your custom text, visit www.pearsoncustomlibrary.com.

▶ MyEconLab

The Parkin-Bade MyEconLab has been designed and refined with a single purpose in mind: to create those moments of understanding that transform the difficult into the clear and obvious. With homework, quiz, test, activity, and tutorial options, instructors can manage all their assessment needs in one program.

- All of the Review Quiz questions and end-of-chapter Problems and Applications were recreated as assignable auto-graded exercises with targeted feedback and related "Help Me Solve This" tools by Robin Bade, Jeannie Gillmore of the University of Western Ontario, and Sharmistha Nag of Fairleigh Dickinson University, and were reviewed for accuracy by Trevor Collier of the University of Dayton.
- All of the Review Quiz questions and end-of chapter Problems and Applications are assignable and automatically graded in MyEconLab.
- The Review Quiz questions and end-of-chapter Study Plan Problems and Applications are available for students to work in the adaptive Study Plan.
- The end-of-chapter Additional Problems and Applications are not available to students in MyEconLab unless assigned by the instructor.
- Many of the problems and applications are algorithmic, draw-graph, and numerical exercises.
- Problems and applications that use real-time data continuously update.
- The Custom Exercise Builder enables instructors to create their own problems for assignment.
- The Gradebook records each student's performance and time spent on the Tests and Study Plan and generates reports by student or by chapter.
- Test Bank questions are also assignable for test, quiz, or homework and auto-graded in MyEconLab.

Enhanced Pearson eText and New Interactive Features

New for the ninth edition is an enhanced Pearson eText that integrates directly with MyEconLab's Study Plan, now powered by Knewton Adaptive Learning, and with MyEconLab's Gradebook.

The enhanced Pearson eText is available within the online course materials and offline via an iPad app.

The eText also allows instructors and students to highlight, bookmark, and take notes. In addition, instructors can create notes and push them out to students.

The new eText includes videos, animations, and problem-solving tools designed to aid comprehension and bring those moments of discovery that stick in the memory.

The features of the enhanced eText include:

- Embedded MyEconLab Study Plan and assessment
- Figure animations
- Interactive graph-drawing exercises
- More *Economics in the News*
- Worked problems
- Automatic real-time updating
- Key terms quizzes

Embedded MyEconLab Study Plan and Assessment In the enhanced eText, every Review Quiz question and Study Plan Problem and Application exercise can be worked by the student directly from the eText page on which it occurs. These exercises are auto-graded and feed into MyEconLab's Adaptive Study Plan, where students receive recommendations based upon their performance. Study Plan links provide opportunities for more practice with problems similar to those in the text and give targeted feedback to guide the student in answering the exercises.

Figure Animations Every textbook figure can be worked through using a step-by-step animation, with audio, to help students learn the intuition behind reading and interpreting graphs. These animations may be used for review or as an instructional aid in the classroom.

More Economics in the News Each in-text *Economics in the News* is reinforced through an extended application of the same analysis. These *Economics in the News* problems are auto-graded and feed into MyEconLab's Adaptive Study Plan.

Worked Problems Each chapter concludes with a Worked Problem that consists of questions, solutions, and key figures. These problems can be worked in the enhanced eText directly from the Worked Problem page. As the student works through each problem, feedback and just-in-time learning aids help the student develop proficiency with the concept.

Interactive Draw-Graph Exercises For each major figure, a graph-drawing exercise accompanies the step-by-step animation. The student builds and interprets the key graphs and develops understanding by working a multiple-choice question about the graph. Each graph-drawing exercise is auto-graded and feeds into MyEconLab's Adaptive Study Plan.

Automatic Real-Time Updating Figures labelled *MyEconLab Real-Time Data* update using the most recent data available from the FRED database maintained by the Federal Reserve Bank of St. Louis.

Key Terms Quizzes Key Terms Quiz links provide opportunities for students to check their knowledge of the definitions and uses of the key terms.

Other MyEconLab Features

MyEconLab also includes the following features:

Adaptive Learning MyEconLab's Study Plan is now powered by a sophisticated adaptive learning engine that tailors learning material to meet the unique needs of each student. MyEconLab's new **Adaptive Learning Study Plan** monitors students' performance on homework, quizzes, and tests and continuously makes recommendations based on that performance.

If a student is struggling with a concept such as supply and demand, or having trouble calculating a price elasticity of demand, the Study Plan provides customized remediation activities—a pathway based on personal proficiencies, the number of attempts, or the difficulty of the questions—to get the student back on track. Students will also receive recommendations

for additional practice in the form of rich multimedia learning aids such as videos, an interactive eText, Help Me Solve This tutorials, and graphing tools.

The Study Plan can extrapolate a student's future trouble spots and provide learning material and practice to avoid pitfalls. In addition, students who are showing a high degree of success with the assessment material are offered a chance to work on future topics based on the professor's course coverage preferences. This personalized and adaptive feedback and support ensures that your students are optimizing their current and future course work and mastering the concepts, rather than just memorizing and guessing answers.

You can learn more about adaptive learning at http://www.myeconlab.com/product-info/adaptive.

Real-Time Data Analysis Exercises (FRED) Easy to assign and automatically graded, Real-Time Data Analysis exercises communicate directly with the Federal Reserve Bank of St. Louis's FRED site, so every time FRED posts new data, students can see the most recent data. As a result, Real-Time Data Analysis exercises offer a no-fuss solution for instructors who want to make the most recent data a central part of their macro course.

End-of-chapter exercises accompanied by the Real-Time Data Analysis icon ⬤ include Real-Time Data versions in MyEconLab.

Economics in the News *Economics in the News* is a turnkey solution to bringing current news into the classroom. Updated weekly during the academic year, we upload two relevant articles (one micro, one macro) and provide questions that may be assigned for homework or for classroom discussion.

Current News Each week during the academic year, we upload multi-part microeconomic and macroeconomic exercises, with links to relevant articles, into the MyEconLab assignment manager. These enable instructors to bring current issues and events into the course with easy to assign and auto-graded exercises.

Office Hours Students and instructors can consult the authors using the "Office Hours" links in MyEconLab. The link for students is in Chapter Resources and for Instructors in Instructor Resources/Instructor Tools.

Experiments in MyEconLab Experiments are a fun and engaging way to promote active learning and mastery of important economic concepts. Pearson's Experiments program is flexible and easy for instructors to assign and students to use.

- Available experiments cover competitive market, price floors, price ceilings, taxes, price controls, and public goods.
- Single-player experiments, available to assign, allow your students to play against virtual players from anywhere at any time as long as they have an Internet connection.
- Multi-player experiments allow you to assign and manage a real-time experiment with your class.
- Experiments can be assigned in MyEconLab as homework integrated with pre-questions and post-questions.
- Experiments are auto-graded using algorithms that objectively evaluate a student's economic gain and performance during the experiment.

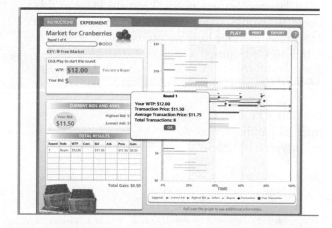

Digital Interactives A Digital Interactive is a simulation game that immerses the student in an activity that leads to the discovery of a fundamental economic idea or principle. Digital Interactives are designed for use in traditional, online, and hybrid courses, and many incorporate real-time data as well as data display and analysis tools. A Digital Interactive can be presented in class as a visually stimulating, engaging lecture tool, and can be assigned with assessment questions for gradinganalysis tools.

Learning Catalytics Learning Catalytics is a web-based system for managing the interactive classroom. It is a "bring your own device" platform that supports the peer-instruction teaching method and can also be used to provide the instructor with real-time feedback during class. Instructors can access 18 different question types among which are multiple choice, numerical, sketching, ranking, and highlighting. For more information, visit learningcatalytics.com.

Dynamic Study Modules Dynamic Study Modules, which focus on key topic areas and are available from within MyEconLab, are an additional way for students to obtain tailored help. These modules work by continuously assessing student performance and activity on discrete topics and provide personalized content in real time to reinforce concepts that target each student's particular strengths and weaknesses.

Each Dynamic Study Module, accessed by computer, smartphone, or tablet, promotes fast learning and long-term retention. Because MyEconLab and Dynamic Study Modules help students stay on track and achieve a higher level of subject-matter mastery, more class time is available for interaction, discussion, collaboration, and exploring applications to current news and events.

Instructors can register, create, and access all of their MyEconLab courses at www.myeconlab.com.

▶ Acknowledgments

We thank our current and former colleagues and friends at the University of Western Ontario who have taught us so much. They are Jim Davies, Jeremy Greenwood, Ig Horstmann, Peter Howitt, Greg Huffman, David Laidler, Phil Reny, Chris Robinson, John Whalley, and Ron Wonnacott. We also thank Doug McTaggart and Christopher Findlay, co-authors of the Australian edition, and Melanie Powell and Kent Matthews, coauthors of the European edition. Suggestions arising from their adaptations of earlier editions have been helpful to us in preparing this edition.

We thank the several thousand students whom we have been privileged to teach. The instant response that comes from the look of puzzlement or enlightenment has taught us how to teach economics.

We thank the management team at Pearson Canada who have built a culture that brings out the best in its editors and authors. They are Jessica Mosher, General Manager Higher Education; Gary Bennett, Vice-President of Cross-Media Production; and Claudine O'Donnell, Editorial Director. Claudine played a major role in shaping this revision and the many outstanding supplements that accompany it. She brings intelligence and insight to her work and is Canada's preeminent economics editor.

It is a special joy to thank the outstanding editors, media specialists, and others at Pearson Canada who contributed to the concerted publishing effort that brought this edition to completion. They are Joel Gladstone, Program Manager; Avinash Chandra, Lead Project Manager; Leanne Rancourt, Developmental Editor; Victoria Naik, Digital Strategist; Joanne Tang, Project Manager, Permissions; Susan Bindernagel, Copy Editor; and Loula March, Marketing Manager.

Leanne Rancourt was our lifeline. She kept the production process on track, provided outstanding management, and gave our manuscript a most thorough proofread and accuracy check.

Anthony Leung designed the cover and package and yet again surpassed the challenge of ensuring that we meet the highest design standards.

We thank the many exceptional reviewers who have shared their insights through the various editions of this book. Their contribution has been invaluable.

We thank the people who work directly with us. Jeannie Gillmore and Sharmistha Nag provided research assistance and created exercises for MyEconLab. Richard Parkin created the electronic art files and offered many ideas that improved the figures in this book.

Classroom experience will test the value of this book. We would appreciate hearing from instructors and students about how we can continue to improve it in future editions.

Michael Parkin
Robin Bade
London, Ontario, Canada
michael.parkin@uwo.ca
robin@econ100.com

Reviewers

Syed Ahmed, Red Deer Community College
Ather H. Akbari, Saint Mary's University
Doug Allen, Simon Fraser University
Benjamin Amoah, University of Guelph
Torben Andersen, Red Deer College
Terri Anderson, Fanshawe College
Syed Ashan, Concordia University
Fred Aswani, McMaster University
Iris Au, University of Toronto, Scarborough
Keith Baxter, Bishop's University
Andy Baziliauskas, University of Winnipeg
Dick Beason, University of Alberta
Karl Bennett, University of Waterloo
Ronald Bodkin, University of Ottawa
Caroline Boivin, Concordia University
Paul Booth, University of Alberta
John Boyd, University of British Columbia
John Brander, University of New Brunswick
Larry Brown, Selkirk College
Sam Bucovetsky, York University
Bogdan Buduru, Concordia University
Lutz-Alexander Busch, University of Waterloo
Beverly J. Cameron, University of Manitoba
Norman Cameron, University of Manitoba
Emanuel Carvalho, University of Waterloo
Francois Casas, University of Toronto
Alan Tak Yan Chan, Atlantic Baptist University
Robert Cherneff, University of Victoria
Jason Childs, University of New Brunswick, Saint John
Saud Choudhry, Trent University
Louis Christofides, University of Guelph
Kam Hon Chu, Memorial University of Newfoundland
George Churchman, University of Manitoba
Avi J. Cohen, York University
Constantin Colonescu, Grant MacEwan University
Ryan A. Compton, University of Manitoba
Marilyn Cottrell, Brock University
Rosilyn Coulson, Douglas College
Brian Coulter, University College of the Fraser Valley
Stanya Cunningham, Concordia University College of Alberta
Douglas Curtis, Trent University
Garth Davies, Olds College
Ajit Dayanandan, University of Northern British Columbia
Carol Derksen, Red River College
David Desjardins, John Abbott College
Vaughan Dickson, University of New Brunswick (Fredericton)
Livio Di Matteo, Lakehead University
Mohammed Dore, Brock University
Torben Drewes, Trent University
Byron Eastman, Laurentian University
Fahira Eston, Humber College

Sigrid Ewender, Kwantlen Polytechnic University
Brian Ferguson, University of Guelph
Len Fitzpatrick, Carleton University
Peter Fortura, Algonquin College
Oliver Franke, Athabasca University
Bruno Fullone, George Brown College
Donald Garrie, Georgian College
Philippe Ghayad, Dawson College and Concordia University
David Gray, University of Ottawa
Sandra Hadersbeck, Okanagan College
Rod Hill, University of New Brunswick
Eric Kam, Ryerson University
Susan Kamp, University of Alberta
Cevat Burc Kayahan, University of Guelph
Peter Kennedy, Simon Fraser University
Harvey King, University of Regina
Patricia Koss, Concordia University
Robert Kunimoto, Mt. Royal University
David Johnson, Wilfrid Laurier University
Cliff Jutlah, York University, Glendon Campus
Michael G. Lanyi, University of Lethbridge
Eva Lau, University of Waterloo
Gordon Lee, University of Alberta
Byron Lew, Trent University
Anastasia M. Lintner, University of Guelph
Scott Lynch, Memorial University
Dan MacKay, SIAST
Leigh MacDonald, University of Western Ontario
Keith MacKinnon, York University
Mohammad Mahbobi, Thompson Rivers University
S. Manchouri, University of Alberta
Christian Marfels, Dalhousie University
Raimo Martalla, Malaspina University College
Perry Martens, University of Regina
Roberto Martínez-Espíneira, St. Francis Xavier University
Dennis McGuire, Okanagan University College
Rob Moir, University of New Brunswick, Saint John
Saeed Moshiri, University of Manitoba
Joseph Muldoon, Trent University
David Murrell, University of New Brunswick, Fredericton
Robin Neill, Carleton University
A. Gyasi Nimarko, Vanier College
Sonia Novkovic, Saint Mary's University
John O'Brien, Concordia University
Arne Paus-Jenssen, University of Saskatchewan
Andrea Podhorsky, York University
Derek Pyne, Memorial University of Newfoundland
Stephen Rakoczy, Humber College
Don Reddick, Kwantlen University College
June Riley, John Abbott College
E. Riser, Memorial University

Roberta Robb, Brock University
Nick Rowe, Carleton University
Michael Rushton, University of Regina
Balbir Sahni, Concordia University
Brian Scarfe, University of Regina
Marlyce Searcy, SIAST Palliser
Jim Sentance, University of Prince Edward Island
Lance Shandler, Kwantlen University College
Stan Shedd, University of Calgary
Chandan Shirvaikar, Red Deer College
Peter Sinclair, Wilfrid Laurier University
Ian Skaith, Fanshawe College
Scott Skjei, Acadia University
Judith Skuce, Georgian College
George Slasor, University of Toronto
Norman Smith, Georgian College
Bert Somers, John Abbott College

Lewis Soroka, Brock University
Glen Stirling, University of Western Ontario
Brennan Thompson, Ryerson University
Irene Trela, University of Western Ontario
Russell Uhler, University of British Columbia
Brian VanBlarcom, Acadia University
Marianne Vigneault, Bishop's University
Jane Waples, Memorial University of Newfoundland
Tony Ward, Brock University
Bruce Wilkinson, University of Alberta
Christopher Willmore, University of Victoria
Andrew Wong, Grant MacEwan University
Peter Wylie, University of British Columbia, Okanagan
Arthur Younger, Humber College Institute of Technology and Advanced Learning
Ayoub Yousefi, University of Western Ontario
Weiqiu Yu, University of New Brunswick, Fredericton

Flexibility

Chapter 1

What Is Economics?

Chapter 2

The Economic Problem

Chapter 3

Demand and Supply

Chapter 31

International Trade Policy

Chapter 20

Measuring GDP and Economic Growth

Chapter 21

Monitoring Jobs and Inflation

Chapter 22

Economic Growth

Chapter 23

Finance, Saving, and Investment

Chapter 26

Aggregate Supply and Aggregate Demand

Chapter 23

Finance, Saving, and Investment

Chapter 24

Money, the Price Level, and Inflation

Chapter 25

The Exchange Rate and the Balance of Payments

Chapter 27

Expenditure Multipliers

Chapter 29

Fiscal Policy

Chapter 28

The Business Cycle, Inflation, and Deflation

Chapter 30

Monetary Policy

Start here ...

... then jump to any of these ...

... and jump to any of these after doing the prerequisites indicated

PART SEVEN
MONITORING MACROECONOMIC
PERFORMANCE 465

PART SEVEN **WRAP-UP** ◆

MACROECONOMICS

CANADA IN THE GLOBAL ENVIRONMENT NINTH EDITION

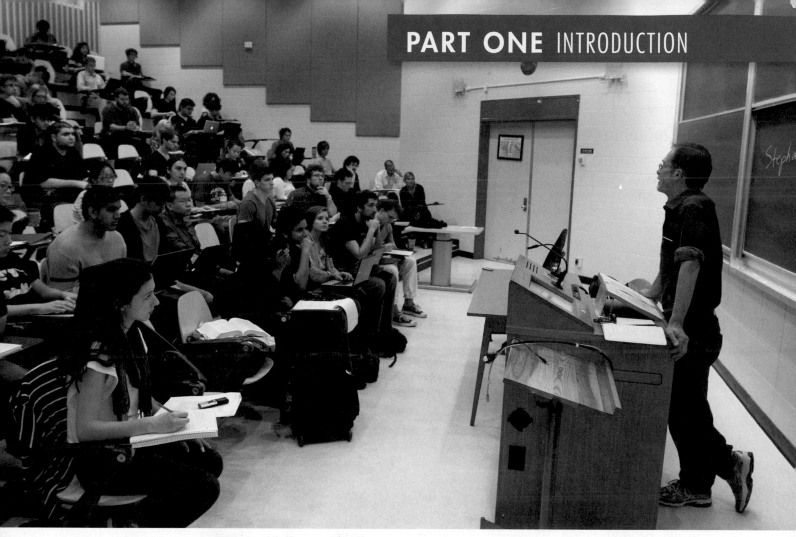

1

WHAT IS ECONOMICS?

After studying this chapter, you will be able to:

◆ Define economics and distinguish between microeconomics and macroeconomics

◆ Explain the two big questions of economics

◆ Explain the key ideas that define the economic way of thinking

◆ Explain how economists go about their work as social scientists and policy advisers

Is economics about money: How people make it and spend it? Is it about business, government, and jobs? Is it about why some people and some nations are rich and others poor? Economics is about all these things. But its core is the study of *choices* and their *consequences.*

Your life will be shaped by the choices that you make and the challenges that you face. To face those challenges and seize the opportunities they present, you must understand the powerful forces at play. The economics that you're about to learn will become your most reliable guide. This chapter gets you started by describing the questions that economists try to answer and looking at how economists think as they search for the answers.

1

Definition of Economics

A fundamental fact dominates our lives: We want more than we can get. Our inability to get everything we want is called **scarcity**. Scarcity is universal. It confronts all living things. Even parrots face scarcity!

Not only do I want a cracker—we all want a cracker!

© The New Yorker Collection 1985
Frank Modell from cartoonbank.com. All Rights Reserved.

Think about the things that *you* want and the scarcity that *you* face. You want to go to a good school, college, or university. You want to live in a well-equipped, spacious, and comfortable home. You want the latest smartphone and the fastest Internet connection for your laptop or iPad. You want some sports and recreational gear—perhaps some new running shoes, or a new bike. You want much more time than is available to go to class, do your homework, play sports and games, read novels, go to the movies, listen to music, travel, and hang out with your friends. And you want to live a long and healthy life.

What you can afford to buy is limited by your income and by the prices you must pay. And your time is limited by the fact that your day has 24 hours.

You want some other things that only governments provide. You want to live in a safe neighbourhood in a peaceful and secure world, and enjoy the benefits of clean air, lakes, rivers, and oceans.

What governments can afford is limited by the taxes they collect. Taxes lower people's incomes and compete with the other things they want to buy.

What *everyone* can get—what *society* can get—is limited by the productive resources available. These resources are the gifts of nature, human labour and ingenuity, and all the previously produced tools and equipment.

Because we can't get everything we want, we must make *choices*. You can't afford *both* a laptop *and* an iPhone, so you must *choose* which one to buy. You can't spend tonight *both* studying for your next test *and* going to the movies, so again, you must *choose* which one to do. Governments can't spend a tax dollar on *both* national defence *and* environmental protection, so they must *choose* how to spend that dollar.

Your choices must somehow be made consistent with the choices of *others*. If you choose to buy a laptop, someone else must choose to sell it. Incentives reconcile choices. An **incentive** is a reward that encourages an action or a penalty that discourages one. Prices act as incentives. If the price of a laptop is too high, more will be offered for sale than people want to buy. And if the price is too low, fewer will be offered for sale than people want to buy. But there is a price at which choices to buy and sell are consistent.

Economics is the social science that studies the *choices* that individuals, businesses, governments, and entire societies make as they cope with *scarcity* and the *incentives* that influence and reconcile those choices.

The subject has two parts:

- Microeconomics
- Macroeconomics

Microeconomics is the study of the choices that individuals and businesses make, the way these choices interact in markets, and the influence of governments. Some examples of microeconomic questions are: Why are people downloading more movies? How would a tax on e-commerce affect eBay?

Macroeconomics is the study of the performance of the national economy and the global economy. Some examples of macroeconomic questions are: Why does the Canadian unemployment rate fluctuate? Can the Bank of Canada make the unemployment rate fall by keeping interest rates low?

◆ REVIEW QUIZ

1 List some examples of the scarcity that you face.
2 Find examples of scarcity in today's headlines.
3 Find an example of the distinction between microeconomics and macroeconomics in today's headlines.

Work these questions in Study Plan 1.1 and get instant feedback. Do a Key Terms Quiz.   *MyEconLab*

Two Big Economic Questions

Two big questions summarize the scope of economics:

- How do choices end up determining *what, how,* and *for whom* goods and services are produced?
- Do choices made in the pursuit of *self-interest* also promote the *social interest*?

What, How, and For Whom?

Goods and services are the objects that people value and produce to satisfy wants. *Goods* are physical objects such as cellphones and automobiles. *Services* are tasks performed for people such as cellphone service and auto-repair service.

What? *What* we produce varies across countries and changes over time. In Canada today, agriculture accounts for 2 percent of total production, manufactured goods for 20 percent, and services (retail and wholesale trade, healthcare, and education are the biggest ones) for 78 percent. In contrast, in China today, agriculture accounts for 10 percent of total production, manufactured goods for 45 percent, and services for 45 percent.

Figure 1.1 shows these numbers and also the percentages for Brazil, which fall between those for Canada and China.

What determines these patterns of production? How do choices end up determining the quantities of cellphones, automobiles, cellphone service, auto-repair service, and the millions of other items that are produced in Canada and around the world?

How? *How* we produce is described by the technologies and resources that we use. The resources used to produce goods and services are called **factors of production**, which are grouped into four categories:

- Land
- Labour
- Capital
- Entrepreneurship

Land The "gifts of nature" that we use to produce goods and services are called **land**. In economics, *land* is what in everyday language we call *natural resources*. It includes land in the everyday sense

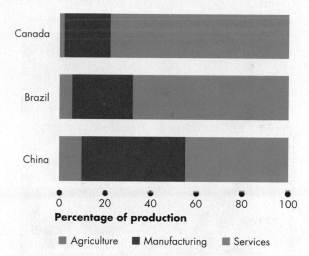

FIGURE 1.1 What Three Countries Produce

Percentage of production

■ Agriculture　■ Manufacturing　■ Services

Agriculture and manufacturing are small percentages of production in rich countries such as Canada and large percentages of production in poorer countries such as China. Most of what is produced in Canada is services.

Source of data: CIA Factbook 2014, Central Intelligence Agency.

───────── MyEconLab Animation ─────────

together with minerals, oil, gas, coal, water, air, forests, and fish.

Our land surface and water resources are renewable, and some of our mineral resources can be recycled. But the resources that we use to create energy are nonrenewable—they can be used only once.

Labour The work time and work effort that people devote to producing goods and services is called **labour**. Labour includes the physical and mental efforts of all the people who work on farms and construction sites and in factories, shops, and offices.

The *quality* of labour depends on **human capital**, which is the knowledge and skill that people obtain from education, on-the-job training, and work experience. You are building your own human capital right now as you work on your economics course, and your human capital will continue to grow as you gain work experience.

Human capital expands over time. Today, 93 percent of the adult population of Canada have completed high school and 23 percent have a college or university degree. Figure 1.2 shows these measures of human capital in Canada and its growth over the past 38 years.

**FIGURE 1.2   A Measure of Human
                Capital**

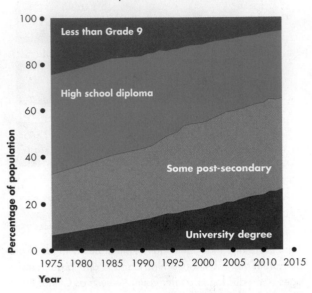

In 2013, 25.3 percent of the adult population had a university degree. A further 39 percent had some post-secondary education, and 93.6 percent had completed high school.

Source of data: Statistics Canada.

——————— MyEconLab Animation ———

Capital The tools, instruments, machines, buildings, and other constructions that businesses use to produce goods and services are called **capital**.

In everyday language, we talk about money, stocks, and bonds as being "capital." These items are *financial capital*. Financial capital plays an important role in enabling businesses to borrow the funds that they use to buy physical capital. But financial capital is not used to produce goods and services and it is not a factor of production.

Entrepreneurship The human resource that organizes labour, land, and capital is called **entrepreneurship**. Entrepreneurs are the drivers of economic progress. They develop new ideas about what and how to produce, make business decisions, and bear the risks that arise from these decisions.

What determines how the factors of production are used to produce each good and service?

For Whom? *Who* consumes the goods and services that are produced depends on the incomes that people earn. People with large incomes can buy a wide range of goods and services. People with small incomes have fewer options and can afford a smaller range of goods and services.

People earn their incomes by selling the services of the factors of production they own:

■ Land earns **rent**.
■ Labour earns **wages**.
■ Capital earns **interest**.
■ Entrepreneurship earns **profit**.

Which factor of production earns the most income? The answer is labour. Wages and fringe benefits are around 70 percent of total income and the incomes from land, capital, and entrepreneurship share the rest. These shares have been remarkably constant over time.

Knowing how income is shared among the factors of production doesn't tell us how it is shared among individuals. And the distribution of income among individuals is extremely unequal. You know of some people who earn very large incomes: Dwayne "The Rock" Johnson (Hercules) earned $46 million in 2013; and Canadian Shea Weber of the Nashville Predators earns $14 million a year.

You know of even more people who earn very small incomes. Servers at Tim Hortons average $9 an hour; checkout clerks, cleaners, and textile and leather workers all earn less than $10 an hour.

You probably know about other persistent differences in incomes. Men, on average, earn more than women; whites earn more than minorities; university graduates earn more than high school graduates.

We can get a good sense of who consumes the goods and services produced by looking at the percentages of total income earned by different groups of people. The 20 percent of people with the lowest incomes earn about 5 percent of total income, while the richest 20 percent earn close to 50 percent of total income. So on average, people in the richest 20 percent earn more than 10 times the incomes of those in the poorest 20 percent. There is even huge inequality within the richest 20 percent, and the top 1 percent earns almost 15 percent of total income.

Why is the distribution of income so unequal?

Economics provides some answers to all these questions about *what, how*, and *for whom* goods and services are produced and much of the rest of this book will help you to understand those answers.

We're now going to look at the second big question of economics: Do choices made in the pursuit of self-interest also promote the social interest?

Do Choices Made in the Pursuit of Self-Interest also Promote the Social Interest?

Every day, you and 35.4 million other Canadians, along with 7.2 billion people in the rest of the world, make economic choices that result in *what, how*, and *for whom* goods and services are produced. These choices are made by people who are pursuing their self-interest.

Self-Interest You make a choice in your **self-interest** if you think that choice is the best one available for you. All the choices that people make about how to use their time and other resources are made in the pursuit of self-interest. When you allocate your time or your budget, you do what makes the most sense to you. You might think about how your choices affect other people and take into account how you feel about that, but it is how *you* feel that influences your choice. You order a home-delivery pizza because you're hungry, not because the delivery person needs a job. And when the pizza delivery person shows up at your door, he's not doing you a favour. He's pursuing *his* self-interest and hoping for a tip and another call next week.

The big question is: Is it possible that all the choices that each one of us makes in the pursuit of self-interest could end up achieving an outcome that is best for everyone?

Social Interest An outcome is in the **social interest** if it is best for society as a whole. It is easy to see how you decide what is in *your* self-interest. But how do we decide if something is in the social interest? To help you answer this question, imagine a scene like that in *Economics in the News* on the next page.

Ted, an entrepreneur, creates a new business. He hires a thousand workers and pays them $20 an hour, $1 an hour more than they earned in their old jobs. Ted's business is extremely profitable and his own earnings increase by $1 million per week.

You can see that Ted's decision to create the business is in his self-interest—he gains $1 million a week. You can also see that for Ted's employees, their decisions to work for Ted are in their self-interest—they gain $1 an hour (say $40 a week). And the decisions of Ted's customers must be in their self-interest, otherwise they wouldn't buy from him. But is this outcome in the social interest?

The economist's answer is "Yes." It is in the social interest because it makes everyone better off. There are no losers.

Efficiency and the Social Interest Economists use the everyday word "efficient" to describe a situation that can't be improved upon. Resource use is **efficient** if it is *not* possible to make someone better off without making someone else worse off. If it *is* possible to make someone better off without making anyone worse off, society can be made better off and the situation is not efficient.

In the Ted story everyone is better off, so it improves efficiency and the outcome is in the social interest. But notice that it would also have been efficient if the workers and customers had gained nothing and Ted had gained even more than $1 million a week. But would that efficient outcome be in the social interest?

Many people have trouble seeing the outcome in which Ted is the only winner as being in the social interest. They say that the social interest requires Ted to share some of his gain either with his workers in higher wages or with his customers in lower prices, or with both groups.

Fair Shares and the Social Interest The idea that the social interest requires "fair shares" is a deeply held one. Think about what you regard as a fair share. To help you, imagine the following game.

I put $100 on the table and tell someone you don't know and who doesn't know you to *propose* a share of the money between the two of you. If you *accept* the proposed share, you each get the agreed upon shares. If you don't accept the proposed share, you both get nothing.

It would be efficient—you would both be better off—if the proposer offered to take $99 and leave you with $1 and you accepted that offer.

But would you accept the $1? If you are like most people, the idea that the other person gets 99 times as much as you is just too much to stomach. "No way," you say and the $100 disappears. That outcome is inefficient. You have both given up something.

When the game I've just described is played in a classroom experiment, about half of the players reject offers of below $30.

So fair shares matter. But what is *fair*? There isn't a crisp definition of fairness to match that of efficiency. Reasonable people have a variety of views about it. Almost everyone agrees that too much inequality is unfair. But how much is too much? And inequality of what: income, wealth, or the *opportunity* to work, earn an income, and accumulate wealth?

You will examine efficiency again in Chapter 2 and efficiency and fairness in Chapter 5.

Questions about the social interest are hard ones to answer and they generate discussion, debate, and disagreement. Four issues in today's world put some flesh on these questions. The issues are:

- Globalization
- Information-age monopolies
- Climate change
- Economic instability

Globalization The term *globalization* means the expansion of international trade, borrowing and lending, and investment.

When Nike produces sports shoes, people in Malaysia get work; and when China Airlines buys new regional jets, Canadians who work at Bombardier build them. While globalization brings expanded production and job opportunities for some workers, it destroys many Canadian jobs. Workers across the manufacturing industries must learn new skills or take service jobs, which are often lower-paid, or retire earlier than previously planned.

Globalization is in the self-interest of those consumers who buy low-cost goods and services produced in other countries; and it is in the self-interest of the multinational firms that produce in low-cost regions and sell in high-price regions. But is globalization in the self-interest of the low-wage worker in Malaysia who sews your new running shoes and the displaced shoemaker in Toronto? Is it in the social interest?

◆ ECONOMICS IN THE NEWS

The Invisible Hand

From Brewer to Bio-Tech Entrepreneur
Kiran Mazumdar-Shaw trained to become a master brewer and learned about enzymes, the stuff from which bio-pharmaceuticals are made. Discovering it was impossible for a woman in India to become a master brewer, the 25-year-old Kiran decided to create a bio-pharmaceutical business.

Kiran's firm, Biocom, employed uneducated workers who loved their jobs and the living conditions made possible by their high wages. But when a labour union entered the scene and unionized the workers, a furious Kiran fired the workers, automated their jobs, and hired a smaller number of educated workers. Biocom continued to grow and today, Kiran's wealth exceeds $1 billion.

Kiran has become wealthy by developing and producing bio-pharmaceuticals that improve people's lives. But Kiran is sharing her wealth in creative ways. She has opened a cancer treatment centre to help thousands of patients who are too poor to pay and created a health insurance scheme.

Source: Ariel Levy, "Drug Test,"
The New Yorker, January 2, 2012.

THE QUESTIONS
- Whose decisions in the story were taken in self-interest?
- Whose decisions turned out to be in the social interest?
- Did any of the decisions harm the social interest?

THE ANSWERS
- All the decisions—Kiran's, the workers', the union's, and the firm's customers'—are taken in the pursuit of self-interest.
- Kiran's decisions serve the social interest: She creates jobs that benefit her workers and products that benefit her customers. And her charitable work brings yet further social benefits.
- The labour union's decision might have harmed the social interest because it destroyed the jobs of uneducated workers.

KIRAN MAZUMDAR-SHAW, FOUNDER AND CEO OF BIOCOM

Information-Age Monopolies The technological change of the past forty years has been called the *Information Revolution*. Bill Gates, a co-founder of Microsoft, held a privileged position in this revolution. For many years, Windows was the only available operating system for the PC. The PC and Mac competed, but the PC had a huge market share.

An absence of competition gave Microsoft the power to sell Windows at prices far above the cost of production. With lower prices, many more people would have been able to afford and buy a computer.

The information revolution has clearly served your self-interest: It has provided your cellphone, laptop, loads of handy applications, and the Internet. It has also served the self-interest of Bill Gates who has seen his wealth soar.

But did the information revolution best serve the social interest? Did Microsoft produce the best possible Windows operating system and sell it at a price that was in the social interest? Or was the quality too low and the price too high?

Climate Change Burning fossil fuels to generate electricity and to power airplanes, automobiles, and trucks pours a staggering 28 billion tonnes—4 tonnes per person—of carbon dioxide into the atmosphere each year. These carbon emissions, two-thirds of which come from the United States, China, the European Union, Russia, and India, bring global warming and climate change.

Every day, when you make self-interested choices to use electricity and gasoline, you leave your carbon footprint. You can lessen this footprint by walking, riding a bike, taking a cold shower, or planting a tree.

But can each one of us be relied upon to make decisions that affect the Earth's carbon-dioxide concentration in the social interest? Must governments change the incentives we face so that our self-interested choices are also in the social interest? How can governments change incentives? How can we

encourage the use of wind and solar power to replace the burning of fossil fuels that brings climate change?

Economic Instability In 2008, U.S. banks were in trouble. They had made loans that borrowers couldn't repay and they were holding securities the values of which had crashed.

Banks' choices to take deposits and make loans are made in self-interest, but does this lending and borrowing serve the social interest? Do banks lend too much in the pursuit of profit?

When U.S. banks got into trouble in 2008, the U.S. Federal Reserve (the Fed) bailed them out with big loans backed by taxpayer dollars. Did the Fed's bailout of troubled banks serve the social interest? Or might the Fed's rescue action encourage banks to repeat their dangerous lending in the future?

We've looked at four topics and asked many questions that illustrate the potential conflict between the pursuit of self-interest and the social interest. We've asked questions but not answered them because we've not yet explained the economic principles needed to do so. We answer these questions in future chapters.

◢ REVIEW QUIZ

1 Describe the broad facts about *what*, *how*, and *for whom* goods and services are produced.
2 Use headlines from the recent news to illustrate the potential for conflict between self-interest and the social interest.

Work these questions in Study Plan 1.2 and get instant feedback. Do a Key Terms Quiz.   MyEconLab

◆ AT **ISSUE**

The Protest Against Market Capitalism

Market capitalism is an economic system in which individuals own land and capital and are free to buy and sell land, capital, and goods and services in markets. Markets for goods and services, along with markets for land and capital, coordinate billions of self-interested choices, which determine what, how, and for whom goods and services are produced. A few people earn enormous incomes, many times the average income. There is no supreme planner guiding the use of scarce resources and the outcome is unintended and unforeseeable.

Centrally planned socialism is an economic system in which the government owns all the land and capital, directs workers to jobs, and decides what, how, and for whom to produce. The Soviet Union, several Eastern European countries, and China have used this system in the past but have now abandoned it. Only Cuba and North Korea use this system today. A few bureaucrats in positions of great power receive huge incomes, many times that of an average person.

Our economy today is a **mixed economy**, which is market capitalism with government regulation.

The Protest

The protest against market capitalism takes many forms. Historically, **Karl Marx** and other communist and socialist thinkers wanted to replace it with *socialism* and *central planning*. Today, thousands of people who feel let down by the economic system want less market capitalism and more government regulation. The **Occupy Wall Street** movement, with its focus on the large incomes of the top 1 percent, is a visible example of today's protest. Protesters say:

- Big corporations (especially big banks) have too much power and influence on governments.

- Democratically elected governments can do a better job of allocating resources and distributing income than uncoordinated markets.

- More regulation in the social interest is needed— to serve "human need, not corporate greed."

- In a market, for every winner, there is a loser.

- Big corporations are the winners. Workers and unemployed people are the losers.

The Economist's Response

Economists agree that market capitalism isn't perfect. But they argue that it is the best system available and while some government intervention and regulation can help, government attempts to serve the social interest often end up harming it.

Adam Smith (see p. 53), who gave the first systematic account of how market capitalism works, says:

- The self-interest of big corporations is *maximum profit*.

- But an *invisible hand* leads production decisions made in pursuit of self-interest to *unintentionally* promote the social interest.

- Politicians are ill-equipped to regulate corporations or to intervene in markets, and those who think they can improve on the market outcome are most likely wrong.

- In a market, buyers get what they want for less than they would be willing to pay and sellers earn a profit. Both buyers and sellers gain. A market transaction is a "win-win" event.

An Occupy Wall Street protester

"It is not from the benevolence of the butcher, the brewer, or the baker that we expect our dinner, but from their regard to their own interest."
The Wealth of Nations,
1776

Adam Smith

◢ The Economic Way of Thinking

The questions that economics tries to answer tell us about the *scope of economics,* but they don't tell us how economists *think* and go about seeking answers to these questions. You're now going to see how economists go about their work.

We're going to look at six key ideas that define the *economic way of thinking*. These ideas are:

- A choice is a *tradeoff.*
- People make *rational choices* by comparing *benefits* and *costs.*
- *Benefit* is what you *gain* from something.
- *Cost* is what you *must give up* to get something.
- Most choices are *"how-much"* choices made at the *margin.*
- Choices respond to *incentives.*

A Choice Is a Tradeoff

Because we face scarcity, we must make choices. And when we make a choice, we select from the available alternatives. For example, you can spend Saturday night studying for your next test or having fun with your friends, but you can't do both of these activities at the same time. You must choose how much time to devote to each. Whatever choice you make, you could have chosen something else.

You can think about your choices as tradeoffs. A **tradeoff** is an exchange—giving up one thing to get something else. When you choose how to spend your Saturday night, you face a tradeoff between studying and hanging out with your friends.

Making a Rational Choice

Economists view the choices that people make as rational. A **rational choice** is one that compares costs and benefits and achieves the greatest benefit over cost for the person making the choice.

Only the wants of the person making a choice are relevant to determine its rationality. For example, you might like your coffee black and strong but your friend prefers his milky and sweet. So it is rational for you to choose espresso and for your friend to choose cappuccino.

The idea of rational choice provides an answer to the first question: *What* goods and services will be produced and in what quantities? The answer is those that people rationally choose to buy!

But how do people choose rationally? Why do more people choose an iPhone rather than a BlackBerry? Why don't CN and CPR build high-speed tracks so that VIA Rail can run Bombardier super-fast trains like those used in Europe? The answers turn on comparing benefits and costs.

Benefit: What You Gain

The **benefit** of something is the gain or pleasure that it brings and is determined by **preferences**—by what a person likes and dislikes and the intensity of those feelings. If you get a huge kick out of "Leagues of Legends," that video game brings you a large benefit. And if you have little interest in listening to Yo-Yo Ma playing a Vivaldi cello concerto, that activity brings you a small benefit.

Some benefits are large and easy to identify, such as the benefit that you get from being in school. A big piece of that benefit is the goods and services that you will be able to enjoy with the boost to your earning power when you graduate. Some benefits are small, such as the benefit you get from a slice of pizza.

Economists measure benefit as the most that a person is *willing to give up* to get something. You are willing to give up a lot to be in school. But you would give up only an iTunes download for a slice of pizza.

Cost: What You *Must* Give Up

The **opportunity cost** of something is the highest-valued alternative that must be given up to get it.

To make the idea of opportunity cost concrete, think about *your* opportunity cost of being in school. It has two components: the things you can't afford to buy and the things you can't do with your time.

Start with the things you can't afford to buy. You've spent all your income on tuition, residence fees, books, and a laptop. If you weren't in school, you would have spent this money on tickets to ball games and movies and all the other things that you enjoy. But that's only the start of your opportunity cost.

You've also given up the opportunity to get a job and earn an income. Suppose that the best job you could get if you weren't in school is working at CIBC as a teller earning $25,000 a year. Another part of your opportunity cost of being in school is all the things that you could buy with the extra $25,000 you would have.

As you well know, being a student eats up many hours in class time, doing homework assignments, preparing for tests, and so on. To do all these school activities, you must give up many hours of what would otherwise be leisure time spent with your friends.

So the opportunity cost of being in school is all the good things that you can't afford and don't have the spare time to enjoy. You might want to put a dollar value on that cost or you might just list all the items that make up the opportunity cost.

The examples of opportunity cost that we've just considered are all-or-nothing costs—you're either in school or not in school. Most situations are not like this one. They involve choosing *how much* of an activity to do.

How Much? Choosing at the Margin

You can allocate the next hour between studying and chatting online with your friends, but the choice is not all or nothing. You must decide how many minutes to allocate to each activity. To make this decision, you compare the benefit of a little bit more study time with its cost—you make your choice at the **margin**.

The benefit that arises from an increase in an activity is called **marginal benefit**. For example, your marginal benefit from one more night of study before a test is the boost it gives to your grade. Your marginal benefit doesn't include the grade you're already achieving without that extra night of work.

The *opportunity cost* of an *increase* in an activity is called **marginal cost**. For you, the marginal cost of studying one more night is the cost of not spending that night on your favourite leisure activity.

To make your decisions, you compare marginal benefit and marginal cost. If the marginal benefit from an extra night of study exceeds its marginal cost, you study the extra night. If the marginal cost exceeds the marginal benefit, you don't study the extra night.

Choices Respond to Incentives

Economists take human nature as given and view people as acting in their self-interest. All people— you, other consumers, producers, politicians, and public servants—pursue their self-interest.

Self-interested actions are not necessarily *selfish* actions. You might decide to use your resources in ways that bring pleasure to others as well as to yourself. But a self-interested act gets the most benefit for *you* based on *your* view about benefit.

The central idea of economics is that we can predict the self-interested choices that people make by looking at the *incentives* they face. People undertake those activities for which marginal benefit exceeds marginal cost; and they reject options for which marginal cost exceeds marginal benefit.

For example, your economics instructor gives you a problem set and tells you these problems will be on the next test. Your marginal benefit from working these problems is large, so you diligently work them. In contrast, your math instructor gives you a problem set on a topic that she says will never be on a test. You get little marginal benefit from working these problems, so you decide to skip most of them.

Economists see incentives as the key to reconciling self-interest and social interest. When our choices are *not* in the social interest, it is because of the incentives we face. One of the challenges for economists is to figure out the incentives that result in self-interested choices being in the social interest.

Economists emphasize the crucial role that institutions play in influencing the incentives that people face as they pursue their self-interest. Laws that protect private property and markets that enable voluntary exchange are the fundamental institutions. You will learn as you progress with your study of economics that where these institutions exist, self-interest can indeed promote the social interest.

REVIEW QUIZ

1 Explain the idea of a tradeoff and think of three tradeoffs that you have made today.

2 Explain what economists mean by rational choice and think of three choices that you've made today that are rational.

3 Explain why opportunity cost is the best forgone alternative and provide examples of some opportunity costs that you have faced today.

4 Explain what it means to choose at the margin and illustrate with three choices at the margin that you have made today.

5 Explain why choices respond to incentives and think of three incentives to which you have responded today.

Work these questions in Study Plan 1.3 and get instant feedback. Do a Key Terms Quiz.   MyEconLab

Economics as Social Science and Policy Tool

Economics is both a social science and a toolkit for advising on policy decisions.

Economist as Social Scientist

As social scientists, economists seek to discover how the economic world works. In pursuit of this goal, like all scientists, economists distinguish between positive and normative statements.

Positive Statements   A *positive* statement is about what *is*. It says what is currently believed about the way the world operates. A positive statement might be right or wrong, but we can test it by checking it against the facts. "Our planet is warming because of the amount of coal that we're burning" is a positive statement. We can test whether it is right or wrong.

A central task of economists is to test positive statements about how the economic world works and to weed out those that are wrong. Economics first got off the ground in the late 1700s, so it is a young science compared with, for example, physics, and much remains to be discovered.

Normative Statements   A *normative* statement is about what *ought to be*. It depends on values and cannot be tested. Policy goals are normative statements. For example, "We ought to cut our use of coal by 50 percent" is a normative policy statement. You may agree or disagree with it, but you can't test it. It doesn't assert a fact that can be checked.

Unscrambling Cause and Effect   Economists are particularly interested in positive statements about cause and effect. Are computers getting cheaper because people are buying them in greater quantities? Or are people buying computers in greater quantities because they are getting cheaper? Or is some third factor causing both the price of a computer to fall and the quantity of computers bought to increase?

To answer such questions, economists create and test economic models. An **economic model** is a description of some aspect of the economic world that includes only those features that are needed for the purpose at hand. For example, an economic model of a cellphone network might include features such as the prices of calls, the number of cellphone users, and the volume of calls. But the model would ignore cellphone colours and ringtones.

A model is tested by comparing its predictions with the facts. But testing an economic model is difficult because we observe the outcomes of the simultaneous change of many factors. To cope with this problem, economists look for natural experiments (situations in the ordinary course of economic life in which the one factor of interest is different and other things are equal or similar); conduct statistical investigations to find correlations; and perform economic experiments by putting people in decision-making situations and varying the influence of one factor at a time to discover how they respond.

Economist as Policy Adviser

Economics is useful. It is a toolkit for advising governments and businesses and for making personal decisions. Some of the most famous economists work partly as policy advisers.

Many leading Canadian economists have advised governments and other organizations on a wide range of economic policy issues. Among them are David Laidler of the University of Western Ontario, Christopher Ragan of McGill University, and Angela Reddish of the University of British Columbia, all of whom have spent time advising the Bank of Canada and the Department of Finance.

All the policy questions on which economists provide advice involve a blend of the positive and the normative. Economics can't help with the normative part—the policy goal. But it can help to clarify the goal. And for a given goal, economics provides the tools for evaluating alternative solutions—comparing marginal benefits and marginal costs and finding the solution that makes the best use of the available resources.

◆ REVIEW QUIZ

1   Distinguish between a positive statement and a normative statement and provide examples.

2   What is a model? Can you think of a model that you might use in your everyday life?

3   How do economists try to disentangle cause and effect?

4   How is economics used as a policy tool?

Work these questions in Study Plan 1.4 and get instant feedback. Do a Key Terms Quiz.   MyEconLab

ECONOMICS IN THE NEWS

The Internet for Everyone

Mark Zuckerberg's Big Idea: The "Next 5 Billion"

Facebook founder Mark Zuckerberg wants to make it so that anyone, anywhere, can get online. To achieve this goal, he has created internet.org, "a global partnership between technology leaders, nonprofits, local communities, and experts who are working together to bring the Internet to the two-thirds of the world's population that don't have it."

Sources: CNN Money, August 21, 2013, and internet.org

THE DATA

- The figure shows that almost 80 percent of Americans and Canadians have Internet access compared to only 16 percent of Africans and 28 percent of Asians.

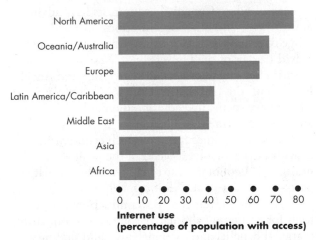

**Internet use
(percentage of population with access)**

Internet Access by Region

- Of the 5 billion people who Mark Zuckerberg wants to have Internet access, 1 billion live in Africa and 2.8 billion live in Asia.
- To figure out what it would take for everyone to have Internet access, we must make an assumption about how many people share resources.
- If four people shared, it would cost about $285 billion for computers and $115 billion a year for Internet access for everyone to get online.
- Satisfying Mark Zuckerberg's want would cost the equivalent of 400 years of Facebook's 2012 profit, or 1,600 Boeing 787 Dreamliners, or 90 aircraft carriers, or 87 billion Big Macs.

THE QUESTIONS

- What is the fundamental economic problem and how does this news clip illustrate it?
- What are some of the things that might be forgone for more people to get online?
- Why don't more people make the tradeoffs needed to get online?
- Why might it be in Mark Zuckerberg's self-interest to get everyone online?
- Why might it not be in the social interest for everyone to get online?

In Africa, 4 in 5 people lack Internet access.

THE ANSWERS

- The fundamental economic problem is scarcity—the fact that wants exceed the resources available to satisfy them. The news clip illustrates scarcity because Mark Zuckerberg's want for everyone to get online *exceeds* the resources available to satisfy it.
- Some of the scarce resources that are used to produce airplanes, war ships, and Big Macs could be reallocated and used to produce more computers and Internet service.
- People don't make the tradeoffs needed to get online because for them the marginal cost of doing so would exceed the marginal benefit.
- It might be in Mark Zuckerberg's self-interest to get everyone online because that would increase the number of Facebook users and increase the firm's advertising revenues.
- It would not be in the social interest to get everyone online if the marginal cost of an Internet connection exceeded its marginal benefit.

SUMMARY

Key Points

Definition of Economics (p. 2)

- All economic questions arise from scarcity—from the fact that wants exceed the resources available to satisfy them.
- Economics is the social science that studies the choices that people make as they cope with scarcity.
- The subject divides into microeconomics and macroeconomics.

Working Problem 1 will give you a better understanding of the definition of economics.

Two Big Economic Questions (pp. 3–8)

- Two big questions summarize the scope of economics:

  1. How do choices end up determining *what, how*, and *for whom* goods and services are produced?
  2. When do choices made in the pursuit of *self-interest* also promote the *social interest*?

Working Problems 2 and 3 will give you a better understanding of the two big questions of economics.

The Economic Way of Thinking (pp. 9–10)

- Every choice is a tradeoff—exchanging more of something for less of something else.
- People make rational choices by comparing benefit and cost.
- Cost—*opportunity cost*—is what you must give up to get something.
- Most choices are "how much" choices made at the *margin* by comparing marginal benefit and marginal cost.
- Choices respond to incentives.

Working Problems 4 and 5 will give you a better understanding of the economic way of thinking.

Economics as Social Science and Policy Tool (p. 11)

- Economists distinguish between positive statements—what is—and normative statements—what ought to be.
- To explain the economic world, economists create and test economic models.
- Economics is a toolkit used to provide advice on government, business, and personal economic decisions.

Working Problem 6 will give you a better understanding of economics as social science and policy tool.

Key Terms

Benefit, 9
Capital, 4
Economic model, 11
Economics, 2
Efficient, 5
Entrepreneurship, 4
Factors of production, 3
Goods and services, 3
Human capital, 3
Incentive, 2

Interest, 4
Labour, 3
Land, 3
Macroeconomics, 2
Margin, 10
Marginal benefit, 10
Marginal cost, 10
Microeconomics, 2
Opportunity cost, 9
Preferences, 9

Profit, 4
Rational choice, 9
Rent, 4
Scarcity, 2
Self-interest, 5
Social interest, 5
Tradeoff, 9
Wages, 4

STUDY PLAN PROBLEMS AND APPLICATIONS

MyEconLab   You can work Problems 1 to 6 in MyEconLab Chapter 1 Study Plan and get instant feedback.

Definition of Economics (Study Plan 1.1)

1. Apple Inc. decides to make iTunes freely available in unlimited quantities.
   a. Does Apple's decision change the incentives that people face?
   b. Is Apple's decision an example of a microeconomic or a macroeconomic issue?

Two Big Economic Questions (Study Plan 1.2)

2. Which of the following pairs does not match?
   a. Labour and wages
   b. Land and rent
   c. Entrepreneurship and profit
   d. Capital and profit

3. Explain how the following news headlines concern self-interest and the social interest.
   a. Starbucks Expands in China
   b. McDonald's Moves into Gourmet Coffee
   c. Food Must Be Labelled with Nutrition Data

The Economic Way of Thinking (Study Plan 1.3)

4. The night before an economics test, you decide to go to the movies instead of staying home and working your MyEconLab Study Plan. You get 50 percent on your test compared with the 70 percent that you normally score.
   a. Did you face a tradeoff?
   b. What was the opportunity cost of your evening at the movies?

5. **Cost of Sochi Winter Olympics**
   The Russian government spent $6.7 billion on Olympic facilities and $16.7 billion upgrading Sochi area infrastructure. Sponsors spent $27.6 billion on hotels and facilities hoping to turn Sochi into a year-round tourist magnet.
   Source: *The Washington Post*, February 11, 2014
   Was the opportunity cost of the Sochi Olympics $6.7, $23.4, or $51 billion? Explain your answer.

Economics as Social Science and Policy Tool
(Study Plan 1.4)

6. Which of the following statements is positive, which is normative, and which can be tested?
   a. Canada should cut its imports.
   b. China is Canada's largest trading partner.
   c. The federal government should increase the production of biofuels.

ADDITIONAL PROBLEMS AND APPLICATIONS

MyEconLab   You can work these problems in MyEconLab if assigned by your instructor.

Definition of Economics

7. **Rapper Offers Free Tickets for Concert**
   Eminem will hit the road with Rihanna offering an awesome deal—buy one and get one free!
   Source: *Mstars News*, February 24, 2014
   When Eminem gave away tickets, what was free and what was scarce? Explain your answer.

Two Big Economic Questions

8. How does the creation of a successful movie influence *what, how*, and *for whom* goods and services are produced?

9. How does a successful movie illustrate self-interested choices that are also in the social interest?

The Economic Way of Thinking

10. When Costco opened a gas bar just off Highway 401, the neighbourhood was swamped with cars as drivers lined up to get the discount of 10 cents a litre.
    a. What is the opportunity cost of a litre of gas? Explain.
    b. To control the crowd, Costco hires traffic police. What is the tradeoff that Costco faces?

11. What might be an incentive for you to take a class in summer school? List some of the benefits and costs involved in your decision. Would your choice be rational?

Economics as Social Science and Policy Tool

12. Look at today's *National Post*. What is the leading economic news story? With which of the big economic questions does it deal and what tradeoffs does it discuss or imply?

13. Provide two microeconomic statements and two macroeconomic statements. Classify your statements as positive or normative. Explain why.

APPENDIX

Graphs in Economics

After studying this appendix, you will be able to:

♦ Make and interpret a scatter diagram

♦ Identify linear and nonlinear relationships and relationships that have a maximum and a minimum

♦ Define and calculate the slope of a line

♦ Graph relationships among more than two variables

▶ Graphing Data

A graph represents a quantity as a distance on a line. In Fig. A1.1, a distance on the horizontal line represents temperature, measured in degrees Celsius. A movement from left to right shows an increase in temperature. The point 0 represents zero degrees Celsius. To the right of 0, the temperature is positive. To the left of 0, the temperature is negative (as indicated by the minus sign). A distance on the vertical line represents height, measured in thousands of metres. The point 0 represents sea level. Points above 0 represent metres above sea level. Points below 0 represent metres below sea level (indicated by a minus sign).

In Fig. A1.1, the two scale lines are perpendicular to each other and are called *axes*. The vertical line is the *y*-axis, and the horizontal line is the *x*-axis. Each axis has a zero point, which is shared by the two axes and called the *origin*.

To make a two-variable graph, we need two pieces of information: the value of the variable *x* and the value of the variable *y*. For example, off the coast of British Columbia, the temperature is 10 degrees—the value of *x*. A fishing boat is located at 0 metres above sea level—the value of *y*. These two bits of information appear as point *A* in Fig. A1.1. A climber at the top of Mount McKinley on a cold day is 6,194 metres above sea level in a zero-degree gale. These two pieces of information appear as point *B*. On a warmer day, a climber might be at the peak of Mt. McKinley when the temperature is 10 degrees, at point *C*.

We can draw two lines, called *coordinates*, from point *C*. One, called the *x*-coordinate, runs from *C* to

FIGURE A1.1   Making a Graph

Graphs have axes that measure quantities as distances. Here, the horizontal axis (*x*-axis) measures temperature, and the vertical axis (*y*-axis) measures height. Point *A* represents a fishing boat at sea level (0 on the *y*-axis) on a day when the temperature is 10°C. Point *B* represents a climber at the top of Mt. McKinley, 6,194 metres above sea level at a temperature of 0°F. Point *C* represents a climber at the top of Mt. McKinley, 6,194 metres above sea level at a temperature of 10°C.

—— **MyEconLab** Animation ——

the vertical axis. This line is called "the *x*-coordinate" because its length is the same as the value marked off on the *x*-axis. The other, called the *y*-coordinate, runs from *C* to the horizontal axis. This line is called "the *y*-coordinate" because its length is the same as the value marked off on the *y*-axis.

We describe a point on a graph by the values of its *x*-coordinate and its *y*-coordinate. For example, at point *C*, *x* is 10 degrees and *y* is 6,194 metres.

A graph like that in Fig. A1.1 can be made using any quantitative data on two variables. The graph can show just a few points, like Fig. A1.1, or many points. Before we look at graphs with many points, let's reinforce what you've just learned by looking at two graphs made with economic data.

Economists measure variables that describe *what*, *how*, and *for whom* goods and services are produced. These variables are quantities produced and prices. Figure A1.2 shows two examples of economic graphs.

FIGURE A1.2   Two Graphs of Economic Data

(a) Movie tickets: quantity and price

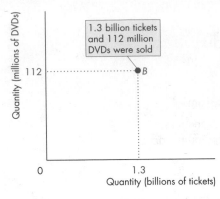

(b) Movies: tickets and DVDs

The graph in part (a) tells us that in 2013, 1.3 billion movie tickets were sold at an average price of $8.16 per ticket.

The graph in part (b) tells us that in 2013, 1.3 billion movie tickets and 112 million DVDs were sold.

MyEconLab Animation

Figure A1.2(a) is a graph about movie tickets in 2013. The *x*-axis measures the quantity of movie tickets sold and the *y*-axis measures the average price of a ticket. Point *A* tells us what the quantity and price were. You can "read" this graph as telling you that in 2013, 1.3 billion movie tickets were sold at an average ticket price of $8.16.

Figure A1.2(b) is a graph about movie-going and DVD buying. The *x*-axis measures the quantity of movie tickets sold in 2013 and the *y*-axis measures the quantity of DVDs sold in the same year. Point *B* tells us what these quantities were. You can "read" this graph as telling you that in 2013, 1.3 billion movie tickets and 112 million DVDs were sold.

The three graphs that you've just seen tell you how to make a graph and how to read a data point on a graph, but they don't improve on the raw data. Graphs become interesting and revealing when they contain a number of data points because then you can visualize the data.

Economists create graphs based on the principles in Figs. A1.1 and A1.2 to reveal, describe, and visualize the relationships among variables. We're now going to look at some examples. These graphs are called scatter diagrams.

Scatter Diagrams

A **scatter diagram** is a graph that plots the value of one variable against the value of another variable for a number of different values of each variable. Such a graph reveals whether a relationship exists between two variables and describes their relationship.

The table in Fig. A1.3 shows some data on two variables: the number of tickets sold at the box office and the number of DVDs sold for nine of the most popular movies in 2013.

What is the relationship between these two variables? Does a big box office success generate a large volume of DVD sales? Or does a box office success mean that fewer DVDs are sold?

We can answer these questions by making a scatter diagram. We do so by graphing the data in the table. In the graph in Fig. A1.3, each point shows the number of box office tickets sold (the *x* variable) and the number of DVDs sold (the *y* variable) of one of the movies. There are nine movies, so there are nine points "scattered" within the graph.

The point labelled *A* tells us that *Monsters University* sold 33 million tickets at the box office and 2.3 million DVDs. The points in the graph don't form a distinct pattern. They suggest that large box office sales do not directly bring large DVD sales. If you want to predict a movie's DVD sales in a given year with any confidence, you need to know more than the number of tickets sold at the box office in that year.

Figure A1.4 shows two scatter diagrams of economic variables. Part (a) shows the relationship between income and expenditure, on average, from 2003 to 2013. Each point represents income and expenditure in a given year. For example, point *A* shows that in 2006, income was $35,000 and expenditure was $25,000. This graph shows that as income increases, so does expenditure, and the relationship is a close one.

FIGURE A1.3   A Scatter Diagram

Movie	Tickets	DVDs
	(millions)	
Iron Man 3	50	1.1
The Hunger Games: Catching Fire	49	1.3
Despicable Me 2	45	1.8
Man of Steel	36	1.2
Frozen	34	0
Monsters University	33	2.3
Gravity	31	0
Fast and Furious 6	29	0
Oz the Great and Powerful	29	1.4

The table lists the number of tickets sold at the box office and the number of DVDs sold for nine popular movies.

The scatter diagram reveals the relationship between these two variables. Each point shows the values of the variables for a specific movie. For example, point *A* shows the point for *Monsters University*, which sold 33 million tickets at the box office and 2.3 million DVDs.

The pattern formed by the points shows no tendency for large box office sales to bring greater DVD sales. You cannot predict how many DVDs of a movie will sell in a given year just by knowing its box office sales in that year.

MyEconLab Animation

Figure A1.4(b) shows a scatter diagram of inflation and unemployment in Canada from 2003 to 2013. Here, the points show no relationship between the two variables. For example, when unemployment was high, the inflation rate was high in 2003 and low in 2013.

You can see that a scatter diagram conveys a wealth of information, and it does so in much less space than we have used to describe only some of its features. But you do have to "read" the graph to obtain all this information.

FIGURE A1.4   Two Economic Scatter Diagrams

(a) Income and expenditure

(b) Unemployment and inflation

The scatter diagram in part (a) shows the relationship between income and expenditure from 2003 to 2013. Point *A* shows that in 2006, income was $35,000 on the *x*-axis and expenditure was $25,000 on the *y*-axis. This graph shows that as income rises, so does expenditure, and the relationship is a close one.

The scatter diagram in part (b) shows a weak relationship between unemployment and inflation in Canada during most of the years.

MyEconLab Animation

Breaks in the Axes The graph in Fig. A1.4(a) has breaks in its axes, as shown by the small gaps. The breaks indicate that there are jumps from the origin, 0, to the first values recorded.

The breaks are used because the lowest value of income is $30,000 and the lowest value of expenditure exceeds $22,000. If we made this graph with no breaks in its axes, there would be a lot of empty space, the points would be crowded into the top right corner, and it would be difficult to see whether a relationship exists between these two variables. By breaking the axes, we are able to bring the relationship into view.

Putting a break in one or both axes is like using a zoom lens to bring the relationship into the centre of the graph and magnify it so that the relationship fills the graph.

Misleading Graphs Breaks can be used to highlight a relationship, but they can also be used to mislead—to make a graph that lies. The most common way of making a graph lie is to put a break in the axis and either stretch or compress the scale. For example, suppose that in Fig. A1.4(a), the y-axis that measures expenditure ran from zero to $28,000 while the x-axis was the same as the one shown. The graph would now create the impression that despite a huge increase in income, expenditure had barely changed.

To avoid being misled, it is a good idea to get into the habit of always looking closely at the values and the labels on the axes of a graph before you start to interpret it.

Correlation and Causation A scatter diagram that shows a clear relationship between two variables, such as Fig. A1.4(a), tells us that the two variables have a high correlation. When a high correlation is present, we can predict the value of one variable from the value of the other variable. But correlation does not imply causation.

Sometimes a high correlation does arise from a causal relationship. It is likely that rising income causes rising expenditure (Fig. A1.4a). But a high correlation can mean that two variables have a common cause. For example, ice cream sales and pool drownings are correlated not because one causes the other, but because both are caused by hot weather.

You've now seen how we can use graphs in economics to show economic data and to reveal relationships. Next, we'll learn how economists use graphs to construct and display economic models.

◢ Graphs Used in Economic Models

The graphs used in economics are not always designed to show real-world data. Often they are used to show general relationships among the variables in an economic model.

An *economic model* is a stripped-down, simplified description of an economy or of a component of an economy such as a business or a household. It consists of statements about economic behaviour that can be expressed as equations or as curves in a graph. Economists use models to explore the effects of different policies or other influences on the economy in ways that are similar to the use of model airplanes in wind tunnels and models of the climate.

You will encounter many different kinds of graphs in economic models, but there are some repeating patterns. Once you've learned to recognize these patterns, you will instantly understand the meaning of a graph. Here, we'll look at the different types of curves that are used in economic models, and we'll see some everyday examples of each type of curve. The patterns to look for in graphs are the four cases in which:

- Variables move in the same direction.
- Variables move in opposite directions.
- Variables have a maximum or a minimum.
- Variables are unrelated.

Let's look at these four cases.

Variables That Move in the Same Direction

Figure A1.5 shows graphs of the relationships between two variables that move up and down together. A relationship between two variables that move in the same direction is called a **positive relationship** or a **direct relationship**. A line that slopes upward shows such a relationship.

Figure A1.5 shows three types of relationships: one that has a straight line and two that have curved lines. All the lines in these three graphs are called curves. Any line on a graph—no matter whether it is straight or curved—is called a *curve*.

A relationship shown by a straight line is called a **linear relationship**. Figure A1.5(a) shows a linear relationship between the number of kilometres travelled

FIGURE A1.5   Positive (Direct) Relationships

(a) Positive, linear relationship

(b) Positive, becoming steeper

(c) Positive, becoming less steep

Each part shows a positive (direct) relationship between two variables. That is, as the value of the variable measured on the *x*-axis increases, so does the value of the variable measured on the *y*-axis. Part (a) shows a linear positive relationship—as the two variables increase together, we move along a straight line.

Part (b) shows a positive relationship such that as the two variables increase together, we move along a curve that becomes steeper.

Part (c) shows a positive relationship such that as the two variables increase together, we move along a curve that becomes flatter.

MyEconLab Animation

in 5 hours and speed. For example, point *A* shows that you will travel 200 kilometres in 5 hours if your speed is 40 kilometres an hour. If you double your speed to 80 kilometres an hour, you will travel 400 kilometres in 5 hours.

Figure A1.5(b) shows the relationship between distance sprinted and recovery time (the time it takes the heart rate to return to its normal resting rate). This relationship is an upward-sloping one that starts out quite flat but then becomes steeper as we move along the curve away from the origin. The reason this curve becomes steeper is that the additional recovery time needed from sprinting an additional 100 metres increases. It takes less than 5 minutes to recover from sprinting 100 metres but more than 10 minutes to recover from 200 metres.

Figure A1.5(c) shows the relationship between the number of problems worked by a student and the amount of study time. This relationship is an upward-sloping one that starts out quite steep and becomes flatter as we move along the curve away from the origin. Study time becomes less productive as the student spends more hours studying and becomes more tired.

Variables That Move in Opposite Directions

Figure A1.6 shows relationships between things that move in opposite directions. A relationship between variables that move in opposite directions is called a **negative relationship** or an **inverse relationship**.

Figure A1.6(a) shows the relationship between the hours spent playing squash and the hours spent playing tennis when the total time available is 5 hours. One extra hour spent playing tennis means one hour less spent playing squash and vice versa. This relationship is negative and linear.

Figure A1.6(b) shows the relationship between the cost per kilometre travelled and the length of a journey. The longer the journey, the lower is the cost per kilometre. But as the journey length increases, even though the cost per kilometre decreases, the fall in the cost per kilometre is smaller, the longer the journey. This feature of the relationship is shown by the fact that the curve slopes downward, starting out steep at a short journey length and then becoming flatter as the journey length increases. This relationship arises because some of the costs are fixed, such as auto insurance, and the fixed costs are spread over a longer journey.

FIGURE A1.6   Negative (Inverse) Relationships

(a) Negative, linear relationship

(b) Negative, becoming less steep

(c) Negative, becoming steeper

Each part shows a negative (inverse) relationship between two variables. Part (a) shows a linear negative relationship. The total time spent playing tennis and squash is 5 hours. As the time spent playing tennis increases, the time spent playing squash decreases, and we move along a straight line.

Part (b) shows a negative relationship such that as the journey length increases, the travel cost decreases as we move along a curve that becomes less steep.

Part (c) shows a negative relationship such that as leisure time increases, the number of problems worked decreases as we move along a curve that becomes steeper.

MyEconLab Animation

Figure A1.6(c) shows the relationship between the amount of leisure time and the number of problems worked by a student. Increasing leisure time produces an increasingly large reduction in the number of problems worked. This relationship is a negative one that starts out with a gentle slope at a small number of leisure hours and becomes steeper as the number of leisure hours increases. This relationship is a different view of the idea shown in Fig. A1.5(c).

Variables That Have a Maximum or a Minimum

Many relationships in economic models have a maximum or a minimum. For example, firms try to make the maximum possible profit and to produce at the lowest possible cost. Figure A1.7 shows relationships that have a maximum or a minimum.

Figure A1.7(a) shows the relationship between rainfall and wheat yield. When there is no rainfall, wheat will not grow, so the yield is zero. As the rainfall increases up to 10 days a month, the wheat yield increases. With 10 rainy days each month, the wheat

yield reaches its maximum at 2 tonnes per hectare (point *A*). Rain in excess of 10 days a month starts to lower the yield of wheat. If every day is rainy, the wheat suffers from a lack of sunshine and the yield decreases to zero. This relationship is one that starts out sloping upward, reaches a maximum, and then slopes downward.

Figure A1.7(b) shows the reverse case—a relationship that begins sloping downward, falls to a minimum, and then slopes upward. Most economic costs are like this relationship. An example is the relationship between the cost per kilometre and the speed of the car. At low speeds, the car is creeping in a traffic snarl-up. The number of kilometres per litre is low, so the gasoline cost per kilometre is high. At high speeds, the car is travelling faster than its efficient speed, using a large quantity of gasoline, and again the number of kilometres per litre is low and the gasoline cost per kilometre is high. At a speed of 100 kilometres an hour, the gasoline cost per kilometre is at its minimum (point *B*). This relationship is one that starts out sloping downward, reaches a minimum, and then slopes upward.

FIGURE A1.7 Maximum and Minimum Points

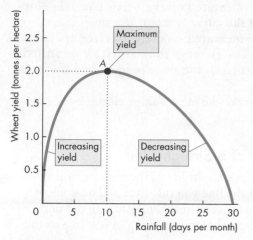

(a) Relationship with a maximum

(b) Relationship with a minimum

Part (a) shows a relationship that has a maximum point, *A*. The curve slopes upward as it rises to its maximum point, is flat at its maximum, and then slopes downward.

Part (b) shows a relationship with a minimum point, *B*. The curve slopes downward as it falls to its minimum, is flat at its minimum, and then slopes upward.

MyEconLab Animation

Variables That Are Unrelated

There are many situations in which no matter what happens to the value of one variable, the other variable remains constant. Sometimes we want to show the independence between two variables in a graph, and Fig. A1.8 shows two ways of achieving this.

In describing the graphs in Fig. A1.5 through Fig. A1.7, we have talked about curves that slope upward or slope downward and curves that become less steep or steeper. Let's spend a little time discussing exactly what we mean by *slope* and how we measure the slope of a curve.

FIGURE A1.8 Variables That Are Unrelated

(a) Unrelated: *y* constant

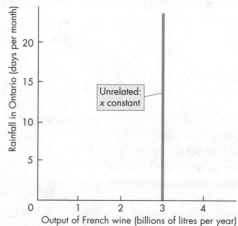

(b) Unrelated: *x* constant

This figure shows how we can graph two variables that are unrelated. In part (a), a student's grade in economics is plotted at 75 percent on the *y*-axis regardless of the price of bananas on the *x*-axis. The curve is horizontal.

In part (b), the output of the vineyards of France on the *x*-axis does not vary with the rainfall in Ontario on the *y*-axis. The curve is vertical.

MyEconLab Animation

◢ The Slope of a Relationship

We can measure the influence of one variable on another by the slope of the relationship. The **slope** of a relationship is the change in the value of the variable measured on the y-axis divided by the change in the value of the variable measured on the x-axis. We use the Greek letter Δ (*delta*) to represent "change in." Thus Δy means the change in the value of the variable measured on the y-axis, and Δx means the change in the value of the variable measured on the x-axis. Therefore the slope of the relationship is

$$\text{Slope} = \frac{\Delta y}{\Delta x}.$$

If a large change in the variable measured on the y-axis (Δy) is associated with a small change in the variable measured on the x-axis (Δx), the slope is large and the curve is steep. If a small change in the variable measured on the y-axis (Δy) is associated with a large change in the variable measured on the x-axis (Δx), the slope is small and the curve is flat.

We can make the idea of slope clearer by doing some calculations.

The Slope of a Straight Line

The slope of a straight line is the same regardless of where on the line you calculate it. The slope of a straight line is constant. Let's calculate the slope of the positive relationship in Fig. A1.9. In part (a),

FIGURE A1.9   The Slope of a Straight Line

(a) Positive slope

(b) Negative slope

To calculate the slope of a straight line, we divide the change in the value of the variable measured on the y-axis (Δy) by the change in the value of the variable measured on the x-axis (Δx) as we move along the line.

Part (a) shows the calculation of a positive slope. When x increases from 2 to 6, Δx equals 4. That change in

x brings about an increase in y from 3 to 6, so Δy equals 3. The slope (Δy/Δx) equals 3/4.

Part (b) shows the calculation of a negative slope. When x increases from 2 to 6, Δx equals 4. That increase in x brings about a decrease in y from 6 to 3, so Δy equals −3. The slope (Δy/Δx) equals −3/4.

MyEconLab Animation

when x increases from 2 to 6, y increases from 3 to 6. The change in x is $+4$—that is, Δx is 4. The change in y is $+3$—that is, Δy is 3. The slope of that line is

$$\frac{\Delta y}{\Delta x} = \frac{3}{4}.$$

In part (b), when x increases from 2 to 6, y decreases from 6 to 3. The change in y is *minus* 3—that is, Δy is -3. The change in x is *plus* 4—that is, Δx is 4. The slope of the curve is

$$\frac{\Delta y}{\Delta x} = \frac{-3}{4}.$$

Notice that the two slopes have the same magnitude (3/4), but the slope of the line in part (a) is positive ($+3/+4 = 3/4$) while that in part (b) is negative ($-3/+4 = -3/4$). The slope of a positive relationship is positive; the slope of a negative relationship is negative.

The Slope of a Curved Line

The slope of a curved line is trickier. The slope of a curved line is not constant, so the slope depends on where on the curved line we calculate it. There are two ways to calculate the slope of a curved line: You can calculate the slope at a point, or you can calculate the slope across an arc of the curve. Let's look at the two alternatives.

Slope at a Point To calculate the slope at a point on a curve, you need to construct a straight line that has the same slope as the curve at the point in question. Figure A1.10 shows how this is done. Suppose you want to calculate the slope of the curve at point A. Place a ruler on the graph so that the ruler touches point A and no other point on the curve, then draw a straight line along the edge of the ruler. The straight red line is this line, and it is the tangent to the curve at point A. If the ruler touches the curve only at point A, then the slope of the curve at point A must be the same as the slope of the edge of the ruler. If the curve and the ruler do not have the same slope, the line along the edge of the ruler will cut the curve instead of just touching it.

Now that you have found a straight line with the same slope as the curve at point A, you can calculate the slope of the curve at point A by calculating the slope of the straight line. Along the straight

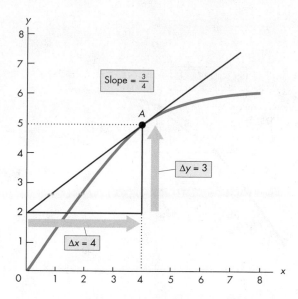

FIGURE A1.10   Slope at a Point

Slope $= \frac{3}{4}$

$\Delta y = 3$

$\Delta x = 4$

To calculate the slope of the curve at point A, draw the red line that just touches the curve at A—the tangent. The slope of this straight line is calculated by dividing the change in y by the change in x along the red line. When x increases from 0 to 4, Δx equals 4. That change in x is associated with an increase in y from 2 to 5, so Δy equals 3. The slope of the red line is 3/4, so the slope of the curve at point A is 3/4.

MyEconLab Animation

line, as x increases from 0 to 4 (Δx is 4) y increases from 2 to 5 (Δy is 3). Therefore the slope of the straight line is

$$\frac{\Delta y}{\Delta x} = \frac{3}{4}.$$

So the slope of the curve at point A is 3/4.

Slope Across an Arc An arc of a curve is a piece of a curve. Figure A1.11 shows the same curve as in Fig. A1.10, but instead of calculating the slope at point A, we are now going to calculate the slope across the arc from point B to point C. You can see that the slope of the curve at point B is greater than at point C. When we calculate the slope across an arc, we are calculating the average slope between two points. As we move along the arc from B to C, x increases from 3 to 5 and y increases from 4.0 to 5.5. The change in x is 2 (Δx is 2), and the change in y is 1.5 (Δy is 1.5).

FIGURE A1.11   Slope Across an Arc

To calculate the average slope of the curve along the arc
BC, draw a straight line from point *B* to point *C*. The slope
of the line *BC* is calculated by dividing the change in *y* by
the change in *x*. In moving from *B* to *C*, the increase in *x* is
2 (Δx equals 2) and the change in *y* is 1.5 (Δy equals 1.5).
The slope of the line *BC* is 1.5 divided by 2, or 3/4. So the
slope of the curve across the arc *BC* is 3/4.

—— MyEconLab Animation ——

Therefore the slope is

$$\frac{\Delta y}{\Delta x} = \frac{1.5}{2} = \frac{3}{4}.$$

So the slope of the curve across the arc *BC* is 3/4.

This calculation gives us the slope of the curve
between points *B* and *C*. The actual slope calculated
is the slope of the straight line from *B* to *C*. This
slope approximates the average slope of the curve
along the arc *BC*. In this particular example, the
slope across the arc *BC* is identical to the slope of the
curve at point *A*, but the calculation of the slope of a
curve does not always work out so neatly. You might
have fun constructing some more examples and a few
counter examples.

You now know how to make and interpret a
graph. So far, we've limited our attention to graphs of
two variables. We're now going to learn how to graph
more than two variables.

Graphing Relationships Among More Than Two Variables

We have seen that we can graph the relationship
between two variables as a point formed by the *x*-
and *y*-coordinates in a two-dimensional graph. You
might be thinking that although a two-dimensional
graph is informative, most of the things in which
you are likely to be interested involve relationships
among many variables, not just two. For example,
the amount of ice cream consumed depends on the
price of ice cream and the temperature. If ice cream
is expensive and the temperature is low, people eat
much less ice cream than when ice cream is inex-
pensive and the temperature is high. For any given
price of ice cream, the quantity consumed varies
with the temperature; and for any given temperature, the quantity of ice cream consumed varies with
its price.

Figure A1.12 shows a relationship among three
variables. The table shows the number of litres of ice
cream consumed each day at two different temperatures and at a number of different prices of ice cream.
How can we graph these numbers?

To graph a relationship that involves more than
two variables, we use the *ceteris paribus* assumption.

Ceteris Paribus

Ceteris paribus (often shortened to *cet par*) means "if
all other relevant things remain the same." To isolate
the relationship of interest in a laboratory experiment, a scientist holds everything constant except for
the variable whose effect is being studied. Economists
use the same method to graph a relationship that has
more than two variables.

Figure A1.12 shows an example. There, you can
see what happens to the quantity of ice cream consumed when the price of ice cream varies but the
temperature is held constant.

The curve labelled 21°C shows the relationship
between ice cream consumption and the price of ice
cream if the temperature remains at 21°C. The numbers used to plot that curve are those in the first two
columns of the table. For example, if the temperature
is 21°C, 10 litres of ice cream are consumed when
the price is $2.75 a scoop and 18 litres are consumed
when the price is $2.25 a scoop.

The curve labelled 32°C shows the relationship
between ice cream consumption and the price of
ice cream if the temperature remains at 32°C. The
numbers used to plot that curve are those in the first

FIGURE A1.12   Graphing a Relationship Among Three Variables

Price (dollars per scoop)	Ice cream consumption (litres per day)	
	21°C	32°C
2.00	25	50
2.25	18	36
2.50	13	26
2.75	**10**	**20**
3.00	7	14
3.25	5	10
3.50	3	6

Ice cream consumption depends on its price and the temperature. The table tells us how many litres of ice cream are consumed each day at different prices and two different temperatures. For example, if the price is $2.75 a scoop and the temperature is 21°C, 10 litres of ice cream are consumed. But if the temperature is 32°C, 20 litres are consumed.

To graph a relationship among three variables, the value of one variable is held constant. The graph shows the relationship between price and consumption when

the temperature is held constant. One curve holds the temperature at 21°C and the other holds it at 32°C.

A change in the price of ice cream brings a movement along one of the curves—along the blue curve at 21°C and along the red curve at 32°C.

When the temperature *rises* from 21°C to 32°C, the curve that shows the relationship between consumption and the price *shifts* rightward from the blue curve to the red curve.

MyEconLab Animation

and third columns of the table. For example, if the temperature is 32°C, 20 litres are consumed when the price is $2.75 a scoop and 36 litres are consumed when the price is $2.25 a scoop.

When the price of ice cream changes but the temperature is constant, you can think of what happens in the graph as a movement along one of the curves. At 21°C there is a movement along the blue curve, and at 32°C there is a movement along the red curve.

When Other Things Change

The temperature is held constant along each of the curves in Fig. A1.12, but in reality the temperature changes. When that event occurs, you can think of

what happens in the graph as a shift of the curve. When the temperature rises from 21°C to 32°C, the curve that shows the relationship between ice cream consumption and the price of ice cream shifts rightward from the blue curve to the red curve.

You will encounter these ideas of movements along and shifts of curves at many points in your study of economics. Think carefully about what you've just learned and make up some examples (with assumed numbers) about other relationships.

With what you have learned about graphs, you can move forward with your study of economics. There are no graphs in this book that are more complicated than those that have been explained in this appendix.

MATHEMATICAL NOTE

Equations of Straight Lines

If a straight line in a graph describes the relationship between two variables, we call it a linear relationship. Figure 1 shows the *linear relationship* between a person's expenditure and income. This person spends $100 a week (by borrowing or spending previous savings) when income is zero. Out of each dollar earned, this person spends 50 cents (and saves 50 cents).

All linear relationships are described by the same general equation. We call the quantity that is measured on the horizontal axis (or *x*-axis) *x,* and we call the quantity that is measured on the vertical axis (or *y*-axis) *y.* In the case of Fig. 1, *x* is income and *y* is expenditure.

A Linear Equation

The equation that describes a straight-line relationship between *x* and *y* is

$$y = a + bx.$$

In this equation, *a* and *b* are fixed numbers and they are called *constants.* The values of *x* and *y* vary, so these numbers are called *variables.* Because the equation describes a straight line, the equation is called a *linear equation.*

The equation tells us that when the value of *x* is zero, the value of *y* is *a.* We call the constant *a* the *y*-axis intercept. The reason is that on the graph the straight line hits the *y*-axis at a value equal to *a.* Figure 1 illustrates the *y*-axis intercept.

For positive values of *x,* the value of *y* exceeds *a.* The constant *b* tells us by how much *y* increases above *a* as *x* increases. The constant *b* is the slope of the line.

Slope of the Line

As we explain in the chapter, the *slope* of a relationship is the change in the value of *y* divided by the change in the value of *x.* We use the Greek letter Δ (delta) to represent "change in." So Δy means the change in the value of the variable measured on the *y*-axis, and Δx means the change in the value of the variable measured on the *x*-axis. Therefore the slope of the relationship is

$$\text{Slope} = \frac{\Delta y}{\Delta x}.$$

To see why the slope is *b,* suppose that initially the value of *x* is x_1, or $200 in Fig. 2. The corresponding value of *y* is y_1, also $200 in Fig. 2. The equation of the line tells us that

$$y_1 = a + bx_1. \tag{1}$$

Now the value of *x* increases by Δx to $x_1 + \Delta x$ (or $400 in Fig. 2). And the value of *y* increases by Δy to $y_1 + \Delta y$ (or $300 in Fig. 2).

The equation of the line now tells us that

$$y_1 + \Delta y = a + b(x_1 + \Delta x). \tag{2}$$

Figure 1 Linear Relationship

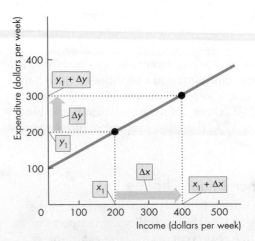

Figure 2 Calculating Slope

To calculate the slope of the line, subtract equation (1) from equation (2) to obtain

$$\Delta y = b\Delta x \qquad (3)$$

and now divide equation (3) by Δx to obtain

$$\Delta y/\Delta x = b.$$

So the slope of the line is b.

Position of the Line

The y-axis intercept determines the position of the line on the graph. Figure 3 illustrates the relationship between the y-axis intercept and the position of the line. In this graph, the y-axis measures saving and the x-axis measures income.

When the y-axis intercept, a, is positive, the line hits the y-axis at a positive value of y—as the blue line does. Its y-axis intercept is 100. When the y-axis intercept, a, is zero, the line hits the y-axis at the origin—as the purple line does. Its y-axis intercept is 0. When the y-axis intercept, a, is negative, the line hits the y-axis at a negative value of y—as the red line does. Its y-axis intercept is -100.

As the equations of the three lines show, the value of the y-axis intercept does not influence the slope of the line. All three lines have a slope equal to 0.5.

Positive Relationships

Figure 1 shows a positive relationship—the two variables x and y move in the same direction. All positive relationships have a slope that is positive. In the

equation of the line, the constant b is positive. In this example, the y-axis intercept, a, is 100. The slope b equals $\Delta y/\Delta x$, which in Fig. 2 is 100/200 or 0.5. The equation of the line is

$$y = 100 + 0.5x.$$

Negative Relationships

Figure 4 shows a negative relationship—the two variables x and y move in the opposite direction. All negative relationships have a slope that is negative. In the equation of the line, the constant b is negative. In the example in Fig. 4, the y-axis intercept, a, is 30. The slope, b, equals $\Delta y/\Delta x$, which is $-20/2$ or -10. The equation of the line is

$$y = 30 + (-10)x$$

or

$$y = 30 - 10x.$$

Example

A straight line has a y-axis intercept of 50 and a slope of 2. What is the equation of this line?

The equation of a straight line is

$$y = a + bx$$

where a is the y-axis intercept and b is the slope. So the equation is

$$y = 50 + 2x.$$

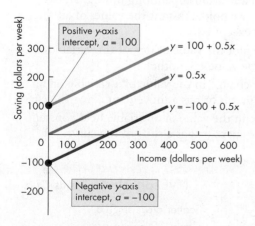

Figure 3 The y-Axis Intercept

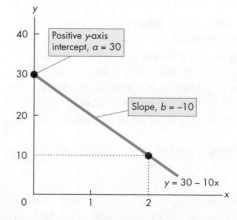

Figure 4 Negative Relationship

REVIEW QUIZ

1 Explain how we "read" the three graphs in Figs. A1.1 and A1.2.

2 Explain what scatter diagrams show and why we use them.

3 Explain how we "read" the three scatter diagrams in Figs. A1.3 and A1.4.

4 Draw a graph to show the relationship between two variables that move in the same direction.

5 Draw a graph to show the relationship between two variables that move in opposite directions.

6 Draw a graph of two variables whose relationship shows (i) a maximum and (ii) a minimum.

7 Which of the relationships in Questions 4 and 5 is a positive relationship and which is a negative relationship?

8 What are the two ways of calculating the slope of a curved line?

9 How do we graph a relationship among more than two variables?

10 Explain what change will bring a *movement along* a curve.

11 Explain what change will bring a *shift* of a curve.

Work these questions in Study Plan 1.A and get instant feedback. Do a Key Terms Quiz.   MyEconLab

SUMMARY

Key Points

Graphing Data (pp. 15–18)

■ A graph is made by plotting the values of two variables *x* and *y* at a point that corresponds to their values measured along the *x*-axis and the *y*-axis.

■ A scatter diagram is a graph that plots the values of two variables for a number of different values of each.

■ A scatter diagram shows the relationship between the two variables. It shows whether they are positively related, negatively related, or unrelated.

Graphs Used in Economic Models (pp. 18–21)

■ Graphs are used to show relationships among variables in economic models.

■ Relationships can be positive (an upward-sloping curve), negative (a downward-sloping curve), positive and then negative (have a maximum point), negative and then positive (have a minimum point), or unrelated (a horizontal or vertical curve).

The Slope of a Relationship (pp. 22–24)

■ The slope of a relationship is calculated as the change in the value of the variable measured on the *y*-axis divided by the change in the value of the variable measured on the *x*-axis—that is, $\Delta y / \Delta x$.

■ A straight line has a constant slope.

■ A curved line has a varying slope. To calculate the slope of a curved line, we calculate the slope at a point or across an arc.

Graphing Relationships Among More Than Two Variables (pp. 24–25)

■ To graph a relationship among more than two variables, we hold constant the values of all the variables except two.

■ We then plot the value of one of the variables against the value of another.

■ A *cet par* change in the value of a variable on an axis of a graph brings a movement along the curve.

■ A change in the value of a variable held constant along the curve brings a shift of the curve.

Key Terms

MyEconLab Key Terms Quiz

Ceteris paribus, 24
Direct relationship, 18
Inverse relationship, 19
Linear relationship, 18
Negative relationship, 19
Positive relationship, 18
Scatter diagram, 16
Slope, 22

STUDY PLAN PROBLEMS AND APPLICATIONS

MyEconLab   You can work Problems 1 to 11 in Chapter 1A Study Plan and get instant feedback.

Use the following spreadsheet to work Problems 1 to 3. The spreadsheet provides the economic data: Column A is the year, column B is the inflation rate, column C is the interest rate, column D is the growth rate, and column E is the unemployment rate.

	A	B	C	D	E
1	2003	1.6	1.0	2.8	6.0
2	2004	2.3	1.4	3.8	5.5
3	2005	2.7	3.2	3.4	5.1
4	2006	3.4	4.9	2.7	4.6
5	2007	3.2	4.5	1.8	4.6
6	2008	2.9	1.4	-0.3	5.8
7	2009	3.8	0.2	-2.8	9.3
8	2010	-0.3	0.1	2.5	9.6
9	2011	1.6	0.1	1.8	8.9
10	2012	3.1	0.1	2.8	8.1
11	2013	2.1	0.1	1.9	7.4

1. Draw a scatter diagram of the inflation rate and the interest rate. Describe the relationship.

2. Draw a scatter diagram of the growth rate and the unemployment rate. Describe the relationship.

3. Draw a scatter diagram of the interest rate and the unemployment rate. Describe the relationship.

Use the following news clip to work Problems 4 to 6.

LEGO **Tops the Box Office**

Movie	Theatres (number)	Revenue (dollars per theatre)
The LEGO Movie	3,775	$16,551
About Last Night	2,253	$12,356
RoboCop	3,372	$7,432
The Monuments Men	3,083	$5,811

Source: boxofficemojo.com,
Data for weekend of February 14–17, 2014

4. Draw a graph of the relationship between the revenue per theatre on the *y*-axis and the number of theatres on the *x*-axis. Describe the relationship.

5. Calculate the slope of the relationship in Problem 4 between 3,775 and 2,253 theatres.

6. Calculate the slope of the relationship in Problem 4 between 2,253 and 3,372 theatres.

7. Calculate the slope of the following relationship.

Use the following relationship to work Problems 8 and 9.

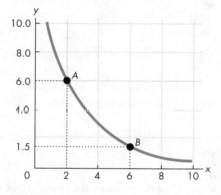

8. Calculate the slope of the relationship at point *A* and at point *B*.

9. Calculate the slope across the arc *AB*.

Use the following table to work Problems 10 and 11. The table gives the price of a balloon ride, the temperature, and the number of rides a day.

Price (dollars per ride)	Balloon rides (number per day)		
	10°C	20°C	30°C
5	32	40	50
10	27	32	40
15	18	27	32

10. Draw a graph to show the relationship between the price and the number of rides when the temperature is 20°C. Describe this relationship.

11. What happens in the graph in Problem 10 if the temperature rises to 30°C?

ADDITIONAL PROBLEMS AND APPLICATIONS

MyEconLab   You can work these problems in MyEconLab if assigned by your instructor.

Use the following spreadsheet to work Problems 12 to 14. The spreadsheet provides data on oil and gasoline: Column A is the year, column B is the price of oil (dollars per barrel), column C is the price of gasoline (cents per litre), column D is oil production, and column E is the quantity of gasoline refined (both in millions of barrels per day).

	A	B	C	D	E
1	2003	31	42	5.7	8.9
2	2004	42	50	5.4	9.1
3	2005	57	61	5.2	9.2
4	2006	66	69	5.1	9.3
5	2007	72	75	5.1	9.3
6	2008	100	87	5.0	9.0
7	2009	62	64	5.4	9.0
8	2010	79	75	5.5	9.0
9	2011	95	94	5.7	9.1
10	2012	94	96	6.5	9.0
11	2013	98	93	7.5	9.1

12. Draw a scatter diagram of the price of oil and the quantity of oil produced. Describe the relationship.

13. Draw a scatter diagram of the price of gasoline and the quantity of gasoline refined. Describe the relationship.

14. Draw a scatter diagram of the quantity of oil produced and the quantity of gasoline refined. Describe the relationship.

Use the following data to work Problems 15 to 17. Draw a graph that shows the relationship between the two variables x and y:

x	0	1	2	3	4	5
y	25	24	22	18	12	0

15. a. Is the relationship positive or negative?
    b. Does the slope of the relationship become steeper or flatter as the value of x increases?
    c. Think of some economic relationships that might be similar to this one.

16. Calculate the slope of the relationship between x and y when x equals 3.

17. Calculate the slope of the relationship across the arc as x increases from 4 to 5.

18. Calculate the slope of the curve in the figure in the next column at point A.

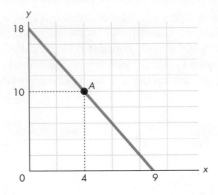

Use the following relationship to work Problems 19 and 20.

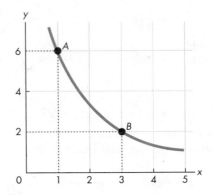

19. Calculate the slope at point A and at point B.

20. Calculate the slope across the arc AB.

Use the following table to work Problems 21 to 23. The table gives data about umbrellas: price, the number purchased, and rainfall in millimetres (mm).

Price	Umbrellas (number purchased per day)		
(dollars per umbrella)	0 mm	200 mm	400 mm
20	4	7	8
30	2	4	7
40	1	2	4

21. Draw a graph to show the relationship between the price and the number of umbrellas purchased, holding the amount of rainfall constant at 200 mm. Describe this relationship.

22. What happens in the graph in Problem 21 if the price rises and rainfall is constant?

23. What happens in the graph in Problem 21 if the rainfall increases from 200 mm to 400 mm?

2

THE ECONOMIC PROBLEM

After studying this chapter, you will be able to:

◆ Define the production possibilities frontier and use it to calculate opportunity cost

◆ Distinguish between production possibilities and preferences and describe an efficient allocation of resources

◆ Explain how current production choices expand future production possibilities

◆ Explain how specialization and trade expand production possibilities

◆ Describe the economic institutions that coordinate decisions

Canada has vast oil and natural gas resources and we produce much more energy than we consume. We are an energy-exporting nation. Should we produce and export even more oil and gas? How do we know when we are using our energy and other resources efficiently?

In this chapter, you study an economic model that answers questions about the efficiency of production and trade.

At the end of the chapter, in *Economics in the News*, we'll apply what you learn to explain why it is smart to export some of our oil and gas, but why it might not be smart to increase our energy production.

▶ Production Possibilities and Opportunity Cost

Every working day, in mines, factories, shops, and offices and on farms and construction sites across Canada, 18 million people produce a vast variety of goods and services valued at $60 billion. But the quantities of goods and services that we can produce are limited by our available resources and by technology. And if we want to increase our production of one good, we must decrease our production of something else—we face a tradeoff. You are now going to study the limits to production.

The **production possibilities frontier** (*PPF*) is the boundary between those combinations of goods and services that can be produced and those that cannot. To illustrate the *PPF*, we look at a *model economy* in which the quantities produced of only two goods change, while the quantities produced of all the other goods and services remain the same.

Let's look at the production possibilities frontier for cola and pizza, which represent *any* pair of goods or services.

Production Possibilities Frontier

The *production possibilities frontier* for cola and pizza shows the limits to the production of these two goods, given the total resources and technology available to produce them. Figure 2.1 shows this production possibilities frontier. The table lists combinations of the quantities of pizza and cola that can be produced in a month and the figure graphs these combinations. The *x*-axis shows the quantity of pizzas produced, and the *y*-axis shows the quantity of cola produced.

The *PPF* illustrates *scarcity* because the points outside the frontier are *unattainable*. These points describe wants that can't be satisfied.

We can produce at any point *inside* the *PPF* or *on* the *PPF*. These points are *attainable*. For example, we can produce 4 million pizzas and 5 million cans of cola. Figure 2.1 shows this combination as point *E* in the graph and as possibility *E* in the table.

Moving along the *PPF* from point *E* to point *D* (possibility *D* in the table) we produce more cola and less pizza: 9 million cans of cola and 3 million pizzas. Or moving in the opposite direction from point *E* to point *F* (possibility *F* in the table), we produce more pizza and less cola: 5 million pizzas and no cola.

FIGURE 2.1   Production Possibilities Frontier

Possibility	Pizzas (millions)		Cola (millions of cans)
A	0	and	15
B	1	and	14
C	2	and	12
D	3	and	9
E	4	and	5
F	5	and	0

The table lists six production possibilities for cola and pizzas. Row *A* tells us that if we produce no pizzas, the maximum quantity of cola we can produce is 15 million cans. Points *A*, *B*, *C*, *D*, *E*, and *F* in the figure represent the rows of the table. The curve passing through these points is the production possibilities frontier (*PPF*).

The *PPF* separates the attainable from the unattainable. Production is possible at any point *inside* the orange area or *on* the frontier. Points outside the frontier are unattainable. Points inside the frontier, such as point *Z*, are inefficient because resources are wasted or misallocated. At such points, it is possible to use the available resources to produce more of either or both goods.

——— **MyEconLab Animation and Draw Graph** ———

Production Efficiency

We achieve **production efficiency** if we produce goods and services at the lowest possible cost. This outcome occurs at all the points *on* the *PPF.* At points *inside* the *PPF,* production is inefficient because we are giving up more than necessary of one good to produce a given quantity of the other good.

For example, at point *Z* in Fig. 2.1, we produce 3 million pizzas and 5 million cans of cola, but we have enough resources to produce 3 million pizzas and 9 million cans of cola. Our pizzas cost more cola than necessary. We can get them for a lower cost. Only when we produce *on* the *PPF* do we incur the lowest possible cost of production.

Production inside the *PPF* is *inefficient* because resources are either *unused* or *misallocated* or both.

Resources are *unused* when they are idle but could be working. For example, we might leave some of the factories idle or some workers unemployed.

Resources are *misallocated* when they are assigned to tasks for which they are not the best match. For example, we might assign skilled pizza chefs to work in a cola factory and skilled cola workers to cook pizza in a pizzeria. We could get more pizzas *and* more cola if we reassigned these workers to the tasks that more closely match their skills.

Tradeoff Along the *PPF*

A choice *along* the *PPF* involves a *tradeoff.* Tradeoffs like that between cola and pizza arise in every imaginable real-world situation in which a choice must be made. At any given time, we have a fixed amount of labour, land, capital, and entrepreneurship and a given state of technology. We can employ these resources and technology to produce goods and services, but we are limited in what we can produce.

When doctors want to spend more on AIDS and cancer research, they face a tradeoff: more medical research for less of some other things. When Parliament wants to spend more on education and healthcare, it faces a tradeoff: more education and healthcare for less national defence. When an environmental group argues for less logging, it is suggesting a tradeoff: greater conservation of endangered wildlife for less paper. When you want a higher grade on your next test, you face a tradeoff: spend more time studying and less leisure or sleep time.

All the tradeoffs you've just considered involve a cost—an opportunity cost.

Opportunity Cost

The **opportunity cost** of an action is the highest-valued alternative forgone. The *PPF* makes this idea precise and enables us to calculate opportunity cost. Along the *PPF,* there are only two goods, so there is only one alternative forgone: some quantity of the other good. To produce more pizzas we must produce less cola. The opportunity cost of producing an additional pizza is the cola we *must* forgo. Similarly, the opportunity cost of producing an additional can of cola is the quantity of pizza we must forgo.

In Fig. 2.1, if we move from point *C* to point *D,* we produce an additional 1 million pizzas but 3 million fewer cans of cola. The additional 1 million pizzas *cost* 3 million cans of cola. Or 1 pizza costs 3 cans of cola. Similarly, if we move from *D* to *C,* we produce an additional 3 million cans of cola but 1 million fewer pizzas. The additional 3 million cans of cola *cost* 1 million pizzas. Or 1 can of cola costs 1/3 of a pizza.

Opportunity Cost Is a Ratio Opportunity cost is a ratio. It is the decrease in the quantity produced of one good divided by the increase in the quantity produced of another good as we move along the production possibilities frontier.

Because opportunity cost is a ratio, the opportunity cost of producing an additional can of cola is equal to the *inverse* of the opportunity cost of producing an additional pizza. Check this proposition by returning to the calculations we've just done. In the move from *C* to *D,* the opportunity cost of a pizza is 3 cans of cola. And in the move from *D* to *C,* the opportunity cost of a can of cola is 1/3 of a pizza. So the opportunity cost of pizza is the inverse of the opportunity cost of cola.

Increasing Opportunity Cost The opportunity cost of a pizza increases as the quantity of pizzas produced increases. The outward-bowed shape of the *PPF* reflects increasing opportunity cost. When we produce a large quantity of cola and a small quantity of pizza— between points *A* and *B* in Fig. 2.1—the frontier has a gentle slope. An increase in the quantity of pizzas costs a small decrease in the quantity of cola—the opportunity cost of a pizza is a small quantity of cola.

When we produce a large quantity of pizzas and a small quantity of cola—between points *E* and *F* in Fig. 2.1—the frontier is steep. A given increase in the quantity of pizzas *costs* a large decrease in the quantity of cola, so the opportunity cost of a pizza is a large quantity of cola.

ECONOMICS IN THE NEWS

Opportunity Cost of Cocoa

World's Sweet Tooth Heats Up Cocoa

Chocolate consumption is soaring as people in developing countries are getting wealthier. Cocoa farmers are ramping up production to keep the chocolate flowing, but the price of cocoa keeps rising.

Source: *The Wall Street Journal,* February 13, 2014

THE QUESTIONS

- How does the *PPF* illustrate (1) the limits to cocoa production; (2) the tradeoff we must make to increase cocoa production; and (3) the effect of increased chocolate consumption on the cost of producing cocoa?

THE ANSWERS

- The figure shows the global *PPF* for cocoa and other goods and services. Point *A* on the *PPF* tells us that if 4 million tonnes of cocoa are produced, a maximum of 96 units of other goods and services can be produced.

- The movement along the *PPF* from *A* to *B* shows the tradeoff we must make to increase cocoa production.

- The slope of the *PPF* measures the opportunity cost of cocoa. If cocoa production increases from zero to 4 million tonnes, the production of other goods and services decreases from 100 units to 96 units. The opportunity cost of 1 tonne of cocoa is 1 unit of other goods and services.

- But if cocoa production increases from 4 million tonnes to 8 million tonnes, the production of other goods and services decreases from 96 units to 80 units. The opportunity cost of 1 tonne of cocoa is now 4 units of other goods and services.

- As resources are moved into producing cocoa, labour, land, and capital less suited to the task of cocoa production are used and the cost of the additional cocoa produced increases.

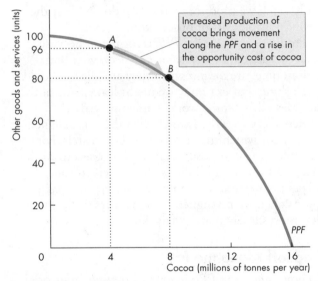

Increased production of cocoa brings movement along the *PPF* and a rise in the opportunity cost of cocoa

PPF for Cocoa and Other Goods and Services

The *PPF* is bowed outward because resources are not all equally productive in all activities. People with many years of experience working for PepsiCo are good at producing cola but not very good at making pizzas. So if we move some of these people from PepsiCo to Domino's, we get a small increase in the quantity of pizzas but a large decrease in the quantity of cola.

Similarly, people who have spent years working at Domino's are good at producing pizzas, but they have no idea how to produce cola. So if we move some people from Domino's to PepsiCo, we get a small increase in the quantity of cola but a large decrease in the quantity of pizzas. The more we produce of either good, the less productive are the additional resources we use and the larger is the opportunity cost of a unit of that good.

How do we choose among the points on the *PPF*? How do we know which point is the best?

MyEconLab More Economics in the News

REVIEW QUIZ

1 How does the production possibilities frontier illustrate scarcity?

2 How does the production possibilities frontier illustrate production efficiency?

3 How does the production possibilities frontier show that every choice involves a tradeoff?

4 How does the production possibilities frontier illustrate opportunity cost?

5 Why is opportunity cost a ratio?

6 Why does the *PPF* bow outward and what does that imply about the relationship between opportunity cost and the quantity produced?

Work these questions in Study Plan 2.1 and get instant feedback. Do a Key Terms Quiz.   MyEconLab

Using Resources Efficiently

We achieve *production efficiency* at every point on the *PPF*, but which of these points is best? The answer is the point on the *PPF* at which goods and services are produced in the quantities that provide the greatest possible benefit. When goods and services are produced at the lowest possible cost and in the quantities that provide the greatest possible benefit, we have achieved **allocative efficiency**.

The questions that we raised when we reviewed the four big issues in Chapter 1 are questions about allocative efficiency. To answer such questions, we must measure and compare costs and benefits.

The *PPF* and Marginal Cost

The **marginal cost** of a good is the opportunity cost of producing one more unit of it. We calculate marginal cost from the slope of the *PPF*. As the quantity of pizzas produced increases, the *PPF* gets steeper and the marginal cost of a pizza increases. Figure 2.2 illustrates the calculation of the marginal cost of a pizza.

Begin by finding the opportunity cost of pizza in blocks of 1 million pizzas. The cost of the first million pizzas is 1 million cans of cola; the cost of the second million pizzas is 2 million cans of cola; the cost of the third million pizzas is 3 million cans of cola, and so on. The bars in part (a) illustrate these calculations.

The bars in part (b) show the cost of an average pizza in each of the 1 million pizza blocks. Focus on the third million pizzas—the move from *C* to *D* in part (a). Over this range, because 1 million pizzas cost 3 million cans of cola, one of these pizzas, on average, costs 3 cans of cola—the height of the bar in part (b).

Next, find the opportunity cost of each additional pizza—the marginal cost of a pizza. The marginal cost of a pizza increases as the quantity of pizzas produced increases. The marginal cost at point *C* is less than it is at point *D*. On average over the range from *C* to *D*, the marginal cost of a pizza is 3 cans of cola. But it exactly equals 3 cans of cola only in the middle of the range between *C* and *D*.

The red dot in part (b) indicates that the marginal cost of a pizza is 3 cans of cola when 2.5 million pizzas are produced. Each black dot in part (b) is interpreted in the same way. The red curve that passes through these dots, labelled *MC*, is the marginal cost curve. It shows the marginal cost of a pizza at each quantity of pizzas as we move along the *PPF*.

FIGURE 2.2 The *PPF* and Marginal Cost

(a) *PPF* and opportunity cost

(b) **Marginal cost**

Marginal cost is calculated from the slope of the *PPF*. As the quantity of pizzas produced increases, the *PPF* gets steeper and the marginal cost of a pizza increases. The bars in part (a) show the opportunity cost of pizza in blocks of 1 million pizzas. The bars in part (b) show the cost of an average pizza in each of these 1 million blocks. The red curve, *MC*, shows the marginal cost of a pizza at each point along the *PPF*. This curve passes through the centre of each of the bars in part (b).

——— MyEconLab Animation ———

Preferences and Marginal Benefit

The **marginal benefit** from a good or service is the benefit received from consuming one more unit of it. This benefit is subjective. It depends on people's **preferences**—people's likes and dislikes and the intensity of those feelings.

Marginal benefit and *preferences* stand in sharp contrast to *marginal cost* and *production possibilities*. Preferences describe what people like and want and the production possibilities describe the limits or constraints on what is feasible.

We need a concrete way of illustrating preferences that parallels the way we illustrate the limits to production using the *PPF*.

The device that we use to illustrate preferences is the **marginal benefit curve**, which is a curve that shows the relationship between the marginal benefit from a good and the quantity consumed of that good. Note that the *marginal benefit curve* is *unrelated* to the *PPF* and cannot be derived from it.

We measure the marginal benefit from a good or service by the most that people are *willing to pay* for an additional unit of it. The idea is that you are willing to pay less for a good than it is worth to you but you are not willing to pay more: The most you are willing to pay for something is its marginal benefit.

It is a general principle that the more we have of any good or service, the smaller is its marginal benefit and the less we are willing to pay for an additional unit of it. This tendency is so widespread and strong that we call it a principle—the *principle of decreasing marginal benefit*.

The basic reason why marginal benefit decreases is that we like variety. The more we consume of any one good or service, the more we tire of it and would prefer to switch to something else.

Think about your willingness to pay for a pizza. If pizza is hard to come by and you can buy only a few slices a year, you might be willing to pay a high price to get an additional slice. But if pizza is all you've eaten for the past few days, you are willing to pay almost nothing for another slice.

You've learned to think about cost as opportunity cost, not as a dollar cost. You can think about marginal benefit and willingness to pay in the same way. The marginal benefit, measured by what you are willing to pay for something, is the quantity of other goods and services that you are willing to forgo. Let's continue with the example of cola and pizza and illustrate preferences this way.

FIGURE 2.3   Preferences and the Marginal Benefit Curve

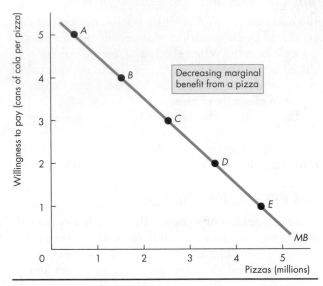

Possibility	Pizzas (millions)	Willingness to pay (cans of cola per pizza)
A	0.5	5
B	1.5	4
C	2.5	3
D	3.5	2
E	4.5	1

The smaller the quantity of pizzas available, the more cola people are willing to give up for an additional pizza. With 0.5 million pizzas available, people are willing to pay 5 cans of cola per pizza. But with 4.5 million pizzas, people are willing to pay only 1 can of cola per pizza. Willingness to pay measures marginal benefit. A universal feature of people's preferences is that marginal benefit decreases.

MyEconLab Animation

Figure 2.3 illustrates preferences as the willingness to pay for pizza in terms of cola. In row *A*, with 0.5 million pizzas available, people are willing to pay 5 cans of cola per pizza. As the quantity of pizzas increases, the amount that people are willing to pay for a pizza falls. With 4.5 million pizzas available, people are willing to pay only 1 can of cola per pizza.

Let's now use the concepts of marginal cost and marginal benefit to describe allocative efficiency.

FIGURE 2.4   Efficient Use of Resources

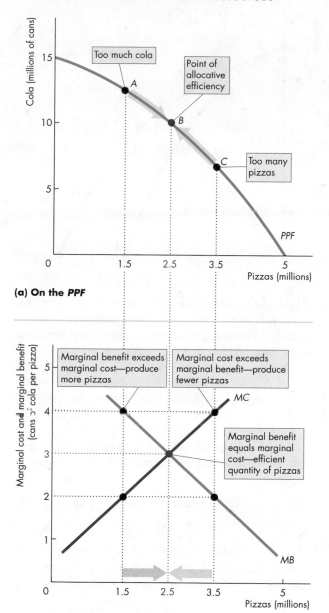

(a) On the PPF

(b) Marginal benefit equals marginal cost

The greater the quantity of pizzas produced, the smaller is the marginal benefit (*MB*) from pizza—the less cola people are willing to give up to get an additional pizza. But the greater the quantity of pizzas produced, the greater is the marginal cost (*MC*) of a pizza—the more cola people must give up to get an additional pizza. When marginal benefit equals marginal cost, resources are being used efficiently.

————— MyEconLab Animation —————

Allocative Efficiency

At *any* point on the *PPF*, we cannot produce more of one good without giving up some other good. At the *best* point on the *PPF*, we cannot produce more of one good without giving up some other good that provides greater benefit. We are producing at the point of allocative efficiency—the point on the *PPF* that we prefer above all other points.

Suppose in Fig. 2.4 we produce 1.5 million pizzas. In part (b), the marginal cost of a pizza is 2 cans of cola and the marginal benefit from a pizza is 4 cans of cola. Because someone values an additional pizza more highly than it costs to produce, we can get more value from our resources by moving some of them out of producing cola and into producing pizza.

Now suppose we produce 3.5 million pizzas. The marginal cost of a pizza is now 4 cans of cola, but the marginal benefit from a pizza is only 2 cans of cola. Because the additional pizza costs more to produce than anyone thinks it is worth, we can get more value from our resources by moving some of them away from producing pizza and into producing cola.

Suppose we produce 2.5 million pizzas. Marginal cost and marginal benefit are now equal at 3 cans of cola. This allocation of resources between pizzas and cola is efficient. If more pizzas are produced, the forgone cola is worth more than the additional pizzas. If fewer pizzas are produced, the forgone pizzas are worth more than the additional cola.

REVIEW QUIZ

1 What is marginal cost? How is it measured?
2 What is marginal benefit? How is it measured?
3 How does the marginal benefit from a good change as the quantity produced of that good increases?
4 What is allocative efficiency and how does it relate to the production possibilities frontier?
5 What conditions must be satisfied if resources are used efficiently?

Work these questions in Study Plan 2.2 and get instant feedback. Do a Key Terms Quiz.   MyEconLab

You now understand the limits to production and the conditions under which resources are used efficiently. Your next task is to study the expansion of production possibilities.

◢ Economic Growth

During the past 30 years, production per person in Canada has doubled. The expansion of production possibilities is called **economic growth**. Economic growth increases our *standard of living,* but it doesn't overcome scarcity and avoid opportunity cost. To make our economy grow, we face a tradeoff—the faster we make production grow, the greater is the opportunity cost of economic growth.

The Cost of Economic Growth

Economic growth comes from technological change and capital accumulation. **Technological change** is the development of new goods and of better ways of producing goods and services. **Capital accumulation** is the growth of capital resources, including *human capital.*

Technological change and capital accumulation have vastly expanded our production possibilities. We can produce automobiles that provide us with more transportation than was available when we had only horses and carriages. We can produce satellites that provide global communications on a much larger scale than that available with the earlier cable technology. But if we use our resources to develop new technologies and produce capital, we must decrease our production of consumption goods and services. New technologies and new capital have an opportunity cost. Let's look at this opportunity cost.

Instead of studying the *PPF* of pizzas and cola, we'll hold the quantity of cola produced constant and examine the *PPF* for pizzas and pizza ovens. Figure 2.5 shows this *PPF* as the blue curve PPF_0. If we devote no resources to producing pizza ovens, we produce at point *A*. If we produce 3 million pizzas, we can produce 6 pizza ovens at point *B*. If we produce no pizza, we can produce 10 ovens at point *C*.

The amount by which our production possibilities expand depends on the resources we devote to technological change and capital accumulation. If we devote no resources to this activity (point *A*), our *PPF* remains the blue curve PPF_0 in Fig. 2.5. If we cut the current pizza production and produce 6 ovens (point *B*), then in the future, we'll have more capital and our *PPF* will rotate outward to the position shown by the red curve PPF_1. The fewer resources we use for producing pizza and the more resources we use for producing ovens, the greater is the expansion of our future production possibilities.

MyEconLab Animation and Draw Graph

FIGURE 2.5   Economic Growth

PPF_0 shows the limits to the production of pizzas and pizza ovens, with the production of all other goods and services remaining the same. If we devote no resources to producing pizza ovens and produce 5 million pizzas, our production possibilities will remain the same at PPF_0. But if we decrease pizza production to 3 million and produce 6 ovens, at point *B*, our production possibilities expand. After one period, the *PPF* rotates outward to PPF_1 and we can produce at point *B'*, a point outside the original PPF_0. We can rotate the *PPF* outward, but we cannot avoid opportunity cost. The opportunity cost of producing more pizzas in the future is fewer pizzas today.

Economic growth brings enormous benefits in the form of increased consumption in the future, but economic growth is not free and it doesn't abolish scarcity.

In Fig. 2.5, to make economic growth happen we must use some resources to produce new ovens, which leaves fewer resources to produce pizzas. To move to *B'* in the future, we must move from *A* to *B* today. The opportunity cost of more pizzas in the future is fewer pizzas today. Also, on the new *PPF*, we still face a tradeoff and opportunity cost.

The ideas about economic growth that we have explored in the setting of the pizza industry also apply to nations. Hong Kong and Canada provide a striking case study.

Economics in Action
Hong Kong Overtakes Canada

In 1963, the production possibilities per person in Canada were more than three times those in Hong Kong (see the figure). Canada devotes one-fifth of its resources to accumulating capital, and in 1963, Canada was at point *A* on its *PPF*. Hong Kong devotes one-third of its resources to accumulating capital, and in 1963, Hong Kong was at point *A* on its *PPF*.

Since 1963, both economies have experienced economic growth, but because Hong Kong devotes a bigger fraction of its resources to accumulating capital, its production possibilities have expanded more quickly.

By 2013, production possibilities per person in Hong Kong had *overtaken* those in Canada. If Hong Kong continues to devote more resources to accumulating capital (at point *B* on its 2013 *PPF*) than Canada does, Hong Kong will continue to grow more rapidly than Canada. But if Hong Kong decreases its capital accumulation (moving to point *D* on its 2013 *PPF*), then its rate of economic growth will slow.

Hong Kong is typical of the fast-growing Asian economies, which include Taiwan, Thailand, South Korea, China, and India. Production possibilities

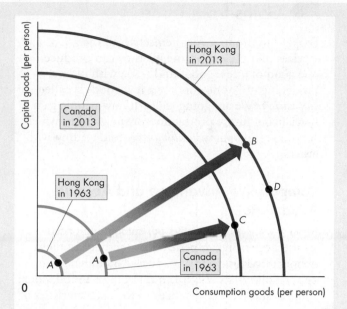

Economic Growth in Canada and Hong Kong

expand in these countries by between 5 percent and almost 10 percent a year.

If such high economic growth rates are maintained, these other Asian countries will continue to catch up with and eventually overtake Canada, as Hong Kong has done.

A Nation's Economic Growth

The experiences of Canada and Hong Kong make a striking example of the effects of our choices about consumption and capital accumulation on the rate of economic growth.

If an economy devotes all its factors of production to producing consumption goods and services and none to advancing technology and accumulating capital, its production possibilities in the future will be the same as they are today.

To expand production possibilities in the future, a nation or an economy must devote fewer resources to producing current consumption goods and services and some resources to accumulating capital and developing new technologies. As production possibilities expand, consumption in the future can increase. The decrease in today's consumption is the opportunity cost of tomorrow's increase in consumption.

REVIEW QUIZ

1 What generates economic growth?
2 How does economic growth influence the production possibilities frontier?
3 What is the opportunity cost of economic growth?
4 Explain why Hong Kong has experienced faster economic growth than Canada.
5 Does economic growth overcome scarcity?

Work these questions in Study Plan 2.3 and get instant feedback. Do a Key Terms Quiz.   MyEconLab

Next, we're going to study another way in which we expand our production possibilities—the amazing fact that *both* buyers and sellers gain from specialization and trade.

Gains from Trade

People can produce for themselves all the goods and services that they consume, or they can produce one good or a few goods and trade with others. Producing only one good or a few goods is called *specialization*. We are going to learn how people gain by specializing in the production of the good in which they have a *comparative advantage* and trading with others.

Comparative Advantage and Absolute Advantage

A person has a **comparative advantage** in an activity if that person can perform the activity at a lower opportunity cost than anyone else. Differences in opportunity costs arise from differences in individual abilities and from differences in the characteristics of other resources.

No one excels at everything. One person is an outstanding pitcher but a poor catcher; another person is a brilliant lawyer but a poor teacher. In almost all human endeavours, what one person does easily, someone else finds difficult. The same applies to land and capital. One plot of land is fertile but has no mineral deposits; another plot of land has outstanding views but is infertile. One machine has great precision but is difficult to operate; another is fast but often breaks down.

Although no one excels at everything, some people excel and can outperform others in a large number of activities—perhaps even in all activities. A person who is more productive than others has an **absolute advantage**.

Absolute advantage involves comparing productivities—production per hour—whereas comparative advantage involves comparing opportunity costs.

A person who has an absolute advantage does not have a *comparative* advantage in every activity. John Grisham is a better lawyer and a better author of fast-paced thrillers than most people. He has an absolute advantage in these two activities. But compared to others, he is a better writer than lawyer, so his *comparative* advantage is in writing.

Because ability and resources vary from one person to another, people have different opportunity costs of producing various goods. These differences in opportunity cost are the source of comparative advantage.

Let's explore the idea of comparative advantage by looking at two smoothie bars: one operated by Liz and the other operated by Joe.

Joe's Smoothie Bar Joe produces smoothies and salads in a small, low-tech bar. He has only one blender, and it's a slow, old machine that keeps stopping. Even if Joe uses all his resources to produce smoothies, he can produce only 6 an hour—see Table 2.1. But Joe is good at making salads, and if he uses all his resources in this activity, he can produce 30 salads an hour.

Joe's ability to make smoothies and salads is the same regardless of how he splits an hour between the two tasks. He can make a salad in 2 minutes or a smoothie in 10 minutes. For each additional smoothie Joe produces, he must decrease his production of salads by 5. And for each additional salad he produces, he must decrease his production of smoothies by 1/5 of a smoothie. So

> Joe's opportunity cost of producing 1 smoothie is 5 salads,

and

> Joe's opportunity cost of producing 1 salad is 1/5 of a smoothie.

Joe's customers buy smoothies and salads in equal quantities. So Joe spends 50 minutes of each hour making smoothies and 10 minutes of each hour making salads. With this division of his time, Joe produces 5 smoothies and 5 salads an hour.

Figure 2.6(a) illustrates the production possibilities at Joe's smoothie bar—Joe's *PPF*.

Joe's *PPF* is linear (not outward bowed) because his ability to produce salads and smoothies is the same no matter how he divides his time between the two activities. Joe's opportunity cost of a smoothie is constant—it is the same at all quantities of smoothies produced.

TABLE 2.1   Joe's Production Possibilities

Item	Minutes to produce 1	Quantity per hour
Smoothies	10	6
Salads	2	30

Liz's Smoothie Bar Liz also produces smoothies and salads but in a high-tech bar that is much more productive than Joe's. Liz can turn out either a smoothie or a salad every 2 minutes—see Table 2.2.

If Liz spends all her time making smoothies, she can produce 30 an hour. And if she spends all her time making salads, she can also produce 30 an hour.

Liz's ability to make smoothies and salads, like Joe's, is the same regardless of how she divides her time between the two tasks. She can make a salad in 2 minutes or a smoothie in 2 minutes. For each additional smoothie Liz produces, she must decrease her production of salads by 1. And for each additional salad she produces, she must decrease her production of smoothies by 1. So

> Liz's opportunity cost of producing 1 smoothie is 1 salad,

and

> Liz's opportunity cost of producing 1 salad is 1 smoothie.

TABLE 2.2   Liz's Production Possibilities

Item	Minutes to produce 1	Quantity per hour
Smoothies	2	30
Salads	2	30

Liz's customers buy smoothies and salads in equal quantities, so she splits her time equally between the two items and produces 15 smoothies and 15 salads an hour.

Figure 2.6(b) illustrates the production possibilities at Liz's smoothie bar—Liz's *PPF*.

Like Joe's, Liz's *PPF* is linear because her ability to produce salads and smoothies is the same no matter how she divides her time between the two activities. Liz's opportunity cost of a smoothie is 1 salad at all quantities of smoothies produced.

FIGURE 2.6   The Production Possibilities Frontiers

(a) Joe

(b) Liz

Joe can produce 30 salads per hour, 1 every two minutes, if he produces no smoothies. Or, he can produce 6 smoothies per hour, 1 every 10 minutes, if he produces no salads. Joe's customers buy equal quantities of salads and smoothies, so Joe produces 5 of each. His opportunity cost of a smoothie is 5 salads.

Liz can produce 30 salads or 30 smoothies per hour, 1 of either item every two minutes. Liz's customers buy equal quantities of salads and smoothies, so she produces 15 of each. Liz's opportunity cost of a smoothie is 1 salad.

Joe's Comparative Advantage In which of the two activities does Joe have a comparative advantage? To answer this question, first recall the definition of comparative advantage. A person has a comparative advantage when that person's opportunity cost of producing a good is lower than another person's opportunity cost of producing that same good.

Joe's opportunity cost of producing a salad is only 1/5 of a smoothie, while Liz's opportunity cost of producing a salad is 1 smoothie. So Joe has a comparative advantage in producing salads.

Liz's Comparative Advantage If Joe has a comparative advantage in producing salads, Liz must have a comparative advantage in producing smoothies. Check the numbers. For Joe, a smoothie costs 5 salads, and for Liz, a smoothie costs only 1 salad. So Liz has a comparative advantage in making smoothies.

Achieving the Gains from Trade

Liz and Joe run into each other one evening in a singles bar. After a few minutes of getting acquainted, Liz tells Joe about her amazing smoothie business. Her only problem, she tells Joe, is that she would like to produce more because potential customers leave when her lines get too long.

Joe doesn't want to risk spoiling a blooming relationship by telling Liz about his own struggling business, but he takes the risk. Joe explains to Liz that he spends 50 minutes of every hour making 5 smoothies and 10 minutes making 5 salads. Liz's eyes pop. "Have I got a deal for you!" she exclaims.

Liz's Proposal Here's the deal that Liz sketches on a paper napkin. Joe stops making smoothies and allocates all his time to producing salads; Liz stops making salads and allocates all her time to producing smoothies. That is, they both specialize in producing the good in which they have a comparative advantage. Together they produce 30 smoothies and 30 salads—see Table 2.3(b).

They then trade. Liz suggests trading at a price of 2 salads per smoothie. For her, that is a good deal because she can produce a smoothie at a cost of 1 salad and sell it to Joe for 2 salads. It is also a good deal for Joe because he can produce a salad at a cost of 1/5th of a smoothie and sell it to Liz for 1/2 a smoothie.

Liz explains that any price above 1 salad per smoothie is good for her and any price below 5 salads per smoothie is good for Joe, so a price of 2 salads per smoothie lets them both gain, as she now describes.

TABLE 2.3 Liz and Joe Gain from Trade

(a) Before trade	Liz	Joe
Smoothies	15	5
Salads	15	5

(b) Specialization	Liz	Joe
Smoothies	30	0
Salads	0	30

(c) Trade	Liz	Joe
Smoothies	sell 10	buy 10
Salads	buy 20	sell 20

(d) After trade	Liz	Joe
Smoothies	20	10
Salads	20	10

(e) Gains from trade	Liz	Joe
Smoothies	+5	+5
Salads	+5	+5

At the proposed price, Liz offers to sell Joe 10 smoothies in exchange for 20 salads. Equivalently, Joe sells Liz 20 salads in exchange for 10 smoothies.—see Table 2.3(c).

After this trade, Joe has 10 salads—the 30 he produces minus the 20 he sells to Liz. He also has the 10 smoothies that he buys from Liz. So Joe now has increased the quantities of smoothies and salads that he can sell to his customers—see Table 2.3(d).

Liz has 20 smoothies—the 30 she produces minus the 10 she sells to Joe. She also has the 20 salads that she buys from Joe. Liz has increased the quantities of smoothies and salads that she can sell to her customers—see Table 2.3(d). Both Liz and Joe gain 5 smoothies and 5 salads an hour—see Table 2.3(e).

Illustrating Liz's Idea To illustrate her idea, Liz grabs a fresh napkin and draws the graphs in Fig. 2.7. First, she sketches Joe's *PPF* in part (a) and shows the point at which he is producing before they meet.

FIGURE 2.7   The Gains from Trade

(a) Joe

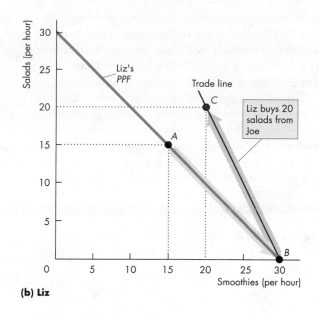

(b) Liz

Initially, Joe produces at point *A* on his *PPF* in part (a), and Liz produces at point *A* on her *PPF* in part (b). Joe's opportunity cost of producing a salad is less than Liz's, so Joe has a comparative advantage in producing salads. Liz's opportunity cost of producing a smoothie is less than Joe's, so Liz has a comparative advantage in producing smoothies.

If Joe specializes in making salads, he produces 30 salads and no smoothies at point *B* on his *PPF*. If Liz specializes

in making smoothies, she produces 30 smoothies and no salads at point *B* on her *PPF*. They exchange salads for smoothies along the red "Trade line." Liz buys salads from Joe for less than her opportunity cost of producing them. Joe buys smoothies from Liz for less than his opportunity cost of producing them. Each goes to point *C*—a point outside his or her *PPF*. With specialization and trade, Joe and Liz gain 5 smoothies and 5 salads each with no extra resources.

────────── **MyEconLab** Animation and Draw Graph ──────────

Recall that he is producing 5 smoothies and 5 salads an hour at point *A*.

She then sketches her own *PPF* in part (b), and marks the point *A* at which she is producing 15 smoothies and 15 salads an hour.

She then shows what happens when they each specialize in producing the good in which they have a comparative advantage. Joe specializes in producing salads and produces 30 salads and no smoothies at point *B* on his *PPF*. Liz specializes in producing smoothies and produces 30 smoothies and no salads at point *B* on her *PPF*.

They then trade smoothies and salads at a price of 2 salads per smoothie or 1/2 a smoothie per salad. The red "Trade line" that Liz draws on each part of the figure illustrates the tradeoff that each faces at the proposed price.

Liz now shows Joe the amazing outcome of her idea. After specializing and trading, Joe gets 10 smoothies and 10 salads at point *C*—a gain of 5 smoothies and 5 salads. He moves to a point *outside*

his *PPF*. And Liz gets 20 smoothies and 20 salads at point *C*—also a gain of 5 smoothies and 5 salads— and moves to a point *outside* her *PPF*.

Despite Liz being more productive than Joe, both gain from specializing at producing the good in which they have a comparative advantage and trading.

◆ REVIEW QUIZ

1   What gives a person a comparative advantage?
2   Distinguish between comparative advantage and absolute advantage.
3   Why do people specialize and trade?
4   What are the gains from specialization and trade?
5   What is the source of the gains from trade?

Work these questions in Study Plan 2.4 and get instant feedback. Do a Key Terms Quiz.   MyEconLab

Economic Coordination

For 7 billion people to specialize and produce millions of different goods and services, individual choices must somehow be coordinated. Two competing coordination systems have been used: central economic planning and markets (see *At Issue*, p. 8).

Central economic planning works badly because economic planners don't know people's production possibilities and preferences, so production ends up *inside* the *PPF* and the wrong things are produced.

Decentralized coordination works best, but to do so it needs four complementary social institutions. They are:

- Firms
- Markets
- Property rights
- Money

Firms

A **firm** is an economic unit that hires factors of production and organizes them to produce and sell goods and services.

Firms coordinate a huge amount of economic activity. For example, Loblaws buys or rents large buildings, equips them with storage shelves and checkout lanes, and hires labour. Loblaws directs the labour and decides what goods to buy and sell.

But Galen Weston would not have become one of the wealthiest people in Canada if Loblaws produced everything that it sells. He became rich by specializing in providing retail services and buying from other firms that specialize in producing goods (just as Liz and Joe did). This trade needs markets.

Markets

In ordinary speech, the word *market* means a place where people buy and sell goods such as fish, meat, fruits, and vegetables.

In economics, a **market** is any arrangement that enables buyers and sellers to get information and to do business with each other. An example is the world oil market, which is not a place but a network of producers, consumers, wholesalers, and brokers who buy and sell oil. In the world oil market, decision makers make deals by using the Internet. Enterprising individuals and firms, each pursuing their own self-interest, have profited by making markets—by

standing ready to buy or sell items in which they specialize. But markets can work only when property rights exist.

Property Rights

The social arrangements that govern the ownership, use, and disposal of anything that people value are called **property rights**. *Real property* includes land and buildings—the things we call property in ordinary speech—and durable goods such as plant and equipment. *Financial property* includes stocks and bonds and money in the bank. *Intellectual property* is the intangible product of creative effort. This type of property includes books, music, computer programs, and inventions of all kinds and is protected by copyrights and patents.

Where property rights are enforced, people have the incentive to specialize and produce the goods and services in which they have a comparative advantage. Where people can steal the production of others, resources are devoted not to production but to protecting possessions.

Money

Money is any commodity or token that is generally acceptable as a means of payment. Liz and Joe don't need money. They can exchange salads and smoothies. In principle, trade in markets can exchange any item for any other item. But you can perhaps imagine how complicated life would be if we exchanged goods for other goods. The "invention" of money makes trading in markets much more efficient.

Circular Flows Through Markets

Trading in markets for goods and services and factors of production creates a circular flow of expenditures and incomes. Figure 2.8 shows the circular flows. Households specialize and choose the quantities of labour, land, capital, and entrepreneurial services to sell or rent to firms. Firms choose the quantities of factors of production to hire. These (red) flows go through the *factor markets*. Households choose the quantities of goods and services to buy, and firms choose the quantities to produce. These (red) flows go through the *goods markets*. Households receive incomes and make expenditures on goods and services (the green flows).

How do markets coordinate all these decisions?

FIGURE 2.8   Circular Flows in the Market Economy

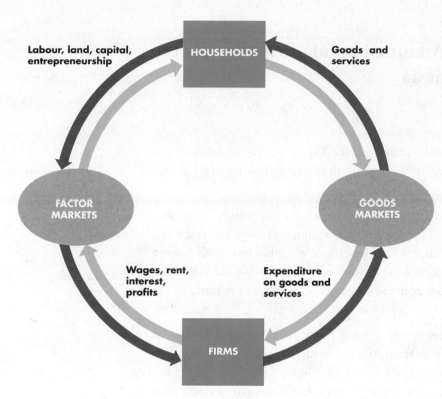

Households and firms make economic choices and markets coordinate these choices.

Households choose the quantities of labour, land, capital, and entrepreneurial services to sell or rent to firms in exchange for wages, rent, interest, and profits. Households also choose how to spend their incomes on the various types of goods and services available.

Firms choose the quantities of factors of production to hire and the quantities of goods and services to produce.

Goods markets and factor markets coordinate these choices of households and firms.

The counterclockwise red flows are real flows—the flow of factors of production from households to firms and the flow of goods and services from firms to households.

The clockwise green flows are the payments for the red flows. They are the flow of incomes from firms to households and the flow of expenditure on goods and services from households to firms.

——— MyEconLab Animation ———

Coordinating Decisions

Markets coordinate decisions through price adjustments. Suppose that some people who want to buy hamburgers are not able to do so. To make buying and selling plans the same, either more hamburgers must be offered for sale or buyers must scale down their appetites (or both). A rise in the price of a hamburger produces this outcome. It encourages producers to offer more hamburgers for sale and encourages some people to change their lunch plans. When the price is right, buying plans and selling plans match.

Alternatively, suppose that more hamburgers are available than people want to buy. In this case, more hamburgers must be bought or fewer hamburgers must be offered for sale (or both). A fall in the price of a hamburger achieves this outcome. It encourages people to buy more hamburgers and it encourages firms to produce a smaller quantity of hamburgers.

REVIEW QUIZ

1 Why are social institutions such as firms, markets, property rights, and money necessary?
2 What are the main functions of markets?
3 What are the flows in the market economy that go from firms to households and the flows from households to firms?

Work these questions in Study Plan 2.5 and get instant feedback. Do a Key Terms Quiz.   MyEconLab

◆ You have now begun to see how economists approach economic questions. You can see all around you the lessons you've learned in this chapter. *Economics in the News* on pp. 46–47 provides an opportunity to apply the *PPF* model to deepen your understanding of why Canada produces more energy than it consumes and exports the rest.

Expanding Production Possibilities

Husky Energy Inc Eyes Atlantic Canada LNG Project to Export to Europe, Indonesia

Financial Post
April 3, 2014

Husky Energy Inc. is mulling a liquefied natural gas (LNG) project in Canada's Atlantic Coast amid interest from European countries looking to diversify their natural gas supplies away from Russia.

"We are constantly looking at ways to monetize some of our gas discoveries," Malcolm Maclean, Husky's senior vice-president for the Atlantic region, said in an interview on the sidelines of a conference in Toronto. "We are looking at a world-class LNG project exporting to Europe or even Indonesia. We are in very early [stages]. We are looking at preliminary studies and need to further appraise some of the discoveries to date. In the Atlantic region, the focus has been very much on oil, not really gas." ...

Natural gas production from the Atlantic may present a new growth avenue for Husky, which has seen its oil production decline from Atlantic fields, despite significant new discoveries. Husky's production from the Atlantic fell to 40,800 barrels per day in the fourth quarter, from 45,700 [barrels a day] during the same period in 2012, partly due to the maturing White Rose fields.

Last year, the company made major discoveries at Bay du Nord and Harpoon in the Atlantic region along with its Norwegian partner Statoil SA.

The companies are accelerating appraisal of the two discoveries, along with the Mizzen field discovery, which is expected to contain as much as 200 million barrels of oil. The Bay du Nord alone may contain 400 million barrels of crude oil, according to a company presentation. ...

Written by Yadullah Hussain. Material reprinted with the express permission of National Post, a division of Postmedia Network Inc.

ESSENCE OF THE STORY

- Husky Energy Inc. is thinking about producing liquefied natural gas (LNG) on the Atlantic Coast for export to Europe and Indonesia.

- The firm's production of oil from its existing Atlantic field is shrinking, but it expects both natural gas and oil production to expand.

- Husky and a partner say they have discovered new Atlantic reserves they believe contain up to 600 million barrels of crude oil.

MyEconLab More Economics in the News

ECONOMIC ANALYSIS

- Husky Energy Inc. is Canada's third-largest producer of oil and gas.

- Canada has hundreds of oil and gas producers, and in 2013 the industry's output was the equivalent of 7 million barrels per day.

- Canada consumed 5 million barrels per day and exported 2 million barrels.

- We can explain Canada's oil and gas production, consumption, and exports using the ideas you have learned in this chapter.

- Figure 1 shows how the discovery of new oil and gas reserves changes Canada's production possibilities.

- The blue curve PPF_0 shows what our production possibilities would be without the discovery of new reserves.

- The discovery of new reserves expands production possibilities and the PPF becomes the red PPF_{2013}. At each quantity of other goods and services (measured on the y-axis), Canada can produce more oil and gas (measured on the x-axis).

- Figure 2 shows the point on PPF_{2013} at which Canada produced in 2013. It produced 7 million barrels (equivalent) of oil and gas and 30 units of other goods and services a day at point A.

- The slope of the PPF at point A measures the opportunity cost of oil and gas—the units of other goods and services that must be forgone to get another million barrels per day.

- Canada can sell oil and gas to other countries and the terms on which that trade occurs is shown by the red "Trade line." This line is like that for trade between Joe and Liz in Fig. 2.7.

- In 2013, Canada consumed 5 million barrels of oil and gas a day at point B, a point outside its PPF, and exported 2 million barrels a day, as shown by the blue arrow.

Figure 1 Oil and Gas Production Possibilities Expand

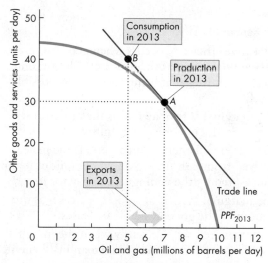

Figure 2 Production, Exports, and Consumption of Oil and Gas in 2013

SUMMARY

Key Points

Production Possibilities and Opportunity Cost (pp. 32–34)

- The production possibilities frontier is the boundary between production levels that are attainable and those that are not attainable when all the available resources are used to their limits.
- Production efficiency occurs at points on the production possibilities frontier.
- Along the production possibilities frontier, the opportunity cost of producing more of one good is the amount of the other good that must be given up.
- The opportunity cost of all goods increases as the production of the good increases.

Working Problems 1 to 3 will give you a better understanding of production possibilities and opportunity cost.

Using Resources Efficiently (pp. 35–37)

- Allocative efficiency occurs when goods and services are produced at the least possible cost and in the quantities that bring the greatest possible benefit.
- The marginal cost of a good is the opportunity cost of producing one more unit of it.
- The marginal benefit from a good is the benefit received from consuming one more unit of it and is measured by the willingness to pay for it.
- The marginal benefit of a good decreases as the amount of the good available increases.
- Resources are used efficiently when the marginal cost of each good is equal to its marginal benefit.

Working Problems 4 to 6 will give you a better understanding of the efficient use of resources.

Economic Growth (pp. 38–39)

- Economic growth, which is the expansion of production possibilities, results from capital accumulation and technological change.
- The opportunity cost of economic growth is forgone current consumption.
- The benefit of economic growth is increased future consumption.

Working Problem 7 will give you a better understanding of economic growth.

Gains from Trade (pp. 40–43)

- A person has a comparative advantage in producing a good if that person can produce the good at a lower opportunity cost than everyone else.
- People gain by specializing in the activity in which they have a comparative advantage and trading with others.

Working Problems 8 and 9 will give you a better understanding of the gains from trade.

Economic Coordination (pp. 44–45)

- Firms coordinate a large amount of economic activity, but there is a limit to the efficient size of a firm.
- Markets coordinate the economic choices of people and firms.
- Markets can work efficiently only when property rights exist.
- Money makes trading in markets more efficient.

Working Problem 10 will give you a better understanding of economic coordination.

Key Terms

Absolute advantage, 40
Allocative efficiency, 35
Capital accumulation, 38
Comparative advantage, 40
Economic growth, 38
Firm, 44

Marginal benefit, 36
Marginal benefit curve, 36
Marginal cost, 35
Market, 44
Money, 44
Opportunity cost, 33

MyEconLab Key Terms Quiz

Preferences, 36
Production efficiency, 33
Production possibilities frontier, 32
Property rights, 44
Technological change, 38

WORKED PROBLEM

MyEconLab   You can work this problem in Chapter 2 Study Plan.

Leisure Island has 50 hours of labour a day that it can use to produce entertainment and good food. The table shows the maximum quantity of each good that it can produce with different quantities of labour.

Labour (hours)	Entertainment (shows per week)		Good food (meals per week)
0	0	or	0
10	2	or	5
20	4	or	9
30	6	or	12
40	8	or	14
50	10	or	15

Questions

1. Can Leisure Island produce 4 shows and 14 meals a week?

2. If Leisure Island produces 4 shows and 9 meals a week, is production efficient?

3. If Leisure Island produces 8 shows and 5 meals a week, do the people of Leisure Island face a tradeoff?

4. Suppose that Leisure Island produces 4 shows and 12 meals a week. Calculate the opportunity cost of producing 2 additional shows a week.

Solutions

1. To produce 4 shows it would use 20 hours and to produce 14 meals it would use 40 hours, so to produce 4 shows and 14 meals a week, Leisure Island would use 60 hours of labour. Leisure Island has only 50 hours of labour available, so it cannot produce 4 shows and 14 meals a week.

Key Point: Production is *unattainable* if it uses more resources than are available.

2. When Leisure Island produces 4 shows it uses 20 hours of labour and when it produces 9 meals it uses 20 hours. In total, it uses 40 hours, which is *less than* the 50 hours of labour available. So Leisure Island's production is not efficient.

Key Point: Production is *efficient* only if the economy uses all its resources.

3. When Leisure Island produces 8 shows and 5 meals, it uses 50 hours of labour. Leisure Island is using all its resources, so to produce more of either good, it would face a tradeoff.

Key Point: An economy faces a *tradeoff* only when it uses all the available resources.

4. When Leisure Island produces 4 shows and 12 meals a week, it uses 50 hours of labour. To produce 2 additional shows a week, Leisure Island faces a tradeoff and incurs an opportunity cost.

To produce 2 additional shows a week, Leisure Island moves 10 hours of labour from good food production, which decreases the quantity of meals from 12 to 9 a week—a decrease of 3 meals. That is, to get 2 additional shows a week Leisure Island *must give up* 3 meals a week. The opportunity cost of the 2 additional shows is 3 meals a week.

Key Point: When an economy is using all its resources and it decides to increase production of one good, it incurs an opportunity cost equal to the quantity of the good that it *must* forgo.

Key Figure

Each row of the following table sets out the combination of shows and meals that Leisure Island can produce in a week when it uses 50 hours of labour.

	Entertainment (shows per week)		Good food (meals per week)
A	0	and	15
B	2	and	14
C	4	and	12
D	6	and	9
E	8	and	5
F	10	and	0

Points *A* through *F* plot these combinations of shows and meals. The blue curve through these points is Leisure Island's *PPF*. Point *X* (4 shows and 14 meals in Question 1) is unattainable; Point *Y* (4 shows and 9 meals in Question 2) is inefficient. Point *E* (8 shows and 5 meals in Question 3) is on the *PPF* and the arrow illustrates the tradeoff and the calculation of opportunity cost of 2 additional shows a week.

MyEconLab Interactive Animation

STUDY PLAN PROBLEMS AND APPLICATIONS

MyEconLab   You can work Problems 1 to 10 in Chapter 2 Study Plan and get instant feedback.

Production Possibilities and Opportunity Cost (Study Plan 2.1)

Use the following information to work Problems 1 to 3. Brazil produces ethanol from sugar, and the land used to grow sugar can be used to grow food crops. The table sets out Brazil's production possibilities for ethanol and food crops:

Ethanol (barrels per day)		Food crops (tonnes per day)
70	and	0
64	and	1
54	and	2
40	and	3
22	and	4
0	and	5

1. a. Draw a graph of Brazil's *PPF* and explain how your graph illustrates scarcity.

    b. If Brazil produces 40 barrels of ethanol a day, how much food must it produce to achieve production efficiency?

    c. Why does Brazil face a tradeoff on its *PPF*?

2. a. If Brazil increases ethanol production from 40 barrels per day to 54 barrels a day, what is the opportunity cost of the additional ethanol?

    b. If Brazil increases food production from 2 tonnes per day to 3 tonnes per day, what is the opportunity cost of the additional food?

    c. What is the relationship between your answers to parts (a) and (b)?

3. Does Brazil face an increasing opportunity cost of ethanol? What feature of Brazil's *PPF* illustrates increasing opportunity cost?

Using Resources Efficiently (Study Plan 2.2)

Use the table above to work Problems 4 and 5.

4. Define marginal cost and calculate Brazil's marginal cost of producing a tonne of food when the quantity produced is 2.5 tonnes per day.

5. Define marginal benefit. Explain how it is measured and why the data in the table does not enable you to calculate Brazil's marginal benefit from food.

6. Distinguish between *production efficiency* and *allocative efficiency*. Explain why many production possibilities achieve production efficiency but only one achieves allocative efficiency.

Economic Growth (Study Plan 2.3)

7. A farm grows wheat and produces pork. The marginal cost of producing each of these products increases as more of it is produced.

    a. Make a graph that illustrates the farm's *PPF*.

    b. The farm adopts a new technology that allows it to use fewer resources to fatten pigs. On your graph sketch the impact of the new technology on the farm's *PPF*.

    c. With the farm using the new technology described in part (b), has the opportunity cost of producing a tonne of wheat increased, decreased, or remained the same? Explain and illustrate your answer.

    d. Is the farm more efficient with the new technology than it was with the old one? Why?

Gains from Trade (Study Plan 2.4)

8. In an hour, Sue can produce 40 caps or 4 jackets and Tessa can produce 80 caps or 4 jackets.

    a. Calculate Sue's opportunity cost of producing a cap.

    b. Calculate Tessa's opportunity cost of producing a cap.

    c. Who has a comparative advantage in producing caps?

    d. If Sue and Tessa specialize in producing the good in which they have a comparative advantage and then trade 1 jacket for 15 caps, who gains from the specialization and trade?

9. Suppose that Tessa buys a new machine that enables her to make 20 jackets an hour. (She can still make only 80 caps per hour.)

    a. Who now has a comparative advantage in producing jackets?

    b. Can Sue and Tessa still gain from trade?

    c. Would Sue and Tessa still be willing to trade 1 jacket for 15 caps? Explain your answer.

Economic Coordination (Study Plan 2.5)

10. For 50 years, Cuba has had a centrally planned economy in which the government makes the big decisions on how resources will be allocated.

    a. Why would you expect Cuba's production possibilities (per person) to be smaller than those of Canada?

    b. What are the social institutions that Cuba might lack that help Canada to achieve allocative efficiency?

ADDITIONAL PROBLEMS AND APPLICATIONS

MyEconLab   You can work these problems in MyEconLab if assigned by your instructor.

Production Possibilities and Opportunity Cost

Use the following table to work Problems 11 and 12.
Suppose that Yucatan's production possibilities are:

Food (kilograms per month)		Sunscreen (litres per month)
300	and	0
200	and	50
100	and	100
0	and	150

11. a. Draw a graph of Yucatan's *PPF* and explain how your graph illustrates a tradeoff.
    b. If Yucatan produces 150 kilograms of food per month, how much sunscreen must it produce if it achieves production efficiency?
    c. What is Yucatan's opportunity cost of producing (i) 1 kilogram of food and (ii) 1 litre of sunscreen?
    d. What is the relationship between your answers to part (c)?

12. What feature of a *PPF* illustrates increasing opportunity cost? Explain why Yucatan's opportunity cost does or does not increase.

Using Resources Efficiently

13. In Problem 11, what is the marginal cost of 1 kilogram of food in Yucatan when the quantity produced is 150 kilograms per day? What is special about the marginal cost of food in Yucatan?

14. The table describes the preferences in Yucatan.

Sunscreen (litres per month)	Willingness to pay (kilograms of food per litre)
25	3
75	2
125	1

    a. What is the marginal benefit from sunscreen and how is it measured?
    b. Use the table in Problem 11. What does Yucatan produce to achieve allocative efficiency?

15. **Downtown Music Stores Squeezed out of Business**
    Music retailing is changing: Sony Music and Amazon are selling online, discount stores are selling at low prices, and downtown music retailers are all struggling.
    Source: *The Economist*, January 20, 2007
    a. Draw the *PPF* curves for downtown music retailers and online music retailers before and after the Internet became available.

    b. Draw the marginal cost and marginal benefit curves for downtown music retailers and online music retailers before and after the Internet became available.
    c. Explain how changes in production possibilities, preferences, or both have changed the way in which recorded music is retailed.

Use the following news clip to work Problems 16 and 17.

Malaria Eradication Back on the Table

In response to the Gates Malaria Forum in October 2007, countries are debating the pros and cons of eradication. Dr. Arata Kochi of the World Health Organization believes that with enough money malaria cases could be cut by 90 percent, but it would be very expensive to eliminate the remaining 10 percent of cases, so countries should not strive to eradicate malaria.
    Source: *The New York Times*, March 4, 2008

16. Is Dr. Kochi talking about *production efficiency* or *allocative efficiency* or both?

17. Make a graph with the percentage of malaria cases eliminated on the *x*-axis and the marginal cost and marginal benefit of driving down malaria cases on the *y*-axis. On your graph:
    (i) Draw a marginal cost curve and marginal benefit curve that are consistent with Dr. Kochi's opinion.
    (ii) Identify the quantity of malaria eradicated that achieves allocative efficiency.

Economic Growth

18. Capital accumulation and technological change bring economic growth: Production that was unattainable yesterday becomes attainable today; production that is unattainable today will become attainable tomorrow. Why doesn't economic growth bring an end to scarcity one day?

19. **Toyota Plans to Build a Better Company**
    Toyota will continue to produce 3 million cars per year and will use the balance of its resources to upgrade its workers' skills and create new technology. In three years' time, Toyota plans to produce better cars and be more productive.
    Source: *Financial Post*, April 7, 2014
    a. What is the opportunity cost of Toyota upgrading its workers' skills and creating new technology?

b. Sketch Toyota's *PPF* and mark its production point in 2014. Now show on your graph Toyota's *PPF* in 2018.

Gains from Trade

Use the following data to work Problems 20 and 21.

Kim can produce 40 pies or 400 cakes an hour. Liam can produce 100 pies or 200 cakes an hour.

20. a. Calculate Kim's opportunity cost of a pie and Liam's opportunity cost of a pie.
    b. If each spends 30 minutes of each hour producing pies and 30 minutes producing cakes, how many pies and cakes does each produce?
    c. Who has a comparative advantage in producing (i) pies and (ii) cakes?

21. a. Draw a graph of Kim's *PPF* and Liam's *PPF* and show the point at which each produces when they spend 30 minutes of each hour producing pies and 30 minutes producing cakes.
    b. On your graph, show what Kim produces and what Liam produces when they specialize.
    c. When they specialize and trade, what are the total gains from trade?
    d. If Kim and Liam share the total gains equally, what trade takes place between them?

22. Tony and Patty produce skis and snowboards. The tables show their production possibilities. Tony produces 5 snowboards and 40 skis a week; Patty produces 10 snowboards and 5 skis a week.

Tony's Production Possibilities

Snowboards (units per week)		Skis (units per week)
25	and	0
20	and	10
15	and	20
10	and	30
5	and	40
0	and	50

Patty's Production Possibilities

Snowboards (units per week)		Skis (units per week)
20	and	0
10	and	5
0	and	10

a. Who has a comparative advantage in producing (i) snowboards and (ii) skis?
b. If Tony and Patty specialize and trade 1 snowboard for 1 ski, what are the gains from trade?

Economic Coordination

23. On a graph of the circular flows in the market economy indicate the real and money flows in which the following items belong:
    a. You buy an iPad from the Apple Store.
    b. Apple Inc. pays the designers of the iPad.
    c. Apple Inc. decides to expand and rents an adjacent building.
    d. You buy a new e-book from Amazon.
    e. Apple Inc. hires a student as an intern during the summer.

Economics in the News

24. After you have studied *Economics in the News* on pp. 46–47, answer the following questions.
    a. How does the discovery of new oil and gas reserves change Canada's *PPF*?
    b. How do technological advances in the production of other goods and services change Canada's *PPF*?
    c. How are Husky's discoveries changing Canada's opportunity cost of producing oil and gas?
    d. When technological advances in the production of other goods and services occur, how does the opportunity cost of producing oil and gas change? Does it increase or decrease?

25. **Lots of Little Screens**

    Inexpensive broadband access has created a generation of television producers for whom the Internet is their native medium. As they redirect the focus from TV to computers, cellphones, and iPods, the video market is developing into an open digital network.

    Source: *The New York Times,* December 2, 2007

    a. How has inexpensive broadband changed the production possibilities of video entertainment and other goods and services?
    b. Sketch a *PPF* for video entertainment and other goods and services before broadband.
    c. Show how the arrival of inexpensive broadband has changed the *PPF*.
    d. Sketch a marginal benefit curve for video entertainment.
    e. Show how the new generation of TV producers for whom the Internet is their native medium might have changed the marginal benefit from video entertainment.
    f. Explain how the efficient quantity of video entertainment has changed.

Your Economic Revolution

Three periods in human history stand out as ones of economic revolution. The first, the *Agricultural Revolution,* occurred 10,000 years ago. In what is today Iraq, people learned to domesticate animals and plant crops. People stopped roaming in search of food and settled in villages, towns, and cities where they specialized in the activities in which they had a comparative advantage and developed markets in which to exchange their products. Wealth increased enormously.

Economics was born during the *Industrial Revolution,* which began in England during the 1760s. For the first time, people began to apply science and create new technologies for the manufacture of textiles and iron, to create steam engines, and to boost the output of farms.

You are studying economics at a time that future historians will call the *Information Revolution.* Over the entire world, people are embracing new information technologies and prospering on an unprecedented scale.

During all three economic revolutions, many have prospered but others have been left behind. It is the range of human progress that poses the greatest question for economics and the one that Adam Smith addressed in the first work of economic science: What causes the differences in wealth among nations?

Many people had written about economics before **Adam Smith**, *but he made economics a science. Born in 1723 in Kirkcaldy, a small fishing town near Edinburgh, Scotland, Smith was the only child of the town's customs officer. Lured from his professorship (he was a full professor at 28) by a wealthy Scottish duke who gave him a pension of £300 a year—10 times the average income at that time—Smith devoted 10 years to writing his masterpiece:* An Inquiry into the Nature and Causes of the **Wealth of Nations***, published in 1776.*

Why, Adam Smith asked, are some nations wealthy while others are poor? He was pondering these questions at the height of the Industrial Revolution, and he answered by emphasizing the power of the division of labour and free markets in raising labour productivity.

To illustrate his argument, Adam Smith described two pin factories. In the first, one person, using the hand tools available in the 1770s, could make 20 pins a day. In the other, by using those same hand tools but breaking the process into a number of individually small operations in which people specialize—by the division of labour—10 people could make a staggering 48,000 pins a day. One draws out

Every individual who intends only his own gain is led by an invisible hand to promote an end (the public good) which was no part of his intention.

ADAM SMITH
The Wealth of Nations

the wire, another straightens it, a third cuts it, a fourth points it, a fifth grinds it. Three specialists make the head, and a fourth attaches it. Finally, the pin is polished and packaged.

But a large market is needed to support the division of labour: One factory employing 10 workers would need to sell more than 15 million pins a year to stay in business!

ESTHER DUFLO is the Abdul Latif Jameel Professor of Poverty Alleviation and Development Economics at the Massachusetts Institute of Technology. Among her many honours are the 2010 John Bates Clark Medal for the best economist under 40 and the Financial Times and Goldman Sachs Business Book of the Year Award in 2011 for her book (with Abhijit Banerjee) *Poor Economics: A Radical Rethinking of the Way to Fight Global Poverty*. Professor Duflo's research seeks to advance our understanding of the economic choices of the extremely poor by conducting massive real-world experiments.

Professor Duflo was an undergraduate student of history and economics at École Normale Supérieure and completed a master's degree at DELTA in Paris before moving to the United States. She earned her Ph.D. in economics at MIT in 1999.

Michael Parkin and Robin Bade talked with her about her work, which advances our understanding of the economic choices and condition of the very poor.

Professor Duflo, what's the story about how you became an economist and in particular the architect of experiments designed to understand the economic choices of the very poor?

When I was a kid, I was exposed to many stories and images of poor children: through my mothers' engagement as a doctor in a small NGO dealing with child victims of war and through books and stories about children living all around the world. I remember asking myself how I could justify my luck of being born where I was. I had a very exaggerated idea of what it was to be poor, but this idea caused sufficient discomfort that I knew I had to do something about it, if I could. Quite by accident, I discovered that economics was the way in which I could actually be useful: While spending a year in Russia teaching French and studying history, I realized that academic economists have the ability to intervene in the world while keeping enough sanity to analyze it. I thought this would be ideal for me and I have never regretted it. I have the best job in the world.

> ... imagine living on under a dollar a day after your rent is paid in Seattle or Denver. Not easy!

The very poor who you study are people who live on $1 a day or $2 a day. ... Is $1 a day a true measure that includes everything these poor people consume?

For defining the poverty line, we don't include the cost of housing. The poor also get free goods, sometimes of bad quality (education, healthcare) and the value of those is also not included. Other than that, yes, it is everything.

Moreover, you have to realize this is everything, taking into account the fact that life is much cheaper in many poor countries because salaries are lower, so anything that is made and consumed locally (e.g., a haircut) is cheaper.

For example, in India, the purchasing power of a dollar (in terms of the real goods you can buy) is about 3 times what it is in the United States. So the poverty line we use for India is 33 cents per day, not a dollar.

All told, you really have to imagine living on under a dollar a day after your rent is paid in Seattle or Denver. Not easy!

*Read the full interview with Esther Duflo in MyEconLab.

3

DEMAND AND SUPPLY

After studying this chapter, you will be able to:

◆ Describe a competitive market and think about a price as an opportunity cost

◆ Explain the influences on demand

◆ Explain the influences on supply

◆ Explain how demand and supply determine prices and quantities bought and sold

◆ Use the demand and supply model to make predictions about changes in prices and quantities

A disease that kills banana trees is jumping continents and left unchecked will bring a big drop in banana production. What will happen to the price of bananas if the disease isn't contained? The demand and supply model answers this question.

This model that you're about to study is the main tool of economics. It explains how prices are determined and how they guide the use of resources to influence *What*, *How*, and *For Whom* goods and services are produced.

Economics in the News at the end of the chapter answers the question about the price of bananas.

◢ Markets and Prices

When you need a new pair of running shoes, want a bagel and a latte, plan to upgrade your cellphone, or need to fly home for Thanksgiving, you must find a place where people sell those items or offer those services. The place in which you find them is a *market*. You learned in Chapter 2 (p. 44) that a market is any arrangement that enables buyers and sellers to get information and to do business with each other.

A market has two sides: buyers and sellers. There are markets for *goods* such as apples and hiking boots, for *services* such as haircuts and tennis lessons, for *factors of production* such as computer programmers and earthmovers, and for other manufactured *inputs* such as memory chips and auto parts. There are also markets for money such as Japanese yen and for financial securities such as Yahoo! stock. Only our imagination limits what can be traded in markets.

Some markets are physical places where buyers and sellers meet and where an auctioneer or a broker helps to determine the prices. Examples of this type of market are live car and house auctions and the wholesale fish, meat, and produce markets.

Some markets are groups of people spread around the world who never meet and know little about each other but are connected through the Internet or by telephone and fax. Examples are the e-commerce markets and the currency markets.

But most markets are unorganized collections of buyers and sellers. You do most of your trading in this type of market. An example is the market for basketball shoes. The buyers in this $3 billion-a-year market are the 45 million Canadians and Americans who play basketball (or who want to make a fashion statement). The sellers are the tens of thousands of retail sports equipment and foot-wear stores. Each buyer can visit several different stores, and each seller knows that the buyer has a choice of stores.

Markets vary in the intensity of competition that buyers and sellers face. In this chapter, we're going to study a **competitive market**—a market that has many buyers and many sellers, so no single buyer or seller can influence the price.

Producers offer items for sale only if the price is high enough to cover their opportunity cost. And consumers respond to changing opportunity cost by seeking cheaper alternatives to expensive items.

We are going to study how people respond to *prices* and the forces that determine prices. But to pursue these tasks, we need to understand the relationship between a price and an opportunity cost.

In everyday life, the *price* of an object is the number of dollars that must be given up in exchange for it. Economists refer to this price as the **money price**.

The *opportunity cost* of an action is the highest-valued alternative forgone. If, when you buy a cup of coffee, the highest-valued thing you forgo is some gum, then the opportunity cost of the coffee is the *quantity* of gum forgone. We can calculate the quantity of gum forgone from the money prices of the coffee and the gum.

If the money price of coffee is $1 a cup and the money price of gum is 50¢ a pack, then the opportunity cost of one cup of coffee is two packs of gum. To calculate this opportunity cost, we divide the price of a cup of coffee by the price of a pack of gum and find the *ratio* of one price to the other. The ratio of one price to another is called a **relative price**, and a *relative price is an opportunity cost*.

We can express the relative price of coffee in terms of gum or any other good. The normal way of expressing a relative price is in terms of a "basket" of all goods and services. To calculate this relative price, we divide the money price of a good by the money price of a "basket" of all goods (called a *price index*). The resulting relative price tells us the opportunity cost of the good in terms of how much of the "basket" we must give up to buy it.

The demand and supply model that we are about to study determines *relative prices,* and the word "price" means *relative* price. When we predict that a price will fall, we do not mean that its *money* price will fall—although it might. We mean that its *relative* price will fall. That is, its price will fall *relative* to the average price of other goods and services.

◢ REVIEW QUIZ

1 What is the distinction between a money price and a relative price?
2 Explain why a relative price is an opportunity cost.
3 Think of examples of goods whose relative price has risen or fallen by a large amount.

Work these questions in Study Plan 3.1 and get instant feedback. Do a Key Terms Quiz. MyEconLab

Let's begin our study of demand and supply, starting with demand.

Demand

If you demand something, then you:

1. Want it.
2. Can afford it.
3. Plan to buy it.

Wants are the unlimited desires or wishes that people have for goods and services. How many times have you thought that you would like something "if only you could afford it" or "if it weren't so expensive"? Scarcity guarantees that many—perhaps most—of our wants will never be satisfied. Demand reflects a decision about which wants to satisfy.

The **quantity demanded** of a good or service is the amount that consumers plan to buy during a given time period at a particular price. The quantity demanded is not necessarily the same as the quantity actually bought. Sometimes the quantity demanded exceeds the amount of goods available, so the quantity bought is less than the quantity demanded.

The quantity demanded is measured as an amount per unit of time. For example, suppose that you buy one cup of coffee a day. The quantity of coffee that you demand can be expressed as 1 cup per day, 7 cups per week, or 365 cups per year.

Many factors influence buying plans, and one of them is the price. We look first at the relationship between the quantity demanded of a good and its price. To study this relationship, we keep all other influences on buying plans the same and we ask: How, other things remaining the same, does the quantity demanded of a good change as its price changes?

The law of demand provides the answer.

The Law of Demand

The **law of demand** states:

> Other things remaining the same, the higher the price of a good, the smaller is the quantity demanded; and the lower the price of a good, the greater is the quantity demanded.

Why does a higher price reduce the quantity demanded? For two reasons:

- Substitution effect
- Income effect

Substitution Effect When the price of a good rises, other things remaining the same, its *relative* price—its opportunity cost—rises. Although each good is unique, it has *substitutes*—other goods that can be used in its place. As the opportunity cost of a good rises, the incentive to economize on its use and switch to a substitute becomes stronger.

Income Effect When a price rises, other things remaining the same, the price rises *relative* to income. Faced with a higher price and an unchanged income, people cannot afford to buy all the things they previously bought. They must decrease the quantities demanded of at least some goods and services. Normally, the good whose price has increased will be one of the goods that people buy less of.

To see the substitution effect and the income effect at work, think about the effects of a change in the price of an energy bar. Several different goods are substitutes for an energy bar. For example, an energy drink could be consumed instead of an energy bar.

Suppose that an energy bar initially sells for $3 and then its price falls to $1.50. People now substitute energy bars for energy drinks—the substitution effect. And with a budget that now has some slack from the lower price of an energy bar, people buy even more energy bars—the income effect. The quantity of energy bars demanded increases for these two reasons.

Now suppose that an energy bar initially sells for $3 and then the price doubles to $6. People now buy fewer energy bars and more energy drinks—the substitution effect. And faced with a tighter budget, people buy even fewer energy bars—the income effect. The quantity of energy bars demanded decreases for these two reasons.

Demand Curve and Demand Schedule

You are now about to study one of the two most used curves in economics: the demand curve. You are also going to encounter one of the most critical distinctions: the distinction between *demand* and *quantity demanded*.

The term **demand** refers to the entire relationship between the price of a good and the quantity demanded of that good. Demand is illustrated by the demand curve and the demand schedule. The term *quantity demanded* refers to a point on a demand curve—the quantity demanded at a particular price.

Figure 3.1 shows the demand curve for energy bars. A **demand curve** shows the relationship between the quantity demanded of a good and its price when all other influences on consumers' planned purchases remain the same.

The table in Fig. 3.1 is the demand schedule for energy bars. A *demand schedule* lists the quantities demanded at each price when all the other influences on consumers' planned purchases remain the same. For example, if the price of a bar is 50¢, the quantity demanded is 22 million a week. If the price is $2.50, the quantity demanded is 5 million a week. The other rows of the table show the quantities demanded at prices of $1.00, $1.50, and $2.00.

We graph the demand schedule as a demand curve with the quantity demanded on the *x*-axis and the price on the *y*-axis. The points on the demand curve labelled *A* through *E* correspond to the rows of the demand schedule. For example, point *A* on the graph shows a quantity demanded of 22 million energy bars a week at a price of 50¢ a bar.

Willingness and Ability to Pay Another way of looking at the demand curve is as a willingness-and-ability-to-pay curve. The willingness and ability to pay is a measure of *marginal benefit.*

If a small quantity is available, the highest price that someone is willing and able to pay for one more unit is high. But as the quantity available increases, the marginal benefit of each additional unit falls and the highest price that someone is willing and able to pay also falls along the demand curve.

In Fig. 3.1, if only 5 million energy bars are available each week, the highest price that someone is willing to pay for the 5 millionth bar is $2.50. But if 22 million energy bars are available each week, someone is willing to pay 50¢ for the last bar bought.

A Change in Demand

When any factor that influences buying plans changes, other than the price of the good, there is a **change in demand**. Figure 3.2 illustrates an increase in demand. When demand increases, the demand curve shifts rightward and the quantity demanded at each price is greater. For example, at $2.50 a bar, the quantity demanded on the original (blue) demand curve is 5 million energy bars a week. On the new (red) demand curve, at $2.50 a bar, the quantity demanded is 15 million bars a week. Look closely at the numbers in the table and check that the quantity demanded at each price is greater.

FIGURE 3.1   The Demand Curve

	Price (dollars per bar)	Quantity demanded (millions of bars per week)
A	0.50	22
B	1.00	15
C	1.50	10
D	2.00	7
E	2.50	5

The table shows a demand schedule for energy bars. At a price of 50¢ a bar, 22 million bars a week are demanded; at a price of $1.50 a bar, 10 million bars a week are demanded. The demand curve shows the relationship between quantity demanded and price, other things remaining the same. The demand curve slopes downward: As the price falls, the quantity demanded increases.

The demand curve can be read in two ways. For a given price, the demand curve tells us the quantity that people plan to buy. For example, at a price of $1.50 a bar, people plan to buy 10 million bars a week. For a given quantity, the demand curve tells us the maximum price that consumers are willing and able to pay for the last bar available. For example, the maximum price that consumers will pay for the 15 millionth bar is $1.00.

FIGURE 3.2   An Increase in Demand

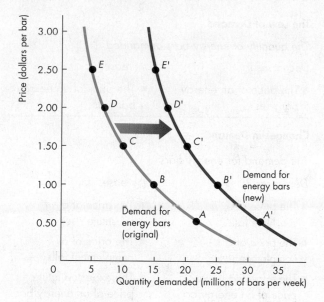

Original demand schedule Original income		New demand schedule New higher income	
Price (dollars per bar)	**Quantity demanded** (millions of bars per week)	**Price** (dollars per bar)	**Quantity demanded** (millions of bars per week)
A 0.50	22	A' 0.50	32
B 1.00	15	B' 1.00	25
C 1.50	10	C' 1.50	20
D 2.00	7	D' 2.00	17
E 2.50	5	E' 2.50	15

A change in any influence on buying plans other than the price of the good itself results in a new demand schedule and a shift of the demand curve. A change in income changes the demand for energy bars. At a price of $1.50 a bar, 10 million bars a week are demanded at the original income (row C of the table) and 20 million bars a week are demanded at the new higher income (row C'). A rise in income increases the demand for energy bars. The demand curve shifts *rightward*, as shown by the shift arrow and the resulting red curve.

_____ **MyEconLab** Animation _____

Six main factors bring changes in demand. They are changes in:

- The prices of related goods
- Expected future prices
- Income
- Expected future income and credit
- Population
- Preferences

Prices of Related Goods The quantity of energy bars that consumers plan to buy depends in part on the prices of substitutes for energy bars. A **substitute** is a good that can be used in place of another good. For example, a bus ride is a substitute for a train ride; a hamburger is a substitute for a hot dog; and an energy drink is a substitute for an energy bar. If the price of a substitute for an energy bar rises, people buy less of the substitute and more energy bars. For example, if the price of an energy drink rises, people buy fewer energy drinks and more energy bars. The demand for energy bars increases.

The quantity of energy bars that people plan to buy also depends on the prices of complements with energy bars. A **complement** is a good that is used in conjunction with another good. Hamburgers and fries are complements, and so are energy bars and exercise. If the price of an hour at the gym falls, people buy more gym time *and more* energy bars.

Expected Future Prices If the expected future price of a good rises and if the good can be stored, the opportunity cost of obtaining the good for future use is lower today than it will be in the future when people expect the price to be higher. So people retime their purchases—they substitute over time. They buy more of the good now before its price is expected to rise (and less afterward), so the demand for the good today increases.

For example, suppose that a Florida frost damages the season's orange crop. You expect the price of orange juice to rise, so you fill your freezer with enough frozen juice to get you through the next six months. Your current demand for frozen orange juice has increased, and your future demand has decreased.

Similarly, if the expected future price of a good falls, the opportunity cost of buying the good today is high relative to what it is expected to be in the future. So again, people retime their purchases. They buy less of the good now before its price is expected to fall, so the demand for the good decreases today and increases in the future.

Computer prices are constantly falling, and this fact poses a dilemma. Will you buy a new computer now, in time for the start of the school year, or will you wait until the price has fallen some more? Because people expect computer prices to keep falling, the current demand for computers is less (and the future demand is greater) than it otherwise would be.

Income Consumers' income influences demand. When income increases, consumers buy more of most goods; and when income decreases, consumers buy less of most goods. Although an increase in income leads to an increase in the demand for *most* goods, it does not lead to an increase in the demand for *all* goods. A **normal good** is one for which demand increases as income increases. An **inferior good** is one for which demand decreases as income increases. As incomes increase, the demand for air travel (a normal good) increases and the demand for long-distance bus trips (an inferior good) decreases.

Expected Future Income and Credit When expected future income increases or credit becomes easier to get, demand for a good might increase now. For example, a salesperson gets the news that she will receive a big bonus at the end of the year, so she goes into debt and buys a new car right now, rather than waiting until she receives the bonus.

Population Demand also depends on the size and the age structure of the population. The larger the population, the greater is the demand for all goods and services; the smaller the population, the smaller is the demand for all goods and services.

For example, the demand for parking spaces, running shoes, movies, or just about anything that you can imagine is much greater in the Greater Toronto Area (population 6 million) than it is in Thunder Bay, Ontario (population 146,000).

Also, the larger the proportion of the population in an age group, the greater is the demand for the goods and services used by that group. For example, in 2010, there were 2.3 million 20-to-24-year-olds in Canada compared with 2.1 million in 2000. As a result, the demand for university places in 2010 was greater than in 2000. During this period, the number of Canadians aged 90 years more than doubled and the demand for nursing home services increased.

TABLE 3.1   The Demand for Energy Bars

The Law of Demand

The quantity of energy bars demanded

Decreases if:	Increases if:
■ The price of an energy bar rises	■ The price of an energy bar falls

Changes in Demand

The demand for energy bars

Decreases if:	Increases if:
■ The price of a substitute falls	■ The price of a substitute rises
■ The price of a complement rises	■ The price of a complement falls
■ The expected future price of an energy bar falls	■ The expected future price of an energy bar rises
■ Income falls*	■ Income rises*
■ Expected future income falls or credit becomes harder to get*	■ Expected future income rises or credit becomes easier to get*
■ The population decreases	■ The population increases

*An energy bar is a normal good.

Preferences Demand depends on preferences. *Preferences* determine the value that people place on each good and service. Preferences depend on such things as the weather, information, and fashion. For example, greater health and fitness awareness has shifted preferences in favour of energy bars, so the demand for energy bars has increased.

Table 3.1 summarizes the influences on demand and the direction of those influences.

A Change in the Quantity Demanded Versus a Change in Demand

Changes in the influences on buying plans bring either a change in the quantity demanded or a change in demand. Equivalently, they bring either a movement along the demand curve or a shift of the demand curve. The distinction between a change in the quantity demanded and a change in demand is the same as that between a movement along the demand curve and a shift of the demand curve.

A point on the demand curve shows the quantity demanded at a given price, so a movement along the demand curve shows a **change in the quantity demanded**. The entire demand curve shows demand, so a shift of the demand curve shows a *change in demand*. Figure 3.3 illustrates these distinctions.

Movement Along the Demand Curve If the price of the good changes but no other influence on buying plans changes, we illustrate the effect as a movement along the demand curve.

A fall in the price of a good increases the quantity demanded of it. In Fig. 3.3, we illustrate the effect of a fall in price as a movement down along the demand curve D_0.

A rise in the price of a good decreases the quantity demanded of it. In Fig. 3.3, we illustrate the effect of a rise in price as a movement up along the demand curve D_0.

A Shift of the Demand Curve If the price of a good remains constant but some other influence on buying plans changes, there is a change in demand for that good. We illustrate a change in demand as a shift of the demand curve. For example, if more people work out at the gym, consumers buy more energy bars regardless of the price of a bar. That is what a rightward shift of the demand curve shows—more energy bars are demanded at each price.

In Fig. 3.3, there is a *change in demand* and the demand curve shifts when any influence on buying plans changes, other than the price of the good. Demand *increases* and the demand curve *shifts rightward* (to the red demand curve D_1) if the price of a substitute rises, the price of a complement falls, the expected future price of the good rises, income increases (for a normal good), expected future income or credit increases, or the population increases. Demand *decreases* and the demand curve *shifts leftward* (to the red demand curve D_2) if the price of a substitute falls, the price of a complement rises, the expected future price of the good falls, income decreases (for a normal good), expected future income or credit decreases, or the population decreases. (For an inferior good, the effects of changes in income are in the opposite direction to those described above.)

FIGURE 3.3 A Change in the Quantity Demanded Versus a Change in Demand

When the price of the good changes, there is a movement along the demand curve and *a change in the quantity demanded*, shown by the blue arrows on demand curve D_0. When any other influence on buying plans changes, there is a shift of the demand curve and a *change in demand*. An increase in demand shifts the demand curve rightward (from D_0 to D_1). A decrease in demand shifts the demand curve leftward (from D_0 to D_2).

MyEconLab Animation and Draw Graph

REVIEW QUIZ

1 Define the quantity demanded of a good or service.
2 What is the law of demand and how do we illustrate it?
3 What does the demand curve tell us about the price that consumers are willing to pay?
4 List all the influences on buying plans that change demand, and for each influence, say whether it increases or decreases demand.
5 Why does demand not change when the price of a good changes with no change in the other influences on buying plans?

Work these questions in Study Plan 3.2 and get instant feedback. Do a Key Terms Quiz. MyEconLab

Supply

If a firm supplies a good or service, the firm:

1. Has the resources and technology to produce it.
2. Can profit from producing it.
3. Plans to produce it and sell it.

A supply is more than just having the *resources* and the *technology* to produce something. *Resources and technology* are the constraints that limit what is possible.

Many useful things can be produced, but they are not produced unless it is profitable to do so. Supply reflects a decision about which technologically feasible items to produce.

The **quantity supplied** of a good or service is the amount that producers plan to sell during a given time period at a particular price. The quantity supplied is not necessarily the same amount as the quantity actually sold. Sometimes the quantity supplied is greater than the quantity demanded, so the quantity sold is less than the quantity supplied.

Like the quantity demanded, the quantity supplied is measured as an amount per unit of time. For example, suppose that GM produces 1,000 cars a day. The quantity of cars supplied by GM can be expressed as 1,000 a day, 7,000 a week, or 365,000 a year. Without the time dimension, we cannot tell whether a particular quantity is large or small.

Many factors influence selling plans, and again one of them is the price of the good. We look first at the relationship between the quantity supplied of a good and its price. Just as we did when we studied demand, to isolate the relationship between the quantity supplied of a good and its price, we keep all other influences on selling plans the same and ask: How does the quantity supplied of a good change as its price changes when other things remain the same?

The law of supply provides the answer.

The Law of Supply

The **law of supply** states:

> Other things remaining the same, the higher the price of a good, the greater is the quantity supplied; and the lower the price of a good, the smaller is the quantity supplied.

Why does a higher price increase the quantity supplied? It is because *marginal cost increases.* As the quantity produced of any good increases, the marginal cost of producing the good increases. (See Chapter 2, p. 35 to review marginal cost.)

It is never worth producing a good if the price received for the good does not at least cover the marginal cost of producing it. When the price of a good rises, other things remaining the same, producers are willing to incur a higher marginal cost, so they increase production. The higher price brings forth an increase in the quantity supplied.

Let's now illustrate the law of supply with a supply curve and a supply schedule.

Supply Curve and Supply Schedule

You are now going to study the second of the two most used curves in economics: the supply curve. You're also going to learn about the critical distinction between *supply* and *quantity supplied.*

The term **supply** refers to the entire relationship between the price of a good and the quantity supplied of it. Supply is illustrated by the supply curve and the supply schedule. The term *quantity supplied* refers to a point on a supply curve—the quantity supplied at a particular price.

Figure 3.4 shows the supply curve of energy bars. A **supply curve** shows the relationship between the quantity supplied of a good and its price when all other influences on producers' planned sales remain the same. The supply curve is a graph of a supply schedule.

The table in Fig. 3.4 sets out the supply schedule for energy bars. A *supply schedule* lists the quantities supplied at each price when all the other influences on producers' planned sales remain the same. For example, if the price of an energy bar is 50¢, the quantity supplied is zero—in row *A* of the table. If the price of an energy bar is $1.00, the quantity supplied is 6 million energy bars a week—in row *B*. The other rows of the table show the quantities supplied at prices of $1.50, $2.00, and $2.50.

To make a supply curve, we graph the quantity supplied on the *x*-axis and the price on the *y*-axis. The points on the supply curve labelled *A* through *E* correspond to the rows of the supply schedule. For example, point *A* on the graph shows a quantity supplied of zero at a price of 50¢ an energy bar. Point *E* shows a quantity supplied of 15 million bars at $2.50 an energy bar.

FIGURE 3.4 The Supply Curve

	Price (dollars per bar)	Quantity supplied (millions of bars per week)
A	0.50	0
B	1.00	6
C	1.50	10
D	2.00	13
E	2.50	15

The table shows the supply schedule of energy bars. For example, at a price of $1.00, 6 million bars a week are supplied; at a price of $2.50, 15 million bars a week are supplied. The supply curve shows the relationship between the quantity supplied and the price, other things remaining the same. The supply curve slopes upward: As the price of a good increases, the quantity supplied increases.

A supply curve can be read in two ways. For a given price, the supply curve tells us the quantity that producers plan to sell at that price. For example, at a price of $1.50 a bar, producers are planning to sell 10 million bars a week. For a given quantity, the supply curve tells us the minimum price at which producers are willing to sell one more bar. For example, if 15 million bars are produced each week, the lowest price at which a producer is willing to sell the 15 millionth bar is $2.50.

——— MyEconLab Animation ———

Minimum Supply Price The supply curve can be interpreted as a minimum-supply-price curve—a curve that shows the lowest price at which someone is willing to sell. This lowest price is the *marginal cost*.

If a small quantity is produced, the lowest price at which someone is willing to sell one more unit is low. But as the quantity produced increases, the marginal cost of each additional unit rises, so the lowest price at which someone is willing to sell an additional unit rises along the supply curve.

In Fig. 3.4, if 15 million bars are produced each week, the lowest price at which someone is willing to sell the 15 millionth bar is $2.50. But if 10 million bars are produced each week, someone is willing to accept $1.50 for the last bar produced.

A Change in Supply

When any factor that influences selling plans other than the price of the good changes, there is a **change in supply**. Six main factors bring changes in supply. They are changes in:

- The prices of factors of production
- The prices of related goods produced
- Expected future prices
- The number of suppliers
- Technology
- The state of nature

Prices of Factors of Production The prices of the factors of production used to produce a good influence its supply. To see this influence, think about the supply curve as a minimum-supply-price curve. If the price of a factor of production rises, the lowest price that a producer is willing to accept for that good rises, so supply decreases. For example, during 2008, as the price of jet fuel increased, the supply of air travel decreased. Similarly, a rise in the minimum wage decreases the supply of hamburgers.

Prices of Related Goods Produced The prices of related goods that firms produce influence supply. For example, if the price of an energy drink rises, firms switch production from bars to drinks. The supply of energy bars decreases. Energy bars and energy drinks are *substitutes in production*—goods that can be produced by using the same resources. If the price of beef rises, the supply of cowhide increases. Beef and cowhide are *complements in production*—goods that must be produced together.

Expected Future Prices If the expected future price of a good rises, the return from selling the good in the future increases and is higher than it is today. So supply decreases today and increases in the future.

The Number of Suppliers The larger the number of firms that produce a good, the greater is the supply of the good. As new firms enter an industry, the supply in that industry increases. As firms leave an industry, the supply in that industry decreases.

Technology The term "technology" is used broadly to mean the way that factors of production are used to produce a good. A technology change occurs when a new method is discovered that lowers the cost of producing a good. For example, new methods used in the factories that produce computer chips have lowered the cost and increased the supply of chips.

The State of Nature The state of nature includes all the natural forces that influence production. It includes the state of the weather and, more broadly, the natural environment. Good weather can increase the supply of many agricultural products and bad weather can decrease their supply. Extreme natural events such as earthquakes, tornadoes, and hurricanes can also influence supply.

Figure 3.5 illustrates an increase in supply. When supply increases, the supply curve shifts rightward and the quantity supplied at each price is larger. For example, at $1.00 per bar, on the original (blue) supply curve, the quantity supplied is 6 million bars a week. On the new (red) supply curve, the quantity supplied is 15 million bars a week. Look closely at the numbers in the table in Fig. 3.5 and check that the quantity supplied is larger at each price.

Table 3.2 summarizes the influences on supply and the directions of those influences.

A Change in the Quantity Supplied Versus a Change in Supply

Changes in the influences on selling plans bring either a change in the quantity supplied or a change in supply. Equivalently, they bring either a movement along the supply curve or a shift of the supply curve.

A point on the supply curve shows the quantity supplied at a given price. A movement along the supply curve shows a **change in the quantity supplied**. The entire supply curve shows supply. A shift of the supply curve shows a *change in supply*.

FIGURE 3.5   An Increase in Supply

Original supply schedule Old technology			New supply schedule New technology		
	Price (dollars per bar)	Quantity supplied (millions of bars per week)		Price (dollars per bar)	Quantity supplied (millions of bars per week)
A	0.50	0	A'	0.50	7
B	1.00	6	B'	1.00	15
C	1.50	10	C'	1.50	20
D	2.00	13	D'	2.00	25
E	2.50	15	E'	2.50	27

A change in any influence on selling plans other than the price of the good itself results in a new supply schedule and a shift of the supply curve. For example, a new, cost-saving technology for producing energy bars changes the supply of energy bars. At a price of $1.50 a bar, 10 million bars a week are supplied when producers use the old technology (row C of the table) and 20 million energy bars a week are supplied when producers use the new technology (row C'). An advance in technology *increases* the supply of energy bars. The supply curve shifts *rightward*, as shown by the shift arrow and the resulting red curve.

————— MyEconLab Animation —————

Figure 3.6 illustrates and summarizes these distinctions. If the price of the good changes and other things remain the same, there is a *change in the quantity supplied* of that good. If the price of the good falls, the quantity supplied decreases and there is a movement down along the supply curve S_0. If the price of the good rises, the quantity supplied increases and there is a movement up along the supply curve S_0. When any other influence on selling plans changes, the supply curve shifts and there is a *change in supply*. If supply increases, the supply curve shifts rightward to S_1. If supply decreases, the supply curve shifts leftward to S_2.

TABLE 3.2 The Supply of Energy Bars

The Law of Supply

The quantity of energy bars supplied

Decreases if:	Increases if:
■ The price of an energy bar falls	■ The price of an energy bar rises

Changes in Supply

The supply of energy bars

Decreases if:	Increases if:
■ The price of a factor of production used to produce energy bars rises	■ The price of a factor of production used to produce energy bars falls
■ The price of a substitute in production rises	■ The price of a substitute in production falls
■ The price of a complement in production falls	■ The price of a complement in production rises
■ The expected future price of an energy bar rises	■ The expected future price of an energy bar falls
■ The number of suppliers of bars decreases	■ The number of suppliers of bars increases
■ A technology change decreases energy bar production	■ A technology change increases energy bar production
■ A natural event decreases energy bar production	■ A natural event increases energy bar production

FIGURE 3.6 A Change in the Quantity Supplied Versus a Change in Supply

When the price of the good changes, there is a movement along the supply curve and a *change in the quantity supplied*, shown by the blue arrows on supply curve S_0. When any other influence on selling plans changes, there is a shift of the supply curve and a *change in supply*. An increase in supply shifts the supply curve rightward (from S_0 to S_1), and a decrease in supply shifts the supply curve leftward (from S_0 to S_2).

MyEconLab Animation and Draw Graph

REVIEW QUIZ

1 Define the quantity supplied of a good or service.
2 What is the law of supply and how do we illustrate it?
3 What does the supply curve tell us about the producer's minimum supply price?
4 List all the influences on selling plans, and for each influence, say whether it changes supply.
5 What happens to the quantity of cellphones supplied and the supply of cellphones if the price of a cellphone falls?

Work these questions in Study Plan 3.3 and get instant feedback. Do a Key Terms Quiz.   MyEconLab

Now we're going to combine demand and supply and see how prices and quantities are determined.

Market Equilibrium

We have seen that when the price of a good rises, the quantity demanded *decreases* and the quantity supplied *increases*. We are now going to see how the price adjusts to coordinate buying plans and selling plans and achieve an equilibrium in the market.

An *equilibrium* is a situation in which opposing forces balance each other. Equilibrium in a market occurs when the price balances buying plans and selling plans. The **equilibrium price** is the price at which the quantity demanded equals the quantity supplied. The **equilibrium quantity** is the quantity bought and sold at the equilibrium price. A market moves toward its equilibrium because

- Price regulates buying and selling plans.
- Price adjusts when plans don't match.

Price as a Regulator

The price of a good regulates the quantities demanded and supplied. If the price is too high, the quantity supplied exceeds the quantity demanded. If the price is too low, the quantity demanded exceeds the quantity supplied. There is one price at which the quantity demanded equals the quantity supplied. Let's work out what that price is.

Figure 3.7 shows the market for energy bars. The table shows the demand schedule (from Fig. 3.1) and the supply schedule (from Fig. 3.4). If the price is 50¢ a bar, the quantity demanded is 22 million bars a week but no bars are supplied. There is a shortage of 22 million bars a week. The final column of the table shows this shortage. At a price of $1.00 a bar, there is still a shortage but only of 9 million bars a week.

If the price is $2.50 a bar, the quantity supplied is 15 million bars a week but the quantity demanded is only 5 million. There is a surplus of 10 million bars a week.

The one price at which there is neither a shortage nor a surplus is $1.50 a bar. At that price, the quantity demanded equals the quantity supplied: 10 million bars a week. The equilibrium price is $1.50 a bar, and the equilibrium quantity is 10 million bars a week.

Figure 3.7 shows that the demand curve and the supply curve intersect at the equilibrium price of $1.50 a bar. At each price *above* $1.50 a bar, there is a surplus of bars. For example, at $2.00 a bar, the surplus is

FIGURE 3.7   Equilibrium

Price (dollars per bar)	Quantity demanded	Quantity supplied	Shortage (–) or surplus (+)
	(millions of bars per week)		
0.50	22	0	–22
1.00	15	6	–9
1.50	10	10	0
2.00	7	13	+6
2.50	5	15	+10

The table lists the quantity demanded and the quantity supplied as well as the shortage or surplus of bars at each price. If the price is $1.00 a bar, 15 million bars a week are demanded and 6 million bars are supplied. There is a shortage of 9 million bars a week, and the price rises.

If the price is $2.00 a bar, 7 million bars a week are demanded and 13 million bars are supplied. There is a surplus of 6 million bars a week, and the price falls.

If the price is $1.50 a bar, 10 million bars a week are demanded and 10 million bars are supplied. There is neither a shortage nor a surplus, and the price does not change. The price at which the quantity demanded equals the quantity supplied is the equilibrium price, and 10 million bars a week is the equilibrium quantity.

—— MyEconLab Animation and Draw Graph ——

6 million bars a week, as shown by the blue arrow. At each price *below* $1.50 a bar, there is a shortage of bars. For example, at $1.00 a bar, the shortage is 9 million bars a week, as shown by the red arrow.

Price Adjustments

You've seen that if the price is below equilibrium there is a shortage, and that if the price is above equilibrium there is a surplus. But can we count on the price to change and eliminate a shortage or a surplus? We can, because such price changes are beneficial to both buyers and sellers. Let's see why the price changes when there is a shortage or a surplus.

A Shortage Forces the Price Up Suppose the price of an energy bar is $1. Consumers plan to buy 15 million bars a week, and producers plan to sell 6 million bars a week. Consumers can't force producers to sell more than they plan, so the quantity that is actually offered for sale is 6 million bars a week. In this situation, powerful forces operate to increase the price and move it toward the equilibrium price. Some producers, noticing lines of unsatisfied consumers, raise the price. Some producers increase their output. As producers push the price up, the price rises toward its equilibrium. The rising price reduces the shortage because it decreases the quantity demanded and increases the quantity supplied. When the price has increased to the point at which there is no longer a shortage, the forces moving the price stop operating and the price comes to rest at its equilibrium.

A Surplus Forces the Price Down Suppose the price of a bar is $2. Producers plan to sell 13 million bars a week, and consumers plan to buy 7 million bars a week. Producers cannot force consumers to buy more than they plan, so the quantity that is actually bought is 7 million bars a week. In this situation, powerful forces operate to lower the price and move it toward the equilibrium price. Some producers, unable to sell the quantities of energy bars they planned to sell, cut their prices. In addition, some producers scale back production. As producers cut the price, the price falls toward its equilibrium. The falling price decreases the surplus because it increases the quantity demanded and decreases the quantity supplied. When the price has fallen to the point at which there is no longer a surplus, the forces moving the price stop operating and the price comes to rest at its equilibrium.

The Best Deal Available for Buyers and Sellers

When the price is below equilibrium, it is forced upward. Why don't buyers resist the increase and refuse to buy at the higher price? The answer is because they value the good more highly than its current price and they can't satisfy their demand at the current price. In some markets—for example, the markets that operate on eBay—the buyers might even be the ones who force the price up by offering to pay a higher price.

When the price is above equilibrium, it is bid downward. Why don't sellers resist this decrease and refuse to sell at the lower price? The answer is because their minimum supply price is below the current price and they cannot sell all they would like to at the current price. Sellers willingly lower the price to gain market share.

At the price at which the quantity demanded and the quantity supplied are equal, neither buyers nor sellers can do business at a better price. Buyers pay the highest price they are willing to pay for the last unit bought, and sellers receive the lowest price at which they are willing to supply the last unit sold.

When people freely make offers to buy and sell and when demanders try to buy at the lowest possible price and suppliers try to sell at the highest possible price, the price at which trade takes place is the equilibrium price—the price at which the quantity demanded equals the quantity supplied. The price coordinates the plans of buyers and sellers, and no one has an incentive to change it.

> ### ◀ REVIEW QUIZ
>
> 1 What is the equilibrium price of a good or service?
> 2 Over what range of prices does a shortage arise? What happens to the price when there is a shortage?
> 3 Over what range of prices does a surplus arise? What happens to the price when there is a surplus?
> 4 Why is the price at which the quantity demanded equals the quantity supplied the equilibrium price?
> 5 Why is the equilibrium price the best deal available for both buyers and sellers?
>
> Work these questions in Study Plan 3.4 and get instant feedback. Do a Key Terms Quiz.   MyEconLab

Predicting Changes in Price and Quantity

The demand and supply model that we have just studied provides us with a powerful way of analyzing influences on prices and the quantities bought and sold. According to the model, a change in price stems from a change in demand, a change in supply, or a change in both demand and supply. Let's look first at the effects of a change in demand.

An Increase in Demand

If more people join health clubs, the demand for energy bars increases. The table in Fig. 3.8 shows the original and new demand schedules for energy bars as well as the supply schedule of energy bars.

The increase in demand creates a shortage at the original price, and to eliminate the shortage the price must rise.

Figure 3.8 shows what happens. The figure shows the original demand for and supply of energy bars. The original equilibrium price is $1.50 an energy bar, and the equilibrium quantity is 10 million energy bars a week. When demand increases, the demand curve shifts rightward. The equilibrium price rises to $2.50 an energy bar, and the quantity supplied increases to 15 million energy bars a week, as highlighted in the figure. There is an *increase in the quantity supplied* but *no change in supply*—a movement along, but no shift of, the supply curve.

A Decrease in Demand

We can reverse this change in demand. Start at a price of $2.50 a bar with 15 million energy bars a week being bought and sold, and then work out what happens if demand decreases to its original level. Such a decrease in demand might arise if people switch to energy drinks (a substitute for energy bars). The decrease in demand shifts the demand curve leftward. The equilibrium price falls to $1.50 a bar, the quantity supplied decreases, and the equilibrium quantity decreases to 10 million bars a week.

We can now make our first two predictions:

1. When demand increases, the price rises and the quantity increases.
2. When demand decreases, the price falls and the quantity decreases.

FIGURE 3.8 The Effects of a Change in Demand

Price (dollars per bar)	Quantity demanded (millions of bars per week)		Quantity supplied (millions of bars per week)
	Original	New	
0.50	22	32	0
1.00	15	25	6
1.50	**10**	20	**10**
2.00	7	17	13
2.50	5	**15**	**15**

Initially, the demand for energy bars is the blue demand curve. The equilibrium price is $1.50 a bar, and the equilibrium quantity is 10 million bars a week. When more health-conscious people do more exercise, the demand for energy bars increases and the demand curve shifts rightward to become the red curve.

At $1.50 a bar, there is now a shortage of 10 million bars a week. The price of a bar rises to a new equilibrium of $2.50. As the price rises to $2.50, the quantity supplied increases—shown by the blue arrow on the supply curve—to the new equilibrium quantity of 15 million bars a week. Following an increase in demand, the quantity supplied increases but supply does not change—the supply curve does not shift.

—— **MyEconLab** Animation and Draw Graph ——

ECONOMICS IN THE NEWS

The Markets for Chocolate and Cocoa

World's Sweet Tooth Heats Up Cocoa

With rising incomes in China and other fast-growing economies, the consumption of chocolate and the cocoa from which it is made is soaring. And the price of cocoa is soaring too.

Source: *The Wall Street Journal*, February 3, 2014

THE DATA

Year	Quantity of Cocoa (millions of tonnes per year)	Price (dollars per tonne)
2010	4	1,500
2014	5	3,000

THE QUESTIONS

- What does the data table tell us?
- Why did the price of cocoa increase? Is it because demand changed or supply changed, and in which direction?

THE ANSWERS

- The data table tells us that from 2010 to 2014, both the quantity of cocoa produced and the price of cocoa increased.
- An increase in demand brings an increase in the quantity and a rise in the price.
- An increase in supply brings an increase in the quantity and a fall in the price.
- Because both the quantity of cocoa and the price of cocoa increased, there must have been in increase in the demand for cocoa.
- The demand for cocoa increases if cocoa is a normal good and incomes increase.
- Cocoa is a normal good and the news clip says that incomes are rising fast in China and some other countries. These increases in income have brought an increase in the demand for cocoa.
- The figure illustrates the market for cocoa in 2010 and 2014. The supply curve S shows the supply of cocoa.
- In 2010, the demand curve was D_{2010}, the price was $1,500 per tonne, and the quantity of cocoa traded was 4 million tonnes.

- By 2014, the higher incomes in China and other countries had increased the demand for cocoa to D_{2014}. The price rose to $3,000 per tonne and the quantity traded increased to 5 million tonnes.
- The higher price brought an increase in the quantity of cocoa supplied, which is shown by the movement upward along the supply curve.

The Market for Cocoa Beans

An Increase in Supply

When Nestlé (the producer of PowerBar) and other energy bar producers switch to a new cost-saving technology, the supply of energy bars increases. Figure 3.9 shows the new supply schedule (the same one that was shown in Fig. 3.5). What are the new equilibrium price and quantity? The price falls to $1.00 a bar, and the quantity increases to 15 million bars a week. You can see why by looking at the quantities demanded and supplied at the old price of $1.50 a bar. The new quantity supplied at that price is 20 million bars a week, and there is a surplus. The price falls. Only when the price is $1.00 a bar does the quantity supplied equal the quantity demanded.

Figure 3.9 illustrates the effect of an increase in supply. It shows the demand curve for energy bars and the original and new supply curves. The initial equilibrium price is $1.50 a bar, and the equilibrium quantity is 10 million bars a week. When supply increases, the supply curve shifts rightward. The equilibrium price falls to $1.00 a bar, and the quantity demanded increases to 15 million bars a week, highlighted in the figure. There is an *increase in the quantity demanded* but *no change in demand*—a movement along, but no shift of, the demand curve.

A Decrease in Supply

Start out at a price of $1.00 a bar with 15 million bars a week being bought and sold. Then suppose that the cost of labour or raw materials rises and the supply of energy bars decreases. The decrease in supply shifts the supply curve leftward. The equilibrium price rises to $1.50 a bar, the quantity demanded decreases, and the equilibrium quantity decreases to 10 million bars a week.

We can now make two more predictions:

1. When supply increases, the price falls and the quantity increases.
2. When supply decreases, the price rises and the quantity decreases.

You've now seen what happens to the price and the quantity when either demand or supply changes while the other one remains unchanged. In real markets, both demand and supply can change together. When this happens, to predict the changes in price and quantity, we must combine the effects that you've just seen. That is your final task in this chapter.

FIGURE 3.9 The Effects of a Change in Supply

Price (dollars per bar)	Quantity demanded (millions of bars per week)	Quantity supplied (millions of bars per week)	
		Original	New
0.50	22	0	7
1.00	15	6	15
1.50	10	10	20
2.00	7	13	25
2.50	5	15	27

Initially, the supply of energy bars is shown by the blue supply curve. The equilibrium price is $1.50 a bar, and the equilibrium quantity is 10 million bars a week. When the new cost-saving technology is adopted, the supply of energy bars increases and the supply curve shifts rightward to become the red curve.

At $1.50 a bar, there is now a surplus of 10 million bars a week. The price of an energy bar falls to a new equilibrium of $1.00 a bar. As the price falls to $1.00, the quantity demanded increases—shown by the blue arrow on the demand curve—to the new equilibrium quantity of 15 million bars a week. Following an increase in supply, the quantity demanded increases but demand does not change—the demand curve does not shift.

MyEconLab Animation and Draw Graph

ECONOMICS IN THE NEWS

The Market for Coffee

Coffee Price Slides

With plentiful crops in Brazil and a recovery in Colombian production, the price of arabica beans has fallen.

Source: *The Financial Times*, October 24, 2013

THE DATA

Year	Quantity (millions of tonnes per year)	Price (dollars per kilogram)
2013	134	12.00
2014	145	10.00

THE QUESTIONS

- What does the data table tell us?
- Why did the price of coffee decrease? Is it because demand changed or supply changed, and in which direction?

THE ANSWERS

- The data table tells us that during 2014, the quantity of coffee produced increased and the average price of coffee fell.
- An increase in demand brings an increase in the quantity and a rise in the price.
- An increase in supply brings an increase in the quantity and a fall in the price.
- Because the quantity of coffee increased and the price fell, there must have been in increase in the supply of coffee.
- The supply of coffee increases if the crop yields increase or if producers increase their plantings.
- The news clip says Brazilian crop was plentiful and Colombian production recovered. These increases in production brought an increase in the supply of coffee.
- The figure illustrates the market for coffee in 2013 and 2014. The demand curve D shows the demand for coffee.
- In 2013, the supply curve was S_{13}, the average price was $12.00 per kilogram, and the quantity of coffee traded was 134 million tonnes.
- In 2014, the increased coffee production in Brazil and Colombia increased the supply of coffee to S_{14}.

- The average price fell to $10.00 per kilogram and the quantity traded increased to 145 million tonnes.
- The lower price brought an increase in the quantity of coffee demanded, which is shown by the movement along the demand curve.

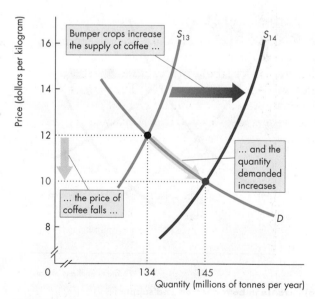

The Market for Coffee in 2013–2014

Changes in Both Demand and Supply

You now know how a change in demand or a change in supply changes the equilibrium price and quantity. But sometimes, events occur that change both demand and supply. When both demand and supply change, we find the resulting change in the equilibrium price and equilibrium quantity by combining the separate cases you've just studied.

Four cases need to be considered. Both demand and supply might increase or decrease, and demand or supply might increase and the other decrease.

Both Demand and Supply Change in the Same Direction When demand and supply change in the *same* direction, the equilibrium quantity changes in that same direction, but to predict whether the price rises or falls, we need to know the magnitudes of the changes in demand and supply.

If demand increases by more than supply increases, the price rises. But if supply increases by more than demand increases, the price falls.

Figure 3.10(a) shows the case when both demand and supply increase and by the same amount. The equilibrium quantity increases. But because the increase in demand equals the increase in supply, neither a shortage nor a surplus arises so the price doesn't change. A bigger increase in demand would have created a shortage and a rise in the price; a bigger increase in supply would have created a surplus and a fall in the price.

Figure 3.10(b) shows the case when both demand and supply decrease by the same amount. Here the equilibrium quantity decreases and again the price might either rise or fall.

Both Demand and Supply Change in Opposite Directions When demand and supply change in *opposite* directions, we can predict how the price changes, but we need to know the magnitudes of the changes in demand and supply to say whether the equilibrium quantity increases or decreases.

If demand changes by more than supply, the equilibrium quantity changes in the same direction as the change in demand. But if supply changes by more than demand, the equilibrium quantity changes in the same direction as the change in supply.

FIGURE 3.10   The Effects of Changes in Both Demand and Supply in the Same Direction

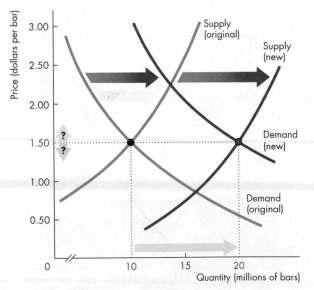

(a) Increase in both demand and supply

(b) Decrease in both demand and supply

An increase in demand shifts the demand curve rightward to become the red new demand curve and an increase in supply shifts the supply curve rightward to become the red new supply curve. The price might rise or fall, but the quantity increases.

A decrease in demand shifts the demand curve leftward to become the red new demand curve and a decrease in supply shifts the supply curve leftward to become the red new supply curve. The price might rise or fall, but the quantity decreases.

MyEconLab Animation

FIGURE 3.11 The Effects of Changes in Both Demand and Supply in Opposite Directions

(a) Decrease in demand; increase in supply

A decrease in demand shifts the demand curve leftward to become the red new demand curve and an increase in supply shifts the supply curve rightward to become the red new supply curve. The price falls, but the quantity might increase or decrease.

(b) Increase in demand; decrease in supply

An increase in demand shifts the demand curve rightward to become the red new demand curve and a decrease in supply shifts the supply curve leftward to become the red new supply curve. The price rises, but the quantity might increase or decrease.

——— MyEconLab Animation ———

Figure 3.11(a) illustrates what happens when demand decreases and supply increases by the *same* amount. At the initial price, there is a surplus, so the price falls. A decrease in demand decreases the quantity and an increase in supply increases the quantity, so when these changes occur together, we can't say what happens to the quantity unless we know the magnitudes of the changes.

Figure 3.11(b) illustrates what happens when demand increases and supply decreases by the same amount. In this case, at the initial price, there is a shortage, so the price rises. An increase in demand increases the quantity and a decrease in supply decreases the quantity, so again, when these changes occur together, we can't say what happens to the quantity unless we know the magnitudes of the changes in demand and supply.

For all the cases in Figures 3.10 and 3.11 where you "can't say" what happens to price or quantity, draw some examples that go in each direction.

REVIEW QUIZ

What is the effect on the price and quantity of MP3 players (such as the iPod) if:

1 The price of a PC falls or the price of an MP3 download rises? (Draw the diagrams!)

2 More firms produce MP3 players or electronics workers' wages rise? (Draw the diagrams!)

3 Any two of the events in questions 1 and 2 occur together? (Draw the diagrams!)

Work these questions in Study Plan 3.5 and get instant feedback.   MyEconLab

◆ To complete your study of demand and supply, take a look at *Economics in the News* on pp. 74–75, which explains what would happen to the price of bananas if a disease that kills plants were to jump continents to Central America. Try to get into the habit of using the demand and supply model to understand the changes in prices in your everyday life.

Demand and Supply: The Market for Bananas

Banana Supply Seen at Risk as Disease Spreads

Bloomberg News
April 9, 2014

A disease damaging banana crops in Southeast Asia has spread to the Middle East and Africa, posing risks to world supply and trade totaling $8.9 billion, according to the United Nations' Food and Agriculture Organization.

The TR4 strain of Panama disease, a soil-born fungus that attacks plant roots, is deadly for the Cavendish banana that makes up about 95 percent of supplies to importers, including North America and Europe, Fazil Dusunceli, an agriculture officer at the FAO, said. ...

While the disease hasn't reached top Latin America exporters such as Ecuador, Costa Rica or Colombia, TR4 was discovered in Jordan and Mozambique, indicating it moved beyond Asia, he said.

"The export market is dominated by the Cavendish, and it is unfortunately susceptible to this particular race of the disease," Dusunceli said. "This is serious for the medium term, but at the same time we should avoid panicking too."

Global exports reached a record value in 2011 and totaled 18.7 million tonnes, making bananas the world's most widely-traded fruit, according to the most recent FAO data. The U.S. is the top importer, followed by Belgium, the data show. Belgium's Port of Antwerp is the world's largest banana port, it says.

Consumer prices for bananas were 131.8 cents a kilogram in February, 2.2 percent higher than an almost three-year low reached in October at 128.9 cents a kilogram, according to data from the Bureau of Labor Statistics. The export price of bananas from Ecuador, the world's biggest shipper, and Central America for North American destinations was $966.85 a tonne in March, the highest in 18 months, according to the International Monetary Fund. ...

Written by Whitney McFerron. Copyright © 2014. Used by permission of Bloomberg News. All rights reserved.

ESSENCE OF THE STORY

- The consumer price of bananas was 131.8 cents per kilogram in February 2014.

- About 95 percent of bananas traded are a variety called Cavendish.

- Cavendish banana plants can be destroyed by the TR4 strain of Panama disease.

- TR4 hasn't reached Latin America, but it has jumped from Asia to the Middle East and Africa.

- Fazil Dusunceli of the United Nations' Food and Agriculture Organization says "This is serious for the medium term, but at the same time we should avoid panicking too."

MyEconLab More Economics in the News

ECONOMIC ANALYSIS

- In the market for bananas, a decrease in world production would decrease supply.

- A decrease in the supply of bananas would raise their price, decrease the equilibrium quantity, and decrease the quantity of bananas demanded.

- We can see the likely price increase by looking at previous events in the banana market.

- Figure 1 shows the price of bananas since 2004. You can see that there was a big temporary jump in the price in 2008.

- That jump in price was *not* caused by a decrease in banana production because as Fig. 2 shows, banana production has increased every year since 2004 except for 2012.

- What happened in 2008? The answer is a spike in the price of oil.

- Transporting bananas from plantations in Central and South America to your neighbourhood grocery store uses a lot of fuel. So when the cost of fuel increased in 2008, the cost of delivering bananas increased, and the consumer price of bananas increased.

- A decrease in supply caused by the TR4 disease would have a similar effect on the banana market to what happened in 2008.

- Figure 3 illustrates this effect. The supply of bananas decreases from S_N (normal) to S_D (disease), the price rises, the equilibrium quantity decreases, and the quantity of bananas demanded decreases.

Figure 1 The Price of Bananas: 2004–2014

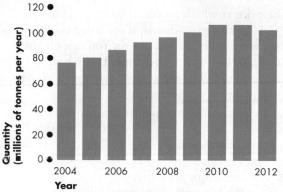

Figure 2 Banana Production: 2004–2012

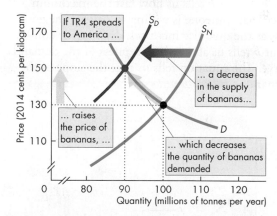

Figure 3 The Market for Bananas

75

MATHEMATICAL NOTE
Demand, Supply, and Equilibrium

Demand Curve

The law of demand says that as the price of a good or service falls, the quantity demanded of that good or service increases. We can illustrate the law of demand by drawing a graph of the demand curve or writing down an equation. When the demand curve is a straight line, the following equation describes it:

$$P = a - bQ_D,$$

where P is the price and Q_D is the quantity demanded. The a and b are positive constants.

The demand equation tells us three things:

1. The price at which no one is willing to buy the good (Q_D is zero). That is, if the price is a, then the quantity demanded is zero. You can see the price a in Fig. 1. It is the price at which the demand curve hits the y-axis—what we call the demand curve's "y-intercept."

2. As the price falls, the quantity demanded increases. If Q_D is a positive number, then the price P must be less than a. As Q_D gets larger, the price P becomes smaller. That is, as the quantity increases, the maximum price that buyers are willing to pay for the last unit of the good falls.

3. The constant b tells us how fast the maximum price that someone is willing to pay for the good falls as the quantity increases. That is, the constant b tells us about the steepness of the demand curve. The equation tells us that the slope of the demand curve is $-b$.

Supply Curve

The law of supply says that as the price of a good or service rises, the quantity supplied of that good or service increases. We can illustrate the law of supply by drawing a graph of the supply curve or writing down an equation. When the supply curve is a straight line, the following equation describes it:

$$P = c + dQ_S,$$

where P is the price and Q_S is the quantity supplied. The c and d are positive constants.

The supply equation tells us three things:

1. The price at which sellers are not willing to supply the good (Q_S is zero). That is, if the price is c, then no one is willing to sell the good. You can see the price c in Fig. 2. It is the price at which the supply curve hits the y-axis—what we call the supply curve's "y-intercept."

2. As the price rises, the quantity supplied increases. If Q_S is a positive number, then the price P must be greater than c. As Q_S increases, the price P becomes larger. That is, as the quantity increases, the minimum price that sellers are willing to accept for the last unit rises.

3. The constant d tells us how fast the minimum price at which someone is willing to sell the good rises as the quantity increases. That is, the constant d tells us about the steepness of the supply curve. The equation tells us that the slope of the supply curve is d.

Figure 1 Demand Curve

Figure 2 Supply Curve

Market Equilibrium

Demand and supply determine market equilibrium. Figure 3 shows the equilibrium price (P^*) and equilibrium quantity (Q^*) at the intersection of the demand curve and the supply curve.

We can use the equations to find the equilibrium price and equilibrium quantity. The price of a good adjusts until the quantity demanded Q_D equals the quantity supplied Q_S. So at the equilibrium price (P^*) and equilibrium quantity (Q^*),

$$Q_D = Q_S = Q^*.$$

To find the equilibrium price and equilibrium quantity, substitute Q^* for Q_D in the demand equation and Q^* for Q_S in the supply equation. Then the price is the equilibrium price (P^*), which gives

$$P^* = a - bQ^*$$
$$P^* = c + dQ^*.$$

Notice that

$$a - bQ^* = c + dQ^*.$$

Now solve for Q^*:

$$a - c = bQ^* + dQ^*$$
$$a - c = (b + d)Q^*$$
$$Q^* = \frac{a - c}{b + d}.$$

To find the equilibrium price P^*, substitute for Q^* in either the demand equation or the supply equation.

Figure 3 Market Equilibrium

Using the demand equation, we have

$$P^* = a - b\left(\frac{a - c}{b + d}\right)$$
$$P^* = \frac{a(b + d) - b(a - c)}{b + d}$$
$$P^* = \frac{ad + bc}{b + d}.$$

Alternatively, using the supply equation, we have

$$P^* = c + d\left(\frac{a - c}{b + d}\right)$$
$$P^* = \frac{c(b + d) + d(a - c)}{b + d}$$
$$P^* = \frac{ad + bc}{b + d}.$$

An Example

The demand for ice-cream cones is

$$P = 800 - 2Q_D.$$

The supply of ice-cream cones is

$$P = 200 + 1Q_S.$$

The price of a cone is expressed in cents, and the quantities are expressed in cones per day.

To find the equilibrium price (P^*) and equilibrium quantity (Q^*), substitute Q^* for Q_D and Q_S and P^* for P. That is,

$$P^* = 800 - 2Q^*$$
$$P^* = 200 + 1Q^*.$$

Now solve for Q^*:

$$800 - 2Q^* = 200 + 1Q^*$$
$$600 = 3Q^*$$
$$Q^* = 200.$$

And

$$P^* = 800 - 2(200)$$
$$= 400.$$

The equilibrium price is $4 a cone, and the equilibrium quantity is 200 cones per day.

SUMMARY

Key Points

Markets and Prices (p. 56)

- A competitive market is one that has so many buyers and sellers that no single buyer or seller can influence the price.
- Opportunity cost is a relative price.
- Demand and supply determine relative prices.

Working Problem 1 will give you a better understanding of markets and prices.

Demand (pp. 57–61)

- Demand is the relationship between the quantity demanded of a good and its price when all other influences on buying plans remain the same.
- The higher the price of a good, other things remaining the same, the smaller is the quantity demanded—the law of demand.
- Demand depends on the prices of related goods (substitutes and complements), expected future prices, income, expected future income and credit, the population, and preferences.

Working Problems 2 to 4 will give you a better understanding of demand.

Supply (pp. 62–65)

- Supply is the relationship between the quantity supplied of a good and its price when all other influences on selling plans remain the same.
- The higher the price of a good, other things remaining the same, the greater is the quantity supplied—the law of supply.

- Supply depends on the prices of factors of production used to produce a good, the prices of related goods produced, expected future prices, the number of suppliers, technology, and the state of nature.

Working Problems 5 and 6 will give you a better understanding of supply.

Market Equilibrium (pp. 66–67)

- At the equilibrium price, the quantity demanded equals the quantity supplied.
- At any price above the equilibrium price, there is a surplus and the price falls.
- At any price below the equilibrium price, there is a shortage and the price rises.

Working Problem 7 will give you a better understanding of market equilibrium.

Predicting Changes in Price and Quantity (pp. 68–73)

- An increase in demand brings a rise in the price and an increase in the quantity supplied. A decrease in demand brings a fall in the price and a decrease in the quantity supplied.
- An increase in supply brings a fall in the price and an increase in the quantity demanded. A decrease in supply brings a rise in the price and a decrease in the quantity demanded.
- An increase in demand and an increase in supply bring an increased quantity but an uncertain price change. An increase in demand and a decrease in supply bring a higher price but an uncertain change in quantity.

Working Problems 8 to 10 will give you a better understanding of predicting changes in price and quantity.

Key Terms

Change in demand, 58
Change in supply, 63
Change in the quantity demanded, 61
Change in the quantity supplied, 64
Competitive market, 56
Complement, 59
Demand, 57

Demand curve, 58
Equilibrium price, 66
Equilibrium quantity, 66
Inferior good, 60
Law of demand, 57
Law of supply, 62
Money price, 56
Normal good, 60

MyEconLab Key Terms Quiz

Quantity demanded, 57
Quantity supplied, 62
Relative price, 56
Substitute, 59
Supply, 62
Supply curve, 62

WORKED PROBLEM

MyEconLab   You can work this problem in Chapter 3 Study Plan.

The table sets out the demand and supply schedules for roses on a normal weekend.

Price	Quantity demanded	Quantity supplied
(dollars per rose)	(roses per week)	
6.00	150	60
7.00	100	100
8.00	70	130
9.00	50	150

Questions

1. If the price of a rose is $6, describe the situation in the rose market. Explain how the price adjusts.
2. If the price of a rose is $9, describe the situation in the rose market. Explain how the price adjusts.
3. What is the market equilibrium?
4. Rose sellers know that Mother's Day is next weekend and they expect the price to be higher, so they withhold 60 roses from the market this weekend. What is the price this weekend?
5. On Mother's Day, demand increases by 160 roses What is the price of a rose on Mother's Day?

Solutions

1. At $6 a rose, the quantity demanded is 150 and the quantity supplied is 60. The quantity demanded exceeds the quantity supplied and there is a *shortage* of 90 roses. With people lining up and a shortage, the price rises above $6 a rose.

Key Point: When a shortage exists, the price rises.

2. At $9 a rose, the quantity demanded is 50 and the quantity supplied is 180. The quantity supplied exceeds the quantity demanded and there is a *surplus* of 130 roses. With slow sales of roses and a surplus, the price falls to below $9 a rose.

Key Point: When a surplus exists, the price falls.

3. Market equilibrium occurs at the price at which the quantity demanded *equals* the quantity supplied. That price is $7 a rose. The equilibrium quantity of roses is 100 a week. Point *A* on the figure.

Key Point: At market equilibrium, there is no shortage or surplus.

4. Sellers expect a higher price next weekend, so they decrease the supply this weekend by 60 roses at each price. Create the new table:

Price	Quantity demanded	Quantity supplied
(dollars per rose)	(roses per week)	
6.00	150	0
7.00	**100**	**40**
8.00	**70**	**70**
9.00	50	90

At $7 a rose, there was a shortage of 60 roses, so the price rises to $8 a rose at which the quantity demanded equals the quantity supplied (Point *B*).

Key Point: When supply decreases, the price rises.

5. Demand increases by 160 roses. Sellers plan to increase the normal supply by the 60 roses withheld last weekend. Create the new table:

Price	Quantity demanded	Quantity supplied
(dollars per rose)	(roses per week)	
6.00	310	120
7.00	**260**	**160**
8.00	230	190
9.00	**210**	**210**

At $7 a rose, there is a shortage of 100 roses, so the price rises. It rises until at $9 a rose, the quantity demanded equals the quantity supplied. The price on Mother's Day is $9 a rose. (Point *C*)

Key Point: When demand increases by more than supply, the price rises.

Key Figure

MyEconLab Interactive Animation

STUDY PLAN PROBLEMS AND APPLICATIONS

MyEconLab   You can work Problems 1 to 10 in Chapter 3 Study Plan and get instant feedback.

Markets and Prices (Study Plan 3.1)

1. In April 2014, the money price of a litre of milk was $2.01 and the money price of a litre of gasoline was $1.30. Calculate the real price of a litre of gasoline in terms of milk.

Demand (Study Plan 3.2)

2. The price of food increased during the past year.
   a. Explain why the law of demand applies to food just as it does to other goods and services.
   b. Explain how the substitution effect influences food purchases when the price of food rises and other things remain the same.
   c. Explain how the income effect influences food purchases and provide some examples of the income effect.

3. Which of the following goods are likely substitutes and which are likely complements? (You may use an item more than once.)

   coal, oil, natural gas, wheat, corn, pasta, pizza, sausage, skateboard, roller blades, video game, laptop, iPad, cellphone, text message, email

4. As the average income in China continues to increase, explain how the following would change:
   a. The demand for beef
   b. The demand for rice

Supply (Study Plan 3.3)

5. In 2013, the price of corn fell and some corn farmers switched from growing corn in 2014 to growing soybeans.
   a. Does this fact illustrate the law of demand or the law of supply? Explain your answer.
   b. Why would a corn farmer grow soybeans?

6. Dairies make low-fat milk from full-cream milk, and in the process they produce cream, which is made into ice cream. The following events occur one at a time:
   (i)   The wage rate of dairy workers rises.
   (ii)   The price of cream rises.
   (iii) The price of low-fat milk rises.
   (iv)   With a drought forecasted, dairies raise their expected price of low-fat milk next year.
   (v)   New technology lowers the cost of producing ice cream.

   Explain the effect of each event on the supply of low-fat milk.

Market Equilibrium (Study Plan 3.4)

7. The demand and supply schedules for gum are:

Price (cents per pack)	Quantity demanded	Quantity supplied
	(millions of packs a week)	
20	180	60
40	140	100
60	100	140
80	60	180

   a. Suppose that the price of gum is 70¢ a pack. Describe the situation in the gum market and explain how the price adjusts.
   b. Suppose that the price of gum is 30¢ a pack. Describe the situation in the gum market and explain how the price adjusts.

Predicting Changes in Price and Quantity
(Study Plan 3.5)

8. The following events occur one at a time:
   (i)   The price of crude oil rises.
   (ii)   The price of a car rises.
   (iii) All speed limits on highways are abolished.
   (iv)   Robots cut car production costs.

   Explain the effect of each of these events on the market for gasoline.

9. In Problem 7, a fire destroys some factories that produce gum and the quantity of gum supplied decreases by 40 million packs a week at each price.
   a. Explain what happens in the market for gum and draw a graph to illustrate the changes.
   b. If, at the same time as the fire, the teenage population increases and the quantity of gum demanded increases by 40 million packs a week at each price. What is the new market equilibrium? Illustrate these changes on your graph.

10. **Tim Hortons' Risks**
    Tim Hortons has exploded to become a dominant player among quick-serve restaurants. In 2001, it took the risk by switching to centralized production of baked goods, which lowered its labour costs and increased its sales volume.

    Source: *Financial Post*, August 12, 2010

    Draw a graph to show the effect of lower labour costs on the price of Tim's baked goods and the quantity sold.

ADDITIONAL PROBLEMS AND APPLICATIONS

MyEconLab   You can work these problems in MyEconLab if assigned by your instructor.

Markets and Prices

11. What features of the world market for crude oil make it a competitive market?

12. The money price of a textbook is $90 and the money price of the Wii game *Super Mario Galaxy* is $45.
    a. What is the opportunity cost of a textbook in terms of the Wii game?
    b. What is the relative price of the Wii game in terms of textbooks?

Demand

13. The price of gasoline has increased during the past year.
    a. Explain why the law of demand applies to gasoline just as it does to all other goods and services.
    b. Explain how the substitution effect influences gasoline purchases and provide some examples of substitutions that people might make when the price of gasoline rises and other things remain the same.
    c. Explain how the income effect influences gasoline purchases and provide some examples of the income effects that might occur when the price of gasoline rises and other things remain the same.

14. Think about the demand for the three game consoles: Xbox One, PlayStation 4, and Wii U. Explain the effect of each of the following events on the demand for Xbox One games and the quantity of Xbox One games demanded, other things remaining the same. The events are:
    a. The price of an Xbox One falls.
    b. The prices of a PlayStation 4 and a Wii U fall.
    c. The number of people writing and producing Xbox One games increases.
    d. Consumers' incomes increase.
    e. Programmers who write code for Xbox One games become more costly to hire.
    f. The expected future price of an Xbox One game falls.
    g. A new game console that is a close substitute for Xbox One comes onto the market.

Supply

15. Classify the following pairs of goods and services as substitutes in production, complements in production, or neither.
    a. Bottled water and health club memberships
    b. French fries and baked potatoes
    c. Leather boots and leather shoes
    d. Hybrids and SUVs
    e. Diet coke and regular coke

16. When a timber mill makes logs from trees it also produces sawdust, which is used to make plywood.
    a. Explain how a rise in the price of sawdust influences the supply of logs.
    b. Explain how a rise in the price of sawdust influences the supply of plywood.

17. **New Maple Syrup Sap Method**

    With the new way to tap maple trees, farmers could produce 10 times as much maple syrup per acre.

    Source: cbc.ca, February 5, 2014

    Will the new method change the supply of maple syrup or the quantity supplied of maple syrup, other things remaining the same? Explain.

Market Equilibrium

Use the following figure to work Problems 18 and 19.

18. a. Label the curves. Which curve shows the willingness to pay for a pizza?
    b. If the price of a pizza is $16, is there a shortage or a surplus and does the price rise or fall?

c. Sellers want to receive the highest possible price, so why would they be willing to accept less than $16 a pizza?

19. a. If the price of a pizza is $12, is there a shortage or a surplus and does the price rise or fall?

b. Buyers want to pay the lowest possible price, so why would they be willing to pay more than $12 for a pizza?

20. The demand and supply schedules for potato chips are:

Price (cents per bag)	Quantity demanded	Quantity supplied
	(millions of bags per week)	
50	160	130
60	150	140
70	140	150
80	130	160
90	120	170
100	110	180

a. Draw a graph of the potato chip market and mark in the equilibrium price and quantity.

b. If the price is 60¢ a bag, is there a shortage or a surplus, and how does the price adjust?

Predicting Changes in Price and Quantity

21. In Problem 20, a new dip increases the quantity of potato chips that people want to buy by 30 million bags per week at each price.
    a. Does the demand for chips change? Does the supply of chips change? Describe the change.
    b. How do the equilibrium price and equilibrium quantity of chips change?

22. In Problem 20, if a virus destroys potato crops and the quantity of potato chips produced decreases by 40 million bags a week at each price, how does the supply of chips change?

23. If the virus in Problem 22 hits just as the new dip in Problem 21 comes onto the market, how do the equilibrium price and equilibrium quantity of chips change?

24. **Strawberry Prices Drop as Late Harvest Hits Market**

Shoppers bought strawberries in March for $1.25 a pound rather than the $3.49 a pound they paid last year. With the price so low, some growers removed their strawberry plants to make way for spring melons; others froze their harvests and sold them to juice and jam makers.

Source: *USA Today*, April 5, 2010

a. Explain how the market for strawberries would have changed if growers had not removed their plants but offered locals "you pick for free."

b. Describe the changes in demand and supply in the market for strawberry jam.

25. **"Popcorn Movie" Experience Gets Pricier**

Cinemas are raising the price of popcorn. Demand for field corn, which is used for animal feed, corn syrup, and ethanol, has increased and its price has exploded. That's caused some farmers to shift from growing popcorn to easier-to-grow field corn.

Source: *USA Today*, May 24, 2008

Explain and illustrate graphically the events described in the news clip in the market for

a. Popcorn

b. Movie tickets

26. **Watch Out for Rising Dry-Cleaning Bills**

In the past year, the price of dry-cleaning solvent doubled. More than 4,000 dry cleaners across the United States disappeared as budget-conscious consumers cut back. This year the price of hangers used by dry cleaners is expected to double.

Source: CNN Money, June 4, 2012

a. Explain the effect of rising solvent prices on the market for dry cleaning.

b. Explain the effect of consumers becoming more budget conscious along with the rising price of solvent on the price of dry cleaning.

c. If the price of hangers does rise this year, do you expect additional dry cleaners to disappear? Explain why or why not.

Economics in the News

27. After you have studied *Economics in the News* on pp. 74–75, answer the following questions.
    a. What would happen to the price of bananas if TR4 spread to Central America?
    b. What are some of the substitutes for bananas and what would happen to demand, supply, price, and quantity in the markets for these items if TR4 spread to Central America?
    c. What are some of the complements of bananas and what would happen to demand, supply, price, and quantity in the markets for these items if TR4 spread to Central America?
    d. When the price of bananas increased in 2008, did it rise by as much as the rise in the price of oil? Why or why not?
    e. Why would the expectation of the future arrival of TR4 in Central Americas have little of no effect on today's price of bananas?

The Amazing Market

PART TWO

The five chapters that you've just studied explain how markets work. The market is an amazing instrument. It enables people who have never met and who know nothing about each other to interact and do business. It also enables us to allocate our scarce resources to the uses that we value most highly. Markets can be very simple or highly organized. Markets are ancient and they are modern.

A simple and ancient market is one that the American historian Daniel J. Boorstin describes in *The Discoverers* (p. 161). In the late fourteenth century,

> *The Muslim caravans that went southward from Morocco across the Atlas Mountains arrived after twenty days at the shores of the Senegal River. There the Moroccan traders laid out separate piles of salt, of beads from Ceutan coral, and cheap manufactured goods. Then they retreated out of sight. The local tribesmen, who lived in the strip mines where they dug their gold, came to the shore and put a heap of gold beside each pile of Moroccan goods. Then they, in turn, went out of view, leaving the Moroccan traders either to take the gold offered for a particular pile or to reduce the pile of their merchandise to suit the offered price in gold. Once again the Moroccan traders withdrew, and the process went on. By this system of commercial etiquette, the Moroccans collected their gold.*

Auctions on eBay and government auction of the airwaves that cellphone companies use are organized and modern markets. Susan Athey, whom you will meet on the following page, is a world-renowned expert on the design of auctions.

Everything and anything that can be exchanged is traded in markets to the benefit of both buyers and sellers.

Alfred Marshall *(1842–1924) grew up in an England that was being transformed by the railroad and by the expansion of manufacturing. Mary Paley was one of Marshall's students at Cambridge, and when Alfred and Mary married in 1877, celibacy rules barred Alfred from continuing to teach at Cambridge. By 1884, with more liberal rules, the Marshalls returned to Cambridge, where Alfred became Professor of Political Economy.*

Many economists had a hand in refining the demand and supply model, but the first thorough and complete statement of the model as we know it today was set out by Alfred Marshall, with the help of Mary Paley Marshall. Published in 1890, this monumental treatise, The Principles of Economics, *became the textbook on economics on both sides of the Atlantic for almost half a century.*

"The forces to be dealt with are ... so numerous, that it is best to take a few at a time. ... Thus we begin by isolating the primary relations of supply, demand, and price."

ALFRED MARSHALL
The Principles of Economics

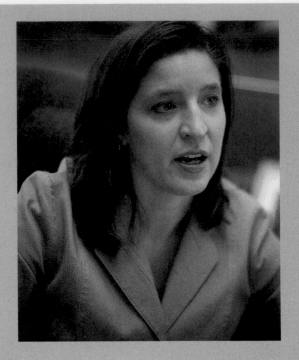

SUSAN ATHEY is Professor of Economics at Harvard University. Born in 1970, she completed high school in three years, wrapped up three majors—in economics, mathematics, and computer science—at Duke University at 20, completed her Ph.D. at Stanford University at 24, and was voted tenure at MIT and Stanford at 29. After teaching at MIT for six years and Stanford for five years, she moved to Harvard in 2006. Among her many honours and awards, the most prestigious is the John Bates Clark Medal given to the best economist under 40. She is the first woman to receive this award.

Professor Athey's research is broad both in scope and style. A government that wants to auction natural resources will turn to her fundamental discoveries (and possibly consult with her) before deciding how to organize the auction. An economist who wants to test a theory using a large data set will use her work on statistics and econometrics.

Michael Parkin and Robin Bade talked with Susan Athey about her research, what economists have learned about designing markets, and her advice to students.

Professor Athey, what sparked your interest in economics?

I was studying mathematics and computer science, but I felt that the subjects were not as relevant as I would like. I discovered economics through a research project with a professor who was working on auctions. I had a summer job working for a firm that sold computers to the government through auctions. Eventually my professor, Bob Marshall, wrote two articles on the topic and testified before Congress to help reform the system for government procurement of computers. That really inspired me and showed me the power of economic ideas to change the world and to make things work more efficiently.

What is the connection between an auction and the supply and demand model?

The basic laws of supply and demand can be seen in evidence in an auction market like eBay. The more sellers that are selling similar products, the lower the prices they can expect to achieve. Similarly the more buyers there are demanding those objects, the higher the prices the sellers can achieve.

An important thing for an auction marketplace is to attract a good balance of buyers and sellers so that both the buyers and the sellers find it more profitable to transact in that marketplace rather than using some other mechanism. From a seller's perspective, the more bidders there are on the platform, the greater the demand and the higher the prices. And from the buyer's perspective, the more sellers there are on the platform, the greater the supply and the lower the prices.

> The basic laws of supply and demand can be seen in evidence in an auction market like eBay.

Can we think of an auction as a mechanism for finding the equilibrium price and quantity?

Exactly. We can think of the whole collection of auctions on eBay as being a mechanism to discover a market-clearing price, and individual items might sell a little higher or a little lower but overall we believe that the prices on eBay auctions will represent equilibrium prices.

*Read the full interview with Susan Athey in MyEconLab.

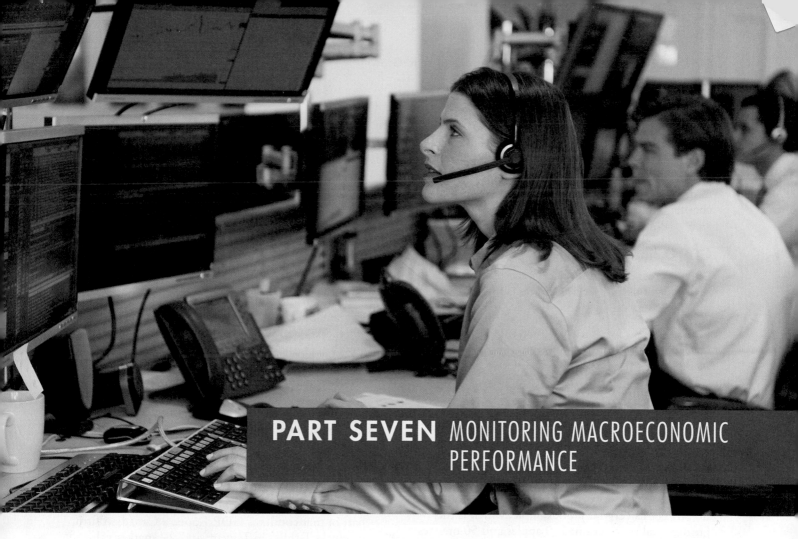

20

MEASURING GDP AND ECONOMIC GROWTH

After studying this chapter, you will be able to:

- ◆ Define GDP and explain why GDP equals aggregate expenditure and aggregate income
- ◆ Explain how Statistics Canada measures Canadian GDP and real GDP
- ◆ Explain the uses and limitations of real GDP as a measure of economic well-being

Will our economy expand more rapidly next year or will it sink into a "double-dip" recession? Many Canadian businesses want to know the answer to this question. To assess the state of the economy and to make big decisions about business expansion, firms such as BlackBerry Ltd. and Rogers Communications use forecasts of GDP. What exactly is GDP and what does it tell us about the state of the economy?

In this chapter, you will find out how Statistics Canada measures GDP. You will also learn about the uses and the limitations of GDP. In *Economics in the News* at the end of the chapter, we look at GDP linkages between Canada and the United States as both economies emerge from recession.

Gross Domestic Product

What exactly is GDP, how is it calculated, what does it mean, and why do we care about it? You are going to discover the answers to these questions in this chapter. First, what *is* GDP?

GDP Defined

GDP, or **gross domestic product**, is the market value of the final goods and services produced within a country in a given time period. This definition has four parts:

- Market value
- Final goods and services
- Produced within a country
- In a given time period

We'll examine each in turn.

Market Value To measure total production, we must add together the production of apples and oranges, computers and popcorn. Just counting the items doesn't get us very far. For example, which is the greater total production: 100 apples and 50 oranges or 50 apples and 100 oranges?

GDP answers this question by valuing items at their *market values*—the prices at which items are traded in markets. If the price of an apple is 10¢, then the market value of 50 apples is $5. If the price of an orange is 20¢, then the market value of 100 oranges is $20. By using market prices to value production, we can add the apples and oranges together. The market value of 50 apples and 100 oranges is $5 plus $20, or $25.

Final Goods and Services To calculate GDP, we value the *final goods and services* produced. A **final good** (or service) is an item that is bought by its final user during a specified time period. It contrasts with an **intermediate good** (or service), which is an item that is produced by one firm, bought by another firm, and used as a component of a final good or service.

For example, a new Ford truck is a final good, but a Firestone tire on that truck is an intermediate good. Your new iPad is a final good, but the chip inside it is an intermediate good.

If we were to add the value of intermediate goods and services produced to the value of final goods and services, we would count the same thing many times—a problem called *double counting*. The value of a truck already includes the value of the tires, and the value of an iPad already includes the value of the chip inside it.

Some goods can be an intermediate good in some situations and a final good in other situations. For example, the ice cream that you buy on a hot summer day is a final good, but the ice cream that a restaurant buys and uses to make sundaes is an intermediate good. The sundae is the final good. So whether a good is an intermediate good or a final good depends on what it is used for, not what it is.

Some items that people buy are neither final goods nor intermediate goods and they are not part of GDP. Examples of such items include financial assets—stocks and bonds—and secondhand goods—used cars or existing homes. A secondhand good was part of GDP in the year in which it was produced, but not in GDP this year.

Produced Within a Country Only goods and services that are produced *within a country* count as part of that country's GDP. Roots, a Canadian firm, produces T-shirts in Taiwan, and the market value of those shirts is part of Taiwan's GDP, not part of Canada's GDP. Toyota, a Japanese firm, produces automobiles in Cambridge, Ontario, and the value of this production is part of Canada's GDP, not part of Japan's GDP.

In a Given Time Period GDP measures the value of production *in a given time period*—normally either a quarter of a year—called the quarterly GDP data—or a year—called the annual GDP data.

GDP measures not only the value of total production but also total income and total expenditure. The equality between the value of total production and total income is important because it shows the direct link between productivity and living standards. Our standard of living rises when our incomes rise and we can afford to buy more goods and services. But we must produce more goods and services if we are to be able to buy more goods and services.

Rising incomes and a rising value of production go together. They are two aspects of the same phenomenon: increasing productivity. To see why, we study the circular flow of expenditure and income.

GDP and the Circular Flow of Expenditure and Income

Figure 20.1 illustrates the circular flow of expenditure and income. The economy consists of households, firms, governments, and the rest of the world (the rectangles), which trade in factor markets and goods (and services) markets. We focus first on households and firms.

Households and Firms Households sell and firms buy the services of labour, capital, and land in factor markets. For these factor services, firms pay income to households: wages for labour services, interest for the use of capital, and rent for the use of land. A fourth factor of production, entrepreneurship, receives profit.

Firms' retained earnings—profits that are not distributed to households—are part of the household sector's income. You can think of retained earnings as being income that households save and lend back to firms. Figure 20.1 shows the total income—*aggregate income*—received by households, including retained earnings, as the blue flow labelled *Y*.

Firms sell and households buy consumer goods and services—such as inline skates and haircuts—in the goods market. The total payment for these goods and services is **consumption expenditure**, shown by the red flow labelled *C*.

Firms buy and sell new capital equipment—such as computer systems, airplanes, trucks, and assembly line equipment—in the goods market. Some of what firms produce is not sold but is added to inventory. For example, if GM produces 1,000 cars and sells 950 of them, the other 50 cars remain in GM's inventory of unsold cars, which increases by 50 cars. When a firm adds unsold output to inventory, we can think of the firm as buying goods from itself. The

---

FIGURE 20.1   The Circular Flow of Expenditure and Income

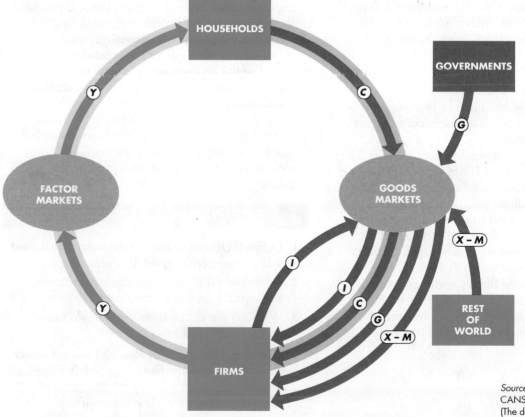

Households make consumption expenditures (*C*); firms make investments (*I*); governments buy goods and services (*G*); and the rest of the world buys net exports (*X* − *M*). Firms pay incomes (*Y*) to households. Aggregate income equals aggregate expenditure.

Billions of dollars in 2013

C =	1,048
I =	379
G =	486
X − *M* =	−32
Y =	1,881

Source of data: Statistics Canada, CANSIM Table 380-0064. (The data are for 2013.)

purchase of new plant, equipment, and buildings and the additions to inventories are **investment**, shown by the red flow labelled *I*.

Governments Governments buy goods and services from firms and their expenditure on goods and services is called **government expenditure**. In Fig. 20.1, government expenditure is shown as the red flow *G*.

Governments finance their expenditure with taxes. But taxes are not part of the circular flow of expenditure and income. Governments also make financial transfers to households, such as social security benefits and unemployment benefits, and pay subsidies to firms. These financial transfers, like taxes, are not part of the circular flow of expenditure and income.

Rest of the World Firms in Canada sell goods and services to the rest of the world—**exports**—and buy goods and services from the rest of the world—**imports**. The value of exports (*X*) minus the value of imports (*M*) is called **net exports** (*NX*), the red flow *X – M* in Fig. 20.1. If net exports are positive, the net flow of goods and services is from Canadian firms to the rest of the world. If net exports are negative, the net flow of goods and services is from the rest of the world to Canadian firms.

GDP Equals Expenditure Equals Income Gross domestic product can be measured in two ways: by the total expenditure on goods and services or by the total income earned producing goods and services.

The total expenditure—*aggregate expenditure*—is the sum of the red flows in Fig. 20.1. Aggregate expenditure equals consumption expenditure plus investment plus government expenditure plus net exports.

Aggregate income is equal to the total amount paid for the services of the factors of production used to produce final goods and services—wages, interest, rent, and profit. The blue flow in Fig. 20.1 shows aggregate income. Because firms pay out as incomes (including retained profits) everything they receive from the sale of their output, aggregate income (the blue flow) equals aggregate expenditure (the sum of the red flows). That is,

$$Y = C + I + G + X - M$$

The table in Fig. 20.1 shows the values of the expenditures for 2013 and that their sum is $1,881 billion, which also equals aggregate income.

Because aggregate expenditure equals aggregate income, the two methods of measuring GDP give the same answer. So

GDP equals aggregate expenditure and equals aggregate income.

The circular flow model is the foundation on which the national economic accounts are built.

Why Is Domestic Product "Gross"?

"Gross" means before subtracting the depreciation of capital. The opposite of "gross" is "net," which means after subtracting the depreciation of capital.

Depreciation is the decrease in the value of a firm's capital that results from wear and tear and obsolescence. The total amount spent both buying new capital and replacing depreciated capital is called **gross investment**. The amount by which the value of capital increases is called **net investment**. Net investment equals gross investment minus depreciation.

For example, if an airline buys 5 new airplanes and retires 2 old airplanes from service, its gross investment is the value of the 5 new airplanes, depreciation is the value of the 2 old airplanes retired, and net investment is the value of 3 new airplanes.

Gross investment is one of the expenditures included in the expenditure approach to measuring GDP. So the resulting value of total product is a gross measure.

Gross profit, which is a firm's profit before subtracting depreciation, is one of the incomes included in the income approach to measuring GDP. So again, the resulting value of total product is a gross measure.

◆ REVIEW QUIZ

1 Define GDP and distinguish between a final good and an intermediate good. Provide examples.
2 Why does GDP equal aggregate income and also equal aggregate expenditure?
3 What are the distinctions between domestic and national, and gross and net?

Work these questions in Study Plan 20.1 and get instant feedback. Do a Key Terms Quiz.   MyEconLab

Let's now see how the ideas that you've just studied are used in practice. We'll see how GDP and its components are measured in Canada today.

Measuring Canada's GDP

Statistics Canada uses the concepts in the circular flow model to measure GDP and its components in the *National Income and Expenditure Accounts*. Because the value of aggregate production equals aggregate expenditure and aggregate income, there are two approaches available for measuring GDP, and both are used. They are:

- The expenditure approach
- The income approach

The Expenditure Approach

The *expenditure approach* measures GDP as the sum of consumption expenditure (C), investment (I), government expenditure on goods and services (G), and net exports of goods and services ($X - M$). These expenditures correspond to the red flows through the goods markets in the circular flow model in Fig. 20.1. Table 20.1 shows these expenditures and the calculation of GDP for 2013.

Consumption expenditure is the expenditure by Canadian households on goods and services produced in Canada and in the rest of the world and is shown by the red flow C in Fig. 20.2. They include goods such as pop and books and services such as banking and legal advice. They also include the purchase of consumer durable goods, such as

TABLE 20.1   GDP: The Expenditure Approach

Item	Symbol	Amount in 2013 (billions of dollars)	Percentage of GDP
Consumption expenditure	C	1,048	55.7
Investment	I	379	20.2
Government expenditure on goods and services	G	486	25.8
Net exports of goods and services	X – M	–32	– 1.7
Gross domestic product	**Y**	**1,881**	**100.0**

The expenditure approach measures GDP as the sum of consumption expenditures, *C*, investment, *I*, government expenditure on goods and services, *G*, and net exports, *X – M*. In 2013, GDP measured by the expenditure approach was $1,881 billion. Some 56 percent of aggregate expenditure is expenditure by Canadian households on consumption goods and services.

Source of data: Statistics Canada, CANSIM Table 380-0064.

FIGURE 20.2   Aggregate Expenditure

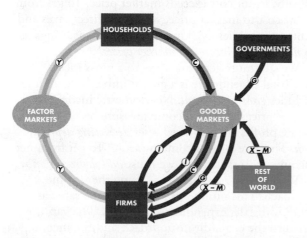

Aggregate expenditure is the sum of the red flows.

MyEconLab Animation

computers and microwave ovens. But they do *not* include the purchase of new homes, which Statistics Canada counts as part of investment.

Investment is the expenditure on capital equipment and buildings by firms and the additions to business inventories. It also includes expenditure on new homes by households. Investment is the red flow *I* in Fig. 20.2.

Government expenditure on goods and services is the expenditure by all levels of government on goods and services, such as national defence and garbage collection. It does *not* include *transfer payments*, such as unemployment benefits, because they are not expenditures on goods and services. Government expenditure is the red flow *G* in Fig. 20.2.

Net exports of goods and services are the value of exports minus the value of imports. This item includes telephone equipment that Nortel sells to AT&T (a Canadian export), and Japanese DVD players that Sears buys from Sony (a Canadian import) and is shown by the red flow *X – M* in Fig. 20.2.

Table 20.1 shows the relative magnitudes of the four items of aggregate expenditure.

The Income Approach

The *income approach* measures GDP by summing the incomes that firms pay households for the factors of production they hire—wages for labour, interest for capital, rent for land, and profit for entrepreneurship. These incomes sum to the blue flows through the goods markets in the circular flow model in Fig. 20.1. We divide the incomes in the *National Income and Expenditure Accounts* into two broad categories:

1. Wages, salaries, and supplementary labour income
2. Other factor incomes

Wages, salaries, and supplementary labour income is the payment for labour services. It includes gross wages plus benefits such as pension contributions and is shown by the blue flow *W* in Fig. 20.3.

Other factor incomes include corporate profits, interest, farmers' income, and income from non-farm unincorporated businesses. These incomes are a mixture of interest, rent, and profit and include some labour income from self-employment. They are included in the blue flow *OFI* in Fig. 20.3.

Table 20.2 shows these incomes and their relative magnitudes. They sum to net domestic income at factor cost.

An *indirect tax* is a tax paid by consumers when they buy goods and services. (In contrast, a *direct tax* is a tax on income.) An indirect tax makes the market price exceed factor cost. A *subsidy* is a payment by the government to a producer. With a

TABLE 20.2   GDP: The Income Approach

Item	Amount in 2013 (billions of dollars)	Percentage of GDP
Wages, salaries, and supplementary labour income	957	50.9
Other factor incomes	408	21.7
Net domestic income at factor cost	1,365	72.6
Indirect taxes *less* subsidies	191	10.1
Net domestic income at market prices	1,556	82.7
Depreciation	324	17.2
GDP (income approach)	**1,880**	**99.9**
Statistical discrepancy	1	0.1
GDP (expenditure approach)	**1,881**	**100.0**

The sum of factor incomes equals *net domestic income at factor cost*. GDP equals net domestic income at factor cost plus indirect taxes less subsidies plus depreciation.

In 2013, GDP measured by the income approach was $1,880 billion. This amount is $1 billion less than GDP measured by the expenditure approach—a statistical discrepancy of $1 billion, or 0.1 percent of GDP.

Wages, salaries, and supplementary labour income is by far the largest component of aggregate income.

Source of data: Statistics Canada, CANSIM Table 380-0063.

FIGURE 20.3   Aggregate Income

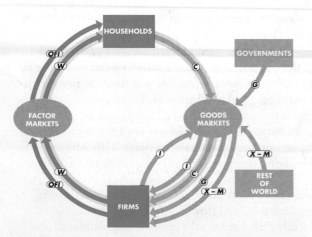

Aggregate income is the sum of the blue flows.

MyEconLab Animation

subsidy, factor cost exceeds market price. To get from factor cost to market price, we add indirect taxes and subtract subsidies. Making this adjustment brings us to *net domestic income at market prices*.

We still must get from a net to a gross measure. Total expenditure is a *gross* number because it includes *gross investment*. Net domestic income at market prices is a net income measure because corporate profits are measured *after deducting depreciation*. They are a net income measure. To get from net income to gross income, we must *add depreciation*.

We've now arrived at GDP using the income approach. This number is not exactly the same as GDP using the expenditure approach. The gap between the expenditure approach and the income approach is called the *statistical discrepancy* and it is calculated as the GDP expenditure total minus the GDP income total. The discrepancy is never large. In 2013, it was 0.1 percent of GDP.

Nominal GDP and Real GDP

Often, we want to *compare* GDP in two periods, say 2003 and 2013. In 2003, GDP was $1,244 billion, and in 2013 it was $1,881 billion—51 percent higher than in 2003. This increase in GDP is a combination of an increase in production and a rise in prices. To isolate the increase in production from the rise in prices, we distinguish between *real* GDP and *nominal* GDP.

Real GDP is the value of final goods and services produced in a given year when *valued at the prices of a reference base year*. By comparing the value of production in the two years at the same prices, we reveal the change in production.

Currently, the reference base year is 2007 and we describe real GDP as measured in 2007 dollars—in terms of what the dollar would buy in 2007.

Nominal GDP is the value of final goods and services produced in a given year when valued at the prices of that year. Nominal GDP is just a more precise name for GDP.

Economists at Statistics Canada calculate real GDP using the method described in the Mathematical Note on pp. 482–483. Here, we'll explain the basic idea but not the technical details.

Calculating Real GDP

We'll calculate real GDP for an economy that produces one consumption good, one capital good, and one government service. Net exports are zero.

Table 20.3 shows the quantities produced and the prices in 2007 (the base year) and in 2014. In part (a), we calculate nominal GDP in 2007. For each item, we multiply the quantity produced in 2007 by its price in 2007 to find the total expenditure on the item. We sum the expenditures to find nominal GDP, which in 2007 is $100 million. Because 2007 is the base year, both real GDP and nominal GDP equal $100 million.

In Table 20.3(b), we calculate nominal GDP in 2014, which is $300 million. Nominal GDP in 2014 is three times its value in 2007. But by how much has production increased? Real GDP will tell us.

In Table 20.3(c), we calculate real GDP in 2014. The quantities of the goods and services produced are those of 2014, as in part (b). The prices are those in the reference base year—2007, as in part (a).

For each item, we multiply the quantity produced in 2014 by its price in 2007. We then sum these expenditures to find real GDP in 2014, which is $160 million. This number is what total

TABLE 20.3   Calculating Nominal GDP and Real GDP

Item	Quantity (millions)	Price (dollars)	Expenditure (millions of dollars)
(a) In 2007			
C T-shirts	10	5	50
I Computer chips	3	10	30
G Security services	1	20	20
Y Real GDP in 2007			100
(b) In 2014			
C T-shirts	4	5	20
I Computer chips	2	20	40
G Security services	6	40	240
Y Nominal GDP in 2014			300
(c) Quantities of 2014 valued at prices of 2007			
C T-shirts	4	5	20
I Computer chips	2	10	20
G Security services	6	20	120
Y Real GDP in 2014			160

In 2007, the reference base year, real GDP equals nominal GDP and was $100 million. In 2014, nominal GDP increased to $300 million, but real GDP, which is calculated by using the quantities in 2014 in part (b) and the prices in 2007 in part (a), was only $160 million—a 60 percent increase from 2007.

expenditure would have been in 2014 if prices had remained the same as they were in 2007.

Nominal GDP in 2014 is three times its value in 2007, but real GDP in 2014 is only 1.6 times its 2007 value—a 60 percent increase in production.

◢ REVIEW QUIZ

1 What is the expenditure approach to measuring GDP?
2 What is the income approach to measuring GDP?
3 What adjustments must be made to total income to make it equal GDP?
4 What is the distinction between nominal GDP and real GDP?
5 How is real GDP calculated?

Work these questions in Study Plan 20.2 and get instant feedback. Do a Key Terms Quiz.   MyEconLab

The Uses and Limitations of Real GDP

Economists use estimates of real GDP for two main purposes:

- To compare the standard of living over time
- To compare the standard of living across countries

The Standard of Living over Time

One method of comparing the standard of living over time is to calculate real GDP per person in different years. **Real GDP per person** is real GDP divided by the population. Real GDP per person tells us the value of goods and services that the average person can enjoy. By using *real* GDP, we remove any influence that rising prices and a rising cost of living might have had on our comparison.

We're interested in both the long-term trends and the shorter-term cycles in the standard of living.

Long-Term Trend A handy way of comparing real GDP per person over time is to express it as a ratio of some reference year. For example, in 1969, real GDP per person was $19,000, and in 2010 it was $38,000 (both rounded to the nearest thousand). So real GDP per person in 2010 was double its 1969 level. To the extent that real GDP per person measures the standard of living, people were twice as well off in 2010 as their grandparents had been in 1969.

Figure 20.4 shows the path of Canadian real GDP per person from 1961 to 2010 and highlights two features of our expanding living standard:

- The growth of potential GDP per person
- Fluctuations of real GDP per person

The Growth of Potential GDP Potential GDP is the maximum level of real GDP that can be produced while avoiding shortages of labour, capital, land, and entrepreneurial ability that would bring rising inflation. Potential GDP per person, the smoother black line in Fig. 20.4, grows at a steady pace because the quantities of the factors of production and their productivities grow at a steady pace.

But potential GDP per person doesn't grow at a *constant* pace. During the 1960s, it grew at 3.4 percent per year but slowed to only 2.4 percent per year during the 1970s. This slowdown might seem small, but it had big consequences, as you'll soon see.

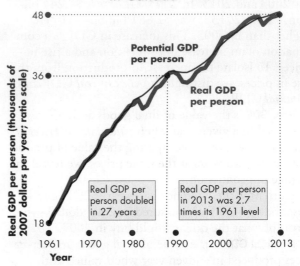

FIGURE 20.4   Rising Standard of Living in Canada

Real GDP per person in Canada doubled between 1961 and 1988 and almost tripled between 1961 and 2013. Real GDP per person, the red line, fluctuates around potential GDP per person, the black line. (The y-axis is a ratio scale—see the Appendix, pp. 480–481.)

Sources of data: Statistics Canada, CANSIM Tables 380-0064 and 051-0001. International Monetary Fund World Economic Outlook output gap data used to calculate potential GDP.

MyEconLab   Real-time data

Fluctuations of Real GDP You can see that real GDP per person shown by the red line in Fig. 20.4 fluctuates around potential GDP per person, and sometimes real GDP per person shrinks.

Let's take a closer look at the two features of our expanding living standard that we've just outlined.

Productivity Growth Slowdown How costly was the slowdown in productivity growth after 1970? The answer is provided by the *Lucas wedge*, which is the dollar value of the accumulated gap between what real GDP per person would have been if the growth rate of the 1960s had persisted and what real GDP per person turned out to be. (Nobel Laureate Robert E. Lucas Jr. drew attention to this gap.)

Figure 20.5 illustrates the Lucas wedge. The wedge started out small during the 1970s, but by 2013 real GDP per person was $45,000 per year lower than it would have been with no growth slowdown, and the accumulated gap was an astonishing $640,000 per person.

FIGURE 20.5   The Cost of Slower Growth: The Lucas Wedge

The black line projects the 1960s growth rate of real GDP per person to 2013. The Lucas wedge arises from the slowdown of productivity growth that began during the 1970s. The cost of the slowdown is $640,000 per person.

Sources of data: Statistics Canada, CANSIM Tables 380-0064 and 051-0001 and authors' calculations.

================= MyEconLab Real-time data =================

Real GDP Fluctuations—The Business Cycle We call the fluctuations in the pace of expansion of real GDP the **business cycle**. The business cycle is a periodic but irregular up-and-down movement of total production and other measures of economic activity. The business cycle isn't a regular predictable cycle like the phases of the moon, but every cycle has two phases:

1. Expansion
2. Recession

and two turning points:

1. Peak
2. Trough

Figure 20.6 shows these features of the most recent Canadian business cycle.

An **expansion** is a period during which real GDP increases. In the early stage of an expansion real GDP returns to potential GDP, and as the expansion progresses potential GDP grows, and real GDP eventually exceeds potential GDP.

A common definition of **recession** is a period during which real GDP decreases—its growth rate is negative—for at least two successive quarters. A more general definition of recession and one used by the U.S. National Bureau of Economic Research is "a period of significant decline in total output, income, employment, and trade, usually lasting from six months to a year, and marked by contractions in many sectors of the economy."

An expansion ends and recession begins at a business cycle *peak*, which is the highest level that real GDP has attained up to that time. A recession ends at a *trough*, when real GDP reaches a temporary low point and from which the next expansion begins.

In 2008, Canada went into an unusually severe recession. Starting from a long way below potential GDP, a new expansion began in mid-2009. Real GDP returned to potential GDP in 2013 but then slipped back to a bit below potential GDP in 2012 and 2013.

FIGURE 20.6   The Most Recent Canadian Business Cycle

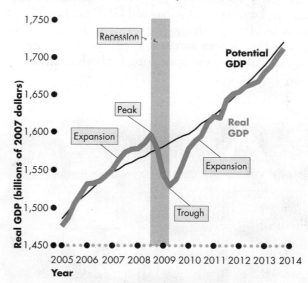

A recession began at a peak in the third quarter of 2008 and ended at a trough in the second quarter of 2009. A slow expansion then began and real GDP remained below potential GDP until 2011. Real GDP slipped below potential GDP again in 2012 and 2013.

Sources of data: Statistics Canada, CANSIM Table 380-0064 and Bank of Canada quarterly output gap data used to calculate potential GDP.

================= MyEconLab Real-time data =================

The Standard of Living Across Countries

Two problems arise in using real GDP to compare living standards across countries. First, the real GDP of one country must be converted into the same currency units as the real GDP of the other country. Second, the goods and services in both countries must be valued at the same prices. Comparing China and the United States provides a striking example of these two problems.

China and the United States in U.S. Dollars In 2013, nominal GDP per person in the United States was $53,000 and in China it was 42,000 yuan. The yuan is the currency of China, and the price at which the dollar and the yuan exchanged, the *market exchange rate*, was 6.2 yuan per $1 U.S. Using this exchange rate, 42,000 yuan converts to $6,775. On these numbers, GDP per person in the United States in 2014 was 7.9 times that in China.

The red line in Fig. 20.7 shows *real* GDP per person in China from 1980 to 2013 when the market exchange rate is used to convert yuan to U.S. dollars.

China and the United States at PPP Figure 20.7 shows a second estimate of China's real GDP per person that values China's production on the same terms as U.S. production. It uses *purchasing power parity* or *PPP* prices, which are the *same prices* for both countries.

FIGURE 20.7   Two Views of Real GDP in China

Real GDP per person in China has grown rapidly. But how rapidly it has grown and to what level depends on how real GDP is valued. When GDP in 2013 is valued at the market exchange rate (the red curve), U.S. income per person is 7.9 times that in China. China looks like a poor developing country. But the comparison is misleading. When GDP is valued at purchasing power parity prices (the green curve), U.S. income per person is only 5.4 times that in China.

Source of data: International Monetary Fund, *World Economic Outlook database*, April 2014.

MyEconLab Animation

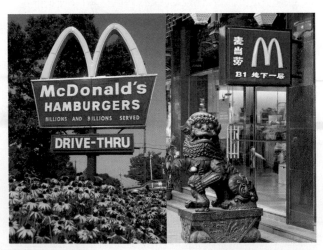

In July 2014, a Big Mac cost $4.80 in Chicago and 16.93 yuan or $2.73 in Shanghai. To compare real GDP in China and the United States, we must value China's Big Macs at the $4.80 U.S. price—the PPP price.

The prices of some goods are higher in the United States than in China, so in calculating real GDP these items get a smaller weight in China's real GDP than they get in U.S. real GDP. An example is a Big Mac that costs $4.80 in Chicago. In Shanghai, a Big Mac costs 16.93 yuan which is the equivalent of $2.73. So in China's real GDP, a Big Mac gets about half the weight that it gets in U.S. real GDP.

Some prices in China are higher than in the United States but more prices are lower, so Chinese prices put a lower value on China's production than do U.S. prices.

According to the PPP comparisons, real GDP per person in the United States in 2013 was 5.4 times that of China, not 7.9 times.

You've seen how real GDP is used to make standard of living comparisons over time and across countries. But real GDP isn't a perfect measure of the standard of living, and we'll now examine its limitations.

Limitations of Real GDP

Real GDP measures the value of goods and services that are bought in markets. Some of the factors that influence the standard of living and that are not part of GDP are:

- Household production
- Underground economic activity
- Leisure time
- Environmental quality

Household Production Preparing meals, changing a light bulb, mowing a lawn, washing a car, and caring for a child are all examples of household production. Because these productive activities are not traded in markets, they are not included in GDP.

The omission of household production from GDP means that GDP *underestimates* total production. But it also means that the growth rate of GDP *overestimates* the growth rate of total production. The reason is that some of the growth rate of market production (included in GDP) is a replacement for home production. So part of the increase in GDP arises from a decrease in home production.

Underground Economic Activity The *underground economy* is economic activity hidden from the view of the government to avoid taxes and regulations or because the activity is illegal. Because underground economic activity is unreported, it is omitted from GDP. The Canadian underground economy is estimated to range between 5 and 15 percent of GDP ($90 billion to $270 billion).

Leisure Time Leisure time is an economic good that adds to our economic well-being and the standard of living. Other things remaining the same, the more leisure we have, the better off we are. Our working time is valued as part of GDP, but our leisure time is not. Yet that leisure time must be at least as valuable to us as the wage that we earn for the last hour worked. If it were not, we would work instead of taking leisure. Over the years, leisure time has steadily increased. The workweek has become shorter, more people take early retirement, and the number of vacation days has increased. These improvements in economic well-being are not reflected in real GDP.

Environmental Quality Economic activity directly influences the quality of the environment. The burning of hydrocarbon fuels is the most visible activity that damages our environment, but it is not the only example. The depletion of nonrenewable natural resources, the mass clearing of forests, and the pollution of lakes and rivers are other major environmental consequences of industrial production.

Resources used to protect the environment are valued as part of GDP. For example, the value of catalytic converters that protect the atmosphere from automobile emissions is part of GDP.

An industrial society possibly produces more atmospheric pollution than an agricultural society does. But pollution does not always increase as we become wealthier. Wealthy people value a clean environment and are willing to pay for one. Compare the pollution in China today with pollution in Canada. The air in Beijing is much more polluted than that of Toronto or Montreal.

Whose production is more valuable: the chef's whose work gets counted in GDP ...

... or the busy mother's whose dinner preparation and child minding don't get counted?

AT **ISSUE**

Should GNNP Replace GDP?

The standard view of economists is that despite its limitations, GDP is a useful measure of the value of production and the overall level of economic activity in a country or region.

But a prominent economist, Joseph Stiglitz, has argued that GDP is dangerously misleading and needs to be replaced by a measure that he calls Green Net National Product (or GNNP).

Let's look at both sides of this issue.

Joe Stiglitz says . . .

- GDP has passed its use-by date.

- A *gross* measure is wrong because it ignores the depreciation of assets.

- A *domestic* measure is wrong because it ignores the incomes paid to foreigners who exploit a nation's resources.

- A *green* measure is needed to take account of the environmental damage that arises from production.

- GNNP subtracts from GDP incomes paid to foreigners, depreciation, the value of depleted natural resources, and the cost of a degraded environment.

- The existence of a market price for carbon emissions makes it possible to measure the cost of these emissions and subtract them from GDP.

- A bad accounting framework is likely to lead to bad decisions.

- America's "drain America first" energy policy is an example of a bad decision. It increases GDP but decreases GNNP and makes Americans poorer.

The Mainstream View

- As a measure of the value of market production in an economy, GDP does a good job.

- GDP is used to track the ups and downs of economic activity and it is a useful indicator for making macroeconomic stabilization policy decisions.

- GDP is *not* used to measure net national economic well-being nor to guide microeconomic resource allocation decisions.

- There is no disagreement that a *net national* measure is appropriate for measuring national economic well-being.

- There is no disagreement that "negative externalities" arising from carbon emissions and other pollution detract from economic well-being.

- The omissions from GDP of household production and underground production are *bigger* problems than those emphasized by Stiglitz.

- It isn't clear that depleting oil and coal resources is costly and misguided because advances in green energy technology will eventually make oil and coal of little value. The stone-age didn't end because we ran out of stone, and the carbon-age won't end because we run out of oil and coal!

Bad accounting frameworks are likely to lead to bad decisions. A government focused on GDP might be encouraged to give away mining or oil concessions; a focus on green NNP might make it realize that the country risks being worse off.

Joseph Stiglitz,
"Good Numbers Gone Bad,"
Fortune, September 25, 2006

When Anglo-Australian company BHP Billiton mines copper in Papua New Guinea, the country's GDP rises, but profits go abroad and 40,000 who live by a polluted river lose their means of earning a living. GNNP measures that loss.

Economics in Action
A Broader Indicator of Economic Well-Being

The limitations of real GDP reviewed in this chapter affect the standard of living and general well-being of every country. So to make international comparisons of the general state of economic well-being, we must look at real GDP and other indicators.

The United Nations has constructed a broader measure called the Human Development Index (HDI), which combines real GDP, life expectancy and health, and education. Real GDP per person (measured on the PPP basis—the same prices in all countries) is a major component of the HDI so, as you can see in the figure, the two are strongly correlated.

The figure shows the data for 2012. In that year, Norway had the highest HDI and Australia had the second highest but Qatar had the highest real GDP per person. Canada had the tenth-highest real GDP per person and the eighth-highest HDI.

The HDI of Canada is lower than that of Norway and Australia mainly because the people of those countries have a longer life expectancy than do Canadians.

African nations have the lowest levels of economic well-being. Niger had the lowest HDI and the

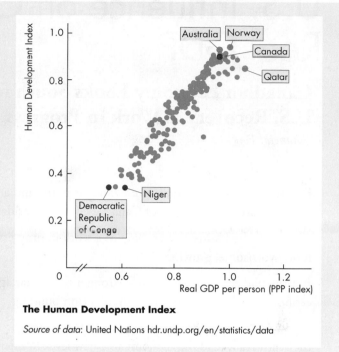

The Human Development Index

Source of data: United Nations hdr.undp.org/en/statistics/data

Democratic Republic of Congo had the lowest real GDP per person.

The Bottom Line Do we get the wrong message about the level and growth in economic well-being and the standard of living by looking at the growth of real GDP? The influences that are omitted from real GDP are probably large. Developing countries have a larger amount of household production than do developed countries, so the gap between their living standards is exaggerated. Also, as real GDP grows, part of the growth is a switch from home production to market production. This switch overstates the growth in economic well-being and the improvement in the standard of living.

It is possible to construct broader measures that combine the many influences that contribute to human happiness. The United Nations' Human Development Index or HDI (above) and Green Net National Product or GNNP (previous page) are two examples of dozens of other measures that have been proposed.

Despite all the alternatives, real GDP per person remains the most widely used indicator of economic well-being.

REVIEW QUIZ

1 Distinguish between real GDP and potential GDP and describe how each grows over time.
2 How does the growth rate of real GDP contribute to an improved standard of living?
3 What is a business cycle and what are its phases and turning points?
4 What is PPP and how does it help us to make valid international comparisons of real GDP?
5 Explain why real GDP might be an unreliable indicator of the standard of living.

Work these questions in Study Plan 20.3 and get instant feedback. Do a Key Terms Quiz.   MyEconLab

◆ You now know how economists measure GDP and what the GDP data tell us. *Economics in the News* on pp. 478–479 uses GDP to look at linkages between Canada and the United States as both economies emerge from recession.

U.S. Influence on Canadian Real GDP

Canadian Economy Looks South for Support—But U.S. Recovery Is Work in Progress

Financial Post
June 30, 2014

Forget the bad-weather effect, mediocre exports, and a recent resurgence of inflation. The most important barometer of Canada's economy resides—as always—to the south.

That said, the United States remains a work in progress and not without its own, perhaps more worrisome, growing pains.

But the two economies are likely stronger than what appears on the surface, according to economists who see underlying momentum building.

"Most of the domestic sources have run their course, and can grind out modest gains, but they can't really lead the economy to a new level. We definitely need exports now. And exports equals the United States," said Douglas Porter, chief economist at BMO Capital Markets.

"The view is that the U.S. economy will start to improve, and a somewhat weaker Canadian dollar will offer a bit of support. But in terms of actual hard data, we're not seeing signs of that yet."

There are hints of that in the United States, with improving consumer confidence, auto sales, home sales, and job growth. Add to that a jump in equity markets on both sides of the border, also pointing to a turnaround.

"But it's certainly not a done deal," Mr. Porter said. "But I think there's a pretty good case for improvement in the second half of the year."

So far in 2014, the Canadian and U.S. economies have fallen short of forecasts.

The Bank of Canada, in its most recent outlook published in April, predicted 1.5% annualized growth in the first quarter of this year. Instead, the economy delivered a 1.2% gain. For the second quarter, the central bank has called for 2.5% growth, but most analysts have penciled in a weaker increase of between 2% and 2.4%. ...

Written by Gordon Isfeld. Material reprinted with the express permission of *National Post*, a division of Postmedia Network Inc.

ESSENCE OF THE STORY

- U.S. economic performance influences Canada's economic performance.

- The United States has been expanding very slowly, which has subdued Canada's exports.

- There are hints that the U.S. economy will expand more quickly, but so far in 2014 the Canadian and U.S. economies have fallen short of forecasts.

- In the first quarter of 2014, Canadian real GDP increased at a 1.2 percent annualized rate against the Bank of Canada's predicted rate of 1.5 percent.

- For the second quarter of 2014, Canadian real GDP is expected to increase at a 2 to 2.4 percent annualized rate.

ECONOMIC ANALYSIS

- Canada's economic performance is strongly influenced by events in the United States and the rest of the world.

- The past few years have seen unusually large swings in real GDP.

- In 2008 and 2009, an unusually deep global recession occurred and the United States was hardest hit.

- In the U.S. recession, which started at a peak at the end of 2007 and ended at a trough in mid-2009, real GDP fell by 5.5 percent.

- Figure 1 illustrates the U.S. recession. This figure is the U.S. version of Fig. 20.6 (p. 473), which shows the Canadian recession.

- Figure 1 also shows the U.S. expansion that started from the 2009 trough alongside the official U.S. estimate of its potential GDP.

- Two features of the graph in Fig. 1 stand out: A slow expansion and a persistently large gap between potential and actual real GDP.

- It is this poor performance of the U.S. economy that the news article describes as a "work in progress."

- Figure 2 compares the recession and subsequent expansion in Canada and the United States.

- To compare the two economies with U.S. real GDP about 10 times Canada's, the graph measures all the variables as percentages of their levels in 2005.

- You can see that the Canadian recession started one quarter later than the U.S. recession and was less severe.

- You can see that Canada's real GDP expanded more rapidly than U.S. real GDP and returned to potential GDP by 2013.

- So although it is true that the U.S. economy has a large influence on Canada, the Canadian economy has performed much better than the U.S. economy.

- A key reason for Canada's better performance is the fact that we export oil, gas, and mineral resources to a more rapidly growing Asia.

- Canada has returned to potential GDP faster than the United States for another reason: Canada's estimated potential GDP growth has slowed.

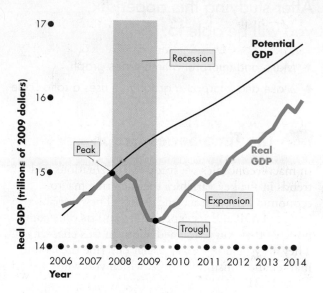

Figure 1 The U.S. Economy in Weak Expansion

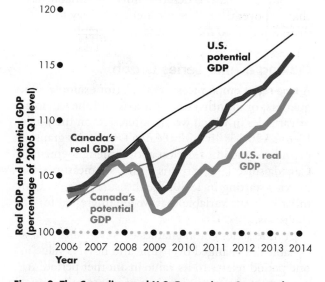

Figure 2 The Canadian and U.S. Expansions Compared

- Potential GDP is estimated and based on assumptions. The U.S. assumptions look incorrect. But more time is needed to be sure.

APPENDIX

Graphs in Macroeconomics

After studying this appendix, you will be able to:

◆ Make and interpret a time-series graph
◆ Make and interpret a graph that uses a ratio scale

◢ The Time-Series Graph

In macroeconomics we study the fluctuations and trends in the key variables that describe macroeconomic performance and policy. These variables include GDP and its expenditure and income components that you've learned about in this chapter. They also include variables that describe the labour market and consumer prices, which you will study in Chapter 21.

Regardless of the variable of interest, we want to be able to compare its value today with that in the past; and we want to describe how the variable has changed over time. The most effective way to do these things is to make a time-series graph.

Making a Time-Series Graph

A **time-series graph** measures time (for example, years, quarters, or months) on the *x*-axis and the variable or variables in which we are interested on the *y*-axis. Figure A20.1 is an example of a time-series graph. It provides some information about unemployment in Canada since 1980. In this figure, we measure time in years starting in 1980. We measure the unemployment rate (the variable that we are interested in) on the *y*-axis.

A time-series graph enables us to visualize how a variable has changed over time and how its value in one period relates to its value in another period. It conveys an enormous amount of information quickly and easily.

Let's see how to "read" a time-series graph.

Reading a Time-Series Graph

To practise reading a time-series graph, take a close look at Fig. A20.1. The graph shows the level, change, and speed of change of the variable.

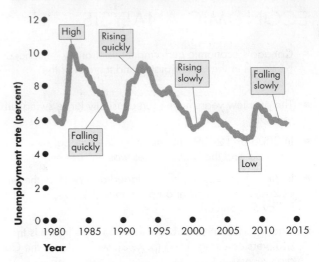

FIGURE A20.1   A Time-Series Graph

A time-series graph plots the level of a variable on the *y*-axis against time (here measured in years) on the *x*-axis. This graph shows the unemployment rate each year from 1980 to 2014. The graph shows when unemployment was high, when it was low, when it increased, when it decreased, and when it changed quickly and slowly.

——— MyEconLab Animation ———

■ The *level* of the variable: It tells us when unemployment is *high* and *low*. When the line is a long distance above the *x*-axis, the unemployment rate is high, as it was, for example, in 1983. When the line is close to the *x*-axis, the unemployment rate is low, as it was, for example, in 2007.

■ The *change* in the variable: It tells us how unemployment *changes*—whether it *increases* or *decreases*. When the line slopes upward, as it did in 2008 and 2009, the unemployment rate is rising. When the line slopes downward, as it did in 1984 and 1997, the unemployment rate is falling.

■ The *speed of change* in the variable: It tells us whether the unemployment rate is rising or falling *quickly* or *slowly*. If the line is very steep, then the unemployment rate increases or decreases quickly. If the line is not steep, the unemployment rate increases or decreases slowly. For example, the unemployment rate rose quickly in 1994 and slowly in 2003, and it fell quickly in 1987 and slowly in 2013.

Ratio Scale Reveals Trend

A time-series graph also reveals whether a variable has a **cycle**, which is a tendency for a variable to alternate between upward and downward movements, or a **trend**, which is a tendency for a variable to move in one general direction.

The unemployment rate in Fig. A20.1 has a cycle but no trend. When a trend is present, a special kind of time-series graph, one that uses a ratio scale on the *y*-axis, reveals the trend.

A Time-Series with a Trend

Many macroeconomics variables, among them GDP and the average level of prices, have an upward trend. Figure A20.2 shows an example of such a variable: the average prices paid by consumers.

In Fig. A20.2(a), Canadian consumer prices since 1970 are graphed on a normal scale. In 1970 the level is 100. In other years, the average level of prices is measured as a percentage of the 1970 level.

The graph clearly shows the upward trend of prices. But it doesn't tell us when prices were rising fastest or whether there was any change in the trend. Just looking at the upward-sloping line in Fig. A20.2(a) gives the impression that the pace of growth of consumer prices was constant.

Using a Ratio Scale

On a graph axis with a normal scale, the gap between 1 and 2 is the same as that between 3 and 4. On a graph axis with a ratio scale, the gap between 1 and 2 is the same as that between 2 and 4. The ratio 2 to 1 equals the ratio 4 to 2. By using a ratio scale, we can "see" when the growth rate (the percentage change per unit of time) changes.

Figure A20.2(b) shows an example of a ratio scale. Notice that the values on the *y*-axis get closer together but the gap between 400 and 200 equals the gap between 200 and 100: The ratio gaps are equal.

Graphing the data on a ratio scale reveals the trends. In the case of consumer prices, the trend is much steeper during the 1970s and early 1980s than in the later years. The steeper the line in the ratio-scale graph in part (b), the faster are prices rising. Prices rose rapidly during the 1970s and early 1980s and more slowly in the later 1980s and the 1990s. The ratio-scale graph reveals this fact. We use ratio-scale graphs extensively in macroeconomics.

FIGURE A20.2   Ratio Scale Reveals Trend

(a) Normal scale

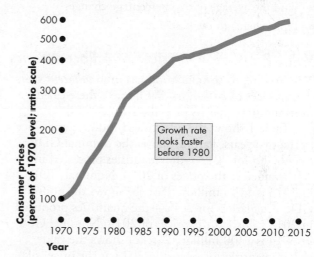

(b) Ratio scale

The graph shows the average of consumer prices from 1970 to 2014. The level is 100 in 1970 and the value for other years are percentages of the 1970 level. Consumer prices normally rise each year, so the line slopes upward. In part (a), where the *y*-axis scale is normal, the rate of increase appears to be constant.

In part (b), where the *y*-axis is a ratio scale (the ratio of 400 to 200 equals the ratio 200 to 100), prices rose faster during the 1970s and early 1980s and slower in the later years. The ratio scale reveals this trend.

MyEconLab Animation

MATHEMATICAL NOTE

Chained-Dollar Real GDP

In the real GDP calculation on p. 471, real GDP in 2014 is 1.6 times its value in 2007. But suppose that we use 2014 as the reference base year and value real GDP in 2007 at 2014 prices. If you do the math, you will see that real GDP in 2007 is $150 million at 2014 prices. GDP in 2014 is $300 million (in 2014 prices), so now the numbers say that real GDP has doubled. Which is correct: Did real GDP increase 1.6 times or double? Should we use the prices of 2007 or 2014? The answer is that we need to use *both* sets of prices.

Statistics Canada uses a measure of real GDP called *chained-dollar real GDP*. Three steps are needed to calculate this measure:

- Value production in the prices of adjacent years
- Find the average of two percentage changes
- Link (chain) to the base year

Value Production in Prices of Adjacent Years

The first step is to value production in *adjacent* years at the prices of *both* years. We'll make these calculations for 2014 and its preceding year, 2013.

Table 1 shows the quantities produced and prices in the two years. Part (a) shows the nominal GDP calculation for 2013—the quantities produced in 2013 valued at the prices of 2013. Nominal GDP in 2013 is $145 million. Part (b) shows the nominal GDP calculation for 2014—the quantities produced in 2014 valued at the prices of 2014. Nominal GDP in 2014 is $300 million. Part (c) shows the value of the quantities produced in 2014 at the prices of 2013. This total is $160 million. Finally, part (d) shows the value of the quantities produced in 2013 at the prices of 2014. This total is $275 million.

Find the Average of Two Percentage Changes

The second step is to find the percentage change in the value of production based on the prices in the two adjacent years. Table 2 summarizes these calculations.

Part (a) shows that, valued at the prices of 2013, production increased from $145 million in 2013 to $160 million in 2014, an increase of 10.3 percent.

TABLE 1   Real GDP Calculation Step 1: Value Production in Adjacent Years at Prices of Both Years

Item		Quantity (millions)	Price (dollars)	Expenditure (millions of dollars)
(a) In 2013				
C	T-shirts	3	5	15
I	Computer chips	3	10	30
G	Security services	5	20	100
Y	Nominal GDP in 2013			**145**
(b) In 2014				
C	T-shirts	4	5	20
I	Computer chips	2	20	40
G	Security services	6	40	240
Y	Nominal GDP in 2014			**300**
(c) Quantities of 2014 valued at prices of 2013				
C	T-shirts	4	5	20
I	Computer chips	2	10	20
G	Security services	6	20	120
Y	2014 production at 2013 prices			**160**
(d) Quantities of 2013 valued at prices of 2014				
C	T-shirts	3	5	15
I	Computer chips	3	20	60
G	Security services	5	40	200
Y	2013 production at 2014 prices			**275**

Step 1 is to value the production of adjacent years at the prices of both years. Here, we value the production of 2013 and 2014 at the prices of both 2013 and 2014. The value of 2013 production at 2013 prices, in part (a), is nominal GDP in 2013. The value of 2014 production at 2014 prices, in part (b), is nominal GDP in 2014. Part (c) calculates the value of 2014 production at 2013 prices, and part (d) calculates the value of 2013 production at 2014 prices. We use these numbers in Step 2.

Part (b) shows that, valued at the prices of 2014, production increased from $275 million in 2013 to $300 million in 2014, an increase of 9.1 percent. Part (c) shows that the average of these two percentage changes in the value of production is 9.7. That is, $(10.3 + 9.1) \div 2 = 9.7$.

What we've just calculated is the *growth rate of real GDP* in 2014. But what is the *level* of real GDP? Finding the level of real GDP is what happens in Step 3 that we'll now describe.

TABLE 2 Real GDP Calculation Step 2: Find Average of Two Percentage Changes

Value of Production	Millions of dollars
(a) At 2013 prices	
Nominal GDP in 2013	145
2014 production at 2013 prices	160
Percentage change in production at 2013 prices	10.3
(b) At 2014 prices	
2013 production at 2014 prices	275
Nominal GDP in 2014	300
Percentage change in production at 2014 prices	9.1
(c) Average percentage change in 2014	**9.7**

Using the numbers calculated in Step 1, the change in production from 2013 to 2014 valued at 2013 prices is 10.3 percent, in part (a). The change in production from 2013 to 2014 valued at 2014 prices is 9.1 percent, in part (b). The average of these two percentage changes is 9.7 percent in part (c).

Link (Chain) to the Base Year

The third step is to measure real GDP in the prices of the *reference base year*. To do this, Statistics Canada selects a base year (currently 2007) in which, *by definition*, real GDP equals nominal GDP. Statistics Canada performs calculations like the ones that you've just worked through for 2014 to find the percentage change in real GDP in each pair of adjacent years. Finally, it uses the percentage changes calculated in Step 2 to find real GDP in 2007 prices for each year.

Figure 1 illustrates these Step 3 calculations to chain link to the base year. In the reference base year, 2007, real GDP equals nominal GDP, which we'll assume is $125 million (highlighted in the chain). Using the same methods that we've just described for 2013 and 2014, we'll assume that the growth rate of real GDP from 2007 to 2008 is 4 percent (also shown in the chain). If real GDP in 2007 is $125 million and the growth rate in 2007 is 4 percent, then real GDP in 2008 is $130 million—4 percent higher than real GDP in 2007.

By repeating these calculations for each year, we obtain *chained-dollar real GDP* in 2007 dollars for each year. The growth rates shown in the table for 2005 to 2014 take real GDP in 2013 to $182 million. That is, the 2013 *chained-dollar real GDP* in 2007 dollars is $182 million.

We've calculated the growth rate for 2014, which is highlighted in Fig. 1 as 9.7 percent. Applying this growth rate to the $182 million level of real GDP in 2013 gives real GDP in 2014 as $200 million.

Notice that the growth rates depend only on prices and quantities produced in adjacent years and do not depend on what the reference base year is. Changing the reference base year changes the *level* of real GDP in each year, but it does not change the *growth rates*.

Year	2005	2006	2007	2008	2009	2010	2011	2012	2013	2014
Growth rate (percent per year)		7	6	4	5	8	9	6	7	9.7
Chained-dollar real GDP (millions of 2007 dollars)	110	118	125	130	136	147	160	170	182	200

Figure 1 Real GDP Calculation Step 3: Repeat Growth Rate Calculations and Chain Link

Exercise

The table provides data on the economy of Tropical Republic, which produces only bananas and coconuts.

Use this data to calculate Tropical Republic's nominal GDP in 2013 and 2014 and its chained-dollar real GDP in 2014 expressed in 2013 dollars.

Table

Quantities	2013	2014
Bananas	1,000 bunches	1,100 bunches
Coconuts	500 bunches	525 bunches
Prices		
Bananas	$2 a bunch	$3 a bunch
Coconuts	$10 a bunch	$8 a bunch

SUMMARY

Key Points

Gross Domestic Product (pp. 466–468)

- GDP, or gross domestic product, is the market value of all the final goods and services produced in a country during a given period.
- A final good is an item that is bought by its final user, and it contrasts with an intermediate good, which is a component of a final good.
- GDP is calculated by using either the expenditure or income totals in the circular flow model.
- Aggregate expenditure on goods and services equals aggregate income and GDP.

Working Problems 1 to 4 will give you a better understanding of gross domestic product.

Measuring Canada's GDP (pp. 469–471)

- Because aggregate expenditure, aggregate income, and the value of aggregate production are equal, we can measure GDP by using the expenditure approach or the income approach.
- The expenditure approach sums consumption expenditure, investment, government expenditure on goods and services, and net exports.
- The income approach sums wages, interest, rent, and profit (plus indirect taxes less subsidies plus depreciation).

- Real GDP is measured using a common set of prices to remove the effects of inflation from GDP.

Working Problems 5 to 8 will give you a better understanding of measuring Canada's GDP.

The Uses and Limitations of Real GDP (pp. 472–477)

- Real GDP is used to compare the standard of living over time and across countries.
- Real GDP per person grows and fluctuates around the more smoothly growing potential GDP.
- Incomes would be much higher today if the growth rate of real GDP per person had not slowed during the 1970s.
- International real GDP comparisons use PPP prices.
- Real GDP is not a perfect measure of the standard of living because it excludes household production, the underground economy, health and life expectancy, leisure time, security, environmental quality, and political freedom and social justice.

Working Problem 9 will give you a better understanding of the uses and limitations of real GDP.

Key Terms

MyEconLab Key Terms Quiz

WORKED PROBLEM

MyEconLab   You can work this problem in Chapter 20 Study Plan.

Items in Dreamland's national accounts include:

- Government expenditure on goods and services: $600
- Consumption expenditure: $1,950
- Rent and interest: $400
- Indirect taxes less subsidies: $350
- Investment: $550
- Wages: $1,600
- Profit: $500
- Net exports: $200
- Depeciation: $450

Questions

1. Use the expenditure approach to calculate GDP.
2. Calculate net domestic income at factor cost.
3. Calculate net domestic income at market prices.
4. Use the income approach to calculate GDP.

Solutions

1. The expenditure approach sums the expenditure on final goods and services. That is, GDP is the sum of consumption expenditure, investment, government expenditure, and net exports. That is, GDP = $1,950 + $550 + $600 + $200 = $3,300.

Key Point: GDP equals aggregate expenditure on final goods produced in Dreamland, which equals C + I + G + NX. See the figure.

2. Net domestic income at factor cost is the income paid to factors of production (labour, land, capital, and entrepreneurship): wages, rent, interest, and profit. Net domestic income at factor cost equals $1,600 + $400 + $500 = $2,500.

Key Point: The incomes earned by the factors of production sum to net domestic incomes at factor cost. See the figure.

3. Expenditure on goods and services equals the quantity bought multiplied by the market price. Incomes are total factor costs. The market price of a good or service equals the cost of the factors of production used to produce it if production is not subsidized and sale of the good is not taxed.

   If the producer of a good receives a subsidy, then the market price of the good is less than the cost of producing it. If a tax is imposed on the sale of the good, then the market price exceeds the cost of producing it. So

   Market price = Factor cost + Indirect taxes less subsidies.

   Net domestic income at factor cost is $2,500, so net domestic income at market prices equals $2,500 + $350 = $2,850.

Key Point: To convert from factor cost to market prices, add indirect taxes less subsidies. See the figure.

4. GDP is a gross measure of total production at market prices while net domestic income at market prices is a net measure. So using the income approach to measuring GDP, depreciation must be added to net domestic income at market prices to convert it to GDP. That is, using the incomes approach, GDP = $2,850 + $450 = $3,300.

Key Point: To convert net domestic income at market prices into GDP, add depreciation. See the figure.

Key Figure

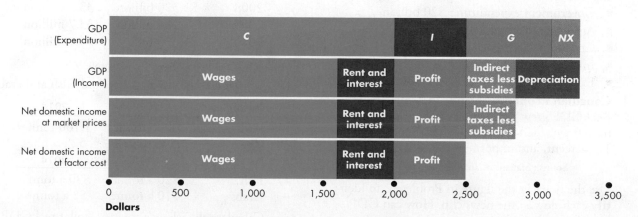

STUDY PLAN PROBLEMS AND APPLICATIONS

MyEconLab   You can work Problems 1 to 10 in Chapter 20 Study Plan and get instant feedback.

Gross Domestic Product (Study Plan 20.1)

1. Classify each of the following items as a final good or service or an intermediate good or service and identify each item as a component of consumption expenditure, investment, or government expenditure on goods and services:
   - Banking services bought by a student.
   - New cars bought by Hertz, the car rental firm.
   - Newsprint bought by the *National Post*.
   - A new limo bought for the prime minister.
   - New house bought by Alanis Morissette.

2. Use the following figure, which illustrates the circular flow model.

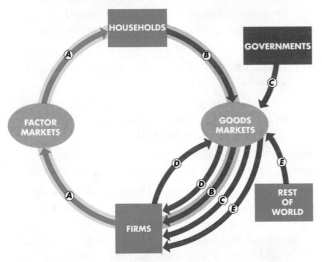

During 2014, flow *A* was $13.0 billion, flow *B* was $9.1 billion, flow *D* was $3.3 billion, and flow *E* was –$0.8 billion. Calculate (i) GDP and (ii) government expenditure.

3. Use the following data to calculate aggregate expenditure and imports of goods and services:
   - Government expenditure: $20 billion
   - Aggregate income: $100 billion
   - Consumption expenditure: $67 billion
   - Investment: $21 billion
   - Exports of goods and services: $30 billion

4. **Canadian Economy Shrinks in May**
   Real GDP grew 1 percent in 2013. Business investment increased 3.2 percent, exports grew 1.6 percent, and imports rose by 2.2 percent.
   Source: Statistics Canada, *The Daily*, July 29, 2013

   Use the flows in the figure in Problem 2 to identify each flow in the news clip. How can GDP have grown by only 1 percent with investment and exports growing by more than 1 percent?

Measuring Canada's GDP (Study Plan 20.2)

Use the following data to work Problems 5 and 6. The table lists some data for Canada in 2008.

Item	Billions of dollars
Wages paid to labour	815
Consumption expenditure	885
Net domestic income at factor cost	1,210
Investment	304
Government expenditure	357
Net exports	32
Depreciation	202

5. Calculate Canada's GDP in 2008.

6. Explain the approach (expenditure or income) that you used to calculate GDP.

Use the following data to work Problems 7 and 8. Tropical Republic produces only bananas and coconuts. The base year is 2013.

Quantities	2013	2014
Bananas	800 bunches	900 bunches
Coconuts	400 bunches	500 bunches

Prices	2013	2014
Bananas	$2 a bunch	$4 a bunch
Coconuts	$10 a bunch	$5 a bunch

7. Calculate nominal GDP in 2013 and 2014.

8. Calculate real GDP in 2014 in base-year prices.

The Uses and Limitations of Real GDP (Study Plan 20.3)

9. Explain in which of the years Canada's standard of living (i) increased and (ii) decreased.

Year	Real GDP	Population
2007	$1,311 billion	32.9 million
2008	$1,320 billion	33.3 million
2009	$1,284 billion	33.7 million
2010	$1,325 billion	34.1 million

Mathematical Note (Study Plan 20.MN)

10. An island economy produces only fish and crabs.

Quantities	2013	2014
Fish	1,000 tonnes	1,100 tonnes
Crabs	500 tonnes	525 tonnes

Prices	2013	2014
Fish	$20 a tonne	$30 a tonne
Crabs	$10 a tonne	$8 a tonne

Calculate the island's chained-dollar real GDP in 2014 expressed in 2013 dollars.

ADDITIONAL PROBLEMS AND APPLICATIONS

MyEconLab   You can work these problems in MyEconLab if assigned by your instructor.

Gross Domestic Product

11. Classify each of the following items as a final good or service or an intermediate good or service and identify which is a component of consumption expenditure, investment, or government expenditure on goods and services:
    - Banking services bought by Loblaws.
    - Security system bought by the TD Bank.
    - Coffee beans bought by Tim Hortons.
    - New coffee grinders bought by Second Cup.
    - Starbucks grande mocha frappuccino bought by a student at a campus coffee bar.
    - New helicopters bought by Canada's army.

Use the figure in Problem 2 to work Problems 12 and 13.

12. In 2013, flow *A* was $1,000 billion, flow *C* was $250 billion, flow *B* was $650 billion, and flow *E* was $50 billion. Calculate investment.

13. In 2014, flow *D* was $2 trillion, flow *E* was –$1 trillion, flow *A* was $10 trillion, and flow *C* was $4 trillion. Calculate consumption expenditure.

Use the following information to work Problems 14 and 15.

The components and robots for Toyota's auto assembly lines in Canada are built in Japan. Toyota assembles cars for the Canadian market in Ontario.

14. Explain where these activities appear in Canada's *National Income and Expenditure Accounts*.

15. Explain where these activities appear in Japan's *National Income and Expenditure Accounts*.

Use the following news clip to work Problems 16 and 17, and use the circular flow model to illustrate your answers.

Boeing Bets the House

Boeing is producing some components of its new 787 Dreamliner in Japan and is assembling it in the United States. Much of the first year's production will be sold to ANA (All Nippon Airways), a Japanese airline.

Source: *The New York Times*, May 7, 2006

16. Explain how Boeing's activities and its transactions affect U.S. and Japanese GDP.

17. Explain how ANA's activities and its transactions affect U.S. and Japanese GDP.

Measuring Canada's GDP

Use the following data to work Problems 18 and 19. The table lists some data for Xanadu in 2014.

Item	Billions of dollars
Wages paid to labour	800
Consumption expenditure	1,000
Profit, interest, and rents	340
Investment	150
Government expenditure	290
Net exports	–34

18. Calculate Xanadu's GDP in 2014.

19. Explain the approach (expenditure or income) that you used to calculate GDP.

Use the following data to work Problems 20 and 21. An economy produces only apples and oranges. The base year is 2013, and the table gives the quantities produced and the prices.

Quantities	2013	2014
Apples	60	160
Oranges	80	220
Prices	**2013**	**2014**
Apples	$0.50	$1.00
Oranges	$0.25	$2.00

20. Calculate nominal GDP in 2013 and 2014.

21. Calculate real GDP in 2013 and 2014 expressed in base-year prices.

22. **GDP Expands 11.4 Percent, Fastest in 13 Years**
    China's gross domestic product grew 11.4 percent last year and marked a fifth year of double-digit growth. The increase was especially remarkable given that the United States is experiencing a slowdown due to the sub-prime crisis and housing slump. Citigroup estimates that each 1 percent drop in the U.S. economy will shave 1.3 percent off China's growth, because Americans are heavy users of Chinese products. In spite of the uncertainties, China is expected to post its sixth year of double-digit growth next year.

    Source: *The China Daily*, January 24, 2008

    Use the expenditure approach for calculating China's GDP to explain why "each 1 percent drop in the U.S. economy will shave 1.3 percent off China's growth."

The Uses and Limitations of Real GDP

23. The United Nations' Human Development Index (HDI) is based on real GDP per person, life expectancy at birth, and indicators of the quality and quantity of education.

    a. Explain why the HDI might be better than real GDP as a measure of economic welfare.

    b. Which items in the HDI are part of real GDP and which items are not in real GDP?

    c. Do you think the HDI should be expanded to include items such as pollution, resource depletion, and political freedom? Explain.

    d. What other influences on economic welfare should be included in a comprehensive measure?

24. **U.K. Living Standards Outstrip U.S.**
    Oxford analysts report that living standards in Britain are set to rise above those in America for the first time since the nineteenth century. Real GDP per person in Britain will be £23,500 this year, compared with £23,250 in America, but also the U.K. economy has had a record run of growth since 2001. But the Oxford analysts also point out that Americans benefit from lower prices than those in Britain.

    Source: *The Sunday Times*, January 6, 2008

    If real GDP per person is greater in the United Kingdom than in the United States but Americans benefit from lower prices, does this comparison of real GDP per person really tell us which country has the higher standard of living?

25. Use the news clip in Problem 22.

    a. Why might China's recent GDP growth rates overstate the actual increase in the level of production taking place in China?

    b. Explain the complications involved with attempting to compare the economic welfare in China and the United States by using the GDP for each country.

26. **Poor India Makes Millionaires at Fastest Pace**
    India, with the world's largest population of poor people, created millionaires at the fastest pace in the world in 2007. India added another 23,000 millionaires in 2007 to its 2006 tally of 100,000 millionaires measured in dollars. That is 1 millionaire for about 7,000 people living on less than $2 a day.

    Source: *The Times of India*, June 25, 2008

    a. Why might real GDP per person misrepresent the standard of living of the average Indian?

    b. Why might $2 a day underestimate the standard of living of the poorest Indians?

Economics in the News

27. After you have studied *Economics in the News* on pp. 478–479, answer the following questions.

    a. Which economy—the Canadian or the U.S.—had the longer and deeper recession in 2008–2009?

    b. Which economy—the Canadian or the U.S.—had the lower estimated growth rate of potential GDP?

    c. Why does the news article describe the U.S. economy as a "work in progress"?

    d. What features of the Canadian economy provide some immunity from U.S. economic ills?

28. **Totally Gross**
    GDP has proved useful in tracking both short-term fluctuations and long-run growth. Which isn't to say GDP doesn't miss some things. Amartya Sen, at Harvard, helped create the United Nations' Human Development Index, which combines health and education data with per capita GDP to give a better measure of the wealth of nations. Joseph Stiglitz, at Columbia, advocates a "green net national product" that takes into account the depletion of natural resources. Others want to include happiness in the measure. These alternative benchmarks have merit, but can they be measured with anything like the frequency, reliability, and impartiality of GDP?

    Source: *Time*, April 21, 2008

    a. Explain the factors that the news clip identifies as limiting the usefulness of GDP as a measure of economic welfare.

    b. What are the challenges involved in trying to incorporate measurements of those factors in an effort to better measure economic welfare?

    c. What does the ranking of Canada in the Human Development Index (see p. 477) imply about the levels of health and education relative to other nations?

Mathematical Note

29. Use the information in Problem 20 to calculate the chained-dollar real GDP in 2014 expressed in 2013 dollars.

21

MONITORING JOBS AND INFLATION

After studying this chapter, you will be able to:

◆ Explain why unemployment is a problem and how we measure the unemployment rate and other labour market indicators

◆ Explain why unemployment occurs and why it is present even at full employment

◆ Explain why inflation is a problem and how we measure the inflation rate

Each month, we chart the course of unemployment and inflation as measures of Canadian economic health. How do we measure the unemployment rate and the inflation rate and are they reliable vital signs?

As the Canadian economy slowly expanded after a recession in 2008 and 2009, job growth was weak and questions about the health of the labour market became of vital importance to millions of Canadian families. *Economics in the News*, at the end of this chapter, compares the Canadian and U.S. labour markets through recession and a weak 2010–2014 expansion.

◆ Employment and Unemployment

What kind of job market will you enter when you graduate? Will there be plenty of good jobs to choose among, or will jobs be so hard to find that you end up taking one that doesn't use your education and pays a low wage? The answer depends, to a large degree, on the total number of jobs available and on the number of people competing for them.

The class of 2014 had a tough time in the jobs market. In July 2014, four years after a recession, 1.4 million Canadians wanted a job but couldn't find one, and another 600,000 had given up the search for a job or had reluctantly settled for a part-time job.

Despite the high unemployment, the Canadian economy is an incredible job-creating machine. Even in 2009 at the depths of recession, 16.8 million people had jobs—5 million more than in 1989. But in recent years, population growth has outstripped jobs growth, so unemployment is a serious problem.

Why Unemployment Is a Problem

Unemployment is a serious personal and social economic problem for two main reasons. It results in:

- Lost incomes and production
- Lost human capital

Lost Incomes and Production The loss of a job brings a loss of income and lost production. These losses are devastating for the people who bear them and they make unemployment a frightening prospect for everyone. Unemployment benefits create a safety net, but they don't fully replace lost earnings.

Lost production means lower consumption and a lower investment in capital, which lowers the living standard in both the present and the future.

Lost Human Capital Prolonged unemployment permanently damages a person's job prospects by destroying human capital.

Economics in Action
What Kept Ben Bernanke Awake at Night

The Great Depression began in October 1929, when the U.S. stock market crashed. It reached its deepest point in 1933, when 25 percent of the labour force was unemployed, and lasted until 1941, when the United States entered World War II. The depression quickly spread globally to envelop most nations.

The 1930s were and remain the longest and worst period of high unemployment in history. Failed banks, shops, farms, and factories left millions of Americans and Canadians without jobs, homes, and food. Without the support of government and charities, millions would have starved.

The Great Depression was an enormous political event: It fostered the rise of the German and Japanese militarism that was to bring the most devastating war humans have ever fought. It also led to a "New Deal" proposed first by President Franklin D. Roosevelt and then by Prime Minister R. B. Bennett, which expanded government intervention in markets and questioned the efficiency and equity of the market economy.

The Great Depression also brought a revolution in economics. British economist John Maynard Keynes published his *General Theory of Employment, Interest, and Money* and created what we now call macroeconomics.

Many economists have studied the Great Depression and tried to determine why what started out as an ordinary recession became so devastating. Among them is Ben Bernanke, the former chairman of the U.S. Federal Reserve.

One of the reasons the U.S. Federal Reserve was so aggressive in 2008–2009 in cutting interest rates and saving banks from going under is that Ben Bernanke is so vividly aware of the horrors of total economic collapse and was determined to avoid any risk of a repeat of the Great Depression.

Think about a manager who loses his job when his employer downsizes. The only work he can find is driving a taxi. After a year in this work, he discovers that he can't compete with new MBA graduates. Eventually, he gets hired as a manager but in a small firm and at a lower wage than before. He has lost some of his human capital. The cost of lost human capital is particularly acute for older workers.

Governments make strenuous efforts to measure unemployment accurately and to adopt policies to moderate its level and ease its pain. Let's see how the Canadian government monitors unemployment.

Labour Force Survey

Every month, Statistics Canada conducts a *Labour Force Survey* in which it asks 54,000 households a series of questions about the age and job market status of the members of each household during a previous week called the *reference week*.

Figure 21.1 shows the population categories used by Statistics Canada and the relationships among the categories.

The population divides into two broad groups: the working-age population and others who are too young to work or who live in institutions and are unable to work. The **working-age population** is the total number of people aged 15 years and over. The working-age population is also divided into two groups: those in the labour force and those not in the labour force. Members of the labour force are either employed or unemployed. So the **labour force** is the sum of the employed and the unemployed. The employed are either full-time or part-time workers; and part-time workers either want part-time work (voluntary part time) or want full-time work (involuntary part time).

To be counted as employed in the Labour Force Survey, a person must have either a full-time job or a part-time job. To be counted as unemployed, a person must be *available for work* and must be in one of three categories:

1. On temporary layoff with an expectation of recall
2. Without work but has looked for work in the past four weeks
3. Has a new job to start within four weeks

People who satisfy one of these three criteria are counted as unemployed. People in the working-age population who are neither employed nor unemployed are classified as *not in the labour force*.

FIGURE 21.1   Population Labour Force Categories

The total population is divided into the working-age population and others. The working-age population is divided into those in the labour force and those not in the labour force. The labour force is divided into the employed and the unemployed. And the employed are either full time or part time, and the part-time employed are either voluntary or involuntary part time.

Source of data: Statistics Canada, CANSIM Tables 051-0005, 282-0002, and 282-0014.

— MyEconLab Animation —

In 2013, the population of Canada was 35.4 million; the working-age population was 28.7 million. Of this number, 9.6 million were not in the labour force. Most of these people were in school full time or had retired from work. The remaining 19.1 million people made up the Canadian labour force. Of these, 17.7 million were employed and 1.4 million were unemployed. Of the 17.7 million employed, 3.4 million had part-time jobs, and of these, 0.9 million wanted a full-time job but couldn't find one.

Four Labour Market Indicators

Statistics Canada calculates four indicators of the state of the labour market. They are:

- The unemployment rate
- The involuntary part-time rate
- The labour force participation rate
- The employment-to-population ratio

The Unemployment Rate The amount of unemployment is an indicator of the extent to which people who want jobs can't find them. The **unemployment rate** is the percentage of the people in the labour force who are unemployed. That is,

$$\text{Unemployment rate} = \frac{\text{Number of people unemployed}}{\text{Labour force}} \times 100.$$

People in the labour force are either employed or unemployed, so

$$\text{Labour force} = \frac{\text{Number of people}}{\text{employed}} + \frac{\text{Number of people}}{\text{unemployed}}$$

In 2013, the number of people employed was 17.73 million and the number unemployed was 1.35 million. By using the above equations, you can verify that the labour force was 19.08 million (17.73 million plus 1.35 million) and the unemployment rate was 7.1 percent (1.35 million divided by 19.08 million, multiplied by 100).

Figure 21.2 shows the unemployment rate from 1960 to 2014. The average during this period is 7.6 percent. The unemployment rate fluctuates over the business cycle. It increases as a recession deepens, reaches a peak value after a recession ends, and decreases as the expansion gets underway.

The Involuntary Part-Time Rate Many part-time workers want part-time jobs, but some want full-time work and the *involuntary part-time rate* is the percentage of the people in the labour force who work part time but want full-time jobs.

$$\frac{\text{Involuntary}}{\text{part-time rate}} = \frac{\text{Number of involuntary part-time workers}}{\text{Labour force}} \times 100.$$

In 2013, with 913,600 involuntary part-time workers and a labour force of 19.08 million, the involuntary part-time rate was 4.8 percent.

The Labour Force Participation Rate Statistics Canada measures the **labour force participation rate** as the percentage of the working-age population who are members of the labour force. That is,

$$\frac{\text{Labour force}}{\text{participation rate}} = \frac{\text{Labour force}}{\text{Working-age population}} \times 100.$$

In 2013, the labour force was 19.08 million and the working-age population was 28.67 million. By using the above equation, you can verify that the labour force participation rate was 66.5 percent (19.08 million divided by 28.67 million, multiplied by 100).

FIGURE 21.2   The Unemployment Rate: 1960–2014

The average unemployment rate from 1960 to 2014 was 7.6 percent. The unemployment rate increases in a recession, peaks after the recession ends, and decreases in an expansion. The unemployment rate was unusually high following the recessions of 1982 and 1991. The unemployment rate following the recession of 2008–2009 was less severe than that following the two earlier recessions.

Source of data: Statistics Canada, CANSIM Table 282-0002.

FIGURE 21.3 Labour Force Participation and Employment: 1960–2014

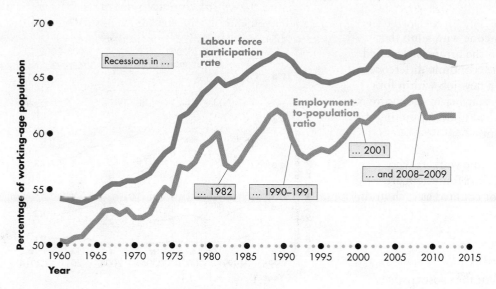

The labour force participation rate and the employment-to-population ratio increased rapidly before 1990 and slowly after 1990. They fluctuate with the business cycle.

The employment-to-population ratio fluctuates more than the labour force participation rate and reflects cyclical fluctuations in the unemployment rate.

Source of data: Statistics Canada, CANSIM Table 282-0002.

MyEconLab Real-time data

The Employment-to-Population Ratio

The number of people of working age who have jobs is an indicator of the availability of jobs and the match of skills to jobs. The **employment-to-population ratio** is the percentage of people of working age who have jobs. That is,

$$\text{Employment-to-population ratio} = \frac{\text{Number of people employed}}{\text{Working-age population}} \times 100.$$

In 2013, the number of people employed was 17.73 million and the working-age population was 28.67 million. By using the above equation, you can verify that the employment-to-population ratio was 61.8 percent (17.73 million divided by 28.67 million, multiplied by 100).

Figure 21.3 shows the labour force participation rate and the employment-to-population ratio. These indicators follow an upward trend before 1990 and then flatten off. The increase before 1990 means that the Canadian economy created jobs at a faster rate than the working-age population grew.

The employment-to-population ratio fluctuates with the business cycle: It falls in a recession and rises in an expansion. The labour force participation rate has milder business cycle swings that reflect movements into and out of the labour force.

Other Definitions of Unemployment

You've seen that to be counted as unemployed, a person must be available for work and either be on temporary layoff with an expectation of recall; or be without work and have looked for work in the past four weeks; or have a new job to start within four weeks. Some people without a job might want one but not meet the strict criteria for being counted as unemployed. Also, people who have part-time jobs but want to work full time might be regarded as part-time unemployed.

Statistics Canada believes that the official definition of unemployment is the correct measure, but recognizes other wider definitions that bring in three types of *underemployed* labour excluded from the official measure. They are:

- Discouraged searchers
- Long-term future starts
- Involuntary part-timers

Discouraged Searchers A **discouraged searcher** is a person who currently is neither working nor looking for work but has indicated that he or she wants a job, is available for work, and has looked for work sometime in the recent past but has stopped looking because of repeated failure. The official unemployment measure excludes discouraged searchers because they haven't made specific efforts to find a job within the past four weeks. In all other respects, they are unemployed.

Long-Term Future Starts Someone with a job that starts more than four weeks in the future is classified as not in the labour force. The economic difference between someone who starts a new job within four weeks and someone who starts farther in the future is slight and is a potential source of underestimating the true amount of unemployment.

Involuntary Part-Timers Part-time workers who would like full-time jobs and can't find them are part-time unemployed but not counted as such in the official statistics.

Most Costly Unemployment

All unemployment is costly, but the most costly is long-term unemployment that results from job loss.

People who are unemployed for a few weeks and then find another job bear some costs of unemployment. But these costs are low compared to those borne by people who remain unemployed for many weeks. The unemployment rate doesn't distinguish among the different lengths of unemployment spells. If most unemployment is long term, the situation is worse than if most are short-term job searchers.

Alternative Measures of Unemployment

To provide information about the aspects of unemployment that we've just discussed, Statistics Canada reports eight alternative measures of the unemployment rate: three that are narrower than the official rate and four that are broader. The narrower measures focus on the personal cost of unemployment and the broader measures focus on assessing the full amount of underemployed labour resources.

Figure 21.4 shows these measures from 1996 (the first year for which all eight are available) to 2014. R4 is the official rate and R3 is comparable to the official U.S. rate. Long-term unemployment (R1) is a small part of total unemployment. Short-term unemployment (R2) is more than double that of long term. Adding discouraged searchers (R5) makes very little difference to the unemployment rate, but adding long-term future starts (R6) makes a bigger difference and adding involuntary part-timers (R7) makes a big difference. R8 is the total *underemployment rate*.

FIGURE 21.4 Eight Alternative Measures of Unemployment

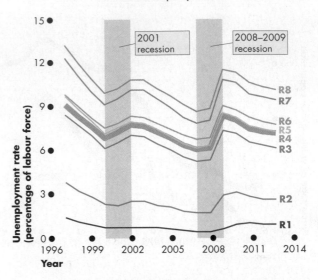

R1 are those unemployed for 1 year or more, and R2 are those unemployed for 3 months or less. R3 is comparable to the official U.S. rate. R4 is Canada's official rate. R5 adds discourged searchers, R6 adds long-term future starts, and R7 adds involuntary part-timers to R4. R8 adds all three groups added separately in R5, R6, and R7. Fluctuations in all alternative measures are similar to those in the official rate, R4.

Source of data: Statistics Canada, CANSIM Table 282-0086.

MyEconLab Real-time data

REVIEW QUIZ

1 What distinguishes an unemployed person from one who is not in the labour force?

2 Describe the trends and fluctuations in the Canadian unemployment rate since 1960.

3 Describe the trends and fluctuations in the Canadian employment-to-population ratio and labour force participation rate since 1960.

4 Describe the alternative measures of unemployment.

Work these questions in Study Plan 21.1 and get instant feedback. Do a Key Terms Quiz.   MyEconLab

You've seen how we measure employment and unemployment. Your next task is to see what we mean by full employment and how unemployment and real GDP fluctuate over the business cycle.

Unemployment and Full Employment

There is always someone without a job who is searching for one, so there is always some unemployment. The key reason is that the economy is a complex mechanism that is always changing—it experiences frictions, structural change, and cycles.

Frictional Unemployment

There is an unending flow of people into and out of the labour force as people move through the stages of life—from being in school to finding a job, to working, perhaps to becoming unhappy with a job and looking for a new one, and finally, to retiring from full-time work.

There is also an unending process of job creation and job destruction as new firms are born, firms expand or contract, and some firms fail and go out of business.

The flows into and out of the labour force and the processes of job creation and job destruction create the need for people to search for jobs and for businesses to search for workers. Businesses don't usually hire the first person who applies for a job, and unemployed people don't usually take the first job that comes their way. Instead, both firms and workers spend time searching for what they believe will be the best available match. By this process of search, people can match their own skills and interests with the available jobs and find a satisfying job and a good income.

The unemployment that arises from the normal labour turnover we've just described—from people entering and leaving the labour force and from the ongoing creation and destruction of jobs—is called **frictional unemployment**. Frictional unemployment is a permanent and healthy phenomenon in a dynamic, growing economy.

Structural Unemployment

The unemployment that arises when changes in technology or international competition change the skills needed to perform jobs or change the locations of jobs is called **structural unemployment**. Structural unemployment usually lasts longer than frictional unemployment because workers must retrain and possibly relocate to find a job. When a steel plant in Hamilton, Ontario, is automated, some jobs in that city disappear. Meanwhile, new jobs for security guards, retail clerks, and life-insurance salespeople are created in Toronto and Vancouver. The unemployed former steelworkers remain unemployed for several months until they move, retrain, and get new jobs. Structural unemployment is painful, especially for older workers for whom the best available option might be to retire early or take a lower-skilled, lower-paying job.

Cyclical Unemployment

The higher-than-normal unemployment at a business cycle trough and the lower-than-normal unemployment at a business cycle peak is called **cyclical unemployment**. A worker who is laid off because the economy is in a recession and who gets rehired some months later when the expansion begins has experienced cyclical unemployment.

"Natural" Unemployment

Natural unemployment is the unemployment that arises from frictions and structural change when there is no cyclical unemployment—when all the unemployment is frictional and structural. Natural unemployment as a percentage of the labour force is called the **natural unemployment rate**.

Full employment is defined as a situation in which the unemployment rate equals the natural unemployment rate.

What determines the natural unemployment rate? Is it constant or does it change over time?

The natural unemployment rate is influenced by many factors but the most important ones are:

- The age distribution of the population
- The scale of structural change
- The real wage rate
- Unemployment benefits

The Age Distribution of the Population An economy with a young population has a large number of new job seekers every year and has a high level of frictional unemployment. An economy with an aging population has fewer new job seekers and a low level of frictional unemployment.

The Scale of Structural Change The scale of structural change is sometimes small. The same jobs using the same machines remain in place for many years. But sometimes there is a technological upheaval.

The old ways are swept aside and millions of jobs are lost and the skill to perform them loses value. The amount of structural unemployment fluctuates with the pace and volume of technological change and the change driven by fierce international competition, especially from fast-changing Asian economies. A high level of structural unemployment is present in many parts of Canada today (as you can see in *Economics in Action*).

The Real Wage Rate The natural unemployment rate is influenced by the level of the real wage rate. Real wage rates that bring unemployment are a *minimum wage* and an *efficiency wage*. Chapter 6 (see pp. 131–133) explains how the minimum wage creates unemployment. An *efficiency wage* is a wage set above the going market wage to enable firms to attract the most productive workers, get them to work hard, and discourage them from quitting.

Unemployment Benefits Unemployment benefits increase the natural unemployment rate by lowering the opportunity cost of job search. Canada and European countries have more generous unemployment benefits and higher natural unemployment rates than the United States. Extending unemployment benefits increases the natural unemployment rate.

There is no controversy about the existence of a natural unemployment rate. Nor is there disagreement that the natural unemployment rate changes. But economists don't know its exact size or the extent to which it fluctuates. Canada has no official estimates of the natural unemployment rate, but a reasonable guess is that it is 7 percent—a bit less than the 2013 unemployment rate.

Real GDP and Unemployment over the Cycle

The quantity of real GDP at full employment is *potential GDP* (Chapter 20, p. 472). Over the business cycle, real GDP fluctuates around potential GDP. The gap between real GDP and potential GDP is called the **output gap**. As the output gap fluctuates over the business cycle, the unemployment rate fluctuates around the natural unemployment rate.

Figure 21.5 illustrates these fluctuations in Canada between 1980 and 2014—the output gap in part (a) and the unemployment rate and natural unemployment rate in part (b).

When the economy is at full employment, the unemployment rate equals the natural

Economics in Action
Structural Unemployment in Canada

If all unemployment were frictional, arising from the ongoing flow of people into and out of the labour force and creation and destruction of firms and jobs, we would expect all Canada's provinces to exhibit similar unemployment rates. They wouldn't be exactly equal, but the ranking of provinces would change randomly over time. But that is not what the data say.

Provincial unemployment rates are extremely unequal, and the ranking of provinces is persistent.

In 2013, provincial unemployment rates ranged from 11.5 percent in Prince Edward Island to 4 percent in Saskachewan. All the provinces west of Ontario had unemployment rates below the national average, Ontario and Quebec were close to the national average at 8 percent, and the Maritime provinces were above the national average.

This range of unemployment rates across the provinces can only be accounted for by structural features of the Canadian economy.

The West in general is growing rapidly based largely on the extraction of resources. The Maritimes and to a lesser extent Quebec and Ontario are growing more slowly. People must leave the eastern provinces and move westward to find work. A reluctuance to uproot keeps the unemployment rates widely dispersed.

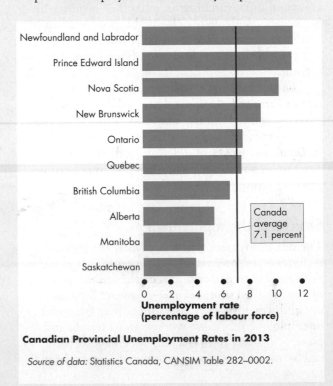

Canadian Provincial Unemployment Rates in 2013

Source of data: Statistics Canada, CANSIM Table 282–0002.

FIGURE 21.5   The Output Gap and the Unemployment Rate

(a) Output gap

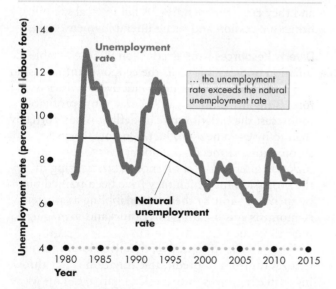

(b) Unemployment rate

As real GDP fluctuates around potential GDP in part (a), the unemployment rate fluctuates around the natural unemployment rate in part (b). In recessions, cyclical unemployment increases and the output gap becomes negative. At business cycle peaks, the unemployment rate falls below the natural rate and the output gap becomes positive. The natural unemployment rate decreased during the 1990s.

Sources of data: Statistics Canada, CANSIM Table 282-0002 and Bank of Canada output gap estimates. The natural unemployment rate is the authors' estimate.

MyEconLab Real-time data

unemployment rate and real GDP equals potential GDP, so the output gap is zero. When the unemployment rate is less than the natural unemployment rate, real GDP is greater than potential GDP and the output gap is positive. And when the unemployment rate is greater than the natural unemployment rate, real GDP is less than potential GDP and the output gap is negative.

The Changing Natural Unemployment Rate

Figure 21.5(b) shows our estimate of the natural unemployment rate since 1980. This estimate puts the natural unemployment rate at 9 percent during the 1980s, falling steadily through the 1990s to 7.0 percent by around 2000, and remaining at around 7 percent since 2000. This view of the natural unemployment rate is consistent with the Bank of Canada's estimate of the output gap in Fig. 21.5(a).

REVIEW QUIZ

1 Why does unemployment arise and what makes some unemployment unavoidable?
2 Define frictional unemployment, structural unemployment, and cyclical unemployment. Give examples of each type of unemployment.
3 What is the natural unemployment rate?
4 How does the natural unemployment rate change and what factors might make it change?
5 Why is the unemployment rate never zero, even at full employment?
6 What is the output gap? How does it change when the economy goes into recession?
7 How does the unemployment rate fluctuate over the business cycle?

Work these questions in Study Plan 21.2 and get instant feedback. Do a Key Terms Quiz.   MyEconLab

Your next task is to see how we monitor the price level and the inflation rate. You will learn about the Consumer Price Index (CPI), which is monitored every month. You will also learn about other measures of the price level and the inflation rate.

The Price Level, Inflation, and Deflation

What will it *really* cost you to pay off your student loan? What will your parents' life savings buy when they retire? The answers depend on what happens to the **price level**, the average level of prices, and the value of money. A persistently rising price level is called **inflation**; a persistently falling price level is called **deflation**.

We are interested in the price level, inflation, and deflation for two main reasons. First, we want to measure the annual percentage change of the price level—the inflation rate or deflation rate. Second, we want to distinguish between the money values and real values of economic variables such as your student loan and your parents' savings.

We begin by explaining why inflation and deflation are problems. Then we'll look at how we measure the price level and the inflation rate. Finally, we'll return to the task of distinguishing real values from money values.

Why Inflation and Deflation Are Problems

Low, steady, and anticipated inflation or deflation isn't a problem, but an unexpected burst of inflation or period of deflation brings big problems and costs. An unexpected inflation or deflation:

- Redistributes income
- Redistributes wealth
- Lowers real GDP and employment
- Diverts resources from production

Redistributes Income Workers and employers sign wage contracts that last for a year or more. An unexpected burst of inflation raises prices but doesn't immediately raise wages. Workers are worse off because their wages buy less than they bargained for and employers are better off because their profits rise.

An unexpected period of deflation has the opposite effect. Wage rates don't fall but prices fall. Workers are better off because their fixed wages buy more than they bargained for and employers are worse off with lower profits.

Redistributes Wealth People enter into loan contracts that are fixed in money terms and that pay an interest rate agreed as a percentage of the money borrowed and lent. With an unexpected burst of inflation, the money that the borrower repays to the lender buys less than the money originally loaned. The borrower wins and the lender loses. The interest paid on the loan doesn't compensate the lender for the loss in the value of the money loaned. With an unexpected deflation, the money that the borrower repays to the lender buys *more* than the money originally loaned. The borrower loses and the lender wins.

Lowers Real GDP and Employment Unexpected inflation that raises firms' profits brings a rise in investment and a boom in production and employment. Real GDP rises above potential GDP and the unemployment rate falls below the natural rate. But this situation is *temporary*. Profitable investment dries up, spending falls, real GDP falls below potential GDP, and the unemployment rate rises. Avoiding these swings in production and jobs means avoiding unexpected swings in the inflation rate.

An unexpected deflation has even greater consequences for real GDP and jobs. Businesses and households that are in debt (borrowers) are worse off and they cut their spending. A fall in total spending brings a recession and rising unemployment.

Diverts Resources from Production Unpredictable inflation or deflation turns the economy into a casino and diverts resources from productive activities to forecasting inflation. It can become more profitable to forecast the inflation rate or deflation rate correctly than to invent a new product. Doctors, lawyers, accountants, farmers—just about everyone—can make themselves better off, not by specializing in the profession for which they have been trained but by spending more of their time dabbling as amateur economists and inflation forecasters and managing their investments.

From a social perspective, the diversion of talent that results from unpredictable inflation is like throwing scarce resources onto a pile of garbage. This waste of resources is a cost of inflation.

At its worst, inflation becomes **hyperinflation**—an inflation rate of 50 percent a month or higher that grinds the economy to a halt and causes a society to collapse. Hyperinflation is rare, but Zimbabwe in recent years and several European and Latin American countries have experienced it.

We pay close attention to the inflation rate, even when its rate is low, to avoid its consequences. We monitor the price level every month and devote considerable resources to measuring it accurately. You're now going to see how we do this.

The Consumer Price Index

Every month, Statistics Canada measures the price level by calculating the **Consumer Price Index (CPI)**, which is a measure of the average of the prices paid by urban consumers for a fixed basket of consumer goods and services. What you learn here will help you to make sense of the CPI and relate it to your own economic life. The CPI tells you about the *value* of the money in your pocket.

Reading the CPI Numbers

The CPI is defined to equal 100 for a period called the *reference base period*. Currently, the reference base period is 2002. That is, for the average of the 12 months of 2002, the CPI equals 100.

In June 2014, the CPI was 125.6. This number tells us that the average of the prices paid by urban consumers for a fixed market basket of consumer goods and services was 25.6 percent *higher* in June 2014 than it was on average during 2002.

Constructing the CPI

Constructing the CPI involves three stages:

- Selecting the CPI basket
- Conducting the monthly price survey
- Calculating the CPI

The CPI Basket The first stage in constructing the CPI is to select what is called the *CPI basket*. This basket contains the goods and services represented in the index, each weighted by its relative importance. The idea is to make the relative importance of the items in the CPI basket the same as that in the budget of an average urban household. For example, because people spend more on housing than on bus rides, the CPI places more weight on the price of housing than on the price of a bus ride.

To determine the CPI basket, Statistics Canada conducts a survey of consumer expenditures. Today's CPI basket is based on data gathered in a 2011 survey valued at the prices in January 2013.

Figure 21.6 shows the CPI basket. As you look at the relative importance of the items in the CPI basket, remember that it applies to the *average* household. *Individual* household's baskets are spread around the average. Think about what you buy and compare *your* basket with the CPI basket.

FIGURE 21.6   The CPI Basket

The CPI basket consists of the items that an average urban household buys. The figure shows the percentages.

Sources of data: Statistics Canada, Weighting Diagram of the Consumer Price Index   2011 Basket at January 2013 prices.

────────── **MyEconLab** Animation ──────────

The Monthly Price Survey Each month, Statistics Canada employees check the prices of the goods and services in the CPI basket in the major cities. Because the CPI aims to measure price *changes*, it is important that the prices recorded each month refer to exactly the same item. For example, suppose the price of a box of jelly beans has increased but a box now contains more beans. Has the price of jelly beans increased? Statistics Canada employees must record the details of changes in quality or packaging so that price changes can be isolated from other changes.

Once the raw price data are in hand, the next task is to calculate the CPI.

Calculating the CPI To calculate the CPI, we:

1. Find the cost of the CPI basket at base-period prices.
2. Find the cost of the CPI basket at current-period prices.
3. Calculate the CPI for the base period and the current period.

We'll work through these three steps for the simple artificial economy in Table 21.1, in which the base year is 2012 and the current year is 2015. The table shows the quantities in the CPI basket and the prices in these two years.

Part (a) contains the data for the base period. In that period, consumers bought 10 oranges at $1 each and 5 haircuts at $8 each. To find the cost of the CPI basket in the base-period prices, multiply the quantities in the CPI basket by the base-period prices. The cost of oranges is $10 (10 at $1 each), and the cost of haircuts is $40 (5 at $8 each). So the total cost of the CPI basket in the base period at base-period prices is $50 ($10 + $40).

Part (b) contains the price data for the current period. The price of an orange increased from $1 to $2, which is a 100 percent increase—($1 ÷ $1) × 100 = 100. The price of a haircut increased from $8 to $10, which is a 25 percent increase—($2 ÷ $8) × 100 = 25.

The CPI provides a way of averaging these price increases by comparing the cost of the basket rather than the price of each item. To find the cost of the CPI basket in the current period, 2015, multiply the quantities in the basket by their 2015 prices. The cost of

oranges is $20 (10 at $2 each), and the cost of haircuts is $50 (5 at $10 each). So total cost of the fixed CPI basket at current-period prices is $70 ($20 + $50).

You've now taken the first two steps toward calculating the CPI: calculating the cost of the CPI basket in the base period and the current period. The third step uses the numbers you've just calculated to find the CPI for 2012 and 2015.

The formula for the CPI is

$$\text{CPI} = \frac{\text{Cost of CPI basket at current-period prices}}{\text{Cost of CPI basket at base-period prices}}$$

In Table 21.1, you established that in 2012 (the base period), the cost of the CPI basket was $50 and in 2015, it was $70. If we use these numbers in the CPI formula, we can find the CPI for 2012 and 2015. For 2012, the CPI is

$$\text{CPI in 2012} = \frac{\$50}{\$50} \times 100 = 100.$$

For 2015, the CPI is

$$\text{CPI in 2015} = \frac{\$70}{\$50} \times 100 = 140.$$

The principles that you've applied in this simplified CPI calculation apply to the more complex calculations performed every month by Statistics Canada.

Measuring the Inflation Rate

A major purpose of the CPI is to measure changes in the cost of living and in the value of money. To measure these changes, we calculate the *inflation rate* as the annual percentage change in the CPI. To calculate the inflation rate, we use the formula:

$$\text{Inflation rate} = \frac{\text{CPI this year} - \text{CPI last year}}{\text{CPI last year}} \times 100.$$

We can use this formula to calculate the inflation rate in 2014. The CPI in June 2014 was 125.6, and the CPI in June 2013 was 122.9. So the inflation rate during the 12 months to June 2014 was

$$\text{Inflation rate} = \frac{(125.6 - 122.9)}{122.9} \times 100 = 2.2\%$$

TABLE 21.1   The CPI:
              A Simplified Calculation

(a) The cost of the CPI basket at base-period prices: 2012

Item	CPI basket Quantity	Price	Cost of CPI Basket
Oranges	10	$1	$10
Haircuts	5	$8	$40
Cost of CPI basket at base-period prices			$50

(b) The cost of the CPI basket at current-period prices: 2015

Item	CPI basket Quantity	Price	Cost of CPI Basket
Oranges	10	$2	$20
Haircuts	5	$10	$50
Cost of CPI basket at current-period prices			$70

Distinguishing High Inflation from a High Price Level

Figure 21.7 shows the CPI and the inflation rate in Canada between 1970 and 2014. The two parts of the figure are related and emphasize the distinction between high inflation and high prices.

When the price level in part (a) *rises rapidly*, (1970 through 1982), the inflation rate in part (b) is *high*. When the price level in part (a) *rises slowly*, (after 1982), the inflation rate in part (b) is *low*.

A high inflation rate means that the price level is rising rapidly. A high price level means that there has been a sustained period of rising prices.

When the price level in part (a) *falls (2009)*, the inflation rate in part (b) is negative—deflation.

The CPI is not a perfect measure of the price level and changes in the CPI probably overstate the inflation rate. Let's look at the sources of bias.

The Biased CPI

The main sources of bias in the CPI are:

- New goods bias
- Quality change bias
- Commodity substitution bias
- Outlet substitution bias

New Goods Bias If you want to compare the price level in 2014 with that in 1970, you must somehow compare the price of a computer today with that of a typewriter in 1970. Because a PC is more expensive than a typewriter was, the arrival of the PC puts an upward bias into the CPI and its inflation rate.

Quality Change Bias Cars and many other goods get better every year. Part of the rise in the prices of these goods is a payment for improved quality and is not inflation. But the CPI counts the entire price rise as inflation and so overstates inflation.

Commodity Substitution Bias Changes in relative prices lead consumers to change the items they buy. For example, if the price of beef rises and the price of chicken remains unchanged, people buy more chicken and less beef. This switch from beef to chicken might provide the same amount of meat and the same enjoyment as before and expenditure is the same as before. The price of meat has not changed. But because the CPI ignores the substitution of chicken for beef, it says the price of meat has increased.

FIGURE 21.7   The CPI and the Inflation Rate

(a) CPI

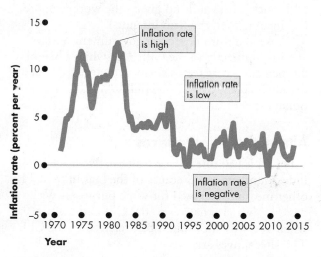

(b) Inflation rate

When the price level rises rapidly, the inflation rate is high; and when the price level rises slowly, the inflation rate is low. When the price level falls, the inflation rate is negative.

From 1970 through 1982, the price level increased rapidly in part (a) and the inflation rate was high in part (b). After 1982, the price level rose slowly in part (a) and the inflation rate was low in part (b). In 2009, the price level fell and the inflation rate was negative—there was deflation.

Source of data: Statistics Canada, CANSIM Table 326-0020.

MyEconLab Real-time data

Outlet Substitution Bias When confronted with higher prices, people use discount stores more frequently and convenience stores less frequently. This phenomenon is called *outlet substitution*. The CPI surveys do not monitor outlet substitutions.

The Magnitude of the Bias

You've reviewed the sources of bias in the CPI. But how big is the bias? This question is addressed periodically and the most recent estimate is provided in a study by Bank of Canada economist James Rossiter at about 0.6 percent per year.

Some Consequences of the Bias

The bias in the CPI distorts private contracts and increases government outlays. Many private agreements, such as wage contracts, are linked to the CPI. For example, a firm and its workers might agree to a three-year wage deal that increases the wage rate by 2 percent a year plus the percentage increase in the CPI. Such a deal ends up giving the workers more real income than the firm intended.

Close to a third of federal government outlays are linked directly to the CPI. And while a bias of 0.6 percent a year seems small, accumulated over a decade it adds up to several billion dollars of additional expenditures.

Alternative Price Indexes

The CPI is just one of many alternative price level index numbers, and because of the bias in the CPI other measures are used for some purposes. We'll describe two alternatives to the CPI and explain when and why they might be preferred to the CPI. The alternatives are:

- GDP deflator
- Chained price index for consumption

GDP Deflator The *GDP deflator* is an index of the prices of all the items included in GDP and is the ratio of nominal GDP to real GDP. That is,

$$\text{GDP deflator} = \frac{\text{Nominal GDP}}{\text{Real GDP}} \times 100.$$

Because real GDP includes consumption expenditure, investment, government expenditure, and net exports, the GDP deflator is an index of the prices of all these items.

Real GDP is calculated using the chained-dollar method (see Chapter 20, pp. 482–483), which means that the weights attached to each item in the GDP deflator are the components of GDP in both the current year and the preceding year.

Because it uses current period and previous period quantities rather than fixed quantities from an earlier period, a chained-dollar price index incorporates substitution effects and new goods and overcomes the sources of bias in the CPI.

Over the period 2000 to 2014, the GDP deflator has increased at an average rate of 2.2 percent per year, which is 0.3 percentage points *above* the CPI inflation rate.

The GDP deflator is appropriate for macroeconomics because, like GDP, it is a comprehensive measure of the cost of the real GDP basket of goods and services. But as a measure of the cost of living, it is too broad—it includes items that consumers don't buy.

Chained Price Index for Consumption The *chained price index for consumption (CPIC)* is an index of the prices of all the items included in consumption expenditure in GDP and is the ratio of nominal consumption expenditure to real consumption expenditure. That is,

$$\text{CPIC} = \frac{\text{Nominal consumption expenditure}}{\text{Real consumption expenditure}} \times 100.$$

Like the GDP deflator, because the CPIC uses current-period and previous-period quantities rather than fixed quantities from an earlier period, it incorporates substitution effects and new goods and overcomes the sources of bias in the CPI.

Over the period 2000 to 2014, the CPIC has increased at an average rate of 1.5 percent per year, which is 0.4 percentage points *below* the CPI inflation rate.

Core Inflation

No matter whether we calculate the inflation rate using the CPI, the GDP deflator, or the CPIC, the number bounces around a good deal from month to month or quarter to quarter. To determine whether the inflation rate is trending upward or downward, we need to strip the raw numbers of their volatility. The **core inflation rate**, which is the inflation rate excluding volatile elements, attempts to do just that and reveal the underlying inflation trend.

The most commonly used measure of core inflation is the core CPI inflation rate and, as a practical matter, the core CPI inflation rate is calculated as the percentage change in the CPI excluding food and fuel. The prices of these two items are among the most volatile.

While the core CPI inflation rate removes the volatile elements in inflation, it can give a misleading view of the true underlying inflation rate. If the relative prices of the excluded items are changing, the core inflation rate will give a biased measure of the true underlying inflation rate.

Such a misleading account was given during the years between 2000 and 2011 when the relative prices of food and fuel were rising. The result was a core CPI inflation rate that was systematically *below* the CPI rate by an average of 0.3 percentage points.

Figure 21.8 shows the two inflation series from 1984 to 2014. More refined measures of core inflation that eliminate the bias have been suggested but are not in common use.

The Real Variables in Macroeconomics

You saw in Chapter 3 the distinction between a money price and a relative price (see p. 56). Another name for a money price is a nominal price. In macroeconomics, we often want to distinguish between a real variable and its corresponding nominal variable. We want to distinguish a real price from its corresponding nominal price because a real price is an opportunity cost that influences choices. And we want to distinguish a real quantity (like real GDP) from a nominal quantity (like nominal GDP) because we want to see what is "really" happening to variables that influence the standard of living.

You've seen in this chapter how we view real GDP as nominal GDP deflated by the GDP deflator. Viewing real GDP in this way opens up the idea of using the same method to calculate other real variables. By using the GDP deflator, we can deflate any nominal variable and find its corresponding real values. An important example is the wage rate, which is the price of labour. We measure the economy's real wage rate as the nominal wage rate divided by the GDP deflator.

There is one variable that is a bit different—an interest rate. A real interest rate is not a nominal interest rate divided by the price level. You'll learn how to adjust interest rates for inflation to find a real interest rate in Chapter 23. But all the other real variables of macroeconomics are calculated by dividing a nominal variable by the price level.

FIGURE 21.8   Core Inflation

The core inflation rate excludes volatile price changes of food and fuel. Since 2000, the core inflation rate has mostly been below the CPI inflation rate because the relative prices of food and fuel have been rising.

Source of data: Statistics Canada, CANSIM Table 380-0020.

———— MyEconLab Real-time data ————

REVIEW QUIZ

1 What is the price level?
2 What is the CPI and how is it calculated?
3 How do we calculate the inflation rate and what is its relationship with the CPI?
4 What are the four main ways in which the CPI is an upward-biased measure of the price level?
5 What problems arise from the CPI bias?
6 What are the alternative measures of the price level and how do they address the problem of bias in the CPI?

Work these questions in Study Plan 21.3 and get instant feedback. Do a Key Terms Quiz.   MyEconLab

◆ You've now completed your study of the measurement of macroeconomic performance. Your next task is to learn what determines that performance and how policy actions might improve it. But first, compare the Canadian and U.S. labour markets in *Economics in the News* on pp. 504–505.

Jobs Growth in Recovery

Why the U.S. Recouping Jobs Lost in Recession Is Also Good News for Canada

The Financial Post
June 6, 2014

While Canada's engine for job creation is sputtering, take some solace in the fact that U.S. employment growth is gaining traction.

Like so many elements of the economy, we will benefit from the hiring gains made by our giant neighbour. Just not yet.

For now, we'll have to contend with what we can get.

In May, what we got was 25,800 new jobs—after all the gains and losses are tallied up—and that's a big swing back from April's net loss of 28,900 positions, according to a Statistics Canada report on Friday.

Still, the unemployment [rate] increased to 7% in May from 6.9% a month earlier, the federal agency said. But that's usually a sign that more people are feeling better about their chances of landing a job and are out looking for one. ...

In the United States, meanwhile, employers added 217,000 positions in May—lifting job growth past the pre-recession peak for the first time, reclaiming the 8.7 million jobs lost since the downturn struck in 2008.

Their unemployment gauge remained at 6.3% in May, the lowest level in more than five years. ...

But backing up a bit, Canada's recovery has not been without its own milestones.

True, the United States retraced all its recession-driven job losses last month. Canada, on the other hand, accomplished the same task much earlier—in July 2009, clawing back 431,300 lost positions—admittedly a smaller pool to draw from and a shorter downturn than in the United States.

Put another way, Canadian employment totalled 17.18 million in October 2008. The labour force surpassed that in January 2011, when jobs amounted 17.24 million. It's now running at 17.8 million. ...

Overall, the majority of those additional workers, 54,900, were part time—many of those traditionally being students straight out of school—while full-time employment fell by 29,100, the agency said. ...

Written by Gordon Isfeld. Material reprinted with the express permission of *National Post*, a division of Postmedia Network Inc.

ESSENCE OF THE STORY

- In May 2014, Canadian employment was rising slowly, most of the jobs created were part time, and the unemployment rate increased.

- Canadian employment returned to its 2008 pre-recession peak in July 2009.

- In May 2014, U.S. employment was increasing more quickly and returned to its 2008 pre-recession peak for the first time.

- The U.S. unemployment rate at 6.3 percent was at its lowest level in more than five years.

MyEconLab More Economics in the News

ECONOMIC ANALYSIS

- This news article reports some Canadian and U.S. labour market data for May 2014 and says that the United States returned from recession more slowly than Canada but is now creating jobs at a faster pace.

- The global recession of 2008–2009 had a bigger effect on the U.S. economy than on the Canadian economy, and the recovery during 2010 and 2011 was weaker in the United States than in Canada.

- The three figures compare the labour markets of Canada and the United States during 2008–2014.

- Figure 1 shows that the employment-to-population ratio in the United States is lower than in Canada and that it fell more steeply in the United States during the recession.

- Figure 1 also shows that the Canadian employment-to-population ratio increased through 2013 before starting to fall slightly; and in contrast, the U.S. ratio was stagnant through 2013 and only in 2014 did it begin to rise.

- Figure 2 shows the unemployment rates. Before the recession and in 2014, Canada had a higher unemployment rate than the United States.

- But during 2008, the U.S. unemployment rate climbed steeply, and by the end of 2008 the U.S. unemployment rate was above the Canadian rate, where it remained until 2014.

- Figure 3 shows that during the 2008–2009 recession, part-time employment expanded as a percentage of total employment.

- Figure 3 also shows that Canada started the recession with more employment in part-time jobs (as a percentage of total jobs) than the United States, but during the expansion of 2010 and 2011, the part-time employment was a similar percentage in the two economies.

- Canada's relatively stronger performance during 2010 and 2011 is driven by the strength of the Asian economies—China and India in particular—and the resource exports to these economies.

- If the United States continues to expand more rapidly, it is likely that Canada will also create jobs at a faster pace and see its unemployment rate fall.

Figure 1 Employment

Figure 2 Unemployment

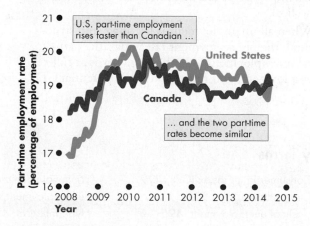

Figure 3 Part-Time Employment

505

SUMMARY

Key Points

Employment and Unemployment (pp. 490–494)

- Unemployment is a serious personal, social, and economic problem because it results in lost output and income and a loss of human capital.
- The unemployment rate averaged 7.6 percent between 1960 and 2014. It increases in recessions and decreases in expansions.
- The labour force participation rate and the employment-to-population ratio have an upward trend and fluctuate with the business cycle.
- Two alternative measures of unemployment, narrower than the official measure, include the long-term unemployed and short-term unemployed.
- Three alternative measures of unemployment, broader than the official measure, include discouraged searchers, long-term future starts, and part-time workers who want full-time jobs.

Working Problems 1 to 5 will give you a better understanding of employment and unemployment.

Unemployment and Full Employment (pp. 495–497)

- Some unemployment is unavoidable because people are constantly entering and leaving the labour force and losing or quitting jobs; also, firms that create jobs are constantly being born, expanding, contracting, and dying.
- Unemployment can be frictional, structural, or cyclical.
- When all unemployment is frictional and structural, the unemployment rate equals the natural unemployment rate, the economy is at full employment, and real GDP equals potential GDP.

- Over the business cycle, real GDP fluctuates around potential GDP and the unemployment rate fluctuates around the natural unemployment rate.

Working Problems 6 and 7 will give you a better understanding of unemployment and full employment.

The Price Level, Inflation, and Deflation (pp. 498–503)

- Inflation and deflation that are unexpected redistribute income and wealth and divert resources from production.
- The Consumer Price Index (CPI) is a measure of the average of the prices paid by urban consumers for a fixed basket of consumer goods and services.
- The CPI is defined to equal 100 for a reference base period—currently 2002.
- The inflation rate is the percentage change in the CPI from one period to the next.
- Changes in the CPI probably overstate the inflation rate because of the bias that arises from new goods, quality changes, commodity substitution, and outlet substitution.
- The bias in the CPI distorts private contracts and increases government outlays.
- Alternative price level measures such as the GDP deflator and the CPIC avoid the bias of the CPI but do not make a large difference to the measured inflation rate.
- Real economic variables (except the real interest rate) are calculated by dividing nominal variables by the price level.

Working Problems 8 to 11 will give you a better understanding of the price level, inflation, and deflation.

Key Terms

MyEconLab Key Terms Quiz

Consumer Price Index (CPI), 499
Core inflation rate, 502
Cyclical unemployment, 495
Deflation, 498
Discouraged searcher, 493
Employment-to-population ratio, 493

Frictional unemployment, 495
Full employment, 495
Hyperinflation, 498
Inflation, 498
Labour force, 491
Labour force participation rate, 492

Natural unemployment rate, 495
Output gap, 496
Price level, 498
Structural unemployment, 495
Unemployment rate, 492
Working-age population, 491

WORKED PROBLEM

MyEconLab   You can work this problem in Chapter 21 Study Plan.

Statistics Canada's Labour Force Survey (LFS) reported the following situations in July 2014:

- Sarah works 10 hours a week at McDonald's. She is available to work more hours but hasn't looked for extra work.
- Kevin spent the first six months of 2014 actively searching for a job but he didn't get hired. He believes there are no jobs, so he has given up looking.
- Pat quit the job he had for the past two years and is actively looking for a better paying job. He is available to work and is still searching for a job.
- Mary is a new graduate who was hired while she was a student to start a job in August.
- Johnnie quit his band in June, has no job in July, and is not looking for work.

Questions

1. Who does the LFS classify as being unemployed, a part-time worker, an employed person, a discouraged worker, and not in the labour force? Explain your classification.

2. How will the labour force change if Sarah starts a second job, Pat finds a good job and is hired, and Mary takes a job at McDonald's while she waits to start her new job?

3. How will the unemployment rate change if Sarah quits and starts to search for a full-time job?

4. How will the labour force participation rate change if Kevin starts creating football apps in his garage and they turn out to be very popular?

Solutions

1. Sarah is a part-time worker, so the LFS classifies her as employed. She doesn't need to be looking for extra work.

   Kevin is a discouraged searcher. In the past he searched for a job but now he has given up. He is not unemployed because he didn't look for work in July, is not laid off, and is not waiting to start a new job within four weeks. The labour force includes only those employed and those unemployed, so Kevin is not in the labour force.

   Pat is unemployed. He has no job, is available to work, and has looked for work during July.

   Mary doesn't have a job, but she is available for work and will start a job within four weeks, so she is classified as unemployed.

Johnnie is not in the labour force. When he played in the band he was employed, but now he is not employed. He is not unemployed because he is not looking for a job.

Key Point: To be counted in the labour force a person must be either employed or unemployed. To be counted as employed, a person must have a job. To be counted as unemployed, a person must have looked for a job in the last four weeks and be available for work or be starting one within four weeks.

2. The labour force consists of the people who are counted by the LFS as employed or unemployed.

   Sarah is already counted as employed, so when she starts a second job the labour force does not change.

   Pat is currently unemployed, so when he is hired he transfers from being unemployed to being employed. So his change of status does not change the labour force.

   Mary is currently counted as unemployed, so taking on a part-time job at McDonald's while she waits to start the new job does not change the labour force.

Key Point: The labour force will change if working-age people not currently in the labour force start to look for work and become unemployed or start a job and become employed.

3. The unemployment rate is the percentage of the labour force who are classified as unemployed. If Sarah quits her job and searches for a full-time job, she becomes unemployed. The labour force doesn't change, so the unemployment rate rises.

Key Point: The unemployment rate rises when people quit their jobs and start searching for new ones.

4. The labour force participation rate is the percentage of the working-age population who are in the labour force. Kevin is currently not in the labour force because he is a discouraged searcher. When Kevin starts creating football apps in his garage and they turn out to be very popular, Kevin has created a job and is counted as employed. He is now in the labour force, so the labour force participation rate rises.

Key Point: The labour force participation rate changes as working-age people enter and exit the labour force.

STUDY PLAN PROBLEMS AND APPLICATIONS

MyEconLab   You can work Problems 1 to 11 in Chapter 21 Study Plan and get instant feedback. Problems marked 🌐 update with real-time data.

Employment and Unemployment (Study Plan 21.1)

🌐 1. Statistics Canada reported the following data for 2013:

Labour force: 19.4 million
Employment: 18.0 million
Working-age population: 26.7 million

Calculate the:

a. Unemployment rate.

b. Labour force participation rate.

c. Employment-to-population ratio.

2. In July 2014, in the economy of Sandy Island, 10,000 people were employed, 1,000 were unemployed, and 5,000 were not in the labour force. During August 2014, 80 people lost their jobs and didn't look for new ones, 20 people quit their jobs and retired, 150 unemployed people were hired, 50 people quit the labour force, and 40 people entered the labour force to look for work. Calculate for July 2014:

a. The unemployment rate.

b. The employment-to-population ratio.

And calculate for the end of August 2014:

c. The number of people unemployed, the number employed, and the unemployment rate.

🌐 Use the following data to work Problems 3 and 4. In July 2011, the Canadian unemployment rate was 7.2 percent. In January 2012, the unemployment rate was 7.6 percent. Predict what happened to:

3. Unemployment between July 2011 and January 2012 if the labour force was constant.

4. The labour force between July 2011 and January 2012, if unemployment was constant.

5. **Shrinking Labour Force Keeps Unemployment Rate Steady**

An exodus of discouraged searchers from the job market kept the unemployment rate from climbing above 10 percent. Had the labour force not decreased by 661,000, the unemployment rate would have been 10.4 percent. The number of discouraged searchers rose to 929,000 last month.

Source: Bloomberg, January 9, 2010

What is a discouraged searcher? Explain how an increase in discouraged searchers influences the official unemployment rate and the R5 unemployment rate.

Unemployment and Full Employment (Study Plan 21.2)

Use the following news clip to work Problems 6 and 7.

Firms Struggle to Hire Despite High Unemployment

Matching people with available jobs is always difficult after a recession as the economy remakes itself. But labour market data suggest the disconnect is particularly acute this time. Since the recovery began, the number of job openings has risen twice as fast as actual hires. If the job market were working normally, openings would be filled as they appear. Some 5 million more would be employed and the unemployment rate would be 6.8%, instead of 9.5%.

Source: *The Wall Street Journal*, August 9, 2010

6. If the labour market is working properly, why would there be any unemployment at all?

7. Are the 5 million workers who cannot find jobs because of mismatching in the labour market counted as part of the economy's structural unemployment or part of its cyclical unemployment?

The Price Level, Inflation, and Deflation

(Study Plan 21.3)

Use the following data to work Problems 8 and 9. The people on Coral Island buy only juice and cloth. The CPI basket contains the quantities bought in 2013. The average household spent $60 on juice and $30 on cloth in 2013 when juice was $2 a bottle and cloth was $5 a metre. In 2014, juice is $4 a bottle and cloth is $6 a metre.

8. Calculate the CPI basket and the percentage of the household's budget spent on juice in 2013.

9. Calculate the CPI and the inflation rate in 2014.

🌐 Use the following data to work Problems 10 and 11. Statistics Canada reported the following CPI data:

June 2008	217.3
June 2009	214.6
June 2010	216.9

10. Calculate the inflation rates for the years ended June 2009 and June 2010. How did the inflation rate change in 2010?

11. Why might these CPI numbers be biased? How can alternative price indexes avoid this bias?

ADDITIONAL PROBLEMS AND APPLICATIONS

MyEconLab   You can work these problems in MyEconLab if assigned by your instructor.
Problems marked ⊕ update with real-time data.

Employment and Unemployment

12. What is the unemployment rate supposed to measure and why is it an imperfect measure?

⊕ 13. Statistics Canada reported the following data for July 2014:

> Labour force participation rate: 67.4 percent
> Working-age population: 29.0 million
> Employment-to-population ratio: 62.5

Calculate the:

a. Labour force.

b. Employment.

c. Unemployment rate.

14. **Jobs Report: Hiring Up, Unemployment Down**

The Labor Department reported that hiring accelerated in November, and the unemployment rate fell to 8.6 percent from 9 percent in October. Two reasons for the fall are that more Americans got jobs, but even more people gave up on their job searches altogether.

> Source: CNNMoney, December 2, 2011

Explain how the labour force and unemployment would have changed if the only change were that:

a. All the newly hired people had been unemployed in October.

b. People gave up on their job searches.

15. In Canada between June and July in 2014, the number of full-time jobs fell by 59,700 while part-time jobs increased by 60,000. The unemployment rate fell 0.1 percent to 7 percent as some workers left the job market. The participation rate fell to 65.9 percent from 66.1 percent.

a. Explain the link between the fall in the participation rate and the fall in the unemployment rate.

b. If all the workers who left the job market were discouraged searchers, explain how the R5 unemployment would have changed.

16. A high unemployment rate tells us that a large percentage of the labour force is unemployed but not why the unemployment rate is high. What unemployment measure tells us if (i) people are searching longer than usual to find a job, (ii) more people are involuntary part-time workers, or (iii) more unemployed people are discouraged searchers?

17. With about 1.3 million Canadians looking for work, some employers are swamped with job applicants, but many employers can't hire enough workers. The job market has changed. During the recession, millions of middle-skill, middle-wage jobs disappeared. Now with the recovery, these people can't find the skilled jobs that they seek and have a hard time adjusting to lower-skilled work with less pay.

Why might the unemployment rate underestimate the underutilization of labour resources?

Unemployment and Full Employment

Use the following data to work Problems 18 to 20. The IMF *World Economic Outlook* reports the following unemployment rates:

Region	2010	2011
United States	9.6	9.0
Euro area	10.1	10.9
Japan	5.1	4.5

18. What do these numbers tell us about the phase of the business cycle in the three regions in 2011?

19. What do these numbers tell us about the relative size of their natural unemployment rates?

20. Do these numbers tell us anything about the relative size of their labour force participation rates and employment-to-population ratios?

Use the following news clip to work Problems 21 to 23.

Economic Conditions at the Cycle Bottom

Employment rebounded by 0.1 percent in August 2008, its first gain in four months. All of the increase was in full-time jobs. The unemployment rate in August 2008 was unchanged at 6.1 percent.

> Source: *Canadian Economic Observer*,
> September 2008

21. How did the unemployment rate in August 2008 compare to the unemployment rate during the recessions of the early 1980s and early 1990s?

22. How can the unemployment rate not change when employment rises?

23. Compare the unemployment rate in August 2008 to the estimated natural unemployment rate. What does this imply about the relationship between real GDP and potential GDP at this time?

24. CNN reported that for the first six months of 2008, the U.S. economy lost 438,000 jobs. The job losses in June were concentrated in manufacturing and construction, two sectors that have been badly battered in the recession.
    a. Based on the report, what might be the main source of increased unemployment?
    b. Based on the report, what might be the main type of increased unemployment?

25. **Governor Plans to Boost Economy with Eco-Friendly Jobs**

    Oregon's 5.6 percent unemployment rate is close to the national average of 5.5 percent. A few years ago, Oregon had one of the highest unemployment rates in the nation. To avoid rising unemployment, Oregon Governor Kulongoski's plan is to provide public schools and universities with enough state funds to meet growing demand for skilled workers. Also, Kulongoski wants to use government money for bridges, roads, and buildings to stimulate more construction jobs.

    Source: *The Oregonian*, July 8, 2008

    a. What is the main type of unemployment that Governor Kulongoski is using policies to avoid? Explain.
    b. How might these policies impact Oregon's natural unemployment rate? Explain.

The Price Level, Inflation, and Deflation

26. A typical family on Sandy Island consumes only juice and cloth. Last year, which was the base year, the family spent $40 on juice and $25 on cloth. In the base year, juice was $4 a bottle and cloth was $5 a length. This year, juice is $4 a bottle and cloth is $6 a length. Calculate:
    a. The CPI basket.
    b. The CPI in the current year.
    c. The inflation rate in the current year.

27. Amazon.com agreed to pay its workers $20 an hour in 1999 and $22 an hour in 2001. The price level for these years was 166 in 1999 and 180 in 2001. Calculate the real wage rate in each year. Did these workers really get a pay raise between 1999 and 2001?

28. **News release**

    Real consumption expenditure in 2002 chained dollars was $814.2 billion in 2009 and $841.5 billion in 2010. In current dollars, it was $898.2 billion in 2009 and $940.6 billion in 2011.

    Source: Statistics Canada

    a. Calculate the chained price index for consumption (CPIC) for 2009 and 2010.
    b. Calculate the CPIC inflation rate for 2010.
    c. Why might the CPIC inflation rate be preferred to the CPI inflation rate?
    d. Did real consumption expenditure increase by more or by less than nominal consumption expenditure? Why?

Economics in the News

29. After you have studied *Economics in the News* on pp. 504–505, answer the following questions.
    a. Describe the key differences in performance of the U.S. and Canadian job markets during 2008–2014.
    b. How do the part-time employment rates of the two countries compare?
    c. Why might the U.S. job market have been so much weaker than the Canadian job market during 2008–2010?
    d. Do you think the differences between the U.S. and Canadian job markets in 2008–2014 were frictional, structural, or cyclical?

30. **Out of a Job and Out of Luck at 54**

    Too young to retire, too old to get a new job. That's how many older workers feel after getting laid off and spending time on the unemployment line. Many lack the skills to craft resumes and search online, experts say. Older workers took an average of 21.1 weeks to land a new job in 2007, about 5 weeks longer than younger people. "Older workers will be more adversely affected because of the time it takes to transition into another job," said Deborah Russell, AARP's director of workforce issues.

    Source: CNN, May 21, 2008

    a. What type of unemployment might older workers be more prone to experience?
    b. Explain how the unemployment rate of older workers is influenced by the business cycle.
    c. Why might older unemployed workers become discouraged searchers during a recession?

The Big Picture

Macroeconomics is a large and controversial subject that is interlaced with political ideological disputes. And it is a field in which charlatans as well as serious thinkers have much to say.

You have just learned in Chapters 20 and 21 how we monitor and measure the main macroeconomic variables. We use real GDP to calculate the rate of economic growth and business cycle fluctuations. And we use the CPI and other measures of the price level to calculate the inflation rate and to "deflate" nominal values to find *real* values.

In the chapters that lie ahead, you will learn the theories that economists have developed to explain economic growth, fluctuations, and inflation.

First, in Chapters 22 to 25, you will study the long-term trends. This material is central to the oldest question in macroeconomics that Adam Smith tried to answer: What are the causes of the wealth of nations? You will also study three other old questions that Adam Smith's contemporary and friend David Hume first addressed: What causes inflation? What causes international deficits and surpluses? And why do exchange rates fluctuate?

In Chapters 26 to 28, you will study macroeconomic fluctuations.

Finally, in Chapters 29 and 30, you will study the policies that the federal government and the Bank of Canada might adopt to make the economy perform well.

David Hume, *a Scot who lived from 1711 to 1776, did not call himself an economist. "Philosophy and general learning" is how he described the subject of his life's work. Hume was an extraordinary thinker and writer. Published in 1742, his* Essays, Moral and Political, *range across economics, political science, moral philosophy, history, literature, ethics, and religion and explore such topics as love, marriage, divorce, suicide, death, and the immortality of the soul!*

His economic essays provide astonishing insights into the forces that cause inflation, business cycle fluctuations, balance of payments deficits, and interest rate fluctuations; and they explain the effects of taxes and government deficits and debts.

Data were scarce in Hume's day, so he was not able to draw on detailed evidence to support his analysis. But he was empirical. He repeatedly appealed to experience and observation as the ultimate judge of the validity of an argument. Hume's fundamentally empirical approach dominates macroeconomics today.

"... in every kingdom into which money begins to flow In greater abundance than formerly, everything takes a new face: labour and industry gain life; the merchant becomes more enterprising, the manufacturer more diligent and skillful, and even the farmer follows his plow with greater alacrity and attention."

DAVID HUME
Essays, Moral and Political

DAVID CARD is Class of 1950 Professor of Economics and Director of the Center for Labor Economics at the University of California, Berkeley, and Faculty Research Associate at the National Bureau of Economic Research.

Born in Canada, Professor Card obtained his B.A. at Queen's University, Kingston, Ontario, and his Ph.D. at Princeton University. He has received many honours, the most notable of which is the American Economic Association's John Bates Clark Prize, awarded to the best economist under 40.

Professor Card's research on labour markets and the effects of public policies on earnings, jobs, and the distribution of income is published in more than 100 articles and several books. His most recent books include two volumes of the *Handbook of Labor Economics* (co-edited with Orley Ashenfelter). An earlier book (co-authored with Alan B. Krueger), *Myth and Measurement: The New Economics of the Minimum Wage* (Princeton, NJ: Princeton University Press, 1995), made a big splash and upset one of the most fundamental beliefs about the effects of minimum wages.

Michael Parkin and Robin Bade talked with David Card about his work and the progress that economists have made in understanding how public policies can influence the distribution of income and economic well-being.

> The ... most difficult thing that empirical economists try to do is infer a causal relationship.

Almost all your work is grounded in data. You are an empirical economist. How do you go about your work, where do your data come from, and how do you use data?

The data I use come from many different sources. I have collected my own data from surveys; transcribed data from historical sources and government publications; and used computerized data files based on records from censuses and surveys in the United States, Canada, Britain, and other countries.

An economist can do three things with data. The first is to develop simple statistics on basic questions such as "What fraction of families live in poverty?" For this, one needs to understand how the data were collected and processed and how the questions were asked. For example, the poverty rate depends on how you define a "family." If a single mother and her child live with the mother's parents, the income of the mother and the grandparents is counted as "family income."

The second thing economists do with data is develop descriptive comparisons. For example, I have compared the wage differences between male and female workers. Again, the details are important. For example, the male–female wage differential is much bigger if you look at annual earnings than at earnings per hour, because women work fewer hours per year.

Once you've established some simple facts, you start to get ideas for possible explanations. You can also rule out a lot of other ideas.

The third and most difficult thing that empirical economists try to do is infer a causal relationship. In rare instances, we have a true experiment in which a random subgroup of volunteers is enrolled in a "treatment group" and the remainder become the "control group." ...

*Read the full interview with David Card in MyEconLab.

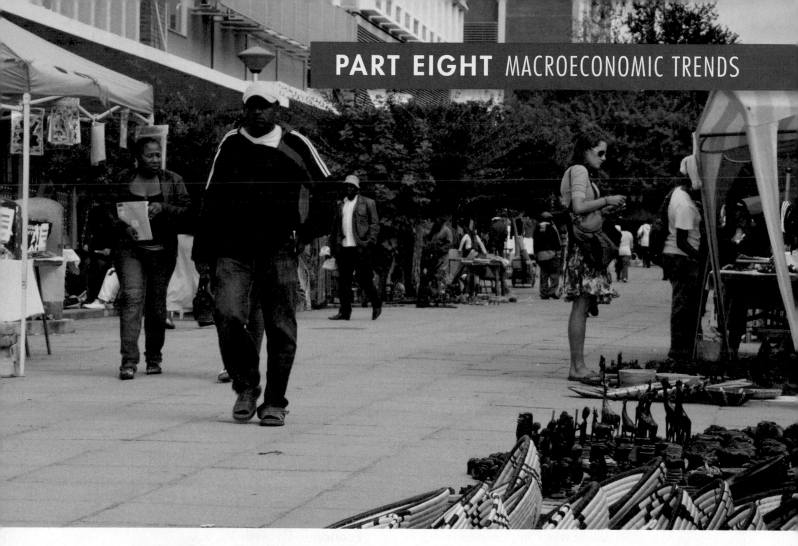

22

ECONOMIC GROWTH

After studying this chapter, you will be able to:

◆ Define and calculate the economic growth rate and explain the implications of sustained growth

◆ Describe the economic growth trends in Canada and other countries and regions

◆ Explain what makes potential GDP grow

◆ Explain the sources of labour productivity growth

◆ Explain the theories of economic growth and policies to increase its rate

Canadian real GDP per person and the standard of living tripled between 1964 and 2014. We see even more dramatic change in China, where incomes have tripled not in 50 years but in the 14 years since 2000. Incomes are also growing rapidly in some African economies, one of which is the small but dynamic Botswana.

In this chapter, we study the forces that make real GDP grow. In *Economics in the News* at the end of the chapter, we look at lessons we can learn from the slow growth of South Africa and its fast-growing neighbour, Botswana.

513

◆ The Basics of Economic Growth

Economic growth is the expansion of production possibilities. A rapid pace of economic growth maintained over a number of years can transform a poor nation into a rich one. Such have been the stories of Hong Kong, South Korea, and some other Asian economies. Slow economic growth or the absence of growth can condemn a nation to devastating poverty. Such has been the fate of Sierra Leone, Somalia, Zambia, and much of the rest of Africa.

The goal of this chapter is to help you understand why some economies expand rapidly and others stagnate. We'll begin by learning how to calculate a growth rate, by distinguishing between economic growth and a business cycle expansion, and by discovering the magic of sustained growth.

Calculating Growth Rates

We express a **growth rate** as the annual percentage change of a variable—the change in the level expressed as a percentage of the initial level. The growth rate of real GDP, for example, is calculated as:

$$\text{Real GDP growth rate} = \frac{\text{Real GDP in current year} - \text{Real GDP in previous year}}{\text{Real GDP in previous year}} \times 100.$$

Using some numbers, if real GDP in the current year is $1,650 billion and if real GDP in the previous year was $1,500 billion, then the economic growth rate is 10 percent.

The growth rate of real GDP tells us how rapidly the *total* economy is expanding. This measure is useful for telling us about potential changes in the balance of economic power among nations. But it does not tell us about changes in the standard of living.

The standard of living depends on **real GDP per person** (also called *per capita* real GDP), which is real GDP divided by the population. So the contribution of real GDP growth to the change in the standard of living depends on the growth rate of real GDP per person. We use the above formula to calculate this growth rate, replacing real GDP with real GDP per person.

Suppose, for example, that in the current year, when real GDP is $1,650 billion, the population is 30.3 million. Then real GDP per person is $1,650 billion divided by 30.3 million, which equals $54,455. And suppose that in the previous year,

when real GDP was $1,500 billion, the population was 30 million. Then real GDP per person in that year was $1,500 billion divided by 30 million, which equals $50,000.

Use these two values of real GDP per person with the growth formula above to calculate the growth rate of real GDP per person. That is,

$$\text{Real GDP per person growth rate} = \frac{\$54,455 - \$50,000}{\$50,000} \times 100 = 8.9 \text{ percent.}$$

The growth rate of real GDP per person can also be calculated (approximately) by subtracting the population growth rate from the real GDP growth rate. In the example you've just worked through, the growth rate of real GDP is 10 percent. The population changes from 30 million to 30.3 million, so the population growth rate is 1 percent. The growth rate of real GDP per person is approximately equal to 10 percent minus 1 percent, which equals 9 percent.

Real GDP per person grows only if real GDP grows faster than the population grows. If the growth rate of the population exceeds the growth of real GDP, then real GDP per person falls.

Economic Growth Versus Business Cycle Expansion

Real GDP can increase for two distinct reasons: The economy might be returning to full employment in an expansion phase of the business cycle or *potential* GDP might be increasing.

The return to full employment in an expansion phase of the business cycle isn't economic growth. It is just taking up the slack that resulted from the previous recession. The expansion of potential GDP is economic growth.

Figure 22.1 illustrates this distinction using the production possibilities frontier (the *PPF* that you studied in Chapter 2, p. 32). A return to full employment in a business cycle expansion is a movement from inside the *PPF* at a point such as *A* to a point on the *PPF* such as *B*.

Economic growth is the expansion of production possibilities. It is an outward movement of the *PPF* such as the shift from PPF_0 to PPF_1 and the movement from point *B* on PPF_0 to point *C* on PPF_1.

The growth rate of potential GDP measures the pace of expansion of production possibilities and smoothes out the business cycle fluctuations in the growth rate of real GDP.

FIGURE 22.1 Economic Growth and a Business Cycle Expansion

The increase in aggregate production in the move from point A inside PPF_0 to point B on PPF_0 is an expansion phase of the business cycle and it occurs with no change in production possibilities. Such an expansion is not economic growth. The increase in aggregate production in the move from point B on PPF_0 to point C on PPF_1 is economic growth—an expansion of production possibilities shown by an outward shift of the PPF.

——— MyEconLab Animation ———

FIGURE 22.2 Growth Rates of Real GDP and Potential GDP

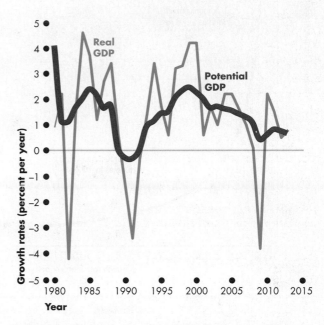

The annual growth rate of real GDP fluctuates widely over the business cycle and masks changes in the underlying trend growth rate. The annual growth rate of potential GDP provides information about changes in the trend growth rate. Both the growth rate of potential GDP and the trend growth rate of real GDP have fallen since 2000.

Sources of data: Statistics Canada, CANSIM Table 282-0002 and Bank of Canada output gap estimates used to calculate the growth rate of potential GDP.

——— MyEconLab Real-time data ———

Figure 22.2 shows how the growth rate of potential GDP (red curve) smoothes the more erratic fluctuations in the growth rate of real GDP. Business cycle fluctuations in the real GDP growth rate mask the underlying *trend* growth rate revealed by the growth rate of *potential* GDP.

The Magic of Sustained Growth

Sustained growth of real GDP per person can transform a poor society into a wealthy one. The reason is that economic growth is like compound interest.

Compound Interest Suppose that you put $100 in the bank and earn 5 percent a year interest on it. After one year, you have $105. If you leave that $105

in the bank for another year, you earn 5 percent interest on the original $100 *and on the $5 interest that you earned last year*. You are now earning interest on interest! The next year, things get even better. Then you earn 5 percent on the original $100 and on the interest earned in the first year and the second year. You are even earning interest on the interest that you earned on the interest of the first year.

Your money in the bank is growing at a rate of 5 percent a year. Before too many years have passed, your initial deposit of $100 will have grown to $200. But after how many years?

The answer is provided by a formula called the **Rule of 70**, which states that the number of years it takes for the level of any variable to double is approximately

FIGURE 22.3   The Rule of 70

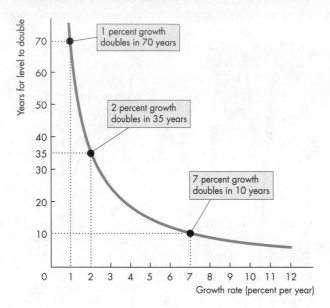

Growth rate (percent per year)	Years for level to double
1	70.0
2	35.0
3	23.3
4	17.5
5	14.0
6	11.7
7	10.0
8	8.8
9	7.8
10	7.0
11	6.4
12	5.8

The number of years it takes for the level of a variable to double is approximately 70 divided by the annual percentage growth rate of the variable.

MyEconLab Animation

---

70 divided by the annual percentage growth rate of the variable. Using the Rule of 70, you can now calculate how many years it takes your $100 to become $200. It is 70 divided by 5, which is 14 years.

Applying the Rule of 70

The Rule of 70 applies to any variable, so it applies to real GDP per person. Figure 22.3 shows the doubling time for growth rates of 1 percent per year to 12 percent per year.

You can see that real GDP per person doubles in 70 years (70 divided by 1)—an average human life span—if the growth rate is 1 percent a year. It doubles in 35 years if the growth rate is 2 percent a year and in just 10 years if the growth rate is 7 percent a year.

We can use the Rule of 70 to answer other questions about economic growth. For example, in 2014, Canadian real GDP per person was approximately 4 times that of China. China's recent growth rate of real GDP per person was 10 percent a year. If this growth rate were maintained, how long would it take China's real GDP per person to reach that of Canada in 2014? The answer, provided by the Rule of 70, is 14 years. China's real GDP per person doubles in 7 years

(70 divided by 10). It doubles again to 4 times its current level in another 7 years. So after 14 years of growth at 10 percent a year, China's real GDP per person is 4 times its current level and equals that of Canada in 2014. Of course, after 14 years, Canadian real GDP per person would have increased, so China would still not have caught up to Canada. But at the current growth rates, China's real GDP per person will equal that of Canada by the late 2020s.

REVIEW QUIZ

1 What is economic growth and how do we calculate its rate?
2 What is the relationship between the growth rate of real GDP and the growth rate of real GDP per person?
3 Use the Rule of 70 to calculate the growth rate that leads to a doubling of real GDP per person in 20 years.

Work these questions in Study Plan 22.1 and get instant feedback. Do a Key Terms Quiz.   MyEconLab

Long-Term Growth Trends

You have just seen the power of economic growth to increase incomes. At a 1 percent growth rate, it takes a human life span to double the standard of living. But at a 7 percent growth rate, the standard of living doubles every decade. How fast has our economy grown over the long term? How fast are other economies growing? Are poor countries catching up to rich ones, or do the gaps between the rich and poor persist or even widen? Let's answer these questions.

Long-Term Growth in Canada

Figure 22.4 shows *real GDP per person* in Canada for the 88 years from 1926 to 2014. The average growth rate over this period was 2 percent a year.

The earliest years in the graph are dominated by two extraordinary events: the Great Depression of the 1930s and World War II in the 1940s. The fall in real GDP during the depression and the bulge during the war obscure the changes in the long-term growth trend that occurred within these years. Averaging out the depression and the war, the long-term growth rate was close to its 88-year average of 2 percent a year.

The 1950s had slow growth but then, during the 1960s, the growth rate speeded up and averaged 3.3 percent a year. The 1970s growth rate slowed to 2.0 percent a year, and in the late 1980s the growth rate slowed to a crawl of 0.5 percent a year. In the 1990s the growth rate increased again to 1.8 percent a year, but after 1996 it slowed to 0.9 percent a year.

A major goal of this chapter is to explain why our economy grows and why the long-term growth rate varies. Why did growth speed up during the 1960s, slow through the 1970s and 1980s, and then speed up again during the late 1990s? Another goal is to explain variations in the growth rate across countries.

Let's look at some facts about the growth rates of other nations and compare them with Canada's growth rates.

FIGURE 22.4 Economic Growth in Canada: 1926–2014

During the 88 years from 1926 to 2014, real GDP per person in Canada grew by 2 percent a year, on average. The growth rate was most rapid during the 1960s and slowest during the 1980s.

Sources of data: F. H. Leacy (ed.), *Historical Statistics of Canada*, 2nd edition, catalogue 11-516, series A1, F32, F55, Statistics Canada, Ottawa, 1983. Statistics Canada, Tables 380-0002 and 051-0005

MyEconLab Real-time data

Real GDP Growth in the World Economy

Figure 22.5 shows real GDP per person in Canada, the United States, and in other countries between 1960 and 2010. Part (a) looks at the seven richest countries—known as the G7 nations. Among these nations, the United States has the highest real GDP per person. In 2010, Canada had the second-highest real GDP per person, ahead of Japan and France, Germany, Italy, and the United Kingdom (collectively the Europe Big 4).

During the fifty years shown here, the gaps between the United States, Canada, and the Europe Big 4 have been almost constant. But starting from a long way below, Japan grew fastest. It caught up to Europe in 1970 and to Canada in 1990. But during the 1990s, Japan's economy stagnated.

Many other countries are growing more slowly than, and falling farther behind, both the United States and Canada. Figure 22.5(b) looks at some of these countries.

Real GDP per person in Central and South America was 28 percent of the Canadian level in 1960. It grew more quickly than Canada and reached 30 percent of the Canadian level by 1980, but then growth slowed and by 2010, real GDP per person in these countries was 23 percent of the Canadian level.

In Eastern Europe, real GDP per person has grown more slowly than anywhere except Africa, and fell from 32 percent of the Canadian level in 1980 to 19 percent in 2003 and then increased again to 22 percent in 2010.

Real GDP per person in Africa, the world's poorest continent, fell from 10 percent of the Canadian level

FIGURE 22.5   Economic Growth Around the World: Catch-Up or Not?

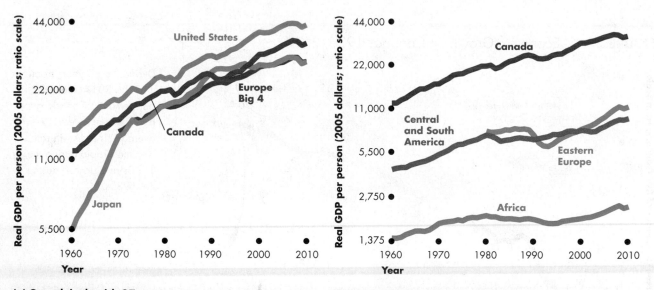

(a) Growth in the rich G7

Real GDP per person has grown throughout the world. Among the rich industrial countries in part (a), real GDP per person has grown slightly faster in the United States than in Canada and the four big countries of Europe (France, Germany, Italy, and the United Kingdom). Japan had the fastest growth rate before 1973 but then growth slowed and Japan's economy stagnated during the 1990s.

(b) Persistent gaps between rich and poor

Among a wider range of countries shown in part (b), growth rates have been slower than that of Canada. The gaps between the real GDP per person in Canada and in these countries have widened. The gap between the real GDP per person in Canada and Africa has widened by a large amount.

Sources of data: Alan Heston, Robert Summers, and Bettina Aten, Penn World Table Version 7.1, Center for International Comparisons of Production, Income and Prices at the University of Pennsylvania, July 2012.

Economics in Action
Fast Trains on the Same Track

Five Asian economies, Hong Kong, Korea, Singapore, Taiwan, and China, have experienced spectacular growth, which you can see in the figure. During the 1960s, real GDP per person in these economies ranged from 3 to 25 percent of that in Canada. But by 2010, real GDP per person in Singapore and Hong Kong had surpassed that of Canada.

The figure also shows that China is catching up rapidly but from a long way behind. China's real GDP per person increased from 3 percent of the Canadian level in 1960 to 15 percent in 2010.

The Asian economies shown here are like fast trains running on the same track at similar speeds and with a roughly constant gap between them. Singapore and Hong Kong are hooked together as the lead train, which runs about 20 years in front of Taiwan and Korea and 40 years in front of China.

Real GDP per person in Korea in 2010 was similar to that in Hong Kong in 1988, and real GDP in China in 2010 was similar to that of Hong Kong in 1976. Between 1976 and 2010, Hong Kong transformed itself from a poor developing economy into one of the richest economies in the world.

The rest of China is now doing what Hong Kong has done. China has a population 200 times that of Hong Kong and more than 4 times that of the United States. So if China continues its rapid growth, the world economy will change dramatically.

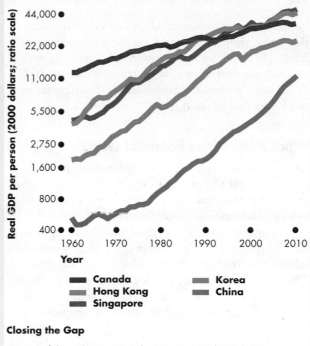

Closing the Gap

Sources of data: Alan Heston, Robert Summers, and Bettina Aten, Penn World Table Version 7.1, Center for International Comparisons of Production, Income, and Prices at the University of Pennsylvania, July 2012.

As these fast-growing Asian economies catch up with Canada, we can expect their growth rates to slow. But it will be surprising if China's growth rate slows much before it has closed the gap on Canada.

in 1960 to 5 percent in 2007 and then increased slightly to 6 percent in 2010.

Even modest differences in growth rates sustained over a number of years bring big differences in the standard of living. So the facts about economic growth raise some big questions.

What are the preconditions for economic growth? What sustains economic growth once it gets going? How can we identify the sources of economic growth and measure the contribution that each source makes? What can we do to increase the sustainable rate of economic growth?

We're now going to address these questions and discover the causes of economic growth. We start by seeing how potential GDP is determined and what makes it grow. You will see that labour productivity growth is the key to rising living standards and go on to explore the sources of this growth.

REVIEW QUIZ

1 What has been the average growth rate of Canadian real GDP per person over the past 86 years? In which periods was growth most rapid and in which periods was it slowest?

2 Describe the gaps between real GDP per person in Canada and in other countries. For which countries is the gap narrowing? For which is it widening? For which is it the same?

3 Compare the growth rates in Hong Kong, Korea, Singapore, Taiwan, China, and Canada. In terms of real GDP per person, how far is China behind these others?

Work these questions in Study Plan 22.2 and get instant feedback.   MyEconLab

How Potential GDP Grows

Economic growth occurs when real GDP increases. But a one-shot rise in real GDP or a recovery from recession isn't economic growth. Economic growth is a sustained, year-after-year increase in *potential GDP*.

So what determines potential GDP and what are the forces that make it grow?

What Determines Potential GDP?

Labour, capital, land, and entrepreneurship produce real GDP, and the productivity of the factors of production determines the quantity of real GDP that can be produced.

The quantity of land is fixed, and on any given day the quantities of entrepreneurial ability and capital are also fixed and their productivities are given. The quantity of labour employed is the only *variable* factor of production. Potential GDP is the level of real GDP when the quantity of labour employed is the full-employment quantity.

To determine potential GDP, we use a model with two components:

- An aggregate production function
- An aggregate labour market

Aggregate Production Function When you studied the limits to production in Chapter 2 (see p. 32), you learned that the *production possibilities frontier* is the boundary between the combinations of goods and services that can be produced and those that cannot. We're now going to think about the production possibilities frontier for two special "goods": real GDP and the quantity of leisure time.

Think of real GDP as a number of big shopping carts. Each cart contains some of each kind of different goods and services produced, and one cartload of items costs $1 billion. To say that real GDP is $1,400 billion means that it is 1,440 very big shopping carts of goods and services.

The quantity of leisure time is the number of hours spent not working. Each leisure hour could be spent working. If we spent all our time taking leisure, we would do no work and produce nothing. Real GDP would be zero. The more leisure we forgo, the greater is the quantity of labour we supply and the greater is the quantity of real GDP produced.

But labour hours are not all equally productive. We use our most productive hours first, and as more

hours are worked, these hours are increasingly less productive. So for each additional hour of leisure forgone (each additional hour of labour), real GDP increases but by successively smaller amounts.

The **aggregate production function** is the relationship that tells us how real GDP changes as the quantity of labour changes when all other influences on production remain the same. Figure 22.6 shows this relationship—the curve labelled *PF*. An increase in the quantity of labour (and a corresponding decrease in leisure hours) brings a movement along the production function and an increase in real GDP.

Aggregate Labour Market In macroeconomics, we pretend that there is one large labour market that determines the quantity of labour employed and the quantity of real GDP produced. To see how this aggregate labour market works, we study the demand for labour, the supply of labour, and labour market equilibrium.

The Demand for Labour The *demand for labour* is the relationship between the quantity of labour demanded and the real wage rate. The quantity of labour demanded is the number of labour hours hired by all the firms in the economy during a given

---

FIGURE 22.6   The Aggregate Production Function

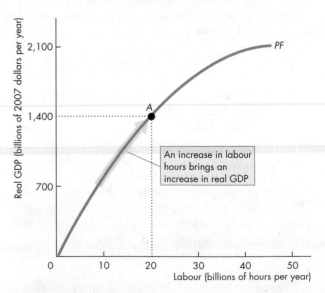

At point *A* on the aggregate production function *PF*, 20 billion hours of labour produce $1,400 billion of real GDP.

──────── **MyEconLab** Animation ────────

period. This quantity depends on the price of labour, which is the real wage rate.

The **real wage rate** is the money wage rate divided by the price level. The real wage rate is the quantity of goods and services that an hour of labour earns. It contrasts with the money wage rate, which is the number of dollars that an hour of labour earns.

The *real* wage rate influences the quantity of labour demanded because what matters to firms is not the number of dollars they pay (money wage rate) but how much output they must sell to earn those dollars.

The quantity of labour demanded *increases* as the real wage rate *decreases*—the demand for labour curve slopes downward. Why? The answer lies in the shape of the production function.

You've seen that along the production function, each additional hour of labour increases real GDP by successively smaller amounts. This tendency has a name: the *law of diminishing returns*. Because of diminishing returns, firms will hire more labour only if the real wage rate falls to match the fall in the extra output produced by that labour.

The Supply of Labour The *supply of labour* is the relationship between the quantity of labour supplied and the real wage rate. The quantity of labour supplied is the number of labour hours that all the households in the economy plan to work during a given period. This quantity depends on the real wage rate.

The *real* wage rate influences the quantity of labour supplied because what matters to households is not the number of dollars they earn (money wage rate) but what they can buy with those dollars.

The quantity of labour supplied *increases* as the real wage rate *increases*—the supply of labour curve slopes upward. At a higher real wage rate, more people choose to work and more people choose to work longer hours if they can earn more per hour.

Labour Market Equilibrium The price of labour is the real wage rate. The forces of supply and demand operate in labour markets just as they do in the markets for goods and services to eliminate a shortage or a surplus. But a shortage or a surplus of labour brings only a gradual change in the real wage rate. If there is a shortage of labour, the real wage rate rises to eliminate it; and if there is a surplus of labour, the real wage rate eventually falls to eliminate it. When there is neither a shortage nor a surplus, the labour market is in equilibrium—a full-employment equilibrium.

FIGURE 22.7 Labour Market Equilibrium

Labour market equilibrium occurs when the quantity of labour demanded equals the quantity of labour supplied. The equilibrium real wage rate is $35 an hour, and equilibrium employment is 20 billion hours per year.

At a wage rate above $35 an hour, there is a surplus of labour and the real wage rate falls to eliminate the surplus. At a wage rate below $35 an hour, there is a shortage of labour and the real wage rate rises to eliminate the shortage.

MyEconLab Animation

Figure 22.7 illustrates labour market equilibrium. The demand for labour curve is *LD* and the supply of labour curve is *LS*. This labour market is in equilibrium at a real wage rate of $35 an hour and 20 billion hours a year are employed.

If the real wage rate exceeds $35 an hour, the quantity of labour supplied exceeds the quantity demanded and there is a surplus of labour. When there is a surplus of labour, the real wage rate falls toward the equilibrium real wage rate where the surplus is eliminated.

If the real wage rate is less than $35 an hour, the quantity of labour demanded exceeds the quantity supplied and there is a shortage of labour. When there is a shortage of labour, the real wage rate rises toward the equilibrium real wage rate where the shortage is eliminated.

If the real wage rate is $35 an hour, the quantity of labour demanded equals the quantity supplied and there is neither a shortage nor a surplus of labour. In this situation, there is no pressure in either direction on the real wage rate. So the real wage rate remains constant and the market is in equilibrium. At this equilibrium real wage rate and level of employment, the economy is at *full employment.*

Potential GDP You've seen that the production function tells us the quantity of real GDP that a given amount of labour can produce—see Fig. 22.6. The quantity of real GDP produced increases as the quantity of labour increases. At the equilibrium quantity of labour, the economy is at full employment, and the quantity of real GDP at full employment is potential GDP. So the full-employment quantity of labour produces potential GDP.

Figure 22.8 illustrates the determination of potential GDP. Part (a) shows labour market equilibrium. At the equilibrium real wage rate, equilibrium employment is 20 billion hours. Part (b) shows the production function. With 20 billion hours of labour, the economy can produce a real GDP of $1,400 billion. This amount is potential GDP.

What Makes Potential GDP Grow?

We can divide all the forces that make potential GDP grow into two categories:

- Growth of the supply of labour
- Growth of labour productivity

Growth of the Supply of Labour When the supply of labour grows, the supply of labour curve shifts rightward. The quantity of labour at a given real wage rate increases.

The quantity of labour is the number of workers employed multiplied by average hours per worker. The number employed equals the employment-to-population ratio multiplied by the working-age population, divided by 100 (Chapter 21, p. 493). So the quantity of labour changes as a result of changes in:

1. Average hours per worker
2. The employment-to-population ratio
3. The working-age population

Average hours per worker have decreased as the workweek has become shorter, and the employment-to-population ratio has increased as more women have entered the labour force. The combined effect of

FIGURE 22.8 The Labour Market and Potential GDP

(a) The labour market

(b) Potential GDP

The economy is at full employment when the quantity of labour demanded equals the quantity of labour supplied, in part (a). The real wage rate is $35 an hour, and employment is 20 billion hours a year. Part (b) shows potential GDP. It is the quantity of real GDP determined by the production function at the full-employment quantity of labour.

———— MyEconLab Animation and Draw Graph ————

these two factors has kept the average hours per working-age person (approximately) constant.

Growth in the supply of labour has come from growth in the working-age population. In the long run, the working-age population grows at the same rate as the total population.

The Effects of Population Growth Population growth brings growth in the supply of labour, but it does not change the demand for labour or the production function. The economy can produce more output by using more labour, but there is no change in the quantity of real GDP that a given quantity of labour can produce.

With an increase in the supply of labour and no change in the demand for labour, the real wage rate falls and the equilibrium quantity of labour increases. The increased quantity of labour produces more output and potential GDP increases.

Illustrating the Effects of Population Growth Figure 22.9 illustrates the effects of an increase in the population. In Fig. 22.9(a), the demand for labour curve is *LD* and initially the supply of labour curve is *LS*₀. The equilibrium real wage rate is $35 an hour and the quantity of labour is 20 billion hours a year. In Fig. 22.9(b), the production function (*PF*) shows that with 20 billion hours of labour employed, potential GDP is $1,400 billion at point *A*.

An increase in the population increases the supply of labour and the supply of labour curve shifts rightward to *LS*₁. At a real wage rate of $35 an hour, there is now a surplus of labour, so the real wage rate falls. In this example, the real wage rate will fall until it reaches $25 an hour. At $25 an hour, the quantity of labour demanded equals the quantity of labour supplied. The equilibrium quantity of labour increases to 30 billion hours a year.

Figure 22.9(b) shows the effect on real GDP. As the equilibrium quantity of labour increases from 20 billion to 30 billion hours, potential GDP increases along the production function from $1,400 billion to $1,750 billion at point *B*.

So an increase in the population increases the full-employment quantity of labour and potential GDP and lowers the real wage rate. But the population increase *decreases* potential GDP per hour of labour. Initially, it was $70 ($1,400 billion divided by 20 billion). With the population increase, potential GDP per hour of labour is $58.33 ($1,750 billion divided by 30 billion). Diminishing returns are the source of the decrease in potential GDP per hour of labour.

FIGURE 22.9   The Effects of an Increase in Population

(a) The labour market

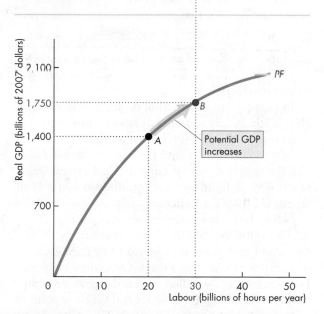

(b) Potential GDP

An increase in the population increases the supply of labour. In part (a), the supply of labour curve shifts rightward. The real wage rate falls and aggregate labour hours increase. In part (b), the increase in aggregate labour hours brings an increase in potential GDP. But diminishing returns bring a decrease in potential GDP per hour of labour.

MyEconLab Animation

Growth of Labour Productivity **Labour productivity** is the quantity of real GDP produced by an hour of labour. It is calculated by dividing real GDP by aggregate labour hours. For example, if real GDP is $1,400 billion and aggregate hours are 20 billion, labour productivity is $65 per hour.

When labour productivity grows, real GDP per person grows and brings a rising standard of living. Let's see how an increase in labour productivity changes potential GDP.

Effects of an Increase in Labour Productivity If labour productivity increases, production possibilities expand. The quantity of real GDP that any given quantity of labour can produce increases. If labour is more productive, firms are willing to pay more for a given number of hours of labour so the demand for labour also increases.

With an increase in the demand for labour and *no change in the supply of labour*, the real wage rate rises and the quantity of labour supplied increases. The equilibrium quantity of labour also increases.

So an increase in labour productivity increases potential GDP for two reasons: Labour is more productive and more labour is employed.

Illustrating the Effects of an Increase in Labour Productivity Figure 22.10 illustrates the effects of an increase in labour productivity.

In part (a), the production function initially is PF_0. With 20 billion hours of labour employed, potential GDP is $1,400 billion at point A.

In part (b), the demand for labour curve is LD_0 and the supply of labour curve is LS. The real wage rate is $35 an hour, and the equilibrium quantity of labour is 20 billion hours a year.

Now labour productivity increases. In Fig. 22.10(a), the increase in labour productivity shifts the production function upward to PF_1. At each quantity of labour, more real GDP can be produced. For example, at 20 billion hours, the economy can now produce $2,000 billion of real GDP at point B.

In Fig. 22.10(b), the increase in labour productivity increases the demand for labour and the demand for labour curve shifts rightward to LD_1. At the initial real wage rate of $35 an hour, there is now a shortage of labour. The real wage rate rises. In this example, the real wage rate will rise until it reaches $45 an hour. At $45 an hour, the quantity of labour demanded equals the quantity of labour supplied. The equilibrium quantity of labour is 22.5 billion hours a year.

FIGURE 22.10 The Effects of an Increase in Labour Productivity

(a) Potential GDP

(b) The labour market

An increase in labour productivity shifts the production function upward from PF_0 to PF_1 in part (a) and shifts the demand for labour curve rightward from LD_0 to LD_1 in part (b). The real wage rate rises to $45 an hour, and aggregate labour hours increase from 20 billion to 22.5 billion. Potential GDP increases from $1,400 billion to $2,100 billion.

MyEconLab Animation and Draw Graph

Figure 22.10(a) shows the effects of the increase in labour productivity on potential GDP. There are two effects. At the initial quantity of labour, real GDP increases to point *B* on the new production function. But as the equilibrium quantity of labour increases from 20 billion to 22.5 billion hours, potential GDP increases to $2,100 billion at point *C*.

Potential GDP per hour of labour also increases. Initially, it was $65 ($1,400 billion divided by 20 billion). With the increase in labour productivity, potential GDP per hour of labour is $84.44 ($2,100 billion divided by 22.5 billion).

The increase in aggregate labour hours that you have just seen is a consequence of an increase in labour productivity. This increase in aggregate labour hours and labour productivity is an example of the interaction effects that economists seek to identify in their search for the ultimate *causes* of economic growth. In the case that we've just studied, aggregate labour hours increase but that increase is a *consequence*, not a cause, of the growth of potential GDP. The source of the increase in potential GDP is an increase in labour productivity.

Labour productivity is the key to increasing output per hour of labour and raising living standards. But what brings an increase in labour productivity? The next section answers this question.

REVIEW QUIZ

1 What is the aggregate production function?
2 What determines the demand for labour, the supply of labour, and labour market equilibrium?
3 What determines potential GDP?
4 What are the two broad sources of potential GDP growth?
5 What are the effects of an increase in the population on potential GDP, the quantity of labour, the real wage rate, and potential GDP per hour of labour?
6 What are the effects of an increase in labour productivity on potential GDP, the quantity of labour, the real wage rate, and potential GDP per hour of labour?

Work these questions in Study Plan 22.3 and get instant feedback. Do a Key Terms Quiz.   MyEconLab

Why Labour Productivity Grows

You've seen that labour productivity growth makes potential GDP grow; and you've seen that labour productivity growth is essential if real GDP per person and the standard of living are to grow. But why does labour productivity grow? What are the preconditions that make labour productivity growth possible and what are the forces that make it grow? Why does labour productivity grow faster at some times and in some places than others?

Preconditions for Labour Productivity Growth

The fundamental precondition for labour productivity growth is the *incentive* system created by firms, markets, property rights, and money. These four social institutions are the same as those described in Chapter 2 (see pp. 44–45) that enable people to gain by specializing and trading.

It was the presence of secure property rights in Britain in the middle 1700s that got the Industrial Revolution going (see *Economics in Action* on p. 527). And it is their absence in some parts of Africa today that is keeping labour productivity stagnant.

With the preconditions for labour productivity growth in place, three things influence its pace:

■ Physical capital growth
■ Human capital growth
■ Technological advances

Physical Capital Growth

As the amount of capital per worker increases, labour productivity also increases. Production processes that use hand tools can create beautiful objects, but production methods that use large amounts of capital per worker are much more productive. The accumulation of capital on farms, in textile factories, in iron foundries and steel mills, in coal mines, on building sites, in chemical plants, in auto plants, in banks and insurance companies, and in shopping malls has added incredibly to the labour productivity of our economy. The next time you see a movie that is set in the Old West or colonial times, look carefully at the small amount of capital around. Try to imagine how productive you would be in such circumstances compared with your productivity today.

Economics in Action
Women Are the Better Borrowers

Economic growth is driven by the decisions of billions of individuals to save and invest, and to borrow and lend. In developing countries, most people are too poor to save and too big a risk to be able to borrow from a bank. But they can get a *microloan* to start a business, employ a few people, and earn an income. And many of the most successful microloan borrowers are women.

Microloans originated in Bangladesh and have spread throughout the developing world. Kiva.org and MicroPlace.com (owned by eBay) are Web sites that enable people to lend money that is used to make microloans in developing economies.

Microloans are helping many women to feed and clothe their families and to grow their businesses. But not all microloan-financed businesses succeed. And the evidence from controlled experiments conducted by Esther Duflo* and her colleagues in the Abdul Latif Jameel Poverty Action Lab is that gains in consumption are temporary. A few years after getting a microloan, borrowers are no better off, on average, than they were before taking a loan. Making poor people less poor requires more than access to microloans.

This woman was able to set up her seamstress business with a microloan.

Human Capital Growth

Human capital—the accumulated skill and knowledge of human beings—is the fundamental source of labour productivity growth. Human capital grows when a new discovery is made and it grows as more and more people learn how to use past discoveries.

The development of one of the most basic human skills—writing—was the source of some of the earliest major gains in productivity. The ability to keep

*See Talking with Esther Duflo on p. 54.

written records made it possible to reap ever-larger gains from specialization and trade. Imagine how hard it would be to do any kind of business if all the accounts, invoices, and agreements existed only in people's memories.

Later, the development of mathematics laid the foundation for the eventual extension of knowledge about physical forces and chemical and biological processes. This base of scientific knowledge was the foundation for the technological advances of the Industrial Revolution and of today's information revolution.

But a lot of human capital that is extremely productive is much more humble. It takes the form of millions of individuals learning and becoming remarkably more productive by repetitively doing simple production tasks. One much-studied example of this type of human capital growth occurred in World War II. With no change in physical capital, thousands of workers and managers in U.S. shipyards learned from experience and accumulated human capital that more than doubled their productivity in less than two years.

Technological Advances

The accumulation of physical capital and human capital has made large contributions to labour productivity growth. But technologial change—the discovery and the application of new technologies—has made an even greater contribution.

Labour is many times more productive today than it was a hundred years ago but not because we have more steam engines and more horse-drawn carriages per person. Rather, it is because we have transportation equipment that uses technologies that were unknown a hundred years ago and that are more productive than the old technologies were.

Technological advance arises from formal research and development programs and from informal trial and error, and it involves discovering new ways of getting more out of our resources.

To reap the benefits of technological change, capital must increase. Some of the most powerful and far-reaching fundamental technologies are embodied in human capital—for example, language, writing, and mathematics. But most technologies are embodied in physical capital. For example, to reap the benefits of the internal combustion engine, millions of horse-drawn carriages had to be replaced with automobiles; and to reap the benefits of digital music, millions of Discmans had to be replaced by iPods.

Economics in Action
Intellectual Property Rights Propel Growth

In 1760, when what is now Canada and the United States of America were developing agricultural economies, England was on the cusp of an economic revolution, the *Industrial Revolution.*

For 70 dazzling years, technological advances in the use of steam power; the manufacture of cotton, wool, iron, and steel; and in transportation, accompanied by massive capital investment associated with these technologies, transformed the economy of England. Incomes rose and brought an explosion in an increasingly urbanized population.

By 1825, advances in steam technology had reached a level of sophistication that enabled Robert Stevenson to build the world's first steam-powered rail engine (the Rocket pictured here in the Science Museum, London) and the birth of the world's first railroad.

Why did the Industrial Revolution happen? Why did it start in 1760? And why in England?

Economic historians say that intellectual property rights—England's patent system—provides the answer.

England's patent system began with the Statute of Monopolies of 1624, which gave inventors a monopoly to use their idea for a term of 14 years. For about 100 years, the system was used to reward friends of the royal

court rather than true inventors. But from around 1720 onward, the system started to work well. To be granted a 14-year monopoly, an inventor only had to pay the required £100 fee (about $22,000 in today's money) and register his or her invention. The inventor was not required to describe the invention in too much detail, so registering and getting a patent didn't mean sharing the invention with competitors.

This patent system, which is essentially the same as today's, aligned the self-interest of entrepreneurial inventors with the social interest and unleashed a flood of inventions, the most transformative of which was steam power and, by 1825, the steam locomotive.

FIGURE 22.11   The Sources of Economic Growth

Change in average hours per worker
Change in employment-to-population ratio
Working-age population growth
→ Labour supply growth

Physical capital growth
Human capital growth
■ Education and training
■ Job experience
Technological advances
→ Labour productivity growth

→ Real GDP growth

Population growth

Real GDP per person growth

Labour supply growth and labour productivity growth combine to determine real GDP growth. Real GDP per person growth depends on real GDP growth and population growth.

MyEconLab Animation

Figure 22.11 summarizes the sources of labour productivity growth and, more broadly, of real GDP growth. The figure also emphasizes that for real GDP per person to grow, real GDP must grow faster than the population.

Economics in the News on the next page provides an example of today's labour productivity growth arising from the spread of robot technologies.

REVIEW QUIZ

1 What are the preconditions for labour productivity growth?
2 Explain the influences on the pace of labour productivity growth.

Work these questions in Study Plan 22.4 and get instant feedback.   MyEconLab

◆ ECONOMICS IN THE NEWS

Robots as Skilled Workers

Skilled Work, Without the Worker
A new wave of robots, far more adept than those now commonly used by automakers and other heavy goods manufacturers, are replacing workers around the world in both manufacturing and distribution.

Source: *The New York Times*, August 18, 2012

SOME FACTS

"The Robot Report" (www.therobotreport.com) agrees with the news clip. The auto industry has been the main customer for industrial robots, but the scene is changing. Robot manufacturers are creating equipment tailored to the requirements of producers of a wide range of items, just a few of which are metals, food and drink, glass, pharmaceuticals, medical devices, and solar panels.

Around 200 established firms worldwide specialize in the design and production of robots, and more than 147 start-up companies have entered this industry in the past year. Almost 2,000 firms have some connection with industrial robots.

THE QUESTIONS

- How will the adoption of industrial robots change employment, the real wage rate, and potential GDP?
- Do robots kill jobs and create unemployment?

THE ANSWERS

- Robots make workers more productive. One person working with a robot can produce as much as hundreds of workers with non-robot technology.
- Robots replace some workers but create a demand for other workers to design, produce, install, and maintain robots.
- In aggregate, robots increase the productivity of labour. The production function shifts upward and the demand for labour curve shifts rightward.
- The equilibrium real wage rate rises, employment increases, and potential GDP increases.
- As robot production technologies spread, many jobs will disappear, but many new jobs will be created.
- Some displaced workers will take new jobs with lower wages. Others will take jobs as skilled robot technicians and producers with higher wages. Average wages will rise.

A robot arm seals a box of Lego building toys for shipping.

(a) Potential GDP

(b) The labour market

The Effects of Robots on Employment and GDP

◆ Is Economic Growth Sustainable? Theories, Evidence, and Policies

You've seen how population growth and labour productivity growth make potential GDP grow. You've also seen that the growth of physical capital and human capital and technological advances make labour productivity grow. But what *causes* economic growth? Why do growth rates vary? How do population growth, capital accumulation, and technoloical change interact to determine the economic growth rate? What can we say about the future of economic growth? Is growth sustainable? Will the rich economies and the economies of the developing world keep growing, or will growth end to be followed by stagnation or even a falling standard of living?

Economists have wrestled with these questions for the past 250 years and made progress in answering them. We're now going to look at the evolution of ideas about the sustainability of economic growth and the policies that might achieve faster growth.

We start by studying the three main theories about the process of economic growth:

- Classical growth theory
- Neoclassical growth theory
- New growth theory

Classical Growth Theory

Classical growth theory is the view that the growth of real GDP per person is temporary and that when it rises above the subsistence level, a population explosion eventually brings it back to the subsistence level. Adam Smith, Thomas Robert Malthus, and David Ricardo—the leading economists of the late eighteenth and early nineteenth centuries—proposed this theory, but the view is most closely associated with the name of Malthus and is sometimes called the *Malthusian theory*. Charles Darwin's ideas about evolution by natural selection were inspired by the insights of Malthus.

Modern-Day Malthusians Many people today are Malthusians. They say that if today's global population of 7.2 billion explodes to 11 billion by 2050 and perhaps 35 billion by 2300, we will run out of resources, real GDP per person will decline, and we will return to a primitive standard of living. We must, say Malthusians, contain population growth.

Modern-day Malthusians also point to global warming and climate change as reasons to believe that, eventually, real GDP per person will decrease.

Neoclassical Growth Theory

Neoclassical growth theory is the proposition that real GDP per person grows because technological change induces saving and investment that make capital per hour of labour grow. Growth ends if technological change stops because of diminishing marginal returns to both labour and capital. Robert Solow of MIT suggested the most popular version of this growth theory in the 1950s.

Neoclassical growth theory's big break with its classical predecessor is its view about population growth.

Neoclassical Theory of Population Growth The population explosion of eighteenth-century Europe that created the classical theory of population growth eventually ended. The birth rate fell, and while the population continued to increase, its rate of increase moderated.

The key economic influence that slows the population growth rate is the opportunity cost of a woman's time. As women's wage rates increase and their job opportunities expand, the opportunity cost of having children increases. Faced with a higher opportunity cost, families choose to have fewer children and the birth rate falls.

Technological advances that bring higher incomes also bring advances in healthcare that extend lives. So as incomes increase, both the birth rate and the death rate decrease. These opposing forces offset each other and result in a slowly rising population.

This modern view of population growth and the historical trends that support it contradict the views of the classical economists. They also call into question the modern doomsday view that the planet will be swamped with more people than it can support.

Technological Change and Diminishing Returns In neoclassical growth theory, the pace of technological change influences the economic growth rate but economic growth does not influence the pace of technological change. It is assumed that technological change results from chance. When we're lucky, we have rapid technological change, and when bad luck strikes, the pace of technological advance slows.

To understand neoclassical growth theory, imagine the world of the mid-1950s, when Robert Solow is explaining his idea. Income per person is around $12,000 a year in today's money. The population is growing at about 1 percent a year. Saving and investment are about 20 percent of GDP, enough to keep the quantity of capital per hour of labour constant. Income per person is growing but not very fast.

Then technology begins to advance at a more rapid pace across a range of activities. The transistor revolutionizes an emerging electronics industry. New plastics revolutionize the manufacture of household appliances. The interstate highway system revolutionizes road transportation. Jet airliners start to replace piston-engine airplanes and speed air transportation.

These technological advances bring new profit opportunities. Businesses expand, and new businesses are created to exploit the newly available profitable technologies. Investment and saving increase. The economy enjoys new levels of prosperity and growth. But will the prosperity last? And will the growth last? Neoclassical growth theory says that the *prosperity* will last but the *growth* will not last unless technology keeps advancing.

According to neoclassical growth theory, the prosperity will persist because there is no classical population growth to induce the wage rate to fall. So the gains in income per person are permanent.

But growth will eventually stop if technology stops advancing because of diminishing marginal returns to capital. The high profit rates that result from technological change bring increased saving and capital accumulation. But as more capital is accumulated, more and more projects are undertaken that have lower rates of return—diminishing marginal returns. As the return on capital falls, the incentive to keep investing weakens. With weaker incentives to save and invest, saving decreases and the rate of capital accumulation slows. Eventually, the pace of capital accumulation slows so that it is only keeping up with population growth. Capital per worker remains constant.

A Problem with Neoclassical Growth Theory All economies have access to the same technologies, and capital is free to roam the globe, seeking the highest available real interest rate. Capital will flow until rates of return are equal, and rates of return will be equal when capital per hour of labour are equal across regions. Real GDP growth rates and income levels per person around the world will converge. Figure 22.5 on p. 518 shows that while there is some sign of convergence among the rich countries in part (a), convergence is slow, and part (b) shows that it does not appear to be imminent for all countries. New growth theory overcomes this shortcoming of neoclassical growth theory. It also explains what determines the pace of technological change.

New Growth Theory

New growth theory holds that real GDP per person grows because of the choices people make in the pursuit of profit and that growth will persist indefinitely. Paul Romer of Stanford University developed this theory during the 1980s, based on ideas of Joseph Schumpeter during the 1930s and 1940s.

According to the new growth theory, the pace at which new discoveries are made—and at which technology advances—is not determined by chance. It depends on how many people are looking for a new technology and how intensively they are looking. The search for new technologies is driven by incentives.

Profit is the spur to technological change. The forces of competition squeeze profits, so to increase profit, people constantly seek either lower-cost methods of production or new and better products for which people are willing to pay a higher price. Inventors can maintain a profit for several years by taking out a patent or a copyright, but eventually, a new discovery is copied, and profits disappear. So more research and development is undertaken in the hope of creating a new burst of profitable investment and growth.

Two facts about discoveries and technological knowledge play a key role in the new growth theory: Discoveries are (at least eventually) a public capital good; and knowledge is capital that is not subject to diminishing marginal returns.

Economists call a good a *public good* when no one can be excluded from using it and when one person's use does not prevent others from using it. National defence is the classic example of a public good. The programming language used to write apps for the iPhone is another.

Because knowledge is a public good, as the benefits of a new discovery spread, free resources become available. Nothing is given up when they are used: They have a zero opportunity cost. When a student in Waterloo writes a new iPhone app, his use of the programming language doesn't prevent another student in Calgary from using it.

Knowledge is even more special because it is *not* subject to diminishing returns. But increasing the stock of knowledge makes both labour and machines more productive. Knowledge capital does not bring diminishing returns. Biotech knowledge illustrates this idea well. Biologists have spent a lot of time developing DNA sequencing technology. As more has been discovered, the productivity of this knowledge capital has relentlessly increased. In 1990, it cost about $50 to sequence one DNA base pair. That cost had fallen to $1 by 2000 and to 1/10,000th of a penny by 2010.

The implication of this simple and appealing observation is astonishing. Unlike the other two theories, new growth theory has no growth-stopping mechanism. As physical capital accumulates, the return to capital—the real interest rate—falls. But the incentive to innovate and earn a higher profit becomes stronger. So innovation occurs, capital becomes more productive, the demand for capital increases, and the real interest rate rises again.

Labour productivity grows indefinitely as people discover new technologies that yield a higher real interest rate. The growth rate depends only on people's incentives and ability to innovate.

A Perpetual Motion Economy New growth theory sees the economy as a perpetual motion machine, which Fig. 22.12 illustrates.

No matter how rich we become, our wants exceed our ability to satisfy them. We always want a higher standard of living. In the pursuit of a higher standard of living, human societies have developed incentive systems—markets, property rights, and money—that enable people to profit from innovation. Innovation leads to the development of new and better techniques of production and new and better products. To take advantage of new techniques and to produce new products, new firms start up and old firms go out of business—firms are born and die. As old firms die and new firms are born, some jobs are destroyed and others are created. The new jobs created are better than the old ones and they pay higher real wage rates. Also, with higher wage rates and more productive techniques, leisure increases. New and better jobs and new and better products lead to more consumption goods and services and, combined with increased leisure, bring a higher standard of living.

But our insatiable wants are still there, so the process continues: Wants and incentives create innovation, new and better products, and a yet higher standard of living.

FIGURE 22.12   A Perpetual Motion Machine

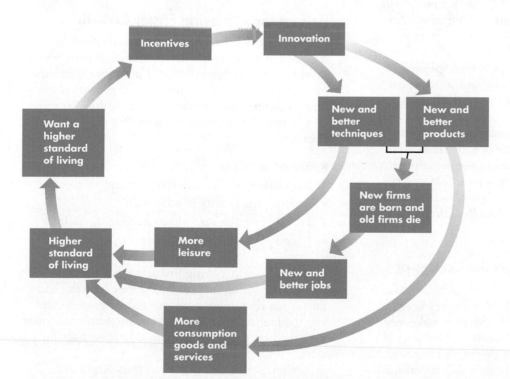

People want a higher standard of living and are spurred by profit incentives to make the innovations that lead to new and better techniques and new and better products.

These new and better techniques and products, in turn, lead to the birth of new firms and the death of some old firms, new and better jobs, and more leisure and more consumption goods and services.

The result is a higher standard of living, but people want a still higher standard of living, and the growth process continues.

Source: Based on a similar figure in *These Are the Good Old Days: A Report on U.S. Living Standards,* Federal Reserve Bank of Dallas 1993 Annual Report.

MyEconLab Animation

New Growth Theory Versus Malthusian Theory

The contrast between the Malthusian theory and new growth theory couldn't be more sharp. Malthusians see the end of prosperity as we know it today and new growth theorists see unending plenty. The contrast becomes clearest by thinking about the differing views about population growth.

To a Malthusian, population growth is part of the problem. To a new growth theorist, population growth is part of the solution. People are the ultimate economic resource. A larger population brings forth more wants, but it also brings a greater amount of scientific discovery and technological advance. So rather than being the source of falling real GDP per person, population growth generates faster labour productivity growth and rising real GDP per person. Resources are limited, but the human imagination and ability to increase productivity are unlimited.

Sorting Out the Theories

Which theory is correct? None of them tells us the whole story, but each teaches us something of value.

Classical growth theory reminds us that our physical resources are limited and that without advances in technology, we must eventually hit diminishing returns.

Neoclassical growth theory reaches the same conclusion but not because of a population explosion. Instead, it emphasizes diminishing returns to capital and reminds us that we cannot keep growth going just by accumulating physical capital. We must also advance technology and accumulate human capital. We must become more creative in our use of scarce resources.

New growth theory emphasizes the capacity of human resources to innovate at a pace that offsets diminishing returns. New growth theory fits the facts of today's world more closely than do either of the other two theories.

The Empirical Evidence on the Causes of Economic Growth

Economics makes progress by the interplay between theory and empirical evidence. A theory makes predictions about what we will observe if the theory is correct. Empirical evidence, the data generated by history and the natural experiments that it performs, provide the data for testing the theory.

Economists have done an enormous amount of research confronting theories of growth with the empirical evidence. The way in which this research has been conducted has changed over the years.

In 1776, when Adam Smith wrote about "the nature and causes of the Wealth of Nations" in his celebrated book, empirical evidence took the form of carefully selected facts described in words and stories. Today, large databases, sophisticated statistical methods, and fast computers provide numerical measurements of the causes of economic growth.

Economists have looked at the growth rate data for more than 100 countries for the period since 1960 and explored the correlations between the growth rate and more than 60 possible influences on it. The conclusion of this data crunching is that most of these possible influences have variable and unpredictable effects, but a few of them have strong and clear effects. Table 22.1 summarizes these more robust influences. They are arranged in order of difficulty (or in the case of region, impossibility) of changing. Political and economic systems are hard to change, but market distortions, investment, and openness to international trade are features of a nation's economy that can be influenced by policy.

Let's now look at growth policies.

Policies for Achieving Faster Growth

Growth theory supported by empirical evidence tells us that to achieve faster economic growth, we must increase the growth rate of physical capital, the pace of technological advance, or the growth rate of human capital and openness to international trade.

The main suggestions for achieving these objectives are:

- Stimulate saving
- Stimulate research and development
- Improve the quality of education
- Provide international aid to developing nations
- Encourage international trade

Stimulate Saving Saving finances investment, so stimulating saving increases economic growth. The East Asian economies have the highest growth rates and the highest saving rates. Some African economies have the lowest growth rates and the lowest saving rates.

Tax incentives can increase saving. Registered Retirement Savings Plans (RRSPs) are a tax incentive to save. Economists claim that a tax on consumption rather than income provides the best saving incentive.

TABLE 22.1 The Influences on Economic Growth

Influence	Good for Economic Growth	Bad for Economic Growth
Region	■ Far from equator	■ Sub-Saharan Africa
Politics	■ Rule of law	■ Revolutions
	■ Civil liberties	■ Military coups
		■ Wars
Economic system	■ Capitalist	
Market distortions		■ Exchange rate distortions
		■ Price controls and black markets
Investment	■ Human capital	
	■ Physical capital	
International trade	■ Open to trade	

Source of data: Xavier Sala-i-Martin, "I Just Ran Two Million Regressions," *The American Economic Review*, Vol. 87, No. 2 (May 1997), pp. 178–183.

Stimulate Research and Development Everyone can use the fruits of *basic* research and development efforts. For example, all biotechnology firms can use advances in gene-splicing technology. Because basic inventions can be copied, the inventor's profit is limited and the market allocates too few resources to this activity. Governments can direct public funds toward financing basic research, but this solution is not foolproof. It requires a mechanism for allocating the public funds to their highest-valued use.

Improve the Quality of Education The free market produces too little education because it brings benefits beyond those valued by the people who receive the education. By funding basic education and by ensuring high standards in basic skills such as language, mathematics, and science, governments can contribute to a nation's growth potential. Education can also be stimulated and improved by using tax incentives to encourage improved private provision.

Provide International Aid to Developing Nations It seems obvious that if rich countries give financial aid to developing countries, investment and growth will increase in the recipient countries. Unfortunately, the obvious does not routinely happen. A large amount of data-driven research on the effects of aid on growth has turned up a zero and even negative effect. Aid often gets diverted and spent on consumption.

Encourage International Trade Trade, not aid, stimulates economic growth. It works by extracting the available gains from specialization and trade. The fastest-growing nations are those most open to trade. If the rich nations truly want to aid economic development, they will lower their trade barriers against developing nations, especially in farm products. The World Trade Organization's efforts to achieve more open trade are being resisted by the richer nations.

REVIEW QUIZ

1 What is the key idea of classical growth theory that leads to the dismal outcome?

2 What, according to neoclassical growth theory, is the fundamental cause of economic growth?

3 What is the key proposition of new growth theory that makes economic growth persist?

Work these questions in Study Plan 22.5 and get instant feedback. Do a Key Terms Quiz.   MyEconLab

◆ To complete your study of economic growth, take a look at *Economics in the News* on pp. 534–535, which compares the contrasting growth performance of two African nations.

Making an Economy Grow

How to Make South Africa's Economy Roar

Financial Times
July 27, 2012

It is clear South Africa needs a radical change in direction. This weekend the opposition Democratic Alliance aims to show how this is possible, launching a strategy to accelerate annual growth to 8 percent. In particular, it proposes tough reforms to labour laws by removing the automatic extension of collective bargaining agreements across sectors; establishing "jobs zones" featuring special exemptions from restrictive regulations; and lifting administrative requirements for small businesses.

These changes will reduce barriers to entry, encourage flexibility, and stimulate productivity in ... mining, manufacturing, and agriculture. Combined with focused employment incentives such as a youth wage subsidy and market-driven skills development programs, the plan provides a radical overhaul of the country's labour market. ...

Our plan contains ... policies to distribute shares in state-owned companies; introduce tax deductions to incentivize employee shared-ownership schemes; promote a joint ownership model in the agricultural sector; and lower the cost barriers facing first-time homeowners.

These measures are essential for facilitating broad-based participation in the economy. ...

Although international rankings such as the World Economic Forum's Global Competitiveness report praise the country's sophisticated financial sector and sound legal environment, South Africa falls short when it comes to the ease of doing business, and the barriers caused by excessive regulation and state inefficiency. My party's proposals in this area will cut the tax and regulatory burdens inhibiting new business growth.

Seven of the 10 fastest-growing economies in the world are in Africa. ... High growth is resulting in rapidly declining poverty and unemployment in the developing world. With the right policies in place, South Africa can be part of this story.

Copyright © 2012 by Helen Zille. Used by permission of the author.

MyEconLab More Economics in the News

ESSENCE OF THE STORY

- South Africa's opposition Democratic Alliance wants to accelerate real GDP growth to 8 percent per year.

- Labour market reforms would limit union agreements, establish "jobs zones" with exemptions from restrictive regulations, subsidize youth wages, and develop market-driven skills.

- Capital market reforms would ease small-business regulation, cut taxes, distribute shares in state-owned companies, provide tax incentives for employee shared-ownership schemes, and make homeownership easier.

- The reforms aim to reduce barriers to entry and boost labour productivity in all parts of the economy.

ECONOMIC ANALYSIS

- South Africa's economic growth rate has not been spectacular.

- Before 1994, South Africa's economy was hit by sanctions aimed at ending apartheid. Real GDP per person decreased.

- Since 1995, real GDP per person has increased but at a rate of 3.4 percent per year.

- South Africa's growth compares unfavourably with that of some other African nations, one of which is its neighbour Botswana, that are growing more rapidly.

- Figure 1 shows real GDP per person in South Africa and Botswana from 1980 to 2012. You can see that real GDP per person in Botswana has grown much more quickly than in South Africa.

- A key reason Botswana's real GDP per person has grown more rapidly than South Africa's is the pace of investment in new capital.

- Figure 2 shows that Botswana invests double the percentage of GDP invested by South Africa.

- The growth of physical capital and human capital and technological change are proceeding at a rapid pace in Botswana and bringing rapid growth in real GDP per person.

- Figure 3 illustrates how the production function is changing in these economies. It is shifting upward at a more rapid pace in Botswana than in South Africa.

- Why is Botswana more successful than South Africa and are the policies proposed in the news article enough to raise South Africa's growth rate to the desired 8 percent per year?

- Economists Daron Acemoglu, Simon Johnson, and James Robinson say that Botswana had the right institutions for growth—well defined and widely respected private property rights.

- The proposals in the news article don't directly address strengthening private property rights but they do have that effect.

- The labour market reforms described in the article would increase human capital and labour productivity.

- The labour market and capital market reforms together would make capital accumulation and technological change more profitable and further contribute to labour productivity growth.

- The specific target for growth of 8 percent per year is probably too ambitious.*

*Daron Acemoglu, Simon Johnson, and James Robinson, "An African Success Story: Botswana," in *In Search of Prosperity: Analytic Narratives on Economic Growth*, edited by Dani Rodrik, Princeton University Press, 2003, pp. 80–122.

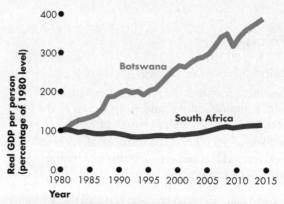

Figure 1 Real GDP in Two African Economies

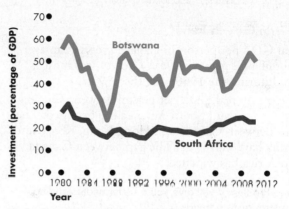

Figure 2 Investment in Two African Economies

Figure 3 Labour Productivity Growth in Two African Economies

Sources of data: (1980–2010) Alan Heston, Robert Summers, and Bettina Aten, Penn World Table Version 7.1, Center for International Comparisons of Production, Income, and Prices at the University of Pennsylvania, July 2012; and (2011–2012) International Monetary Fund, *World Economic Outlook*, April 2012.

SUMMARY

Key Points

The Basics of Economic Growth (pp. 514–516)

- Economic growth is the sustained expansion of production possibilities and is measured as the annual percentage rate of change of real GDP.
- The Rule of 70 tells us the number of years in which real GDP doubles—70 divided by the annual percentage growth rate.

Working Problems 1 to 3 will give you a better understanding of the basics of economic growth.

Long-Term Growth Trends (pp. 517–519)

- Real GDP per person in Canada grows at an average rate of 2 percent a year. Growth was most rapid during the 1960s and the 1990s.
- The gap in real GDP per person between Canada and Central and South America has persisted. The gaps between Canada and Hong Kong, Korea, and China have narrowed. The gap between Canada and Africa has widened.

Working Problem 4 will give you a better understanding of long-term growth trends.

How Potential GDP Grows (pp. 520–525)

- The aggregate production function and equilibrium in the aggregate labour market determine potential GDP.
- Potential GDP grows if the labour supply grows or if labour productivity grows.

- Only labour productivity growth makes real GDP per person and the standard of living grow.

Working Problems 5 to 7 will give you a better understanding of how potential GDP grows.

Why Labour Productivity Grows (pp. 525–528)

- Labour productivity growth requires an incentive system created by firms, markets, property rights, and money.
- The sources of labour productivity growth are growth of physical capital and human capital and advances in technology.

Working Problem 8 will give you a better understanding of why labour productivity grows.

Is Economic Growth Sustainable? Theories, Evidence, and Policies (pp. 529–533)

- In classical theory, real GDP per person keeps returning to the subsistence level.
- In neoclassical growth theory, diminishing returns to capital limit economic growth.
- In new growth theory, economic growth persists indefinitely at a rate determined by decisions that lead to innovation and technological change.
- Policies for achieving faster growth include stimulating saving and research and development, encouraging international trade, and improving the quality of education.

Working Problem 9 will give you a better understanding of growth theories, evidence, and policies.

Key Terms

MyEconLab Key Terms Quiz

Aggregate production function, 520
Classical growth theory, 529
Economic growth, 514
Growth rate, 514

Labour productivity, 524
Neoclassical growth theory, 529
New growth theory, 530
Real GDP per person, 514

Real wage rate, 521
Rule of 70, 515

WORKED PROBLEM

MyEconLab   You can work this problem in Chapter 22 Study Plan.

The *World Economic Outlook* reports the following information:

- China's real GDP was 17.9 trillion yuan in 2012 and 19.3 trillion yuan in 2013.
- China's population was 1,361 million in 2012 and 1,368 million in 2013.

Questions

1. Calculate China's real GDP growth rate and its population growth rate during 2013.
2. Calculate the growth rate of China's standard of living during 2013.
3. If the growth rate of China's standard of living during 2013 is maintained, how many years will it take to double?

Solutions

1. The growth of a variable equals the change in the value from 2012 to 2013 calculated as a percentage of the value in 2012.

   China's growth rate of real GDP during 2013 equals (19.3 trillion yuan – 17.9 trillion yuan) divided by 17.9 trillion yuan, multiplied by 100. That is, China's real GDP growth rate equals:

   $(1.4 \div 17.9) \times 100 = 7.8$ percent.

   China's population growth rate equals (1,368 million – 1,361 million) divided by 1,361 million, multiplied by 100. That is, China's population growth rate equals:

   $(7 \div 1,361) \times 100 = 0.5$ percent.

Key Point: The growth rate of a variable equals the annual percentage change in the value of the variable.

2. Real GDP per person measures the standard of living.

   In 2012, real GDP per person was 17.9 trillion yuan divided by 1,361 million, which equals 13,152 yuan.

   In 2013, real GDP per person was 19.3 trillion yuan divided by 1,368 million, which equals 14,108 yuan.

The growth rate of real GDP per person equals (14,108 yuan – 13,152 yuan) ÷ 13,152 yuan, multiplied by 100.

The growth rate of real GDP per person equals $(956 \div 13,152) \times 100$, which is 7.3 percent.

So during 2013, China's standard of living increased by 7.3 percent.

An alternative way of calculating the growth rate of the standard of living is to compare the growth rates of real GDP and the population.

Notice that a higher real GDP growth rate increases the growth rate of real GDP per person, but a higher population growth rate lowers the growth rate of real GDP per person.

So when real GDP grows by 7.8 percent and the population doesn't change, the standard of living grows by 7.8 percent.

When the population grows by 0.5 percent and real GDP doesn't change, the standard of living falls by 0.5 percent.

That is, the growth rate of China's standard of living during 2013 is approximately equal to the growth rate of real GDP minus the population growth rate, which equals 7.8 percent minus 0.5 percent, or 7.3 percent.

Key Point: The growth rate of the standard of living equals the growth rate of real GDP minus the growth rate of the population.

3. The number of years it will take for the standard of living to double its 2013 level is given by the Rule of 70.

   China's standard of living is growing at 7.3 percent a year. The Rule of 70 says that if this growth rate is sustained, China's standard of living will double in 70 years divided by 7.3, which equals 9.6 years.

   China's standard of living will be twice what it was in 2013 sometime during 2023.

Key Point: The time it takes for the standard of living to double equals 70 years divided by the sustained growth rate of the standard of living.

STUDY PLAN PROBLEMS AND APPLICATIONS

MyEconLab   You can work Problems 1 to 9 in Chapter 22 Study Plan and get instant feedback.

The Basics of Economic Growth (Study Plan 22.1)

1. Brazil's real GDP was 1,180 trillion reais in 2013 and 1,202 trillion reais in 2014. Brazil's population was 198 million in 2013 and 200 million in 2014. Calculate:
   a. The growth rate of real GDP.
   b. The growth rate of real GDP per person.
   c. The approximate number of years it takes for real GDP per person in Brazil to double if the 2014 growth rate of real GDP and the population growth rate are maintained.

2. The IMF projects that China's real GDP per person will be 15,040 yuan in 2015 and 16,010 yuan in 2016 and that India's real GDP per person will be 54,085 rupees in 2015 and 56,840 rupees in 2016. By maintaining their current growth rates, which country will be first to double its standard of living?

3. The Asian Development Bank reported that Myanmar's GDP growth accelerated to 7.5% in 2013 from 7.3% in 2012. Growth was supported by rising investment, improved business confidence, commodity exports, and buoyant tourism. Is this expansion more likely to be a business cycle expansion or economic growth? Explain your answer.

Long-Term Growth Trends (Study Plan 22.2)

4. China was the largest economy for centuries because everyone had the same type of economy—subsistence—and so the country with the most people would be economically biggest. Then the Industrial Revolution sent the West on a more prosperous path. Now the world is returning to a common economy, this time technology- and information-based, so once again population triumphs.
   a. Why was China the world's largest economy until 1890?
   b. Why did the United States surpass China in 1890 to become the world's largest economy?

How Potential GDP Grows (Study Plan 22.3)

Use the tables in the next column to work Problems 5 to 7.
The tables describe an economy's labour market and its production function in 2014.

Real wage rate (dollars per hour)	Labour hours supplied	Labour hours demanded
80	45	5
70	40	10
60	35	15
50	30	20
40	25	25
30	20	30
20	15	35

Labour (hours)	Real GDP (2007 dollars)
5	425
10	800
15	1,125
20	1,400
25	1,625
30	1,800
35	1,925
40	2,000

5. What are the equilibrium real wage rate, the quantity of labour employed in 2014, labour productivity, and potential GDP in 2014?

6. In 2015, the population increases and labour hours supplied increase by 10 at each real wage rate. What are the equilibrium real wage rate, labour productivity, and potential GDP in 2015?

7. In 2015, the population increases and labour hours supplied increase by 10 at each real wage rate. Does the standard of living in this economy increase in 2015? Explain why or why not.

Why Labour Productivity Grows (Study Plan 22.4)

8. For three years, there was no technological change in Longland but capital per hour of labour increased from $10 to $20 to $30 and real GDP per hour of labour increased from $3.80 to $5.70 to $7.13. Then, in the fourth year, capital per hour of labour remained constant, but real GDP per hour of labour increased to $10. Does Longland experience diminising returns? Explain why or why not.

Is Economic Growth Sustainable? Theories, Evidence, and Policies (Study Plan 22.5)

9. Explain the processes that will bring the growth of real GDP per person to a stop according to the classical, neoclassical, and new growth theories.

ADDITIONAL PROBLEMS AND APPLICATIONS

MyEconLab   You can work these problems in MyEconLab if assigned by your instructor.

The Basics of Economic Growth

10. In 2014, China's real GDP is growing at 7 percent a year and its population is growing at 0.5 percent a year. If these growth rates continue, in what year will China's real GDP per person be twice what it is in 2014?

11. Mexico's real GDP was 13,405 trillion pesos in 2013 and 13,805 trillion pesos in 2014. Mexico's population was 118.4 million in 2013 and 119.5 million in 2014. Calculate:
    a. The growth rate of real GDP.
    b. The growth rate of real GDP per person.
    c. The approximate number of years it takes for real GDP per person in Mexico to double if the 2014 growth rate of real GDP and the population growth rate are maintained.

12. South Africa's real GDP was 1,900 billion rand in 2011 and 1,970 billion rand in 2012. South Africa's population was 50.5 million in 2011 and 51.0 million in 2012. Calculate:
    a. The growth rate of real GDP.
    b. The growth rate of real GDP per person.
    c. The approximate number of years it will take for real GDP per person in South Africa to double if the current growth rate of real GDP is maintained.

Long-Term Growth Trends

13. **The New World Order**

    While gross domestic product growth is picking up a bit in emerging market economies, it is picking up even more in the advanced economies. Real GDP in the emerging market economies is forecasted to grow at 5.4% in 2015 up from 4.9% in 2012. In the advanced economies, real GDP is expected to grow at 2.3% in 2015 up from 1.4% in 2012. The difference in growth rates means that the large spread between emerging market economies and advanced economies of the past 40 years will continue for many more years.

    Source: *World Economic Outlook*, January 2014

    Do the growth rates over the past few decades indicate that gaps in real GDP per person around the world are shrinking, growing, or staying the same? Explain.

How Potential GDP Grows

14. If a large increase in investment increases labour productivity, explain what happens to:
    a. Potential GDP.
    b. Employment.
    c. The real wage rate.

15. If a severe drought decreases labour productivity, explain what happens to:
    a. Potential GDP.
    b. Employment.
    c. The real wage rate.

Use the following tables to work Problems 16 to 18. The first table describes an economy's labour market in 2014 and the second table describes its production function in 2014.

Real wage rate (dollars per hour)	Labour hours supplied	Labour hours demanded
80	55	15
70	50	20
60	45	25
50	40	30
40	35	35
30	30	40
20	25	45

Labour (hours)	Real GDP (2007 dollars)
15	1,425
20	1,800
25	2,125
30	2,400
35	2,625
40	2,800
45	2,925
50	3,000

16. What are the equilibrium real wage rate and the quantity of labour employed in 2014?

17. What are labour productivity and potential GDP in 2014?

18. Suppose that labour productivity increases in 2014. What effect does the increased labour productivity have on the demand for labour, the supply of labour, potential GDP, and real GDP per person?

Why Labour Productivity Grows

19. **India's Economy Hits the Wall**

    Just six months ago, India was looking good. Annual growth was 9%, consumer demand was huge, and foreign investment was growing. But now most economic forecasts expect growth to slow to 7%—a big drop for a country that needs to accelerate growth. India needs urgently to upgrade its infrastructure and education and healthcare facilities. Agriculture is unproductive and needs better technology. The legal system needs to be strengthened with more judges and courtrooms.

    Source: *BusinessWeek*, July 1, 2008

    Explain five potential sources for faster economic growth in India suggested in this news clip.

Is Economic Growth Sustainable? Theories, Evidence, and Policies

20. **The Productivity Watch**

    According to former Federal Reserve chairman Alan Greenspan, IT investments in the 1990s boosted productivity, which boosted corporate profits, which led to more IT investments, and so on, leading to a nirvana of high growth.

    Source: *Fortune*, September 4, 2006

    Which of the growth theories that you've studied in this chapter best corresponds to the explanation given by Mr. Greenspan?

21. Is faster economic growth always a good thing? Argue the case for faster growth and the case for slower growth. Then reach a conclusion on whether growth should be increased or slowed.

22. **Why Canada's Industry Leaders Need to Embrace the Technology Mindset**

    We are at a tipping point where technology—from software to hardware and everything in between—is weaving its way into all that we do and is about to touch every industry. Every day, we are reminded how quickly things are changing, from connected cars, to wearable devices, to manufacturing. Just look at the rapid advance in China's economy and standard of living driven in large part by an innovative spirit unleashed in the late 1990s.

    Source: *Financial Post*, July 11, 2014

    Explain which growth theory best describes the news clip.

Economics in the News

23. After you have studied *Economics in the News* on pp. 534–535, answer the following questions.

    a. How do South Africa and Botswana compare on economic growth rates?

    b. For South Africa to grow faster, how would the percentage of GDP invested in new capital need to change?

    c. If South Africa is able to achieve a growth rate of 8 percent per year, in how many years will real GDP have doubled?

    d. Describe the policies proposed by the author of the news article and explain how they might change labour productivity.

    e. What is the source of Botswana's growth success story and what must South Africa do to replicate that success?

    f. Draw a *PPF* graph to show what has happened in Botswana and South Africa since 1980.

24. **Make Way for India—The Next China**

    China grows at around 9 percent a year, but its one-child policy will start to reduce the size of China's working-age population within the next 10 years. India, by contrast, will have an increasing working-age population for another generation at least.

    Source: *The Independent*, March 1, 2006

    a. Given the expected population changes, do you think China or India will have the greater economic growth rate? Why?

    b. Would China's growth rate remain at 9 percent a year without the restriction on its population growth rate?

    c. India's population growth rate is 1.6 percent a year, and in 2005 its economic growth rate was 8 percent a year. China's population growth rate is 0.6 percent a year, and in 2005 its economic growth rate was 9 percent a year. In what year will real GDP per person double in each country?

ABN·AMRO

23

FINANCE, SAVING, AND INVESTMENT

After studying this chapter, you will be able to:

◆ Describe the flows of funds in financial markets

◆ Explain how saving and investment decisions interact in financial markets

◆ Explain how governments influence financial markets

Interest rates fell during 2014 and by mid-year, the government of Canada could borrow at 2.2 percent. In 2012, when the economy was still feeling the effects of a financial meltdown in which billions of dollars had been lost, interest rates were even lower.

Behind the drama and headlines they create, financial markets play a crucial unseen role funnelling funds from savers and lenders to investors and borrowers. This chapter explains how financial markets work, and *Economics in the News* at the end of the chapter looks at the forces at work during 2014 that led to lower interest rates.

Financial Institutions and Financial Markets

The financial institutions and markets that we study in this chapter play a crucial role in the economy. They provide the channels through which saving flows to finance the investment in new capital that makes the economy grow.

In studying the economics of financial institutions and markets, we distinguish between:

- Finance and money
- Physical capital and financial capital

Finance and Money

In economics, we use the term *finance* to describe the activity of providing the funds that finance expenditures on capital. The study of finance looks at how households and firms obtain and use financial resources and how they cope with the risks that arise in this activity.

Money is what we use to pay for goods and services and factors of production and to make financial transactions. The study of money looks at how households and firms use it, how much of it they hold, how banks create and manage it, and how its quantity influences the economy.

In the economic lives of individuals and businesses, finance and money are closely interrelated. And some of the main financial institutions, such as banks, provide both financial services and monetary services. Nevertheless, by distinguishing between *finance* and *money* and studying them separately, we will better understand our financial and monetary markets and institutions.

For the rest of this chapter, we study finance. Money is the topic of the next chapter.

Physical Capital and Financial Capital

Economists distinguish between physical capital and financial capital. *Physical capital* is the tools, instruments, machines, buildings, and other items that have been produced in the past and that are used today to produce goods and services. Inventories of raw materials, semifinished goods, and components are part of physical capital. When economists use the term capital, they mean *physical* capital. The funds that firms use to buy physical capital are called **financial capital**.

Along the *aggregate production function* in Chapter 22 (see p. 520), the quantity of capital is fixed. An increase in the quantity of capital increases production possibilities and shifts the aggregate production function upward. You're going to see, in this chapter, how investment, saving, borrowing, and lending decisions influence the quantity of capital and make it grow and, as a consequence, make real GDP grow.

We begin by describing the links between capital and investment and between wealth and saving.

Capital and Investment

The quantity of capital changes because of investment and depreciation. *Investment* increases the quantity of capital and *depreciation* decreases it (see Chapter 20, p. 468). The total amount spent on new capital is called **gross investment**. The change in the value of capital is called **net investment**. Net investment equals gross investment minus depreciation.

Figure 23.1 illustrates these terms. On January 1, 2014, Ace Bottling Inc. had machines worth $30,000—Ace's initial capital. During 2014, the market value of Ace's machines fell by 67 percent—$20,000. After this depreciation, Ace's machines were valued at $10,000. During 2014, Ace spent $30,000 on new machines. This amount is Ace's gross investment. By December 31, 2014, Ace Bottling had capital valued at $40,000, so its capital had increased by $10,000. This amount is Ace's net investment. Ace's net investment equals its gross investment of $30,000 minus depreciation of its initial capital of $20,000.

Wealth and Saving

Wealth is the value of all the things that people own. What people own is related to what they earn, but it is not the same thing. People earn an *income*, which is the amount they receive during a given time period from supplying the services of the resources they own. **Saving** is the amount of income that is not paid in taxes or spent on consumption goods and services. Saving increases wealth. Wealth also increases when the market value of assets rises—called *capital gains*—and decreases when the market value of assets falls—called *capital losses*.

For example, if at the end of the school year you have $250 in the bank and a coin collection worth $300, then your wealth is $550. During the summer,

FIGURE 23.1   Capital and Investment

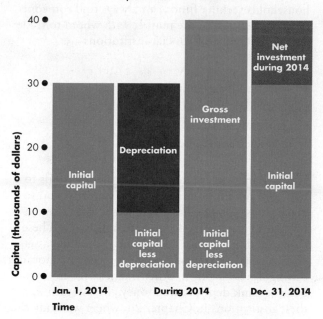

On January 1, 2014, Ace Bottling had capital worth $30,000. During the year, the value of Ace's capital fell by $20,000—depreciation—and it spent $30,000 on new capital—gross investment. Ace's net investment was $10,000 ($30,000 gross investment minus $20,000 depreciation) so that at the end of 2014, Ace had capital worth $40,000.

——————————— MyEconLab Animation ——

suppose that you earn $5,000 (net of taxes) and spend $1,000 on consumption goods and services, so your saving is $4,000. Your bank account increases to $4,250 and your wealth becomes $4,550. The $4,000 increase in wealth equals saving. If coins rise in value and your coin collection is now worth $500, you have a capital gain of $200, which is also added to your wealth.

National wealth and national saving work like this personal example. The wealth of a nation at the end of a year equals its wealth at the start of the year plus its saving during the year, which equals income minus consumption expenditure.

To make real GDP grow, saving and wealth must be transformed into investment and capital. This transformation takes place in the markets for financial capital and through the activities of financial institutions. We're now going to describe these markets and institutions.

Financial Capital Markets

Saving is the source of the funds that are used to finance investment, and these funds are supplied and demanded in three types of financial markets:

- Loan markets
- Bond markets
- Stock markets

Loan Markets Businesses often want short-term finance to buy inventories or to extend credit to their customers. Sometimes they get this finance in the form of a loan from a bank. Households often want finance to purchase big ticket items, such as automobiles or household furnishings and appliances. They get this finance as bank loans, often in the form of outstanding credit card balances.

Households also get finance to buy new homes. (Expenditure on new homes is counted as part of investment.) These funds are usually obtained as a loan that is secured by a **mortgage**—a legal contract that gives ownership of a home to the lender in the event that the borrower fails to meet the agreed loan payments (repayments and interest). In 2007–2008, U.S. mortgages were at the centre of a global credit crisis. See *Economics in Action* on p. 545.

All of these types of financing take place in loan markets.

Bond Markets When Walmart expands its business and opens new stores, it gets the finance it needs by selling bonds. Governments—federal, provincial, and municipal—also raise finance by issuing bonds.

A **bond** is a promise to make specified payments on specified dates. For example, you can buy a McDonald's Corporation bond that promises to pay $3.50 every year until 2020 and then to make a final payment of $100 on July 15, 2020.

The buyer of a bond from McDonald's makes a loan to the company and is entitled to the payments promised by the bond. When a person buys a newly issued bond, he or she may hold the bond until the borrower has repaid the amount borrowed or sell it to someone else. Bonds issued by corporations and governments are traded in the **bond market**.

The term of a bond might be long (decades) or short (just a month or two). Corporations often issue very short-term bonds as a way of getting paid for their sales before the buyer is able to pay. For example, suppose that Bombardier sells $100 million of railway locomotives to VIA Rail. Bombardier wants to be paid when the items are shipped, but VIA Rail doesn't want to pay until the locomotives are earning an income. So VIA Rail promises to pay Bombardier $101 million three months in the future. A bank is willing to buy Bombardier's promise for (say) $100 million. Bombardier gets $100 million immediately and the bank gets $101 million in three months when VIA Rail honours its promise. The Government of Canada issues promises of this type, called Treasury bills.

Another type of bond is a **mortgage-backed security**, which entitles its holder to the income from a package of mortgages. Mortgage lenders create mortgage-backed securities. They make mortgage loans to home buyers and then create securities that they sell to obtain more funds to make more mortgage loans. The holder of a mortgage-backed security is entitled to receive payments that derive from the payments received by the mortgage lender from the home buyer–borrower.

Mortgage-backed securities created in the United States were at the centre of the storm in the financial markets in 2007–2008 that brought a global financial crisis. *Economics in Action* on p. 545 provides a brief account of the origins of this event.

Stock Markets   When Petro-Canada wants finance to expand its business, it issues stock. A **stock** is a certificate of ownership and claim to the firm's profits. Petro-Canada has issued 484 million shares of its stock. So if you owned 484 Petro-Canada shares, you would own one-millionth of the firm and be entitled to receive one-millionth of its profits.

Unlike a stockholder, a bondholder does not own part of the firm that issued the bond.

A **stock market** is a financial market in which shares of stocks of corporations are traded. The Toronto Stock Exchange, the New York Stock Exchange, the London Stock Exchange (in England), and the Tokyo Stock Exchange (in Japan) are all examples of stock markets.

Financial Institutions

Financial markets are highly competitive because of the role played by financial institutions in those markets. A **financial institution** is a firm that operates on both sides of the markets for financial capital. The financial institution is a borrower in one market and a lender in another.

Financial institutions also stand ready to trade so that households with funds to lend and firms or households seeking funds can always find someone on the other side of the market with whom to trade. The key Canadian financial institutions are:

- Banks
- Trust and loan companies
- Credit unions and caisses populaires
- Pension funds
- Insurance companies

Banks   Banks accept deposits and use the funds to buy government bonds and other securities and to make loans. Canada has 14 domestic banks, and a further 33 foreign banks operate in Canada. These banks hold more than 70 percent of the total assets of the Canadian financial services sector. Economists distinguish banks from other financial institutions because bank deposits are money. We'll return to these institutions in Chapter 24, where we study the role of money in our economy.

Trust and Loan Companies   Trust and loan companies provide similar services to banks and the largest of them are owned by banks. They accept deposits and make personal loans and mortgage loans. They also administer estates, trusts, and pension plans.

Credit Unions and Caisses Populaires   Credit unions and caisses populaires are banks that are owned and controlled by their depositors and borrowers, are regulated by provincial rules, and operate only inside their own provincial boundaries. These institutions are large in number but small in size.

Pension Funds   Pension funds are financial institutions that receive the pension contributions of firms and workers. They use these funds to buy a diversified portfolio of bonds and stocks that they expect to generate an income that balances risk and return. The income is used to pay pension benefits.

Pension funds can be very large and play an active role in the firms whose stock they hold.

Insurance Companies   Insurance companies provide risk-sharing services. They enter into agreements with households and firms to provide compensation in the event of accident, theft, fire, and a host of other misfortunes. They receive premiums from their customers and make payments against claims.

Economics in Action
The Financial Crisis

Bear Stearns: absorbed by JPMorgan Chase with help from the Federal Reserve. Lehman Brothers: gone. Fannie Mae and Freddie Mac: taken into government oversight. Merrill Lynch: absorbed by Bank of America. AIG: given an $85 billion lifeline by the Federal Reserve and sold off in parcels to financial institutions around the world. Wachovia: taken over by Wells Fargo. Washington Mutual: taken over by JPMorgan Chase. Morgan Stanley: 20 percent bought by Mitsubishi, a large Japanese bank. These are some of the events in the financial crisis of 2008. What was going on?

What Was Going On?

Between 2002 and 2006, U.S. mortgage borrowing to buy a home exploded and home prices rocketed. You can see the rise in U.S. mortgage borrowing in Fig. 1. Mortgages increased from 65 percent of income in 2000 to more than 100 percent in 2006. And you can see the rocketing home prices in Fig. 2. Between 2000 and 2006, home prices doubled. In 2007 they crashed.

Banks and other financial institutions that had made mortgage loans to home buyers sold the loans to Fannie Mae, Freddie Mac, and other large banks who bundled these loans into *mortgage-backed securities* and sold them to eager buyers around the world.

When home prices began to fall in 2007, many home owners found themselves with mortages that were bigger than the value of their home. The mortage default rate jumped and the prices of mortage-backed securities and more widely of other assets fell sharply. Financial institutions took big losses. Some losses were too big to bear and big-name institutions became insolvent.

Figure 1   U.S. Household Debt

Figure 2   U.S. Home Prices

Insurance companies use the funds they have received but not paid out as claims to buy bonds and stocks on which they earn an interest income.

Some insurance companies also insure corporate bonds and other risky financial assets. They provide insurance that pays out if a firm fails and cannot meet its bond obligations. Some insurance companies insure other insurers in a complex network of reinsurance.

In normal times, insurance companies have a steady flow of funds coming in from premiums and interest on the financial assets they hold and a steady, but smaller, flow of funds paying claims. Their profit is the gap between the two flows. But in unusual times, when large and widespread losses are being incurred, insurance companies can run into difficulty in meeting their obligations. Such a situation arose in 2008 for one of the world's biggest insurers, AIG, and the firm was taken into public ownership.

Canadian insurance companies have very large international operations and earn 70 percent of their income outside Canada.

All financial institutions face risk, which poses two problems: solvency and liquidity problems.

Insolvency and Illiquidity

A financial institution's **net worth** is the market value of what it has lent minus the market value of what it has borrowed. If net worth is positive, the institution is *solvent*. But if net worth is negative, the institution is *insolvent*. An insolvent business cannot pay its debts and must go out of business. The owners of an insolvent financial institution—usually its stockholders—bear the loss but the firms and individuals who are owed payments by an insolvent firm also incur losses.

A financial institution both borrows and lends, so it is exposed to the risk that its net worth might become negative. To limit that risk, financial institutions are regulated and a minimum amount of their lending must be backed by their net worth.

Sometimes, a financial institution is solvent but illiquid. A firm is *illiquid* if it has made long-term loans with borrowed funds and is faced with a sudden demand to repay more of what it has borrowed than its available cash. In normal times, a financial institution that is illiquid can borrow from another institution. But if all the financial institutions are short of cash, the market for loans among financial institutions dries up.

Both insolvency and illiquidity were at the core of the financial meltdown of 2007–2008.

Interest Rates and Asset Prices

Stocks, bonds, short-term securities, and loans are collectively called *financial assets*. The interest rate on a financial asset is the interest received expressed as a percentage of the price of the asset.

Because the interest rate is a percentage of the price of an asset, if the asset price rises, other things remaining the same, the interest rate falls. Conversely, if the asset price falls, other things remaining the same, the interest rate rises.

To see this inverse relationship between an asset price and the interest rate, let's look at an example. We'll consider a bond that promises to pay its holder $5 a year forever. What is the rate of return—the interest rate—on this bond? The answer depends on the price of the bond. If you could buy this bond for $50, the interest rate would be 10 percent per year:

Interest rate = ($5 ÷ $50) × 100 = 10 percent.

But if the price of this bond increased to $200, its rate of return or interest rate would be only 2.5 percent per year. That is,

Interest rate = ($5 ÷ $200) × 100 = 2.5 percent.

This relationship means that the price of an asset and the interest rate on that asset are determined simultaneously—one implies the other.

This relationship also means that if the interest rate on the asset rises, the price of the asset falls, debts become harder to pay, and the net worth of the financial institution falls. Insolvency can arise from a previously unexpected large rise in the interest rate.

In the next part of this chapter, we learn how interest rates and asset prices are determined in the financial markets.

REVIEW QUIZ

1 Distinguish between physical capital and financial capital and give two examples of each.
2 What is the distinction between gross investment and net investment?
3 What are the three main types of markets for financial capital?
4 Explain the connection between the price of a financial asset and its interest rate.

Work these questions in Study Plan 23.1 and get instant feedback. Do a Key Terms Quiz.   MyEconLab

The Loanable Funds Market

In macroeconomics, we group all the financial markets that we described in the previous section into a single loanable funds market. The **loanable funds market** is the aggregate of all the individual financial markets.

The circular flow model of Chapter 20 (see p. 467) can be extended to include flows in the loanable funds market that finance investment.

Funds that Finance Investment

Figure 23.2 shows the flows of funds that finance investment. They come from three sources:

1. Household saving
2. Government budget surplus
3. Borrowing from the rest of the world

Households' income, Y, is spent on consumption goods and services, C, saved, S, or paid in net taxes, T. **Net taxes** are the taxes paid to governments minus the cash transfers received from governments (such as social security and unemployment benefits). So

income is equal to the sum of consumption expenditure, saving, and net taxes:

$$Y = C + S + T.$$

You saw in Chapter 20 (p. 468) that Y also equals the sum of the items of aggregate expenditure: consumption expenditure, C, investment, I, government expenditure, G, and exports, X, minus imports, M. That is:

$$Y = C + I + G + X - M.$$

By using these two equations, you can see that

$$I + G + X = M + S + T.$$

Subtract G and X from both sides of the last equation to obtain:

$$I = S + (T - G) + (M - X).$$

This equation tells us that investment, I, is financed by household saving, S, the government budget surplus, $(T - G)$, and borrowing from the rest of the world, $(M - X)$.

The sum of private saving, S, and government saving, $(T - G)$, is called **national saving**.

FIGURE 23.2   Financial Flows and the Circular Flow of Expenditure and Income

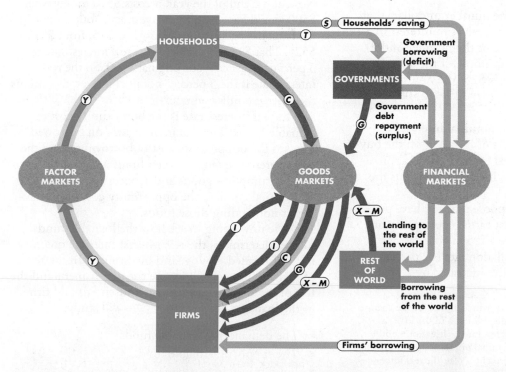

Households use their income for consumption expenditure (C), saving (S), and net taxes (T). Firms borrow to finance their investment expenditure. Governments borrow to finance a budget deficit or repay debt if they have a budget surplus. The rest of the world borrows to finance its deficit or lends its surplus.

National saving and foreign borrowing finance investment. In 2014, Canadian investment was $394 billion. Governments (federal, provincial, and local combined) had a deficit of $56 billion. This total of $450 billion was financed by private saving of $421 billion and borrowing from the rest of the world (negative net exports) of $29 billion.

In the rest of this chapter, we focus on the influences on national saving and the effects of a government budget deficit (or surplus) in the loanable funds market. We broaden our view to examine the influences on and the effects of borrowing from the rest of the world in Chapter 25. You can think of this chapter as an account of the Canadian loanable funds market when exports equal imports, $(X = M)$ or as an account of the global loanable funds market.

You're going to see how investment and saving and the flows of loanable funds—all measured in constant 2007 dollars—are determined. The price in the loanable funds market that achieves equilibrium is an interest rate, which we also measure in real terms as the *real* interest rate. In the loanable funds market, there is just one interest rate, which is an average of the interest rates on all the different types of financial securities that we described earlier. Let's see what we mean by the real interest rate.

The Real Interest Rate

The **nominal interest rate** is the number of dollars that a borrower pays and a lender receives in interest in a year expressed as a percentage of the number of dollars borrowed and lent. For example, if the annual interest paid on a $500 loan is $25, the nominal interest rate is 5 percent per year: $25 ÷ $500 × 100 or 5 percent.

The **real interest rate** is the nominal interest rate adjusted to remove the effects of inflation on the buying power of money. The real interest rate is approximately equal to the nominal interest rate minus the inflation rate.

You can see why if you suppose that you have put $500 in a savings account that earns 5 percent a year. At the end of a year, you have $525 in your savings account. Suppose that the inflation rate is 2 percent per year—during the year, all prices increased by 2 percent.

---

[1] The *exact* real interest rate formula, which allows for the change in the purchasing power of both the interest and the loan, is Real interest rate = (Nominal interest rate − Inflation rate) ÷ (1 + Inflation rate/100). If the nominal interest rate is 5 percent a year and the inflation rate is 2 percent a year, the real interest rate is (5 − 2) ÷ (1 + 0.02) = 2.94 percent a year.

Economics in Action
Nominal and Real Interest Rates

Nominal and real interest rates were extremely high during the 1980s. They have trended downward for the past 30 years. Where will they go next? See *Economics in the News* on pp 556–557.

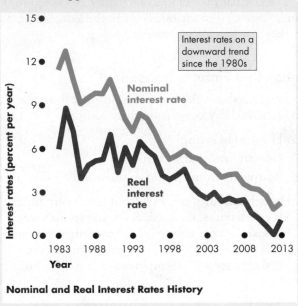

Nominal and Real Interest Rates History

Now, at the end of the year, it costs $510 to buy what $500 would have bought one year ago. Your money in the bank has really only increased by $15, from $510 to $525. That $15 is equivalent to a real interest rate of 3 percent a year on your original $500. So the real interest rate is the 5 percent nominal interest rate minus the 2 percent inflation rate.[1]

The real interest rate is the opportunity cost of loanable funds. The real interest *paid* on borrowed funds is the opportunity cost of borrowing. And the real interest rate *forgone* when funds are used either to buy consumption goods and services or to invest in new capital goods is the opportunity cost of not saving or not lending those funds.

We're now going to see how the loanable funds market determines the real interest rate, the quantity of funds loaned, saving, and investment. In the rest of this section, we will ignore the government and the rest of the world and focus on households and firms in the loanable funds market. We will study:

- The demand for loanable funds
- The supply of loanable funds
- Equilibrium in the loanable funds market

Economics in Action
The Total Quantities Supplied and Demanded

Around $7,300 billion of loanable funds have been supplied and demanded, and the figure shows who supplies and who demands. About 40 percent of the funds get supplied to banks and other financial institutions.

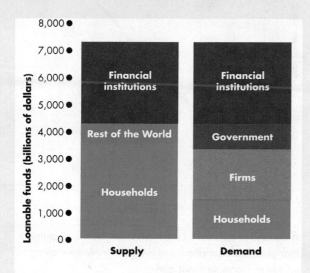

Supply and Demand in the Loanable Funds Market

The Demand for Loanable Funds

The *quantity of loanable funds demanded* is the total quantity of funds demanded to finance investment, the government budget deficit, and international investment or lending during a given period. Our focus here is on investment. We'll bring the budget deficit into the picture later in this chapter.

What determines investment and the demand for loanable funds to finance it? Many details influence this decision, but we can summarize them in two factors:

1. The real interest rate
2. Expected profit

Firms invest in capital only if they expect to earn a profit, and fewer projects are profitable at a high real interest rate than at a low real interest rate, so:

Other things remaining the same, the higher the real interest rate, the smaller is the quantity of loanable funds demanded; and the lower the real interest rate, the greater the quantity of loanable funds demanded.

FIGURE 23.3   The Demand for Loanable Funds

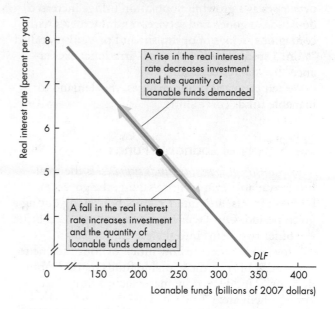

A change in the real interest rate changes the quantity of loanable funds demanded and brings a movement along the demand for loanable funds curve.

MyEconLab Animation

Demand for Loanable Funds Curve The **demand for loanable funds** is the relationship between the quantity of loanable funds demanded and the real interest rate, when all other influences on borrowing plans remain the same. The demand curve *DLF* in Fig. 23.3 is a demand for loanable funds curve.

To understand the demand for loanable funds, think about Amazon.com's decision to borrow $100 million to build some new warehouses. If Amazon expects to get a return of $5 million a year from this investment before paying interest costs and the interest rate is less than 5 percent a year, Amazon would make a profit, so it builds the warehouses. But if the interest rate is more than 5 percent a year, Amazon would incur a loss, so it doesn't build the warehouses. The quantity of loanable funds demanded is greater the lower is the real interest rate.

Changes in the Demand for Loanable Funds When the expected profit changes, the demand for loanable funds changes. Other things remaining the same, the greater the expected profit from new capital, the greater is the amount of investment and the greater the demand for loanable funds.

Expected profit rises during a business cycle expansion and falls during a recession; rises when technological change creates profitable new products; rises as a growing population brings increased demand for goods and services; and fluctuates with contagious swings of optimism and pessimism, called "animal spirits" by Keynes and "irrational exuberance" by Alan Greenspan.

When expected profit changes, the demand for loanable funds curve shifts.

The Supply of Loanable Funds

The *quantity of loanable funds supplied* is the total funds available from private saving, the government budget surplus, and international borrowing during a given period. Our focus here is on saving. We'll bring the other two items into the picture later.

How do you decide how much of your income to save and supply in the loanable funds market? Your decision is influenced by many factors, but chief among them are:

1. The real interest rate
2. Disposable income
3. Expected future income
4. Wealth
5. Default risk

We begin by focusing on the real interest rate.

> Other things remaining the same, the higher the real interest rate, the greater is the quantity of loanable funds supplied; and the lower the real interest rate, the smaller is the quantity of loanable funds supplied.

The Supply of Loanable Funds Curve The **supply of loanable funds** is the relationship between the quantity of loanable funds supplied and the real interest rate when all other influences on lending plans remain the same. The curve *SLF* in Fig. 23.4 is a supply of loanable funds curve.

Think about a student's decision to save some of what she earns from her summer job. With a real interest rate of 2 percent a year, she decides that it is not worth saving much—better to spend the income and take a student loan if funds run out during the semester. But if the real interest rate jumped to 10 percent a year, the payoff from saving would be high enough to encourage her to cut back on spending and increase the amount she saves.

FIGURE 23.4   The Supply of Loanable Funds

A rise in the real interest rate increases saving and the quantity of loanable funds supplied

A fall in the real interest rate decreases saving and the quantity of loanable funds supplied

A change in the real interest rate changes the quantity of loanable funds supplied and brings a movement along the supply of loanable funds curve.

MyEconLab Animation

Changes in the Supply of Loanable Funds A change in disposable income, expected future income, wealth, or default risk changes the supply of loanable funds.

Disposable Income A household's *disposable income* is the income earned minus net taxes. When disposable income increases, other things remaining the same, consumption expenditure increases but by less than the increase in income. Some of the increase in income is saved. So the greater a household's disposable income, other things remaining the same, the greater is its saving.

Expected Future Income The higher a household's expected future income, other things remaining the same, the smaller is its saving today.

Wealth The higher a household's wealth, other things remaining the same, the smaller is its saving. If a person's wealth increases because of a capital gain, the person sees less need to save. For example, from 2002 through 2006, when house prices were rising rapidly, wealth increased despite the fact that personal saving decreased.

Default Risk The risk that a loan will not be repaid is called **default risk**. The greater that risk, the higher is the interest rate needed to induce a person to lend and the smaller is the supply of loanable funds.

Shifts of the Supply of Loanable Funds Curve When any of the four influences on the supply of loanable funds changes, the supply of loanable funds changes and the supply curve shifts. An increase in disposable income, a decrease in expected future income, a decrease in wealth, or a fall in default risk increases saving and increases the supply of loanable funds.

Equilibrium in the Loanable Funds Market

You've seen that, other things remaining the same, the higher the real interest rate, the greater is the quantity of loanable funds supplied and the smaller is the quantity of loanable funds demanded. There is one real interest rate at which the quantities of loanable funds demanded and supplied are equal, and that interest rate is the equilibrium real interest rate.

Figure 23.5 shows how the demand for and supply of loanable funds determine the real interest rate. The *DLF* curve is the demand curve and the *SLF* curve is the supply curve. If the real interest rate exceeds 6 percent a year, the quantity of loanable funds supplied exceeds the quantity demanded—a surplus of funds. Borrowers find it easy to get funds, but lenders are unable to lend all the funds they have available. The real interest rate falls and continues to fall until the quantity of funds supplied equals the quantity of funds demanded.

If the real interest rate is less than 6 percent a year, the quantity of loanable funds supplied is less than the quantity demanded—a shortage of funds. Borrowers can't get the funds they want, but lenders are able to lend all the funds they have. So the real interest rate rises and continues to rise until the quantity of funds supplied equals the quantity demanded.

Regardless of whether there is a surplus or a shortage of loanable funds, the real interest rate changes and is pulled toward an equilibrium level. In Fig. 23.5, the equilibrium real interest rate is 6 percent a year. At this interest rate, there is neither a surplus nor a shortage of loanable funds. Borrowers can get the funds they want, and lenders can lend all the funds they have available. The investment plans of borrowers and the saving plans of lenders are consistent with each other.

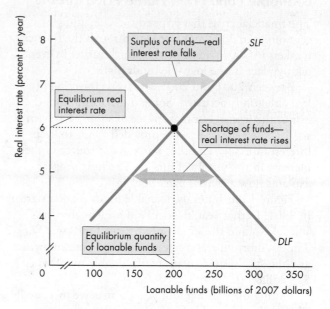

FIGURE 23.5 Equilibrium in the Loanable Funds Market

A surplus of funds lowers the real interest rate and a shortage of funds raises it. At an interest rate of 6 percent a year, the quantity of funds demanded equals the quantity supplied and the market is in equilibrium.

———— MyEconLab Animation and Draw Graph ————

Changes in Demand and Supply

Financial markets are highly volatile in the short run but remarkably stable in the long run. Volatility in the market comes from fluctuations in either the demand for loanable funds or the supply of loanable funds. These fluctuations bring fluctuations in the real interest rate and in the equilibrium quantity of funds lent and borrowed. They also bring fluctuations in asset prices.

Here we'll illustrate the effects of *increases* in demand and supply in the loanable funds market.

An Increase in Demand If the profits that firms expect to earn increase, they increase their planned investment and increase their demand for loanable funds to finance that investment. With an increase in the demand for loanable funds, but no change in the supply of loanable funds, there is a shortage of funds. As borrowers compete for funds, the interest rate rises and lenders increase the quantity of funds supplied.

Figure 23.6(a) illustrates these changes. An increase in the demand for loanable funds shifts the demand curve rightward from DLF_0 to DLF_1. With

Economics in Action

Loanable Funds Fuel Home Price Bubble

The financial crisis that gripped the U.S. and global economies in 2007 and cascaded through the financial markets in 2008 had its origins much earlier in events taking place in the loanable funds market.

Between 2001 and 2005, a massive injection of loanable funds occurred. Some funds came from the rest of the world, but that source of supply has been stable. The Federal Reserve provided funds to keep interest rates low, and that was a major source of the increase in the supply of funds. (The next chapter explains how a central bank does this.)

Figure 1 illustrates the loanable funds market starting in 2001. In that year, the demand for loanable funds was DLF_{01} and the supply of loanable funds was SLF_{01}. The equilibrium real interest rate was 4 percent a year and the equilibrium quantity of loanable funds was $29 trillion (in 2009 U.S. dollars).

During the ensuing four years, a massive increase in the supply of loanable funds shifted the supply curve rightward to SLF_{05}. A smaller increase in demand shifted the demand for loanable funds curve to DLF_{05}. The real interest rate fell to 1 percent a year and the quantity of loanable funds increased to $36 trillion—a 24 percent increase in just four years.

With this large increase in available funds, much of it in the form of mortgage loans to home buyers, the demand for homes increased by more than the increase in the supply of homes. Home prices rose and the expectation of further increases fuelled the demand for loanable funds.

By 2006, the expectation of continued rapidly rising home prices brought a very large increase in the demand for loanable funds. At the same time, the Federal Reserve began to tighten credit. (Again, you'll learn how this is done in the next chapter.) The result of the Fed's tighter credit policy was a slowdown in the pace of increase in the supply of loanable funds.

Figure 2 illustrates these events. In 2006, the demand for loanable funds increased from DLF_{05} to DLF_{06} and the supply of loanable funds increased by a smaller amount from SLF_{05} to SLF_{06}. The real interest rate increased to 3 percent a year.

The rise in the real interest rate (and a much higher rise in the nominal interest rate) put many home owners in financial difficulty. Mortgage payments increased and some borrowers stopped repaying their loans.

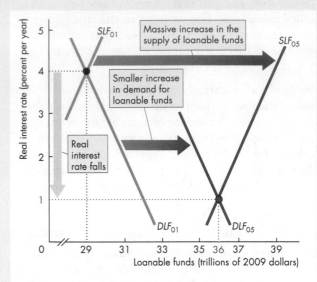

Figure 1 The Foundation of the Crisis: 2001–2005

Figure 2 The Start of the Crisis: 2005–2006

By August 2007, the damage from mortgage default and foreclosure was so large that the credit market began to dry up. A large decrease in both demand and supply kept interest rates roughly constant but decreased the quantity of new business.

The total quantity of loanable funds didn't decrease, but the rate of increase slowed to a snail's pace and financial institutions most exposed to the bad mortgage debts and the securities that they backed (described on p. 545) began to fail.

These events illustrate the crucial role played by the loanable funds market in our economy.

FIGURE 23.6   Changes in Demand and Supply

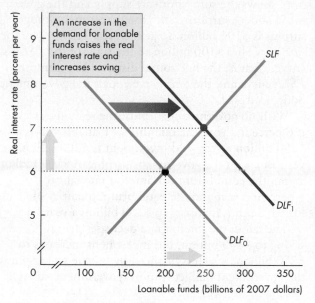

An increase in the demand for loanable funds raises the real interest rate and increases saving

(a) An increase in demand

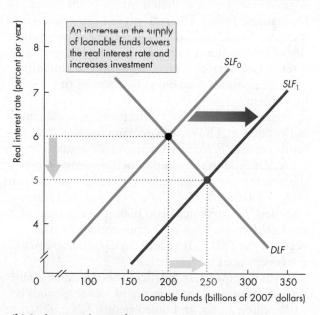

An increase in the supply of loanable funds lowers the real interest rate and increases investment

(b) An increase in supply

In part (a), the demand for loanable funds increases and supply doesn't change. The real interest rate rises (financial asset prices fall) and the quantity of funds increases. In part (b), the supply of loanable funds increases and demand doesn't change. The real interest rate falls (financial asset prices rise) and the quantity of funds increases.

MyEconLab Animation and Draw Graph

no change in the supply of loanable funds, there is a shortage of funds at a real interest rate of 6 percent a year. The real interest rate rises until it is 7 percent a year. Equilibrium is restored and the equilibrium quantity of funds has increased.

An Increase in Supply If one of the influences on saving plans changes and increases saving, the supply of loanable funds increases. With no change in the demand for loanable funds, the market is flush with loanable funds. Borrowers find bargains and lenders find themselves accepting a lower interest rate. At the lower interest rate, borrowers find additional investment projects profitable and increase the quantity of loanable funds that they borrow.

Figure 23.6(b) illustrates these changes. An increase in supply shifts the supply curve rightward from SLF_0 to SLF_1. With no change in demand, there is a surplus of funds at a real interest rate of 6 percent a year. The real interest rate falls until it is 5 percent a year. Equilibrium is restored and the equilibrium quantity of funds has increased.

Long-Run Growth of Demand and Supply Over time, both demand and supply in the loanable funds market fluctuate and the real interest rate rises and falls. Both the supply of loanable funds and the demand for loanable funds tend to increase over time. On the average, they increase at a similar pace, so although demand and supply trend upward, the real interest rate has no trend. It fluctuates around a constant average level.

◆ REVIEW QUIZ

1 What is the loanable funds market?
2 Why is the real interest rate the opportunity cost of loanable funds?
3 How do firms make investment decisions?
4 What determines the demand for loanable funds and what makes it change?
5 How do households make saving decisions?
6 What determines the supply of loanable funds and what makes it change?
7 How do changes in the demand for and supply of loanable funds change the real interest rate and quantity of loanable funds?

Work these questions in Study Plan 23.2 and get instant feedback. Do a Key Terms Quiz.   **MyEconLab**

Government in the Loanable Funds Market

Government enters the loanable funds market when it has a budget surplus or budget deficit. A government budget surplus increases the supply of loanable funds and contributes to financing investment; a government budget deficit increases the demand for loanable funds and competes with businesses for funds. Let's study the effects of government on the loanable funds market.

A Government Budget Surplus

A government budget surplus increases the supply of loanable funds. The real interest rate falls, which decreases household saving and decreases the quantity of private funds supplied. The lower real interest rate increases the quantity of loanable funds demanded and increases investment.

FIGURE 23.7   A Government Budget Surplus

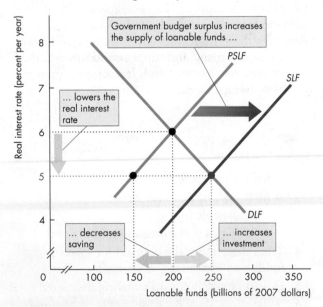

A government budget surplus of $100 billion adds to private saving and the private supply of loanable funds curve, *PSLF*, to determine the supply of loanable funds curve, *SLF*. The real interest rate falls to 5 percent a year, private saving decreases, but investment increases to $250 billion.

MyEconLab Animation

Figure 23.7 shows these effects of a government budget surplus. The private supply of loanable funds curve is *PSLF*. The supply of loanable funds curve, *SLF*, shows the sum of private supply and the government budget surplus. Here, the government budget surplus is $100 billion, so at each real interest rate the *SLF* curve lies $100 billion to the right of the *PSLF* curve. That is, the horizontal distance between the *PSLF* curve and the *SLF* curve equals the government budget surplus.

With no government surplus, the real interest rate is 6 percent a year, the quantity of loanable funds is $200 billion a year, and investment is $200 billion a year. But with the government surplus of $100 billion a year, the equilibrium real interest rate falls to 5 percent a year and the equilibrium quantity of loanable funds increases to $250 billion a year.

The fall in the interest rate decreases private saving to $150 billion, but investment increases to $250 billion, which is financed by private saving plus the government budget surplus (government saving).

A Government Budget Deficit

A government budget deficit increases the demand for loanable funds. The real interest rate rises, which increases household saving and increases the quantity of private funds supplied. But the higher real interest rate decreases investment and the quantity of loanable funds demanded by firms to finance investment.

Figure 23.8 shows these effects of a government budget deficit. The private demand for loanable funds curve is *PDLF*. The demand for loanable funds curve, *DLF*, shows the sum of private demand and the government budget deficit. Here, the government budget deficit is $100 billion, so at each real interest rate the *DLF* curve lies $100 billion to the right of the *PDLF* curve. That is, the horizontal distance between the *PDLF* curve and the *DLF* curve equals the government budget deficit.

With no government deficit, the real interest rate is 6 percent a year, the quantity of loanable funds is $200 billion a year, and investment is $200 billion a year. But with the government budget deficit of $100 billion a year, the equilibrium real interest rate rises to 7 percent a year and the equilibrium quantity of loanable funds increases to $250 billion a year.

The rise in the real interest rate increases private saving to $250 billion, but investment decreases to $150 billion because $100 billion of private saving must finance the government budget deficit.

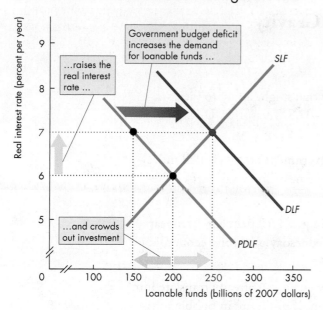

FIGURE 23.8 A Government Budget Deficit

A government budget deficit adds to the private demand for loanable funds curve, *PDLF*, to determine the demand for loanable funds curve, *DLF*. The real interest rate rises, saving increases, but investment decreases—a crowding-out effect.

——— MyEconLab Animation ———

The Crowding-Out Effect The tendency for a government budget deficit to raise the real interest rate and decrease investment is called the **crowding-out effect**. The crowding-out effect does not decrease investment by the full amount of the government budget deficit because a higher real interest rate induces an increase in private saving that partly contributes toward financing the deficit.

The Ricardo-Barro Effect First suggested by the English economist David Ricardo in the eighteenth century and refined by Robert J. Barro of Harvard University, the Ricardo-Barro effect holds that both of the effects we've just shown are wrong and the government budget has no effect on either the real interest rate or investment.

Barro says that taxpayers are rational and can see that a budget deficit today means that future taxes must be higher and future disposable incomes smaller. With smaller expected future disposable incomes, saving increases today. The private supply of loanable funds increases to match the quantity of loanable funds demanded by the government. So the budget deficit has no effect on either the real interest rate or investment. Figure 23.9 shows this outcome.

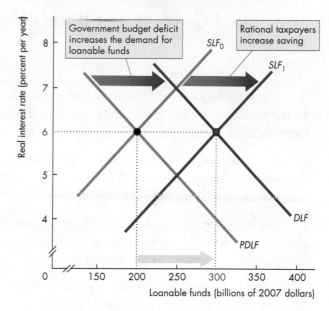

FIGURE 23.9 The Ricardo-Barro Effect

A budget deficit increases the demand for loanable funds. Rational taxpayers increase saving, which shifts the supply of loanable funds curve from SLF_0 to SLF_1. Crowding out is avoided: Increased saving finances the budget deficit.

——— MyEconLab Animation ———

Most economists regard the Ricardo-Barro view as extreme. But there might be some change in private saving that goes in the direction suggested by the Ricardo-Barro effect that lessens the crowding-out effect.

REVIEW QUIZ

1 How does a government budget surplus or deficit influence the loanable funds market?
2 What is the crowding-out effect and how does it work?
3 What is the Ricardo-Barro effect and how does it modify the crowding-out effect?

Work these questions in Study Plan 23.3 and get instant feedback. Do a Key Terms Quiz.   MyEconLab

◆ To complete your study of financial markets, take a look at *Economics in the News* on pp. 556–557 and see how you can use the model of the loanable funds market to understand why interest rates fell in 2014.

Interest Rates Low but Fall

Top-Rated Government Bonds Defy Gravity

The Financial Times
June 20, 2014

When you hit rock bottom, the only way is up. One day that might apply to yields on the world's safest and most liquid government bonds—U.S. Treasuries, U.K. gilts, German Bunds, and Japanese government bonds.

One day—but maybe not yet. Ten-year yields on core government bonds, which move inversely with prices, have edged lower in 2014—defying a near-universal start-of-the-year consensus that the only way was up.

German Bund 10-year yields this week hit a record low of just 1.12 per cent. Ten-year U.S. Treasuries yields rose back above 2.5 per cent on Wednesday on strong economic data but were 3 per cent at the start of 2014.

Such historically meagre rates worry some investors. Low yields can already translate into negative real interest rates after taking account of inflation. If prices are in bubble territory, a correction could inflict heavy capital losses on bond portfolios.

Yields have already risen this year on two-year U.S. Treasuries and U.K. gilts, which track closely expectations about central bank interest rate moves.

Among strategists and analysts, it is hard to sense a bubble about to burst, however. "For there to be a bubble, there has to be irrational behaviour," says Steven Major, global head of fixed income research at HSBC. "I don't see people borrowing to buy bonds—and I don't think values are far from fundamentals."

Instead, core government bonds offer havens in still-uncertain times—Russia's tensions with the west are escalating—while yields are held in check by ultra-loose central bank monetary policies and a global glut in savings.

Low yields also reflect global economic prospects. From Japan to the eurozone, growth remains weak. While U.K. gilts in particular may be vulnerable to sudden changes in interest rate expectations, it is arguably too early to claim the U.S. and U.K. recoveries will be sustained.

"We are unlikely to see U.S. bond yields rise in isolation; we should expect a synchronised move higher once the global economy is fully recovering," says Zach Pandl, portfolio manager at Columbia Management. ...

Written by Ralph Atkins, Michael MacKenzie, and Ben McLannahan. Copyright © 2014 by Financial Times. Used under licence from *The Financial Times*. All rights reserved.

ESSENCE OF THE STORY

- Interest rates on government bonds fell during the first half of 2014.

- The interest rate on a German government 10-year bond was at a record low of 1.12 percent and the rate on a 10-year U.S. government bond fell from 3 percent to 2.5 percent during the first half of 2014.

- Real interest rates could become negative.

- When interest rates rise, bond prices will fall.

- Economic growth is weak in Japan and Europe and it is uncertain whether the U.S. and U.K. expansions will be sustained.

MyEconLab More Economics in the News

ECONOMIC ANALYSIS

- The news article reports that government bond interest rates fell from an already low level and bond prices increased. (Canadian interest rates also fell.)

- Government bonds, called treasuries in the United States, gilts in the United Kingdom, and bunds in Germany, are the safest securities in the loanable funds market.

- They are also easily traded, so they can be sold at a moment's notice, which makes them highly liquid.

- Because they are safe and liquid, government bonds have a lower interest rate than corporate bonds—bonds issued by corporations.

- Although the level of an interest rate depends on the safety and liquidity of a security, on average, interest rates move up and down together and are influenced by common forces that change the supply of and demand for loanable funds.

- Figure 1 shows the interest rate on U.S. government 10-year bonds from 2010 to mid-2014 (both the nominal rate and the real rate.)

- The striking feature of this graph is that although the interest rate was low in 2014, it was not as low as it had been in 2012, when the real interest rate was close to zero for two years and briefly negative at the end of 2012.

- The news article says that the falling rate in 2014 risks making the real rate negative again, but that would require a full 1 percentage point fall in the nominal interest rate or a 1 percentage point rise in the inflation rate.

- The news article says that the U.S. government bond rate fell from 3 percent to 2.5 percent per year. With inflation a constant 1.4 percent per year, these numbers translate to a fall in the real interest rate from 1.6 percent to 1.1 percent per year.

- Figure 2 illustrates why the real interest rate fell. In January 2014, the demand for loanable funds was DLF_{Jan} and the supply of loanable funds was SLF_{Jan}. The equilibrium interest rate was 1.6 percent per year.

- During 2014, the factors described in the news article increased the supply of loanable funds to SLF_{Jun}.

- A key influence on the interest rate is missing from the news article: In 2014, the German, U.S., and U.K. government budget deficits shrank, which decreased the demand for loanable funds to DLF_{Jun}.

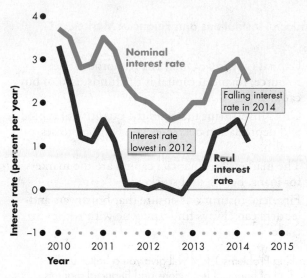

Figure 1 Interest Rates 2010 to 2014

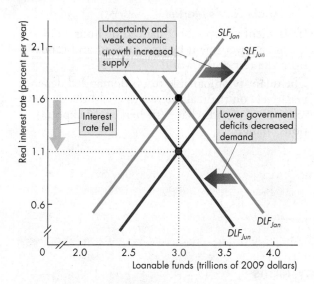

Figure 2 The Loanable Funds Market in 2014

- With an increase in supply and a decrease in demand, the equilibrium real interest rate fell from 1.6 percent to 1.1 percent.

- The news article speculates that bond prices will fall and interest rates will rise as economic expansion increases the demand for loanable funds.

557

SUMMARY

Key Points

Financial Institutions and Financial Markets

(pp. 542–546)

- Capital (*physical capital*) is a real productive resource; financial capital is the funds used to buy capital.
- Gross investment increases the quantity of capital and depreciation decreases it. Saving increases wealth.
- The markets for financial capital are the markets for loans, bonds, and stocks.
- Financial institutions ensure that borrowers and lenders can always find someone with whom to trade.

Working Problems 1 to 4 will give you a better understanding of financial institutions and financial markets.

The Loanable Funds Market (pp. 547–553)

- Investment in capital is financed by household saving, a government budget surplus, and funds from the rest of the world.
- The quantity of loanable funds demanded depends negatively on the real interest rate and the demand for loanable funds changes when profit expectations change.

- The quantity of loanable funds supplied depends positively on the real interest rate and the supply of loanable funds changes when disposable income, expected future income, wealth, and default risk change.
- Equilibrium in the loanable funds market determines the real interest rate and quantity of funds.

Working Problems 5 to 7 will give you a better understanding of the loanable funds market.

Government in the Loanable Funds Market

(pp. 554–555)

- A government budget surplus increases the supply of loanable funds, lowers the real interest rate, and increases investment and the equilibrium quantity of loanable funds.
- A government budget deficit increases the demand for loanable funds, raises the real interest rate, and increases the equilibrium quantity of loanable funds, but decreases investment in a crowding-out effect.
- The Ricardo-Barro effect is the response of rational taxpayers to a budget deficit: Private saving increases to finance the budget deficit. The real interest rate remains constant and the crowding-out effect is avoided.

Working Problems 8 to 11 will give you a better understanding of government in the loanable funds market.

Key Terms

Bond, 543
Bond market, 543
Crowding-out effect, 555
Default risk, 551
Demand for loanable funds, 549
Financial capital, 542
Financial institution, 544
Gross investment, 542

Loanable funds market, 547
Mortgage, 543
Mortgage-backed security, 544
National saving, 547
Net investment, 542
Net taxes, 547
Net worth, 546
Nominal interest rate, 548

MyEconLab Key Terms Quiz

Real interest rate, 548
Saving, 542
Stock, 544
Stock market, 544
Supply of loanable funds, 550
Wealth, 542

WORKED PROBLEM

MyEconLab   You can work this problem in Chapter 23 Study Plan.

Some facts about an economy are:

- In 2005, the nominal interest rate on bonds was 5 percent a year and the real interest rate was 2 percent a year. Investment was $2.7 billion and the government budget deficit was $0.5 billion.

- By 2009, the real interest rate had increased to 5 percent a year, but the nominal interest rate was unchanged at 5 percent a year. Investment had crashed to $1.8 billion and the government budget deficit had climbed to $1.8 billion.

Assume that the private demand for and private supply of loanable funds did not change between 2005 and 2009.

Questions

1. What was the inflation rate in 2005 and 2009? How do you know?
2. What happened to the price of a bond between 2005 and 2009? How do you know?
3. What happened to the demand for loanable funds between 2005 and 2009? How do you know?
4. Did the change in the government budget deficit crowd out some investment?
5. What happened to the quantity of saving and investment?

Solutions

1. The real interest rate equals the nominal interest rate minus the inflation rate. So the inflation rate equals the nominal interest rate minus the real interest rate. In 2005, the inflation rate was 3 percent a year, and in 2009 the inflation rate was zero.

Key Point: The nominal interest rate minus the real interest rate equals the inflation rate.

2. The price of a bond is inversely related to the nominal interest rate. Between 2005 and 2009, the nominal interest rate did not change—it remained at 5 percent a year. With the nominal interest rate unchanged, the price of a bond was also unchanged.

Key Point: The price of a bond is inversely related to the nominal interest rate.

3. The demand for loanable funds is the relationship between the quantity of loanable funds demanded and the real interest rate.

An increase in the government budget deficit increases the demand for loanable funds. Between 2005 and 2009, the government budget deficit increased from $0.5 billion to $1.8 billion, so the demand for loanable funds increased.

Key Point: An increase in the government budget deficit increases the demand for loanable funds.

4. The increase in the government budget deficit increased the demand for loanable funds. With no change in the supply of loanable funds, the real interest rate increases.

Between 2005 and 2009, the real interest rate increased from 2 percent a year to 5 percent a year. As the real interest rate increased, the quantity of loanable funds demanded by firms decreased from $2.7 billion to $1.8 billion. Crowding out occurred.

Key Point: With no change in the supply of loanable funds, an increase in the government budget deficit increases the real interest rate and crowds out investment.

5. Saving and investment plans depend on the real interest rate. Between 2005 and 2009, the real interest rate increased, which increased saving and decreased investment. The increase in saving increased the quantity supplied of loanable funds. The decrease in investment decreased the quantity demanded of loanable funds.

Key Point: A change in the real interest rate does not change the supply of or demand for loanable funds: It changes the quantities supplied and demanded.

Key Figure   MyEconLab Interactive Animation

STUDY PLAN PROBLEMS AND APPLICATIONS

MyEconLab   You can work Problems 1 to 11 in Chapter 23 Study Plan and get instant feedback.

Financial Institutions and Financial Markets

(Study Plan 23.1)

Use the following data to work Problems 1 and 2.
Michael is an Internet service provider. On December 31, 2014, he bought an existing business with servers and a building worth $400,000. During 2015, his business grew and he bought new servers for $500,000. The market value of some of his older servers fell by $100,000.

1. What was Michael's gross investment, depreciation, and net investment during 2015?

2. What is the value of Michael's capital at the end of 2015?

3. Lori is a student who teaches golf on Saturdays. In a year, she earns $20,000 after paying her taxes. At the beginning of 2014, Lori owned $1,000 worth of books, DVDs, and golf clubs and she had $5,000 in a savings account at the bank. During 2014, the interest on her savings account was $300 and she spent a total of $15,300 on consumption goods and services. There was no change in the market values of her books, DVDs, and golf clubs.
   a. How much did Lori save in 2014?
   b. What was her wealth at the end of 2014?

4. **Treasury Yields Fall to Two-Week Low**
   Treasury bond prices rose on Monday, pushing interest rates down. The interest rate on 10-year bonds fell 4 basis points to 1.65%.
      Source: *The Wall Street Journal*, August 27, 2012
   What is the relationship between the price of a Treasury bond and its interest rate? Why does the interest rate move inversely to price?

The Loanable Funds Market (Study Plan 23.2)

Use the following data to work Problems 5 and 6.
First Call, Inc., a smartphone company, plans to build an assembly plant that costs $10 million if the real interest rate is 6 percent a year or a larger plant that costs $12 million if the real interest rate is 5 percent a year or a smaller plant that costs $8 million if the real interest rate is 7 percent a year.

5. Draw a graph of First Call's demand for loanable funds curve.

6. First Call expects its profit to double next year. Explain how this increase in expected profit influences First Call's demand for loanable funds.

7. The table sets out the data for an economy when the government's budget is balanced.

Real interest rate	Loanable funds demanded	Loanable funds supplied
(percent per year)	(billions of 2007 dollars)	
4	8.5	5.5
5	8.0	6.0
6	7.5	6.5
7	7.0	7.0
8	6.5	7.5
9	6.0	8.0
10	5.5	8.5

   a. Calculate the equilibrium real interest rate, investment, and private saving.
   b. If planned saving increases by $0.5 billion at each real interest rate, explain the change in the real interest rate.
   c. If planned investment increases by $1 billion at each real interest rate, explain the change in saving and the real interest rate.

Government in the Loanable Funds Market

(Study Plan 23.3)

Use the data in Problem 7 to work Problems 8 and 9.

8. If the government's budget becomes a deficit of $1 trillion, what are the real interest rate and investment? Does crowding out occur?

9. If the government's budget becomes a deficit of $1 trillion and the Ricardo-Barro effect occurs, what are the real interest rate and investment?

Use the table in Problem 7 and the following data to work Problems 10 and 11.

Suppose that the quantity of loanable funds demanded increases by $1 trillion at each real interest rate and the quantity of loanable funds supplied increases by $2 trillion at each interest rate.

10. If the government budget remains balanced, what are the real interest rate, investment, and private saving? Does any crowding out occur?

11. If the government's budget becomes a deficit of $1 trillion, what are the real interest rate, investment, and private saving? Does any crowding out occur?

ADDITIONAL PROBLEMS AND APPLICATIONS

MyEconLab   You can work these problems in MyEconLab if assigned by your instructor.

Financial Institutions and Financial Markets

12. On January 1, 2014, Terry's Towing Service owned 4 tow trucks valued at $300,000. During 2014, Terry's bought 2 new trucks for a total of $180,000. At the end of 2014, the market value of all of the firm's trucks was $400,000. What was Terry's gross investment? Calculate Terry's depreciation and net investment.

Use the following information to work Problems 13 and 14.

An economy's capital stock was $46.3 billion at the end of 2010, $46.6 billion at the end of 2011, and $47.0 billion at the end of 2012. Depreciation in 2011 was $2.4 billion, and gross investment during 2012 was $2.8 billion (all in 2007 dollars).

13. Calculate net investment and gross investment during 2011.

14. Calculate depreciation and net investment during 2012.

15. Annie runs a fitness centre. On December 31, 2014, she bought an existing business with exercise equipment and a building worth $300,000. During 2015, business improved and she bought some new equipment for $50,000. At the end of 2015, her equipment and buildings were worth $325,000. Calculate Annie's gross investment, depreciation, and net investment during 2015.

16. Karrie is a golf pro, and after she paid taxes, her income from golf and interest from financial assets was $1,500,000 in 2013. At the beginning of 2013, she owned $900,000 worth of financial assets. At the end of 2013, Karrie's financial assets were worth $1,900,000.

    a. How much did Karrie save during 2013?

    b. How much did she spend on consumption goods and services?

The Loanable Funds Market

17. **Canadians Saving More**

    Recent data indicate that Canadians are saving more. Statistics Canada reports that the Household Savings Rate is currently 5.4%, a 0.4% increase from the previous year. Likewise, a recent Bank of Montreal study found that

48% of Canadians are now investing in Tax-Free Savings Accounts (TFSAs), a 23% increase from 2012.

>   Source: *Financial Post*, January 15, 2014

    a. Is investing in TFSAs part of household consumption or saving? Explain your answer.

    b. Explain how an increase in saving influences the loanable funds market and its equilibrium.

18. Draw a graph to illustrate the effect of an increase in the demand for loanable funds and an even larger increase in the supply of loanable funds on the real interest rate and the equilibrium quantity of loanable funds.

19. Draw a graph to illustrate how an increase in the supply of loanable funds and a decrease in the demand for loanable funds can lower the real interest rate and leave the equilibrium quantity of loanable funds unchanged.

Use the following data to work Problems 20 and 21.

In 2012, the Lee family had disposable income of $80,000, wealth of $140,000, and an expected future income of $80,000 a year. At a real interest rate of 4 percent a year, the Lee family saves $15,000 a year; at a real interest rate of 6 percent a year, they save $20,000 a year; and at a real interest rate of 8 percent, they save $25,000 a year.

20. Draw a graph of the Lee family's supply of loanable funds curve.

21. In 2013, suppose that the stock market crashes and the default risk increases. Explain how this increase in default risk influences the Lee family's supply of loanable funds curve.

22. **Keystone Pipeline Clears a Hurdle**

    A judge in Lamar County, Texas, ruled that TransCanada has permission to build its Keystone XL pipeline from Cushing, Oklahoma, to Port Arthur, Texas. TransCanada has said it will start building as soon as possible.

>   Source: CNN, August 23, 2012

    Show on a graph the effect of TransCanada going to the loanable funds market to finance the building of its pipeline. Explain the effect on the real interest rate, private saving, and investment.

23. The table sets out the data for an economy when the government's budget is balanced.

Real interest rate	Loanable funds demanded	Loanable funds supplied
(percent per year)	(billions of 2007 dollars)	
2	8.0	4.0
3	7.0	5.0
4	6.0	6.0
5	5.0	7.0
6	4.0	8.0
7	3.0	9.0
8	2.0	10.0

a. Calculate the equilibrium real interest rate, investment, and private saving.

b. If planned saving decreases by $1 billion at each real interest rate, explain the change in the real interest rate and investment.

c. If planned investment decreases by $1 billion at each real interest rate, explain the change in saving and the real interest rate.

Government in the Loanable Funds Market

Use the following information to work Problems 24 and 25.

India's Economy Hits the Wall

At the start of 2008, India had an annual growth of 9 percent, huge consumer demand, and increasing investment. But by July 2008, India had large government deficits and rising interest rates. Economic growth is expected to fall to 7 percent by the end of 2008. A Goldman Sachs report suggests that India needs to lower the government's deficit and raise educational achievement.

Source: *BusinessWeek*, July 1, 2008

24. If the Indian government reduces its deficit and returns to a balanced budget, how will the demand for or supply of loanable funds in India change?

25. With economic growth forecasted to slow, future incomes are expected to fall. If other things remain the same, how will the demand or supply of loanable funds in India change?

26. **Canadian Budget Deficit Narrows**

The deficit in the first 10 months of the year from April 2013 to January 2014 totalled $10.54 billion, down from $13.87 billion in the same period a year earlier.

Source: Reuters, March 28, 2014

a. Explain the effect of the decrease in the budget deficit on the loanable funds market.

b. What effect does the smaller budget deficit have on the real interest rate, private saving, and investment?

Economics in the News

27. After you have studied *Economics in the News* on pp. 556–557, answer the following questions.

a. Why does the news article say that bond prices and interest rates move in opposite directions? Is it correct? Explain.

b. How does a government budget deficit influence the loanable funds market, and why does a decrease in the deficit lower the real interest rate?

c. When an economic expansion gets going, what happens to the demand for loanable funds and the real interest rate?

d. If an expanding economy increases government tax revenue, how will that affect the loanable funds market and the real interest rate?

e. Looking at Fig. 1 on p. 557, what must have happened to either the demand for or the supply of loanable funds during 2011, 2012, and 2013?

28. **G20 Vows to Boost World GDP by $2 trillion**

The centrepiece of the 2014 G20 meeting is for all 20 countries to boost investment, create new jobs, and together boost world income by $2 trillion over 5 years.

Source: Associated Press, February 23, 2014

a. Explain the effect of an increase in planned investment on the demand for or supply of loanable funds.

b. If G20 countries do increase global income, how will the world real interest rate, saving, and investment change? Explain your answer.

c. On a graph of the global loanable funds market, illustrate your answer to part (b).

24

MONEY, THE PRICE LEVEL, AND INFLATION

After studying this chapter, you will be able to:

◆ Define money and describe its functions

◆ Explain the economic functions of banks

◆ Describe the structure and functions of the Bank of Canada

◆ Explain how the banking system creates money

◆ Explain what determines the quantity of money and the nominal interest rate

◆ Explain how the quantity of money influences the price level and the inflation rate

Money, like fire and the wheel, has been around for a long time, and it has taken many forms. It was beads made from shells for North American Indians and tobacco for early American colonists. Today, we use dollar bills or swipe a card or, in some places, tap a cellphone. Are all these things money?

In this chapter, we study money, its functions, how it gets created, how the Bank of Canada regulates its quantity, and what happens when its quantity changes. In *Economics in the News* at the end of the chapter, we look at the growth of Canadian money in recent years and ask whether there is a risk of inflation.

What Is Money?

What do beads, tobacco, and nickels and dimes have in common? They are all examples of **money**, which is defined as any commodity or token that is generally acceptable as a means of payment. A **means of payment** is a method of settling a debt. When a payment has been made, there is no remaining obligation between the parties to a transaction. So what wampum, tobacco, and nickels and dimes have in common is that they have served (or still do serve) as the means of payment. Money serves three other functions:

- Medium of exchange
- Unit of account
- Store of value

Medium of Exchange

A *medium of exchange* is any object that is generally accepted in exchange for goods and services. Without a medium of exchange, goods and services must be exchanged directly for other goods and services—an exchange called *barter*. Barter requires a *double coincidence of wants*, a situation that rarely occurs. For example, if you want a hamburger, you might offer a CD in exchange for it. But you must find someone who is selling hamburgers and wants your CD.

A medium of exchange overcomes the need for a double coincidence of wants. Money acts as a medium of exchange because people with something to sell will always accept money in exchange for it. But money isn't the only medium of exchange. You can buy with a credit card, but a credit card isn't money. It doesn't make a final payment, and the debt it creates must eventually be settled by using money.

Unit of Account

A *unit of account* is an agreed measure for stating the prices of goods and services. To get the most out of your budget, you have to figure out whether seeing one more movie is worth its opportunity cost. But that cost is not dollars and cents. It is the number of ice-cream cones, sodas, or cups of coffee that you must give up. It's easy to do such calculations when all these goods have prices in terms of dollars and cents (see Table 24.1). If the price of a movie is $8 and the price of a cappuccino is $4, you know right away that seeing one movie costs you 2 cappuccinos. If jelly beans are $1 a pack, one movie costs

TABLE 24.1 The Unit of Account Function of Money Simplifies Price Comparisons

Good	Price in money units	Price in units of another good
Movie	$8.00 each	2 cappuccinos
Cappuccino	$4.00 each	2 ice-cream cones
Ice cream	$2.00 per cone	2 packs of jelly beans
Jelly beans	$1.00 per pack	2 sticks of gum
Gum	$0.50 per stick	

Money as a unit of account: The price of a movie is $8 and the price of a stick of gum is 50¢, so the opportunity cost of a movie is 16 sticks of gum ($8.00 ÷ 50¢ = 16).

No unit of account: You go to a movie theatre and learn that the cost of seeing a movie is 2 cappuccinos. You go to a grocery store and learn that a pack of jelly beans costs 2 sticks of gum. But how many sticks of gum does seeing a movie cost you? To answer that question, you go to the coffee shop and find that a cappuccino costs 2 ice-cream cones. Now you head for the ice-cream shop, where an ice-cream cone costs 2 packs of jelly beans. Now you get out your pocket calculator: 1 movie costs 2 cappuccinos, or 4 ice-cream cones, or 8 packs of jelly beans, or 16 sticks of gum!

8 packs of jelly beans. You need only one calculation to figure out the opportunity cost of any pair of goods and services.

Imagine how troublesome it would be if your local movie theatre posted its price as 2 cappuccinos, the coffee shop posted the price of a cappuccino as 2 ice-cream cones, the ice-cream shop posted the price of an ice-cream cone as 2 packs of jelly beans, and the grocery store priced a pack of jelly beans as 2 sticks of gum! Now how much running around and calculating will you have to do to find out how much that movie is going to cost you in terms of the cappuccinos, ice-cream cones, jelly beans, or gum that you must give up to see it? You get the answer for cappuccinos right away from the sign posted on the movie theatre. But for all the other goods, you're going to have to visit many different stores to establish the price of each good in terms of another and then calculate the prices in units that are relevant for your own decision. The hassle of doing all this research might be enough to make a person swear off movies! You can see how much simpler it is if all the prices are expressed in dollars and cents.

Store of Value

Money is a *store of value* in the sense that it can be held and exchanged later for goods and services. If money were not a store of value, it could not serve as a means of payment.

Money is not alone in acting as a store of value. A house, a car, and a work of art are other examples.

The more stable the value of a commodity or token, the better it can act as a store of value and the more useful it is as money. No store of value has a completely stable value. The value of a house, a car, or a work of art fluctuates over time. The values of the commodities and tokens that are used as money also fluctuate over time.

Inflation lowers the value of money and the values of other commodities and tokens that are used as money. To make money as useful as possible as a store of value, a low inflation rate is needed.

Money in Canada Today

In Canada today, money consists of:

- Currency
- Deposits at banks and other depository institutions

Currency The notes and coins held by individuals and businesses are known as **currency**. Notes are money because the government declares them so with the words "Ce billet a cours légal—this note is legal tender." Notes and coins inside banks are not counted as currency because they are not held by individuals and businesses. Currency is convenient for settling small debts and buying low-priced items.

Deposits Deposits of individuals and businesses at banks and other depository institutions, such as trust and mortgage companies, credit unions, and caisses populaires, are also counted as money. Deposits are money because the owners of the deposits can use them to make payments. Deposits owned by the Government of Canada are not counted as money because they are not held by individuals and businesses.

Official Measures of Money Two official measures of money in Canada today are known as M1 and M2. **M1** consists of currency held by individuals and businesses plus chequable deposits owned by individuals and businesses. **M2** consists of M1 plus all other deposits—non-chequable deposits and fixed term deposits—held by individuals and businesses.

Economics in Action
Official Measures of Canadian Money

The figure shows the relative magnitudes of the items that make up M1 and M2. Notice that currency is a small part of our money.

	$ billions in May 2014
M2	1,261
Comprises all in M1, plus...	
Fixed term deposits	312
Non-chequable deposits, non-personal	39
Non-chequable deposits, personal	238
M1	672
Chequable deposits, non-personal	361
Chequable deposits, personal	244
Currency outside banks	67

Two Official Measures of Money

M1
- Currency held by individuals and businesses
- Personal chequable deposits
- Non-personal chequable deposits

M2
- M1
- Personal non-chequable deposits
- Non-personal non-chequable deposits
- Fixed term deposits

Source of data: Statistics Canada, CANSIM Table 176-0020. M1 is M1+ (gross), and M2 is M2 (gross). The data are for May 2014.

Are M1 and M2 Really Money? Money is the means of payment. So the test of whether an asset is money is whether it serves as a means of payment. Currency passes the test. But what about deposits? Chequable deposits are money because they can be transferred from one person to another by writing a cheque or using a debit card. Such a transfer of ownership is equivalent to handing over currency. Because M1 consists of currency plus chequable deposits and each of these is a means of payment, *M1 is money.*

But what about M2? Some of the savings deposits in M2 are just as much a means of payment as the chequable deposits in M1. You can use an ATM to get funds from your savings account to pay for your purchase at the grocery store or the gas station. But some savings deposits are not means of payment. These deposits are known as liquid assets. *Liquidity* is the property of being easily convertible into a means of payment without loss in value. Because the deposits in M2 that are not means of payment are quickly and easily converted into a means of payment— currency or chequable deposits—they are counted as money.

Deposits Are Money but Cheques Are Not In defining money, we include, along with currency, deposits at banks and other depository institutions. But the cheques that people write are not counted as money. Why are deposits money and cheques not?

To see why deposits are money but cheques are not, think about what happens when Colleen buys some roller-blades for $100 from Rocky's Rollers. When Colleen goes to Rocky's shop, she has $500 in her deposit account at the Laser Bank. Rocky has $1,000 in his deposit account—at the same bank, as it happens. The deposits of these two people total $1,500. Colleen writes a cheque for $100. Rocky takes the cheque to the bank right away and deposits it. Rocky's bank balance rises from $1,000 to $1,100, and Colleen's balance falls from $500 to $400. The deposits of Colleen and Rocky still total $1,500. Rocky now has $100 more than before, and Colleen has $100 less.

This transaction has transferred money from Colleen to Rocky, but the cheque itself was never money. There wasn't an extra $100 of money while the cheque was in circulation. The cheque instructs the bank to transfer money from Colleen to Rocky.

If Colleen and Rocky use different banks, there is an extra step. Rocky's bank credits $100 to Rocky's account and then takes the cheque to a cheque-clearing centre. The cheque is then sent to Colleen's bank, which pays Rocky's bank $100 and then debits Colleen's account $100. This process can take a few days, but the principles are the same as when two people use the same bank.

Credit Cards Are Not Money You've just seen that cheques are not money, but what about credit cards? Isn't having a credit card in your wallet and presenting the card to pay for your roller-blades the same thing as using money? Why aren't credit cards somehow valued and counted as part of the quantity of money?

When you pay by cheque, you are frequently asked to show your driver's licence. It would never occur to you to think of your driver's licence as money. It's just an ID card. A credit card is also an ID card, but one that lets you take out a loan at the instant you buy something. When you swipe your credit card and key in your pin, you are saying, "I agree to pay for these goods when the credit card company bills me." Once you get your statement from the credit card company, you must make at least the minimum payment due. To make that payment, you need money—you need to have currency or a chequable deposit to pay the credit card company. So although you use a credit card when you buy something, the credit card is not the *means of payment* and it is not money.

◤ **REVIEW QUIZ**

1 What makes something money? What functions does money perform? Why do you think packs of chewing gum don't serve as money?

2 What are the problems that arise when a commodity is used as money?

3 What are the main components of money in Canada today?

4 What are the official measures of money? Are all the measures really money?

5 Why are cheques and credit cards not money?

Work these questions in Study Plan 24.1 and get instant feedback. Do a Key Terms Quiz.   MyEconLab

We've seen that the main component of money in Canada is deposits held by individuals and businesses at banks and other depository institutions. Let's take a closer look at these institutions.

◼▶ Depository Institutions

A **depository institution** is a financial firm that takes deposits from households and firms. These deposits are components of M1 and M2. You will learn what these institutions are, what they do, the economic benefits they bring, how they are regulated, and how they innovate and create new financial products.

Types of Depository Institutions

The deposits of three types of depository institution make up Canada's money. They are:

- Chartered banks
- Credit unions and caisses populaires
- Trust and mortgage loan companies

Chartered Banks A **chartered bank** is a private firm, chartered under the Bank Act of 1991 to receive deposits and make loans. The chartered banks are by far the largest institutions in the banking system and conduct all types of banking and financial business. In 2008, 14 Canadian-owned banks (including the Royal Bank of Canada, CIBC, Bank of Montreal, Bank of Nova Scotia, National Bank of Canada, and TD Canada Trust) and 33 foreign-owned banks had the bulk of the deposits in M1 and M2.

Credit Unions and Caisses Populaires A *credit union* is a cooperative organization that operates under the Cooperative Credit Associations Act of 1991 and that receives deposits from and makes loans to its members. A caisse populaire is a similar type of institution that operates in Quebec.

Trust and Mortgage Loan Companies A trust and mortgage loan company is a privately owned depository institution that operates under the Trust and Loan Companies Act of 1991. These institutions receive deposits, make loans, and act as trustee for pension funds and for estates.

All Banks Now Historically, Canada has made a sharp legal distinction between banks and other depository institutions. But the economic functions of all depository institutions have grown increasingly similar. This fact is recognized in laws governing these institutions that became effective in 1991. Because they all perform the same essential economic functions, we'll call all these institutions banks unless we need to distinguish among them.

What Depository Institutions Do

Depository institutions provide services such as cheque clearing, account management, credit cards, and Internet banking, all of which provide an income from service fees.

But depository institutions earn most of their income by using the funds they receive from depositors to make loans and buy securities that earn a higher interest rate than that paid to depositors. In this activity, a depository institution must perform a balancing act weighing return against risk. To see this balancing act, we'll focus on the chartered banks.

A chartered bank puts the funds it receives from depositors and other funds that it borrows into four types of assets:

- Reserves
- Liquid assets
- Securities
- Loans

Reserves A depository institution's **reserves** are notes and coins in its vault or its deposit account at the Bank of Canada. (We study the Bank of Canada later in this chapter.) These funds are used to meet depositors' currency withdrawals and to make payments to other banks. In normal times, a bank keeps about a half of 1 percent of deposits as reserves.

Liquid Assets Liquid assets are Government of Canada Treasury bills and commercial bills. These assets are the banks' first line of defence if they need reserves. Liquid assets can be sold and instantly converted into reserves with virtually no risk of loss. Because they have a low risk, they also earn a low interest rate.

Securities Securities are Government of Canada bonds and other bonds such as mortgage-backed securities. These assets can be converted into reserves but at prices that fluctuate. Because their prices fluctuate, these assets are riskier than liquid assets, but they also have a higher interest rate.

Loans Loans are commitments of funds for an agreed-upon period of time. Banks make loans to corporations to finance the purchase of capital. They also make mortgage loans to finance the purchase of homes, and personal loans to finance consumer durable goods, such as cars or boats. The outstanding balances on credit card accounts are also bank loans.

Loans are the riskiest assets of a bank. They cannot be converted into reserves until they are due to be repaid. Also, some borrowers default and never repay. These assets earn the highest interest rate.

Table 24.2 provides a snapshot of the sources and uses of funds of all the chartered banks in 2014.

Economic Benefits Provided by Depository Institutions

You've seen that a depository institution earns part of its profit because it pays a lower interest rate on deposits than what it receives on loans. What benefits do these institutions provide that make depositors willing to put up with a low interest rate and borrowers willing to pay a higher one?

Depository institutions provide four benefits:

- Create liquidity
- Pool risk
- Lower the cost of borrowing
- Lower the cost of monitoring borrowers

Create Liquidity Depository institutions create liquidity by borrowing short and lending long—taking deposits and standing ready to repay them on short notice or on demand and making loan commitments that run for terms of many years.

TABLE 24.2   Chartered Banks: Sources and Uses of Funds

	$ billions April 2014	Percentage of deposits
Total funds	2,243	151.7
Sources		
Deposits	1,479	100.0
Borrowing	532	36.0
Own capital	232	15.7
Uses		
Reserves	28	1.9
Liquid assets	83	5.6
Securities	340	23.0
Loans	1,792	121.2

Chartered banks get most of their funds from depositors and use most of them to make loans. They hold less than 1 percent of deposits as reserves but hold about a quarter of deposits as liquid assets.

Source of data: Statistics Canada, CANSIM Table 176-0011.

Pool Risk A loan might not be repaid—a default. If you lend to one person who defaults, you lose the entire amount loaned. If you lend to 1,000 people (through a bank) and one person defaults, you lose almost nothing. Depository institutions pool risk.

Lower the Cost of Borrowing Imagine a firm is looking for $1 million to buy a new factory and there are no depository institutions. The firm hunts around for several dozen people from whom to borrow the funds. Depository institutions lower the cost of this search. The firm gets its $1 million from a single institution that gets deposits from a large number of people but spreads the cost of this activity over many borrowers.

Lower the Cost of Monitoring Borrowers By monitoring borrowers, a lender can encourage good decisions that prevent defaults. But this activity is costly. Imagine how costly it would be if each household that lent money to a firm incurred the costs of monitoring that firm directly. Depository institutions can perform this task at a much lower cost.

How Depository Institutions Are Regulated

Responsibility for financial regulation in Canada is shared by the Department of Finance, the Bank of Canada, the Office of the Superintendent of Financial Institutions, the Canada Deposit Insurance Corporation, and provincial agencies. The goal of financial regulation is to identify, evaluate, and lessen the consequences of financial risk.

The Department of Finance bears the ultimate responsibility for regulation but delegates the day-to-day details to the other agencies.

The Bank of Canada ensures that the banks and other depository institutions have adequate liquidity and provides general guidance and advice to government.

The Office of the Superintendent of Financial Institutions supervises the banks and other depository institutions and ensures that their balance sheets have a high enough capital ratio and their assets are sufficiently liquid to withstand stress.

The Canada Deposit Insurance Corporation operates a system of deposit insurance that insures deposits held at Canadian banks up to $100,000 in case of a bank failure.

Provincial government agencies regulate credit unions and caisses populaires.

Canadian financial regulation has successfully avoided major failures at times when U.S. banks have failed.

◆ AT **ISSUE**

Fractional-Reserve Banking Versus 100 Percent Reserve Banking

Fractional-reserve banking, a system in which banks keep a fraction of their depositors' funds as a cash reserve and lend the rest, was invented by goldsmiths in sixteenth-century Europe and is the only system in use today.

This system contrasts with **100 percent reserve banking**, a system in which banks keep the full amount of their depositors' funds as a cash reserve.

The 2008 global financial crisis raises the question: Should banks be required to keep 100 percent cash reserves to prevent them from failing and bringing recession?

Yes

- The most unrelenting advocates of 100 percent reserve banking are a group of economists known as the *Austrian School*, who say that fractional-reserve banking violates property rights.
- Because a deposit is owned by the depositor and not the bank, the bank has no legal right to lend the deposit to someone else.
- Mainstream economists Irving Fisher in the 1930s and Milton Friedman in the 1950s advocated 100 percent reserve banking.
- They said it enables the central bank to exercise more precise control over the quantity of money, and it eliminates the risk of a bank running out of cash.

Irving Fisher of Yale University supported 100 percent reserve banking.

No

- The requirement to hold 100 percent reserves would prevent the banks making loans and lower their profits.
- Lower bank profits weaken rather than strengthen the banks.
- The demand for loans would be met by a supply from unregulated institutions, and they might be riskier than the current fractional-reserve banks.
- Nonetheless, banks do need to be regulated.
- The Financial Stability Board, based in Basel, Switzerland, has drawn up rules, called Basel III, that are designed to eliminate the risk that a major bank will fail.
- Mark Carney, Chairman of the Financial Stability Board and Governor of the Bank of England, wants all banks to adopt the Basel III principles, which increase the amount of a bank's own capital that must be held as a buffer against a fall in asset values.

Mark Carney, Chairman of the Financial Stability Board and Governor of the Bank of England.

"Our destination should be one where financial institutions and markets play critical—and complementary—roles to support long-term economic prosperity. This requires institutions that are adequately capitalized, with sufficient liquidity buffers to manage shocks."
Mark Carney, remarks at the Institute of International Finance, Washington, D.C., September 25, 2011.

Economics in Action
Canadian and U.S. Banks Compared

The figure compares the sources and uses of funds (sources are liabilities and uses are assets) of Canadian and U.S. banks in 2008 and in 2014.

The data are measured as percentages of deposits in 2008, so they enable us to compare the growth and changes in composition in both economies.

The overall growth in the size of banks is slightly larger in the United States, but growth in the two economies is similar.

The big differences are in the composition of the sources and uses of funds. The banks' own capital resources and banks' cash reserves have increased much more in the United States than in Canada.

Canadian bank borrowing has increased much more than that of U.S. banks.

(a) Sources of funds

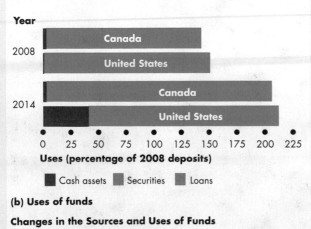

(b) Uses of funds

Changes in the Sources and Uses of Funds

Source of data: Statistics Canada.

Financial Innovation

In the pursuit of larger profits, depository institutions are constantly seeking ways to improve their products in a process called *financial innovation*.

During the late 1970s, a high inflation rate sent the interest rate on home-purchase loans to 15 percent a year. Traditional fixed interest rate mortgages became unprofitable, and variable interest rate mortgages were introduced.

During the 2000s, when interest rates were low and depository institutions were flush with funds, sub-prime mortgages were developed. To avoid the risk of carrying these mortgages, mortgage-backed securities were developed. The original lending institution sold these securities, lowered their own exposure to risk, and obtained funds to make more loans.

The development of low-cost computing and communication brought financial innovations such as credit cards and daily interest deposit accounts.

Financial innovation has brought large changes in the *composition* of money. Since 1989, and expressed as percentages of M2, chequable deposits have shrunk from 48 percent to 14 percent. Non-chequable deposits have increased from 22 percent to 32 percent, and fixed term deposits have expanded from 25 percent to 50 percent. Perhaps surprisingly, the use of currency has not fallen much, but it is down from 5 percent to 4 percent.

REVIEW QUIZ

1 What are depository institutions?
2 What are the functions of depository institutions?
3 How do depository institutions balance risk and return?
4 How do depository institutions create liquidity, pool risks, and lower the cost of borrowing?
5 How have depository institutions made innovations that have influenced the composition of money?

Work these questions in Study Plan 24.2 and get instant feedback. Do a Key Terms Quiz.   MyEconLab

You now know what money is. Your next task is to learn about the Bank of Canada and the ways in which it can influence the quantity of money.

The Bank of Canada

The Bank of Canada is Canada's **central bank**, a public authority that supervises other banks and financial institutions, financial markets, and the payments system, and conducts monetary policy.

The Bank of Canada is a bank. And like all banks, it accepts deposits, makes loans, and holds investment securities. But the Bank of Canada is special in three important ways. It is the:

- Banker to banks and government
- Lender of last resort
- Sole issuer of bank notes

Banker to Banks and Government

The Bank of Canada has a restricted list of customers. They are the chartered banks, credit unions and caisses populaires, and trust and mortgage loan companies that make up the banking system; the Government of Canada; and the central banks of other countries.

The Bank of Canada accepts deposits from these customers. The deposits of depository institutions are part of their reserves.

Lender of Last Resort

The Bank of Canada makes loans to banks. It is the **lender of last resort**, which means that it stands ready to make loans when the banking system as a whole is short of reserves. If some banks are short of reserves while others have surplus reserves, the overnight loan market moves the funds from one bank to another.

Sole Issuer of Bank Notes

The Bank of Canada is the only bank that is permitted to issue bank notes. You might think that such a monopoly is natural, but it isn't. In some banking systems—those of Ireland and Scotland are examples—private banks also issue bank notes. But in Canada and most other countries, the central bank has a monopoly on this activity.

The Bank of Canada's Balance Sheet

The Bank of Canada influences the economy by changing interest rates. You'll learn the details of the Bank's monetary policy strategy in Chapter 30 when you've studied all the tools needed to understand monetary policy. But to influence interest rates, the Bank must change the quantity of money

---

FIGURE 24.1   The Bank of Canada Home Page

The Bank of Canada is located in Ottawa. Its governor, pictured, is Stephen S. Poloz. Its Web site (Home Page shown here) is packed with useful information and data on the Bank's actions and the performance of the economy.

Source: Bank of Canada. Used by permission of Bank of Canada.

in the economy. This quantity depends on the size and composition of the Bank of Canada's balance sheet—its assets and liabilities. Lets look at the Bank of Canada's balance sheet, starting with its assets.

The Bank of Canada's Assets The Bank of Canada has two main assets:

1. Government securities
2. Loans to depository institutions

The Bank of Canada holds Government of Canada securities—Treasury bills—that it buys in the bills market. The Bank of Canada makes loans to depository institutions. When these institutions in aggregate are short of reserves, they can borrow from the Bank of Canada. In normal times this item is small, or zero as it was in 2014 (see Table 24.3).

The Bank of Canada's Liabilities The Bank of Canada has two liabilities:

1. Bank of Canada notes
2. Depository institution deposits

Bank of Canada notes are the dollar bills that we use in our daily transactions. Some of these notes are held by individuals and businesses; others are in the tills and vaults of banks and other depository institutions. Depository institution deposits at the Bank of Canada are part of the reserves of these institutions (see p. 567).

The Monetary Base The Bank of Canada's liabilities together with coins issued by the Royal Canadian Mint (coins are not liabilities of the Bank of Canada) make up the monetary base. That is, the **monetary base** is the sum of Bank of Canada notes, coins, and depository institution deposits at the Bank of Canada. The monetary base is so named because it acts like a base that supports the nation's money. Table 24.3 provides a snapshot of the sources and uses of the monetary base in April 2014.

The Bank of Canada's Policy Tools

The Bank of Canada has two main policy tools:

- Open market operation
- Bank rate

Open Market Operation To change the monetary base, the Bank of Canada conducts an **open market operation**, which is the purchase or sale of government securities by the Bank of Canada in the

TABLE 24.3   The Sources and Uses of the Monetary Base

Sources (billions of dollars)		Uses (billions of dollars)	
Government of Canada securities	64.7	Notes	64.5
Loans to depository institutions	0	Reserves of depository institutions	0.2
Monetary base	64.7	Monetary base	64.7

Source of data: Statistics Canada. The data are for June 2014.

loanable funds market. Let's see how an open market operation works and what it does.

An Open Market Purchase An open market operation changes bank reserves, which changes the monetary base. To see how, suppose the Bank of Canada buys $100 million of government securities from CIBC.

Economics in Action
A Tale of Two Central Banks

Figure 1 shows the balance sheet of the Bank of Canada. Almost all its assets (sources of monetary base) in part (a) are government securities. Almost all of its liabilities (uses of monetary base) in part (b) are notes and coins. The monetary base grew between 2007, the last year before a global financial crisis, and 2014 at an average annual rate of 4.7 percent.

Figure 2 shows the balance sheet of the U.S. Federal Reserve (the Fed). In 2007, before the financial crisis, this balance sheet looked like Canada's. Almost all its assets in part (a) were government securities and almost all of its liabilities in part (b) were notes and coins.

But through the financial crisis and still in place in mid-2014 and expected to be in place well into 2015, the Fed loaned billions of dollars to banks and other troubled institutions and created $3 trillion of monetary base—an increase of 380 percent or 25 percent per year on average. Most of this new monetary base is held by the banks as reserves.

When, and how quickly, the Fed unwinds this large increase in the monetary base and bank reserves will have a major influence on the U.S. and Canadian economies.

When the Bank of Canada makes this transaction, two things happen:

1. CIBC has $100 million less securities. The Bank of Canada has $100 million more securities.
2. The Bank of Canada pays for the securities by placing $100 million in CIBC's reserve deposit at the Bank of Canada.

Figure 24.2 shows the effects of these actions on the balance sheets of the Bank of Canada and CIBC. Ownership of the securities passes from CIBC to the Bank of Canada, so CIBC's assets decrease by $100 million and the Bank of Canada's assets increase by $100 million, as shown by the blue arrow running from CIBC to the Bank of Canada.

The Bank of Canada pays for the securities by placing $100 million in CIBC's reserve deposit at the Bank of Canada, as shown by the green arrow running from the Bank of Canada to CIBC.

The Bank of Canada's assets increase by $100 million and its and liabilities increase by $100 million. The CIBC's total assets are unchanged: It sold securities to increase its reserves.

FIGURE 24.2 The Bank of Canada Buys Securities in the Open Market

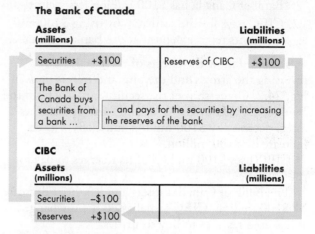

When the Bank of Canada buys securities in the open market, it creates bank reserves. The Bank of Canada's assets and liabilities increase, and CIBC exchanges securities for reserves.

_____ MyEconLab Animation ___

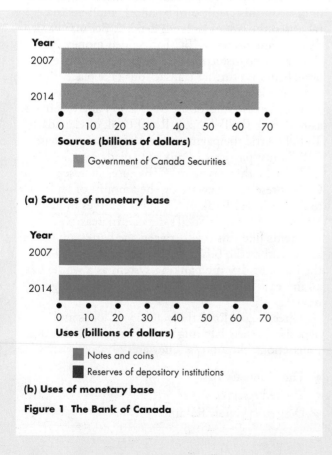

(a) Sources of monetary base

(b) Uses of monetary base

Figure 1 The Bank of Canada

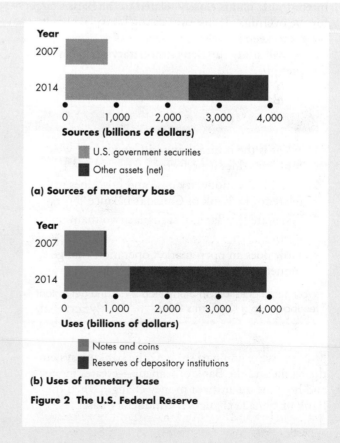

(a) Sources of monetary base

(b) Uses of monetary base

Figure 2 The U.S. Federal Reserve

An Open Market Sale If the Bank of Canada sells $100 million of government securities to CIBC:

1. CIBC has $100 million more securities and the Bank of Canada has $100 million less securities.
2. CIBC pays for the securities by using $100 million of its reserve deposit at the Bank of Canada.

You can follow the effects of these actions by reversing the arrows and the plus and minus signs in Fig. 24.2. Ownership of the securities passes from the Bank of Canada to CIBC, so the Bank of Canada's assets decrease by $100 million and CIBC's assets increase by $100 million.

CIBC uses $100 million of its reserves to pay for the securities.

The Bank of Canada's assets and liabilities decrease by $100 million. CIBC's total assets are unchanged: It has used reserves to buy securities.

Bank Rate The Bank of Canada makes short-term, typically one-day, loans to major depository institutions when the banking system is temporarily short of reserves, and the interest rate that the Bank charges on these loans is called **bank rate.**

Bank rate acts like an anchor for other short-term interest rates and is closely related to the Bank's target for the overnight loans rate among banks, which it targets to keep inflation in check.

You will study the Bank's monetary policy in Chapter 30.

◆ REVIEW QUIZ

1 What is the central bank in Canada and what functions does it perform?
2 What is the monetary base and how does it relate to the Bank of Canada's balance sheet?
3 What are the Bank of Canada's two main policy tools?
4 How does an open market operation change the monetary base?

Work these questions in Study Plan 24.3 and get instant feedback. Do a Key Terms Quiz.   MyEconLab

Next, we're going to see how the banking system—the banks and the Bank of Canada—creates money and how the quantity of money changes when the Bank of Canada changes the monetary base.

 ## How Banks Create Money

Banks create money. But this doesn't mean that they have smoke-filled back rooms in which counterfeiters are busily working. Remember, money is both currency and bank deposits. What banks create is deposits, and they do so by making loans.

Creating Deposits by Making Loans

The easiest way to see that banks create deposits is to think about what happens when Andy, who has a Visa card issued by CIBC, uses his card to buy a tank of gas from Shell. When Andy swipes his card, two financial transactions occur. First, Andy takes a loan from CIBC and obligates himself to repay the loan at a later date. Second, a message is transmitted to Shell's bank and the bank credits Shell's account with the amount of Andy's purchase (minus the bank's commission).

For now, let's assume that Shell, like Andy, banks at CIBC so that the two transactions we've just described both occur at the one bank.

You can see that these transactions have created a bank deposit and a loan. Andy has increased the size of his loan (his credit card balance), and Shell has increased the size of its bank deposit. Because bank deposits are money, CIBC has created money.

If, as we've just assumed, Andy and Shell use the same bank, no further transactions take place. But if two banks are involved, there is another transaction. To see this additional transaction and its effects, assume that Shell's bank is Royal Bank of Canada. To fully settle the payment for Andy's gas purchase, CIBC must pay Royal Bank of Canada.

To make this payment, CIBC uses its reserves. CIBC's reserves decrease by the amount of its loan to Andy; Royal Bank of Canada's reserves increase by the amount that Shell's deposit increases. Payments like this one between the banks are made at the end of the business day. So, at the end of the business day the banking system as a whole has an increase in loans and deposits but no change in reserves.

Three factors limit the quantity of loans and deposits that the banking system can create through transactions like Andy's. They are:

- The monetary base
- Desired reserves
- Desired currency holding

The Monetary Base You've seen that the *monetary base* is the sum of Bank of Canada notes and banks' deposits at the Bank of Canada. The size of the monetary base limits the total quantity of money that the banking system can create. The reason is that banks have a desired level of reserves, households and firms have a desired holding of currency, and both of these desired holdings of the monetary base depend on the quantity of deposits.

Desired Reserves A bank's *desired reserves* are the reserves that it *plans* to hold. They contrast with a bank's *required reserves*, which is the minimum quantity of reserves that a bank *must* hold.

The quantity of desired reserves depends on the level of deposits and is determined by the **desired reserve ratio**—the ratio of reserves to deposits that the banks *plan* to hold. The *desired* reserve ratio exceeds the *required* reserve ratio by an amount that the banks determine to be prudent on the basis of their daily business requirements and in the light of the current outlook in financial markets.

Desired Currency Holding The proportions of money held as currency and bank deposits—the ratio of currency to deposits—depend on how households and firms choose to make payments: whether they plan to use currency or debit cards and cheques.

Choices about how to make payments change slowly, so the ratio of desired currency to deposits also changes slowly, and at any given time this ratio is fixed. If bank deposits increase, desired currency holding also increases. For this reason, when banks make loans that increase deposits, some currency leaves the banks—the banking system leaks reserves. We call the leakage of bank reserves into currency the *currency drain*, and we call the ratio of currency to deposits the **currency drain ratio**.

We've sketched the way that a loan creates a deposit and described the three factors that limit the amount of loans and deposits that can be created. We're now going to examine the money creation process more closely and discover a money multiplier.

The Money Creation Process

The money creation process begins with an increase in the monetary base, which occurs if the Bank of Canada conducts an open market operation in which it buys securities from banks and other institutions.

The Bank of Canada pays for the securities it buys with newly created bank reserves.

When the Bank of Canada buys securities from a bank, the bank's reserves increase but its deposits don't change. So the bank has excess reserves. A bank's **excess reserves** are its actual reserves minus its desired reserves.

When a bank has excess reserves, it makes loans and creates deposits. When the entire banking system has excess reserves, total loans and deposits increase and the quantity of money increases.

One bank can make a loan and get rid of excess reserves. But the banking system as a whole can't get rid of excess reserves so easily. When the banks make loans and create deposits, the extra deposits lower excess reserves for two reasons. First, the increase in deposits increases desired reserves. Second, a currency drain decreases total reserves. But excess reserves don't completely disappear. So the banks lend some more and the process repeats.

As the process of making loans and increasing deposits repeats, desired reserves increase, total reserves decrease through the currency drain, and eventually enough new deposits have been created to use all the new monetary base.

Figure 24.3 summarizes one round in the process we've just described. The sequence has the following eight steps:

1. Banks have excess reserves.
2. Banks lend excess reserves.
3. The quantity of money increases.
4. New money is used to make payments.
5. Some of the new money remains on deposit.
6. Some of the new money is a *currency drain*.
7. Desired reserves increase because deposits have increased.
8. Excess reserves decrease.

If the Bank of Canada *sells* securities in an open market operation, then banks have negative excess reserves—they are short of reserves. When the banks are short of reserves, loans and deposits decrease and the process we've described above works in a downward direction until desired reserves plus desired currency holding has decreased by an amount equal to the decrease in monetary base.

A money multiplier determines the change in the quantity of money that results from a change in the monetary base.

FIGURE 24.3   How the Banking System Creates Money by Making Loans

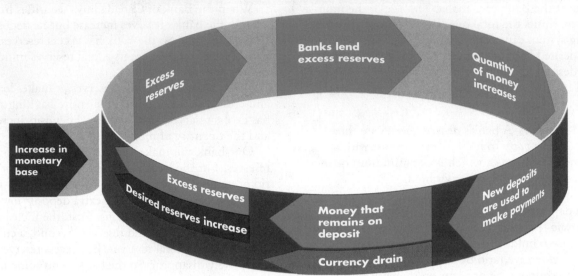

The Bank of Canada increases the monetary base, which increases bank reserves and creates excess reserves. Banks lend the excess reserves, which creates new deposits. The quantity of money increases. New deposits are used to make payments. Some of the new money remains on deposit at banks and some leaves the banks in a currency drain. The increase in bank deposits increases banks' desired reserves. But the banks still have excess reserves, though less than before. The process repeats until excess reserves have been eliminated.

MyEconLab Animation

Economics in Action
The Variable Money Multipliers

We can measure the money multiplier, other things remaining the same, as the ratio of the quantity of money to the monetary base. Because there are two definitions of money, M1 and M2, there are two money multipliers. These money multipliers, it turns out, are not constant.

In 1990, the M1 multiplier—the ratio of M1 to the monetary base—was about 5.5; and the M2 multiplier—the ratio of M2 to the monetary base—was about 16. Through the 1990s and 2000s, the currency drain ratio gradually decreased and so did the desired reserve ratio of the banks. Because these two uses of monetary base decreased relative to deposits, the money multipliers increased.

By 2014, the M1 multiplier was 10.4, almost double its 1990 value, and the M2 multiplier was 19.5.

Because the money multipliers have increased over time, the quantity of monetary base has grown more slowly than the quantities of M1 and M2.

The Money Multiplier

The **money multiplier** is the ratio of the change in the quantity of money to the change in monetary base. For example, if a $1 million increase in the monetary base increases the quantity of money by $2.5 million, then the money multiplier is 2.5.

The smaller the banks' desired reserve ratio and the smaller the currency drain ratio, the larger is the money multiplier. (See the Mathematical Note on pp. 586–587 for details on the money multiplier.)

REVIEW QUIZ

1 How do banks create money?
2 What limits the quantity of money that the banking system can create?
3 A bank manager tells you that she doesn't create money. She just lends the money that people deposit. Explain why she's wrong.

Work these questions in Study Plan 24.4 and get instant feedback. Do a Key Terms Quiz.   MyEconLab

ECONOMICS IN THE NEWS

A Massive Open Market Operation

QE2 Is No Silver Bullet

The U.S. Federal Reserve's $600 billion bond-buying program initiated last year, known as the second round of quantitative easing or QE2, will end on schedule this month with a mixed legacy, having proved to be neither the economy's needed elixir nor the scourge that critics describe.

Source: *The Wall Street Journal*, June 22, 2011

THE QUESTIONS

- What is *quantitative easing*? What transactions did the U.S. Fed undertake?
- How did QE2 affect the quantity of reserves, loans, and deposits of the U.S. banks?
- Why was QE2 neither "elixir" nor "scourge"?

THE ANSWERS

- *Quantitative easing*, or QE, is an open market purchase of securities by the Fed. QE2 was the purchase of $600 billion of long-term securities from businesses, pension funds, and other holders.
- The purchase was an open market operation similar to that described in Fig. 24.2 on p. 573 but with one more step because the Fed buys the securities from holders who are not banks.
- The figure illustrates the QE2 open market operation and the extra step in the chain of transactions.
- When the Fed buys securities, its assets increase. Its liabilities also increase because it creates monetary base to pay for the securities.
- For the businesses that sell bonds, their assets change: Securities decrease and bank deposits increase.
- For the U.S. banks, deposit liabilities increase and reserves, an asset, also increase.
- You saw on pp. 572–573 that the U.S banks are flush with reserves. They held on to the increase in reserves created by QE2. There was no multiplier effect on loans and deposits.
- QE2 would have been an "elixir" if it had resulted in a boost to bank lending, business investment, and economic expansion, and a "scourge" if it had caused inflation.

The New York Fed building where U.S. open market operations are conducted.

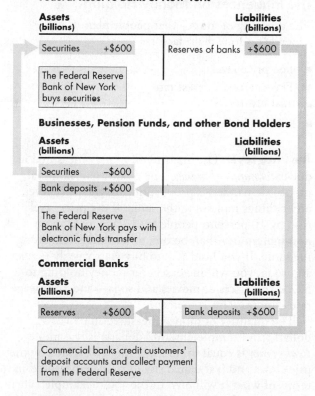

The QE2 Transactions

- QE2 had neither of these effects because the banks held on to the newly created reserves and neither loans nor the quantity of money increased.

The Money Market

There is no limit to the amount of money we would like to *receive* in payment for our labour or as interest on our savings. But there *is* a limit to how big an inventory of money we would like to *hold* and neither spend nor use to buy assets that generate an income. The *quantity of money demanded* is the inventory of money that people plan to hold on any given day. It is the quantity of money in our wallets and in our deposit accounts at banks. The quantity of money held must equal the quantity supplied, and the forces that bring about this equality in the money market have powerful effects on the economy, as you will see in the rest of this chapter.

But first, we need to explain what determines the amount of money that people plan to hold.

The Influences on Money Holding

The quantity of money that people plan to hold depends on four main factors:

- The price level
- The *nominal* interest rate
- Real GDP
- Financial innovation

The Price Level The quantity of money measured in dollars is *nominal money*. The quantity of nominal money demanded is proportional to the price level, other things remaining the same. If the price level rises by 10 percent, people hold 10 percent more nominal money than before, other things remaining the same. If you hold $20 to buy your weekly movies and soda, you will increase your money holding to $22 if the prices of movies and soda—and your wage rate—increase by 10 percent.

The quantity of money measured in constant dollars (for example, in 2007 dollars) is real money. *Real money* is equal to nominal money divided by the price level and is the quantity of money measured in terms of what it will buy. In the above example, when the price level rises by 10 percent and you increase your money holding by 10 percent, your *real* money holding is constant. Your $22 at the new price level buys the same quantity of goods and is the same quantity of *real money* as your $20 at the original price level. The quantity of real money demanded is independent of the price level.

The *Nominal* Interest Rate A fundamental principle of economics is that as the opportunity cost of something increases, people try to find substitutes for it. Money is no exception. The higher the opportunity cost of holding money, other things remaining the same, the smaller is the quantity of real money demanded. The nominal interest rate on other assets minus the nominal interest rate on money is the opportunity cost of holding money.

The interest rate that you earn on currency and chequable deposits is zero. So the opportunity cost of holding these items is the nominal interest rate on other assets such as a savings bond or Treasury bill. By holding money instead, you forgo the interest that you otherwise would have received.

Money loses value because of inflation, so why isn't the inflation rate part of the cost of holding money? It is. Other things remaining the same, the higher the expected inflation rate, the higher is the nominal interest rate.

Real GDP The quantity of money that households and firms plan to hold depends on the amount they are spending. The quantity of money demanded in the economy as a whole depends on aggregate expenditure—real GDP.

Again, suppose that you hold an average of $20 to finance your weekly purchases of movies and soda. Now imagine that the prices of these goods and of all other goods remain constant but that your income increases. As a consequence, you now buy more goods and services and you also keep a larger amount of money on hand to finance your higher volume of expenditure.

Financial Innovation Technological change and the arrival of new financial products influence the quantity of money held. Financial innovations include:

1. Daily interest chequable deposits
2. Automatic transfers between chequable and saving deposits
3. Automatic teller machines
4. Credit cards and debit cards
5. Internet banking and bill paying

These innovations have occurred because of the development of computing power that has lowered the cost of calculations and record keeping.

We summarize the effects of the influences on money holding by using a demand for money curve.

The Demand for Money

The **demand for money** is the relationship between the quantity of real money demanded and the nominal interest rate when all other influences on the amount of money that people wish to hold remain the same.

Figure 24.4 shows a demand for money curve, *MD*. When the interest rate rises, other things remaining the same, the opportunity cost of holding money rises and the quantity of real money demanded decreases—there is a movement up along the demand for money curve. Similarly, when the interest rate falls, the opportunity cost of holding money falls, and the quantity of real money demanded increases—there is a movement down along the demand for money curve.

When any influence on money holding other than the interest rate changes, there is a change in the demand for money and the demand for money curve shifts. Let's study these shifts.

Shifts in the Demand for Money Curve

A change in real GDP or financial innovation changes the demand for money and shifts the demand for money curve.

Figure 24.5 illustrates the change in the demand for money. A decrease in real GDP decreases the demand for money and shifts the demand for money curve leftward from MD_0 to MD_1. An increase in real GDP has the opposite effect: It increases the demand for money and shifts the demand for money curve rightward from MD_0 to MD_2.

The influence of financial innovation on the demand for money curve is more complicated. It decreases the demand for currency and might increase the demand for some types of deposits and decrease the demand for others. But generally, financial innovation decreases the demand for money.

Changes in real GDP and financial innovation have brought large shifts in the demand for money in Canada.

FIGURE 24.4   The Demand for Money

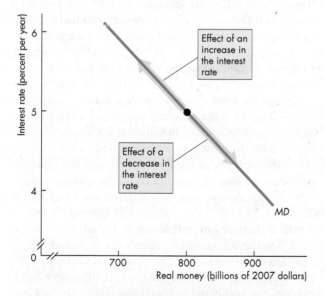

The demand for money curve, *MD*, shows the relationship between the quantity of real money that people plan to hold and the nominal interest rate, other things remaining the same. The interest rate is the opportunity cost of holding money. A change in the interest rate brings a movement along the demand for money curve.

FIGURE 24.5   Changes in the Demand for Money

A decrease in real GDP decreases the demand for money. The demand for money curve shifts leftward from MD_0 to MD_1. An increase in real GDP increases the demand for money. The demand for money curve shifts rightward from MD_0 to MD_2. Financial innovation generally decreases the demand for money.

MyEconLab Animation —   — MyEconLab Animation —

Money Market Equilibrium

You now know what determines the demand for money, and you've seen how the banking system creates money. Let's now see how the money market reaches an equilibrium.

Money market equilibrium occurs when the quantity of money demanded equals the quantity of money supplied. The adjustments that occur to bring money market equilibrium are fundamentally different in the short run and the long run.

Short-Run Equilibrium The quantity of money supplied is determined by the actions of the banks and the Bank of Canada. As the Bank of Canada adjusts the quantity of money, the interest rate changes.

In Fig. 24.6, the Bank of Canada uses open market operations to make the quantity of real money supplied equal to $800 billion and the supply of money curve is *MS*. With demand for money curve *MD*, the equilibrium interest rate is 5 percent a year.

If the interest rate were 4 percent a year, people would want to hold more money than is available.

FIGURE 24.6 Money Market Equilibrium

Money market equilibrium occurs when the quantity of money demanded equals the quantity supplied. In the short run, real GDP determines the demand for money curve, *MD*, and the Bank of Canada determines the quantity of real money supplied and the supply of money curve, *MS*. The interest rate adjusts to achieve equilibrium, here 5 percent a year.

_____ MyEconLab Animation and Draw Graph _____

They would sell bonds, bid down their price, and the interest rate would rise. If the interest rate were 6 percent a year, people would want to hold less money than is available. They would buy bonds, bid up their price, and the interest rate would fall.

The Short-Run Effect of a Change in the Quantity of Money Starting from a short-run equilibrium, if the Bank of Canada increases the quantity of money, people find themselves holding more money than the quantity demanded. With a surplus of money holding, people enter the loanable funds market and buy bonds. The increase in demand for bonds raises the price of a bond and lowers the interest rate (refresh your memory by looking at Chapter 23, p. 546).

If the Bank of Canada decreases the quantity of money, people find themselves holding less money than the quantity demanded. They now enter the loanable funds market to sell bonds. The decrease in the demand for bonds lowers their price and raises the interest rate.

Figure 24.7 illustrates the effects of the changes in the quantity of money that we've just described. When the supply of money curve shifts rightward from MS_0 to MS_1, the interest rate falls to 4 percent a year; when the supply of money curve shifts leftward to MS_2, the interest rate rises to 6 percent a year.

Long-Run Equilibrium You've just seen how the nominal interest rate is determined in the money market at the level that makes the quantity of money demanded equal the quantity supplied by the Bank of Canada. You learned in Chapter 23 (on p. 550) that the real interest rate is determined in the loanable funds market at the level that makes the quantity of loanable funds demanded equal the quantity of loanable funds supplied. You also learned in Chapter 23 (on p. 548) that the real interest rate equals the nominal interest rate minus the inflation rate.

When the inflation rate equals the expected (or forecasted) inflation rate and when real GDP equals potential GDP, the money market, the loanable funds market, the goods market, and the labour market are in long-run equilibrium—the economy is in long-run equilibrium.

An increase in the quantity of money starting and ending in long-run equilibrium returns all the real variables to their original levels. But something does change: the price level. The price level rises by the same percentage as the rise in the quantity of money. Why does this outcome occur in the long run?

FIGURE 24.7   A Change in the Quantity of Money

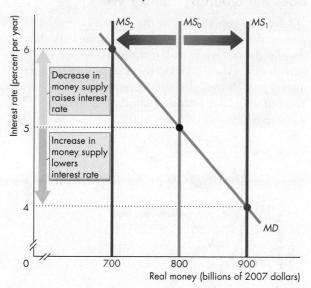

An increase in the quantity of money shifts the supply of money curve from MS_0 to MS_1 and the interest rate falls. A decrease in the quantity of money shifts the supply of money curve from MS_0 to MS_2 and the interest rate rises.

———— MyEconLab Animation and Draw Graph ————

The reason is that real GDP and employment are determined by the demand for labour, the supply of labour, and the production function—the real forces described in Chapter 22 (pp. 520–522); and the real interest rate is determined by the demand for and supply of (real) loanable funds—the real forces described in Chapter 23 (pp. 547–551). The only variable that is free to respond to a change in the supply of money in the long run is the price level. The price level adjusts to make the quantity of real money supplied equal to the quantity demanded.

So when the nominal quantity of money changes, in the long run the price level changes by a percentage equal to the percentage change in the quantity of nominal money. In the long run, the change in the price level is proportional to the change in the quantity of money.

The Transition from the Short Run to the Long Run

How does the economy move from the first short-run response to an increase in the quantity of money to the long-run response?

The adjustment process is lengthy and complex. Here, we'll only provide a sketch of the process. A more thorough account must wait until you've studied Chapter 26.

We start out in long-run equilibrium and the Bank of Canada increases the quantity of money by 10 percent. Here are the steps in what happens next.

First, the nominal interest rate falls (just like you saw on p. 580 and in Fig. 24.6). The real interest rate falls too, as people try to get rid of their excess money holdings and buy bonds.

With a lower real interest rate, people want to borrow and spend more. Firms want to borrow to invest and households want to borrow to invest in bigger homes or to buy more consumer goods.

The increase in the demand for goods cannot be met by an increase in supply because the economy is already at full employment. So there is a general shortage of all kinds of goods and services.

The shortage of goods and services forces the price level to rise.

As the price level rises, the real quantity of money decreases. The decrease in the quantity of real money raises the nominal interest rate and the real interest rate. As the interest rate rises, spending plans are cut back, and eventually the original full-employment equilibrium is restored. At the new long-run equilibrium, the price level has risen by 10 percent and nothing real has changed.

◆ REVIEW QUIZ

1   What are the main influences on the quantity of real money that people and businesses plan to hold?

2   Show the effects of a change in the nominal interest rate and a change in real GDP using the demand for money curve.

3   How is money market equilibrium determined in the short run?

4   How does a change in the supply of money change the interest rate in the short run?

5   How does a change in the supply of money change the interest rate in the long run?

Work these questions in Study Plan 24.5 and get instant feedback. Do a Key Terms Quiz.   MyEconLab

Let's explore the long-run link between money and the price level a bit further.

The Quantity Theory of Money

In the long run, the price level adjusts to make the quantity of real money demanded equal the quantity supplied. A special theory of the price level and inflation—the quantity theory of money—explains this long-run adjustment of the price level.

The **quantity theory of money** is the proposition that, in the long run, an increase in the quantity of money brings an equal percentage increase in the price level. To explain the quantity theory of money, we first need to define *the velocity of circulation*.

The **velocity of circulation** is the average number of times a dollar of money is used annually to buy the goods and services that make up GDP. But GDP equals the price level (P) multiplied by *real* GDP (Y). That is,

$$GDP = PY.$$

Call the quantity of money M. The velocity of circulation, V, is determined by the equation:

$$V = PY/M.$$

For example, if GDP is $1,000 billion ($PY = $1,000 billion) and the quantity of money is $250 billion, then the velocity of circulation is 4.

From the definition of the velocity of circulation, the *equation of exchange* tells us how M, V, P, and Y are connected. This equation is:

$$MV = PY.$$

Given the definition of the velocity of circulation, the equation of exchange is always true—it is true by definition. It becomes the quantity theory of money if the quantity of money does not influence the velocity of circulation or real GDP. In this case, the equation of exchange tells us that in the long run, the price level is determined by the quantity of money. That is,

$$P = M(V/Y),$$

where (V/Y) is independent of M. So a change in M brings a proportional change in P.

We can also express the equation of exchange in growth rates,[1] in which form it states that

$$\frac{\text{Money}}{\text{growth rate}} + \frac{\text{Rate of}}{\text{velocity}} = \frac{\text{Inflation}}{\text{rate}} + \frac{\text{Real GDP}}{\text{growth rate}}$$
$$\text{change}$$

Economics in Action

Does the Quantity Theory Work?

On average, as predicted by the quantity theory of money, the inflation rate fluctuates in line with fluctuations in the money growth rate minus the real GDP growth rate. Figure 1 shows the relationship between money growth (M2 definition) and inflation in Canada. You can see a clear relationship between the two variables.

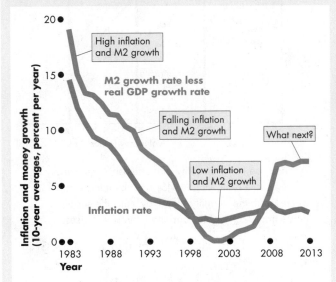

Figure 1 Canadian Money Growth and Inflation

Sources of data: Statistics Canada, CANSIM Tables 176-0020 and 380-0002.

Solving this equation for the inflation rate gives:

$$\frac{\text{Inflation}}{\text{rate}} = \frac{\text{Money}}{\text{growth rate}} + \frac{\text{Rate of}}{\text{velocity}} - \frac{\text{Real GDP}}{\text{growth rate}}$$
$$\text{change}$$

In the long run, the rate of velocity change is not influenced by the money growth rate. More strongly, in the long run, the rate of velocity change

---

[1]To obtain this equation, begin with

$$MV = PY.$$

Then changes in these variables are related by the equation

$$V\Delta M + M\Delta V = Y\Delta P + P\Delta Y.$$

Divide this equation by the equation of exchange to obtain

$$\Delta M/M + \Delta V/V = \Delta P/P + \Delta Y/Y.$$

The term $\Delta M/M$ is the money growth rate, $\Delta V/V$ is the rate of velocity change, $\Delta P/P$ is the inflation rate, and $\Delta Y/Y$ is the real GDP growth rate.

International data also support the quantity theory. Figure 2 shows a scatter diagram of the inflation rate and the money growth rate in 134 countries, and Fig. 3 shows the inflation rate and money growth rate in countries with inflation rates below 20 percent a year. You can see a general tendency for money growth and inflation to be correlated, but the quantity theory (the red line) does not predict inflation precisely.

The correlation between money growth and inflation isn't perfect, and the correlation does not tell us that money growth *causes* inflation. Money growth might cause inflation; inflation might cause money growth; or some third variable might cause both inflation and money growth. Other evidence does confirm, though, that causation runs from money growth to inflation.

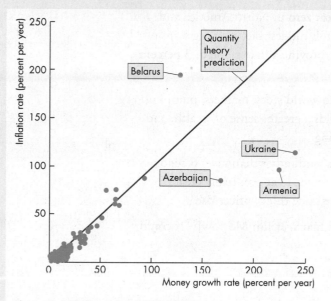

Figure 2 134 Countries: 1990–2005

Figure 3 Lower-Inflation Countries: 1990–2005

Sources of data: International Financial Statistics Yearbook, 2008, and International Monetary Fund, *World Economic Outlook,* October 2008.

is approximately zero. With this assumption, the inflation rate in the long run is determined as

$$\frac{\text{Inflation}}{\text{rate}} = \frac{\text{Money}}{\text{growth rate}} - \frac{\text{Real GDP}}{\text{growth rate}}$$

In the long run, fluctuations in the money growth rate minus the real GDP growth rate bring equal fluctuations in the inflation rate.

Also, in the long run, with the economy at full employment, real GDP equals potential GDP, so the real GDP growth rate equals the potential GDP growth rate. This growth rate might be influenced by inflation, but the influence is most likely small and the quantity theory assumes that it is zero. So the real GDP growth rate is given and doesn't change when the money growth rate changes—inflation is correlated with money growth.

1 What is the quantity theory of money?
2 How is the velocity of circulation calculated?
3 What is the equation of exchange?
4 Does the quantity theory correctly predict the effects of money growth on inflation?

Work these questions in Study Plan 24.6 and get instant feedback. Do a Key Terms Quiz.   MyEconLab

◆ You now know what money is, how the banks create it, and why the quantity of money is important. *Economics in the News* on pp. 584–585 looks at how low interest rates have increased the quantity of money but not brought inflation.

Money and the Interest Rate

Why the Low-Interest-Rate Trap Is Worrying

Toronto Star
August 4, 2014

Adam Mayers, Personal Finance Editor

… After 68 months of central bank interest rates at or near zero in North America and Europe, increases seem to be a year or two away. Inflation is modest but showing signs of stirring. Ontario is Canada's inflation hotspot, where the provincial rate stood at 3 percent in June. …

The low cost of borrowing has sent a flood of money into world stock markets, pumping up prices, helping pension plans recover, giving households a greater sense of wealth, and offering savers a way to keep their nest eggs from shrinking. …

Cheap-money policies encourage people to borrow and spend rather than save. It sends them into the stock market because there's nowhere else to go. That eventually creates inflation and bubbles. When too much money chases the same thing, prices rise.

"Inflation is my single biggest worry," [said Fidelity fund manager Jim Morrow]. "It could cause a real correction."…

As Morrow noted, there's no sign of resource-price inflation and no push for large wage hikes in North America and Europe. Economic growth is low and factory demand slack.

"I look for inflation everywhere," he said, adding that rates will rise, though the current environment could continue for a while to come. …

Our central banker, Stephen Poloz, says the bank rate will remain at 1 percent, where it's been for four years, and things may not change for two more years. If so, housing prices will continue to rise. …

Written by Adam Mayers. Copyright © 2014. Reprinted with permission of Torstar Syndication Services.

MyEconLab More Economics in the News

ESSENCE OF THE STORY

- Interest rates have been near zero in North America and Europe for 68 months and seem set to remain low for another year or two.

- The Ontario inflation rate is 3 percent a year, but resource prices and wages are not rising rapidly.

- Fidelity fund manager Jim Morrow says he looks for inflation everywhere.

- Share prices and house prices are rising rapidly.

ECONOMIC ANALYSIS

- A global financial crisis started quietly in the summer of 2007, when the interest rate on Government of Canada 3-month Treasury bills was a bit more than 4 percent per year, and the quantity of M2 money was a bit below 50 percent of GDP.

- To keep the economy well supplied with cheap money, the Bank of Canada cut the interest rate to almost zero in 2009 and then raised it slightly to 1 percent per year, where it remained in mid-2014.

- With the interest rate falling and then remaining low, the quantity of M2 money increased and by mid-2014 it stood at 65 percent of GDP.

- Figure 1 shows the paths taken by the 3-month Treasury bill rate and the quantity of M2 as a percentage of GDP.

- You've learned in this chapter that the quantity of money demanded depends inversely on the interest rate. So it is to be expected that a falling interest rate would bring an increasing quantity of money.

- Figure 2 shows this inverse relationship in the period 2007 to 2014. The demand for money is influenced by GDP, so the graph removes the influence of GDP by measuring the quantity of M2 as a percentage of GDP.

- The curve MD_0 shows the demand for money before 2010, and the curve MD_1 shows the demand for money in 2012–2014. Demand possibly increased because of financial risk.

- Figure 3 focuses on fund manager Jim Morrow's concern and shows what has been happening to money growth and inflation.

- In the long run, when the velocity of circulation (see p. 582) is constant, the inflation rate should equal the growth rate of M2 money minus the growth rate of real GDP shown in the graph.

- Looking at Fig. 3, there is no tendency for the inflation rate to be aligned with the money growth rate.

- The burst of money growth in 2009 occurred because of the fall in the interest rate and the increase in the quantity of M2 demanded. During this time, the velocity of circulation of M2 decreased.

- Since 2012, the growth rate of M2 minus the growth rate of real GDP has exceeded the inflation rate, and it is this fact that makes Jim Morrow's fear a reasonable one.

- The lag between money growth and inflation is long (and variable), and today's rising share and house prices noted in the news article could portend future inflation.

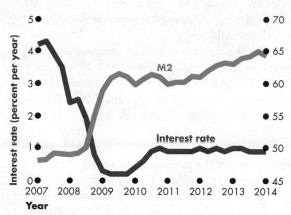

Figure 1 Money Growth and the Interest Rate

Figure 2 The Demand for M2

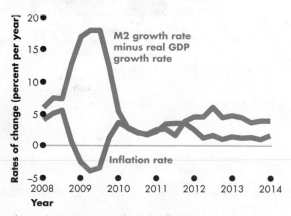

Figure 3 Money Growth and Inflation

MATHEMATICAL NOTE

The Money Multiplier

This note explains the basic math of the money multiplier and shows how the value of the multiplier depends on the banks' desired reserve ratio and the currency drain ratio.

To make the process of money creation concrete, we work through an example for a banking system in which each bank has a desired reserve ratio of 10 percent of deposits and the currency drain ratio is 50 percent of deposits. (Although these ratios are larger than the ones in the Canadian economy, they make the process end more quickly and enable you to see more clearly the principles at work.)

The figure keeps track of the numbers. Before the process begins, all the banks have no excess reserves. Then the monetary base increases by $100,000 and one bank has excess reserves of this amount.

The bank lends the $100,000 of excess reserves. When this loan is made, new money increases by $100,000.

Some of the new money will be held as currency and some as deposits. With a currency drain ratio of

50 percent of deposits, one-third of the new money will be held as currency and two-thirds will be held as deposits. That is, $33,333 drains out of the banks as currency and $66,667 remains in the banks as deposits. The increase in the quantity of money of $100,000 equals the increase in deposits plus the increase in currency holdings.

The increased bank deposits of $66,667 generate an increase in desired reserves of 10 percent of that amount, which is $6,667. Actual reserves have increased by the same amount as the increase in deposits: $66,667. So the banks now have excess reserves of $60,000.

The process we've just described repeats but begins with excess reserves of $60,000. The figure shows the next two rounds. At the end of the process, the quantity of money has increased by a multiple of the increase in the monetary base. In this case, the increase is $250,000, which is 2.5 times the increase in the monetary base.

The sequence in the figure shows the first stages of the process that finally reaches the total shown in the final row of the "money" column.

To calculate what happens at the later stages in the process and the final increase in the quantity of

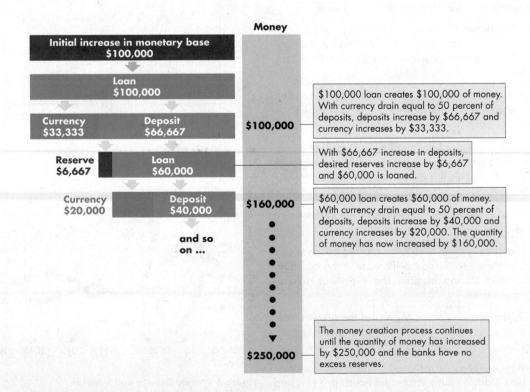

Figure 1 The Money Creation Process

money, look closely at the numbers in the figure. The initial increase in reserves is $100,000 (call it A). At each stage, the loan is 60 percent (0.6) of the previous loan and the quantity of money increases by 0.6 of the previous increase. Call that proportion L ($L = 0.6$). We can write down the complete sequence for the increase in the quantity of money as

$$A + AL + AL^2 + AL^3 + AL^4 + AL^5 + \dots.$$

Remember, L is a fraction, so at each stage in this sequence, the amount of new loans and new money gets smaller. The total value of loans made and money created at the end of the process is the sum of the sequence,[2] which is

$$A/(1 - L).$$

If we use the numbers from the example, the total increase in the quantity of money is

$100,000 + 60,000 + 36,000 + \dots$

$\qquad = \$100,000\,(1 + 0.6 + 0.36 + \dots)$

$\qquad = \$100,000\,(1 + 0.6 + 0.6^2 + \dots)$

$\qquad = \$100,000 \times 1/(1 - 0.6)$

$\qquad = \$100,000 \times 1/(0.4)$

$\qquad = \$100,000 \times 2.5$

$\qquad = \$250,000.$

The magnitude of the money multiplier depends on the desired reserve ratio and the currency drain ratio. Let's explore this relationship.

The money multiplier is the ratio of money to the monetary base. Call the money multiplier mm, the quantity of money M, and the monetary base MB.

---

[2] The sequence of values is called a convergent geometric series. To find the sum of a series such as this, begin by calling the sum S. Then write the sum as

$$S = A + AL + AL^2 + AL^3 + AL^4 + AL^5 + \dots$$

Multiply by L to get

$$LS = AL + AL^2 + AL^3 + AL^4 + AL^5 + \dots$$

and then subtract the second equation from the first to get

$$S(1 - L) = A$$

or

$$S = A/(1 - L).$$

Then

$$mm = M/MB.$$

Next recall that money, M, is the sum of deposits and currency. Call deposits D and currency C. Then

$$M = D + C.$$

The monetary base, MB, is the sum of banks' reserves and currency. Call banks' reserves R. Then

$$MB = R + C.$$

Use the equations for M and MB in the mm equation to give

$$mm = M/MB = (D + C)/(R + C).$$

Now divide all the variables on the right side of the equation by D to give

$$mm = M/MB = (1 + C/D)/(R/D) + C/D).$$

In this equation, C/D is the currency drain ratio and R/D is the banks' reserve ratio. If we use the values in the example on the previous page, C/D is 0.5 and R/D is 0.1, and

$$mm = (1 + 0.5)/(0.1 + 0.5).$$
$$= 1.5/0.6 = 2.5.$$

The Canadian Money Multiplier

The money multiplier in Canada can be found by using the formula above along with the values of C/D and R/D in the Canadian economy. Because we have two definitions of money, M1 and M2, we have two money multipliers. Call the M1 deposits $D1$ and call the M2 deposits $D2$.

The numbers for M1 in 2014 are $C/D1 = 0.1061$ and $R/D1 = 0.0003$. So

M1 multiplier $= (1 + 0.1061)/(0.0003 + 0.1061)$
$$= 10.4.$$

The numbers for M2 in 2014 are $C/D2 = 0.0539$ and $R/D2 = 0.0002$, so

M2 multiplier $= (1 + 0.0539)/(0.0002 + 0.0539)$
$$= 19.5.$$

SUMMARY

Key Points

What Is Money? (pp. 564–566)

- Money is the means of payment. It functions as a medium of exchange, a unit of account, and a store of value.
- Today, money consists of currency and deposits.

Working Problems 1 and 2 will give you a better understanding of what money is.

Depository Institutions (pp. 567–570)

- Chartered banks, credit unions and caisses populaires, and trust and mortgage loan companies are depository institutions whose deposits are money.
- Depository institutions provide four main economic services: They create liquidity, minimize the cost of obtaining funds, minimize the cost of monitoring borrowers, and pool risks.

Working Problem 3 will give you a better understanding of depository institutions.

The Bank of Canada (pp. 571–574)

- The Bank of Canada is the central bank of Canada.
- The Bank of Canada has two main policy tools: open market operations and bank rate.
- When the Bank buys securities in an open market operation, the monetary base increases; when the Bank sells securities, the monetary base decreases.

Working Problem 4 will give you a better understanding of the Bank of Canada.

How Banks Create Money (pp. 574–577)

- Banks create money by making loans.
- The total quantity of money that can be created depends on the monetary base, the desired reserve ratio, and the currency drain ratio.

Working Problems 5 and 6 will give you a better understanding of how banks create money.

The Money Market (pp. 578–581)

- The quantity of money demanded is the amount of money that people plan to hold.
- The quantity of real money equals the quantity of nominal money divided by the price level.
- The quantity of real money demanded depends on the nominal interest rate, real GDP, and financial innovation.
- The nominal interest rate makes the quantity of money demanded equal the quantity supplied.
- When the Bank of Canada increases the quantity of money, the nominal interest rate falls (the short-run effect).
- In the long run, when the Bank of Canada increases the quantity of money, the price level rises and the nominal interest rate returns to its initial level.

Working Problem 7 will give you a better understanding of the money market.

The Quantity Theory of Money (pp. 582–583)

- The quantity theory of money is the proposition that money growth and inflation move up and down together in the long run.

Working Problem 8 will give you a better understanding of the quantity theory of money.

Key Terms

WORKED PROBLEM

MyEconLab   You can work this problem in Chapter 24 Study Plan.

In June 2014, individuals and businesses held:

- $50 billion in currency
- $1,000 billion in chequable deposits
- $5,000 billion in non-chequable deposits
- $750 billion in fixed term deposits and other deposits.

In June 2014, banks held:

- $450 billion in notes and coins
- $100 billion in reserves at the central bank
- $800 billion in loans to households and businesses

Questions

1. Calculate the M1 and M2 measures of money.
2. Calculate the monetary base.
3. What are the currency drain ratio and the banks' reserve ratio?
4. What are the M1 and M2 money multipliers?
5. How is the money multiplier influenced by the banks' reserve ratio?

Solutions

1. M1 is the quantity of money held by individuals and businesses in the form of chequable deposits and currency.

   M1 = $1,000 billion + $50 billion = $1,050 billion.

   M2 is M1 plus non-chequable deposits held by individuals and businesses, fixed term deposits, and other deposits.

   M2 = $1,050 billion + $5,000 billion + $750 billion = $6,800 billion.

Key Point: M1 is a narrow measure of money that consists of chequable deposits and currency held by individuals and businesses.

   M2 is a broad measure of money that consists of M1 plus non-chequable deposits, term deposits, and other deposits of individuals and businesses.

2. Monetary base is the sum of bank reserves held at the central bank and notes and coins outside the central bank.

   Notes and coins outside the central bank are the notes and coins held by individuals, businesses, and banks.

   Monetary base = $100 billion + $450 billion + $50 billion = $600 billion

Key Point: Monetary base equals the central bank's liabilities—bank reserves held at the central bank and notes issued by the central bank—plus coins outside the central bank.

3. Currency drain ratio = (Currency held by individuals and businesses ÷ Chequable deposits) × 100.

   Currency drain ratio = ($50 billion ÷ $1,000 billion) × 100 = 5 percent.

   Banks' reserve ratio = (Bank reserves ÷ Chequable deposits) × 100.

   Bank reserves = Notes and coins held by banks + reserves at the central bank.

   Bank reserves = $450 billion + $100 billion = $550 billion.

   The banks' reserve ratio = ($550 billion ÷ $1,000 billion) × 100 = 55 percent.

Key Point: Currency drain ratio is the ratio of currency to chequable deposits held by individuals and businesses, expressed as a percentage. The banks' reserve ratio is the ratio of bank reserves to bank deposits, expressed as a percentage.

4. M1 Money multiplier = M1 ÷ Monetary base = $1,050 billion ÷ $600 billion = 1.75.

   M2 Money multiplier = M2 ÷ Monetary base = $6,800 billion ÷ $600 billion = 11.33.

Key Point: The money multiplier is the number by which the monetary base is multiplied to equal the quantity of money.

5. Money M is the sum of deposits D and currency C held by individuals and businesses.

   Monetary base MB is the sum of reserves R and currency C.

   Money multiplier = $(D + C) \div (R + C)$

   An increase in the banks' reserves R with no change in D increases the banks' reserves ratio and decreases the money multiplier.

Key Point: The money multiplier equals $(1 + C/D) \div (R/D + C/D)$, where C/D is the currency drain ratio and R/D is the banks' reserve ratio. An increase in the banks' reserve ratio decreases the money multiplier.

STUDY PLAN PROBLEMS AND APPLICATIONS

MyEconLab   You can work Problems 1 to 9 in Chapter 24 Study Plan and get instant feedback.

What Is Money? (Study Plan 24.1)

1. Money in Canada today includes which of the following items? Cash in CIBC's cash machines; Bank of Canada dollar bills in your wallet; your Visa card; your loan to pay for school fees.

2. In July 2011, currency held by individuals and businesses was $57 billion; chequable deposits owned by individuals were $211 billion and owned by businesses were $277 billion; non-chequable personal deposits were $163 billion; non-chequable business deposits were $29 billion; and term deposits and other deposits were $303 billion. Calculate M1 and M2 in July 2011.

Depository Institutions (Study Plan 24.2)

3. **Europe's Banks Must Be Forced to Recapitalize**
   E.U. banks must hold more capital. Where private funding is not forthcoming, recapitalization must be imposed by E.U. governments.
   Source: *The Financial Times*, November 24, 2011

   What is the "capital" referred to in the news clip? How might the requirement to hold more capital make banks safer?

The Bank of Canada (Study Plan 24.3)

4. The Bank of Canada sells $20 million of securities to the Bank of Nova Scotia. Enter the transactions that take place to show the changes in the following balance sheets:

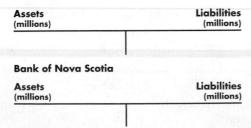

Bank of Canada

Assets (millions)	Liabilities (millions)

Bank of Nova Scotia

Assets (millions)	Liabilities (millions)

How Banks Create Money (Study Plan 24.4)

5. In the economy of Nocoin, bank deposits are $300 billion, bank reserves are $15 billion of which two-thirds are deposits with the central bank. Households and firms hold $30 billion in bank notes. There are no coins. Calculate:
   a. The monetary base and quantity of money.
   b. The banks' desired reserve ratio and the currency drain ratio (as percentages).

6. China Cuts Banks' Reserve Ratios

The People's Bank of China announces it will cut the required reserve ratio.
Source: *The Financial Times*, February 19, 2012

Explain how lowering the required reserve ratio will impact banks' money creation process.

The Money Market (Study Plan 24.5)

7. The spreadsheet provides data about the demand for money in Minland. Columns A and B show the demand for money schedule when real GDP (Y_0) is $10 billion, and Columns A and C show the demand for money schedule when real GDP (Y_1) is $20 billion. The quantity of money is $3 billion.

	A	B	C
1	r	Y_0	Y_1
2	7	1.0	1.5
3	6	1.5	2.0
4	5	2.0	2.5
5	4	2.5	3.0
6	3	3.0	3.5
7	2	3.5	4.0
8	1	4.0	4.5

What is the interest rate when real GDP is $10 billion? Explain what happens in the money market in the short run if real GDP increases to $20 billion.

The Quantity Theory of Money (Study Plan 24.6)

8. In year 1, the economy is at full employment and real GDP is $400 million, the GDP deflator is 200 (the price level is 2), and the velocity of circulation is 20. In year 2, the quantity of money increases by 20 percent. If the quantity theory of money holds, calculate the quantity of money, the GDP deflator, real GDP, and the velocity of circulation in year 2.

Mathematical Note (Study Plan 24.MN)

9. In Problem 5, the banks have no excess reserves. Suppose that the central bank in Nocoin increases bank reserves by $0.5 billion.
   a. Explain what happens to the quantity of money and why the change in the quantity of money is not equal to the change in the monetary base.
   b. Calculate the money multiplier.

ADDITIONAL PROBLEMS AND APPLICATIONS

MyEconLab   You can work these problems in MyEconLab if assigned by your instructor.

What Is Money?

10. Sara withdraws $1,000 from her savings account at the TD Bank, keeps $50 in cash, and deposits the balance in her chequable account at the TD Bank. What is the immediate change in M1 and M2?

11. Rapid inflation in Brazil in the early 1990s caused the cruzeiro to lose its ability to function as money. Which of the following commodities would most likely have taken the place of the cruzeiro in the Brazilian economy? Explain why.
    a. Tractor parts
    b. Packs of cigarettes
    c. Loaves of bread
    d. Impressionist paintings
    e. Baseball trading cards

12. **Are You Ready to Pay by Smartphone?**
    Starbucks customers can now pay for their coffee using their smartphone. Does this mean the move to electronic payments is finally coming?
    Source: *The Wall Street Journal*, January 20, 2011

    If people can use their smartphones to make payments, will currency disappear? How will the components of M1 change?

Depository Institutions

Use the following news clip to work Problems 13 and 14.

Investment in the Future

The RBC says lines of credit for education are popular and the size of loans to students has been going up as tuition costs have increased. Compared to "good debt" like a mortgage, student loan rates are higher because the debt is riskier. Financial institutions know that students need help and have created financial-management Web sites and other educational material to help students.
    Source: *Winnipeg Free Press*, September 17, 2011

13. Explain how this news clip illustrates the attempts by banks to maximize profits. Why are interest rates on student loans higher than those on mortgages?

14. Why would banks create Web sites to educate students about financial management?

15. How does financial regulation in Canada help minimize the cost of bank failure? Does it bring more stability to the banking system?

The Bank of Canada

16. Explain the distinction between a central bank and a chartered bank.

17. If the Bank of Canada makes an open market sale of $1 million of securities to a bank, what initial changes occur in the economy?

18. Set out the transactions that the Bank of Canada undertakes to increase the quantity of money.

19. Describe the Bank of Canada's assets and liabilities. What is the monetary base and how does it relate to the Bank of Canada's balance sheet?

20. **U.S. Federal Reserve Minutes Show Active Discussion of QE3**
    The U.S. Federal Reserve discussed "a new large-scale asset purchase program" commonly called "QE3." Some members said such a program could help the economy by lowering long-term interest rates and making financial conditions, more broadly, easier. They discussed whether a new program should snap up more Treasury bonds or buy mortgage-backed securities issued by the likes of Fannie Mae and Freddie Mac.
    Source: *The Wall Street Journal*, August 22, 2012

    What would the U.S. Federal Reserve do to implement QE3, how would the monetary base change, and how would bank reserves change?

How Banks Create Money

21. Banks in New Transylvania have a desired reserve ratio of 10 percent of deposits and no excess reserves. The currency drain ratio is 50 percent of deposits. Now suppose that the central bank increases the monetary base by $1,200 billion.
    a. How much do the banks lend in the first round of the money creation process?
    b. How much of the initial amount loaned flows back to the banking system as new deposits?
    c. How much of the initial amount loaned does not return to the banks but is held as currency?
    d. Why does a second round of lending occur?

The Money Market

22. Explain the change in the nominal interest rate in the short run if:
    a. Real GDP increases.
    b. The Bank of Canada increases the quantity of money.
    c. The price level rises.

23. The figure shows an economy's demand for money curve.

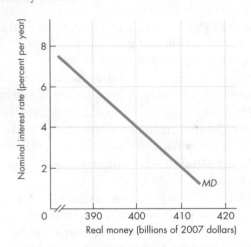

    If the central bank decreases the quantity of real money from $400 billion to $390 billion, explain how the price of a bond will change.

24. Use the data in Problem 7 to work this problem.
    The interest rate is 4 percent a year. Suppose that real GDP decreases from $20 billion to $10 billion and the quantity of money remains unchanged. Do people buy bonds or sell bonds? Explain how the interest rate changes.

The Quantity Theory of Money

25. The table provides some data for the United States in the first decade following the Civil War.

	1869	1879
Quantity of money	$1.3 billion	$1.7 billion
Real GDP (1929 dollars)	$7.4 billion	Z
Price level (1929 = 100)	X	54
Velocity of circulation	4.50	4.61

Source of data: Milton Friedman and Anna J. Schwartz, A Monetary History of the United States 1867–1960

    a. Calculate the value of X in 1869.
    b. Calculate the value of Z in 1879.
    c. Are the data consistent with the quantity theory of money? Explain your answer.

Economics in the News

26. After you have studied *Economics in the News* on pp. 584–585, answer the following questions.
    a. What changes in the interest rate and the quantity of M2 occurred between 2007 and 2014?
    b. When the interest rate fell, why did the quantity of M2 demanded increase?
    c. How would you interpret the growth of M2 and the inflation rate during the years 2009–2014 using the quantity theory of money?
    d. Why does Jim Morrow fear inflation when there was no sign of an upturn in its measured rate in 2014?
    e. Why might Jim Morrow nonetheless be correct in his concern?

27. **U.S. Federal Reserve at Odds with ECB over Value of Policy Tool**

    Financial innovation and the spread of U.S. currency throughout the world has broken down relationships between money, inflation, and output growth, making monetary gauges a less useful tool for policymakers, the U.S. Federal Reserve chairman, Ben Bernanke, said. Many other central banks use monetary aggregates as a guide to policy decision, but Bernanke believes reliance on monetary aggregates would be unwise. "There are differences between the United States and Europe in terms of the stability of money demand," Bernanke said.

    Source: *International Herald Tribune*, November 10, 2006

    a. Explain how the debate surrounding the quantity theory of money could make "monetary gauges a less useful tool for policymakers."
    b. What do Ben Bernanke's statements reveal about his view on the accuracy of the quantity theory of money?

Mathematical Note

28. In the United Kingdom, the currency drain ratio is 38 percent of deposits and the reserve ratio is 2 percent of deposits. In Australia, the quantity of money is $150 billion, the currency drain ratio is 33 percent of deposits, and the reserve ratio is 8 percent of deposits.
    a. Calculate the U.K. money multiplier.
    b. Calculate the monetary base in Australia.

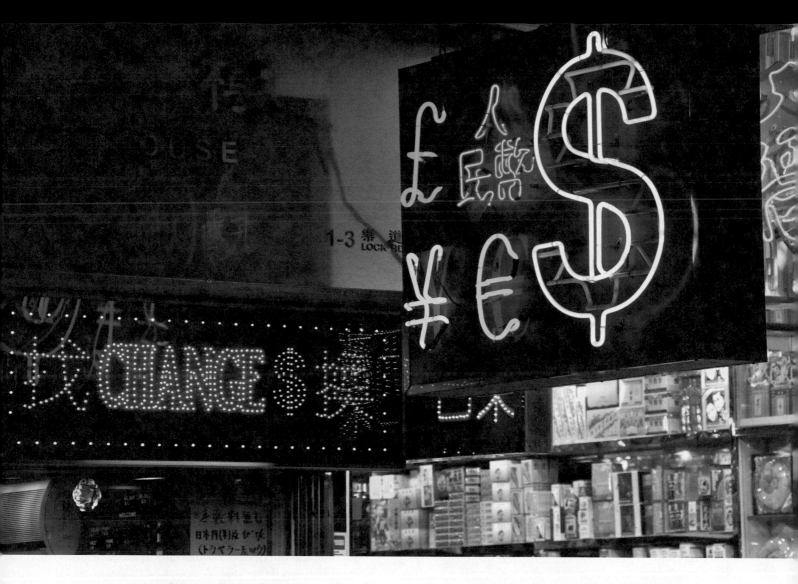

25

THE EXCHANGE RATE AND THE BALANCE OF PAYMENTS

After studying this chapter, you will be able to:

◆ Explain how the exchange rate is determined

◆ Explain interest rate parity and purchasing power parity

◆ Describe the alternative exchange rate policies and explain their effects

◆ Describe the balance of payments accounts and explain what causes an international deficit

The Canadian dollar—the loonie—is one of more than a hundred different monies. But most international payments are made using the U.S. dollar ($), the euro (€), and the Japanese yen (¥). The value of the Canadian dollar rises and falls against these other monies. Why?

Sometimes we borrow from foreigners and at other times we repay our international debts. Why? What causes international deficits and surpluses?

In this chapter, you're going to discover the answers to these questions. In *Economics in the News* we'll look at the rising U.S. dollar in the summer of 2014.

◆ The Foreign Exchange Market

When Canadian Tire imports snow blowers from China, it pays for them using Chinese yuan. And when China Airlines buys an airplane from Bombardier, it pays using Canadian dollars. Whenever people buy things from another country, they use the currency of that country to make the transaction. It doesn't make any difference what the item is that is being traded internationally. It might be a Blu-ray player, an airplane, insurance or banking services, real estate, the shares and bonds of a government or corporation, or even an entire business.

Foreign money is just like Canadian money. It consists of notes and coins issued by a central bank and mint and deposits in banks and other depository institutions. When we described Canadian money in Chapter 24, we distinguished between currency (notes and coins) and deposits. But when we talk about foreign money, we refer to it as foreign currency. **Foreign currency** is the money of other countries regardless of whether that money is in the form of notes, coins, or bank deposits.

We buy these foreign currencies and foreigners buy Canadian dollars in the foreign exchange market.

Trading Currencies

The currency of one country is exchanged for the currency of another in the **foreign exchange market**. The foreign exchange market is not a place like a downtown flea market or a fruit and vegetable market. The foreign exchange market is made up of thousands of people—importers and exporters, banks, international investors and speculators, international travellers, and specialist traders called *foreign exchange brokers*.

The foreign exchange market opens on Monday morning in Sydney, Australia, and Hong Kong, which is still Sunday evening in Toronto. As the day advances, markets open in Singapore, Tokyo, Bahrain, Frankfurt, London, New York, Toronto, Chicago, and San Francisco. As the West Coast markets close, Sydney is only an hour away from opening for the next day of business. The sun barely sets in the foreign exchange market. Dealers around the world are in continual Internet contact, and on a typical day in 2014, $5.3 trillion (of all currencies) were traded in the foreign exchange market—that's $6 million every second.

Exchange Rates

An **exchange rate** is the price at which one currency exchanges for another currency in the foreign exchange market. For example, on September 2, 2014, one Canadian dollar would buy 96 Japanese yen or 70 euro cents. So the exchange rate was 96 yen per dollar or, equivalently, 70 euro cents per dollar.

The exchange rate fluctuates. Sometimes it rises and sometimes it falls. A rise in the exchange rate is called an *appreciation* of the dollar, and a fall in the exchange rate is called a *depreciation* of the dollar. For example, when the exchange rate rises from 96 yen to 98 yen per dollar, the dollar appreciates against the yen; when the exchange rate falls from 96 yen to 94 yen per dollar, the dollar depreciates against the yen.

Economics in Action on p. 595 shows the fluctuations of the Canadian dollar against three currencies.

Questions About the Canadian Dollar Exchange Rate

The performance of the Canadian dollar in the foreign exchange market raises a number of questions that we address in this chapter.

First, how is the exchange rate determined? Why does the Canadian dollar sometimes appreciate and at other times depreciate?

Second, how do the Bank of Canada and other central banks operate in the foreign exchange market? In particular, how was the exchange rate between the U.S. dollar and the Chinese yuan fixed and why did it remain constant for many years?

Third, how do exchange rate fluctuations influence our international trade and international payments? In particular, could we influence our international deficit by changing the exchange rate? Would an appreciation of the yuan change the balance of trade and payments between China and the rest of the world?

We begin by learning how trading in the foreign exchange market determines the exchange rate.

An Exchange Rate Is a Price

An exchange rate is a price—the price of one currency in terms of another. And like all prices, an exchange rate is determined in a market—the *foreign exchange market*.

The Canadian dollar trades in the foreign exchange market and is supplied and demanded by tens of thousands of traders every hour of every

Economics in Action
The Canadian Dollar: More Up than Down

The figure shows the Canadian dollar exchange rate against the three currencies that feature prominently in Canada's imports—the U.S. dollar, the European euro, and the Japanese yen—between 2000 and 2014.

Against the U.S. dollar and the yen, the Canadian dollar has tended to appreciate. It depreciated only in 2008 and 2009 and in 2013 and 2014. The Canadian dollar has fluctuated both up and down against the euro but has had no trend. It depreciated slightly against the euro up to 2005, appreciated slightly from 2005 to 2012, and depreciated from 2012 to 2014.

Notice the high-frequency fluctuations (rapid brief up and down movements) of the Canadian dollar against the other three currencies.

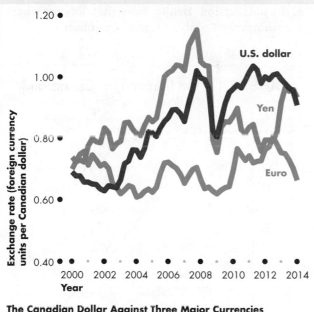

The Canadian Dollar Against Three Major Currencies

Source of data: Pacific Exchange Rate Service.

business day. Because it has many traders and no restrictions on who may trade, the foreign exchange market is a *competitive market*.

In a competitive market, demand and supply determine the price. So to understand the forces that determine the exchange rate, we need to study the factors that influence demand and supply in the foreign exchange market. But there is a feature of the foreign exchange market that makes it special.

The Demand for One Money Is the Supply of Another Money

When people who are holding the money of another country want to exchange it for Canadian dollars, they demand Canadian dollars and supply that other country's money. And when people who are holding Canadian dollars want to exchange them for the money of some other country, they supply Canadian dollars and demand that other country's money.

So the factors that influence the demand for Canadian dollars also influence the supply of euros, or yen, or yuan. And the factors that influence the demand for another country's money also influence the supply of Canadian dollars.

We'll first look at the influences on the demand for Canadian dollars in the foreign exchange market.

Demand in the Foreign Exchange Market

People buy Canadian dollars so that they can buy Canadian-produced goods and services—Canadian exports—or so they can buy Canadian assets such as bonds, stocks, businesses, and real estate or so that they can keep part of their money holding in a Canadian dollar bank account.

The quantity of Canadian dollars demanded in the foreign exchange market is the amount that traders plan to buy during a given time period at a given exchange rate. This quantity depends on many factors, but the main ones are:

1. The exchange rate
2. World demand for Canadian exports
3. Interest rates in the United States and other countries
4. The expected future exchange rate

We look first at the relationship between the quantity of Canadian dollars demanded in the foreign exchange market and the exchange rate when the other three influences remain the same.

The Law of Demand for Foreign Exchange The law of demand applies to Canadian dollars just as it does to anything else that people value. Other things remaining the same, the higher the exchange rate, the smaller is the quantity of Canadian dollars demanded in the foreign exchange market. For example, if the market price of the Canadian dollar rises from 100 yen to 120 yen but nothing else changes, the quantity of Canadian dollars that people plan to buy in the foreign exchange market decreases.

The exchange rate influences the quantity of Canadian dollars demanded for two reasons:

- Exports effect
- Expected profit effect

Exports Effect The larger the value of Canadian exports, the larger is the quantity of Canadian dollars demanded by the buyers of Canadian exports in the foreign exchange market. But the value of Canadian exports depends on the prices of Canadian-produced goods and services *expressed in the currency of the foreign buyer*. And these prices depend on the exchange rate. The lower the exchange rate, other things remaining the same, the lower are the prices of Canadian-produced goods and services to foreigners and the greater is the volume of Canadian exports. So if the exchange rate falls (and other influences remain the same), the quantity of Canadian dollars demanded in the foreign exchange market increases.

To see the exports effect at work, think about orders for Bombardier's regional jet. If the price of this airplane is $8 million and the exchange rate is 75 euro cents per Canadian dollar, its price to KLM, a European airline, is €6 million. KLM decides that this price is too high, so it doesn't buy the airplane. If the exchange rate falls to 60 euro cents, the price of a regional jet falls to €4.8 million, KLM decides to buy the plane and buys Canadian dollars in the foreign exchange market.

Expected Profit Effect The larger the expected profit from holding Canadian dollars, the greater is the quantity of Canadian dollars demanded in the foreign exchange market. But expected profit depends on the exchange rate. For a given expected future exchange rate, the lower the exchange rate today, the larger is the expected profit from buying Canadian dollars today and holding them, so the greater is the quantity of Canadian dollars demanded in the foreign exchange market today. Let's look at an example.

Suppose that Mitsubishi Bank, a Japanese bank, expects the exchange rate to be 120 yen per Canadian dollar at the end of the year. If today's exchange rate is also 120 yen per Canadian dollar, Mitsubishi Bank expects no profit from buying Canadian dollars and holding them until the end of the year. But if today's exchange rate is 100 yen per Canadian dollar and

Mitsubishi Bank buys Canadian dollars, it expects to sell those dollars at the end of the year for 120 yen per dollar and make a profit of 20 yen on each Canadian dollar bought.

The lower the exchange rate today, other things remaining the same, the greater is the expected profit from holding Canadian dollars, so the greater is the quantity of Canadian dollars demanded in the foreign exchange market today.

Demand Curve for Canadian Dollars

Figure 25.1 shows the demand curve for Canadian dollars in the foreign exchange market. A change in the exchange rate, other things remaining the same, brings a change in the quantity of Canadian dollars demanded and a movement along the demand curve. The arrows show such movements.

We will look at the factors that *change* demand in the next section. Before doing that, let's see what determines the supply of Canadian dollars.

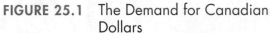

FIGURE 25.1 The Demand for Canadian Dollars

The quantity of Canadian dollars demanded depends on the exchange rate. Other things remaining the same, if the exchange rate rises, the quantity of Canadian dollars demanded decreases and there is a movement up along the demand curve. If the exchange rate falls, the quantity of Canadian dollars demanded increases and there is a movement down along the demand curve.

————— MyEconLab Animation —————

Supply in the Foreign Exchange Market

People and businesses sell Canadian dollars and buy other currencies so that they can buy foreign-produced goods and services—Canadian imports—or so that they can buy foreign assets such as bonds, stocks, businesses, and real estate or so that they can hold part of their money in bank deposits denominated in a foreign currency.

The quantity of Canadian dollars supplied in the foreign exchange market is the amount that traders plan to sell during a given time period at a given exchange rate. This quantity depends on many factors, but the main ones are:

1. The exchange rate
2. Canadian demand for imports
3. Interest rates in the United States and other countries
4. The expected future exchange rate

Let's look at the law of supply in the foreign exchange market—the relationship between the quantity of Canadian dollars supplied in the foreign exchange market and the exchange rate when the other three influences remain the same.

The Law of Supply of Foreign Exchange Other things remaining the same, the higher the exchange rate, the greater is the quantity of Canadian dollars supplied in the foreign exchange market. For example, if the exchange rate rises from 100 yen to 120 yen per Canadian dollar and other things remain the same, the quantity of Canadian dollars that people plan to sell in the foreign exchange market increases.

The exchange rate influences the quantity of dollars supplied for two reasons:

- Imports effect
- Expected profit effect

Imports Effect The larger the value of Canadian imports, the larger is the quantity of Canadian dollars supplied in the foreign exchange market. But the value of Canadian imports depends on the prices of foreign-produced goods and services *expressed in Canadian dollars*. These prices depend on the exchange rate. The higher the exchange rate, other things remaining the same, the lower are the prices of foreign-produced goods and services to Americans and the greater is the volume of Canadian imports. So if the exchange rate rises (and other influences

remain the same), the quantity of Canadian dollars supplied in the foreign exchange market increases.

Expected Profit Effect This effect works just like that on the demand for the Canadian dollar but in the opposite direction. The higher the exchange rate today, other things remaining the same, the larger is the expected profit from selling Canadian dollars today and holding foreign currencies, so the greater is the quantity of Canadian dollars supplied in the foreign exchange market.

Supply Curve for Canadian Dollars

Figure 25.2 shows the supply curve of Canadian dollars in the foreign exchange market. A change in the exchange rate, other things remaining the same, brings a change in the quantity of Canadian dollars supplied and a movement along the supply curve. The arrows show such movements.

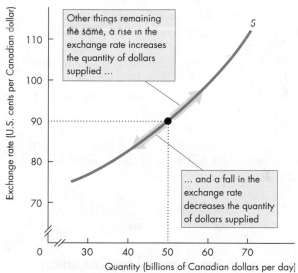

FIGURE 25.2   The Supply of Canadian Dollars

Other things remaining the same, a rise in the exchange rate increases the quantity of dollars supplied ...

... and a fall in the exchange rate decreases the quantity of dollars supplied

The quantity of Canadian dollars supplied depends on the exchange rate. Other things remaining the same, if the exchange rate rises, the quantity of Canadian dollars supplied increases and there is a movement up along the supply curve. If the exchange rate falls, the quantity of Canadian dollars supplied decreases and there is a movement down along the supply curve.

MyEconLab Animation

Market Equilibrium

Equilibrium in the foreign exchange market depends on how the Bank of Canada and other central banks behave. Here, we will study the foreign exchange market with no central bank actions.

Figure 25.3 shows the demand curve for Canadian dollars, D, from Fig. 25.1, the supply curve of Canadian dollars, S, from Fig. 25.2, and the equilibrium exchange rate. The exchange rate acts as a regulator of the quantities demanded and supplied. If the exchange rate is too high, there is a surplus of dollars. For example, in Fig. 25.3, if the exchange rate is 100 U.S. cents per Canadian dollar, there is a surplus of Canadian dollars. If the exchange rate is too low, there is a shortage of dollars. For example, if the exchange rate is 80 U.S. cents per Canadian dollar, there is a shortage of Canadian dollars.

At the equilibrium exchange rate, there is neither a shortage nor a surplus—the quantity supplied equals the quantity demanded. In Fig. 25.3, the equilibrium exchange rate is 90 U.S. cents per Canadian dollar. At this exchange rate, the quantity demanded and the quantity supplied are each $50 billion a day.

The foreign exchange market is constantly pulled to its equilibrium by foreign exchange traders who are constantly looking for the best price they can get. If they are selling, they want the highest price available. If they are buying, they want the lowest price available. Information flows from trader to trader through a worldwide computer network, and the price adjusts minute by minute to keep the exchange rate at its equilibrium.

But as you've seen (in *Economics in Action* on p. 595), the Canadian dollar fluctuates a lot against other currencies. Changes in the demand for Canadian dollars or the supply of Canadian dollars bring these exchange rate fluctuations. We'll now look at the factors that make demand and supply change, starting with the demand side of the market.

Changes in the Demand for Canadian Dollars

The demand for Canadian dollars in the foreign exchange market changes when there is a change in:

- World demand for Canadian exports
- Canadian interest rate relative to the foreign interest rate
- The expected future exchange rate

FIGURE 25.3   Equilibrium Exchange Rate

The demand curve for Canadian dollars is D, and the supply curve of Canadian dollars is S. If the exchange rate is 100 U.S. cents per Canadian dollar, there is a surplus of Canadian dollars and the exchange rate falls. If the exchange rate is 80 U.S. cents per Canadian dollar, there is a shortage of Canadian dollars and the exchange rate rises. If the exchange rate is 90 U.S. cents per Canadian dollar, there is neither a shortage nor a surplus of Canadian dollars and the exchange rate remains constant. The foreign exchange market is in equilibrium.

MyEconLab Animation and Draw Graph

World Demand for Canadian Exports An increase in world demand for Canadian exports increases the demand for Canadian dollars. To see this effect, think about Bombardier's airplane sales. An increase in demand for air travel in Australia sends that country's airlines on a global shopping spree. They decide that Bombardier has the ideal plane, so they order some. The demand for Canadian dollars now increases.

Canadian Interest Rate Relative to the Foreign Interest Rate People and businesses buy financial assets to make a return. The higher the interest rate that people can make on Canadian assets compared with foreign assets, the more Canadian assets they buy.

What matters is not the *level* of the Canadian interest rate, but the Canadian interest rate relative to the foreign interest rate—the Canadian interest rate minus the foreign interest rate, which is called the **Canadian interest rate differential**. If the Canadian interest rate rises and the foreign interest rate remains constant, the Canadian interest rate differential increases. The larger the Canadian interest rate differential, the greater is the demand for Canadian assets and the greater is the demand for Canadian dollars in the foreign exchange market.

The Expected Future Exchange Rate For a given current exchange rate, other things remaining the same, a rise in the expected future exchange rate increases the profit that people expect to make by holding Canadian dollars, so the demand for Canadian dollars increases today.

Figure 25.4 summarizes the influences on the demand for Canadian dollars. An increase in the demand for Canadian exports, a rise in the Canadian interest rate differential, or a rise in the expected future exchange rate increases the demand for Canadian dollars today and shifts the demand curve rightward from D_0 to D_1. A decrease in the demand for Canadian exports, a fall in the Canadian interest rate differential, or a fall in the expected future exchange rate decreases the demand for Canadian dollars today and shifts the demand curve leftward from D_0 to D_2.

Changes in the Supply of Canadian Dollars

The supply of Canadian dollars in the foreign exchange market changes when there is a change in:

- Canadian demand for imports
- Canadian interest rate relative to the foreign interest rate
- The expected future exchange rate

Canadian Demand for Imports An increase in the Canadian demand for imports increases the supply of Canadian dollars in the foreign exchange market. To see why, think about Canadian Tire's purchase of snow blowers. An increase in the demand for snow blowers sends Canadian Tire shopping in China, and the supply of Canadian dollars increases as Canadian Tire buys Chinese yuan.

Canadian Interest Rate Relative to the Foreign Interest Rate The effect of the Canadian interest rate differential on the supply of Canadian dollars is the opposite of its effect on the demand for Canadian dollars. The larger the Canadian interest

FIGURE 25.4   Changes in the Demand for Canadian Dollars

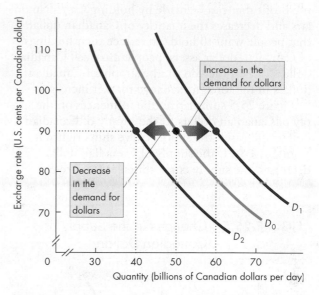

A change in any influence on the quantity of Canadian dollars that people plan to buy, other than the exchange rate, brings a change in the demand for Canadian dollars.

The demand for Canadian dollars

Increases if:

- World demand for Canadian exports increases

- The Canadian interest rate differential rises

- The expected future exchange rate rises

Decreases if:

- World demand for Canadian exports decreases

- The Canadian interest rate differential falls

- The expected future exchange rate falls

—— MyEconLab Animation ——

rate differential, the *smaller* is the supply of Canadian dollars.

With a higher Canadian interest rate differential, people decide to keep more of their funds in Canadian dollar assets and less in foreign currency assets. They buy a smaller quantity of foreign currency and sell a smaller quantity of Canadian dollars.

So, a rise in the Canadian interest rate, other things remaining the same, decreases the supply of Canadian dollars in the foreign exchange market.

The Expected Future Exchange Rate For a given current exchange rate, other things remaining the same, a fall in the expected future exchange rate decreases the profit that can be made by holding Canadian dollars and decreases the quantity of Canadian dollars that people want to hold. To reduce their holdings of Canadian dollar assets, people must sell Canadian dollars. When they do so, the supply of Canadian dollars in the foreign exchange market increases.

Figure 25.5 summarizes the influences on the supply of Canadian dollars. If the supply of Canadian dollars increases, the supply curve shifts rightward from S_0 to S_1. If the supply of Canadian dollars decreases, the supply curve shifts leftward to S_2.

FIGURE 25.5   Changes in the Supply of Canadian Dollars

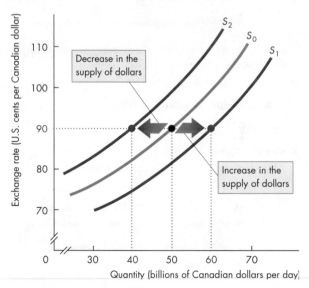

A change in any influence on the quantity of Canadian dollars that people plan to sell, other than the exchange rate, brings a change in the supply of dollars.

The supply of Canadian dollars

Increases if:

- Canadian import demand increases
- The Canadian interest rate differential falls
- The expected future exchange rate falls

Decreases if:

- Canadian import demand decreases
- The Canadian interest rate differential rises
- The expected future exchange rate rises

MyEconLab Animation

Changes in the Exchange Rate

The exchange rate changes when either the demand for dollars or the supply of dollars changes.

An increase in the demand for Canadian dollars raises the exchange rate; and a decrease in the demand for Canadian dollars lowers the exchange rate. Similarly, a decrease in the supply of Canadian dollars raises the exchange rate; and an increase in the supply of Canadian dollars lowers the exchange rate.

These predictions are the same as those for any other market. Two episodes in the life of the Canadian dollar (next page) illustrate these predictions.

Two of the influences on demand and supply—the Canadian interest differential and the expected future exchange rate—change both sides of the foreign exchange market simultaneously. A rise in the Canadian interest rate differential or a rise in the expected future exchange rate increases demand, decreases supply, and raises the exchange rate. Similarly, a fall in the Canadian interest rate differential or a fall in the expected future exchange rate decreases demand, increases supply, and lowers the exchange rate.

We take a closer look at the interest rate differential and expectations in the next section.

REVIEW QUIZ

1 What are the influences on the demand for Canadian dollars in the foreign exchange market?
2 What are the influences on the supply of Canadian dollars in the foreign exchange market?
3 How is the equilibrium exchange rate determined?
4 What happens if there is a shortage or a surplus of Canadian dollars in the foreign exchange market?
5 What makes the demand for Canadian dollars change?
6 What makes the supply of Canadian dollars change?
7 What makes the Canadian dollar exchange rate fluctuate?

Work these questions in Study Plan 25.1 and get instant feedback. Do a Key Terms Quiz.   MyEconLab

Economics in Action

The Canadian Dollar on a Roller Coaster

The foreign exchange market is a striking example of a competitive market. The expectations of thousands of traders around the world influence this market minute-by-minute throughout the 24-hour global trading day.

Demand and supply rarely stand still, and their fluctuations bring a fluctuating exchange rate. Two episodes in the life of the Canadian dollar illustrate these fluctuations: 2007–2009, when the dollar depreciated, and 2009–2011, when the dollar appreciated.

A Depreciating Canadian Dollar: 2007–2009

Between October 2007 and February 2009, the Canadian dollar depreciated against the U.S dollar. It fell from 100 U.S. cents to 80 U.S. cents per Canadian dollar. Part (a) of the figure illustrates this depreciation. In 2007, the demand and supply curves were those labelled D_{07} and S_{07}. The exchange rate was 100 U.S. cents per Canadian dollar.

During the last quarter of 2007 and the whole of 2008, the global economy was in recession. The demand by China and other Asian economies for Canadian energy and raw material exports decreased, which decreased the demand for Canadian dollars. The effect of the global recession on the Canadian dollar was anticipated by foreign exchange traders, who reacted by

selling more Canadian dollars—an increase in the supply of Canadian dollars.

The combination of a decrease in demand for and an increase in supply of Canadian dollars sent the exchange rate down.

In part (a) of the figure, the demand curve shifted leftward from D_{07} to D_{09}, the supply curve shifted rightward from S_{07} to S_{09}, and the exchange rate fell to 80 U.S. cents per Canadian dollar.

An Appreciating Canadian Dollar: 2009–2011

Between February 2009 and May 2011, the Canadian dollar appreciated against the U.S. dollar. It rose from 80 U.S. cents to 103 U.S. cents per Canadian dollar. Part (b) of the figure illustrates this appreciation.

The demand and supply curves labelled D_{09} and S_{09} are the same as in part (a). During 2009 and 2010, the Asian economy began to expand rapidly and lead the world from recession. China's demand for Canadian energy and raw materials increased, and so did the demand for the Canadian dollar.

Again, this increase in demand was anticipated and traders, expecting a higher Canadian dollar, held on to their dollars, so the supply of Canadian dollars decreased. In the figure, the demand curve shifted rightward from D_{09} to D_{11} and the supply curve shifted leftward from S_{09} to S_{11}. The exchange rate rose to 103 U.S. cents per Canadian dollar.

(a) 2007–2009

The Falling and Rising Canadian Dollar

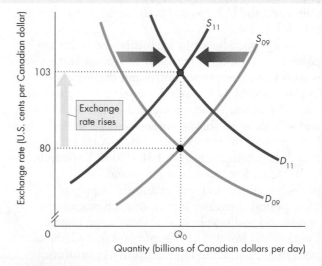

(b) 2009–2011

Arbitrage, Speculation, and Market Fundamentals

You've just seen how an exchange rate is determined. In our example, we used the Canadian dollar–U.S. dollar exchange rate, but exchange rates between the Canadian dollar and all other currencies are determined in a similar way. So are the exchange rates *among* the other currencies such as that of the European euro and U.K. pound. Exchange rates are kept in alignment with each other by a process called *arbitrage*.

Arbitrage

Arbitrage is the practice of seeking to profit by buying in one market and selling for a higher price in another related market. Arbitrage in the foreign exchange market and international loans markets and goods markets achieves three outcomes:

- The law of one price
- No round-trip profit
- Interest rate parity
- Purchasing power parity

The Law of One Price The *law of one price* states that if an item is traded in more than one place, the price will be the same in all locations. An example of this law is that the exchange rate between the Canadian dollar and the U.K. pound is the same in Toronto as it is in London.

You can see why arbitrage brings about this outcome by imagining that the exchange rate in London is 0.60 U.K. pounds per dollar and the price in Toronto is 0.61 U.K. pounds per dollar. In this imaginary sitiuation, a trader who buys dollars in London and sells them in Toronto makes a profit of 0.01 U.K. pounds on every dollar traded. A trade of 1 million dollars brings a profit of 10,000 U.K. pounds.

Within a few seconds, the demand for U.K. pounds increases in London and the supply of U.K. pounds increases in Toronto. These changes in demand and supply raise the exchange rate in London and lower it in Toronto and make it equal in both markets—removing the profit opportunity.

No Round-Trip Profit A round trip is using currency *A* to buy currency *B*, and then using *B* to buy *A*. A round trip might involve more stages, using *B* to buy *C* and then using *C* to buy *A*.

Arbitrage removes profit from all transactions of this type. Any fleeting profit is taken, and the changes in supply and demand induced by the momentarily available profit snap the exchange rates back to levels that remove the profit.

Interest Rate Parity Borrowers and lenders must choose the currency in which to denominate their assets and debts. **Interest rate parity**, which means equal rates of return across currencies, means that for risk-free transactions, there is no gain from choosing one currency over another.

To see why interest rate parity always prevails, suppose a Brazilian real bank deposit in Rio de Janeiro earns 10 percent a year and a Canadian dollar bank deposit in Toronto earns 1 percent a year. Why wouldn't people move their funds from Toronto to Rio?

The answer begins with the fact that to earn 10 percent in Rio, funds must be converted from Canadian dollars to reais at the beginning of the year and from reais back to dollars at the end of the year. This transaction can be done without risk by selling reais for Canadian dollars today for delivery one year from today at an exchange rate agreed on today. Such a transaction is called a *future* or *forward* transaction and it takes place at the *one-year forward exchange rate*.

Suppose that today's exchange rate is 2.30 reais per dollar, and you convert $100 to 230 reais. In one year, you will have 253 reais—your deposit of 230 reais plus interest of 23 reais. If the one-year forward exchange rate is 2.50 reais per Canadian dollar, you can contract today to sell 253 reais for $101 for delivery in one year. But that is exactly the amount you can earn by putting your $100 in the Toronto bank and earning 1 percent a year.

If, for a few seconds, interest rate parity did not hold and it was possible to profit from buying and holding Brazilian reais, traders would flock to the profit opportunity, supply dollars and demand reais, and drive the exchange rate to its interest rate parity level.

Purchasing Power Parity Suppose a camera costs 10,000 yen in Tokyo and $100 in Toronto. If the exchange rate is 100 yen per dollar, the two monies have the same value. You can buy the camera in either Tokyo or Toronto for the same price. You can express that price as either 10,000 yen or $100, but the price is the same in the two currencies.

The situation we've just described is called **purchasing power parity** (or PPP), which means *equal value of money*. PPP is an example of the law of one price, and if it does not prevail, arbitrage forces go to work. To see these forces, suppose that the price of the camera in Toronto is $120, but in Tokyo it remains at 10,000 yen and the exchange rate remains at 100 yen per dollar. In this case, the camera in Tokyo still costs 10,000 yen or $100, but in Toronto, it costs $120 or 12,000 yen. Money buys more in Japan than in Canada: Its value is *not* equal in the two countries.

Arbitrage now kicks in. With the camera cheaper in Toyko than in Toronto, the demand for cameras increases in Tokyo and the supply of cameras increases in Toronto. The Toronto price falls and the Tokyo price rises to eliminate the price difference and restore purchasing power parity.

If most goods and services cost more in one country than another, the currency of the first country is said to be *overvalued*: A depreciation of the currency would restore PPP. Similarly, the currency of the country with the lower prices is said to be *undervalued*: An appreciation of that currency would restore PPP. When goods and services cost the same in two countries, their currencies are said to be at their PPP levels.

Determining whether a currency is overvalued or undervalued based on PPP is not easy, and testing PPP by looking at individual prices requires care to ensure that the goods compared are identical. What is identical isn't always immediately obvious (see *Economics in Action* below).

Speculation

Speculation is trading on the *expectation* of making a profit. Speculation contrasts with arbitrage, which is trading on the certainty of making a profit. Most foreign exchange transactions are based on speculation, which explains why the expected future exchange rate plays such a central role in the foreign exchange market.

The expected future exchange rate influences both supply and demand, so it influences the current equilibrium exchange rate. But what determines the expected future exchange rate?

The Expected Future Exchange Rate An expectation is a forecast. Exchange rate forecasts, like weather forecasts, are made over horizons that run from a few hours to many months and perhaps years. Also, like weather forecasters, exchange rate forecasters use scientific models and data to make their predictions.

But exchange rate forecasting differs from weather forecasting in three ways. First, exchange rate forecasts are hedged with a lot of uncertainty; second, there are many divergent forecasts; and third, the forecasts influence the outcome.

The dependence of today's exchange rate on forecasts of tomorrow's exchange rate can give rise to exchange rate volatility in the short run.

Economics in Action
A Big Mac Index

Because a Big Mac is the same in Chicago as in Beijing, *The Economist* magazine wondered if its price in these cities might tell us how far China's yuan is from its PPP level. In July 2014, the price of a Big Mac was $4.80 in the United States and 16.93 yuan, or $2.73, in China. Does this dollar price difference mean that the yuan is undervalued?

The Big Mac price comparison doesn't answer this question. A Big Mac *looks* the same in all places but most of its value is in its *service*, not its *appearance*.

The figure shows the price of a Big Mac as a percentage of the U.S. price averaged over 2000, 2007, and 2014. It shows that the price is persistently above the U.S. price in a few rich countries and persistently below the U.S. price in lower-income countries.

The persistent differences arise from different relative prices of services, not from over- or undervalued currencies.

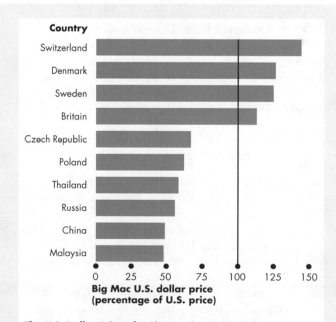

The U.S. Dollar Price of a Big Mac in 10 Countries

Source of data: The Economist, April 2000, June 2007, and July 2014.

Exchange Rate Volatility An exchange rate might rise one day and fall the next, as news about the influences on the exchange rate change the expected future exchange rate. For example, news that the Bank of Canada is going to start to raise interest rates next month brings an immediate increase in the demand for Canadian dollars, decrease in the supply of Canadian dollars, and appreciation of the Canadian dollar. As the news is digested and its expected consequences revised, expectations are revised sometimes upward and sometimes downward, bringing further changes in the exchange rate.

The influences of expectations and the constant arrival of news about the influences on supply and demand make day-to-day and week-to-week changes in the exchange rate impossible to predict. But exchange rate trends are more predictable and depend on market fundamentals.

Market Fundamentals

The market fundamentals that influence the exchange rate are world demand for Canadian exports, Canadian demand for imports, and the Canadian interest rate differential. But how these forces influence the exchange rate is different in the short run and the long run. The short-run influences are those described on pp. 595–597. To understand the long run, we need to define and understand the role played by the real exchange rate.

The Real Exchange Rate The **real exchange rate** is the relative price of Canadian-produced goods and services to foreign-produced goods and services. It is a measure of the quantity of the real GDP of other countries that a unit of Canadian real GDP buys. For example, the real Japanese yen exchange rate, RER, is given by:

$$RER = (E \times P) \div P^*,$$

where E is the exchange rate (yen per Canadian dollar), P is the Canadian price level, and P^* is the Japanese price level.

To understand the real exchange rate, suppose that the exchange rate E is 100 yen per dollar. Canada produces only computer chips priced at $150 each, so P equals $150 and $E \times P$ equals 15,000 yen. Japan produces only iPods priced at 5,000 yen each, so P^* equals 5,000 yen. Then the real Japanese yen exchange rate equals:

$$RER = (100 \times 150) \div 5,000 = 3 \text{ iPods per chip.}$$

If Japan and Canada produced identical goods, the real exchange rate would equal 1 unit of Canadian real GDP per unit of Japanese real GDP.

In reality, Canadian real GDP is a different bundle of goods and services from Japanese real GDP. So the real exchange rate is not 1 and it changes over time. The forces of demand and supply in the markets for the millions of goods and services that make up real GDP determine the relative price of Japanese and Canadian real GDP and the real exchange rate.

Price Levels and Money We can turn the real exchange rate equation around and determine the exchange rate as:

$$E = (RER \times P^*) \div P.$$

This equation says that the exchange rate equals the real exchange rate multiplied by the foreign price level, divided by the domestic price level.

In the long run, the quantity of money determines the price level. But the quantity theory of money applies to all countries, so the quantity of money in Japan determines the price level in Japan, and the quantity of money in Canada determines the price level in Canada.

For a given real exchange rate, a change in the quantity of money brings a change in the price level *and* a change in the exchange rate.

The market fundamentals that determine the exchange rate in the long run are the real exchange rate and the quantities of money in each economy.

◆ REVIEW QUIZ

1 What is arbitrage and what are its effects in the foreign exchange market?

2 What is interest rate parity and what happens when this condition doesn't hold?

3 What makes an exchange rate hard to predict?

4 What is purchasing power parity and what happens when this condition doesn't hold?

5 What determines the real exchange rate and the nominal exchange rate in the short run?

6 What determines the real exchange rate and the nominal exchange rate in the long run?

Work these questions in Study Plan 25.2 and get instant feedback. Do a Key Terms Quiz.   MyEconLab

◢ Exchange Rate Policy

Because the exchange rate is the price of a country's money in terms of another country's money, governments and central banks must have a policy toward the exchange rate. Three possible exchange rate policies are:

- Flexible exchange rate
- Fixed exchange rate
- Crawling peg

Flexible Exchange Rate

A **flexible exchange rate** is an exchange rate that is determined by demand and supply in the foreign exchange market with no direct intervention by the central bank.

Most countries, including Canada, operate a flexible exchange rate, and the foreign exchange market that we have studied so far in this chapter is an example of a flexible exchange rate regime.

But even a flexible exchange rate is influenced by central bank actions. If the Bank of Canada raises the Canadian interest rate and other countries keep their interest rates unchanged, the demand for Canadian dollars increases, the supply of Canadian dollars decreases, and the exchange rate rises. (Similarly, if the Bank of Canada lowers the Canadian interest rate, the demand for Canadian dollars decreases, the supply increases, and the exchange rate falls.)

In a flexible exchange rate regime, when the central bank changes the interest rate, its purpose is not usually to influence the exchange rate, but to achieve some other monetary policy objective. (We return to this topic at length in Chapter 30.)

Fixed Exchange Rate

A **fixed exchange rate** is an exchange rate that is determined by a decision of the government or the central bank and is achieved by central bank intervention in the foreign exchange market to block the unregulated forces of demand and supply.

The world economy operated a fixed exchange rate regime from the end of World War II to the early 1970s. China had a fixed exchange rate until recently. Hong Kong has had a fixed exchange rate for many years and continues with that policy today.

Active intervention in the foreign exchange market is required to achieve a fixed exchange rate.

If the Bank of Canada wanted to fix the Canadian dollar exchange rate against the U.S. dollar, it would have to sell Canadian dollars to prevent the exchange rate from rising above the target value and buy Canadian dollars to prevent the exchange rate from falling below the target value.

There is no limit to the quantity of Canadian dollars that the Bank of Canada can *sell* because it creates Canadian dollars. But there is a limit to the quantity of Canadian dollars the Bank of Canada can *buy*, which is set by Canadian official foreign currency reserves. Intervention to buy Canadian dollars would have to stop when Canadian official foreign currency reserves run out.

Let's look at the foreign exchange interventions that the Bank of Canada can make.

Suppose the Bank of Canada wants the exchange rate to be steady at 90 U.S. cents per Canadian dollar. If the exchange rate rises above 90 U.S. cents, the Bank of Canada sells dollars. If the exchange rate falls below 90 U.S. cents, the Bank of Canada buys dollars. By these actions, the Bank of Canada keeps the exchange rate close to its target rate of 90 U.S. cents per Canadian dollar.

Figure 25.6 shows the Bank of Canada's intervention in the foreign exchange market. The supply of dollars is S and initially the demand for dollars is D_0. The equilibrium exchange rate is 90 U.S. cents per dollar. This exchange rate is also the target exchange rate, shown by the horizontal red line.

When the demand for Canadian dollars increases and the demand curve shifts rightward to D_1, the Bank sells $100 billion. This action prevents the exchange rate from rising. When the demand for Canadian dollars decreases and the demand curve shifts leftward to D_2, the Bank buys $100 billion. This action prevents the exchange rate from falling.

If the demand for Canadian dollars fluctuates between D_1 and D_2 and on average is D_0, the Bank of Canada can repeatedly intervene in the way we've just seen. Sometimes the Bank of Canada buys and sometimes it sells but, on average, it neither buys nor sells.

But suppose the demand for Canadian dollars *increases permanently* from D_0 to D_1. To maintain the exchange rate at 90 U.S. cents per Canadian dollar, the Bank of Canada must sell dollars and buy foreign currency, so Canadian official foreign currency reserves would be increasing. At some point, the Bank of Canada would abandon the exchange rate of 90 U.S. cents per Canadian dollar and stop piling up foreign currency reserves.

FIGURE 25.6   Foreign Exchange Market
                   Intervention

Initially, the demand for Canadian dollars is D_0, the supply of Canadian dollars is S, and the exchange rate is 90 U.S. cents per Canadian dollar. The Bank of Canada can intervene in the foreign exchange market to keep the exchange rate close to its target rate (90 U.S. cents). If the demand for Canadian dollars increases and the demand curve shifts from D_0 to D_1, the Bank of Canada sells Canadian dollars. If the demand for Canadian dollars decreases and the demand curve shifts from D_0 to D_2, the Bank of Canada buys Canadian dollars. Persistent intervention on one side of the market cannot be sustained.

————— MyEconLab Animation —————

Now suppose the demand for Canadian dollars *decreases permanently* from D_0 to D_2. In this situation, the Bank of Canada *cannot* maintain the exchange rate at 90 U.S. cents per Canadian dollar indefinitely. To hold it at 90 U.S. cents, the Bank of Canada must *buy* Canadian dollars using Canada's official foreign currency reserves. So the Bank of Canada's action decreases its foreign currency reserves. Eventually, the Bank of Canada would run out of foreign currency and would then have to abandon the target exchange rate of 90 U.S. cents per Canadian dollar.

Crawling Peg

A **crawling peg** is an exchange rate that follows a path determined by a decision of the government or the central bank and is achieved in a similar way to a fixed exchange rate by central bank intervention in

Economics in Action
The People's Bank of China in the Foreign Exchange Market

The exchange rate between the U.S. dollar and the Chinese yuan was constant for several years before 2005. The reason for this constant exchange rate is that China's central bank, the People's Bank of China, intervened to operate a *fixed exchange rate policy*. From 1997 until 2005, the yuan was pegged at 8.28 yuan per U.S. dollar. Since 2005, the yuan has appreciated slightly, but it has not been permitted to fluctuate freely. Since 2005, the yuan has been on a crawling peg.

Why Does China Manage Its Exchange Rate?   The popular story is that China manages its exchange rate to keep its export prices low and to make it easier to compete in world markets. You've seen that this story is correct *only in the short run*. With prices in China unchanged, a lower yuan–U.S. dollar exchange rate brings lower U.S. dollar prices for China's exports. But the yuan–U.S. dollar exchange rate was fixed for almost 10 years and has been managed for five more years. This long period of a fixed exchange rate has long-run, not short-run, effects. In the long run, the exchange rate has no effect on competitiveness. The reason is that prices adjust to reflect the exchange rate and the real exchange rate is unaffected by the nominal exchange rate.

So why does China fix its exchange rate? The most convincing answer is that China sees a fixed exchange rate as a way of controlling its inflation rate. By making the yuan crawl against the U.S. dollar, China's inflation rate is anchored to the U.S. inflation rate and will depart from U.S. inflation by an amount determined by the speed of the crawl.

the foreign exchange market. A crawling peg works like a fixed exchange rate except that the target value changes. The target might change at fixed intervals (daily, weekly, monthly) or at random intervals.

The Bank of Canada has never operated a crawling peg, but some countries do. When China abandoned its fixed exchange rate, it replaced it with a crawling peg. Developing countries might use a crawling peg as a method of trying to control inflation.

The ideal crawling peg sets a target for the exchange rate equal to the equilibrium exchange rate

The bottom line is that in the long run, exchange rate policy is monetary policy, not foreign trade policy. To change its exports and imports, a country must change its comparative advantage (Chapter 2).

How Does China Manage Its Exchange Rate? The People's Bank manages the exchange rate between the yuan and the U.S. dollar by intervening in the foreign exchange market and buying U.S. dollars. But to do so, it must pile up U.S. dollars.

Part (a) of the figure shows the scale of China's increase in official foreign currency reserves, some of which are euros and yen but most of which are U.S. dollars. You can see that China's reserves increased by more than $400 billion a year in 2007 through 2010.

The demand and supply curves in part (b) of the figure illustrate what is happening in the market for U.S. dollars priced in terms of the yuan and explains why China's reserves have increased. The demand curve D and supply curve S intersect at 5 yuan per U.S. dollar. If the People's Bank of China takes no actions in the market, this exchange rate is the equilibrium rate (an assumed value).

The consequence of the fixed (and crawling peg) yuan exchange rate is that China has piled up U.S. dollar reserves on a huge scale. By mid-2006, China's official foreign currency reserves approached $1 trillion, and by 2014 they had reached $4 trillion!

If the People's Bank stopped buying U.S. dollars, the U.S. dollar would depreciate and the yuan would appreciate—the yuan–U.S. dollar exchange rate would fall— and China would stop piling up U.S. dollar reserves.

In the example in the figure, the dollar would depreciate to 5 yuan per dollar.

(a) Increase in U.S. dollar reserves

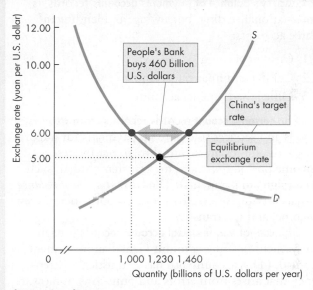

(b) Pegging the yuan

China's Foreign Exchange Market Intervention

Source of data: The People's Bank of China.

on average. The peg seeks only to prevent large swings in the expected future exchange rate that change demand and supply and make the exchange rate fluctuate too wildly.

A crawling peg departs from the ideal if, as often happens with a fixed exchange rate, the target rate departs from the equilibrium exchange rate for too long. When this happens, the country either runs out of reserves or piles up reserves.

In the final part of this chapter, we explain how the balance of international payments is determined.

REVIEW QUIZ

1 What is a flexible exchange rate and how does it work?

2 What is a fixed exchange rate and how is its value fixed?

3 What is a crawling peg and how does it work?

4 How has China operated in the foreign exchange market, why, and with what effect?

Work these questions in Study Plan 25.3 and get instant feedback. Do a Key Terms Quiz. MyEconLab

Financing International Trade

You now know how the exchange rate is determined, but what is the effect of the exchange rate? How does currency depreciation or currency appreciation influence our international trade and payments? We're going to lay the foundation for addressing these questions by looking at the scale of international trading, borrowing, and lending and at the way in which we keep our records of international transactions. These records are called the *balance of payments accounts*.

Balance of Payments Accounts

A country's **balance of payments accounts** records its international trading, borrowing, and lending in three accounts:

1. Current account
2. Capital and financial account
3. Official settlements account

The **current account** records receipts from exports of goods and services sold abroad, payments for imports of goods and services from abroad, net interest income paid abroad, and net transfers abroad (such as foreign aid payments). The *current account balance* equals the sum of exports minus imports, net interest income, and net transfers.

The **capital and financial account** records foreign investment in Canada minus Canadian investment abroad. (This account also has a statistical discrepancy that arises from errors and omissions in measuring international capital transactions.)

The **official settlements account** records the change in **Canadian official reserves**, which are the government's holdings of foreign currency. If Canadian official reserves *increase*, the official settlements account balance is *negative*. The reason is that holding foreign money is like investing abroad. Canadian investment abroad is a minus item in the capital and financial account and in the official settlements account.

The sum of the balances on the three accounts *always* equals zero. That is, to pay for our current account deficit, we must either borrow more from abroad than we lend abroad or use our official reserves to cover the shortfall.

Table 25.1 shows the Canadian balance of payments accounts in 2013. Items in the current account and the capital and financial account that provide foreign currency to Canada have a plus sign; items that cost Canada foreign currency have a minus sign. The table shows that in 2013, Canadian imports exceeded Canadian exports and the current account had a deficit of $60 billion. How do we pay for imports that exceed the value of our exports? That is, how do we pay for our current account deficit?

We pay for our current account deficit by borrowing from the rest of the world. The capital and financial account tells us by how much. We borrowed from the rest of the world (foreign investment in Canada) and we lent to the rest of the world (Canadian investment abroad). Our *net* foreign borrowing was $65 billion. There is almost always a statistical discrepancy between the capital and financial account and current account transactions, and in 2013, the discrepancy was less that half a billion (shown as zero in the table), so the capital and financial account balance was $65 billion.

TABLE 25.1   Canadian Balance of Payments Accounts in 2013

Current account	Billions of dollars
Exports of goods and services	+566
Imports of goods and services	−598
Net interest income	−26
Net transfers	−2
Current account balance	−60

Capital and financial account	
Net foreign investment in Canada	+65
Statistical discrepancy	0
Capital and financial account balance	+65

Official settlements account	0
Offical settlements account balance	−5

Source of data: Statistics Canada, CANSIM Tables 376-0101 and 376-0104.

The capital and financial account balance plus the current account balance equals the change in Canadian official reserves. In 2013, the capital and financial account balance of $65 billion plus the current account balance of −$60 billion equalled $5 billion. Canadian official reserves *increased* in 2013 by $5 billion. Holding more foreign reserves is like lending to the rest of the world, so this amount appears in the official settlements account in Table 25.1 as −$5 billion. The sum of the balances on the three balance of payments accounts equals zero.

To see more clearly what the nation's balance of payments accounts mean, think about your own balance of payments accounts. They are similar to the nation's accounts.

An Individual's Balance of Payments Accounts An individual's current account records the income from supplying the services of factors of production and the expenditure on goods and services. Consider Jackie, for example. She worked in 2014 and earned an income of $25,000. Jackie has $10,000 worth of investments that earned her an interest income of $1,000. Jackie's current account shows an income of $26,000. Jackie spent $18,000 buying consumption goods and services. She also bought a new house, which cost her $60,000. So Jackie's total expenditure was $78,000. Jackie's expenditure minus her income is $52,000 ($78,000 minus $26,000). This amount is Jackie's current account deficit.

Economics in Action
Three Decades of Deficits

The numbers that you reviewed in Table 25.1 give a snapshot of the balance of payments accounts in 2013. The figure below puts that snapshot into perspective by showing the balance of payments between 1985 and the first half of 2013.

Because the economy grows and the price level rises, changes in the dollar value of the balance of payments do not convey much information. To remove the influences of economic growth and inflation, the figure shows the balance of payments expressed as a percentage of nominal GDP.

As you can see, a large current account deficit emerged during the 1980s and declined during the 1990s and moved into surplus in the 2000s before returning to deficit after 2008.

The capital and financial account balance is almost a mirror image of the current account balance. The official settlements balance is very small in comparison with the balances on the other two accounts.

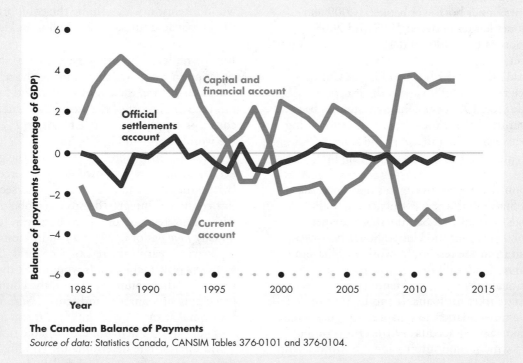

The Canadian Balance of Payments
Source of data: Statistics Canada, CANSIM Tables 376-0101 and 376-0104.

To pay for expenditure of $52,000 in excess of her income, Jackie must either use the money that she has in the bank or take out a loan. Suppose that Jackie took out a loan of $50,000 to help buy her house and that this loan was the only borrowing that she did. Borrowing is an *inflow* in the capital account, so Jackie's capital account *surplus* was $50,000. With a current account deficit of $52,000 and a capital account surplus of $50,000, Jackie was still $2,000 short. She got that $2,000 from her own bank account. Her cash holdings decreased by $2,000.

Jackie's income from her work is like a country's income from its exports. Her income from her investments is like a country's interest income from foreigners. Her purchases of goods and services, including her purchase of a house, are like a country's imports. Jackie's loan—borrowing from someone else—is like a country's borrowing from the rest of the world. The change in Jackie's bank account is like the change in the country's official reserves.

Borrowers and Lenders

A country that is borrowing more from the rest of the world than it is lending to the rest of the world is called a **net borrower**. Similarly, a **net lender** is a country that is lending more to the rest of the world than it is borrowing from the rest of the world.

Canada was a net borrower between 2009 and 2013 and a net lender between 1999 and 2008. Through most of the 1980s and 1990s, Canada was a net borrower.

The world's largest net borrower is the United States. Since the early 1980s, with the exception of only a single year, 1991, the United States has been a net borrower from the rest of the world. And during the years between 1992 and 2008, the scale of U.S. borrowing mushroomed. It has shrunk slightly since 2008.

Most countries are net borrowers like Canada and the United States. But a few countries, including China, Japan, and oil-rich Saudi Arabia, are net lenders. In 2014, when the United States borrowed $397 billion from the rest of the world, China alone lent more than $200 billion.

International borrowing and lending takes place in the global market for loanable funds. You studied the loanable funds market in Chapter 23, but there, we didn't take explicit account of the effects of the balance of payments and international borrowing and lending on the market. That's what we will now do.

The Global Loanable Funds Market

Figure 25.7(a) illustrates the demand for loanable funds, DLF_W, and the supply of loanable funds, SLF_W, in the global loanable funds market. The world equilibrium real interest rate makes the quantity of funds supplied in the world as a whole equal to the quantity demanded. In this example, the equilibrium real interest rate is 5 percent a year and the quantity of funds is $10 trillion.

An International Borrower Figure 25.7(b) shows the loanable funds market in a country that borrows from the rest of the world. The country's demand for loanable funds, DLF, is part of the world demand in Fig. 25.7(a). The country's supply of loanable funds, SLF_D, is part of the world supply.

If this country were isolated from the global market, the real interest rate would be 6 percent a year (where the DLF and SLF_D curves intersect). But if the country is integrated into the global economy, with an interest rate of 6 percent a year, funds would *flood into* it. With a real interest rate of 5 percent a year in the global market, suppliers of loanable funds would seek the higher return in this country. In effect, the country faces the supply of loanable funds curve, SLF, which is horizontal at the world equilibrium real interest rate.

The country's demand for loanable funds and the world interest rate determine the equilibrium quantity of loanable funds—$2.5 billion in Fig. 25.7(b).

An International Lender Figure 25.7(c) shows the situation in a country that lends to the rest of the world. As before, the country's demand for loanable funds, DLF, is part of the world demand and the country's supply of loanable funds, SLF_D, is part of the world supply in Fig. 25.7(a).

If this country were isolated from the global market, the real interest rate would be 4 percent a year (where the DLF and SLF_D curves intersect). But if this country is integrated into the global economy, with an interest rate of 4 percent a year, funds would quickly *flow out* of it. With a real interest rate of 5 percent a year in the rest of the world, domestic suppliers of loanable funds would seek the higher return in other countries. Again, the country faces the supply of loanable funds curve, SLF, which is horizontal at the world equilibrium real interest rate.

The country's demand for loanable funds and the world interest rate determine the equilibrium quantity of loanable funds—$1.5 billion in Fig. 25.7(c).

FIGURE 25.7   Borrowing and Lending in the Global Loanable Funds Market

(a) The global market   **(b) An international borrower**   **(c) An international lender**

In the global loanable funds market in part (a), the demand for loanable funds curve, DLF_W, and the supply of funds curve, SLF_W, determine the world real interest rate. Each country can get funds at the world real interest rate and faces the (horizontal) supply curve SLF in parts (b) and (c).

At the world real interest rate, borrowers in part (b) want more funds than the quantity supplied by domestic

lenders, $1.5 billion on the domestic supply curve SLF_D. The shortage is made up by net foreign borrowing.

Domestic suppliers of funds in part (c) want to lend more than domestic borrowers demand. The excess quantity supplied goes to foreign borrowers.

MyEconLab Animation

Debtors and Creditors

A net borrower might be decreasing its net assets held in the rest of the world, or it might be going deeper into debt. A nation's total stock of foreign investment determines whether it is a debtor or a creditor. A **debtor nation** is a country that during its entire history has borrowed more from the rest of the world than it has lent to it. It has a stock of outstanding debt to the rest of the world that exceeds the stock of its own claims on the rest of the world. A **creditor nation** is a country that during its entire history has invested more in the rest of the world than other countries have invested in it.

Canada is a debtor nation. Throughout the nineteenth century Canada borrowed from Europe to finance its westward expansion, railroads, and industrialization. The capital-hungry developing countries (such as Canada was during the nineteenth century) are among the largest debtor nations in the world. The international debt of these countries grew from less than a third to more than a half of their gross domestic product during the 1980s and created what was called the "Third World debt crisis."

But the United States is the largest debtor nation. Since 1986, the total stock of U.S. borrowing from

the rest of the world has exceeded U.S. lending to the rest of the world by $11.9 trillion (more than five times Canada's gross domestic product).

Should we be concerned that Canada is a net borrower and a debtor? The answer depends on whether the borrowing is financing investment that in turn is generating economic growth and higher income, or financing consumption expenditure. If the borrowed money is used to finance consumption, it will eventually have to be reduced, and the longer it goes on, the greater is the reduction in consumption that will eventually be necessary.

Is Canadian Borrowing for Consumption?

In 2013, Canada borrowed $65 billion from abroad. In that year, private investment in buildings, plant, and equipment was $340 billion and government investment in defence equipment and social projects was $78 billion. All this investment added to Canada's capital and increased productivity. The government also spends on education and healthcare services, which increase *human capital*. Canadian international borrowing is financing private and public investment, not consumption.

Current Account Balance

What determines a country's current account balance and net foreign borrowing? You've seen that net exports (NX) is the main item in the current account. We can define the current account balance (CAB) as:

$$CAB = NX + \text{Net interest income} + \text{Net transfers}.$$

We can study the current account balance by looking at what determines net exports because the other two items are small and do not fluctuate much.

Net Exports

Net exports are determined by the government budget and private saving and investment. To see how net exports are determined, we need to recall some of the things that we learned in Chapter 23 about the flows of funds that finance investment. Table 25.2 refreshes your memory and summarizes some calculations.

Part (a) lists the national income variables that are needed, with their symbols. Part (b) defines three balances: net exports, the government sector balance, and the private sector balance.

Net exports is exports of goods and services minus imports of goods and services.

The **government sector balance** is equal to net taxes minus government expenditure on goods and services. If that number is positive, a government sector surplus is lent to other sectors; if that number is negative, a government deficit must be financed by borrowing from other sectors. The government sector deficit is the sum of the deficits of the Bank of Canada, provincial, and local governments.

The **private sector balance** is saving minus investment. If saving exceeds investment, a private sector surplus is lent to other sectors. If investment exceeds saving, a private sector deficit is financed by borrowing from other sectors.

Part (b) also shows the values of these balances for Canada in 2013. As you can see, net exports were −$32 billion, a deficit of $32 billion. The government sector's revenue from *net* taxes was $429 billion and its expenditure was $486 billion, so the government sector balance was −$57 billion—a deficit of $57 billion. The private sector saved $365 billion and invested $340 billion, so its balance was $25 billion—a surplus of $25 billion.

Part (c) shows the relationship among the three balances. From the national income and expenditure accounts, we know that real GDP, Y, is the sum of

consumption expenditure (C), investment, government expenditure, and net exports. Real GDP also equals the sum of consumption expenditure, saving, and net taxes. Rearranging these equations tells us that net exports is the sum of the government sector balance and the private sector balance. In Canada in 2013, the government sector balance was −$57 billion and the private sector balance was $25 billion.

TABLE 25.2 Net Exports, the Government Budget, Saving, and Investment

	Symbols and equations	Canada in 2013 (billions of dollars)
(a) Variables		
Exports*	X	566
Imports*	M	598
Government expenditure	G	486
Net taxes	T	429
Investment	I	340
Saving	S	365
(b) Balances		
Net exports	$X - M$	$566 - 598 = -32$
Government sector	$T - G$	$429 - 486 = -57$
Private sector	$S - I$	$365 - 340 = +25$
(c) Relationship among balances		
National accounts	$Y = C + I + G + X - M$	
	$= C + S + T$	
Rearranging:	$X - M = S - I + T - G$	
Net exports	$X - M$	−32
equals:		
Government sector	$T - G$	−57
plus		
Private sector	$S - I$	+25

Source of data: Statistics Canada, CANSIM Tables 380-0002, 380-0017, and 380-0064.

* The national income and expenditure accounts measures of exports and imports are slightly different from the balance of payments accounts measures in Table 25.1 on p. 608.

Economics in Action
The Three Sector Balances

You've seen that net exports equal the sum of the government sector balance and the private sector balance. How do these three sector balances fluctuate over time?

The figure answers this question. It shows the government sector balance (the red line), net exports (the blue line), and the private sector balance (the green line).

The private sector balance and the government sector balance move in opposite directions. When the government sector deficit increased during the early 1980s and early 1990s, the private sector surplus increased. And when the government sector deficit decreased during the late 1990s and became a surplus during the early 2000s, the private sector's surplus decreased and became a deficit. In the late 2000s, when the government surplus shrank and became a deficit, the private sector deficit shrank and became a surplus.

Sometimes the government sector deficit and the net export surplus are correlated, but the net export balance does not follow the government sector balance closely. Rather, net exports respond to the sum of the government sector and private sector balances. When the private sector surplus exceeds the government sector

deficit, net exports are positive. When the government sector deficit exceeds the private sector surplus, net exports are negative.

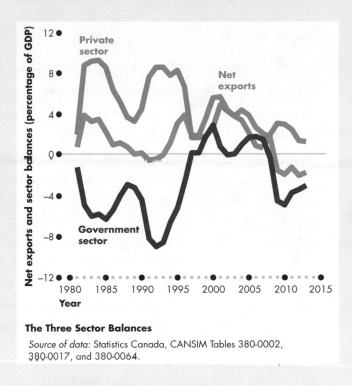

The Three Sector Balances

Source of data: Statistics Canada, CANSIM Tables 380-0002, 380-0017, and 380-0064.

The government sector balance plus the private sector balance equalled net exports of –$32 billion.

Where Is the Exchange Rate?

We haven't mentioned the exchange rate while discussing the balance of payments. Doesn't it play a role? The answer is that in the short run it does but in the long run it doesn't.

In the short run, a fall in the dollar lowers the real exchange rate, which makes Canadian imports more costly and Canadian exports more competitive. A higher price of imported consumption goods and services might induce a decrease in consumption expenditure and an increase in saving. A higher price of imported capital goods might induce a decrease in investment. Other things remaining the same, an increase in saving or a decrease in investment decreases the private sector deficit and decreases the current account deficit.

But in the long run, a change in the nominal exchange rate leaves the real exchange rate unchanged and plays no role in influencing the current account balance.

REVIEW QUIZ

1 What are the transactions that the balance of payments accounts record?
2 Is Canada a net borrower or a net lender? Is it a debtor or a creditor nation?
3 How are net exports and the government sector balance linked?

Work these questions in Study Plan 25.4 and get instant feedback. Do a Key Terms Quiz.   MyEconLab

◆ *Economics in the News* on pp. 614–615 looks at the rising U.S. dollar in the summer of 2014.

The Rising U.S. Dollar

Fed Minutes Lift U.S. Bond Yields and Dollar

The Financial Times
August 20, 2014

… [The] dollar extended its recent advance as the markets took a hawkish view of the minutes of the Federal Reserve's July policy meeting. …

Analysts said the minutes indicated that the U.S. Fed's Open Market Committee (FOMC) had moved closer toward raising interest rates. …

Paul Dales at Capital Economics said the minutes made it very clear that any change in officials' expectations of when the first rate hike would take place depended on incoming economic data. …

"Overall, a lot still depends on whether or not wage growth accelerates as the labor market continues to improve. Nonetheless, the minutes provide some support to our view that rates will first rise in March and will then increase by more than widely expected."…

But the bond and currency markets moved to price in an earlier tightening. The dollar index—a measure of the U.S. currency's value against a basket of its peers—was up 0.5 percent at its highest level in 11 months. The euro was down 0.4 percent at $1.3262—its first break below $1.33 since November—while the dollar was up 0.9 percent versus the yen at a four-month high of ¥103.75. …

This rekindled the prospect of an early U.K. rate rise and drove sterling as high as $1.6678 against the dollar—although it later eased back to $1.6593, down 0.1 percent on the day, as the dollar rose broadly. …

Recent data showing a drop in the annual rate of U.K. inflation last month—and stagnant wage growth—had persuaded some in the markets to push back their expectations of the timing of a rate rise. …

Written by Dave Shellock. Copyright © 2014 by Financial Times. Used under licence from *The Financial Times.* All rights reserved.

MyEconLab More Economics in the News

ESSENCE OF THE STORY

- The minutes of the U.S. Federal Reserve's July FOMC meeting indicated a movement toward raising interest rates.

- When the first increase occurs will depend on wage and employment growth.

- Paul Dales of Capital Economics predicts that interest rates will first rise in March 2015 and then increase by more than most expect.

- Anticipating an earlier interest rate rise, the U.S. dollar strengthened against other currencies.

ECONOMIC ANALYSIS

- The news article says the U.S. dollar rose against "a basket" of other currencies when the Federal Reserve published the minutes of the July meeting of its policy committee on August 20, 2014.

- The main currencies in the "basket" are the Canadian dollar, the Japanese yen, the European euro, and the U.K. pound.

- Figure 1 shows how the U.S dollar exchange rate changed against a basket of the top 10 currencies and separately against the Canadian dollar from July 2 to August 27, 2014.

- You can see that the U.S. dollar increased against all currencies and it increased somewhat more against the Canadian dollar than against the basket of currencies.

- The July minutes indicated that the Fed was moving closer to being ready to raise interest rates, and the news article attributes the stronger U.S. dollar to this news.

- But as you can see in Fig. 1, although the foreign exchange value of the U.S. dollar did rise immediately after the July minutes were released, it had been rising for almost two months.

- Also, after August 21, the U.S. dollar rose by more against the basket (that includes the euro) than it did against the Canadian dollar.

- These facts about the timing of changes in the exchange rate suggests that other forces are at work.

- The summer of 2014 was a time of global tension arising from the political situation in Ukraine. Currency traders sold the Russian ruble and the Ukrainian hryvnia and bought the U.S. dollar rather than currencies such as the euro or the pound.

- The Russia–Ukraine situation and the added effect of the expectation of a U.S. interest rate rise changed the demand for and supply of U.S. dollars in the foreign exchange market.

- The political tensions and predicted future rise in the U.S. interest rate increased the expected future exchange rate.

- With a higher expected future exchange rate, the demand for U.S. dollars increases and the supply of U.S. dollars decreases, and these changes in demand and supply bring an immediate appreciation of the U.S. dollar.

- Figure 2 shows these changes in supply and demand and their effects on the U.S. dollar–Canadian dollar exchange rate. (A similar figure would apply to the exchange rates between the U.S. dollar and other currencies.)

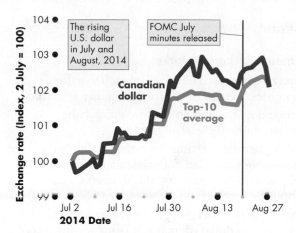

Figure 1 The U.S. Dollar Exchange Rate in July and August 2014

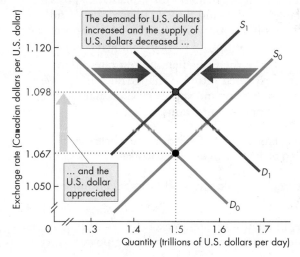

Figure 2 The U.S. Dollar Foreign Exchange Market

- On July 2, demand was D_0 and supply was S_0. The equilibrium exchange rate was 1.067 $C per $US. (The equilibrium quantity of dollars traded is an assumption.)

- On August 22, demand had increased to D_1 and supply had decreased to S_1. The equilibrium exchange rate had risen to 1.098 $C per $US—an appreciation of the U.S. dollar (and a depreciation of the Canadian dollar).

- Although we can explain past changes in the exchange rate, we can't predict the future exchange rate because we can't predict how the factors that influence the exchange rate will change.

SUMMARY

Key Points

The Foreign Exchange Market (pp. 594–601)

- Foreign currency is obtained in exchange for domestic currency in the foreign exchange market.
- Demand and supply in the foreign exchange market determine the exchange rate.
- The higher the exchange rate, the smaller is the quantity of Canadian dollars demanded and the greater is the quantity of Canadian dollars supplied.
- The equilibrium exchange rate makes the quantity of Canadian dollars demanded equal the quantity of Canadian dollars supplied.
- Changes in the demand for Canadian exports change the demand for Canadian dollars, and changes in the Canadian demand for imports change the supply of Canadian dollars.
- Changes in the Canadian interest rate differential or the expected future exchange rate change *both* the demand for and supply of Canadian dollars, but in opposite directions.

Working Problems 1 to 5 will give you a better understanding of the foreign exchange market.

Arbitrage, Speculation, and Market Fundamentals
(pp. 602–604)

- Arbitrage in the foreign exchange market achieves interest rate parity and purchasing power parity.

- Speculation in the foreign exchange market can bring excess volatility to the exchange rate.
- In the long run, the exchange rate is determined by the real exchange rate and the relative quantities of money.

Working Problems 6 to 8 will give you a better understanding of arbitrage, speculation, and market fundamentals.

Exchange Rate Policy (pp. 605–607)

- An exchange rate can be flexible, fixed, or a crawling peg.
- To achieve a fixed or a crawling exchange rate, a central bank must either buy or sell foreign currency in the foreign exchange market.

Working Problem 9 will give you a better understanding of exchange rate policy.

Financing International Trade (pp. 608–613)

- A country's international transactions are recorded in its current account, capital account, and official settlements account.
- The current account balance is similar to net exports and is determined by the government sector balance plus the private sector balance.
- International borrowing and lending take place in the global loanable funds market.

Working Problem 10 will give you a better understanding of financing international trade.

Key Terms   MyEconLab Key Terms Quiz

Arbitrage, 602	Current account, 608	Interest rate parity, 602
Balance of payments accounts, 608	Debtor nation, 611	Net borrower, 610
Canadian interest rate differential, 599	Exchange rate, 594	Net exports, 612
Canadian official reserves, 608	Fixed exchange rate, 605	Net lender, 610
Capital and financial account, 608	Flexible exchange rate, 605	Official settlements account, 608
Crawling peg, 606	Foreign currency, 594	Private sector balance, 612
Creditor nation, 611	Foreign exchange market, 594	Purchasing power parity, 602
	Government sector balance, 612	Real exchange rate, 604

WORKED PROBLEM

MyEconLab   You can work this problem in Chapter 25 Study Plan.

On June 1, 2015, the exchange rate was 101 yen per Canadian dollar. During that day, the Bank of Canada made a surprise announcement that it would raise the interest rate next month by 1 percentage point. At the same moment, the Bank of Japan announced that it would lower the interest rate next month.

On June 2, 2015, the exchange rate was 99 yen per Canadian dollar.

Questions

1. Explain the effect of the Bank of Canada's announcement on the demand for and supply of Canadian dollars.

2. Explain the effect of the Bank of Japan's announcement on the demand for and supply of Canadian dollars.

3. Explain the effect of the two announcements on the Canadian dollar–yen exchange rate: Would the Canadian dollar appreciate or depreciate?

4. Could the change in the exchange rate on June 2 have resulted from the two announcements, or must some other influence have changed too? If so, what might that influence have been?

Solutions

1. The Bank of Canada's announcement of a 1 percentage point rise in the Canadian interest rate next month means that, other interest rates remaining the same, the Canadian interest rate differential will increase next month.

    An increase in the Canadian interest rate differential next month will increase the demand for Canadian dollars and decrease the supply of Canadian dollars next month. The exchange rate next month will increase.

    With the increase in the exchange rate expected next month, the demand for Canadian dollars will increase and the supply of Canadian dollars will decrease on June 2.

Key Point: An expected *future* rise in the interest rate differential increases the demand for Canadian dollars and decreases the supply of Canadian dollars immediately through its effect on the expected future exchange rate.

2. The Bank of Japan's announcement that it will lower the interest rate in Japan next month has the same effect on the Canadian interest rate differential as a rise in the Canadian interest rate.

So the effect of a Japanese interest rate cut reinforces that of a Canadian interest rate increase.

The even-larger increase in the interest rate differential next month will bring a larger increase in the demand for Canadian dollars and decrease in the supply of Canadian dollars next month, and a larger increase in the exchange rate.

The larger increase in the exchange rate expected next month will bring a larger increase in the demand for Canadian dollars and a decrease in the supply of Canadian dollars on June 2.

Key Point: A fall in the foreign interest rate has the same effects on the demand for and supply of Canadian dollars as a rise in the Canadian interest rate.

3. The two interest rate announcements have the same effect: They increase the demand for Canadian dollars and decrease the supply of Canadian dollars.

    An increase in the demand for Canadian dollars raises the exchange rate and a decrease in the supply of Canadian dollars raises the exchange rate, so the announcements would make the dollar appreciate.

Key Point: An increase in demand and a decrease in supply have the same effect on price: They raise the price. The exchange rate is a price.

4. When the Canadian dollar fell from 101 yen on June 1 to 99 yen on June 2, the Canadian dollar depreciated. Other things remaining the same, the two central bank announcements would have appreciated the Canadian dollar.

    Because the exchange rate fell—the Canadian dollar depreciated—either the demand for Canadian dollars must have decreased or the supply of Canadian dollars must have increased.

    The influences on demand and supply that might have changed are Canadian exports or Canadian imports.

    A decrease in Canadian exports would have decreased the demand for Canadian dollars. An increase in Canadian imports would have increased the supply of Canadian dollars.

Key Point: When the Canadian dollar–yen exchange rate falls, either the demand for Canadian dollars has decreased or the supply of Canadian dollars has increased or both have occurred.

STUDY PLAN PROBLEMS AND APPLICATIONS

MyEconLab   You can work Problems 1 to 10 in Chapter 25 Study Plan and get instant feedback. Problems marked 🌐 update with real-time data.

The Foreign Exchange Market (Study Plan 25.1)

Use the following data to work Problems 1 to 3.
The U.S. dollar exchange rate increased from $0.96 Canadian in June 2011 to $1.03 Canadian in June 2012, and it decreased from 81 Japanese yen in June 2011 to 78 yen in June 2012.

🌐 1. Did the U.S. dollar appreciate or depreciate against the Canadian dollar? Did the U.S. dollar appreciate or depreciate against the yen?

🌐 2. What was the value of the Canadian dollar in terms of U.S. dollars in June 2011 and June 2012? Did the Canadian dollar appreciate or depreciate against the U.S. dollar over the year June 2011 to June 2012?

🌐 3. What was the value of 100 yen in terms of U.S. dollars in June 2011 and June 2012? Did the yen appreciate or depreciate against the U.S. dollar over the year June 2011 to June 2012?

🌐 4. On March 30, 2012, the U.S. dollar was trading at 82 yen per U.S. dollar on the foreign exchange market. On August 30, 2012, the U.S. dollar was trading at 79 yen per U.S. dollar.

  a. What events in the foreign exchange market could have brought this fall in the value of the U.S. dollar?

  b. Did the events you've described change the demand for U.S. dollars, the supply of U.S. dollars, or both demand and supply in the foreign exchange market?

5. Colombia is the world's biggest producer of roses. The global demand for roses increases and at the same time Colombia's central bank increases the interest rate. In the foreign exchange market for Colombian pesos, what happens to:

  a. The demand for pesos?

  b. The supply of pesos?

  c. The quantity of pesos demanded?

  d. The quantity of pesos supplied?

  e. The peso–Canadian dollar exchange rate?

Arbitrage, Speculation, and Market Fundamentals
(Study Plan 25.2)

6. If a euro deposit in a bank in France earns interest of 4 percent a year and a yen deposit in Japan earns 0.5 percent a year, other things remaining the same and adjusted for risk, what is the exchange rate expectation of the Japanese yen?

7. The U.K. pound is trading at 1.54 Canadian dollars per U.K. pound and purchasing power parity holds. The Canadian interest rate is 2 percent a year and the U.K. interest rate is 4 percent a year.

  a. Calculate the Canadian interest rate differential.

  b. What is the U.K. pound expected to be worth in terms of Canadian dollars one year from now?

  c. Which country more likely has the lower inflation rate? How can you tell?

8. The Canadian price level is 106.3, the Japanese price level is 95.4, and the real exchange rate is 103.6 Japanese real GDP per unit of Canadian real GDP. What is the nominal exchange rate?

Exchange Rate Policy (Study Plan 25.3)

9. With the strengthening of the yen against other currencies in 2012, Japan's central bank did not take any action. A Japanese politician called on the central bank to take actions to weaken the yen, saying it will help exporters in the short run and have no long-run effects.

  a. What is Japan's current exchange rate policy?

  b. What does the politician want the exchange rate policy to be in the short run? Why would such a policy have no effect on the exchange rate in the long run?

Financing International Trade (Study Plan 25.4)

10. The table gives some information about Canada's international transactions in 2010.

Item	Billions of dollars
Imports of goods and services	508
Net foreign investment in Canada	54
Exports of goods and services	476
Net interest income	16
Net transfers	−3
Statistical discrepancy	1

  a. Calculate the balance on the three balance of payments accounts.

  b. Was Canada a net borrower or a net lender in 2010? Explain your answer.

ADDITIONAL PROBLEMS AND APPLICATIONS

MyEconLab   You can work these problems in MyEconLab if assigned by your instructor.
Problems marked ⊕ update with real-time data.

The Foreign Exchange Market

11. Suppose that yesterday the Canadian dollar was trading on the foreign exchange market at 0.75 euros per Canadian dollar and today the Canadian dollar is trading at 0.80 euros per Canadian dollar. Which of the two currencies (the Canadian dollar or the euro) has appreciated and which has depreciated today?

12. Suppose that the exchange rate fell from 80 yen per Canadian dollar to 70 yen per Canadian dollar. What is the effect of this change on the quantity of Canadian dollars that people plan to buy in the foreign exchange market?

13. Suppose that the exchange rate rose from 80 yen per Canadian dollar to 90 yen per Canadian dollar. What is the effect of this change on the quantity of Canadian dollars that people plan to sell in the foreign exchange market?

14. Today's exchange rate between the yuan and the U.S. dollar is 6.40 yuan per dollar, and the central bank of China is buying U.S. dollars in the foreign exchange market. If the central bank of China did not purchase U.S. dollars would there be excess demand or excess supply of U.S. dollars in the foreign exchange market? Would the exchange rate remain at 6.40 yuan per U.S. dollar? If not, which currency would appreciate?

15. Yesterday, the current exchange rate was $1.05 Canadian per U.S. dollar and traders expected the exchange rate to remain unchanged for the next month. Today, with new information, traders now expect the exchange rate next month to fall to $1 Canadian per U.S. dollar. Explain how the revised expected future exchange rate influences the demand for U.S. dollars, or the supply of U.S. dollars, or both in the foreign exchange market.

16. In 2011, the exchange rate changed from 94 yen per U.S. dollar in January to 84 yen per U.S. dollar in June, and back to 94 yen per dollar in December. What information would you need to determine the factors that caused these changes in the exchange rate? Which factors would change *both* demand and supply?

17. Canada produces natural resources (coal, natural gas, and others), the demand for which has increased rapidly as China and other emerging economies expand.

    a. Explain how growth in the demand for Canada's natural resources would affect the demand for Canadian dollars in the foreign exchange market.

    b. Explain how the supply of Canadian dollars would change.

    c. Explain how the value of the Canadian dollar would change.

    d. Illustrate your answer with a graphical analysis.

Arbitrage, Speculation, and Market Fundamentals

Use the following news clip to work Problems 18 and 19.

Indian Entrepreneur Seeks Opportunities

Rahul Reddy, an Indian real estate entrepreneur, believes that "The United States is good for speculative higher-risk investments." He profited from earlier investment in Australia, and a strong Australian dollar provided him with the funds to enter the U.S. real estate market at prices that he believed "we will probably not see for a long time." He said, "The United States is an economic powerhouse that I think will recover, and if the exchange rate goes back to what it was a few years ago, we will benefit."

Based on an article in *Forbes*, July 10, 2008

18. Explain why Mr. Reddy is investing in the U.S. real estate market.

19. Explain what would happen if the speculation made by Mr. Reddy became widespread. Would expectations become self-fulfilling?

Use the following information to work Problems 20 and 21.

Brazil's Overvalued Real

The Brazilian real has appreciated 33 percent against the U.S. dollar and has pushed up the price of a Big Mac in Sao Paulo to $4.60, higher than the New York price of $3.99. Despite Brazil's interest rate being at 8.75 percent a year compared to the U.S. interest rate at near zero, foreign funds flowing into Brazil surged in October.

Source: Bloomberg News, October 27, 2009

20. Does purchasing power parity hold? If not, does PPP predict that the Brazilian real will appreciate or depreciate against the U.S. dollar? Explain.

21. Does interest rate parity hold? If not, why not? Will the Brazilian real appreciate further or

depreciate against the U.S. dollar if the U.S. Federal Reserve raises the interest rate while the Brazilian interest rate remains at 8.75 percent a year?

22. **When the Chips Are Down**
The Economist magazine uses the price of a Big Mac to determine whether a currency is undervalued or overvalued. In July 2012, the price of a Big Mac was $4.33 in New York, 15.65 yuan in Beijing, and 6.50 Swiss francs in Geneva. The exchange rates were 6.37 yuan per U.S. dollar and 0.98 Swiss francs per U.S. dollar.

Source: *The Economist*, July 25, 2012

a. Was the yuan undervalued or overvalued relative to purchasing power parity?
b. Was the Swiss franc undervalued or overvalued relative to purchasing power parity?
c. Do you think the price of a Big Mac in different countries provides a valid test of purchasing power parity?

Exchange Rate Policy

Use the following news clip to work Problems 23 to 25.

U.S. Declines to Cite China as Currency Manipulator
In 2007, the U.S. trade deficit with China hit $256.3 billion, the largest deficit ever recorded with a single country. Chinese currency, the yuan, has risen in value by 18.4 percent against the U.S. dollar since the Chinese government loosened its currency system in July 2005. However, U.S. manufacturers contend the yuan is still undervalued by about 40 percent, making Chinese goods more competitive in this country and U.S. goods more expensive in China. China buys U.S. dollar-denominated securities to maintain the value of the yuan in terms of the U.S. dollar.

Source: MSN, May 15, 2008

23. What was the exchange rate policy adopted by China until July 2005? Explain how it worked. Draw a graph to illustrate your answer.
24. What was the exchange rate policy adopted by China after July 2005? Explain how it works.
25. Explain how fixed and crawling peg exchange rates can be used to manipulate trade balances in the short run, but not the long run.
26. **Aussie Dollar Hit by Interest Rate Talk**
The Australian dollar fell against the U.S. dollar to its lowest value in the past two weeks. The CPI inflation rate was reported to be generally as

expected but not high enough to justify previous expectations for an aggressive interest rate rise by Australia's central bank next week.

Source: Reuters, October 28, 2009

a. What is Australia's exchange rate policy? Explain why expectations about the Australian interest rate lowered the value of the Australian dollar against the U.S. dollar.
b. To avoid the fall in the value of the Australian dollar against the U.S. dollar, what action could the central bank of Australia have taken? Would such an action signal a change in Australia's exchange rate policy?

Financing International Trade

Use the following table to work Problems 27 and 28. The table gives some data about the U.K. economy:

Item	Billions of U.K. pounds
Consumption expenditure	721
Exports of goods and services	277
Government expenditures	230
Net taxes	217
Investment	181
Saving	162

27. Calculate the private sector and government sector balances.
28. What is the relationship between the government sector balance and net exports?

Economics in the News

29. After you have studied *Economics in the News* on pp. 614–615, answer the following questions.
a. What happened to the foreign exchange value of the U.S. dollar in July and August 2014?
b. What could the Bank of Canada have done to stop the fall in the Canadian dollar?
c. What could the European Central Bank have done that might have stopped the fall in the euro?
d. What can you infer about the changes in the Canadian dollar exchange rate against the basket of currencies during July and August 2014? Can you think of a reason for the behaviour of that exchange rate?
e. If the dollar continues its upward path against the euro, what do you predict will be the consequences for U.S. and European relative inflation rates?

Expanding the Frontier

PART EIGHT

Economics is about how we cope with scarcity. We cope as individuals by making choices that balance marginal benefits and marginal costs so that we use our scarce resources efficiently. We cope as societies by creating incentive systems and social institutions that encourage specialization and exchange.

These choices and the incentive systems that guide them determine what we specialize in; how much work we do; how hard we work at school to learn the mental skills that form our human capital and that determine the kinds of jobs we get and the incomes we earn; how much we save for future big-ticket expenditures; how much businesses and governments spend on new capital—on auto assembly lines, computers and fibre cables for improved Internet services, shopping malls, highways, bridges, and tunnels; how intensively existing capital and natural resources are used and how quickly they wear out or are used up; and the problems that scientists, engineers, and other inventors work on to develop new technologies.

All the choices we've just described combine to determine the standard of living and the rate at which it improves—the economic growth rate.

Money that makes specialization and exchange in markets possible is a huge contributor to economic growth. But too much money brings a rising cost of living with no improvement in the standard of living.

Joseph Schumpeter, *the son of a textile factory owner, was born in Austria in 1883. He moved from Austria to Germany during the tumultuous 1920s when those two countries experienced hyperinflation. In 1932, in the depths of the Great Depression, he came to the United States and became a professor of economics at Harvard University.*

This creative economic thinker wrote about economic growth and development, business cycles, political systems, and economic biography. He was a person of strong opinions who expressed them forcefully and delighted in verbal battles.

Schumpeter saw the development and diffusion of new technologies by profit-seeking entrepreneurs as the source of economic progress. But he saw economic progress as a process of creative destruction—the creation of new profit opportunities and the destruction of currently profitable businesses. For Schumpeter, economic growth and the business cycle were a single phenomenon.

"Economic progress, in capitalist society, means turmoil."

JOSEPH SCHUMPETER
Capitalism, Socialism, and Democracy

XAVIER SALA-I-MARTIN is Professor of Economics at Columbia University. He is also a Research Associate at the National Bureau of Economic Research, Senior Economic Advisor to the World Economic Forum, Associate Editor of the *Journal of Economic Growth,* founder and CEO of Umbele Foundation: A Future for Africa, and President of the Economic Commission of the Barcelona Football Club.

Professor Sala-i-Martin was an undergraduate at Universitat Autonoma de Barcelona and a graduate student at Harvard University, where he obtained his Ph.D. in 1990.

In 2004, he was awarded the Premio Juan Carlos I de Economía, a biannual prize given by the Bank of Spain to the best economist in Spain and Latin America. With Robert Barro, he is the author of *Economic Growth,* Second Edition (MIT Press, 2003), the definitive graduate level text on this topic.

Michael Parkin and Robin Bade talked with Xavier Sala-i-Martin about his work and the progress that economists have made in understanding economic growth.

How did economic growth become your major field of research?

I studied economics. I liked it. I studied mathematical economics. I liked it too, and I went to graduate school. In my second year at Harvard, Jeffrey Sachs hired me to go to Bolivia. I saw poor people for the first time in my life. I was shocked. I decided I should try to answer the question "Why are these people so poor and why are we so rich, and what can we do to turn their state into our state?" We live in a bubble world in the United States and Europe, and we don't realize how poor people really are. When you see poverty at first hand, it is very hard to think about something else. So I decided to study economic growth. Coincidentally, when I returned from Bolivia, I was assigned to be Robert Barro's teaching assistant. He was teaching economic growth, so I studied with him and eventually wrote books and articles with him.

> If there's no investment, there's no growth. ... Incentives are important.

What do we know today about the nature and causes of the wealth of nations that Adam Smith didn't know?

Actually, even though over the last 200 years some of the best minds have looked at the question, we know surprisingly little. We have some general principles that are not very easy to apply in practice. We know, for example, that markets are good. We know that for the economy to work, we need property rights to be guaranteed. If there are thieves—government or private thieves—that can steal the proceeds of the investment, there's no investment and there's no growth. We know that the incentives are very important.

These are general principles. Because we know these principles we should ask: How come Africa is still poor? The answer is, it is very hard to translate "Markets are good" and "Property rights work" into practical actions. We know that Zimbabwe has to guarantee property rights. With the government it has, that's not going to work. The U.S. constitution works in the United States. If you try to copy the constitution and impose the system in Zimbabwe, it's not going to work.

*You can read the full interview with Xavier Sala-i-Martin in MyEconLab.

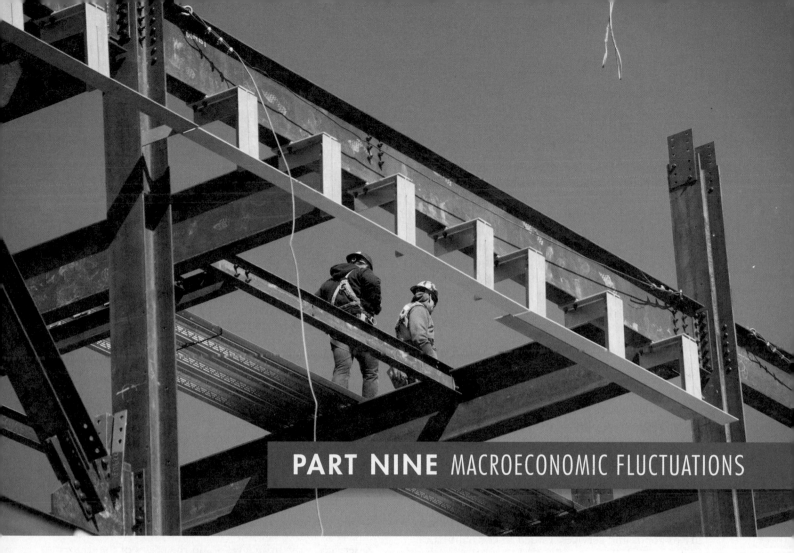

26

AGGREGATE SUPPLY AND AGGREGATE DEMAND

After studying this chapter, you will be able to:

◆ Explain what determines aggregate supply in the long run and in the short run

◆ Explain what determines aggregate demand

◆ Explain how real GDP and the price level are determined and what causes growth, inflation, and cycles

◆ Describe the main schools of thought in macroeconomics today

Real GDP grew by 3.1 percent in the second quarter of 2014, the fastest growth rate for several quarters. The inflation rate also edged upward in 2014. Why do real GDP and inflation fluctuate?

This chapter explains the economic fluctuations that we call the business cycle. You will study the *aggregate supply–aggregate demand model* or *AS-AD model*—a model of real GDP and the price level. And in *Economics in the News* at the end of the chapter, you will use that model to interpret and explain the state of the Canadian economy in 2014.

▶ Aggregate Supply

The purpose of the aggregate supply–aggregate demand model that you study in this chapter is to explain how real GDP and the price level are determined and how they interact. The model uses similar ideas to those that you encountered in Chapter 3 when you learned how the quantity and price in a competitive market are determined. But the *aggregate supply–aggregate* demand model (*AS-AD* model) isn't just an application of the competitive market model. Some differences arise because the *AS-AD* model is a model of an imaginary market for the total of all the final goods and services that make up real GDP. The quantity in this "market" is real GDP and the price is the price level measured by the GDP deflator.

One thing that the *AS-AD* model shares with the competitive market model is that both distinguish between *supply* and the *quantity supplied*. We begin by explaining what we mean by the quantity of real GDP supplied.

Quantity Supplied and Supply

The *quantity of real GDP supplied* is the total quantity of goods and services, valued in constant base-year (2007) dollars, that firms plan to produce during a given period. This quantity depends on the quantity of labour employed, the quantity of physical and human capital, and the state of technology.

At any given time, the quantity of capital and the state of technology are fixed. They depend on decisions that were made in the past. The population is also fixed. But the quantity of labour is not fixed. It depends on decisions made by households and firms about the supply of and demand for labour.

The labour market can be in any one of three states: at full employment, above full employment, or below full employment. At full employment, the quantity of real GDP supplied is *potential GDP*, which depends on the full-employment quantity of labour (see Chapter 22, pp. 521–522). Over the business cycle, employment fluctuates around full employment and the quantity of real GDP supplied fluctuates around potential GDP.

Aggregate supply is the relationship between the quantity of real GDP supplied and the price level. This relationship is different in the long run than in the short run and to study aggregate supply, we distinguish between two time frames:

- Long-run aggregate supply
- Short-run aggregate supply

Long-Run Aggregate Supply

Long-run aggregate supply is the relationship between the quantity of real GDP supplied and the price level when the money wage rate changes in step with the price level to maintain full employment. The quantity of real GDP supplied at full employment equals potential GDP, and this quantity is the same regardless of the price level.

The long-run aggregate supply curve in Fig. 26.1 illustrates long-run aggregate supply as the vertical line at potential GDP labelled *LAS*. Along the long-run aggregate supply curve, as the price level changes, the money wage rate also changes so that the real wage rate remains at the full-employment equilibrium level and real GDP remains at potential GDP. The long-run aggregate supply curve is always vertical and is always located at potential GDP.

The long-run aggregate supply curve is vertical because potential GDP is independent of the price level. The reason for this independence is that a movement along the *LAS* curve is accompanied by a change in *two* sets of prices: the prices of goods and services—the price level—and the prices of the factors of production, most notably, the money wage rate. A 10 percent increase in the prices of goods and services is matched by a 10 percent increase in the money wage rate. Because the price level and the money wage rate change by the same percentage, the *real wage rate* remains unchanged at its full-employment equilibrium level. So when the price level changes and the real wage rate remains constant, employment remains constant and real GDP remains constant at potential GDP.

Production at a Pepsi Plant You can see more clearly why real GDP is unchanged when all prices change by the same percentage by thinking about production decisions at a Pepsi bottling plant. How does the quantity of Pepsi supplied change if the price of Pepsi changes and the wage rate of the workers and prices of all the other resources used vary by the same percentage? The answer is that the quantity supplied doesn't change. The firm produces the quantity that maximizes profit. That quantity depends on the price of Pepsi relative to the cost of producing it. With no change in price *relative to cost*, production doesn't change.

Short-Run Aggregate Supply

Short-run aggregate supply is the relationship between the quantity of real GDP supplied and the price level *when the money wage rate, the prices of other resources, and potential GDP remain constant.* Figure 26.1 illustrates this relationship as the short-run aggregate supply curve *SAS* and the short-run aggregate supply schedule. Each point on the *SAS* curve corresponds to a row of the short-run aggregate supply schedule. For example, point *A* on the *SAS* curve and row *A* of the schedule tell us that if the price level is 100, the quantity of real GDP supplied is $1.5 trillion. In the short run, a rise in the price level brings an increase in the quantity of real GDP supplied. The short-run aggregate supply curve slopes upward.

With a given money wage rate, there is one price level at which the real wage rate is at its full-employment equilibrium level. At this price level, the quantity of real GDP supplied equals potential GDP and the *SAS* curve intersects the *LAS* curve. In this example, that price level is 110. If the price level rises above 110, the quantity of real GDP supplied increases along the *SAS* curve and exceeds potential GDP; if the price level falls below 110, the quantity of real GDP supplied decreases along the *SAS* curve and is less than potential GDP.

Back at the Pepsi Plant You can see why the short-run aggregate supply curve slopes upward by returning to the Pepsi bottling plant. If production increases, marginal cost rises; and if production decreases, marginal cost falls (see Chapter 2, p. 35).

If the price of Pepsi rises with no change in the money wage rate and other costs, Pepsi can increase profit by increasing production. Pepsi is in business to maximize its profit, so it increases production.

Similarly, if the price of Pepsi falls while the money wage rate and other costs remain constant, Pepsi can avoid a loss by decreasing production. The lower price weakens the incentive to produce, so Pepsi decreases production.

What's true for Pepsi bottlers is true for the producers of all goods and services. When all prices rise, the *price level rises.* If the price level rises and the money wage rate and other factor prices remain constant, all firms increase production and the quantity of real GDP supplied increases. A fall in the price level has the opposite effect and decreases the quantity of real GDP supplied.

FIGURE 26.1 Long-Run and Short-Run Aggregate Supply

	Price level (GDP deflator)	Real GDP supplied (trillions of 2007 dollars)
A	100	1.5
B	105	1.6
C	**110**	**1.7**
D	115	1.8
E	120	1.9

In the long run, the quantity of real GDP supplied is potential GDP and the *LAS* curve is vertical at potential GDP. In the short run, the quantity of real GDP supplied increases if the price level rises, while all other influences on supply plans remain the same.

The short-run aggregate supply curve, *SAS*, slopes upward. The short-run aggregate supply curve is based on the aggregate supply schedule in the table. Each point *A* through *E* on the curve corresponds to the row in the table identified by the same letter.

When the price level is 110, the quantity of real GDP supplied is $1.7 trillion, which is potential GDP. If the price level rises above 110, the quantity of real GDP supplied increases and exceeds potential GDP; if the price level falls below 110, the quantity of real GDP supplied decreases below potential GDP.

—————— MyEconLab Animation and Draw Graph ——————

Changes in Aggregate Supply

A change in the price level changes the quantity of real GDP supplied, which is illustrated by a movement along the short-run aggregate supply curve. It does not change aggregate supply. Aggregate supply changes when an influence on production plans other than the price level changes. These other influences include changes in potential GDP and changes in the money wage rate. Let's begin by looking at a change in potential GDP.

Changes in Potential GDP

When potential GDP changes, aggregate supply changes. An increase in potential GDP increases both long-run aggregate supply and short-run aggregate supply.

Figure 26.2 shows the effects of an increase in potential GDP. Initially, potential GDP is $1.7 trillion, the long-run aggregate supply curve is LAS_0, and the short-run aggregate supply curve is SAS_0. If potential GDP increases to $1.9 trillion, long-run aggregate supply increases and the long-run aggregate supply curve shifts rightward to LAS_1. Short-run aggregate supply also increases, and the short-run aggregate supply curve shifts rightward to SAS_1. The two supply curves shift by the same amount only if the full-employment price level remains constant, which we will assume to be the case.

Potential GDP can increase for any of three reasons:

- An increase in the full-employment quantity of labour
- An increase in the quantity of capital
- An advance in technology

Let's look at these influences on potential GDP and the aggregate supply curves.

An Increase in the Full-Employment Quantity of Labour

A Pepsi bottling plant that employs 100 workers bottles more Pepsi than does an otherwise identical plant that employs 10 workers. The same is true for the economy as a whole. The larger the quantity of labour employed, the greater is real GDP.

Over time, potential GDP increases because the labour force increases. But (with constant capital and technology) *potential* GDP increases only if the full-employment quantity of labour increases. Fluctuations in employment over the business cycle bring fluctuations in real GDP. But these changes in real GDP are fluctuations around potential GDP.

FIGURE 26.2   A Change in Potential GDP

An increase in potential GDP increases both long-run aggregate supply and short-run aggregate supply. The long-run aggregate supply curve shifts rightward from LAS_0 to LAS_1, and the short-run aggregate supply curve shifts from SAS_0 to SAS_1.

MyEconLab Animation

They are not changes in potential GDP and long-run aggregate supply.

An Increase in the Quantity of Capital

A Pepsi bottling plant with two production lines bottles more Pepsi than does an otherwise identical plant that has only one production line. For the economy, the larger the quantity of capital, the more productive is the labour force and the greater is its potential GDP. Potential GDP per person in capital-rich Canada is vastly greater than that in capital-poor China or Russia.

Capital includes *human capital*. One Pepsi plant is managed by an economics major with an MBA and has a labour force with an average of 10 years of experience. This plant produces a larger output than does an otherwise identical plant that is managed by someone with no business training or experience and that has a young labour force that is new to bottling. The first plant has a greater amount of human capital than the second. For the economy as a whole, the larger the quantity of *human capital*—the skills that people have acquired in school and through on-the-job training—the greater is potential GDP.

An Advance in Technology A Pepsi plant that has pre-computer age machines produces less than one that uses the latest robot technology. Technological change enables firms to produce more from any given amount of factors of production. So even with fixed quantities of labour and capital, improvements in technology increase potential GDP.

Technological advances are by far the most important source of increased production over the past two centuries. As a result of technological advances, one farmer in Canada today can feed 100 people and in a year one autoworker can produce almost 14 cars and trucks.

Let's now look at the effects of changes in the money wage rate.

Changes in the Money Wage Rate When the money wage rate (or the money price of any other factor of production such as oil) changes, short-run aggregate supply changes but long-run aggregate supply does not change.

Figure 26.3 shows the effect of an increase in the money wage rate. Initially, the short-run aggregate supply curve is SAS_0. A rise in the money wage rate *decreases* short-run aggregate supply and shifts the short-run aggregate supply curve leftward to SAS_2.

A rise in the money wage rate decreases short-run aggregate supply because it increases firms' costs. With increased costs, the quantity that firms are willing to supply at each price level decreases, which is shown by a leftward shift of the SAS curve.

A change in the money wage rate does not change long-run aggregate supply because on the LAS curve, the change in the money wage rate is accompanied by an equal percentage change in the price level. With no change in *relative* prices, firms have no incentive to change production, so real GDP remains constant at potential GDP. With no change in potential GDP, the long-run aggregate supply curve LAS does not shift.

What Makes the Money Wage Rate Change? The money wage rate can change for two reasons: departures from full employment and expectations about inflation. Unemployment above the natural rate puts downward pressure on the money wage rate, and unemployment below the natural rate puts upward pressure on it. An expected rise in the inflation rate makes the money wage rate rise faster, and an expected fall in the inflation rate slows the rate at which the money wage rate rises.

FIGURE 26.3   A Change in the Money Wage Rate

A rise in the money wage rate decreases short-run aggregate supply and shifts the short-run aggregate supply curve leftward from SAS_0 to SAS_2. A rise in the money wage rate does not change potential GDP, so the long-run aggregate supply curve does not shift.

MyEconLab Animation

◢ REVIEW QUIZ

1   If the price level and the money wage rate rise by the same percentage, what happens to the quantity of real GDP supplied? Along which aggregate supply curve does the economy move?

2   If the price level rises and the money wage rate remains constant, what happens to the quantity of real GDP supplied? Along which aggregate supply curve does the economy move?

3   If potential GDP increases, what happens to aggregate supply? Does the LAS curve shift or is there a movement along the LAS curve? Does the SAS curve shift or is there a movement along the SAS curve?

4   If the money wage rate rises and potential GDP remains the same, does the LAS curve or the SAS curve shift or is there a movement along the LAS curve or the SAS curve?

Work these questions in Study Plan 26.1 and get instant feedback. Do a Key Terms Quiz.   **MyEconLab**

Aggregate Demand

The quantity of real GDP demanded (Y) is the sum of real consumption expenditure (C), investment (I), government expenditure (G), and exports (X) minus imports (M). That is,

$$Y = C + I + G + X - M.$$

The *quantity of real GDP demanded* is the total amount of final goods and services produced in Canada that people, businesses, governments, and foreigners plan to buy.

These buying plans depend on many factors. Some of the main ones are:

1. The price level
2. Expectations
3. Fiscal policy and monetary policy
4. The world economy

We first focus on the relationship between the quantity of real GDP demanded and the price level. To study this relationship, we keep all other influences on buying plans the same and ask: How does the quantity of real GDP demanded vary as the price level varies?

The Aggregate Demand Curve

Other things remaining the same, the higher the price level, the smaller is the quantity of real GDP demanded. This relationship between the quantity of real GDP demanded and the price level is called **aggregate demand**. Aggregate demand is described by an *aggregate demand schedule* and an *aggregate demand curve*.

Figure 26.4 shows an aggregate demand curve (AD) and an aggregate demand schedule. Each point on the AD curve corresponds to a row of the schedule. For example, point C' on the AD curve and row C' of the schedule tell us that if the price level is 110, the quantity of real GDP demanded is $1.7 trillion.

The aggregate demand curve slopes downward for two reasons:

- Wealth effect
- Substitution effects

Wealth Effect When the price level rises but other things remain the same, *real* wealth decreases. Real

FIGURE 26.4 Aggregate Demand

	Price level (GDP deflator)	Real GDP demanded (trillions of 2007 dollars)
A'	90	1.9
B'	100	1.8
C'	**110**	**1.7**
D'	120	1.6
E'	130	1.5

The aggregate demand curve (*AD*) shows the relationship between the quantity of real GDP demanded and the price level. The aggregate demand curve is based on the aggregate demand schedule in the table. Each point A' through E' on the curve corresponds to the row in the table identified by the same letter. When the price level is 110, the quantity of real GDP demanded is $1.7 trillion, as shown by point C' in the figure. A change in the price level, when all other influences on aggregate buying plans remain the same, brings a change in the quantity of real GDP demanded and a movement along the AD curve.

MyEconLab Animation

wealth is the amount of money in the bank, bonds, shares, and other assets that people own, measured not in dollars but in terms of the goods and services that the money, bonds, and shares will buy.

People save and hold money, bonds, and shares for many reasons. One reason is to build up funds for education expenses. Another reason is to build up enough funds to meet home renovation expenses or other big bills. But the biggest reason is to build up enough funds to provide a retirement income.

If the price level rises, real wealth decreases. People then try to restore their wealth. To do so, they must increase saving and, equivalently, decrease current consumption. Such a decrease in consumption is a decrease in aggregate demand.

Maria's Wealth Effect You can see how the wealth effect works by thinking about Maria's buying plans. Maria lives in Moscow, Russia. She has worked hard all summer and saved 20,000 rubles (the ruble is the currency of Russia), which she plans to spend attending graduate school when she has finished her economics degree. So Maria's wealth is 20,000 rubles. Maria has a part-time job, and her income from this job pays her current expenses. The price level in Russia rises by 100 percent, and now Maria needs 40,000 rubles to buy what 20,000 once bought. To try to make up some of the fall in value of her savings, Maria saves even more and cuts her current spending to the bare minimum.

Substitution Effects When the price level rises and other things remain the same, interest rates rise. The reason is related to the wealth effect that you've just studied. A rise in the price level decreases the real value of the money in people's pockets and bank accounts. With a smaller amount of real money around, banks and other lenders can get a higher interest rate on loans. But faced with a higher interest rate, people and businesses delay plans to buy new capital and consumer durable goods and cut back on spending.

This substitution effect involves changing the timing of purchases of capital and consumer durable goods and is called an *intertemporal* substitution effect—a substitution across time. Saving increases to increase future consumption.

To see this intertemporal substitution effect more clearly, think about your own plan to buy a new computer. At an interest rate of 5 percent a year, you might borrow $1,000 and buy the new computer. But at an interest rate of 10 percent a year, you might decide that the payments would be too high. You don't abandon your plan to buy the computer, but you decide to delay your purchase.

A second substitution effect works through international prices. When the Canadian price level rises and other things remain the same, Canadian-made goods and services become more expensive relative to foreign-made goods and services. This change in *relative prices* encourages people to spend less on Canadian-made items and more on foreign-made items. For example, if the Canadian price level rises relative to the Japanese price level, Japanese buy fewer Canadian-made cars (Canadian exports decrease) and Canadians buy more Japanese-made cars (Canadian imports increase). Canadian GDP decreases.

Maria's Substitution Effects In Moscow, Russia, Maria makes some substitutions. She was planning to trade in her old motor scooter and get a new one. But with a higher price level and a higher interest rate, she decides to make her old scooter last one more year. Also, with the prices of Russian goods sharply increasing, Maria substitutes a low-cost dress made in Malaysia for the Russian-made dress she had originally planned to buy.

Changes in the Quantity of Real GDP Demanded

When the price level rises and other things remain the same, the quantity of real GDP demanded decreases—a movement up along the *AD* curve as shown by the arrow in Fig. 26.4. When the price level falls and other things remain the same, the quantity of real GDP demanded increases—a movement down along the *AD* curve.

We've now seen how the quantity of real GDP demanded changes when the price level changes. How do other influences on buying plans affect aggregate demand?

Changes in Aggregate Demand

A change in any factor that influences buying plans other than the price level brings a change in aggregate demand. The main factors are:

- Expectations
- Fiscal policy and monetary policy
- The world economy

Expectations An increase in expected future income increases the amount of consumption goods (especially expensive items such as cars) that people plan to buy today and increases aggregate demand today.

An increase in the expected future inflation rate increases aggregate demand today because people decide to buy more goods and services at today's relatively lower prices.

An increase in expected future profits increases the investment that firms plan to undertake today and increases aggregate demand today.

Fiscal Policy and Monetary Policy The government's attempt to influence the economy by setting and changing taxes, making transfer payments, and purchasing goods and services is called **fiscal policy**. A tax cut or an increase in transfer payments—for example, unemployment benefits or welfare payments—increases aggregate demand. Both of these influences operate by increasing households' *disposable* income. **Disposable income** is aggregate income minus taxes plus transfer payments. The greater the disposable income, the greater is the quantity of consumption goods and services that households plan to buy and the greater is aggregate demand.

Government expenditure on goods and services is one component of aggregate demand. So if the government spends more on spy satellites, schools, and highways, aggregate demand increases.

The Bank of Canada's attempt to influence the economy by changing interest rates and the quantity of money is called **monetary policy**. The Bank influences the quantity of money and interest rates by using the tools and methods described in Chapter 24.

An increase in the quantity of money increases aggregate demand through two main channels: It lowers interest rates and makes it easier to get a loan.

With lower interest rates, businesses plan greater investment in new capital and households plan greater expenditure on new homes, on home improvements, on automobiles, and a host of other consumer durable goods. Banks and others eager to lend lower their standards for making loans and more people are able to get home loans and other consumer loans.

A decrease in the quantity of money has the opposite effects and lowers aggregate demand.

The World Economy Two main influences that the world economy has on aggregate demand are the exchange rate and foreign income. The *exchange rate* is the amount of a foreign currency that you can buy with a Canadian dollar. Other things remaining the same, a rise in the exchange rate decreases aggregate

Economics in Action
Central Banks Fight Recession

The global financial crisis of 2008 sent the Canadian and global economies into a deep recession from which recovery was slow. Even six years later, in 2014, no major economy had returned to full employment and the Canadian economy continued to face headwinds from weak U.S. demand and even weaker E.U. demand.

Starting in the fall of 2008, the Bank of Canada, in concert with the U.S. Federal Reserve, the European

Central Bank, and the Bank of England, cut the interest rate and took other measures to ease credit and encourage banks and other financial institutions to increase their lending.

The goal of these central bank actions was to restore business and consumer confidence and provide low-cost financing that might boost investment and consumer spending and increase aggregate demand.

Low interest rate policies helped to avoid a deeper recession, but they had limited success in bringing recovery and were still being pursued at the end of 2014.

Bank of Canada, Ottawa

Federal Reserve, Washington, DC

European Central Bank, Frankfurt, Germany

FIGURE 26.5   Changes in Aggregate Demand

Aggregate demand

Decreases if:

- Expected future income, inflation, or profit decreases

- Fiscal policy decreases government expenditure, increases taxes, or decreases transfer payments

- Monetary policy decreases the quantity of money and increases interest rates

- The exchange rate increases or foreign income decreases

Increases if:

- Expected future income, inflation, or profit increases

- Fiscal policy increases government expenditure, decreases taxes, or increases transfer payments

- Monetary policy increases the quantity of money and decreases interest rates

- The exchange rate decreases or foreign income increases

———— MyEconLab Animation ————

demand. To see how the exchange rate influences aggregate demand, suppose that the exchange rate is 1.20 euros per Canadian dollar. An Airbus plane made in France costs 120 million euros, and an equivalent Bombardier airplane made in Canada costs $110 million. In Canadian dollars, the Airbus

plane costs $100 million, so airlines both in Canada and around the world buy the cheaper airplane from France. Now suppose the exchange rate falls to 1 euro per Canadian dollar. The Airbus airplane now costs $120 million and is more expensive than the Bombardier airplane. Airlines will switch from the Airbus to Bombardier. Canadian exports will increase and Canadian imports will decrease, so Canadian aggregate demand will increase.

An increase in foreign income increases Canadian exports and increases Canadian aggregate demand. For example, an increase in income in China and the United States increases Chinese and U.S. consumers' and producers' planned expenditures on Canadian-produced goods and services.

Shifts of the Aggregate Demand Curve   When aggregate demand changes, the aggregate demand curve shifts. Figure 26.5 shows two changes in aggregate demand and summarizes the factors that bring about such changes.

Aggregate demand increases and the AD curve shifts rightward from AD_0 to AD_1 when expected future income, inflation, or profit increases; government expenditure on goods and services increases; taxes are cut; transfer payments increase; the quantity of money increases and the interest rate falls; the exchange rate falls; or foreign income increases.

Aggregate demand decreases and the AD curve shifts leftward from AD_0 to AD_2 when expected future income, inflation, or profit decreases; government expenditure on goods and services decreases; taxes increase; transfer payments decrease; the quantity of money decreases and the interest rate rises; the exchange rate rises; or foreign income decreases.

REVIEW QUIZ

1   What does the aggregate demand curve show? What factors change and what factors remain the same when there is a movement along the aggregate demand curve?

2   Why does the aggregate demand curve slope downward?

3   How do changes in expectations, fiscal policy and monetary policy, and the world economy change aggregate demand and the aggregate demand curve?

Work these questions in Study Plan 26.2 and get instant feedback. Do a Key Terms Quiz.   MyEconLab

Explaining Macroeconomic Trends and Fluctuations

The purpose of the *AS-AD* model is to explain changes in real GDP and the price level. The model's main purpose is to explain business cycle fluctuations in these variables. But the model also aids our understanding of economic growth and inflation trends. We begin by combining aggregate supply and aggregate demand to determine real GDP and the price level in equilibrium. Just as there are two time frames for aggregate supply, there are two time frames for macroeconomic equilibrium: a long-run equilibrium and a short-run equilibrium. We'll first look at short-run equilibrium.

Short-Run Macroeconomic Equilibrium

The aggregate demand curve tells us the quantity of real GDP demanded at each price level, and the short-run aggregate supply curve tells us the quantity of real GDP supplied at each price level. **Short-run macroeconomic equilibrium** occurs when the quantity of real GDP demanded equals the quantity of real GDP supplied. That is, short-run macroeconomic equilibrium occurs at the point of intersection of the *AD* curve and the *SAS* curve.

Figure 26.6 shows such an equilibrium at a price level of 110 and real GDP of $1.7 trillion (points *C* and *C'*).

To see why this position is the equilibrium, think about what happens if the price level is something other than 110. Suppose, for example, that the price level is 120 and that real GDP is $1.9 trillion (at point *E* on the *SAS* curve). The quantity of real GDP demanded is less than $1.9 trillion, so firms are unable to sell all their output. Unwanted inventories pile up, and firms cut both production and prices. Production and prices are cut until firms can sell all their output. This situation occurs only when real GDP is $1.7 trillion and the price level is 110.

Now suppose the price level is 100 and real GDP is $1.5 trillion (at point *A* on the *SAS* curve). The quantity of real GDP demanded exceeds $1.5 trillion, so firms are unable to meet the demand for their output. Inventories decrease, and customers clamour for goods and services, so firms increase production and raise prices. Production and prices increase until firms can meet the demand for their output. This

FIGURE 26.6 Short-Run Equilibrium

Short-run macroeconomic equilibrium occurs when real GDP demanded equals real GDP supplied—at the intersection of the aggregate demand curve (*AD*) and the short-run aggregate supply curve (*SAS*).

_____ **MyEconLab** Animation and Draw Graph _____

situation occurs only when real GDP is $1.7 trillion and the price level is 110.

In the short run, the money wage rate is fixed. It does not adjust to move the economy to full employment. So in the short run, real GDP can be greater than or less than potential GDP. But in the long run, the money wage rate adjusts and real GDP moves toward potential GDP. Let's look at the long-run equilibrium and see how we get there.

Long-Run Macroeconomic Equilibrium

Long-run macroeconomic equilibrium occurs when real GDP equals potential GDP—equivalently, when the economy is on its *LAS* curve.

When the economy is away from long-run equilibrium, the money wage rate adjusts. If the money wage rate is too high, short-run equilibrium is below potential GDP and the unemployment rate is above the natural rate. With an excess supply of labour, the money wage rate falls. If the money wage rate is too low, short-run equilibrium is above potential GDP and the unemployment rate is below the natural rate.

With an excess demand for labour, the money wage rate rises.

Figure 26.7 shows the long-run equilibrium and how it comes about. If the short-run aggregate supply curve is SAS_1, the money wage rate is too high to achieve full employment. A fall in the money wage rate shifts the SAS curve to SAS^* and brings full employment. If the short-run aggregate supply curve is SAS_2, the money wage rate is too low to achieve full employment. Now, a rise in the money wage rate shifts the SAS curve to SAS^* and brings full employment.

In long-run equilibrium, potential GDP determines real GDP, and potential GDP and aggregate demand together determine the price level. The money wage rate adjusts until the SAS curve passes through the long-run equilibrium point.

Let's now see how the AS-AD model helps us to understand economic growth and inflation.

FIGURE 26.7   Long-Run Equilibrium

In long-run macroeconomic equilibrium, real GDP equals potential GDP. So long-run equilibrium occurs where the aggregate demand curve, AD, intersects the long-run aggregate supply curve, LAS. In the long run, aggregate demand determines the price level and has no effect on real GDP. The money wage rate adjusts in the long run, so that the SAS curve intersects the LAS curve at the long-run equilibrium price level.

MyEconLab Animation and Draw Graph

Economic Growth and Inflation in the *AS-AD* Model

Economic growth results from a growing labour force and increasing labour productivity, which together make potential GDP grow (Chapter 22, pp. 522–525). Inflation results from a growing quantity of money that outpaces the growth of potential GDP (Chapter 24, pp. 582–583).

The *AS-AD* model explains and illustrates economic growth and inflation. It explains economic growth as increasing long-run aggregate supply and it explains inflation as a persistent increase in aggregate demand at a faster pace than that of the increase in potential GDP.

Economics in Action
Canadian Economic Growth and Inflation

The figure is a *scatter diagram* of Canadian real GDP and the price level. The graph has the same axes as those of the *AS-AD* model. Each dot represents a year between 1961 and 2014. The three red dots are recession years. The pattern formed by the dots shows the combination of economic growth and inflation. Economic growth was fastest during the 1960s, and inflation was fastest during the 1970s.

The *AS-AD* model interprets each dot as being at the intersection of the SAS and AD curves.

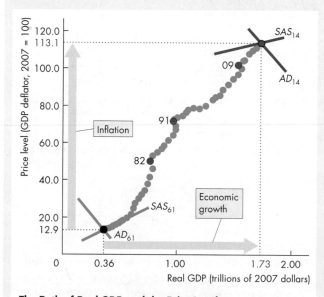

The Path of Real GDP and the Price Level

Source of data: Statistics Canada, CANSIM Table 380-0064.

Figure 26.8 illustrates this explanation in terms of the shifting *LAS* and *AD* curves.

When the *LAS* curve shifts rightward from LAS_0 to LAS_1, potential GDP grows from \$1.7 trillion to \$1.9 trillion. And in long-run equilibrium, real GDP also grows to \$1.9 trillion.

When the *AD* curve shifts rightward from AD_0 to AD_1 and the growth of aggregate demand outpaces the growth of potential GDP, the price level rises from 110 to 120.

If aggregate demand were to increase at the same pace as long-run aggregate supply, real GDP would grow with no inflation.

Our economy experiences periods of growth and inflation, like those shown in Fig. 26.8, but it does not experience *steady* growth and *steady* inflation. Real GDP fluctuates around potential GDP in a business cycle. When we study the business cycle, we ignore economic growth and focus on the fluctuations around the trend growth rate. By doing so, we see the business cycle more clearly. Let's now see how the *AS-AD* model explains the business cycle.

The Business Cycle in the *AS-AD* Model

The business cycle occurs because aggregate demand and short-run aggregate supply fluctuate but the money wage rate does not adjust quickly enough to keep real GDP at potential GDP. Figure 26.9 shows three types of short-run equilibrium.

Figure 26.9(a) shows an above full-employment equilibrium. An **above full-employment equilibrium** is an equilibrium in which real GDP exceeds potential GDP. The gap between real GDP and potential GDP is the **output gap**. When real GDP exceeds potential GDP, the output gap is called an **inflationary gap**.

The above full-employment equilibrium shown in Fig. 26.9(a) occurs where the aggregate demand curve AD_0 intersects the short-run aggregate supply curve SAS_0 at a real GDP of \$1.74 trillion. There is an inflationary gap of \$0.04 trillion.

Economics in Action
The Canadian Business Cycle

The Canadian economy had an inflationary gap in 2000 (at *A* in the figure), full employment in 2007 (at *B*), and a recessionary gap in 2009 (at *C*). The fluctuating output gap in the figure is the real-world version of Fig. 26.9(d) and is generated by fluctuations in aggregate demand and short-run aggregate supply.

FIGURE 26.8   Economic Growth and Inflation

Economic growth results from a persistent increase in potential GDP—a rightward shift of the *LAS* curve. Inflation results from persistent growth in the quantity of money that shifts the *AD* curve rightward at a faster pace than the real GDP growth rate.

MyEconLab Animation and Draw Graph

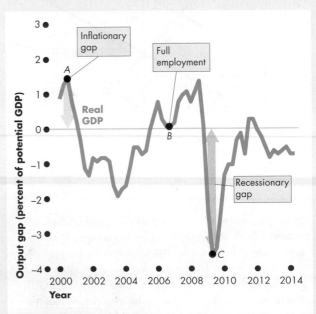

The Canadian Output Gap

Sources of data: Bank of Canada output gap, www.bankofcanada.ca/en/rates/indinf/product_data_en.html.

2. In Fig. 26.9(b), real GDP equals potential GDP and there is a **full-employment equilibrium**. In this example, the equilibrium occurs where the aggregate demand curve AD_1 intersects the short-run aggregate supply curve SAS_1 at a real GDP and potential GDP of $1.7 trillion.

3. In part (c), there is a below full-employment equilibrium. A **below full-employment equilibrium** is an equilibrium in which potential GDP exceeds real GDP. When potential GDP exceeds real GDP, the output gap is called a **recessionary gap**.

The below full-employment equilibrium shown in Fig. 26.9(c) occurs where the aggregate demand curve

AD_2 intersects the short-run aggregate supply curve SAS_2 at a real GDP of $1.66 trillion. Potential GDP is $1.7 trillion, so the recessionary gap is $0.04 trillion.

The economy moves from one type of macroeconomic equilibrium to another as a result of fluctuations in aggregate demand and in short-run aggregate supply. These fluctuations produce fluctuations in real GDP. Figure 26.9(d) shows how real GDP fluctuates around potential GDP.

Let's now look at some of the sources of these fluctuations around potential GDP.

FIGURE 26.9 The Business Cycle

(a) Above full-employment equilibrium

(b) Full-employment equilibrium

(c) Below full-employment equilibrium

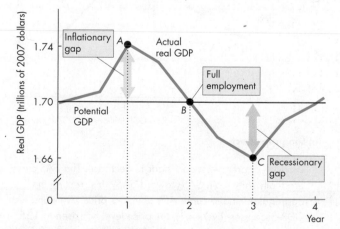

(d) Fluctuations in real GDP

Part (a) shows an above full-employment equilibrium in year 1; part (b) shows a full-employment equilibrium in year 2; and part (c) shows a below full-employment equilibrium in year 3. Part (d) shows how real GDP fluctuates around potential GDP in a business cycle during year 1, year 2, and year 3.

In year 1, an inflationary gap exists and the economy is at point A in parts (a) and (d). In year 2, the economy is at full employment and the economy is at point B in parts (b) and (d). In year 3, a recessionary gap exists and the economy is at point C in parts (c) and (d).

Fluctuations in Aggregate Demand

One reason real GDP fluctuates around potential GDP is that aggregate demand fluctuates. Let's see what happens when aggregate demand increases.

Figure 26.10(a) shows an economy at full employment. The aggregate demand curve is AD_0, the short-run aggregate supply curve is SAS_0, and the long-run aggregate supply curve is LAS. Real GDP equals potential GDP at $1.7 trillion, and the price level is 110.

Now suppose that the world economy expands and that the demand for Canadian-produced goods increases in Asia and Europe. The increase in Canadian exports increases aggregate demand in Canada, and the aggregate demand curve shifts rightward from AD_0 to AD_1 in Fig. 26.10(a).

Faced with an increase in demand, firms increase production and raise prices. Real GDP increases to $1.8 trillion, and the price level rises to 115. The economy is now in an above full-employment equilibrium. Real GDP exceeds potential GDP, and there is an inflationary gap.

The increase in aggregate demand has increased the prices of all goods and services. Faced with higher prices, firms increased their output rates. At this stage, prices of goods and services have increased but the money wage rate has not changed. (Recall that as we move along the SAS curve, the money wage rate is constant.)

The economy cannot produce in excess of potential GDP forever. Why not? What are the forces at work that bring real GDP back to potential GDP?

Because the price level has increased and the money wage rate is unchanged, workers have experienced a fall in the buying power of their wages and firms' profits have increased. Under these circumstances, workers demand higher wages and firms, anxious to maintain their employment and output levels, meet those demands. If firms do not raise the money wage rate, they will either lose workers or have to hire less productive ones.

As the money wage rate rises, the short-run aggregate supply begins to decrease. In Fig. 26.10(b), the short-run aggregate supply curve begins to shift from

---

FIGURE 26.10   An Increase in Aggregate Demand

(a) Short-run effect

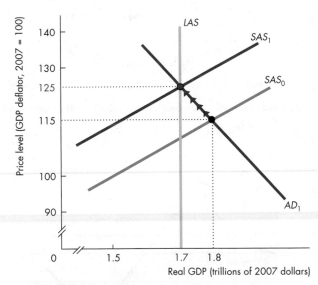

(b) Long-run effect

An increase in aggregate demand shifts the aggregate demand curve from AD_0 to AD_1. In short-run equilibrium, real GDP increases to $1.8 trillion and the price level rises to 115. In this situation, an inflationary gap exists. In the long run in part (b), the money wage rate starts to rise and

short-run aggregate supply starts to decrease. The SAS curve gradually shifts from SAS_0 toward SAS_1, intersecting the aggregate demand curve AD_1 at higher price levels and real GDP decreases. Eventually, the price level has risen to 125 and real GDP has decreased to $1.7 trillion—potential GDP.

MyEconLab Animation

SAS_0 toward SAS_1. The rise in the money wage rate and the shift in the SAS curve produce a sequence of new equilibrium positions. Along the adjustment path, real GDP decreases and the price level rises. The economy moves up along its aggregate demand curve as shown by the arrows in the figure.

Eventually, the money wage rate rises by the same percentage as the price level. At this time, the aggregate demand curve AD_1 intersects SAS_1 at a new full-employment equilibrium. The price level has risen to 125, and real GDP is back where it started, at potential GDP.

A decrease in aggregate demand has effects similar but opposite to those of an increase in aggregate demand. That is, a decrease in aggregate demand shifts the aggregate demand curve leftward. Real GDP decreases to less than potential GDP, and a recessionary gap emerges. Firms cut prices. The lower price level increases the purchasing power of wages and increases firms' costs relative to their output prices because the money wage rate is unchanged. Eventually, the money wage rate falls and the short-run aggregate supply increases.

Let's now work out how real GDP and the price level change when aggregate supply changes.

Fluctuations in Aggregate Supply

Fluctuations in short-run aggregate supply can bring fluctuations in real GDP around potential GDP. Suppose that initially real GDP equals potential GDP. Then there is a large but temporary rise in the price of oil. What happens to real GDP and the price level?

Figure 26.11 answers this question. The aggregate demand curve is AD_0, the short-run aggregate supply curve is SAS_0, and the long-run aggregate supply curve is LAS. Real GDP is $1.7 trillion, which equals potential GDP, and the price level is 110. Then the price of oil rises. Faced with higher energy and transportation costs, firms decrease production. Short-run aggregate supply decreases, and the short-run aggregate supply curve shifts leftward to SAS_1. The price level rises to 120, and real GDP decreases to $1.6 trillion. Because real GDP decreases, the economy experiences recession. Because the price level increases, the economy experiences inflation. A combination of recession and inflation is called **stagflation**. Canada experienced stagflation in the mid-1970s and early 1980s, but events like this are not common.

When the price of oil returns to its original level, the economy returns to full employment.

FIGURE 26.11   A Decrease in Aggregate Supply

An increase in the price of oil decreases short-run aggregate supply and shifts the short-run aggregate supply curve from SAS_0 to SAS_1. Real GDP decreases from $1.7 trillion to $1.6 trillion, and the price level rises from 110 to 120. The economy experiences stagflation.

MyEconLab Animation

REVIEW QUIZ

1 Does economic growth result from increases in aggregate demand, short-run aggregate supply, or long-run aggregate supply?

2 Does inflation result from increases in aggregate demand, short-run aggregate supply, or long-run aggregate supply?

3 Describe three types of short-run macroeconomic equilibrium.

4 How do fluctuations in aggregate demand and short-run aggregate supply bring fluctuations in real GDP around potential GDP?

Work these questions in Study Plan 26.3 and get instant feedback. Do a Key Terms Quiz.   MyEconLab

We can use the *AS-AD* model to explain and illustrate the views of the alternative schools of thought in macroeconomics. That is your next task.

Macroeconomic Schools of Thought

Macroeconomics is an active field of research, and much remains to be learned about the forces that make our economy grow and fluctuate. There is a greater degree of consensus and certainty about economic growth and inflation—the longer-term trends in real GDP and the price level—than there is about the business cycle—the short-term fluctuations in these variables. Here, we'll look only at differences of view about short-term fluctuations.

The *AS-AD* model that you've studied in this chapter provides a good foundation for understanding the range of views that macroeconomists hold about this topic. But what you will learn here is just a glimpse at the scientific controversy and debate. We'll return to these issues at various points later in the text and deepen your appreciation of the alternative views.

Classification usually requires simplification, and classifying macroeconomists is no exception to this general rule. The classification that we'll use here is simple, but it is not misleading. We're going to divide macroeconomists into three broad schools of thought and examine the views of each group in turn. The groups are:

- Classical
- Keynesian
- Monetarist

The Classical View

A **classical** macroeconomist believes that the economy is self-regulating and always at full employment. The term "classical" derives from the name of the founding school of economics that includes Adam Smith, David Ricardo, and John Stuart Mill.

A **new classical** view is that business cycle fluctuations are the efficient responses of a well-functioning market economy that is bombarded by shocks that arise from the uneven pace of technological change.

The classical view can be understood in terms of beliefs about aggregate demand and aggregate supply.

Aggregate Demand Fluctuations In the classical view, technological change is the most significant influence on both aggregate demand and aggregate supply. For this reason, classical macroeconomists don't use the *AS-AD* framework. But their views can be interpreted in this framework. A technological change that increases the productivity of capital brings an increase in aggregate demand because firms increase their expenditure on new plant and equipment. A technological change that lengthens the useful life of existing capital decreases the demand for new capital, which decreases aggregate demand.

Aggregate Supply Response In the classical view, the money wage rate that lies behind the short-run aggregate supply curve is instantly and completely flexible. The money wage rate adjusts so quickly to maintain equilibrium in the labour market that real GDP always adjusts to equal potential GDP.

Potential GDP itself fluctuates for the same reasons that aggregate demand fluctuates: technological change. When the pace of technological change is rapid, potential GDP increases quickly and so does real GDP. And when the pace of technological change slows, so does the growth rate of potential GDP.

Classical Policy The classical view of policy emphasizes the potential for taxes to stunt incentives and create inefficiency. By minimizing the disincentive effects of taxes, employment, investment, and technological advance are at their efficient levels and the economy expands at an appropriate and rapid pace.

The Keynesian View

A **Keynesian** macroeconomist believes that, left alone, the economy would rarely operate at full employment and that to achieve and maintain full employment, active help from fiscal policy and monetary policy is required.

The term "Keynesian" derives from the name of one of the twentieth century's most famous economists, John Maynard Keynes (see p. 701).

The Keynesian view is based on beliefs about the forces that determine aggregate demand and short-run aggregate supply.

Aggregate Demand Fluctuations In the Keynesian view, *expectations* are the most significant influence on aggregate demand. Those expectations are based on herd instinct, or what Keynes himself called "animal spirits." A wave of pessimism about future profit prospects can lead to a fall in aggregate demand and plunge the economy into recession.

Aggregate Supply Response In the Keynesian view, the money wage rate that lies behind the short-run aggregate supply curve is extremely sticky in the downward direction. Basically, the money wage rate doesn't fall. So if there is a recessionary gap, there is no automatic mechanism for getting rid of it. If it were to happen, a fall in the money wage rate would increase short-run aggregate supply and restore full employment. But the money wage rate doesn't fall, so the economy remains stuck in recession.

A modern version of the Keynesian view, known as the **new Keynesian** view, holds not only that the money wage rate is sticky but also that prices of goods and services are sticky. With a sticky price level, the short-run aggregate supply curve is horizontal at a fixed price level.

Policy Response Needed The Keynesian view calls for fiscal policy and monetary policy to actively offset changes in aggregate demand that bring recession.

By stimulating aggregate demand in a recession, full employment can be restored.

The Monetarist View

A **monetarist** is a macroeconomist who believes that the economy is self regulating and that it will normally operate at full employment, provided that monetary policy is not erratic and that the pace of money growth is kept steady.

The term "monetarist" was coined by an outstanding twentieth-century economist, Karl Brunner, to describe his own views and those of Milton Friedman (see p. 773).

The monetarist view can be interpreted in terms of beliefs about the forces that determine aggregate demand and short-run aggregate supply.

Aggregate Demand Fluctuations In the monetarist view, *the quantity of money* is the most significant influence on aggregate demand. The quantity of money is determined by the Bank of Canada. If the Bank of Canada keeps money growing at a steady pace, aggregate demand fluctuations will be minimized and the economy will operate close to full employment. But if the Bank of Canada decreases the quantity of money or even just slows its growth rate too abruptly, the economy will go into recession. In the monetarist view, all recessions result from inappropriate monetary policy.

Aggregate Supply Response The monetarist view of short-run aggregate supply is the same as the Keynesian view: The money wage rate is sticky. If the economy is in recession, it will take an unnecessarily long time for it to return unaided to full employment.

Monetarist Policy The monetarist view of policy is the same as the classical view on fiscal policy. Taxes should be kept low to avoid disincentive effects that decrease potential GDP. Provided that the quantity of money is kept on a steady growth path, no active stabilization is needed to offset changes in aggregate demand.

The Way Ahead

In the chapters that follow, you're going to encounter Keynesian, classical, and monetarist views again. In the next chapter, we study the original Keynesian model of aggregate demand. This model remains useful today because it explains how expenditure fluctuations are magnified and bring changes in aggregate demand that are larger than the changes in expenditure. We then go on to apply the *AS-AD* model to a deeper look at Canadian inflation and business cycle.

Our attention then turns to short-run macroeconomic policy—the fiscal policy of the government and the monetary policy of the Bank of Canada.

◆ **REVIEW QUIZ**

1 What are the defining features of classical macroeconomics and what policies do classical macroeconomists recommend?

2 What are the defining features of Keynesian macroeconomics and what policies do Keynesian macroeconomists recommend?

3 What are the defining features of monetarist macroeconomics and what policies do monetarist macroeconomists recommend?

Work these questions in Study Plan 26.4 and get instant feedback. Do a Key Terms Quiz.   MyEconLab

◆ To complete your study of the *AS-AD* model, *Economics in the News* on pp. 640–641 looks at the Canadian economy in 2014 through the eyes of this model.

Aggregate Supply and Aggregate Demand in Action

Canada "In the Sweet Spot" as Exports, Consumer Spending Boost Economy to Fastest Growth in Almost Three Years

Financial Post
August 29, 2014

The strong second-quarter performance of the Canadian economy provides a welcome reality check after a chilly start to 2014.

Consumers still underpinning growth: Check. Exports and business investment picking up: Check. U.S. expansion back on track: Check. Interest rates at ultra-low levels: Check, for now.

All tallied, not a bad way to kick off the second half of the year.

Gross domestic product climbed at an annualized pace of 3.1 percent between April and June, the strongest performance since a 6.2 percent annualized jump in the first quarter of 2012, Statistics Canada said Friday. ...

There's no denying the Canadian economy is turning around—with growth above the Bank of Canada's own second-quarter forecast of 2.5 percent—as is the United States, which added an even more impressive 4.2 percent in the second quarter, after going into reverse during the previous three months.

"The big story in both countries is that after a struggling start to the year, both economies rebounded with purpose in the spring," said Douglas Porter, chief economist at BMO Capital Markets.

"We could see more of the same in the third quarter. ... We did get a very nice pickup in exports. But we did not get [enough] investment following through. ... There's no doubt that there's still quite a bit of caution among businesses," Mr. Porter said.

"Fortunately enough, filling that void was the consumer, and housing had a nice quarter," he added. "Both are coming back for either sluggish or weak first quarters." ...

Written by Gordon Isfeld. Material reprinted with the express permission of *National Post*, a division of Postmedia Network Inc.

ESSENCE OF THE STORY

- Canadian real GDP grew at an annualized rate of 3.1 percent in the second quarter of 2014.

- Consumption expenditure, exports, and business investment all increased.

- The real GDP growth rate exceeded the Bank of Canada's forecast of 2.5 percent growth.

- U.S. real GDP grew at an annualized rate of 4.2 percent in the second quarter of 2014.

- Douglas Porter, chief economist at BMO Capital Markets, expected the third quarter of 2014 to have strong growth, and noted that caution among businesses was offset by consumer spending and housing investment.

MyEconLab More Economics in the News

ECONOMIC ANALYSIS

- Canadian real GDP grew at an annual rate of 3.1 percent during the second quarter of 2014—a faster growth rate than the Bank of Canada and others had expected.

- In the second quarter of 2014, real GDP was estimated to be $1,729 billion. The price level was 113 (up 13 percent since 2007).

- A year earlier, in the second quarter of 2013, real GDP was $1,688 billion and the price level was 111.

- Figure 1 illustrates the situation in the second quarter of 2013. The aggregate demand curve was AD_{13} and the short-run aggregate supply curve was SAS_{13}. Real GDP ($1,688 billion) and the price level (111) are at the intersection of these curves.

- The Bank of Canada estimated that the output gap in the second quarter of 2013 was –0.7 percent, which implies that *potential* GDP in 2013 was $1,700 billion, so the long-run aggregate supply curve in 2013 was LAS_{13} in Fig. 1.

- Figure 1 shows the output gap in 2013, which was a recessionary gap of $12 billion.

- During the year from June 2013 to June 2014, the labour force increased, the capital stock increased, and labour productivity increased. Potential GDP increased to an estimated $1,741 billion.

- In Fig. 2, the LAS curve shifted rightward to LAS_{14}.

- Also during the year from June 2013 to June 2014, a combination of monetary policy stimulus and an increase in demand from an expanding U.S. economy and world economy increased aggregate demand.

- The increase in aggregate demand exceeded the increase in long-run aggregate supply, and the AD curve shifted rightward to AD_{14}.

- Two forces act on short-run aggregate supply: The increase in potential GDP shifts the SAS curve rightward and a rise in the money wage rate and other factor prices shifts the SAS curve leftward.

- Because potential GDP didn't increase by much, short-run aggregate supply probably didn't change by much, and here we assume it didn't change at all. The SAS curve in 2014, SAS_{14}, was the same as SAS_{13}.

- Real GDP increased to $1,729 billion and the price level increased to 113.

- The output gap remained constant at –0.7 percent of potential GDP.

Figure 1 *AS-AD* in Second Quarter of 2013

Figure 2 *AS-AD* in Second Quarter of 2014

SUMMARY

Key Points

Aggregate Supply (pp. 624–627)

- In the long run, the quantity of real GDP supplied is potential GDP.
- In the short run, a rise in the price level increases the quantity of real GDP supplied.
- A change in potential GDP changes long-run and short-run aggregate supply. A change in the money wage rate changes only short-run aggregate supply.

Working Problems 1 and 2 will give you a better understanding of aggregate supply.

Aggregate Demand (pp. 628–631)

- A rise in the price level decreases the quantity of real GDP demanded.
- Changes in expected future income, inflation, and profits; in fiscal policy and monetary policy; and in foreign income and the exchange rate change aggregate demand.

Working Problems 3 to 5 will give you a better understanding of aggregate demand.

Explaining Macroeconomic Trends and Fluctuations (pp. 632–637)

- Aggregate demand and short-run aggregate supply determine real GDP and the price level.
- In the long run, real GDP equals potential GDP and aggregate demand determines the price level.
- The business cycle occurs because aggregate demand and aggregate supply fluctuate.

Working Problems 6 to 8 will give you a better understanding of macroeconomic trends and fluctuations.

Macroeconomic Schools of Thought (pp. 638–639)

- Classical economists believe that the economy is self-regulating and always at full employment.
- Keynesian economists believe that full employment can be achieved only with active policy.
- Monetarist economists believe that recessions result from inappropriate monetary policy.

Working Problem 9 will give you a better understanding of the macroeconomic schools of thought.

Key Terms

MyEconLab Key Terms Quiz

Above full-employment equilibrium, 634
Aggregate demand, 628
Below full-employment equilibrium, 635
Classical, 638
Disposable income, 630
Fiscal policy, 630

Full-employment equilibrium, 635
Inflationary gap, 634
Keynesian, 638
Long-run aggregate supply, 624
Long-run macroeconomic equilibrium, 632
Monetarist, 639
Monetary policy, 630

New classical, 638
New Keynesian, 639
Output gap, 634
Recessionary gap, 635
Short-run aggregate supply, 625
Short-run macroeconomic equilibrium, 632
Stagflation, 637

WORKED PROBLEM

MyEconLab   You can work this problem in Chapter 26 Study Plan.

The table shows the aggregate demand and short-run aggregate supply schedules of Lizard Island in which potential GDP is $600 billion.

Price level	Real GDP demanded	Real GDP supplied in the short run
	(billions of 2007 dollars)	
100	600	550
110	575	575
120	550	600
130	525	625

Questions

1. Calculate equilibrium real GDP and price level in the short run.
2. Does the country have an inflationary gap or a recessionary gap and what is its magnitude?
3. If aggregate demand increases by $50 billion, what is the new short-run macroeconomic equilibrium and the output gap?

Solutions

1. Short-run macroeconomic equilibrium occurs at the price level at which the quantity of real GDP demanded equals the quantity of real GDP supplied.

    At a price level of 110, the quantity of real GDP demanded is $575 billion and the quantity of real GDP supplied is $575 billion, so equilibrium real GDP is $575 billion and the price level is 110. See the equilibrium in the figure.

Key Point: Aggregate demand and aggregate supply determine the short-run macroeconomic equilibrium.

2. The output gap is the gap between equilibrium real GDP and potential GDP. Equilibrium real GDP is $575 billion and potential GDP is $600 billion, so the output gap is $25 billion. Because potential GDP exceeds equilibrium real GDP, the economy is in a below full-employment equilibrium and the output gap is a recessionary gap.

Key Point: A recessionary gap occurs when the economy is in a below full-employment equilibrium. When the economy is in an above full-employment equilibrium, the output gap is an inflationary gap.

3. The table below shows the new aggregate demand schedule when aggregate demand increases by $50 billion.

Price level	Real GDP demanded	Real GDP supplied in the short run
	(billions of 2007 dollars)	
100	650	550
110	625	575
120	600	600
130	575	675

At a price level of 110, the quantity of real GDP demanded ($625 billion) exceeds the quantity of real GDP supplied ($575 billion). Firms are unable to meet the demand for their output, so inventories start to decline. As people clamour for goods and services, firms increase production and start to raise their prices. Production and prices will continue to increase until a new short-run equilibrium is reached.

At the new equilibrium, real GDP is $600 billion and the price level is 120. Because equilibrium real GDP equals potential GDP of $600 billion, the economy is at full employment and there is no output gap. See the new short-run equilibrium in the figure.

Key Point: An increase in aggregate demand with no change in aggregate supply increases the price level and increases equilibrium real GDP.

Key Figure

MyEconLab Interactive Animation

STUDY PLAN PROBLEMS AND APPLICATIONS

MyEconLab   You can work Problems 1 to 9 in Chapter 26 Study Plan and get instant feedback.

Aggregate Supply (Study Plan 26.1)

1. Explain the influence of each of the following events on the quantity of real GDP supplied and aggregate supply in India and use a graph to illustrate.
   - Canadian firms move their call handling, IT, and data functions to India.
   - Fuel prices rise.
   - Walmart and Starbucks open in India.
   - Universities in India increase the number of engineering graduates.
   - The money wage rate rises.
   - The price level in India increases.

2. Labour productivity is rising at a rapid rate in China and wages are rising at a similar rate. Explain how a rise in labour productivity and wages in China will influence the quantity of real GDP supplied and aggregate supply in China.

Aggregate Demand (Study Plan 26.2)

3. Canada trades with the United States. Explain the effect of each of the following events on Canada's aggregate demand.
   - The government of Canada cuts income taxes.
   - The United States experiences strong economic growth.
   - Canada sets new environmental standards that require power utilities to upgrade their production facilities.

4. The Bank of Canada cuts the quantity of money and all other things remain the same. Explain the effect of the cut in the quantity of money on aggregate demand in the short run.

5. **Gross Domestic Product for the Second Quarter of 2014**
   The increase in real GDP in the second quarter primarily reflected increases in personal consumption expenditure (0.9%), exports (4.2%), and investment (0.8%)—the largest quarterly gain since 2011, mainly due to the increase in consumption expenditure.
        Source: Statistics Canada, August 29, 2014
   Explain how the items in the news clip influence Canada's aggregate demand.

Explaining Macroeconomic Trends and Fluctuations
(Study Plan 26.3)

Use the following graph to work Problems 6 to 8. Initially, the short-run aggregate supply curve is SAS_0 and the aggregate demand curve is AD_0.

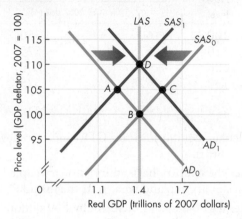

6. Some events change aggregate demand from AD_0 to AD_1. Describe two events that could have created this change in aggregate demand. What is the equilibrium after aggregate demand changed? If potential GDP is unchanged, the economy is at what type of macroeconomic equilibrium?

7. Some events change aggregate supply from SAS_0 to SAS_1. Describe two events that could have created this change in aggregate supply. What is the equilibrium after short-run aggregate supply changed? If potential GDP is unchanged, does the economy have an inflationary gap, a recessionary gap, or no output gap?

8. Some events change aggregate demand from AD_0 to AD_1 and aggregate supply from SAS_0 to SAS_1. What is the new macroeconomic equilibrium?

Macroeconomic Schools of Thought (Study Plan 26.4)

9. Describe the policy change that a classical macroeconomist, a Keynesian, and a monetarist would recommend for Canadian policymakers to adopt in response to each of the following events:
   a. Growth in the world economy slows.
   b. The world price of oil rises.
   c. Canadian labour productivity declines.

ADDITIONAL PROBLEMS AND APPLICATIONS

MyEconLab   You can work these problems in MyEconLab if assigned by your instructor.

Aggregate Supply

10. Explain for each event whether it changes the quantity of real GDP supplied, short-run aggregate supply, long-run aggregate supply, or a combination of them.
    - Automotive firms in Canada switch to a new technology that raises productivity.
    - Toyota and Honda build additional plants in Canada.
    - The prices of auto parts imported from China rise.
    - Autoworkers agree to a lower money wage rate.
    - The Canadian price level rises.

Aggregate Demand

11. Explain for each event whether it changes the quantity of real GDP demanded or aggregate demand in Canada.
    - Canada's exports to the European Union boom.
    - Canadian firms build new pipelines across the nation.
    - Foreign exchange dealers expect the Canadian dollar next year to appreciate against all currencies.

12. **Inventory Investment Decreases**
    When real GDP increased in the second quarter of 2014, consumption expenditure, exports, and fixed investment increased, but business inventory investment fell from $14.5 billion to $7.0 billion.
    Source: Statistics Canada, August 29, 2014

    Explain how a fall in business inventories influences aggregate demand.

13. **Exports and Imports Increase**
    Real exports of goods and services increased 4.2 percent in the second quarter, after falling 0.2 percent in the first quarter. Real imports of goods and services increased 2.7 percent, after falling 1.4 percent in the first quarter.
    Source: Statistics Canada, August 29, 2014

    Explain how the changes in exports and imports reported here influence the quantity of real GDP demanded and aggregate demand. In which of the first two quarters of 2014 did exports and imports contribute more to the change in aggregate demand?

Explaining Macroeconomic Trends and Fluctuations

Use the following information to work Problems 14 to 16.
The following events have occurred at times in the history of Canada:
- The world economy goes into an expansion.
- Canadian businesses expect future profits to rise.
- The government increases its expenditure on goods and services in a time of increased international tension.

14. Explain for each event whether it changes short-run aggregate supply, long-run aggregate supply, aggregate demand, or some combination of them.

15. Explain the separate effects of each event on Canadian real GDP and the price level, starting from a position of long-run equilibrium.

16. Explain the combined effects of these events on Canadian real GDP and the price level, starting from a position of long-run equilibrium.

Use the following information to work Problems 17 and 18.

In Japan, potential GDP is 600 trillion yen. The table shows Japan's aggregate demand and short-run aggregate supply schedules.

Price level	Real GDP demanded	Real GDP supplied in the short run
	(trillions of 2007 yen)	
75	600	400
85	550	450
95	500	500
105	450	550
115	400	600
125	350	650
135	300	700

17. a. Draw a graph of the aggregate demand curve and the short-run aggregate supply curve.
    b. What is the short-run equilibrium real GDP and price level?

18. Does Japan have an inflationary gap or a recessionary gap and what is its magnitude?

Use the following news clip to work Problems 19 and 20.

Spending by Women Jumps

The magazine *Women of China* reported that the percentage of income spent on consumer goods by urban Chinese women increased from 26 percent in 2007 to 63 percent in 2009. China's National Bureau of Statistics reported that in the first six months of 2010, consumption expenditure in rural China grew by 16 percent and in urban China by 19 percent, but GDP grew by 11 percent. A private forecaster expects consumption expenditure to increase from 36 percent of GDP in 2010 to 42 percent in 2020.

Source of information: *The Wall Street Journal*, August 27, 2010

19. Explain the effect of a rise in consumption expenditure on real GDP and the price level in the short run.

20. If the economy had been operating at a full-employment equilibrium,

   a. Describe the macroeconomic equilibrium after the rise in consumer spending.

   b. Explain and draw a graph to illustrate how the economy can adjust in the long run to restore a full-employment equilibrium.

21. Suppose that the E.U. economy goes into an expansion. Explain the effect of the expansion on Canadian real GDP and unemployment in the short run.

22. Explain why changes in consumer spending and business investment play a large role in the business cycle.

23. **How to Avoid Recession? Let the Fed Do Its Work**

   Greg Mankiw wrote in 2007 on the eve of the global financial crisis, "Congress made its most important contribution to taming the business cycle back in 1913, when it created the Federal Reserve System. Today, the Fed remains the first line of defence against recession."

   Source: *The New York Times*, December 23, 2007

   a. Describe the process by which action by the Fed in times of recession flows through the economy.

   b. Draw a graph the illustrate the Fed's action and its effect.

Macroeconomic Schools of Thought

24. **Cut Taxes and Boost Spending? Raise Taxes and Cut Spending? Cut Taxes and Cut Spending?**

   This headline expresses three views about what to do to get an economy growing more rapidly and contribute to closing the recessionary gap.

   Economists from which macroeconomic school of thought would recommend pursuing policies described by each of these views?

Economics in the News

25. After you have studied *Economics in the News* on pp. 640–641, answer the following questions.

   a. What are the main features of the Canadian economy in the second quarter of 2014?

   b. Did Canada have a recessionary gap or an inflationary gap in 2014? How do you know?

   c. Use the *AS-AD* model to show the changes in aggregate demand and aggregate supply that occurred in 2013 and 2014 that brought the economy to its situation in mid-2014.

   d. Use the *AS-AD* model to show the changes in aggregate demand and aggregate supply that will have occurred when full employment is restored.

   e. Use the *AS-AD* model to show the changes in aggregate demand and aggregate supply that would occur if the government increased its expenditure on goods and services or cut taxes by enough to restore full employment.

   f. Use the *AS-AD* model to show the changes in aggregate demand and aggregate supply that would occur if the economy moved into an inflationary gap. Show the short-run and the long-run effects.

26. **Brazil Falls into Recession**

   A decade ago, Brazil had rapid growth but now its economy is experiencing a slowdown with investment falling and inventories increasing. Potential GDP growth rate has slowed. Business and consumer confidence has fallen.

   Source: BBC News, August 29, 2014

   a. Explain the effect of a decrease in investment on real GDP and potential GDP.

   b. Explain how business and consumer confidence influences aggregate expenditure.

27

EXPENDITURE MULTIPLIERS

After studying this chapter, you will be able to:

◆ Explain how expenditure plans are determined when the price level is fixed

◆ Explain how real GDP is determined when the price level is fixed

◆ Explain the expenditure multiplier

◆ Explain the relationship between aggregate expenditure and aggregate demand

Investment and inventories fluctuate like the volume of a rock singer's voice and the uneven surface of a potholed road. How does the economy react to those fluctuations? Does it behave like an amplifier, blowing up the fluctuations and spreading them out to affect the many millions of participants in an economic rock concert? Or does it react like a limousine, absorbing the shocks and providing a smooth ride for the economy's passengers?

You will explore these questions in this chapter, and in *Economics in the News* at the end of the chapter you will see the role played by inventory investment during 2014 as the economy expanded.

◢ Fixed Prices and Expenditure Plans

In the model that we study in this chapter, all the firms are like your grocery store: They set their prices and sell the quantities their customers are willing to buy. If they persistently sell more than they plan to and keep running out of inventory, they eventually raise their prices. And if they persistently sell less than they plan to and have inventories piling up, they eventually cut their prices. But on any given day, their prices are fixed and the quantities they sell depend on demand, not supply.

Because each firm's prices are fixed, for the economy as a whole:

1. The *price level* is fixed, and
2. *Aggregate demand* determines real GDP.

We call this model the *Keynesian model* because it was first suggested by John Maynard Keynes (see p. 701) as a model of persistent depression.

We begin by identifying the forces that determine expenditure plans.

Expenditure Plans

Aggregate expenditure has four components: consumption expenditure, investment, government expenditure on goods and services, and net exports (exports *minus* imports). These four components sum to real GDP (see Chapter 20, pp. 467–468).

Aggregate planned expenditure is equal to the sum of the *planned* levels of consumption expenditure, investment, government expenditure on goods and services, and exports minus imports. Two of these components of planned expenditure, consumption expenditure and imports, change when income changes and so they depend on real GDP.

A Two-Way Link Between Aggregate Expenditure and Real GDP There is a two-way link between aggregate expenditure and real GDP. Other things remaining the same:

- An increase in real GDP increases aggregate expenditure, and
- An increase in aggregate expenditure increases real GDP.

You are now going to study this two-way link.

Consumption and Saving Plans

Several factors influence consumption expenditure and saving plans. The more important ones are:

1. Disposable income
2. Real interest rate
3. Wealth
4. Expected future income

Disposable income is aggregate income minus taxes plus transfer payments. Aggregate income equals real GDP, so disposable income depends on real GDP. To explore the two-way link between real GDP and planned consumption expenditure, we focus on the relationship between consumption expenditure and disposable income when the other three factors listed above are constant.

Consumption Expenditure and Saving The table in Fig. 27.1 lists the consumption expenditure and the saving that people plan at each level of disposable income. Households can only spend their disposable income on consumption or save it, so planned consumption expenditure plus planned saving *always* equals disposable income.

The relationship between consumption expenditure and disposable income, other things remaining the same, is called the **consumption function**. The relationship between saving and disposable income, other things remaining the same, is called the **saving function**.

Consumption Function Figure 27.1(a) shows a consumption function. The *y*-axis measures consumption expenditure, and the *x*-axis measures disposable income. Along the consumption function, the points labelled *A* through *F* correspond to the rows of the table. For example, point *E* shows that when disposable income is $800 billion, consumption expenditure is $750 billion. As disposable income increases, consumption expenditure also increases.

At point *A* on the consumption function, consumption expenditure is $150 billion even though disposable income is zero. This consumption expenditure is called *autonomous consumption*, and it is the amount of consumption expenditure that would take place in the short run even if people had no current income. Consumption expenditure in excess of this amount is called *induced consumption*, which is the consumption expenditure that is induced by an increase in disposable income.

45° Line Figure 27.1(a) also contains a 45° line, the height of which measures disposable income. At each point on this line, consumption expenditure equals disposable income. Between points A and D consumption expenditure exceeds disposable income, between points D and F consumption expenditure is less than disposable income, and at point D consumption expenditure equals disposable income.

Saving Function Figure 27.1(b) shows a saving function. Again, the points A through F correspond to the rows of the table. For example, point E shows that when disposable income is $800 billion, saving is $50 billion. As disposable income increases, saving increases. Notice that when consumption expenditure exceeds disposable income in part (a), saving is negative, called *dissaving,* in part (b).

FIGURE 27.1   Consumption Function and Saving Function

(a) Consumption function

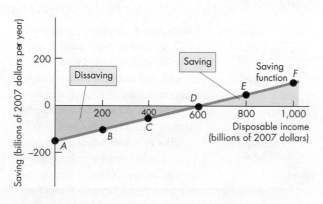

(b) Saving function

	Disposable income	Planned consumption expenditure	Planned saving
		(billions of 2007 dollars)	
A	0	150	−150
B	200	300	−100
C	400	450	−50
D	600	600	0
E	800	750	50
F	1,000	900	100

The table shows consumption expenditure and saving plans at various levels of disposable income. Part (a) of the figure shows the relationship between consumption expenditure and disposable income (the consumption function). The height of the consumption function measures consumption expenditure at each level of disposable income. Part (b) shows the relationship between saving and disposable income (the saving function). The height of the saving function measures saving at each level of disposable income. Points A through F on the consumption and saving functions correspond to the rows in the table.

The height of the 45° line in part (a) measures disposable income. So along the 45° line, consumption expenditure equals disposable income. Consumption expenditure plus saving equals disposable income. When the consumption function is above the 45° line, saving is negative (dissaving occurs). When the consumption function is below the 45° line, saving is positive. At the point where the consumption function intersects the 45° line, all disposable income is spent on consumption and saving is zero.

Marginal Propensities to Consume and Save

The **marginal propensity to consume** (*MPC*) is the fraction of a *change* in disposable income that is spent on consumption. It is calculated as the *change* in consumption expenditure (ΔC) divided by the *change* in disposable income (ΔYD). The formula is

$$MPC = \frac{\Delta C}{\Delta YD}.$$

In the table in Fig. 27.1, when disposable income increases by $200 billion, consumption expenditure increases by $150 billion. The *MPC* is $150 billion divided by $200 billion, which equals 0.75.

The **marginal propensity to save** (*MPS*) is the fraction of a *change* in disposable income that is saved. It is calculated as the *change* in saving (ΔS) divided by the *change* in disposable income (ΔYD). The formula is

$$MPS = \frac{\Delta S}{\Delta YD}.$$

In the table in Fig. 27.1, when disposable income increases by $200 billion, saving increases by $50 billion. The *MPS* is $50 billion divided by $200 billion, which equals 0.25.

Because an increase in disposable income is either spent on consumption or saved, the marginal propensity to consume plus the marginal propensity to save equals 1. You can see why by using the equation

$$\Delta C + \Delta S = \Delta YD.$$

Divide both sides of the equation by the change in disposable income to obtain

$$\frac{\Delta C}{\Delta YD} + \frac{\Delta S}{\Delta YD} = 1.$$

$\Delta C / \Delta YD$ is the marginal propensity to consume (*MPC*), and $\Delta S / \Delta YD$ is the marginal propensity to save (*MPS*), so

$$MPC + MPS = 1.$$

Slopes and Marginal Propensities

The slope of the consumption function is the marginal propensity to consume, and the slope of the saving function is the marginal propensity to save.

Figure 27.2(a) shows the *MPC* as the slope of the consumption function. An increase in disposable income of $200 billion is the base of the red triangle. The increase in consumption expenditure that results from this increase in disposable income is $150 billion and is the height of the triangle. The slope of the consumption function is given by the formula "slope equals rise over run" and is $150 billion divided by $200 billion, which equals 0.75—the *MPC*.

Figure 27.2(b) shows the *MPS* as the slope of the saving function. An increase in disposable income of $200 billion (the base of the red triangle) increases saving by $50 billion (the height of the triangle). The slope of the saving function is $50 billion divided by $200 billion, which equals 0.25—the *MPS*.

FIGURE 27.2   The Marginal Propensities to Consume and Save

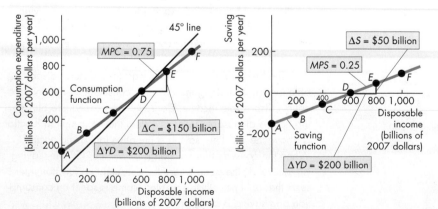

(a) Consumption function   **(b) Saving function**

The marginal propensity to consume, *MPC*, is equal to the change in consumption expenditure divided by the change in disposable income, other things remaining the same. It is measured by the slope of the consumption function. In part (a), the *MPC* is 0.75.

The marginal propensity to save, *MPS*, is equal to the change in saving divided by the change in disposable income, other things remaining the same. It is measured by the slope of the saving function. In part (b), the *MPS* is 0.25.

MyEconLab Animation

Economics in Action
The Canadian Consumption Function

The figure shows the Canadian consumption function. Each point identified by a blue dot represents consumption expenditure and disposable income for a particular year. (The dots are for the years 1981 to 2013, and the dots for five of those years are identified in the figure.)

The Canadian consumption function is CF_{81} in 1981 and CF_{13} in 2013.

The slope of the consumption function in the figure is 0.8, which means that a $1 increase in disposable income increases consumption expenditure by 80 cents. This slope, which is an estimate of the marginal propensity to consume, is an assumption that is at the upper end of the range of values that economists have estimated for the marginal propensity to consume.

The consumption function shifts upward over time as other influences on consumption expenditure change. Of these other influences, the real interest rate and wealth fluctuate and so bring upward and downward shifts in the consumption function.

But increasing wealth and increasing expected future income bring a steady upward shift in the consumption function. As the consumption function shifts upward, autonomous consumption increases.

The Canadian Consumption Function

Source of data: Statistics Canada, CANSIM Tables 380-0002 and 380-0004.

Consumption as a Function of Real GDP

Consumption expenditure changes when disposable income changes, and disposable income changes when real GDP changes. So consumption expenditure depends not only on disposable income but also on real GDP. We use this link between consumption expenditure and real GDP to determine equilibrium expenditure. But before we do so, we need to look at one further component of aggregate expenditure: imports. Like consumption expenditure, imports are influenced by real GDP.

Import Function

Of the many influences on Canadian imports in the short run, Canadian real GDP is the main influence. Other things remaining the same, an increase in Canadian real GDP increases the quantity of Canadian imports.

The relationship between imports and real GDP is determined by the **marginal propensity to import**, which is the fraction of an increase in real GDP that is spent on imports. It is calculated as the change in imports divided by the change in real GDP, other things remaining the same. For example, if an increase in real GDP of $100 billion increases imports by $25 billion, the marginal propensity to import is 0.25.

REVIEW QUIZ

1 Which components of aggregate expenditure are influenced by real GDP?
2 Define and explain how we calculate the marginal propensity to consume and the marginal propensity to save.
3 How do we calculate the effects of real GDP on consumption expenditure and imports by using the marginal propensity to consume and the marginal propensity to import?

Work these questions in Study Plan 27.1 and get instant feedback. Do a Key Terms Quiz.   MyEconLab

Real GDP influences consumption expenditure and imports, which in turn influence real GDP. Your next task is to study this second piece of the two-way link between aggregate expenditure and real GDP and see how all the components of aggregate planned expenditure interact to determine real GDP.

▶ Real GDP with a Fixed Price Level

You are now going to see how, at a given price level, aggregate expenditure plans determine real GDP. We start by looking at the relationship between aggregate planned expenditure and real GDP. This relationship can be described by an aggregate expenditure schedule or an aggregate expenditure curve. The *aggregate expenditure schedule* lists aggregate planned expenditure generated at each level of real GDP. The *aggregate expenditure curve* is a graph of the aggregate expenditure schedule.

Aggregate Planned Expenditure

The table in Fig. 27.3 sets out an aggregate expenditure schedule. To calculate aggregate planned expenditure at a given real GDP, we add the expenditure components together. The first column of the table shows real GDP, and the second column shows the planned consumption at each level of real GDP. A $100 billion increase in real GDP increases consumption expenditure by $70 billion—the *MPC* is 0.7.

The next two columns show investment and government expenditure on goods and services, both of which are independent of the level of real GDP. Investment depends on the real interest rate and the expected profit (see Chapter 23, p. 549). At a given point in time, these factors generate a given level of investment. Suppose this level of investment is $240 billion. Also, suppose that government expenditure is $270 billion.

The next two columns show exports and imports. Exports are influenced by events in the rest of the world, prices of foreign-produced goods and services relative to the prices of similar Canadian-produced goods and services, and exchange rates. But they are not directly affected by Canadian real GDP. Exports are a constant $340 billion. Imports increase as Canadian real GDP increases. A $100 billion increase in Canadian real GDP generates a $20 billion increase in imports—the marginal propensity to import is 0.2.

The final column shows aggregate planned expenditure—the sum of planned consumption expenditure, investment, government expenditure on goods and services, and exports minus imports.

Figure 27.3 plots an aggregate expenditure curve. Real GDP is shown on the *x*-axis, and aggregate planned expenditure is shown on the *y*-axis. The aggregate expenditure curve is the red line *AE*. Points *A* through *F* on that curve correspond to the rows of the table. The *AE* curve is a graph of aggregate planned expenditure (the last column) plotted against real GDP (the first column).

Figure 27.3 also shows the components of aggregate expenditure. The constant components—investment (I), government expenditure on goods and services (G), and exports (X)—are shown by the horizontal lines in the figure. Consumption expenditure (C) is the vertical gap between the lines labelled $I + G + X$ and $I + G + X + C$.

To construct the *AE* curve, subtract imports (M) from the $I + G + X + C$ line. Aggregate expenditure is expenditure on Canadian-produced goods and services. But the components of aggregate expenditure—C, I, and G—include expenditure on imported goods and services. For example, if you buy a new cellphone, your expenditure is part of consumption expenditure. But if the cellphone is a Samsung made in Korea, your expenditure on it must be subtracted from consumption expenditure to find out how much is spent on goods and services produced in Canada—on Canadian real GDP. Money paid to Samsung for cellphone imports from Korea does not add to aggregate expenditure in Canada.

Because imports are only a part of aggregate expenditure, when we subtract imports from the other components of aggregate expenditure, aggregate planned expenditure still increases as real GDP increases, as you can see in Fig. 27.3.

Consumption expenditure minus imports, which varies with real GDP, is called **induced expenditure**. The sum of investment, government expenditure, and exports, which does not vary with real GDP, is called **autonomous expenditure**. Consumption expenditure and imports can also have an autonomous component—a component that does not vary with real GDP. Another way of thinking about autonomous expenditure is that it would be the level of aggregate planned expenditure if real GDP were zero.

In Fig. 27.3, autonomous expenditure is $850 billion—aggregate planned expenditure when real GDP is zero (point *A*). For each $100 billion increase in real GDP, induced expenditure increases by $50 billion.

The aggregate expenditure curve summarizes the relationship between aggregate *planned* expenditure and real GDP. But what determines the point on the aggregate expenditure curve at which the economy operates? What determines *actual* aggregate expenditure?

FIGURE 27.3   Aggregate Planned Expenditure: The AE Curve

Aggregate planned expenditure is the sum of planned consumption expenditure, investment, government expenditure on goods and services, and exports minus imports. For example, in row C of the table, when real GDP is $1,600 billion, planned consumption expenditure is $1,120 billion, planned investment is $240 billion, planned government expenditure is $270 billion, planned exports are $340 billion, and planned imports are $320 billion. So when real GDP is $1,600 billion, aggregate planned expenditure is $1,650 billion ($1,120 + $240 + $270 + $340 − $320).

The schedule shows that aggregate planned expenditure increases as real GDP increases. This relationship is graphed as the aggregate expenditure curve AE. The components of aggregate expenditure that increase with real GDP are consumption expenditure and imports. The other components—investment, government expenditure, and exports—do not vary with real GDP.

			Planned expenditure				
	Real GDP (Y)	Consumption expenditure (C)	Investment (I)	Government expenditure (G)	Exports (X)	Imports (M)	Aggregate planned expenditure (AE = C + I + G + X − M)
				(billions of 2007 dollars)			
A	0	0	240	270	340	0	850
B	1,500	1,050	240	270	340	300	1,600
C	1,600	1,120	240	270	340	320	1,650
D	1,700	1,190	240	270	340	340	1,700
E	1,800	1,260	240	270	340	360	1,750
F	1,900	1,330	240	270	340	380	1,800

MyEconLab Animation

Actual Expenditure, Planned Expenditure, and Real GDP

Actual aggregate expenditure is always equal to real GDP, as we saw in Chapter 20 (p. 468). But aggregate *planned* expenditure is not always equal to actual aggregate expenditure and therefore is not always equal to real GDP. How can actual expenditure and planned expenditure differ? The answer is that firms can end up with inventories that are greater or smaller than planned. People carry out their consumption

expenditure plans, the government implements its planned expenditure on goods and services, and net exports are as planned. Firms carry out their plans to purchase new buildings, plant, and equipment. But one component of investment is the change in firms' inventories. If aggregate planned expenditure is less than real GDP, firms sell less than they planned to sell and end up with unplanned inventories. If aggregate planned expenditure exceeds real GDP, firms sell more than they planned to sell and end up with inventories being too low.

Equilibrium Expenditure

Equilibrium expenditure is the level of aggregate expenditure that occurs when aggregate *planned* expenditure equals real GDP. Equilibrium expenditure is a level of aggregate expenditure and real GDP at which spending plans are fulfilled. At a given price level, equilibrium expenditure determines real GDP. When aggregate planned expenditure and actual aggregate expenditure are unequal, a process of convergence toward equilibrium expenditure occurs. Throughout this process, real GDP adjusts. Let's examine equilibrium expenditure and the process that brings it about.

Figure 27.4(a) illustrates equilibrium expenditure. The table sets out aggregate planned expenditure at various levels of real GDP. These values are plotted

---

FIGURE 27.4   Equilibrium Expenditure

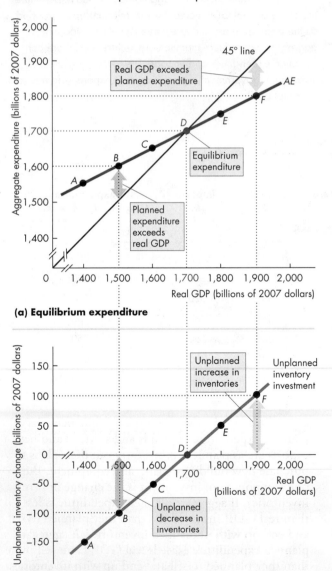

(a) Equilibrium expenditure

(b) Unplanned inventory changes

	Real GDP (Y)	Aggregate planned expenditure (AE)	Unplanned inventory change (Y − AE)
	(billions of 2007 dollars)		
A	1,400	1,550	−150
B	1,500	1,600	−100
C	1,600	1,650	−50
D	**1,700**	**1,700**	**0**
E	1,800	1,750	50
F	1,900	1,800	100

The table shows expenditure plans at different levels of real GDP. When real GDP is $1,700 billion, aggregate planned expenditure equals real GDP.

Part (a) of the figure illustrates equilibrium expenditure, which occurs when aggregate planned expenditure equals real GDP at the intersection of the 45° line and the *AE* curve. Part (b) of the figure shows the forces that bring about equilibrium expenditure.

When aggregate planned expenditure exceeds real GDP, inventories decrease—for example, at point *B* in both parts of the figure. So, firms increase production and real GDP increases.

When aggregate planned expenditure is less than real GDP, inventories increase—for example, at point *F* in both parts of the figure. So, firms cut production and real GDP decreases.

When aggregate planned expenditure equals real GDP, there are no unplanned inventory changes and real GDP remains constant at equilibrium expenditure.

MyEconLab Animation and Draw Graph

as points *A* through *F* along the *AE* curve. The 45°
line shows all the points at which aggregate planned
expenditure equals real GDP. So where the *AE* curve
lies above the 45° line, aggregate planned expenditure
exceeds real GDP; where the *AE* curve lies below the
45° line, aggregate planned expenditure is less than
real GDP; and where the *AE* curve intersects the 45°
line, aggregate planned expenditure equals real GDP.
Point *D* illustrates equilibrium expenditure. At this
point, real GDP is $1,700 billion.

Convergence to Equilibrium

What are the forces that move aggregate expenditure
toward its equilibrium level? To answer this question,
we must look at a situation in which aggregate expenditure is away from its equilibrium level.

From Below Equilibrium Suppose that in Fig. 27.4,
real GDP is $1,500 billion. With real GDP at $1,500
billion, actual aggregate expenditure is also $1,500 bil-
lion. But aggregate *planned* expenditure is $1,600 bil-
lion, point *B* in Fig. 27.4(a). Aggregate planned expenditure exceeds *actual* expenditure. When people spend
$1,600 billion and firms produce goods and services
worth $1,500 billion, firms' inventories fall by
$100 billion, point *B* in Fig. 27.4(b). Because
the change in inventories is part of investment,
actual investment is $100 billion less than *planned*
investment.

Real GDP doesn't remain at $1,500 billion for very
long. Firms have inventory targets based on their sales.
When inventories fall below target, firms increase production to restore inventories to the target level.

To increase inventories, firms hire additional
labour and increase production. Suppose that they
increase production in the next period by $100 bil-
lion. Real GDP increases by $100 billion to
$1,600 billion. But again, aggregate planned expendi-
ture exceeds real GDP. When real GDP is $1,600 bil-
lion, aggregate planned expenditure is $1,650 billion,
point *C* in Fig. 27.4(a). Again, inventories decrease,
but this time by less than before. With real GDP of
$1,600 billion and aggregate planned expenditure of
$1,650 billion, inventories decrease by $50 billion,
point *C* in Fig. 27.4(b). Again, firms hire additional
labour and production increases; real GDP increases
yet further.

The process that we've just described—planned
expenditure exceeds real GDP, inventories decrease,
and production increases to restore inventories—ends

when real GDP has reached $1,700 billion. At
this real GDP, there is equilibrium expenditure.
Unplanned inventory changes are zero. Firms do not
change their production.

From Above Equilibrium If in Fig. 27.4 real GDP is
$1,900 billion, the process that we've just described
works in reverse. With real GDP at $1,900 billion,
actual aggregate expenditure is also $1,900 billion.
But aggregate planned expenditure is $1,800 billion,
point *F* in Fig. 27.4(a). Actual expenditure exceeds
planned expenditure. When people spend
$1,800 billion and firms produce goods and services
worth $1,900 billion, firms' inventories rise by
$100 billion, point *F* in Fig. 27.4(b). Now, real GDP
begins to decrease. As long as actual expenditure
exceeds planned expenditure, inventories rise and
production decreases. Again, the process ends when
real GDP has reached $1,700 billion, the equilibrium
at which unplanned inventory changes are zero and
firms do not change their production.

> ### ◀ REVIEW QUIZ
>
> 1 What is the relationship between aggregate
>   planned expenditure and real GDP at equilib-
>   rium expenditure?
> 2 How does equilibrium expenditure come
>   about? What adjusts to achieve equilibrium?
> 3 If real GDP and aggregate expenditure are less
>   than equilibrium expenditure, what happens to
>   firms' inventories? How do firms change their
>   production? And what happens to real GDP?
> 4 If real GDP and aggregate expenditure are
>   greater than equilibrium expenditure, what
>   happens to firms' inventories? How do firms
>   change their production? And what happens to
>   real GDP?
>
> Work these questions in Study Plan 27.2 and get instant
> feedback. Do a Key Terms Quiz.   MyEconLab

We've learned that when the price level is fixed,
real GDP is determined by equilibrium expenditure.
And we have seen how unplanned changes in inventories and the production response they generate
bring a convergence toward equilibrium expenditure.
We're now going to study *changes* in equilibrium
expenditure and discover an economic amplifier
called the *multiplier*.

◆ The Multiplier

Investment and exports can change for many reasons. A fall in the real interest rate might induce firms to increase their planned investment. A wave of innovation, such as occurred with the spread of multimedia computers in the 1990s, might increase expected future profits and lead firms to increase their planned investment. An economic boom in the United States, the European Union, and Japan might lead to a large increase in their expenditure on Canadian-produced goods and services—on Canadian exports. These are all examples of increases in autonomous expenditure.

When autonomous expenditure increases, aggregate expenditure increases and so does equilibrium expenditure and real GDP. But the increase in real GDP is *larger* than the change in autonomous expenditure. The **multiplier** is the amount by which a change in autonomous expenditure is magnified or multiplied to determine the change in equilibrium expenditure and real GDP.

To get the basic idea of the multiplier, we'll work with an example economy in which there are no income taxes and no imports. So we'll first assume that these factors are absent. Then, when you understand the basic idea, we'll bring these factors back into play and see what difference they make to the multiplier.

The Basic Idea of the Multiplier

Suppose that investment increases. The additional expenditure by businesses means that aggregate expenditure and real GDP increase. The increase in real GDP increases disposable income and, with no income taxes, real GDP and disposable income increase by the same amount. The increase in disposable income brings an increase in consumption expenditure. And the increased consumption expenditure adds even more to aggregate expenditure. Real GDP and disposable income increase further, and so does consumption expenditure.

The initial increase in investment brings an even bigger increase in aggregate expenditure because it induces an increase in consumption expenditure. The magnitude of the increase in aggregate expenditure that results from an increase in autonomous expenditure is determined by the *multiplier*.

The table in Fig. 27.5 sets out an aggregate planned expenditure schedule. Initially, when real GDP is $1,600 billion, aggregate planned expenditure is $1,625 billion. For each $100 billion increase

in real GDP, aggregate planned expenditure increases by $75 billion. This aggregate expenditure schedule is shown in the figure as the aggregate expenditure curve AE_0. Initially, equilibrium expenditure is $1,700 billion. You can see this equilibrium in row B of the table and in the figure where the curve AE_0 intersects the 45° line at the point marked B.

Now suppose that autonomous expenditure increases by $50 billion. What happens to equilibrium expenditure? You can see the answer in Fig. 27.5. When this increase in autonomous expenditure is added to the original aggregate planned expenditure, aggregate planned expenditure increases by $50 billion at each level of real GDP. The new aggregate expenditure curve is AE_1. The new equilibrium expenditure, highlighted in the table (row D'), occurs where AE_1 intersects the 45° line and is $1,900 billion (point D'). At this real GDP, aggregate planned expenditure equals real GDP.

The Multiplier Effect

In Fig. 27.5, the increase in autonomous expenditure of $50 billion increases equilibrium expenditure by $200 billion. That is, the change in autonomous expenditure leads, like a rock singer's electronic equipment, to an amplified change in equilibrium expenditure. This amplified change is the *multiplier effect*—equilibrium expenditure increases by *more than* the increase in autonomous expenditure. The multiplier is greater than 1.

Initially, when autonomous expenditure increases, aggregate planned expenditure exceeds real GDP. As a result, inventories decrease. Firms respond by increasing production so as to restore their inventories to the target level. As production increases, so does real GDP. With a higher level of real GDP, *induced expenditure* increases. Equilibrium expenditure increases by the sum of the initial increase in autonomous expenditure and the increase in induced expenditure. In this example, equilibrium expenditure increases by $200 billion following the increase in autonomous expenditure of $50 billion, so induced expenditure increases by $150 billion.

Although we have just analyzed the effects of an *increase* in autonomous expenditure, this analysis also applies to a decrease in autonomous expenditure. If initially the aggregate expenditure curve is AE_1, equilibrium expenditure and real GDP are $1,900 billion. A decrease in autonomous expenditure of $50 billion shifts the aggregate expenditure curve downward by

FIGURE 27.5 The Multiplier

Real GDP (Y)	Aggregate planned expenditure			
	Original (AE₀)		New (AE₁)	
	(billions of 2007 dollars)			
1,600	A	1,625	A'	1,675
1,700	**B**	**1,700**	**B'**	**1,750**
1,800	C	1,775	C'	1,825
1,900	**D**	**1,850**	**D'**	**1,900**
2,000	E	1,925	E'	1,975

An increase in autonomous expenditure of $50 billion shifts the AE curve upward by $50 billion from AE₀ to AE₁. Equilibrium expenditure increases by $200 billion from $1,700 billion to $1,900 billion. The increase in equilibrium expenditure is 4 times the increase in autonomous expenditure, so the multiplier is 4.

MyEconLab Animation and Draw Graph

$50 billion to AE_0. Equilibrium expenditure decreases from $1,900 billion to $1,700 billion. The decrease in equilibrium expenditure ($200 billion) is larger than the decrease in autonomous expenditure that brought it about ($50 billion).

Why Is the Multiplier Greater Than 1?

We've seen that equilibrium expenditure increases by more than the increase in autonomous expenditure. This makes the multiplier greater than 1. How come? Why does equilibrium expenditure increase by more than the increase in autonomous expenditure?

The multiplier is greater than 1 because induced expenditure increases—an increase in autonomous expenditure *induces* further increases in expenditure. For example, TransCanada will spend $5 billion to build the Prince Rupert Gas Transmission Project. This expenditure adds $5 billion directly to real GDP. But that is not the end of the story. Engineers and construction workers now have more income, and they spend part of the extra income on goods and services. Real GDP now increases by the initial $5 billion plus the extra consumption expenditure induced by the $5 billion increase in income. The producers of cars, TVs, vacation cruises, and other goods and services now have increased incomes, and they, in turn, spend part of the increase in their incomes on consumption goods and services. Additional income induces additional consumption expenditure, which creates additional income.

How big is the multiplier effect?

The Size of the Multiplier

Suppose that the economy is in a recession. Profit prospects start to look better, and firms are planning a large increase in investment. The world economy is also heading toward expansion. The question on everyone's lips is: How strong will the expansion be? This is a hard question to answer, but an important ingredient in the answer is the size of the multiplier.

The *multiplier* is the amount by which a change in autonomous expenditure is multiplied to determine the change in equilibrium expenditure that it generates. To calculate the multiplier, we divide the change in equilibrium expenditure by the change in autonomous expenditure.

Let's calculate the multiplier for the example in Fig. 27.5. Initially, equilibrium expenditure is $1,700 billion. Then autonomous expenditure increases by $50 billion, and equilibrium expenditure increases by $200 billion to $1,900 billion. Then

$$\text{Multiplier} = \frac{\text{Change in equilibrium expenditure}}{\text{Change in autonomous expenditure}}$$

$$\text{Multiplier} = \frac{\$200 \text{ billion}}{\$50 \text{ billion}} = 4.$$

The Multiplier and the Slope of the *AE* Curve

The magnitude of the multiplier depends on the slope of the *AE* curve. In Fig. 27.6, the *AE* curve in part (a) is steeper than the *AE* curve in part (b), and the multiplier is larger in part (a) than in part (b). To see why, let's do a calculation.

Aggregate expenditure and real GDP change because induced expenditure and autonomous expenditure change. The change in real GDP (ΔY) equals the change in induced expenditure (ΔN) plus the change in autonomous expenditure (ΔA). That is,

$$\Delta Y = \Delta N + \Delta A.$$

But the change in induced expenditure is determined by the change in real GDP and the slope of the *AE* curve. To see why, begin with the fact that the slope of the *AE* curve equals the "rise," ΔN, divided by the "run," ΔY. That is,

$$\text{Slope of } AE \text{ curve} = \Delta N \div \Delta Y.$$

So,

$$\Delta N = \text{Slope of } AE \text{ curve} \times \Delta Y.$$

Now, use this equation to replace ΔN in the first equation above to give

$$\Delta Y = \text{Slope of } AE \text{ curve} \times \Delta Y + \Delta A.$$

Now, solve for ΔY as

$$(1 - \text{Slope of } AE \text{ curve}) \times \Delta Y = \Delta A.$$

Now rearrange the equation to give

$$\Delta Y = \frac{\Delta A}{1 - \text{Slope of } AE \text{ curve}}.$$

Finally, divide both sides of this equation by ΔA to give

$$\text{Multiplier} = \frac{\Delta Y}{\Delta A} = \frac{1}{1 - \text{Slope of } AE \text{ curve}}.$$

If we use the example in Fig. 27.5, the slope of the *AE* curve is 0.75, so,

$$\text{Multiplier} = \frac{1}{1 - 0.75} = \frac{1}{0.25} = 4.$$

Where there are no income taxes and no imports, the slope of the *AE* curve equals the marginal propensity to consume (*MPC*). So,

$$\text{Multiplier} = \frac{1}{1 - MPC}.$$

But $(1 - MPC)$ equals *MPS*. So another formula is

$$\text{Multiplier} = \frac{1}{MPS}.$$

Again using the numbers in Fig. 27.5, we have

$$\text{Multiplier} = \frac{1}{0.25} = 4.$$

Because the marginal propensity to save (*MPS*) is a fraction—a number between 0 and 1—the multiplier is greater than 1.

FIGURE 27.6   The Multiplier and the Slope of the *AE* Curve

(a) Multiplier is 4

(b) Multiplier is 2

Imports and income taxes make the *AE* curve less steep and reduce the value of the multiplier. In part (a), with no imports and no income taxes, the slope of the *AE* curve is 0.75 (the marginal propensity to consume) and the multiplier is 4.

But with imports and income taxes, the slope of the *AE* curve is less than the marginal propensity to consume. In part (b), the slope of the *AE* curve is 0.5. In this case, the multiplier is 2.

MyEconLab Animation

Imports and Income Taxes

Imports and income taxes influence the size of the multiplier and make it smaller than it otherwise would be.

To see why imports make the multiplier smaller, think about what happens following an increase in investment. The increase in investment increases real GDP, which in turn increases consumption expenditure. But part of the increase in expenditure is on imported goods and services. Only expenditure on Canadian-produced goods and services increases Canadian real GDP. The larger the marginal propensity to import, the smaller is the change in Canadian real GDP. The Mathematical Note on pp. 668–671 shows the effects of imports and income taxes on the multiplier.

Income taxes also make the multiplier smaller than it otherwise would be. Again, think about what happens following an increase in investment. The increase in investment increases real GDP. Income tax payments increase, so disposable income increases by less than the increase in real GDP and consumption expenditure increases by less than it would if taxes had not changed. The larger the income tax rate, the smaller is the change in real GDP.

The marginal propensity to import and the income tax rate together with the marginal propensity to consume determine the multiplier. And their combined influence determines the slope of the *AE* curve.

Over time, the value of the multiplier changes as tax rates change and as the marginal propensity to consume and the marginal propensity to import change. These ongoing changes make the multiplier hard to predict. But they do not change the fundamental fact that an initial change in autonomous expenditure leads to a magnified change in aggregate expenditure and real GDP.

The Multiplier Process

The multiplier effect isn't a one-shot event. It is a process that plays out over a few months. Figure 27.7 illustrates the multiplier process. Autonomous expenditure increases by $50 billion and real GDP increases by $50 billion (the green bar in round 1). This increase in real GDP increases induced expenditure in round 2. With the slope of the *AE* curve equal to 0.75, induced expenditure increases by 0.75 times the increase in real GDP, so the increase in real GDP of $50 billion induces a further increase in

expenditure of $37.5 billion. This change in induced expenditure (the green bar in round 2) when added to the previous increase in expenditure (the blue bar in round 2) increases real GDP by $87.5 billion. The round 2 increase in real GDP induces a round 3 increase in induced expenditure. The process repeats through successive rounds. Each increase in real GDP is 0.75 times the previous increase and eventually real GDP increases by $200 billion.

FIGURE 27.7   The Multiplier Process

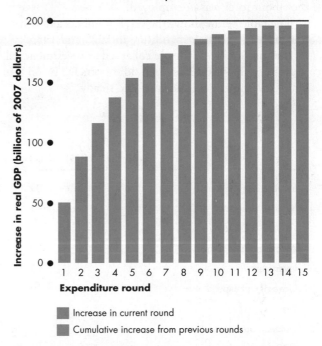

Autonomous expenditure increases by $50 billion. In round 1, real GDP increases by the same amount. With the slope of the *AE* curve equal to 0.75, each additional dollar of real GDP induces an additional 0.75 of a dollar of induced expenditure. The round 1 increase in real GDP brings an increase in induced expenditure of $37.5 billion in round 2. At the end of round 2, real GDP has increased by $87.5 billion.

The extra $37.5 billion of real GDP in round 2 brings a further increase in induced expenditure of $28.1 billion in round 3. At the end of round 3, real GDP has increased by $115.6 billion.

This process continues with real GDP increasing by ever-smaller amounts. When the process comes to an end, real GDP has increased by a total of $200 billion.

MyEconLab Animation

Economics in Action
The Multiplier in the Great Depression

The aggregate expenditure model and its multiplier were developed during the 1930s by John Maynard Keynes to understand the most traumatic event in economic history, the *Great Depression*.

In 1929, the Canadian and global economies were booming. Canadian real GDP and real GDP per person had never been higher. By 1933, real GDP had fallen to 67 percent of its 1929 level and more than a quarter of the labour force was unemployed.

The table below shows the GDP numbers and components of aggregate expenditure in 1929 and 1933.

Autonomous expenditure collapsed as investment fell from $17 billion to $3 billion and exports fell by $3 billion. Government expenditure held steady.

The figure uses the *AE* model to illustrate the Great Depression. In 1929, with autonomous expenditure of $63 billion, the *AE* curve was AE_{29}. Equilibrium expenditure and real GDP were $104 billion.

By 1933, autonomous expenditure had fallen by $17 billion to $46 billion and the *AE* curve had shifted downward to AE_{33}. Equilibrium expenditure and real GDP had fallen to $76 billion.

The decrease in autonomous expenditure of $17 billion brought a decrease in real GDP of $28 billion. The multiplier was $28/$17 = 1.6. The slope of the *AE* curve is 0.39—the fall in induced expenditure, $11 billion, divided by the fall in real GDP, $28 billion. The multiplier formula, $1/(1 - \text{Slope of } AE \text{ curve})$, delivers a multiplier equal to 1.6.

	1929	1933
	(billions of 1929 dollars)	
Induced consumption	47	34
Induced imports	−6	−4
Induced expenditure	41	30
Autonomous consumption	30	30
Investment	17	3
Government expenditure	10	10
Exports	6	3
Autonomous expenditure	63	46
GDP	**104**	**76**

Source of data: Bureau of Economic Analysis.

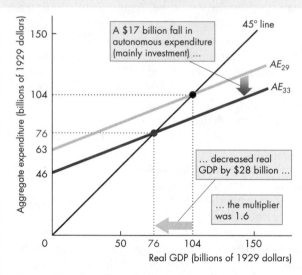

Aggregate Expenditure in the Great Depression

Business Cycle Turning Points

At business cycle turning points, the economy moves from expansion to recession or from recession to expansion. Economists understand these turning points as seismologists understand earthquakes. They know quite a lot about the forces and mechanisms that produce them, but they can't predict them. The forces that bring business cycle turning points are the swings in autonomous expenditure, such as investment and exports. The multiplier that you've just studied is the mechanism that gives momentum to the economy's new direction.

◀ REVIEW QUIZ

1 What is the multiplier? What does it determine? Why does it matter?
2 How do the marginal propensity to consume, the marginal propensity to import, and the income tax rate influence the multiplier?
3 How do fluctuations in autonomous expenditure influence real GDP?

Work these questions in Study Plan 27.3 and get instant feedback. Do a Key Terms Quiz.   MyEconLab

◆ The Multiplier and the Price Level

We have just considered adjustments in spending that occur in the very short run when the price level is fixed. In this time frame, the economy's cobblestones, which are changes in investment and exports, are not smoothed by shock absorbers like those on a limousine. Instead, they are amplified like a rock singer's voice. But these outcomes occur only when the price level is fixed. We now investigate what happens after a long enough time lapse for the price level to change.

Adjusting Quantities and Prices

When firms can't keep up with sales and their inventories fall below target, they increase production, but at some point, they raise their prices. Similarly, when firms find unwanted inventories piling up, they decrease production, but eventually they cut their prices. So far, we've studied the macroeconomic consequences of firms changing their production levels when their sales change, but we haven't looked at the effects of price changes. When individual firms change their prices, the economy's price level changes.

To study the simultaneous determination of real GDP and the price level, we use the *AS-AD model*, which is explained in Chapter 26. But to understand how aggregate demand adjusts, we need to work out the connection between the *AS-AD* model and the aggregate expenditure model that we've used in this chapter. The key to understanding the relationship between these two models is the distinction between aggregate *expenditure* and aggregate *demand* and the related distinction between the aggregate *expenditure curve* and the aggregate *demand curve*.

Aggregate Expenditure and Aggregate Demand

The aggregate expenditure curve is the relationship between the aggregate planned expenditure and real GDP, all other influences on aggregate planned expenditure remaining the same. The aggregate demand curve is the relationship between the aggregate quantity of goods and services demanded and the price level, all other influences on aggregate demand remaining the same. Let's explore the links between these two relationships.

Deriving the Aggregate Demand Curve

When the price level changes, aggregate planned expenditure changes and the quantity of real GDP demanded changes. The aggregate demand curve slopes downward. Why? There are two main reasons:

- Wealth effect
- Substitution effects

Wealth Effect Other things remaining the same, the higher the price level, the smaller is the purchasing power of wealth. For example, suppose you have $100 in the bank and the price level is 105. If the price level rises to 125, your $100 buys fewer goods and services. You are less wealthy. With less wealth, you will probably want to try to spend a bit less and save a bit more. The higher the price level, other things remaining the same, the lower is aggregate planned expenditure.

Substitution Effects For a given expected future price level, a rise in the price level today makes current goods and services more expensive relative to future goods and services and results in a delay in purchases—an *intertemporal substitution*. A rise in the Canadian price level, other things remaining the same, makes Canadian-produced goods and services more expensive relative to foreign-produced goods and services. As a result, Canadian imports increase and Canadian exports decrease—an *international substitution*.

When the price level rises, each of these effects reduces aggregate planned expenditure at each level of real GDP. As a result, when the price level *rises*, the aggregate expenditure curve shifts *downward*. A fall in the price level has the opposite effect. When the price level *falls*, the aggregate expenditure curve shifts *upward*.

Figure 27.8(a) shows the shifts of the *AE* curve. When the price level is 110, the aggregate expenditure curve is AE_0, which intersects the 45° line at point *B*. Equilibrium expenditure is $1,700 billion. If the price level *rises* to 130, the aggregate expenditure curve shifts *downward* to AE_1, which intersects the 45° line at point *A*. Equilibrium expenditure decreases to $1,600 billion. If the price level *falls* to 90, the aggregate expenditure curve shifts *upward* to AE_2, which intersects the 45° line at point *C*. Equilibrium expenditure increases to $1,800 billion.

We've just seen that when the price level changes, other things remaining the same, the aggregate expenditure curve *shifts* and the equilibrium expenditure changes. But when the price level changes and other things remain the same, there is a *movement along* the aggregate demand curve.

Figure 27.8(b) shows the movements along the aggregate demand curve. At a price level of 110, the aggregate quantity of goods and services demanded is $1,700 billion—point *B* on the *AD* curve. If the price level rises to 130, the aggregate quantity of goods and services demanded decreases to $1,600 billion and there is a movement up along the aggregate demand curve to point *A*. If the price level falls to 90, the aggregate quantity of goods and services demanded increases to $1,800 billion and there is a movement down along the aggregate demand curve to point *C*.

Each point on the aggregate demand curve corresponds to a point of equilibrium expenditure. The equilibrium expenditure points *A*, *B*, and *C* in Fig. 27.8(a) correspond to the points *A*, *B*, and *C* on the aggregate demand curve in Fig. 27.8(b).

Changes in Aggregate Expenditure and Aggregate Demand

When any influence on aggregate planned expenditure other than the price level changes, both the aggregate expenditure curve and the aggregate demand curve shift. For example, an increase in investment or exports increases both aggregate planned expenditure and aggregate demand and shifts both the *AE* curve and the *AD* curve. Figure 27.9 illustrates the effect of such an increase.

Initially, the aggregate expenditure curve is AE_0 in part (a) and the aggregate demand curve is AD_0 in part (b). The price level is 110, real GDP is $1,700 billion, and the economy is at point *A* in both parts of Fig. 27.9. Now suppose that investment increases by $100 billion. At a constant price level of 110, the aggregate expenditure curve shifts upward to AE_1. This curve intersects the 45° line at an equilibrium expenditure of $1,900 billion (point *B*). This equilibrium expenditure of $1,900 billion is the aggregate quantity of goods and services demanded at a price level of 110, as shown by point *B* in part (b). Point *B* lies on a new aggregate demand curve. The aggregate demand curve has shifted rightward to AD_1 to pass through point *B*.

But how do we know by how much the *AD* curve shifts? The multiplier determines the answer. The

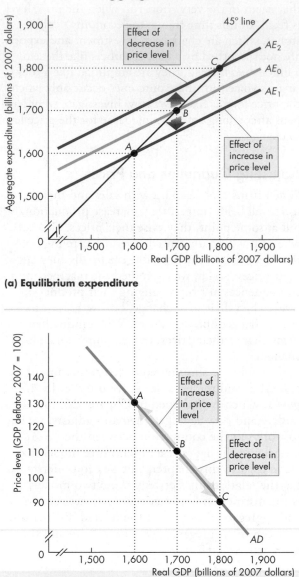

FIGURE 27.8 Equilibrium Expenditure and Aggregate Demand

(a) Equilibrium expenditure

(b) Aggregate demand

A change in the price level *shifts* the *AE* curve and results in a *movement along* the *AD* curve. When the price level is 110, the *AE* curve is AE_0. Equilibrium expenditure is $1,700 billion at point *B*. A rise in the price level from 110 to 130 shifts the *AE* curve downward to AE_1. Equilibrium expenditure decreases to $1,600 billion at point *A*. A fall in the price level from 110 to 90 shifts the *AE* curve upward to AE_2. Equilibrium expenditure increases to $1,800 billion at point *C*. Points *A*, *B*, and *C* on the *AD* curve in part (b) correspond to the equilibrium expenditure points *A*, *B*, and *C* in part (a).

MyEconLab Animation and Draw Graph

FIGURE 27.9   A Change in Aggregate Demand

(a) Aggregate expenditure

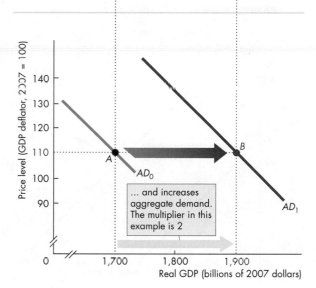

(b) Aggregate demand

An increase in autonomous expenditure increases aggregate demand. The price level is 110. When the aggregate expenditure curve is AE_0 in part (a), the aggregate demand curve is AD_0 in part (b). The economy is at point A in both parts of the figure. An increase in autonomous expenditure shifts the AE curve upward to AE_1. In the new equilibrium, real GDP is $1,900 billion at point B in part (a). Because the quantity of real GDP demanded at a price level of 110 increases from $1,700 billion to $1,900 billion, the AD curve shifts rightward to AD_1.

MyEconLab Animation

larger the multiplier, the larger is the shift in the aggregate demand curve that results from a given change in autonomous expenditure. In this example, the multiplier is 2. A $100 billion increase in investment produces a $200 billion increase in the aggregate quantity of goods and services demanded at each price level. That is, a $100 billion increase in autonomous expenditure shifts the aggregate demand curve rightward by $200 billion.

A decrease in autonomous expenditure shifts the aggregate expenditure curve downward and shifts the aggregate demand curve leftward. You can see these effects by reversing the change that we've just described. If the economy is initially at point B on the aggregate expenditure curve AE_1 and on the aggregate demand curve AD_1, a decrease in autonomous expenditure shifts the aggregate expenditure curve downward to AE_0. The aggregate quantity of goods and services demanded decreases from $1,900 billion to $1,700 billion, and the aggregate demand curve shifts leftward to AD_0.

Let's summarize what we have just discovered:

> If some factor other than a change in the price level increases autonomous expenditure, then the AE curve shifts upward and the AD curve shifts rightward. The size of the AD curve shift equals the change in autonomous expenditure multiplied by the multiplier.

Equilibrium Real GDP and the Price Level

In Chapter 26, we learned that aggregate demand and short-run aggregate supply determine equilibrium real GDP and the price level. We've now put aggregate demand under a more powerful microscope and have discovered that a change in investment (or in any component of autonomous expenditure) changes aggregate demand and shifts the aggregate demand curve. The magnitude of the shift depends on the multiplier. But whether a change in autonomous expenditure results ultimately in a change in real GDP, a change in the price level, or a combination of the two depends on aggregate supply. There are two time frames to consider: the short run and the long run. First we'll see what happens in the short run.

An Increase in Aggregate Demand in the Short Run
Figure 27.10 describes the economy. Initially, in part (a), the aggregate expenditure curve is AE_0 and

equilibrium expenditure is $1,700 billion—point *A*. In part (b), aggregate demand is AD_0 and the short-run aggregate supply curve is *SAS*. (Chapter 26, pp. 625–626, explains the *SAS* curve.) Equilibrium is at point *A* in part (b), where the aggregate demand and short-run aggregate supply curves intersect. The price level is 110, and real GDP is $1,700 billion.

Now suppose that investment increases by $100 billion. With the price level fixed at 110, the aggregate expenditure curve shifts upward to AE_1. Equilibrium expenditure increases to $1,900 billion—point *B* in part (a). In part (b), the aggregate demand curve shifts rightward by $200 billion, from AD_0 to AD_1. How far the aggregate demand curve shifts is determined by the multiplier when the price level is fixed.

But with this new aggregate demand curve, the price level does *not* remain fixed. The price level rises, and as it does, the aggregate expenditure curve shifts downward. The short-run equilibrium occurs when the aggregate expenditure curve has shifted downward to AE_2 and the new aggregate demand curve, AD_1, intersects the short-run aggregate supply curve at point *C* in both part (a) and part (b). Real GDP is $1,830 billion, and the price level is 123.

When price level effects are taken into account, the increase in investment still has a multiplier effect on real GDP, but the multiplier is smaller than it would be if the price level were fixed. The steeper the slope of the short-run aggregate supply curve, the larger is the increase in the price level and the smaller is the multiplier effect on real GDP.

An Increase in Aggregate Demand in the Long Run

Figure 27.11 illustrates the long-run effect of an increase in aggregate demand. In the long run, real GDP equals potential GDP and there is full employment. Potential GDP is $1,700 billion, and the long-run aggregate supply curve is *LAS*. Initially, the economy is at point *A* in parts (a) and (b).

Investment increases by $100 billion. In Fig. 27.11, the aggregate expenditure curve shifts to AE_1 and the aggregate demand curve shifts to AD_1. With no change in the price level, the economy would move to point *B* and real GDP would increase to $1,900 billion. But in the short run, the price level rises to 123 and real GDP increases to only $1,830 billion. With the higher price level, the *AE* curve shifts downward from AE_1 to AE_2. The economy is now in a short-run equilibrium at point *C* in both part (a) and part (b).

FIGURE 27.10   The Multiplier in the Short Run

(a) Aggregate expenditure

(b) Aggregate demand

An increase in investment shifts the *AE* curve from AE_0 to AE_1 and the *AD* curve from AD_0 to AD_1. The price level rises, and the higher price level shifts the *AE* curve downward from AE_1 to AE_2. The economy moves to point *C* in both parts of the figure. In the short run, when prices are flexible, the multiplier effect is smaller than when the price level is fixed.

MyEconLab Animation

FIGURE 27.11   The Multiplier in the Long Run

(a) Aggregate expenditure

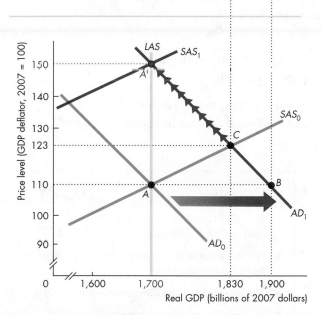

(b) Aggregate demand

Starting from point A, an increase in investment shifts the AE curve upward to AE_1 and the AD curve rightward to AD_1. In the short run, the economy is at point C and at an above full-employment equilibrium. In the long run, the money wage rate rises and the SAS curve shifts leftward toward SAS_1. As the price level rises, the AE curve shifts downward. In the long run, the economy moves to point A' and the multiplier is zero.

MyEconLab Animation

Real GDP now exceeds potential GDP. The labour force is more than fully employed, and in the long run shortages of labour increase the money wage rate. The higher money wage rate increases firms' costs, which decreases short-run aggregate supply and shifts the SAS curve leftward to SAS_1. The price level rises above 123 and real GDP decreases. There is a movement up along AD_1, and the AE curve shifts downward from AE_2 toward AE_0. When the money wage rate and the price level have increased by the same percentage, real GDP is again equal to potential GDP and the economy is at point A'. In the long run, the multiplier is zero.

◆ REVIEW QUIZ

1 How does a change in the price level influence the AE curve and the AD curve?

2 If autonomous expenditure increases with no change in the price level, what happens to the AE curve and the AD curve? Which curve shifts by an amount that is determined by the multiplier and why?

3 How does an increase in autonomous expenditure change real GDP in the short run? Does real GDP change by the same amount as the change in aggregate demand? Explain why or why not.

4 How does real GDP change in the long run when autonomous expenditure increases? Does real GDP change by the same amount as the change in aggregate demand? Why or why not?

Work these questions in Study Plan 27.4 and get instant feedback.   **MyEconLab**

◆ You are now ready to build on what you've learned about aggregate expenditure fluctuations. We'll study the business cycle and the roles of fiscal policy and monetary policy in smoothing the business cycle while achieving price stability and sustained economic growth. In Chapter 28 we study the Canadian business cycle and inflation, and in Chapters 29 and 30 we study fiscal policy and monetary policy, respectively. But before you leave the current topic, look at *Economics in the News* on pp. 666–667 and see the aggregate expenditure model in action in the Canadian economy during 2014.

Expenditure Changes in the 2014 Expansion

Canadian Economic Accounts, Second Quarter 2014

The Daily
August 29, 2014

Real gross domestic product (GDP) rose 0.8 percent in the second quarter, following a 0.2 percent increase in the first quarter. This was the largest quarterly gain since the third quarter of 2011. ...

The quarterly growth was a result of increased economic activity in all sectors of the economy except non-profit institutions serving households. Final domestic demand was up 0.7 percent after a flat first quarter.

The increase was mainly due to higher household final consumption expenditure, [which] increased by 0.9 percent. ...

Business gross fixed capital formation increased 0.8 percent, following two consecutive quarterly declines. Investment in residential structures (+2.9 percent) contributed the most to the overall gain. Ownership transfer costs were up 9.0 percent after declining in the previous two quarters.

Businesses accumulated $7.0 billion in inventories, down from $14.5 billion in the first quarter. Retail trade reduced its inventories of non-durable goods by $2.8 billion.

Exports of goods and services increased 4.2 percent following a 0.2 percent decline in the previous quarter. Exports of goods rose 4.4 percent. Imports of goods and services increased 2.7 percent. ...

Expressed at an annualized rate, real GDP expanded 3.1 percent in the second quarter. By comparison, real GDP in the United States rose 4.2 percent. ...

Imports of goods and services increased 2.7 percent in the second quarter, following a 1.4 percent decrease in the first quarter. This was the largest increase since the second quarter of 2010. ...

Published by Statistics Canada, © 2014.

ESSENCE OF THE STORY

- Real GDP grew at an annual rate of 3.1 percent during the second quarter of 2014.

- The increase was due mainly to an increase in consumer expenditure.

- Exports and business investment increased.

- Business inventories increased.

ECONOMIC ANALYSIS

- Statistics Canada reports that real GDP increased in the second quarter of 2014 and identifies consumer expenditure as being mainly responsible. Exports, business investment, and business inventories also increased.

- Table 1 shows the real GDP and aggregate expenditure numbers for the first two quarters of 2014 along with the change in the second quarter.

- You can see that consumption expenditure increased most and by much more than real GDP, which means that much of the increase must have been autonomous expenditure rather than induced expenditure.

- So much of consumption expenditure, exports, and business investment increased autonomous expenditure.

- The role played by inventories depends on whether their change was planned or unplanned.

- Figure 1 shows the changes in inventories and real GDP. The two variables fluctuate together at some times and move in opposition at other times.

- Most likely, inventories increased by less than planned, and you can see why in Fig. 2, which interprets the data for 2014 using the aggregate expenditure model.

- In 2014 Q1, the AE curve was AE_0 and real GDP was $1,716 billion, which we assume to be equilibrium expenditure at point A.

- The slope of the AE curve is 0.5 (an assumption).

- In Fig. 2(a), an increase in autonomous expenditure shifted the AE curve upward to AE_1 and aggregate planned expenditure temporarily exceeded real GDP at point B.

- In Fig 2(b), an unplanned decrease in inventories occurred as real GDP increased toward its second quarter equilibrium.

- When real GDP reached its second quarter equilibrium at point C, unplanned inventory changes had returned to zero.

Figure 1 Inventories and the Change in Real GDP

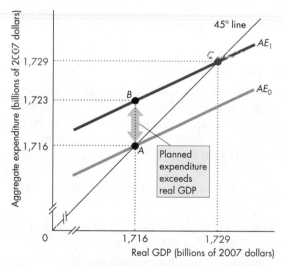

(a) Convergence to equilibrium expenditure in 2014

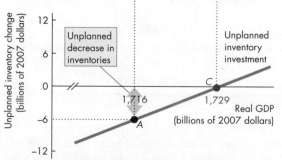

(b) Unplanned inventory change in 2014

Figure 2 Equilibrium Expenditure in 2014

TABLE 1 The Components of Aggregate Expenditure

Item	2014 Q1	2014 Q2	Change
	(billions of 2007 dollars)		
Consumption expenditure	984.4	993.2	8.8
Investment	407.3	402.6	−4.7
Government expenditure	348.4	349.6	1.2
Exports	522.2	544.0	21.8
Imports	551.7	566.4	14.7
Real GDP*	**1,716.0**	**1,729.3**	**13.3**
Change in inventories	14.5	7.1	−7.4

*Chained-dollar real variables are calculated for each expenditure component independently of chained-dollar real GDP and the components don't exactly sum to real GDP.

MATHEMATICAL NOTE

The Algebra of the Keynesian Model

This mathematical note derives formulas for equilibrium expenditure and the multipliers when the price level is fixed. The variables are:

- Aggregate planned expenditure, AE
- Real GDP, Y
- Consumption expenditure, C
- Disposable income, YD
- Investment, I
- Government expenditure, G
- Exports, X
- Imports, M
- Net taxes, T
- Autonomous consumption expenditure, a
- Autonomous taxes, T_a
- Marginal propensity to consume, b
- Marginal propensity to import, m
- Marginal tax rate, t
- Autonomous expenditure, A

Aggregate Expenditure

Aggregate planned expenditure (AE) is the sum of the planned amounts of consumption expenditure (C), investment (I), government expenditure (G), and exports (X) minus the planned amount of imports (M). That is,

$$AE = C + I + G + X - M.$$

Consumption Function Consumption expenditure (C) depends on disposable income (YD), and we write the consumption function as

$$C = a + bYD.$$

Disposable income (YD) equals real GDP minus net taxes ($Y - T$). So if we replace YD with ($Y - T$), the consumption function becomes

$$C = a + b(Y - T).$$

Net taxes, T, equal autonomous taxes (that are independent of income), T_a, plus induced taxes (that vary with income), tY.

So we can write net taxes as

$$T = T_a + tY.$$

Use this last equation to replace T in the consumption function. The consumption function becomes

$$C = a - bT_a + b(1 - t)Y.$$

This equation describes consumption expenditure as a function of real GDP.

Import Function Imports depend on real GDP, and the import function is

$$M = mY.$$

Aggregate Expenditure Curve Use the consumption function and the import function to replace C and M in the AE equation. That is,

$$AE = a - bT_a + b(1 - t)Y + I + G + X - mY.$$

Collect the terms that involve Y on the right side of the equation to obtain

$$AE = (a - bT_a + I + G + X) + [b(1 - t) - m]Y.$$

Autonomous expenditure (A) is ($a - bT_a + I + G + X$), and the slope of the AE curve is $[b(1 - t) - m]$. So the equation for the AE curve, which is shown in Fig. 1, is

$$AE = A + [b(1 - t) - m]Y.$$

Figure 1 The AE Curve

Equilibrium Expenditure

Equilibrium expenditure occurs when aggregate planned expenditure (AE) equals real GDP (Y). That is,

$$AE = Y.$$

In Fig. 2, the scales of the x-axis (real GDP) and the y-axis (aggregate planned expenditure) are identical, so the 45° line shows the points at which aggregate planned expenditure equals real GDP.

Figure 2 shows the point of equilibrium expenditure at the intersection of the AE curve and the 45° line.

To calculate equilibrium expenditure, solve the equations for the AE curve and the 45° line for the two unknown quantities AE and Y. So starting with

$$AE = A + [b(1 - t) - m]Y$$

$$AE = Y,$$

replace AE with Y in the AE equation to obtain

$$Y = A + [b(1 - t) - m]Y.$$

The solution for Y is

$$Y = \frac{1}{1 - [b(1 - t) - m]}A.$$

The Multiplier

The *multiplier* equals the change in equilibrium expenditure and real GDP (Y) that results from a change in autonomous expenditure (A) divided by the change in autonomous expenditure.

A change in autonomous expenditure (ΔA) changes equilibrium expenditure and real GDP by

$$\Delta Y = \frac{1}{1 - [b(1 - t) - m]}\Delta A.$$

$$\text{Multiplier} = \frac{1}{1 - [b(1 - t) - m]}.$$

The size of the multiplier depends on the slope of the AE curve, $b(1 - t) - m$. The larger the slope, the larger is the multiplier. So the multiplier is larger,

- The greater the marginal propensity to consume (b)
- The smaller the marginal tax rate (t)
- The smaller the marginal propensity to import (m)

An economy with no imports and no income taxes has $m = 0$ and $t = 0$. In this special case, the multiplier equals $1/(1 - b)$. If b is 0.75, then the multiplier is 4, as shown in Fig. 3.

In an economy with imports and income taxes, if $b = 0.75$, $t = 0.2$, and $m = 0.1$, the multiplier equals 1 divided by $[1 - 0.75(1 - 0.2) - 0.1]$, which equals 2. Make up some alternative examples to show the effects of b, t, and m on the multiplier.

Figure 2 Equilibrium Expenditure

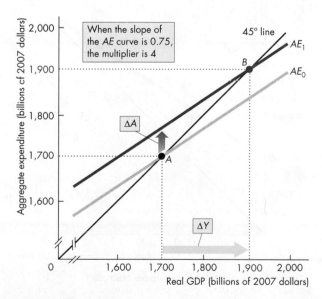

Figure 3 The Multiplier

Government Expenditure Multiplier

The **government expenditure multiplier** equals the change in equilibrium expenditure and real GDP (Y) that results from a change in government expenditure (G) divided by the change in government expenditure. Because autonomous expenditure is equal to

$$A = a - bT_a + I + G + X,$$

the change in autonomous expenditure equals the change in government expenditure. That is,

$$\Delta A = \Delta G.$$

You can see from the solution for equilibrium expenditure Y that

$$\Delta Y = \frac{1}{1 - [b(1 - t) - m]} \Delta G.$$

The government expenditure multiplier equals

$$\frac{1}{1 - [b(1 - t) - m]}.$$

In an economy in which $t = 0$ and $m = 0$, the government expenditure multiplier is $1/(1 - b)$. With $b = 0.75$, the government expenditure multiplier is 4, as Fig. 4 shows. Make up some examples and use the above formula to show how b, m, and t influence the government expenditure multiplier.

Autonomous Tax Multiplier

The **autonomous tax multiplier** equals the change in equilibrium expenditure and real GDP (Y) that results from a change in autonomous taxes (T_a) divided by the change in autonomous taxes. Because autonomous expenditure is equal to

$$A = a - bT_a + I + G + X,$$

the change in autonomous expenditure equals *minus* b multiplied by the change in autonomous taxes. That is,

$$\Delta A = -b\Delta T_a.$$

You can see from the solution for equilibrium expenditure Y that

$$\Delta Y = \frac{-b}{1 - [b(1 - t) - m]} \Delta T_a.$$

The autonomous tax multiplier equals

$$\frac{-b}{1 - [b(1 - t) - m]}.$$

In an economy in which $t = 0$ and $m = 0$, the autonomous tax multiplier is $-b/(1 - b)$. In this special case, with $b = 0.75$, the autonomous tax multiplier equals -3, as Fig. 5 shows. Make up some examples and use the above formula to show how b, m, and t influence the autonomous tax multiplier.

Figure 4 Government Expenditure Multiplier

Figure 5 Autonomous Tax Multiplier

Balanced Budget Multiplier

The **balanced budget multiplier** equals the change in equilibrium expenditure and real GDP (Y) that results from equal changes in government expenditure and lump-sum taxes divided by the change in government expenditure. Because government expenditure and autonomous taxes change by the same amount, the budget balance does not change.

The change in equilibrium expenditure that results from the change in government expenditure is

$$\Delta Y = \frac{1}{1 - [b(1 - t) - m]} \Delta G.$$

And the change in equilibrium expenditure that results from the change in autonomous taxes is

$$\Delta Y = \frac{-b}{1 - [b(1 - t) - m]} \Delta T_a.$$

So the change in equilibrium expenditure resulting from the changes in government expenditure and autonomous taxes is

$$\Delta Y = \frac{1}{1 - [b(1 - t) - m]} \Delta G +$$

$$\frac{-b}{1 - [b(1 - t) - m]} \Delta T_a.$$

Notice that

$$\frac{1}{1 - [b(1 - t) - m]}$$

is common to both terms on the right side. So we can rewrite the equation as

$$\Delta Y = \frac{1}{1 - [b(1 - t) - m]} (\Delta G - b\Delta T_a).$$

The AE curve shifts upward by $\Delta G - b\Delta T_a$ as shown in Fig. 6.

But the change in government expenditure equals the change in autonomous taxes. That is,

$$\Delta G = \Delta T_a.$$

So we can write the equation as

$$\Delta Y = \frac{1 - b}{1 - [b(1 - t) - m]} \Delta G.$$

The balanced budget multiplier equals

$$\frac{1 - b}{1 - [b(1 - t) - m]}.$$

In an economy in which $t - 0$ and $m - 0$, the balanced budget multiplier is $(1 - b)/(1 - b)$, which equals 1, as Fig. 6 shows. Make up some examples and use the above formula to show how b, m, and t influence the balanced budget multiplier.

Exercise

In an economy, autonomous consumption expenditure is $50 billion, investment is $200 billion, and government expenditure is $250 billion. The marginal propensity to consume is 0.7 and net taxes are $250 billion. Exports are $500 billion and imports are $450 billion. Assume that net taxes and imports are autonomous and the price level is fixed.

a. What is the consumption function?
b. What is the equation of the AE curve?
c. Calculate equilibrium expenditure.
d. Calculate the multiplier.
e. If investment decreases to $150 billion, what is the change in equilibrium expenditure?
f. Describe the process in part (e) that moves the economy to its new equilibrium expenditure.

Figure 6 Balanced Budget Multiplier

SUMMARY

Key Points

Fixed Prices and Expenditure Plans (pp. 648–651)

- When the price level is fixed, expenditure plans determine real GDP.
- Consumption expenditure is determined by disposable income, and the marginal propensity to consume (*MPC*) determines the change in consumption expenditure brought about by a change in disposable income. Real GDP determines disposable income.
- Imports are determined by real GDP, and the marginal propensity to import determines the change in imports brought about by a change in real GDP.

Working Problem 1 will give you a better understanding of fixed prices and expenditure plans.

Real GDP with a Fixed Price Level (pp. 652–655)

- Aggregate *planned* expenditure depends on real GDP.
- Equilibrium expenditure occurs when aggregate planned expenditure equals actual expenditure and real GDP.

Working Problems 2 to 5 will give you a better understanding of real GDP with a fixed price level.

The Multiplier (pp. 656–660)

- The multiplier is the magnified effect of a change in autonomous expenditure on equilibrium expenditure and real GDP.

- The multiplier is determined by the slope of the *AE* curve.
- The slope of the *AE* curve is influenced by the marginal propensity to consume, the marginal propensity to import, and the income tax rate.

Working Problems 6 to 8 will give you a better understanding of the multiplier.

The Multiplier and the Price Level (pp. 661–665)

- The *AD* curve is the relationship between the quantity of real GDP demanded and the price level, other things remaining the same.
- The *AE* curve is the relationship between aggregate planned expenditure and real GDP, other things remaining the same.
- At a given price level, there is a given *AE* curve. A change in the price level changes aggregate planned expenditure and shifts the *AE* curve. A change in the price level also creates a movement along the *AD* curve.
- A change in autonomous expenditure that is not caused by a change in the price level shifts the *AE* curve and shifts the *AD* curve. The magnitude of the shift of the *AD* curve depends on the multiplier and on the change in autonomous expenditure.
- The multiplier decreases as the price level changes, and the long-run multiplier is zero.

Working Problems 9 to 14 will give you a better understanding of the multiplier and the price level.

Key Terms

Aggregate planned expenditure, 648
Autonomous expenditure, 652
Autonomous tax multiplier, 670
Balanced budget multiplier, 671

Consumption function, 648
Disposable income, 648
Equilibrium expenditure, 654
Government expenditure multiplier, 670
Induced expenditure, 652

MyEconLab Key Terms Quiz

Marginal propensity to consume, 650
Marginal propensity to import, 651
Marginal propensity to save, 650
Multiplier, 656
Saving function, 648

WORKED PROBLEM

MyEconLab   You can work this problem in Chapter 27 Study Plan.

You are given the following data about an economy that has a fixed price level, no imports, and no taxes:

Disposable income	Consumption expenditure
(billions of dollars per year)	
0	5
100	80
200	155
300	230
400	305

Questions

1. Calculate the marginal propensity to consume.
2. Calculate autonomous consumption expenditure.
3. Calculate saving at each level of disposable income and the marginal propensity to save.
4. Calculate the multiplier.
5. Calculate the increase in real GDP when autonomous spending increases by $5 billion. Why does real GDP increase by more than $5 billion?

Solutions

1. The marginal propensity to consume equals the fraction of an increase in disposable income that is spent on consumption.

    When disposable income increases from $100 billion to $200 billion, consumption expenditure increases from $80 billion to $155 billion. The increase in disposable income of $100 billion increases consumption expenditure by $75 billion. The marginal propensity to consume equals $75 billion ÷ $100 billion, which equals 0.75.

    Key Point: The marginal propensity to consume is the fraction of an increase in disposable income that is spent on consumption.

2. Autonomous consumption expenditure is the amount of consumption expenditure when dispo-sabale income is zero. From the table, autonomous consumption expenditure is $5 billion.

    Key Point: Autonomous consumption expenditure is the amount of consumption expenditure that depends on things other than disposable income.

3. Disposable income is spent on consumption or saved.

    Saving = Disposable income − Consumption expenditure.

For example, when disposable income is $100 billion, consumption expenditure is $80 billion, so saving is $20 billion.

The table below sets out saving at each level of disposable income.

Disposable income	Saving
(billions of dollars per year)	
0	−5
100	20
200	45
300	70
400	95

The marginal propensity to save is the fraction of an increase in disposable income that is saved. When disposable income increases by $100 billion, saving increases by $25 billion, so the marginal propensity to save equals 0.25.

Key Point: The marginal propensity to consume plus the marginal propensity to save equal 1.

4. When the price level is fixed, the multiplier equals $1/(1 −$ Slope of the AE curve). With no income taxes, the slope of the AE curve equals the marginal propensity to consume (MPC), which is 0.75.

    The multiplier $= 1/(1 − 0.75) = 1/0.25 = 4$.

    Because $(1 − MPC) = MPS$, the multiplier also equals $1/MPS$.

Key Point: With a fixed price level, the multiplier equals $1/(1 − MPC)$ or $1/MPS$.

5. The increase in real GDP when the price level is fixed equals the change in autonomous spending multiplied by the multiplier. That is,

    Change in real GDP = Change in autonomous spending × Multiplier

    Change in real GDP = $5 billion × 4
    = $20 billion.

    An increase in autonomous spending increases income, which increases induced consumption, which in turn increases income. The quantity of real GDP demanded increases.

Key Point: With a fixed price level, real GDP increases by more than the increase in autonomous spending because induced consumption expenditure increases.

STUDY PLAN PROBLEMS AND APPLICATIONS

MyEconLab   You can work Problems 1 to 15 in Chapter 27 Study Plan and get instant feedback.

Fixed Prices and Expenditure Plans (Study Plan 27.1)

1. In an economy, when income increases from $400 billion to $500 billion, consumption expenditure increases from $420 billion to $500 billion. Calculate the marginal propensity to consume, the change in saving, and the marginal propensity to save.

Real GDP with a Fixed Price Level (Study Plan 27.2)

Use the following figure to work Problems 2 and 3. The figure illustrates the components of aggregate planned expenditure on Turtle Island. Turtle Island has no imports or exports, no incomes taxes, and the price level is fixed.

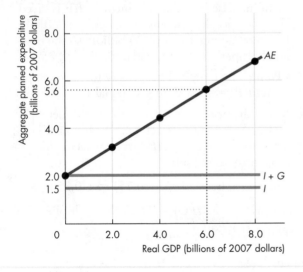

2. Calculate autonomous expenditure and the marginal propensity to consume.
3. a. What is aggregate planned expenditure when real GDP is $6 billion?
   b. If real GDP is $4 billion, what is happening to inventories?
   c. If real GDP is $6 billion, what is happening to inventories?
4. Explain why induced consumption expenditure differs from autonomous consumption expenditure. Why isn't all consumption expenditure induced expenditure?
5. Explain how an increase in business investment at a constant price level changes equilibrium expenditure.

The Multiplier (Study Plan 27.3)

Use the following data to work Problems 6 and 7. An economy has a fixed price level, no imports, and no income taxes. *MPC* is 0.80, and real GDP is $150 billion. Businesses increase investment by $5 billion.

6. Calculate the multiplier and the change in real GDP.
7. Calculate the new real GDP and explain why real GDP increases by more than $5 billion.
8. An economy has a fixed price level, no imports, and no income taxes. An increase in autonomous expenditure of $200 billion increases equilibrium expenditure by $800 billion. Calculate the multiplier and explain what happens to the multiplier if an income tax is introduced.

The Multiplier and the Price Level (Study Plan 27.4)

9. Explain the link between equilibrium expenditure and the quantity of real GDP demanded.

Use the following data to work Problems 10 to 14. Suppose that the economy is at full employment, the price level is 100, and the multiplier is 2. Investment increases by $100 billion.

10. What is the change in equilibrium expenditure if the price level remains at 100?
11. a. What is the immediate change in the quantity of real GDP demanded?
    b. In the short run, does real GDP increase by more than, less than, or the same amount as the immediate change in the quantity of real GDP demanded?
12. In the short run, does the price level remain at 100? Explain why or why not.
13. a. Compare the change in real GDP in the long run with the increase in investment.
    b. Explain how the price level changes in the long run.
14. Are the values of the multipliers in the short run and the long run larger or smaller than 2?

Mathematical Note (Study Plan 27.MN)

15. Use the data in the Worked Problem on p. 673. Calculate the change in equilibrium expenditure when investment decreases by $50 billion.

ADDITIONAL PROBLEMS AND APPLICATIONS

MyEconLab   You can work these problems in MyEconLab if assigned by your instructor.

Fixed Prices and Expenditure Plans

Use the following data to work Problems 16 and 17. You are given the following information about the economy of Australia:

Disposable income	Saving
(billions of dollars per year)	
0	0
100	25
200	50
300	75
400	100

16. Calculate the marginal propensity to save.
17. Calculate consumption at each level of disposable income. Calculate the marginal propensity to consume.

Use the following news clip to work Problems 18 to 20.

Canadians' Wealth Rises

Gains in stock markets and increased house prices boosted Canadians' wealth in the first quarter of 2014. On a per capita basis, household wealth rose to $222,600. Statistics Canada also reported that consumption expenditure increased by $4 billion in the first quarter of 2014.

Sources: *Toronto Star*, September 11, 2014, and Statistics Canada

18. Explain why higher share prices and house prices are equivalent to saving.
19. Explain how a rise in household wealth would be expected to influence consumption expenditure and saving and how the consumption function and the saving function would change.
20. Draw a graph to illustrate how a rise in household wealth would change the consumption function and the saving function.

Real GDP with a Fixed Price Level

Use the spreadsheet in the next column to work Problems 21 and 22.

The spreadsheet lists real GDP (*Y*) and the components of aggregate planned expenditure in billions of dollars.

21. Calculate autonomous expenditure. Calculate the marginal propensity to consume.

	A	B	C	D	E	F	G
1		Y	C	I	G	X	M
2	A	100	110	50	60	60	15
3	B	200	170	50	60	60	30
4	C	300	230	50	60	60	45
5	D	400	290	50	60	60	60
6	E	500	350	50	60	60	75
7	F	600	410	50	60	60	90

22. a. What is aggregate planned expenditure when real GDP is $200 billion?
   b. If real GDP is $200 billion, explain the process that moves the economy toward equilibrium expenditure.
   c. If real GDP is $500 billion, explain the process that moves the economy toward equilibrium expenditure.

23. **Wholesale Inventories Decline, Sales Rise**

The U.S. Commerce Department reported that wholesale inventories fell 1.3 percent in August for a record 12th consecutive month, evidence that companies are trimming orders to factories, which helped depress economic output during the recession. Economists hope that the rising sales will encourage businesses to begin restocking their inventories, which would boost factory production and help bolster broad economic growth in coming months.

Source: *The New York Times*, October 8, 2009

Explain why a fall in inventories is associated with recession and a restocking of inventories might bolster economic growth.

The Multiplier

24. On January 27, 2009, the government announced a stimulus package, which included $12 billion earmarked for infrastructure—the construction of roads, bridges, public transit, broadband Internet access, schools, and social housing in every region of the country.

   If the slope of the *AE* curve is 0.7, calculate the immediate change in aggregate planned expenditure and the change in real GDP in the short run if the price level remains unchanged.

25. **Obama's Economic Recovery Plan**

President Obama's proposal to jolt a listless economic recovery with $180 billion worth of tax breaks and transportation projects left economists largely unimpressed Tuesday.

Source: *USA Today*, September 10, 2010

If taxes fall by $90 billion and the spending on transport projects increases by $90 billion, which component of Obama's recovery plan would have the larger effect on equilibrium expenditure, other things remaining the same?

The Multiplier and the Price Level

Use the following news item to work Problems 26 to 28.

Statistics Canada reported that in the second quarter of 2014 Canadian exports increased by $24 billion.

26. Explain and draw a graph to illustrate the effect of an increase in exports on equilibrium expenditure in the short run.

27. Explain and draw a graph to illustrate the effect of an increase in exports on equilibrium real GDP in the short run.

28. Explain and draw a graph to illustrate the effect of an increase in exports on equilibrium real GDP in the long run.

29. Compare the multiplier in the short run and the long run and explain why they are not identical.

Use the following news clip to work Problems 30 to 32.

Consumer Sentiment Rose to a Three-Month High

Consumer sentiment was up in August, helped by merchant discounts, especially from auto dealerships who received incentives from automakers Honda, General Motors, and Toyota to lower prices.

But consumers are worried about the future. They are worried about tax changes and government budget cuts that are on the horizon. Capital spending fell somewhat.

Source: Bloomberg, September 1, 2012

30. For each of the expenditures listed in the news clip, say which is part of induced expenditure and which is part of autonomous expenditure.

31. Which of the events reported in the news clip would change aggregate demand and which would change the quantity of real GDP demanded? Provide a graphical illustration of the distinction.

32. Explain and draw a graph to illustrate how increasing consumer confidence influences aggregate expenditure and aggregate demand.

33. **Japan Slides Into Recession**

In Japan, consumer prices slid at a faster pace in July and industrial production unexpectedly slumped.

Source: Bloomberg, September 1, 2012

Contrast what the news clip says is happening in Japan with what is happening in Canada in Problem 30 and provide a graphical analysis of the differences.

Economics in the News

34. After you have studied *Economics in the News* on pp. 666–667, answer the following questions.

a. If the second quarter 2014 change in inventories was a planned change, what role did it play in shifting the *AE* curve and changing equilibrium expenditure? Use a two-part figure (similar to that on p. 667) to answer this question.

b. The Statistics Canada report says that an increase in consumption expenditure was the main reason why real GDP increased. How do we know that most of the increase in consumption expenditure was autonomous?

c. Using the assumptions made in Fig. 2 on p. 667, what is the slope of the *AE* curve and what is the value of the autonomous expenditure multiplier?

Mathematical Note

35. In an economy with a fixed price level, autonomous spending is $20 billion and the slope of the *AE* curve is 0.6.

a. What is the equation of the *AE* curve?

b. Calculate equilibrium expenditure.

c. Calculate the multiplier.

d. Calculate the shift of the aggregate demand curve if investment increases by $1 billion.

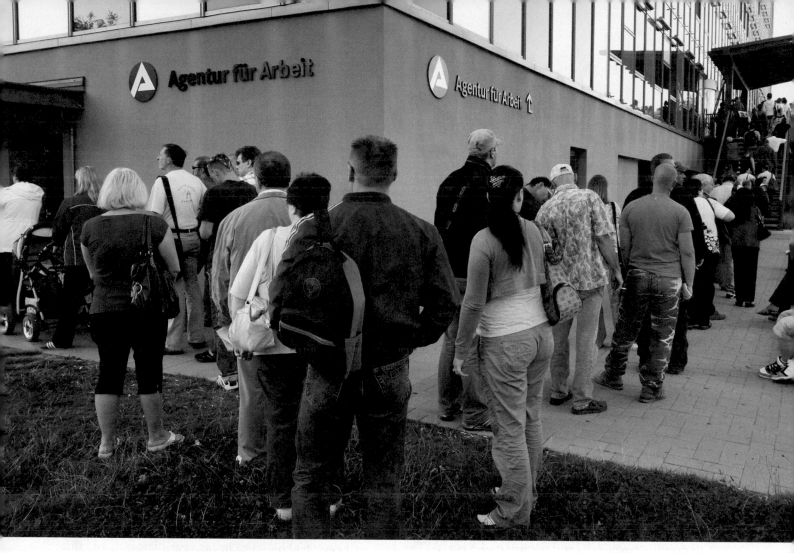

28

THE BUSINESS CYCLE, INFLATION, AND DEFLATION

After studying this chapter, you will be able to:

◆ Explain how aggregate demand shocks and aggregate supply shocks create the business cycle

◆ Explain how demand-pull and cost-push forces bring cycles in inflation and output

◆ Explain the causes and consequences of deflation

◆ Explain the short-run and long-run tradeoff between inflation and unemployment

We fear deflation because it brings stagnant incomes and high unemployment. And we worry about inflation because it raises our cost of living. We want low inflation, low unemployment, and rapid income growth. But can we have all these things at the same time? Or do we face a tradeoff among them? As this chapter explains, we face a tradeoff in the short run but not in the long run.

At the end of the chapter, in *Economics in the News*, we examine a stagnating European economy and the lessons it holds for Canada and other countries.

The Business Cycle

The business cycle is easy to describe but hard to explain and the next peak or trough is impossible to predict. We'll look at two approaches to understanding the business cycle:

- Mainstream business cycle theory
- Real business cycle theory

Mainstream Business Cycle Theory

The mainstream business cycle theory is that potential GDP grows at a steady rate while aggregate demand grows at a fluctuating rate. Because the money wage rate is sticky, if aggregate demand grows faster than potential GDP, real GDP moves above potential GDP and an inflationary gap emerges. And if aggregate demand grows slower than potential GDP, real GDP moves below potential GDP and a recessionary gap emerges. If aggregate demand decreases, real GDP also decreases in a recession.

Figure 28.1 illustrates this business cycle theory. Initially, potential GDP is $1.1 trillion. The long-run aggregate supply curve is LAS_0, the aggregate demand curve is AD_0, and the price level is 100. The economy is at full employment at point A.

An expansion occurs when potential GDP increases and the LAS curve shifts rightward. During an expansion, aggregate demand also increases, and usually by more than potential GDP, so the price level rises. Assume that in the current expansion, the LAS curve shifts rightward to LAS_1, the price level is expected to rise to 110, and the money wage rate has been set based on that expectation. The short-run aggregate supply curve is SAS_1.

If aggregate demand increases to AD_1, real GDP increases from $1.1 trillion to $1.7 trillion, the new level of potential GDP, and the price level rises, as expected, to 110. The economy remains at full employment but now at point B.

If aggregate demand increases more slowly to AD_2, real GDP grows by less than potential GDP and the economy moves to point C, with real GDP at $1.6 trillion and the price level at 107. Real GDP growth is slower and inflation is lower than expected.

If aggregate demand increases more quickly to AD_3, real GDP grows by more than potential GDP and the economy moves to point D. Real GDP is $1.8 trillion and the price level is 113. Real GDP growth is faster and inflation is higher than expected.

Growth, inflation, and the business cycle arise from the relentless increases in potential GDP, faster (on average) increases in aggregate demand, and fluctuations in the pace of aggregate demand growth.

FIGURE 28.1   The Mainstream Business Cycle Theory

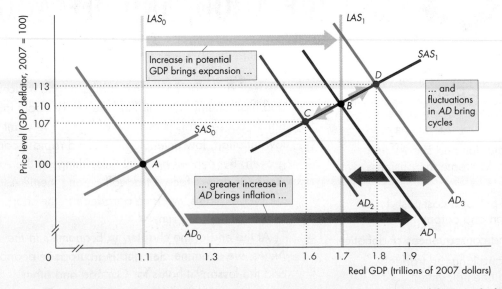

In a business cycle expansion, potential GDP increases and the LAS curve shifts rightward from LAS_0 to LAS_1. A greater than expected increase in aggregate demand brings inflation.

If the aggregate demand curve shifts to AD_1, the economy remains at full employment. If the aggregate demand curve shifts to AD_2, a recessionary gap arises. If the aggregate demand curve shifts to AD_3, an inflationary gap arises.

MyEconLab Animation and Draw Graph

This mainstream theory comes in a number of special forms that differ regarding the source of fluctuations in aggregate demand growth and the source of money wage stickiness.

Keynesian Cycle Theory In **Keynesian cycle theory**, fluctuations in investment driven by fluctuations in business confidence—summarized by the phrase "animal spirits"—are the main source of fluctuations in aggregate demand.

Monetarist Cycle Theory In **monetarist cycle theory**, fluctuations in both investment and consumption expenditure, driven by fluctuations in the growth rate of the quantity of money, are the main source of fluctuations in aggregate demand.

Both the Keynesian and monetarist cycle theories simply assume that the money wage rate is rigid and don't explain that rigidity.

Two newer theories seek to explain money wage rate rigidity and to be more careful about working out its consequences.

New Classical Cycle Theory In **new classical cycle theory**, the rational expectation of the price level, which is determined by potential GDP and *expected* aggregate demand, determines the money wage rate and the position of the *SAS* curve. In this theory, only *unexpected* fluctuations in aggregate demand bring fluctuations in real GDP around potential GDP.

New Keynesian Cycle Theory The **new Keynesian cycle theory** emphasizes the fact that today's money wage rates were negotiated at many past dates, which means that *past* rational expectations of the current price level influence the money wage rate and the position of the *SAS* curve. In this theory, both unexpected and currently expected fluctuations in aggregate demand bring fluctuations in real GDP around potential GDP.

The mainstream cycle theories don't rule out the possibility that aggregate supply shocks might occur. An oil price rise, a widespread drought, a major hurricane, or another natural disaster, could, for example, bring a recession. But supply shocks are not the normal source of fluctuations in the mainstream theories. In contrast, real business cycle theory puts supply shocks at centre stage.

Real Business Cycle Theory

The newest theory of the business cycle, known as **real business cycle theory** (or RBC theory), regards random fluctuations in productivity as the main source of economic fluctuations. These productivity fluctuations are assumed to result mainly from fluctuations in the pace of technological change, but they might also have other sources, such as international disturbances, climate fluctuations, or natural disasters. The origins of RBC theory can be traced to the rational expectations revolution set off by Robert E. Lucas, Jr., but the first demonstrations of the power of this theory were given by Edward Prescott and Finn Kydland and by John Long and Charles Plosser. Today, RBC theory is part of a broad research agenda called dynamic general equilibrium analysis, and hundreds of young macroeconomists do research on this topic.

We'll explore RBC theory by looking first at its impulse and then at the mechanism that converts that impulse into a cycle in real GDP.

The RBC Impulse The impulse in RBC theory is the growth rate of productivity that results from technological change. RBC theorists believe this impulse to be generated mainly by the process of research and development that leads to the creation and use of new technologies (see *Economics in Action*, p. 680).

The pace of technological change and productivity growth is not constant. Sometimes productivity growth speeds up, sometimes it slows, and occasionally it even *falls*—labour and capital become less productive, on average. A period of rapid productivity growth brings a business cycle expansion, and a slowdown or fall in productivity triggers a recession.

It is easy to understand why technological change brings productivity growth, but how does it *decrease* productivity? All technological change eventually increases productivity. But if, initially, technological change makes a sufficient amount of existing capital—especially human capital—obsolete, productivity can temporarily fall. At such a time, more jobs are destroyed than created and more businesses fail than start up.

The RBC Mechanism Two effects follow from a change in productivity that sparks an expansion or a contraction: Investment demand changes and the demand for labour changes. We'll study these effects and their consequences during a recession. In an

Economics in Action
The Real Business Cycle Impulse

To isolate the RBC impulse, economists measure the change in the combined productivity of capital and labour—called *total factor productivity*. The figure shows the RBC impulse for Canada from 1960 through 2010.

You can see that the productivity growth rate fluctuations are not directly correlated with real GDP fluctuations. Their influence on real GDP growth is spread out over time.

You can also see that the fluctuations in real GDP growth have wider swings than those of productivity growth.

Real business cycle theory explains these facts.

Source of data: Centre for the Study of Living Standards (www.csls.ca/data/ipt.asp, Table 4A).

expansion, they work in the direction opposite to what is described here.

Technological change makes some existing capital obsolete and temporarily decreases productivity. Firms expect future profits to fall and see their labour productivity falling. With lower profit expectations, they cut back their purchases of new capital, and with lower labour productivity, they plan to lay off some workers. So the initial effect of a temporary fall in productivity is a decrease in investment demand and a decrease in the demand for labour.

Figure 28.2 illustrates these two initial effects of a decrease in productivity. Part (a) shows the effects of a decrease in investment demand in the loanable funds market. The demand for loanable funds curve is DLF and the supply of loanable funds curve is SLF (both of which are explained in Chapter 23, pp. 549–551). Initially, the demand for loanable

funds curve is DLF_0 and the equilibrium quantity of funds is \$200 billion at a real interest rate of 6 percent a year. A decrease in productivity decreases investment demand, and the demand for loanable funds curve shifts leftward from DLF_0 to DLF_1. The real interest rate falls to 4 percent a year, and the equilibrium quantity of loanable funds decreases to \$170 billion.

Figure 28.2(b) shows the demand for labour and supply of labour (which are explained in Chapter 22, pp. 520–522). Initially, the demand for labour curve is LD_0, the supply of labour curve is LS_0, and equilibrium employment is 20 billion hours a year at a real wage rate of \$35 an hour. The decrease in productivity decreases the demand for labour, and the demand for labour curve shifts leftward from LD_0 to LD_1.

Before we can determine the new level of employment and the real wage rate, we need to look at a ripple effect—the key effect in RBC theory.

FIGURE 28.2   Loanable Funds and Labour Markets in a Real Business Cycle

(a) Loanable funds and interest rate

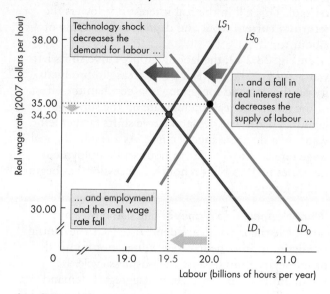

(b) Labour and wage rate

In part (a), the supply of loanable funds SLF and the initial demand for loanable funds DLF₀ determine the real interest rate at 6 percent a year. In part (b), the initial demand for labour LD₀ and the supply of labour LS₀ determine the real wage rate at $35 an hour and employment at 20 billion hours. A technological change temporarily decreases productivity, and both the demand for loanable funds and

the demand for labour decrease. The two demand curves shift leftward to DLF₁ and LD₁. In part (a), the real interest rate falls to 4 percent a year. In part (b), the fall in the real interest rate decreases the supply of labour (the when-to-work decision) and the supply of labour curve shifts leftward to LS₁. Employment decreases to 19.5 billion hours, and the real wage rate falls to $34.50 an hour. A recession is under way.

MyEconLab Animation

The Key Decision: When to Work? According to RBC theory, people decide *when* to work by doing a cost-benefit calculation. They compare the return from working in the current period with the *expected* return from working in a later period. You make such a comparison every day in university. Suppose your goal in this course is to get an A. To achieve this goal, you work hard most of the time. But during the few days before the midterm and final exams, you work especially hard. Why? Because you believe that the return from studying close to the exam is greater than the return from studying when the exam is a long time away. So during the term, you take time off for the movies and other leisure pursuits, but at exam time you study every evening and weekend.

RBC theory says that workers behave like you. They work fewer hours, sometimes zero hours, when the real wage rate is temporarily low, and they work more hours when the real wage rate is temporarily high. But to properly compare the current wage rate

with the expected future wage rate, workers must use the real interest rate.

If the real interest rate is 6 percent a year, a real wage of $1 an hour earned this week will become $1.06 a year from now. If the real wage rate is expected to be $1.05 an hour next year, today's real wage of $1 looks good. By working longer hours now and shorter hours a year from now, a person can get a 1 percent higher real wage. But suppose the real interest rate is 4 percent a year. In this case, $1 earned now is worth $1.04 next year. Working fewer hours now and more next year is the way to get a 1 percent higher real wage.

So the when-to-work decision depends on the real interest rate. The lower the real interest rate, other things remaining the same, the smaller is the supply of labour today. Many economists believe this *intertemporal substitution* effect to be of negligible size. RBC theorists believe that the effect is large, and it is the key feature of the RBC mechanism.

You saw in Fig. 28.2(a) that the decrease in the demand for loanable funds lowers the real interest rate. This fall in the real interest rate lowers the return to current work and decreases the supply of labour today.

In Fig. 28.2(b), the labour supply curve shifts leftward to LS_1. The effect of the decrease in productivity on the demand for labour is larger than the effect of the fall in the real interest rate on the supply of labour. That is, the demand curve shifts farther leftward than does the supply curve. As a result, the real wage rate falls to $34.50 an hour and employment decreases to 19.5 billion hours. A recession has begun and is intensifying.

What Happened to Money? The name *real* business cycle theory is no accident. It reflects the central prediction of the theory. Real things, not nominal or monetary things, cause the business cycle. If the quantity of money changes, aggregate demand changes. But with no real change—with no change in the use of resources or in potential GDP—the change in the quantity of money changes only the price level. In RBC theory, this outcome occurs because the aggregate supply curve is the *LAS* curve, which pins real GDP down at potential GDP. So a change in aggregate demand changes only the price level.

Cycles and Growth The shock that drives the business cycle of RBC theory is the same as the force that generates economic growth: technological change. On average, as technology advances, productivity grows; but as you saw in *Economics in Action* on p. 680 it grows at an uneven pace. Economic growth arises from the upward trend in productivity growth and, according to RBC theory, the mostly positive but occasionally negative higher frequency shocks to productivity bring the business cycle.

Criticisms and Defences of RBC Theory There are three main criticisms of RBC theory:

1. The money wage rate *is* sticky, and to assume otherwise is at odds with a clear fact.
2. Intertemporal substitution is too weak a force to account for large fluctuations in labour supply and employment with small real wage rate changes.
3. Productivity shocks are as likely to be caused by *changes in aggregate demand* as by technological change.

If aggregate demand fluctuations cause the fluctuations in productivity, then the traditional aggregate demand theories are needed to explain them. Fluctuations in productivity do not cause the business cycle but are caused by it!

Building on this theme, the critics point out that the so-called productivity fluctuations that growth accounting measures are correlated with changes in the growth rate of money and other indicators of changes in aggregate demand.

The defenders of RBC theory claim that the theory explains the macroeconomic facts about the business cycle and is consistent with the facts about economic growth. In effect, a single theory explains *both growth and the business cycle*. The growth accounting exercise that explains slowly changing trends also explains the more frequent business cycle swings. Its defenders also claim that RBC theory is consistent with a wide range of *micro*economic evidence about labour supply decisions, labour demand and investment demand decisions, and information on the distribution of income between labour and capital.

REVIEW QUIZ

1 Explain the mainstream theory of the business cycle.
2 What are the four special forms of the mainstream theory of the business cycle and how do they differ?
3 According to RBC theory, what is the source of the business cycle? What is the role of fluctuations in the rate of technological change?
4 According to RBC theory, how does a fall in productivity growth influence investment demand, the market for loanable funds, the real interest rate, the demand for labour, the supply of labour, employment, and the real wage rate?
5 What are the main criticisms of RBC theory and how do its supporters defend it?

Work these questions in Study Plan 28.1 and get instant feedback. Do a Key Terms Quiz.   MyEconLab

In this first section, we've focused on the cycles in real GDP and the loanable funds and labour markets. Next, we're going to look at the causes and effects of cycles in the inflation rate.

Inflation Cycles

In the long run, inflation is a monetary phenomenon. It occurs if the quantity of money grows faster than potential GDP. But in the short run, many factors can start an inflation, and real GDP and the price level interact. To study these interactions, we distinguish between two sources of inflation:

- Demand-pull inflation
- Cost-push inflation

Demand-Pull Inflation

An inflation that starts because aggregate demand increases is called **demand-pull inflation**. Demand-pull inflation can be kicked off by *any* of the factors that change aggregate demand. Examples are a cut in the interest rate, an increase in the quantity of money, an increase in government expenditure, a tax cut, an increase in exports, or an increase in investment stimulated by an increase in expected future profits.

Initial Effect of an Increase in Aggregate Demand
Suppose that last year the price level was 110 and real GDP was $1.7 trillion. Potential GDP was also $1.7 trillion. Figure 28.3(a) illustrates this situation. The aggregate demand curve is AD_0, the short-run aggregate supply curve is SAS_0, and the long-run aggregate supply curve is LAS.

Now suppose that the Bank of Canada cuts the interest rate. The quantity of money increases and the aggregate demand curve shifts from AD_0 to AD_1. With no change in potential GDP and no change in the money wage rate, the long-run aggregate supply curve and the short-run aggregate supply curve remain at LAS and SAS_0, respectively.

The price level and real GDP are determined at the point where the aggregate demand curve AD_1 intersects the short-run aggregate supply curve. The price level rises to 113, and real GDP increases above potential GDP to $1.8 trillion. Unemployment falls below its natural rate. The economy is at an above full-employment equilibrium and there is an inflationary gap. The next step in the unfolding story is a rise in the money wage rate.

FIGURE 28.3   A Demand-Pull Rise in the Price Level

(a) Initial effect

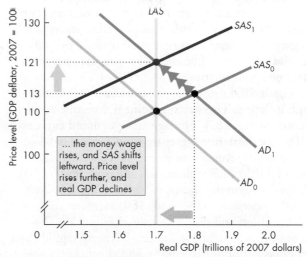

(b) The money wage adjusts

In part (a), the aggregate demand curve is AD_0, the short-run aggregate supply curve is SAS_0, and the long-run aggregate supply curve is LAS. The price level is 110, and real GDP is $1.7 trillion, which equals potential GDP. Aggregate demand increases to AD_1. The price level rises to 113, and real GDP increases to $1.8 trillion.

In part (b), starting from the above full-employment equilibrium, the money wage rate begins to rise and the short-run aggregate supply curve shifts leftward toward SAS_1. The price level rises further, and real GDP returns to potential GDP.

Money Wage Rate Response Real GDP cannot remain above potential GDP forever. With unemployment below its natural rate, there is a shortage of labour. In this situation, the money wage rate begins to rise. As it does so, short-run aggregate supply decreases and the *SAS* curve starts to shift leftward. The price level rises further, and real GDP begins to decrease.

With no further change in aggregate demand—that is, the aggregate demand curve remains at AD_1—this process ends when the short-run aggregate supply curve has shifted to SAS_1 in Fig. 28.3(b). At this time, the price level has increased to 121 and real GDP has returned to potential GDP of $1.7 trillion, the level at which it started.

A Demand-Pull Inflation Process The events that we've just described bring a *one-time rise in the price level*, not an inflation. For inflation to proceed, aggregate demand must *persistently* increase.

The only way in which aggregate demand can persistently increase is if the quantity of money persistently increases. Suppose the government has a budget deficit that it finances by selling bonds. Also suppose that the Bank of Canada buys some of these bonds. When the Bank of Canada buys bonds, it creates more money. In this situation, aggregate demand increases year after year. The aggregate demand curve keeps shifting rightward. This persistent increase in aggregate demand puts continual upward pressure on the price level. The economy now experiences demand-pull inflation.

Figure 28.4 illustrates the process of demand-pull inflation. The starting point is the same as that shown in Fig. 28.3. The aggregate demand curve is AD_0, the short-run aggregate supply curve is SAS_0, and the long-run aggregate supply curve is *LAS*. Real GDP is $1.7 trillion, and the price level is 110. Aggregate demand increases, shifting the aggregate demand curve to AD_1. Real GDP increases to $1.8 trillion, and the price level rises to 113. The economy is at an above full-employment equilibrium. There is a shortage of labour, and the money wage rate rises. The short-run aggregate supply curve shifts to SAS_1. The price level rises to 121, and real GDP returns to potential GDP.

But the Bank of Canada increases the quantity of money again, and aggregate demand continues to increase. The aggregate demand curve shifts rightward to AD_2. The price level rises further to 125, and real GDP again exceeds potential GDP at $1.8 trillion.

FIGURE 28.4   A Demand-Pull Inflation Spiral

Each time the quantity of money increases, aggregate demand increases and the aggregate demand curve shifts rightward from AD_0 to AD_1 to AD_2, and so on. Each time real GDP increases above potential GDP, the money wage rate rises and the short-run aggregate supply curve shifts leftward from SAS_0 to SAS_1 to SAS_2, and so on. The price level rises from 110 to 113, 121, 125, 133, and so on. There is a demand-pull inflation spiral. Real GDP fluctuates between $1.7 trillion and $1.8 trillion.

———— MyEconLab Animation and Draw Graph ————

Yet again, the money wage rate rises and decreases short-run aggregate supply. The *SAS* curve shifts to SAS_2, and the price level rises further, to 133. As the quantity of money continues to grow, aggregate demand increases and the price level rises in an ongoing demand-pull inflation process.

The process you have just studied generates inflation—a persistently rising price level.

Demand-Pull Inflation in Chatham You may better understand the inflation process that we've just described by considering what is going on in an individual part of the economy, such as a Chatham pop-bottling plant. Initially, when aggregate demand increases, the demand for pop increases and the price of pop rises. Faced with a higher price, the bottling plant works overtime and increases production. Conditions are good for workers in Chatham and the pop-bottling factory finds it hard to hang on to its best people. To do so, it offers a higher money wage rate. As the wage rate rises, so do the bottling factory's costs.

What happens next depends on aggregate demand. If aggregate demand remains constant, the firm's costs increase but the price of pop does not increase as quickly as its costs. In this case, the firm cuts production. Eventually, the money wage rate and costs increase by the same percentage as the rise in the price of pop. In real terms, the bottling factory is in the same situation as it was initially. It produces the same amount of pop and employs the same amount of labour as before the increase in demand.

But if aggregate demand continues to increase, so does the demand for pop and the price of pop rises at the same rate as the money wage rate. The bottling factory continues to operate at an above full employment equilibrium and there is a persistent shortage of labour. Prices and the money wage rate chase each other upward in a demand-pull inflation spiral.

Demand-Pull Inflation in Canada A demand-pull inflation like the one you've just studied occurred in Canada during the late 1960s. In 1960, inflation was a moderate 2 percent a year, but its rate increased slowly during the mid-1960s. Then, between 1966 and 1969, the inflation rate surged upward. Inflation then decreased slightly during 1970 and 1971, but it took off again in 1972. By 1973, the inflation rate was almost 10 percent a year.

These increases in inflation resulted from increases in aggregate demand that had two main sources. The first was a large increase in U.S. government expenditure and the quantity of money in the United States, which increased aggregate demand in the entire world economy. The second source was an increase in Canadian government expenditure and the quantity of money.

With unemployment below its natural rate, the money wage rate started to rise more quickly and the *SAS* curve shifted leftward. The Bank of Canada responded with a further increase in the money growth rate, and a demand-pull inflation spiral unfolded. By 1974, the inflation rate had reached double digits.

Next, let's see how shocks to aggregate supply can create cost-push inflation.

Cost-Push Inflation

An inflation that is kicked off by an increase in costs is called **cost-push inflation**. There are two main sources of cost increases:

1. An increase in the money wage rate
2. An increase in the money prices of raw materials

At a given price level, the higher the cost of production, the smaller is the amount that firms are willing to produce. So if the money wage rate rises or if the prices of raw materials (for example, oil) rise, firms decrease their supply of goods and services. Aggregate supply decreases, and the short-run aggregate supply curve shifts leftward.[1] Let's trace the effects of such a decrease in short-run aggregate supply on the price level and real GDP.

Initial Effect of a Decrease in Aggregate Supply
Suppose that last year the price level was 110 and real GDP was $1.7 trillion. Potential real GDP was also $1.7 trillion. Figure 28.5(a) illustrates this situation. The aggregate demand curve was AD_0, the short-run aggregate supply curve was SAS_0, and the long-run aggregate supply curve was LAS. In the current year, the world's oil producers form a price-fixing organization that strengthens their market power and increases the relative price of oil. They raise the price of oil, and this action decreases short-run aggregate supply. The short-run aggregate supply curve shifts leftward to SAS_1. The price level rises to 117, and real GDP decreases to $1.6 trillion. The economy is at a below full-employment equilibrium and there is a recessionary gap.

This event is a *one-time rise in the price level*. It is not inflation. In fact, a supply shock on its own cannot cause inflation. Something more must happen to enable a one-time supply shock, which causes a one-time rise in the price level, to be converted into a process of ongoing inflation. The quantity of money must persistently increase. Sometimes it does increase, as you will now see.

---

[1] Some cost-push forces, such as an increase in the price of oil accompanied by a decrease in the availability of oil, can also decrease long-run aggregate supply. We ignore such effects here and examine cost-push factors that change only short-run aggregate supply. Real business cycle theory that you studied earlier in this chapter emphasizes the effects of shocks to long-run aggregate supply.

FIGURE 28.5   A Cost-Push Rise in the Price Level

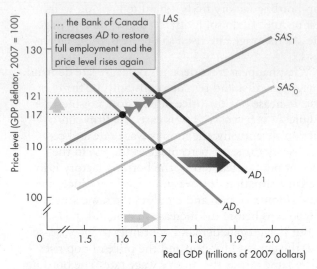

(a) Initial cost push

(b) The Bank of Canada responds

Initially, the aggregate demand curve is AD_0, the short-run aggregate supply curve is SAS_0, and the long-run aggregate supply curve is LAS. A decrease in aggregate supply (for example, resulting from a rise in the world price of oil) shifts the short-run aggregate supply curve to SAS_1. The economy moves to the point where the short-run aggregate supply curve SAS_1 intersects the aggregate demand curve

AD_0. The price level rises to 117, and real GDP decreases to $1.6 trillion.

In part (b), if the Bank of Canada responds by increasing aggregate demand to restore full employment, the aggregate demand curve shifts rightward to AD_1. The economy returns to full employment, but the price level rises further to 121.

MyEconLab Animation

Aggregate Demand Response When real GDP decreases, unemployment rises above its natural rate. In such a situation, there is an outcry of concern and a call for action to restore full employment. Suppose that the Bank of Canada cuts the interest rate and increases the quantity of money. Aggregate demand increases. In Fig. 28.5(b), the aggregate demand curve shifts rightward to AD_1 and full employment is restored. But the price level rises further to 121.

A Cost-Push Inflation Process The oil producers now see the prices of everything they buy increasing, so oil producers increase the price of oil again to restore its new high relative price. Figure 28.6 continues the story. The short-run aggregate supply curve now shifts to SAS_2. The price level rises and real GDP decreases.

The price level rises further, to 129, and real GDP decreases to $1.6 trillion. Unemployment increases above its natural rate. If the Bank of Canada responds

yet again with an increase in the quantity of money, aggregate demand increases and the aggregate demand curve shifts to AD_2. The price level rises even higher—to 133—and full employment is again restored. A cost-push inflation spiral results. The combination of a rising price level and decreasing real GDP is called **stagflation**.

You can see that the Bank of Canada has a dilemma. If it does not respond when producers raise the oil price, the economy remains below full employment. If the Bank of Canada increases the quantity of money to restore full employment, it invites another oil price hike that will call forth yet a further increase in the quantity of money.

If the Bank of Canada responds to each oil price hike by increasing the quantity of money, inflation will rage along at a rate decided by oil producers. But if the Bank of Canada keeps the lid on money growth, the economy remains below full employment.

FIGURE 28.6   A Cost-Push Inflation Spiral

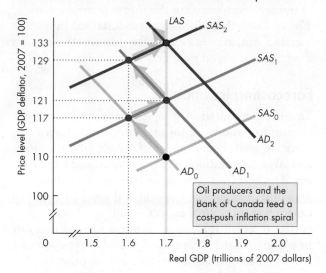

Each time a cost increase occurs, the short-run aggregate supply curve shifts leftward from SAS_0 to SAS_1 to SAS_2, and so on. Each time real GDP decreases to below potential GDP, the Bank of Canada increases the quantity of money and the aggregate demand curve shifts rightward from AD_0 to AD_1 to AD_2, and so on. The price level rises from 110 to 117, 121, 129, 133, and so on. There is a cost-push inflation spiral. Real GDP fluctuates between $1.7 trillion and $1.6 trillion.

———— MyEconLab Animation and Draw Graph ————

Cost-Push Inflation in Chatham What is going on in the Chatham pop-bottling plant when the economy is experiencing cost-push inflation?

When the oil price increases, so do the costs of bottling pop. These higher costs decrease the supply of pop, increasing its price and decreasing the quantity produced. The bottling plant lays off some workers.

This situation persists until either the Bank of Canada increases aggregate demand or the price of oil falls. If the Bank of Canada increases aggregate demand, the demand for pop increases and so does its price. The higher price of pop brings higher profits, and the bottling plant increases its production. The botling factory rehires the laid-off workers.

Cost-Push Inflation in Canada A cost-push inflation like the one you've just studied occurred in Canada during the 1970s. It began in 1974 when the Organization of the Petroleum Exporting Countries (OPEC) raised the price of oil fourfold. The higher oil price decreased aggregate supply, which caused the price level to rise more quickly and real GDP to shrink. The Bank of Canada then faced a dilemma: Would it increase the quantity of money and accommodate the cost-push forces, or would it keep aggregate demand growth in check by limiting money growth? In 1975, 1976, and 1977, the Bank of Canada repeatedly allowed the quantity of money to grow quickly and inflation proceeded at a rapid rate.

In 1979 and 1980, OPEC was again able to push the price of oil higher. On that occasion, the Bank of Canada decided not to respond to the oil price hike with an increase in the quantity of money. The Canadian economy went into a recession but also, eventually, the inflation rate fell.

Expected Inflation

If inflation is expected, the fluctuations in real GDP that accompany demand-pull and cost-push inflation that you've just studied don't occur. Instead, inflation proceeds as it does in the long run, with real GDP equal to potential GDP and unemployment at its natural rate. Figure 28.7 explains why.

Suppose that last year the aggregate demand curve was AD_0, the aggregate supply curve was SAS_0, and the long-run aggregate supply curve was LAS. The price level was 110, and real GDP was $1.7 trillion, which is also potential GDP.

To keep things as simple as possible, suppose that potential GDP does not change, so the LAS curve doesn't shift. Also suppose that aggregate demand is *expected to increase* to AD_1.

In anticipation of this increase in aggregate demand, the money wage rate rises and the short-run aggregate supply curve shifts leftward. If the money wage rate rises by the same percentage as the price level is expected to rise, the short-run aggregate supply curve for next year is SAS_1.

If aggregate demand turns out to be the same as expected, the aggregate demand curve is AD_1. The short-run aggregate supply curve, SAS_1, and AD_1 determine the actual price level at 121. Between last year and this year, the price level increased from 110 to 121 and the economy experienced an inflation rate equal to that expected.

If this inflation is ongoing, aggregate demand increases (as expected) in the following year and the aggregate demand curve shifts to AD_2. The money wage rate rises to reflect the expected inflation, and

FIGURE 28.7   Expected Inflation

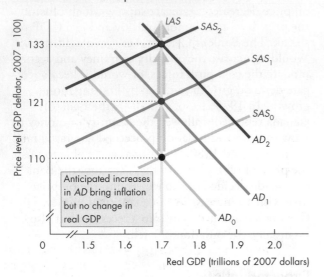

Potential real GDP is $1.7 trillion. Last year, aggregate demand was AD_0 and the short-run aggregate supply curve was SAS_0. The actual price level was the same as the expected price level: 110. This year, aggregate demand is expected to increase to AD_1 and the price level is expected to rise from 110 to 121. As a result, the money wage rate rises and the short-run aggregate supply curve shifts to SAS_1. If aggregate demand actually increases as expected, the actual aggregate demand curve AD_1 is the same as the expected aggregate demand curve. Real GDP is $1.7 trillion and the actual price level rises to 121. The inflation is expected. Next year, the process continues with aggregate demand increasing as expected to AD_2 and the money wage rate rising to shift the short-run aggregate supply curve to SAS_2. Again, real GDP remains at $1.7 trillion and the price level rises, as expected, to 133.

MyEconLab Animation and Draw Graph

the short-run aggregate supply curve shifts to SAS_2. The price level rises, as expected, to 133.

What caused this inflation? The immediate answer is that because people expected inflation, the money wage rate increased and the price level increased. But the expectation was correct. Aggregate demand was expected to increase, and it did increase. It is the actual and expected increase in aggregate demand that caused the inflation.

An expected inflation at full employment is exactly the process that the quantity theory of money predicts. To review the quantity theory of money, see Chapter 24, pp. 582–583.

This broader account of the inflation process and its short-run effects shows why the quantity theory of money doesn't explain the *fluctuations* in inflation. The economy follows the course described in Fig. 28.7 but, as predicted by the quantity theory, only if aggregate demand growth is forecasted correctly.

Forecasting Inflation

To anticipate inflation, people must forecast it. Some economists who work for macroeconomic forecasting agencies, banks, insurance companies, labour unions, and large corporations specialize in inflation forecasting. The best forecast available is one that is based on all the relevant information and is called a **rational expectation**. A rational expectation is not necessarily a correct forecast. It is simply the best forecast that can be made with the information available. The forecast will often turn out to be wrong, but no other forecast that could have been made with the information available could do better.

Inflation and the Business Cycle

When the inflation forecast is correct, the economy operates at full employment. If aggregate demand grows faster than expected, real GDP increases to above potential GDP, the inflation rate exceeds its expected rate, and the economy behaves like it does in a demand-pull inflation. If aggregate demand grows more slowly than expected, real GDP decreases to below potential GDP and the inflation rate slows.

REVIEW QUIZ

1 How does demand-pull inflation begin?
2 What must happen to create a demand-pull inflation spiral?
3 How does cost-push inflation begin?
4 What must happen to create a cost-push inflation spiral?
5 What is stagflation and why does cost-push inflation cause stagflation?
6 How does expected inflation occur?
7 How do real GDP and the price level change if the forecast of inflation is incorrect?

Work these questions in Study Plan 28.2 and get instant feedback. Do a Key Terms Quiz.   MyEconLab

Deflation

An economy experiences *deflation* when it has a persistently *falling* price level. Equivalently, during a period of deflation, the inflation rate is negative.

In most economies and for most of the time, the inflation rate is positive—the price level is rising—and deflation is rare. But deflation does happen, and most recently it was present in Japan (see *Economics in Action* on p. 690).

We're going to answer three questions about deflation:

- What causes deflation?
- What are the consequences of deflation?
- How can deflation be ended?

What Causes Deflation?

The starting point for understanding the cause of deflation is to distinguish between a one-time fall in the price level and a persistently falling price level. A one-time *fall* in the price level is not deflation. Deflation is a persistent and ongoing *falling* price level.

A One-Time Fall in the Price Level The price level can fall either because aggregate demand decreases or because short-run aggregate supply increases. So any of the influences on aggregate demand and short-run aggregate supply that you studied in Chapter 26 can bring a one-time fall in the price level.

Some examples on the demand side are a fall in global demand for a country's exports, or a fall in profit expectations that lowers business investment. Some examples on the supply side are an increase in capital or advance in technology that increases potential GDP, or (unlikely but possible) a fall in the money wage rate.

But none of these sources of a decrease in aggregate demand or increase in aggregate supply can bring a persistently falling price level.

A Persistently Falling Price Level The price level falls persistently if aggregate demand increases at a persistently slower rate than aggregate supply. The trend rate of increase in aggregate supply is determined by the forces that make potential GDP grow. These forces are the growth rates of the labour force and capital stock and the growth rate of productivity that results from technological change. Notice that all these variables are real, not monetary, and they have trends that change slowly.

In contrast, the forces that drive aggregate demand include the quantity of money. And this quantity can grow as quickly or as slowly as the central bank chooses.

In most situations, the central bank doesn't have a target for the money stock or its growth rate and instead sets the interest rate. But the money stock is under central bank control, and its growth rate has a powerful effect on the growth rate of aggregate demand. To see the effect of growth in the money stock in the long term, we need to return to the quantity theory of money.

The Quantity Theory and Deflation The quantity theory of money explains the trends in inflation by focusing on the trend influences on aggregate supply and aggregate demand.

The foundation of the quantity theory is the *equation of exchange* (see Chapter 24, p. 582), which in its growth rate version and solved for the inflation rate states:

$$\text{Inflation rate} = \text{Money growth rate} + \text{Rate of velocity change} - \text{Real GDP growth rate}$$

This equation, true by definition, derives from the fact that the amount of money spent on real GDP, MV, equals the money value of GDP, PY. (M is the money stock, V is its velocity of circulation, P is the price level, and Y is real GDP.)

The quantity theory adds to the equation of exchange two propositons. First, the trend rate of change in the velocity of circulation does not depend on the money growth rate and is determined by decisions about the quantity of money to hold and to spend. Second, the trend growth rate of real GDP equals the growth rate of potential GDP and, again, is independent of the money growth rate.

With these two assumptions, the equation of exchange becomes the quantity theory of money and predicts that a change in the money growth rate brings an equal change in the inflation rate.

For example, suppose velocity increases by 2 percent per year and potential GDP grows by 3 percent per year. Then the quantity theory predicts that the trend inflation rate equals the money growth rate minus 1 percent. If the central bank makes the quantity of money grow by 1 percent, the inflation rate will be zero. If money grows at a rate faster than 1 percent, the economy will experience inflation. And if money grows at a slower rate than 1 percent, the economy will experience deflation.

Economics in Action

Fifteen Years of Deflation in Japan

Japan experienced deflation for the 15 years from 1998 to 2013.

Japan's Deflation Rate

Figure 1 shows the inflation rate in Japan from 1990 to 2015. The inflation rate fluctuated between −1 percent and −2 percent per year and accumulated to a 17 percent fall in the price level.

Cause of Japan's Deflation

Deflation, like its opposite, inflation, is primarily a monetary phenomenon. Japan's money stock grew too slowly during the deflation years.

Figure 2 shows the facts about inflation and money growth in Japan from 1995 to 2013. The relevant money growth rate that brings inflation or deflation is that of money itself *plus* the trend rate of change in the velocity of circulaton *minus* the growth rate of potential GDP. That is the money growth rate shown in Fig. 2, and except for one year, 1997, it is negative, which means that Japan's money stock did not grow fast enough to accommodate the growth of potential GDP and a trend rise in velocity.

Consequences of Japan's Deflation

At first, Japan's deflation was unexpected and loan and wage contracts had been entered into that anticipated on ongoing low but positive inflation rate. So when the price level started to fall, the real value of debt increased and the real wage rate increased.

With higher real debt and wages, businesses cut back on both investment and hiring labour and cut production. Real GDP fell and the recessionary gap increased.

Because investment decreased, the capital stock increased more slowly and the growth rate of potential GDP slowed. From being one of the world's most dynamic rich economies, Japan became the world's most sluggish.

Figure 3 tells the story. The 1960s saw Japan doubling its real GDP in seven years. The growth rate slowed in the 1970s and 1980s but remained one of the world's fastest. Then, during the deflation years, the growth rate dropped to 1.5 percent (in the 1990s) and 0.5 percent (in the 2000s).

Japan's inflation rate turned positive in 2014, and real GDP growth picked up, but money growth rate remained too low. Without a sustained increase in money growth, deflation cannot end.

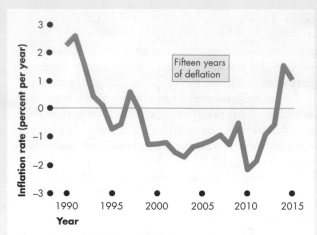

Figure 1 Japan's Long Deflation

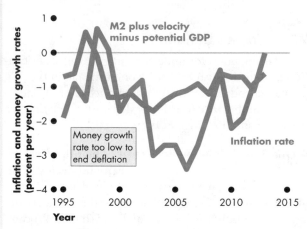

Figure 2 Money Growth Rate Too Low

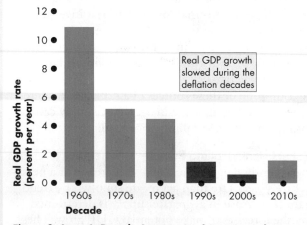

Figure 3 Japan's Decade Average Real GDP Growth Rates

Sources of data: Financial Statistics and World Economic Outlook,
International Monetary Fund, Washington, DC.

Japan Example In the example of Japan during the 1990s and 2000s (see *Economics in Action*), the money (M2) growth rate during the 15 years 1998–2013 was 2.5 percent per year. The velocity growth rate was negative, and it *decreased* at a rate of 3 percent per year. Potential GDP grew at an average rate of 0.8 percent per year. Combining these numbers, the quantity theory predicts an inflation rate equal to −1.3 percent per year:

$$+2.5 + (-3) - 0.8 = -1.3.$$

In fact, the average inflation rate was −1.2 percent per year. So the quantity theory prediction is not exactly correct, but it is close. Its prediction of the deflation rate of 1.3 percent per year is off by only 0.1.

You now know what causes deflation. Let's turn to its consequences.

What Are the Consequences of Deflation?

Chapter 21 (p. 498) discusses why deflation and inflation are problems. But with what you now know about aggregate supply and aggregate demand and the determinants of potential GDP and its growth rate, you can gain deeper insight into the costs of deflation (and the related costs of inflation).

The effects of deflation (like those of inflation) depend on whether it is anticipated or unanticipated. But because inflation is normal and deflation is rare, when deflation occurs it is usually unanticipated.

Unanticipated deflation redistributes income and wealth, lowers real GDP and employment, and diverts resources from production.

Workers with long-term wage contracts find their real wages rising. But on the other side of the labour market, employers respond to a higher and rising real wage by hiring fewer workers. So employment decreases and output falls.

With lower output and profits, firms re-evaluate their investment plans and cut back on projects that they now see as unprofitable. This fall in investment slows the pace of capital accumulation and slows the growth rate of potential GDP.

Another consequence of deflation is a low nominal interest rate, which, in turn, brings an increase in the quantity of money that people plan to hold and a decrease in the velocity of circulation. A lower velocity adds to the deflationary forces and, if unattended to, lowers the inflation rate yet further.

So, what is the cure for deflation?

How Can Deflation Be Ended?

Deflation can be ended by removing its cause: The quantity of money is growing too slowly. If the central bank ensures that the quantity of money grows at the target inflation rate *plus* the growth rate of potential GDP *minus* the growth rate of the velocity of circulation, then, on average, the inflation rate will turn out to be close to target.

In the example of Japan, if the Bank of Japan, the central bank, wanted to get a 2 percent inflation rate, and other things remained the same, it would have needed to make the quantity of money grow at an annual average rate of 5.8 percent. (Money growth of 5.8 *plus* velocity growth of −3 *minus* potential GDP growth of 0.8 equals target inflation of 2 percent.) If raising the inflation rate brought faster potential GDP growth, a yet higher money growth rate would be needed to sustain the higher inflation rate.

Money Growth, Not Quantity Notice that it is an increase in the *growth rate* of the money stock, not a one-time increase in the quantity of money, that is required to end deflation. Central banks sometimes increase the quantity of money and fail to increase its growth rate. An increase in level with no change in the growth rate brings a temporary inflation as the price level adjusts, but not ongoing inflation, so it does not end deflation.

◆ REVIEW QUIZ

1 What is deflation?
2 What is the distinction between deflation and a one-time fall in the price level?
3 What causes deflation?
4 How does the quantity theory of money help us to understand the process of deflation?
5 What are the consequences of deflation?
6 How can deflation be ended?

Work these questions in Study Plan 28.3 and get instant feedback.   MyEconLab

In the final section of this chapter, we're going to look at an alternative model of short-run fluctuations— a model that focuses on the tradeoff between inflation and unemployment.

◆ The Phillips Curve

The *Phillips curve* is a relationship between inflation and unemployment. It is so named because it was first suggested by New Zealand economist A.W. (Bill) Phillips. We distinguish between two time frames for the Phillips curve (similar to the two aggregate supply time frames). We study:

- The short-run Phillips curve
- The long-run Phillips curve

The Short-Run Phillips Curve

The **short-run Phillips curve** is the relationship between inflation and unemployment, when:

1. The expected inflation rate is held constant
2. The natural unemployment rate is constant

You've seen what determines the expected inflation rate earlier in this chapter (p. 688), and the influences on the natural unemployment rate were explained in Chapter 21 (pp. 495–496).

Figure 28.8 shows a short-run Phillips curve, *SRPC*. Suppose that the expected inflation rate is 10 percent a year and the natural unemployment rate is 6 percent, point *A* in the figure. A short-run Phillips curve passes through this point. If inflation rises above its expected rate, unemployment falls below its natural rate in a movement up along the short-run Phillips curve from point *A* to point *B*. Similarly, if inflation falls below its expected rate, unemployment rises above its natural rate in a movement down along the short-run Phillips curve from point *A* to point *C*.

The Long-Run Phillips Curve

The **long-run Phillips curve** is the relationship between inflation and unemployment when the actual inflation rate equals the expected inflation rate. The long-run Phillips curve is vertical at the natural unemployment rate because, in the long run, any expected inflation rate is possible. In Fig. 28.9(a), the long-run Phillips curve is the vertical line *LRPC*.

Change in Expected Inflation A change in the expected inflation rate shifts the short-run Phillips curve, but it does not shift the long-run Phillips curve. In Fig. 28.9(a), if the expected inflation rate is 10 percent a year, the short-run Phillips curve is $SRPC_0$. If the expected inflation rate falls to 6 percent a year, the short-run Phillips curve shifts downward

FIGURE 28.8   A Short-Run Phillips Curve

The short-run Phillips curve, *SRPC*, is the relationship between inflation and unemployment at a given expected inflation rate and a given natural unemployment rate. Here, the expected inflation rate is 10 percent a year and the natural unemployment rate is 6 percent at point *A*.

A change in the actual inflation rate brings a movement along the short-run Phillips curve from *A* to *B* or from *A* to *C*.

— MyEconLab Animation —

to $SRPC_1$. The vertical distance by which the short-run Phillips curve shifts from point *A* to point *D* is equal to the change in the expected inflation rate. If the actual inflation rate also falls from 10 percent to 6 percent, there is a movement down the long-run Phillips curve from *A* to *D*. An increase in the expected inflation rate has the opposite effect to that shown in Fig. 28.9(a).

The other source of a shift in the Phillips curve is a change in the natural unemployment rate.

Change in Natural Unemployment Rate A change in the natural unemployment rate shifts both the short-run and long-run Phillips curves. Figure 28.9(b) illustrates such shifts.

If the natural unemployment rate increases from 6 percent to 9 percent, the long-run Phillips curve shifts from $LRPC_0$ to $LRPC_1$, and if expected inflation is constant at 10 percent a year, the short-run Phillips curve shifts from $SRPC_0$ to $SRPC_1$. Because the expected inflation rate is constant, $SRPC_1$ intersects the long-run curve $LRPC_1$ (point *E*) at the same inflation rate at which $SRPC_0$ intersects the long-run curve $LRPC_0$ (point *A*).

FIGURE 28.9 Short-Run and Long-Run Phillips Curves

(a) A change in expected inflation

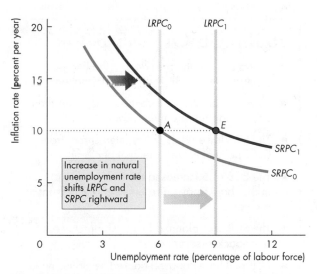

(b) A change in natural unemployment

In part (a), the long-run Phillips curve is *LRPC*. A fall in expected inflation shifts the short-run Phillips curve downward from $SRPC_0$ to $SRPC_1$. The long-run Phillips curve does not shift. In part (b), a change in the natural unemployment rate shifts both the short-run and long-run Phillips curves.

—— MyEconLab Animation ——

Economics in Action on this page looks at the Canadian Phillips curve from 2001 to 2013, a period through which the expected inflation rate and the natural unemployment rate didn't change much. Over longer periods, big changes in the expected inflation rate have shifted the Canadian Phillips curve.

Economics in Action
The Canadian Phillips Curve

The figure is a scatter diagram of the Canadian inflation rate (measured by the GDP deflator) and the unemployment rate from 2001 to 2013. *LRPC* is at a natural unemployment rate of 7 percent and *SRPC* is at an expected inflation rate of 1.7 percent a year. The dots for each year (eight of which are identified) show that the *SRPC* jumps around as inflation expectations change.

The Canadian Phillips Curve in the 2000s

REVIEW QUIZ

1 How would you use the Phillips curve to illustrate an unexpected change in inflation?
2 If the expected inflation rate increases by 10 percentage points, how do the short-run Phillips curve and the long-run Phillips curve change?
3 If the natural unemployment rate increases, what happens to the short-run Phillips curve and the long-run Phillips curve?
4 Does Canada have a stable short-run Phillips curve? Explain why or why not.

Work these questions in Study Plan 28.4 and get instant feedback. Do a Key Terms Quiz.   MyEconLab

◆ *Economics in the News* on pp. 694–695 looks at the stagnating economy of Europe and the plans of the European Central Bank to revive it.

The Stagnating Eurozone

Draghi Launches His Counter Attack

The Financial Times
September 4, 2014

When Mario Draghi departed from his script at the central bankers' gathering at Jackson Hole last month, the world took note.

The president of the European Central Bank [ECB] did not quite promise to do "whatever it takes" to stave off deflation in the Eurozone. But he said enough for investors to believe the Frankfurt-based institution had finally woken up to the threat of stagnation.

Mr. Draghi yesterday threw more troops into his counter-offensive. Admitting that Eurozone inflation would fall short of expectations in each of the next three years, he committed the ECB to a series of measures designed to sustain flagging demand.

Mr. Draghi drew a final line under conventional monetary measures as he announced a cut in the repo rate from 0.15 percent to 0.05 percent and increased the amount the ECB would charge lenders for deposits to 0.2 percent.

More importantly, he said the ECB would launch purchases of asset-backed securities.

While this is not the full-scale quantitative easing which many market observers were looking for, it has merits in a world in which Eurozone banks have yet to restore their balance sheets. Reducing sovereign yields in such circumstances may do little to increase the propensity of financial institutions to lend.

Mr. Draghi's plans are not without their difficulties. Purchases of asset-backed securities will only make a difference if the pool of underlying assets is large enough and if loans are genuinely taken off strained bank balance sheets, freeing space for new lending. ...

Copyright © 2014 by Financial Times. Used under licence from *The Financial Times*. All rights reserved.

ESSENCE OF THE STORY

- Mario Draghi, the president of the European Central Bank (ECB), is fighting stagnation.

- Eurozone inflation is forecast to be lower than desired for the next three years.

- The ECB lowered its policy interest rate from 0.15 percent to 0.05 percent per year.

- The ECB also increased the interest rate it makes banks pay on reserves to 0.2 percent per year.

- The ECB also planned to launch purchases of asset-backed securities.

- ECB purchases of asset-backed securities need to be large enough to take bad assets from the banks and free them to increase loans.

ECONOMIC ANALYSIS

- The Eurozone is the group of 18 European countries that use the euro as their money and for which the European Central Bank (ECB) makes monetary policy decisions.

- The Eurozone economy is stagnating and has a high unemployment rate.

- Figure 1 shows the Eurozone unemployment rate compared with that of Canada.

- The Eurozone unemployment rate has been persistently higher than that of Canada and the average difference is structural, not cyclical.

- A high structural unemployment rate in the Eurozone results from high minimum wages, generous unemployment benefits and welfare payments, and extensive regulation of the labour market.

- ECB monetary policy can do nothing to lower the structural unemployment rate. But it can act to lower the cyclical unemployment rate.

- The Eurozone also has a low inflation rate that is below the ECB target rate of 2 percent per year.

- Figure 2 shows the Eurozone inflation rate compared with that of Canada. Both economies had inflation rates below 2 percent per year in 2013, but in the Eurozone inflation had been below 2 percent for 6 years.

- The high unemployment and stagnating real GDP result from real structural problems that make the Eurozone natural unemployment rate high and from high cyclical unemployment and below-target inflation that result from insufficient aggregate demand.

- The aggregate demand problem arises from the fact that the ECB has not expanded the money stock quickly enough.

- Figure 3 shows the growth rate of money plus the growth rate of velocity minus the growth rate of potential GDP.

- The growth rate of money plus the growth rate of velocity minus the growth rate of potential GDP equals the inflation rate that can be sustained at full employment.

- To lower cyclical unemployment, the growth rate of money plus the growth rate of velocity minus the growth rate of potential GDP must *exceed* the target and expected inflation rate.

- If, as in 2009 and 2010, the growth rate of money plus the growth rate of velocity minus the growth rate of potential GDP decreases, cyclical unemployment will increase and inflation will decrease.

- To end stagnation, the ECB must buy assets and increase the growth rate of money. A big one-off asset purchase will not do the job required.

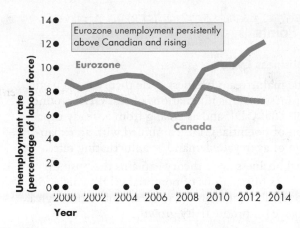

Figure 1 The Stagnating Eurozone Economy

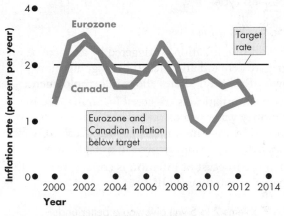

Figure 2 Inflation Rates Miss Targets

Figure 3 Money Growth Rate Too Low

SUMMARY

Key Points

The Business Cycle (pp. 678–682)

- The mainstream business cycle theory explains the business cycle as fluctuations of real GDP around potential GDP and as arising from a steady expansion of potential GDP combined with an expansion of aggregate demand at a fluctuating rate.
- Real business cycle theory explains the business cycle as fluctuations of potential GDP, which arise from fluctuations in the influence of technological change on productivity growth.

Working Problem 1 will give you a better understanding of the business cycle.

Inflation Cycles (pp. 683–688)

- Demand-pull inflation is triggered by an increase in aggregate demand and fuelled by ongoing money growth. Real GDP cycles above full employment.
- Cost-push inflation is triggered by an increase in the money wage rate or raw material prices and is fuelled by ongoing money growth. Real GDP cycles below full employment in a stagflation.
- When the forecast of inflation is correct, real GDP remains at potential GDP.

Working Problems 2 to 5 will give you a better understanding of inflation cycles.

Deflation (pp. 689–691)

- Deflation is a falling price level or negative inflation rate.
- Deflation is caused by a money growth rate that is too low to accommodate the growth of potential GDP and changes in the velocity of circulation.
- Unanticipated deflation brings stagnation.
- Deflation can be ended by increasing the money growth rate to a rate that accommodates the growth of potential GDP and changes in the velocity of circulation.

Working Problem 6 will give you a better understanding of deflation.

The Phillips Curve (pp. 692–693)

- The short-run Phillips curve shows the tradeoff between inflation and unemployment when the expected inflation rate and the natural unemployment rate are constant.
- The long-run Phillips curve, which is vertical, shows that when the actual inflation rate equals the expected inflation rate, the unemployment rate equals the natural unemployment rate.

Working Problems 7 and 8 will give you a better understanding of the Phillips curve.

Key Terms

MyEconLab Key Terms Quiz

Cost-push inflation, 685
Demand-pull inflation, 683
Keynesian cycle theory, 679
Long-run Phillips curve, 692

Monetarist cycle theory, 679
New classical cycle theory, 679
New Keynesian cycle theory, 679
Rational expectation, 688

Real business cycle theory, 679
Short-run Phillips curve, 692
Stagflation, 686

WORKED PROBLEM

MyEconLab   You can work this problem in Chapter 28 Study Plan.

The table shows the aggregate demand and short-run aggregate supply schedules of Shell Island, in which potential GDP is $600 billion. The economy is at full employment.

Price level	Real GDP demanded	Real GDP supplied in the short run
	(billions of 2007 dollars)	
100	650	550
110	625	575
120	600	600
130	575	625
140	550	650

Questions

1. An unexpected increase in exports increases aggregate demand by $50 billion. What happens to the price level and real GDP? Has Shell Island experienced inflation or deflation, and what type of output gap does it now have?

2. The price of oil falls unexpectedly and aggregate supply increases by $50 billion. What type of output gap appears? If the central bank responds to close the output gap, does Shell Island experience inflation or deflation?

3. The government of Shell Island announces an increase in spending of $50 billion a year and the central bank will increase the quantity of money to pay for the spending. Does the economy go into a boom? Will there be inflation?

Solutions

1. When aggregate demand increases by $50 billion, the price level rises from 120 to 130 and real GDP increases from $600 billion to $625 billion and the economy is at an above full-employment equilibrium.

   Shell Island experiences a one-time change in the price level and not inflation. The output gap is an inflationary gap, but demand-pull inflation does not take off until businesses respond to the labour shortage by raising the money wage rate.

Key Point: For an increase in aggregate demand to create demand-pull inflation, the shortage of labour must put pressure on the money wage rate to rise to close the inflationary gap.

2. When the price of oil falls unexpectedly, aggregate supply increases. The price level falls from 120 to 110 and real GDP increases from $600 billion to $625 billion. The economy is at an above full-employment equilibrium. An inflationary gap arises. Shell Island experiences a one-time change in the price level and not inflation.

   If the central bank responds to close the output gap, it cuts the quantity of money. Aggregate demand shifts leftward and a cost-push deflation is created. See the figure.

Key Point: A cost-push deflation is created if the central bank responds to a fall in costs by decreasing the quantity of money.

3. When the government announces an increase in spending of $50 billion a year, aggregate demand increases and the increase in aggregate demand is anticipated. Because the central bank increases the quantity of money, businesses anticipate the rise in the price level, so the money wage rate rises. Aggregate supply decreases.

   Real GDP remains at $600 billion and no output gap is created, but an anticipated inflation occurs.

Key Point: An anticipated increase in aggregate demand accompanied by an increase in the quantity of money created an anticipated inflation spiral with the economy at full employment.

Key Figure

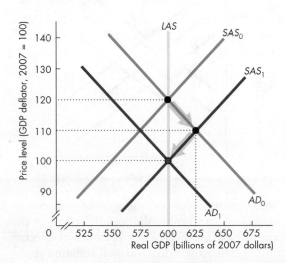

MyEconLab Interactive Animation

STUDY PLAN PROBLEMS AND APPLICATIONS

MyEconLab   You can work Problems 1 to 8 in MyEconLab Chapter 28 Study Plan and get instant feedback.

The Business Cycle (Study Plan 28.1)

1. **Debate on Causes of Joblessness Grows**

   What is the cause of the high unemployment rate? One side says there is not enough government spending. The other says it's a structural problem—people who can't move to take new jobs because they are tied down to burdensome mortgages or firms that can't find workers with the requisite skills to fill job openings.

   Source: *The Wall Street Journal*, September 4, 2010

   Which business cycle theory would say that most of the unemployment is cyclical? Which would say it is an increase in the natural rate? Why?

Inflation Cycles (Study Plan 28.2)

2. **High Food and Energy Prices Here to Stay**

   On top of rising energy prices, a severe drought, bad harvests, and a poor monsoon season in Asia have sent grain prices soaring. Globally, this is the third major food price shock in five years.

   Source: *The Telegraph*, August 29, 2012

   Explain what type of inflation the news clip is describing and provide a graphical analysis of it.

Use the following figure to work Problems 3 to 5.

The economy starts out on the curves labelled AD_0 and SAS_0.

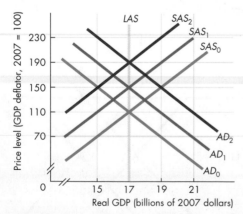

3. Some events occur and the economy experiences a demand-pull inflation. What might those events have been? Describe their initial effects and explain how a demand-pull inflation spiral results.

4. Some events occur and the economy experiences a cost-push inflation. What might those events have been? Describe their initial effects and explain how a cost-push inflation spiral develops.

5. Some events occur and the economy is expected to experience inflation. What might those events have been? Describe their initial effects and what happens as an expected inflation proceeds.

Deflation (Study Plan 28.3)

6. Suppose that the velocity of circulation of money is constant and real GDP is growing at 3 percent a year.
   a. To achieve an inflation target of 2 percent a year, at what rate would the central bank grow the quantity of money?
   b. At what growth rate of the quantity of money would deflation be created?

The Phillips Curve (Study Plan 28.4)

7. **Eurozone Unemployment Hits Record High as Inflation Rises Unexpectedly**

   Eurozone unemployment rose to 10.7 percent. At the same time, Eurozone inflation unexpectedly rose to 2.7 percent a year, up from the previous month's 2.6 percent a year.

   Source: *Huffington Post*, March 1, 2012

   a. How does the Phillips curve model account for a very high unemployment rate?
   b. Explain the change in unemployment and inflation in the Eurozone in terms of what is happening to the short-run and long-run Phillips curves.

8. **From the Fed's Minutes**

   Members expected real GDP growth to be moderate over coming quarters and then to pick up very gradually, with the unemployment rate declining only slowly. With longer-term inflation expectations stable, members anticipated that inflation over the medium run would be at or below 2 percent a year.

   Source: FOMC Minutes, June 2012

   Are FOMC members predicting that the U.S. economy will move along a short-run Phillips curve or that the short-run Phillips curve will shift through 2012 and 2013? Explain.

ADDITIONAL PROBLEMS AND APPLICATIONS

MyEconLab   You can work these problems in MyEconLab if assigned by your instructor.

The Business Cycle

Use the following information to work Problems 9 to 11.

Suppose that the Canadian business cycle is best described by RBC theory and that a new technology increases productivity.

9. Draw a graph to show the effect of the new technology in the market for loanable funds.

10. Draw a graph to show the effect of the new technology in the labour market.

11. Explain the when-to-work decision when technology advances.

12. **Real Wages Fail to Match a Rise in Productivity**

For most of the last century, wages and productivity—the key measure of the economy's efficiency—have risen together, increasing rapidly through the 1950s and '60s and far more slowly in the 1970s and '80s. But in recent years, the productivity gains have continued while the pay increases have not kept up.

Source: *The New York Times,*
August 28, 2006

Explain the relationship between wages and productivity in this news clip in terms of RBC theory.

Inflation Cycles

Use the following news clip to work Problems 13 and 14.

Inflation Should Be Feared

John H. Cochrane, a professor of finance at the University of Chicago, thinks we face the risk of inflation, and if inflation does break out the Fed will not have the ability to stop it and it will "bring stagnation rather than prosperity." The source of the inflation risk that Cochrane fears is not the Fed but fiscal policy. He worries that budget deficits have made U.S. government debt too large, and with no plans to return to budget surplus on the horizon, debt will keep growing. Today, foreigners are happy to hold and to keep buying the debt. But if they decide the risk of continuing to hold the debt is too high, they will dump the debt and buy real assets, whose prices will skyrocket. If inflation takes off, "it will happen with little warning."

Source of information: *The New York Times,*
August 22, 2012

13. What type of inflation process does John Cochrane warn could happen? Explain the role that inflation expectations would play if the outbreak of inflation were to "happen with little warning."

14. Explain why the inflation that John Cochrane fears would "bring stagnation rather than prosperity."

Deflation

15. **Europe's Deflation Risk**

The United States is planning to push Europe towards new and more aggressive efforts to boost aggregate demand given a renewed risk of deflation in the Eurozone.

Source: Reuters, September 12, 2014

a. Explain the process by which deflation occurs.

b. How might Europe boost its aggregate demand? Might the boost to aggregate demand create demand-pull inflation?

The Phillips Curve

Use the following data to work Problems 16 and 17.

An economy has an unemployment rate of 4 percent and an inflation rate of 5 percent a year at point *A* in the figure. Then some events occur that move the economy from *A* to *B* to *D* to *C* and back to *A*.

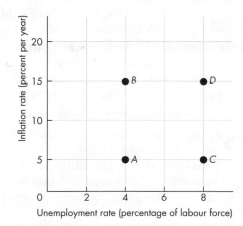

16. Describe the events that could create this sequence. Has the economy experienced demand-pull inflation, cost-push inflation, expected inflation, or none of these?

17. In the graph, draw the sequence of the economy's short-run and long-run Phillips curves.

Use the following information to work Problems 18 and 19.

The Reserve Bank of New Zealand signed an agreement with the New Zealand government in which the Bank agreed to maintain inflation inside a low target range. Failure to achieve the target would result in the governor of the Bank losing his job.

18. Explain how this arrangement might have influenced New Zealand's short-run Phillips curve.

19. Explain how this arrangement might have influenced New Zealand's long-run Phillips curve.

20. **Fed Pause Promises Financial Disaster**

The indication is that inflationary expectations have become entrenched and strongly rooted in world markets. As a result, the risk of global stagflation has become significant. A drawn-out inflationary process always precedes stagflation. Following the attritional effect of inflation, the economy starts to grow below its potential. It experiences a persistent output gap, rising unemployment, and increasingly entrenched inflationary expectations.

Source: *Asia Times Online*, May 20, 2008

Evaluate the claim that if "inflationary expectations" become strongly "entrenched" an economy will experience "a persistent output gap."

21. **Growth Concern**

Despite higher-than-forecast inflation, Bank of Canada Governor Mark Carney said he may keep interest rates low beyond when full output is restored as the domestic recovery is hobbled by a weak economy in the United States, the nation's biggest trade partner. "Given current material headwinds, the policy rate can return to its long-run level after inflation is projected to reach the 2 percent target and output is projected to reach its potential," Carney said.

Source: *Bloomberg*, September 21, 2011

a. Is Mark Carney predicting that the Canadian economy is being pushed along a short-run Phillips curve or that the short-run Phillips curve is shifting? In which direction is the economy moving and how will Carney's plan counter it?

b. Sketch an example of the Phillips curve and show on the graph how the economy is changing.

Economics in the News

22. After you have studied *Economics in the News* on pp. 694–695, answer the following questions.
a. What are the macroeconomic problems in the Eurozone economy that the ECB is seeking to address?
b. Is the European unemployment problem structural, cyclical, or both, and how can we determine its type?
c. Explain which type of unemployment the ECB can help with.
d. Use the *AS-AD* model to show the changes in aggregate demand and/or aggregate supply that created the Eurozone's macroeconomic problems.
e. Use the *AS-AD* model to show the changes in aggregate demand and/or aggregate supply that the ECB must bring about to achieve its goal.

23. **Germany Leads Slowdown in Eurozone**

The pace of German economic growth has weakened "markedly," but the reason is the weaker global prospects. Although German policymakers worry about the country's exposure to a fall in demand for its export goods, evidence is growing that the recovery is broadening with real wage rates rising and unemployment falling, which will lead into stronger consumer spending.

Source: *The Financial Times*, September 23, 2010*

a. How does "exposure to a fall in demand for its export goods" influence Germany's aggregate demand, aggregate supply, unemployment, and inflation?
b. Use the *AS-AD* model to illustrate your answer to part (a).
c. Use the Phillips curve model to illustrate your answer to part (a).
d. What do you think the news clip means by "the recovery is broadening with real wage rates rising and unemployment falling, which will lead into stronger consumer spending"?
e. Use the *AS-AD* model to illustrate your answer to part (d).
f. Use the Phillips curve model to illustrate your answer to part (d).

*Copyright © 2010. Used under licence from *The Financial Times*. All rights reserved.

Boom and Bust

PART NINE

To cure a disease, doctors must first understand how the disease responds to different treatments. It helps to understand the mechanisms that operate to cause the disease, but sometimes a workable cure can be found even before the full story of the causes has been told.

Curing economic ills is similar to curing our medical ills. We need to understand how the economy responds to the treatments we might prescribe for it. And sometimes, we want to try a cure even though we don't fully understand the reasons for the problem we're trying to control.

You've seen how the pace of capital accumulation and technological change determine the long-term growth trend. You've learned how fluctuations around the long-term trend can be generated by changes in aggregate demand and aggregate supply. And you've learned about the key sources of fluctuations in aggregate demand and aggregate supply.

The *AS-AD* model explains the forces that determine real GDP and the price level in the short run. The model also enables us to see the big picture or grand vision of the different schools of macroeconomic thought concerning the sources of aggregate fluctuations. The Keynesian aggregate expenditure model provides an account of the factors that determine aggregate demand and make it fluctuate.

An alternative real business cycle theory puts all the emphasis on fluctuations in long-run aggregate supply. According to this theory, money changes aggregate demand and the price level but leaves the real economy untouched. The events of 2008 and 2009 provide a powerful test of this theory.

John Maynard Keynes, *born in England in 1883, was one of the outstanding minds of the twentieth century. He represented Britain at the Versailles peace conference at the end of World War I, was a master speculator on international financial markets (an activity he conducted from bed every morning and which made and lost him several fortunes), and played a prominent role in creating the International Monetary Fund.*

He was a member of the Bloomsbury Group, a circle of outstanding artists and writers that included E. M. Forster, Bertrand Russell, and Virginia Woolf.

Keynes was a controversial and quick-witted figure. A critic once complained that Keynes had changed his opinion on some matter, to which Keynes retorted: "When I discover I am wrong, I change my mind. What do you do?"

Keynes' book, The General Theory of Employment, Interest and Money, *written during the Great Depression and published in 1936, created macroeconomics and revolutionized the way economists study aggregate fluctuations.*

"The ideas of economists and political philosophers, both when they are right and when they are wrong, are more powerful than is commonly understood. Indeed the world is ruled by little else."

JOHN MAYNARD KEYNES
The General Theory of Employment, Interest and Money

PETER HOWITT is Lyn Crost Professor of Social Sciences in the Department of Economics at Brown University. Born in 1946 in Toronto, he was an undergraduate at McGill University and a graduate student at Northwestern University.

Professor Howitt began his research and teaching career at the University of Western Ontario in 1972, where he spent many productive years before moving to the United States in 1996.

Professor Howitt is a past president of the Canadian Economics Association and is one of the world's leading macroeconomists. He has done research on all aspect of macroeconomics, with a focus in recent years on economic growth.

Michael Parkin and Robin Bade talked with Peter Howitt about his work and the major macroeconomic problems facing Canada today.

Peter, what attracted you to economics?

When I was in high school I had a part-time job as office boy with a small company that imported wool from around the world and sold it to textile mills in Ontario and Quebec. I was fascinated by the way wool prices went up and down all the time, and this curiosity led me to enroll in an honours economics course. My interests soon switched to macroeconomics, but I was always driven by curiosity to find out more about the workings of the human anthill.

You have made outstanding contributions to our understanding of all the major problems of macroeconomics, notably unemployment, economic growth, and inflation. Which of these issues do you believe is the most serious one for Canada today? Can they be separated?

Canada has suffered much less from the global financial crisis than the United States and most other countries. There are a number of reasons for this: Canadian banks have been more prudent in their lending and investment strategies; we did not have the explosion of household debt, especially mortgage debt, or the bubble in housing prices that occurred in the United States; and both the Bank of Canada's inflation-targeting policy and our relatively small government deficits gave our policymakers

*Read the full interview with Peter Howitt in MyEconLab.

more room to stimulate the economy without stoking fears of inflation.

My biggest concern is that Canada seems to be losing many of these advantages, and we may be headed for our own crisis. In particular, household debt is still rising at a rapid rate in Canada, to the

> My biggest concern ... is that we may be headed for a credit crisis that would result in high unemployment and low economic growth.

point where it is now a larger proportion of household income than in the United States. The longer this credit boom continues, the more exposed our financial system becomes in the event of a downturn in housing prices or a rise in unemployment.

Either of these events would lead to a rise in loan defaults, as it has already in the United States where people are walking away from mortgages on houses whose prices have fallen below the amount owed (i.e., mortgages that are "underwater") and where many unemployed people find themselves no longer able to pay back their debts.

29

FISCAL POLICY

After studying this chapter, you will be able to:

◆ Describe the federal budget process and the recent history of outlays, revenues, deficits, and debt

◆ Explain the supply-side effects of fiscal policy

◆ Explain how fiscal stimulus is used to fight a recession

For the past few years, the Government of Canada has had a budget deficit. Does it matter if the government doesn't balance its books? How does a government deficit influence the economy? Does it create jobs, or does it destroy them? Does it speed or slow economic growth?

Like Canada, most countries have a government budget deficit, and that of Japan tops them all and provides a powerful lesson to Canada and others of the consequences of running a persistent and large deficit.

This chapter studies the effects of budget deficits and other fiscal policy actions. And in *Economics in the News* at the end of the chapter, we look at the extreme fiscal policy challenges facing Japan and the lesson they hold for us.

703

◆ The Federal Budget

The annual statement of the outlays and revenues of the Government of Canada, together with the laws and regulations that approve and support those outlays and revenues, make up the **federal budget**. Similarly, a *provincial budget* is an annual statement of the revenues and outlays of a provincial government, together with the laws and regulations that approve or support those revenues and outlays.

Before World War II, the federal budget had no purpose other than to finance the business of government. But since the late 1940s, the federal budget has assumed a second purpose, which is to pursue the government's fiscal policy. **Fiscal policy** is the use of the federal budget to achieve macroeconomic objectives such as full employment, sustained long-term economic growth, and price level stability. Our focus is this second purpose.

Budget Making

The federal government and Parliament make fiscal policy. The process begins with long, drawn-out consultations between the Minister of Finance and Department of Finance officials and their counterparts in the provincial governments. These discussions deal with programs that are funded and operated jointly by the two levels of government. The minister also consults with business and consumer groups on a wide range of issues.

After all these consultations, and using economic projections made by Department of Finance economists, the minister develops a set of proposals, which are discussed in Cabinet and which become government policy. The minister finally presents a budget plan to Parliament, which debates the plan and enacts the laws necessary to implement it.

The Federal Budget in 2013

Table 29.1 shows the main items in the federal budget. The numbers are the amounts for the calendar year 2013 in the *National Income and Expenditure Accounts*. The three main items shown are:

- Revenues
- Outlays
- Budget balance

TABLE 29.1   Federal Budget in 2013

Item	Calendar year 2013 (billions of dollars)
Revenues	**262**
Personal income taxes	130
Corporate income taxes	39
Indirect and other taxes	83
Investment income	10
Outlays	**276**
Transfer payments	179
Expenditure on goods and services	71
Debt interest	26
Deficit	**14**

Source of data: Statistics Canada, CANSIM Table 380-0080.

Revenues Revenues are the federal government's receipts, which were $262 billion. These revenues come from four sources:

1. Personal income taxes
2. Corporate income taxes
3. Indirect and other taxes
4. Investment income

The largest revenue source is personal income taxes. In 2013, personal income taxes were $130 billion. These are the taxes paid by individuals on their incomes. The second largest source of revenue is indirect taxes, which in 2013 were $83 billion. These taxes include the Harmonized Sales Tax (HST) and taxes on the sale of gasoline, alcoholic drinks, and a few other items.

The smallest revenue sources are corporate income taxes, which are the taxes paid by companies on their profits, and investment income, which is the income from government enterprises and investments. In 2013, corporate income taxes were $39 billion and investment income was projected at $10 billion.

Outlays Total federal government outlays in 2013 were $276 billion. Outlays are classified in three categories:

1. Transfer payments
2. Expenditure on goods and services
3. Debt interest

The largest outlay, and by a big margin, is *transfer payments*. Transfer payments are payments to individuals, businesses, other levels of government, and the rest of the world. In 2013, this item was $179 billion. It includes unemployment cheques and welfare payments to individuals, farm subsidies, grants to provincial and local governments, aid to developing countries, and dues to international organizations such as the United Nations.

Expenditure on goods and services is the government's expenditure on final goods and services, and in 2013 this item totalled $71 billion. This expenditure includes the expenditure on national defence, computers for the Canada Revenue Agency, government cars, and highways.

This component of the federal budget is the government expenditure on goods and services that appears in the circular flow of expenditure and income and in the national income and product accounts (see Chapter 20, pp. 467–468).

Debt interest is the interest on the government debt. In 2013, this item was $26 billion. At its peak percentage in 1990, debt interest exceeded government expenditure on goods and services. This interest payment was large because the government has a large debt—$540 billion. The large debt arose because, from the mid-1970s to 1997, the federal government had a large and persistent budget deficit.

Budget Balance The government's budget balance is equal to its revenues minus its outlays. That is,

$$\text{Budget balance} = \text{Revenues} - \text{Outlays}.$$

If revenues exceed outlays, the government has a **budget surplus**. If outlays exceed revenues, the government has a **budget deficit**. If revenues equal outlays, the government has a **balanced budget**.

In 2013, with outlays of $276 billion and revenues of $262 billion, the government had a budget deficit of $14 billion.

How typical is the federal budget of 2013? Let's look at its recent history.

The Budget in Historical Perspective

Figure 29.1 shows the government's revenues, outlays, and budget balance from 1961 to 2013. To get a better sense of the magnitudes of these items, they are shown as percentages of GDP. Expressing them in this way lets us see how large the government is relative to the size of the economy, and also helps us to

---

FIGURE 29.1   The Budget Surplus and Deficit

The figure records the federal government's revenues, outlays, and budget balance as percentages of GDP from 1961 to 2013. During the 1960s, outlays and revenues increased. During the late 1970s and through the 1980s, outlays continued to rise but revenues fell and then remained steady, so a large budget deficit arose. During the 1990s, expenditure cuts eliminated the budget deficit, and after 1997, the federal government had a budget surplus. A deficit re-emerged during the 2008–2009 recession.

Source of data: Statistics Canada, CANSIM Table 380-0080.

MyEconLab Animation

study changes in the scale of government over time. You can think of the percentages of GDP as telling you how many cents of each dollar that Canadians earn get paid to and are spent by the government.

During the 1960s, government expanded but tax revenues and outlays kept pace with each other. But from the mid-1970s through 1996, the federal budget was in deficit, and the average deficit over these years was 4.2 percent of GDP. The deficit climbed to a peak of 6.6 percent of GDP in 1985. It then decreased through the rest of the 1980s. During the recession of 1990–1991, the deficit increased again. The deficit remained above 4 percent of GDP for most of the 1980s and early 1990s.

In 1997, the federal government finally eradicated its deficit. And it did so by cutting outlays, especially transfer payments to provincial governments. But another deficit emerged in the 2008–2009 recession.

Why did the government deficit grow during the early 1980s and remain high through the early 1990s? The immediate answer is that outlays increased while revenues remained relatively constant. But which components of outlays increased? And did all the sources of revenues remain constant?

To answer these questions, we need to examine each of the sources of revenues and outlays in detail. We'll begin by looking at the sources of revenues.

Revenues　Figure 29.2 shows the components of government revenues since 1961. Total revenues have no strong trends. They increased through the 1960s and again through the 1980s, but they decreased during the 1970s and the 2000s.

The main source of the fluctuations in revenues was personal income taxes. Indirect taxes also fluctuated, but corporate income taxes and investment income were more stable than the other two revenue components.

The increase in personal income taxes during the 1980s resulted from increases in tax rates in successive budgets.

Indirect taxes decreased during the 1990s mainly because an old federal sales tax was replaced by the Goods and Services Tax, GST, or the Harmonized Sales Tax, HST. Initially, this switch maintained revenues at a constant level, but gradually, the revenue from indirect taxes (as a percentage of GDP) fell.

Outlays　Figure 29.3 shows the components of government outlays since 1961. Total outlays increased steadily from 1971 through 1985, were relatively high through 1993, and then decreased sharply after 1993. The main source of the changing trends in outlays is transfer payments to provincial governments. These payments swelled during the 1980s and were cut drastically during the mid-1990s.

FIGURE 29.2　Federal Government Revenues

The figure shows four main components of government revenues (as percentages of GDP): personal income taxes, corporate income taxes, indirect taxes, and investment income. Revenues from personal income taxes fluctuate the most. They increased during the 1960s and early 1970s, decreased during the late 1970s, increased again during the 1980s and 1990s, and then decreased again during the 2000s. Indirect taxes have fallen during the 2000s. The other two components of revenues remained steady.

Source of data: Statistics Canada, CANSIM Tables 380-0080 and 380-0064.

MyEconLab Animation

FIGURE 29.3   Federal Government Outlays

The figure shows three components of government outlays (as percentages of GDP): expenditure on goods and services, debt interest, and transfer payments. Expenditure on goods and services have had a downward trend. Transfer payments increased from 1965 to 1990 but decreased sharply during the 1990s and continued to fall until the 2008–2009 recession when they increased. Debt interest increased steadily during the 1980s as the budget deficit fed on itself, but decreased during the late 1990s as surpluses began to reduce the government's debt.

Source of data: Statistics Canada, CANSIM Tables 380-0080 and 380-0064.

—— MyEconLab Animation ——

To understand the changes in debt interest, we need to see the connection between the budget deficit and government debt.

Deficit and Debt The government borrows to finance its deficit. And **government debt** is the total amount of government borrowing, which equals the sum of past deficits minus the sum of past surpluses.

When the government budget is in deficit, government debt increases; and when the government budget is in surplus, government debt decreases.

A persistent budget deficit emerged during the mid-1970s, and in such a situation, the deficit begins to feed on itself. A budget deficit increases borrowing; increased borrowing leads to larger debt; a larger debt leads to larger interest payments; and larger interest payments lead to a larger deficit and yet larger debt. That is the story of the increasing budget deficit and rising debt of the 1980s and early 1990s.

Similarly, a persistent budget surplus creates a virtuous cycle of falling interest payments, larger surpluses, and declining debt.

Figure 29.4 shows the history of the Government of Canada debt since 1970. In 1970, debt (as a percentage of GDP) was at a low of 5 percent. This almost zero debt resulted from 25 years of surpluses to pay off a huge debt built up during World War II that exceeded 100 percent of GDP.

FIGURE 29.4   The Federal Government Debt

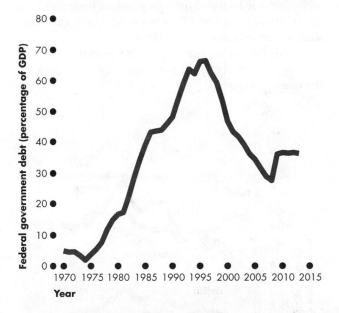

Federal government debt as a percentage of GDP increased from 1974 through 1997 and then began to decrease. It increased slightly during the 2008–2009 recession and has remained constant at a bit more than 36 percent of GDP.

Source of data: Statistics Canada, CANSIM Tables 380-0080 and 191-0002.

—— MyEconLab Animation ——

Economics in Action
Provincial and Local Governments

The total government sector of Canada includes provincial and local governments as well as the federal government. In 2013, when federal government outlays were $276 billion, provincial and local government outlays were $482 billion and total government outlays were $758 billion.

Most provincial and local government outlays are on public hospitals and public schools, colleges, and universities.

Figure 1 shows the revenues, outlays, and deficits of the federal government and of total government from 1961 to 2013.

You can see that federal government outlays and revenues and total government outlays and revenues fluctuate in similar ways, but the total government is much larger than the federal government. In other words, the provincial and local governments are a large component of total government. You can also see that total government outlays fluctuate more than federal government outlays.

Both the federal and total government budgets moved into and out of deficit at similar times, and both were in surplus from the late 1990s to 2008.

Provincial government outlays and revenue sources vary a great deal across the provinces. Figure 2 shows the range of variation.

Part (a) shows outlays as a percentage of provincial GDP. You can see that outlays are greatest in the northern governments (Nunavut, Yukon, and Northwest Territories) and smallest in Alberta, Ontario, and British Columbia.

Part (b) shows the sources of provincial revenues as a percentage of total outlays. Again, the northern governments receive the largest transfers from the federal government. Atlantic provinces receive the next largest transfers from the federal government, while Alberta, Saskatchewan, Ontario, and British Columbia receive the least.

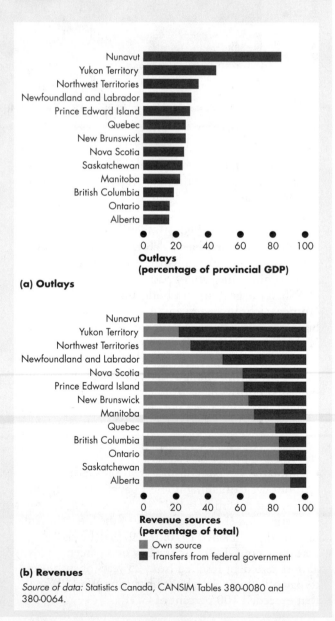

(a) Outlays

(b) Revenues

Source of data: Statistics Canada, CANSIM Tables 380-0080 and 380-0064.

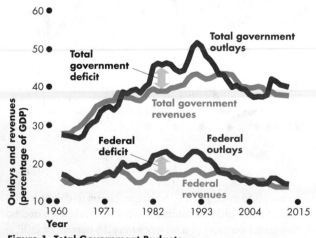

Figure 1   Total Government Budgets

Source of data: Statistics Canada, CANSIM Tables 380-0080 and 380-0064.

Economics in Action
The Canadian Government Budget in Global Perspective

How does the Canadian government budget deficit compare with those of other major economies?

Comparing Like with Like

To compare the budget deficits of governments across economies, we must take into account the fact that some countries, and Canada is one of them, have large provincial and local governments, while others, and the United Kingdom is one, have a large central government and small local governments. These differences make the international comparison more valid at the level of total government.

Deficits Almost Everywhere

The figure shows the budget balances of all levels of government in Canada and other economies in 2014. Fiscal stimulus to fight the global recession of 2008 resulted in deficits almost everywhere. Of the countries shown here, only Germany had a budget surplus in 2014. Japan had the largest deficit and the United States had the second largest. Canada's budget deficit is in the middle of the pack.

Italy and other advanced economies as a group, which includes the newly industrialized economies of Asia (Hong Kong, South Korea, Singapore, and Taiwan), had the smallest deficits.

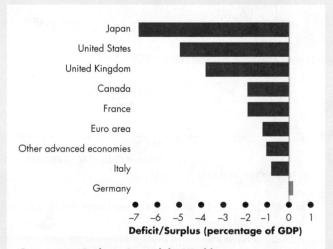

Government Budgets Around the World

Source of data: International Monetary Fund, *World Economic Outlook*, September 2014.

Small budget deficits increased the debt-to-GDP ratio slightly through the 1970s, and large budget deficits increased it dramatically between 1981 and 1986. During the late 1980s, the ratio continued to increase but at a more moderate rate. The debt-to-GDP ratio grew quickly again during the 1990–1991 recession and its growth rate slowed after 1995 and debt interest as a percentage of GDP decreased.

The 2008–2009 recession lowered revenues and increased outlays, so the debt-to GDP ratio increased again and has remained fairly steady.

Debt and Capital When individuals and businesses incur debts, they usually do so to buy capital—assets that yield a return. In fact, the main point of debt is to enable people to buy assets that will earn a return that exceeds the interest paid on the debt. The government is similar to individuals and businesses in this regard. Some government expenditure is investment—the purchase of public capital that yields a return. Highways, major irrigation schemes, public schools and universities, public libraries, and the stock of national defence capital all yield a social rate of return that probably far exceeds the interest rate the government pays on its debt.

But Canadian government debt, which is $680 billion, is much larger than the value of the public capital stock. This fact means that some government debt has been incurred to finance public consumption expenditure.

REVIEW QUIZ

1 What are the main items of government revenues and outlays?
2 Under what circumstances does the government have a budget surplus?
3 Explain the connection between a government budget deficit and a government debt.

Work these questions in Study Plan 29.1 and get instant feedback. Do a Key Terms Quiz.   MyEconLab

It is now time to study the *effects* of fiscal policy. We'll begin by learning about the effects of taxes on employment, aggregate supply, and potential GDP. Then we'll look at fiscal stimulus and see how it might be used to speed recovery from recession and stabilize the business cycle.

Supply-Side Effects of Fiscal Policy

How do taxes on personal and corporate income affect real GDP and employment? The answer to these questions is controversial. Some economists, known as *supply-siders*, believe these effects to be large, and an accumulating body of evidence suggests that they are correct. To see why these effects might be large, we'll begin with a refresher on how full employment and potential GDP are determined in the absence of taxes. Then we'll introduce an income tax and see how it changes the economic outcome.

Full Employment and Potential GDP

You learned in Chapter 22 (pp. 520–522) how the full-employment quantity of labour and potential GDP are determined. At full employment, the real wage rate adjusts to make the quantity of labour demanded equal the quantity of labour supplied. Potential GDP is the real GDP that the full-employment quantity of labour produces.

Figure 29.5 illustrates a full-employment situation. In part (a), the demand for labour curve is *LD*, and the supply of labour curve is *LS*. At a real wage rate of $30 an hour and 25 billion hours of labour a year employed, the economy is at full employment.

In Fig. 29.5(b), the production function is *PF*. When 25 billion hours of labour are employed, real GDP and potential GDP are $1.8 trillion.

Let's now see how an income tax changes potential GDP.

The Effects of the Income Tax

The tax on labour income influences potential GDP and aggregate supply by changing the full-employment quantity of labour. The income tax weakens the incentive to work and drives a wedge between the take-home wage of workers and the cost of labour to firms. The result is a smaller quantity of labour and a lower potential GDP.

Figure 29.5 shows this outcome. In the labour market, the income tax has no effect on the demand for labour, which remains at *LD*. The reason is that the quantity of labour that firms plan to hire depends only on how productive labour is and what it costs—its real wage rate.

FIGURE 29.5 The Effects of the Income Tax on Aggregate Supply

(a) Income tax and the labour market

(b) Income tax and potential GDP

In part (a), with no income tax, the real wage rate is $30 an hour and employment is 25 billion hours. In part (b), potential GDP is $1.8 trillion. An income tax shifts the supply of labour curve leftward to *LS* + *tax*. The before-tax wage rate rises to $35 an hour, the after-tax wage rate falls to $20 an hour, and the quantity of labour employed decreases to 20 billion hours. With less labour, potential GDP decreases.

MyEconLab Animation and Draw Graph

But the supply of labour *does* change. With no income tax, the real wage rate is $30 an hour and 25 billion hours of labour a year are employed. An income tax weakens the incentive to work and decreases the supply of labour. The reason is that for each dollar of before-tax earnings, workers must pay the government an amount determined by the income tax code. So workers look at the after-tax wage rate when they decide how much labour to supply. An income tax shifts the supply curve leftward to *LS* + *tax*. The vertical distance between the *LS* curve and the *LS* + *tax* curve measures the amount of income tax. With the smaller supply of labour, the *before-tax* wage rate rises to $35 an hour but the *after-tax* wage rate falls to $20 an hour. The gap created between the before-tax and after-tax wage rates is called the **tax wedge**.

The new equilibrium quantity of labour employed is 20 billion hours a year—less than in the no-tax case. Because the full-employment quantity of labour decreases, so does potential GDP. And a decrease in potential GDP decreases aggregate supply.

In this example, the tax rate is high—$15 tax on a $35 wage rate is a tax rate of about 43 percent. A lower tax rate would have a smaller effect on employment and potential GDP.

An increase in the tax rate to above 43 percent would decrease the supply of labour by more than the decrease shown in Fig. 29.5. Equilibrium employment and potential GDP would also decrease still further. A tax cut would increase the supply of labour, increase equilibrium employment, and increase potential GDP.

Taxes on Expenditure and the Tax Wedge

The tax wedge that we've just considered is only a part of the wedge that affects labour-supply decisions. Taxes on consumption expenditure add to the wedge. The reason is that a tax on consumption raises the prices paid for consumption goods and services and is equivalent to a cut in the real wage rate.

The incentive to supply labour depends on the goods and services that an hour of labour can buy. The higher the taxes on goods and services and the lower the after-tax wage rate, the less is the incentive to supply labour. If the income tax rate is 25 percent and the tax rate on consumption expenditure is 10 percent, a dollar earned buys only 65 cents worth of goods and services. The tax wedge is 35 percent.

Economics in Action
Some Real-World Tax Wedges

Edward C. Prescott of Arizona State University, who shared the 2004 Nobel Prize for Economic Science, has estimated the tax wedges for three countries: the United States, the United Kingdom, and France. We have estimated the tax wedge for Canada.

The wedges are a combination of taxes on labour income and taxes on consumption. They include all taxes on labour, including social insurance taxes. And the wedges are based on marginal tax rates—the tax rates paid on the marginal dollar earned.

The figure shows the tax wedges in these four countries. In the United States, the consumption tax wedge is 13 percent and the income tax wedge is 32 percent. Canada is very similar. In France, the consumption tax wedge is 33 percent and the income tax wedge is 49 percent. The tax wedges in United Kingdom fall between those of France and Canada.

Does the Tax Wedge Matter?

Differences in potential GDP per person arise partly from productivity differences and partly from choices influenced by the tax wedge. Potential GDP (per person) in France is 30 percent below that of the United States and the entire difference is attributed to the difference in the tax wedge in the two countries. Potential GDP in Canada is 12 percent below that of the United States, but this difference is due to different productivities. Potential GDP in the United Kingdom is 28 percent below that of the United States, and about a third of the difference arises from the different tax wedges and two-thirds from productivity difference.

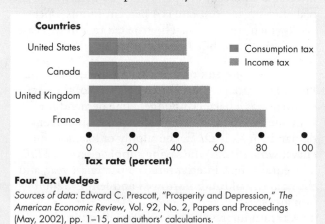

Four Tax Wedges

Sources of data: Edward C. Prescott, "Prosperity and Depression," *The American Economic Review,* Vol. 92, No. 2, Papers and Proceedings (May, 2002), pp. 1–15, and authors' calculations.

Taxes and the Incentive to Save and Invest

A tax on interest income weakens the incentive to save and drives a wedge between the after-tax interest rate earned by savers and the interest rate paid by firms. These effects are analogous to those of a tax on labour income, but they are more serious for two reasons.

First, a tax on labour income lowers the quantity of labour employed and lowers potential GDP, while a tax on capital income lowers the quantity of saving and investment and slows the growth rate of real GDP.

Second, the true tax rate on interest income is much higher than that on labour income because of the way in which inflation and taxes on interest income interact. Let's examine this interaction.

Effect of Tax Rate on Real Interest Rate

The interest rate that influences investment and saving plans is the real after-tax interest rate. The real after-tax interest rate subtracts the income tax rate paid on interest income from the real interest rate. But the taxes depend on the nominal interest rate, not the real interest rate. So the higher the inflation rate, the higher is the true tax rate on interest income. Here is an example. Suppose the real interest rate is 4 percent a year and the tax rate is 40 percent.

If there is no inflation, the nominal interest rate equals the real interest rate. The tax on 4 percent interest is 1.6 percent (40 percent of 4 percent), so the real after-tax interest rate is 4 percent minus 1.6 percent, which equals 2.4 percent.

If the inflation rate is 6 percent a year, the nominal interest rate is 10 percent. The tax on 10 percent interest is 4 percent (40 percent of 10 percent), so the real after-tax interest rate is 4 percent minus 4 percent, which equals zero. The true tax rate in this case is not 40 percent but 100 percent!

Effect of Income Tax on Saving and Investment

In Fig. 29.6, initially there are no taxes. Also, the government has a balanced budget. The demand for loanable funds curve, which is also the investment demand curve, is *DLF*. The supply of loanable funds curve, which is also the saving supply curve, is *SLF*. The equilibrium interest rate is 3 percent a year, and the quantity of funds borrowed and lent is $200 billion a year.

A tax on interest income has no effect on the demand for loanable funds. The quantity of investment and borrowing that firms plan to undertake depends only on how productive capital is and what

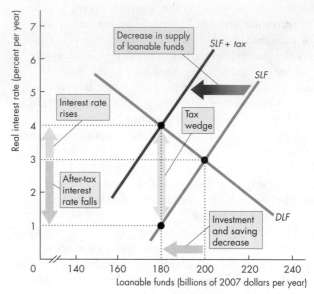

FIGURE 29.6   The Effects of a Tax on Capital Income

The demand for loanable funds and investment demand curve is *DLF*, and the supply of loanable funds and saving supply curve is *SLF*. With no income tax, the real interest rate is 3 percent a year and investment is $200 billion. An income tax shifts the supply curve leftward to *SLF + tax*. The interest rate rises to 4 percent a year, the after-tax interest rate falls to 1 percent a year, and investment decreases to $180 billion. With less investment, the real GDP growth rate decreases.

MyEconLab Animation and Draw Graph

it costs—its real interest rate. But a tax on interest income weakens the incentive to save and lend and decreases the supply of loanable funds. For each dollar of before-tax interest, savers must pay the government an amount determined by the tax code. So savers look at the after-tax real interest rate when they decide how much to save.

When a tax is imposed, saving decreases and the supply of loanable funds curve shifts leftward to *SLF + tax*. The amount of tax payable is measured by the vertical distance between the *SLF* curve and the *SLF + tax* curve. With this smaller supply of loanable funds, the interest rate rises to 4 percent a year but the after-tax interest rate falls to 1 percent a year. A tax wedge is driven between the interest rate and the after-tax interest rate, and the equilibrium quantity of loanable funds decreases. Saving and investment also decrease.

Tax Revenues and the Laffer Curve

An interesting consequence of the effect of taxes on employment and saving is that a higher tax *rate* does not always bring greater tax *revenue*. A higher tax rate brings in more revenue per dollar earned. But because a higher tax rate decreases the number of dollars earned, two forces operate in opposite directions on the tax revenue collected.

The relationship between the tax rate and the amount of tax revenue collected is called the **Laffer curve**. The curve is so named because Arthur B. Laffer, a member of President Reagan's Economic Policy Advisory Board, drew such a curve on a table napkin and launched the idea that tax cuts could increase tax revenue.

Figure 29.7 shows a Laffer curve. The tax rate is on the *x*-axis, and total tax revenue is on the *y*-axis. For tax rates below T^*, an increase in the tax rate increases tax revenue; at T^*, tax revenue is maximized; and a tax rate increase above T^* decreases tax revenue.

Most people think that Canada is on the upward-sloping part of the Laffer curve; so is the United Kingdom. But France might be close to the maximum point or perhaps even beyond it.

The Supply-Side Debate

Before 1980, few economists paid attention to the supply-side effects of taxes on employment and potential GDP. Then, when Ronald Reagan took office as president, a group of supply-siders began to argue the virtues of cutting taxes. Arthur Laffer was one of them. Laffer and his supporters were not held in high esteem among mainstream economists, but they were influential for a period. They correctly argued that tax cuts would increase employment and increase output. But they incorrectly argued that tax cuts would increase tax revenues and decrease the budget deficit. For this prediction to be correct, the United States would have had to be on the "wrong" side of the Laffer curve. Given that U.S. tax rates are among the lowest in the industrial world, it is unlikely that this condition was met. And when the Reagan administration did cut taxes, the budget deficit increased, a fact that reinforces this view.

Supply-side economics became tarnished because of its association with Laffer and came to be called "voodoo economics." But mainstream economists, including Martin Feldstein, a Harvard professor who was Reagan's chief economic advisor, recognized the

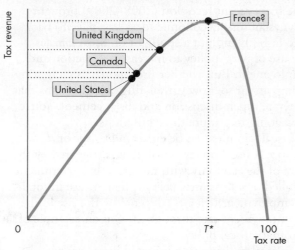

FIGURE 29.7   A Laffer Curve

A Laffer curve shows the relationship between the tax rate and tax revenues. For tax rates below T^*, an increase in the tax rate increases tax revenue. At the tax rate T^*, tax revenue is maximized. For tax rates above T^*, an increase in the tax rate decreases tax revenue.

—— **MyEconLab** Animation ——

power of tax cuts as incentives but took the standard view that tax cuts without spending cuts would swell the budget deficit and bring serious further problems. This view is now widely accepted by economists of all political persuasions.

◆ REVIEW QUIZ

1 How does a tax on labour income influence the equilibrium quantity of employment?
2 How does the tax wedge influence potential GDP?
3 Why are consumption taxes relevant for measuring the tax wedge?
4 Why are income taxes on capital income more powerful than those on labour income?
5 What is the Laffer curve and why is it unlikely that Canada is on the "wrong" side of it?

Work these questions in Study Plan 29.2 and get instant feedback. Do a Key Terms Quiz.   **MyEconLab**

You now know how taxes influence potential GDP and saving and investment. Next, we look at the demand-side effects of fiscal policy.

◆ Fiscal Stimulus

The most recent recession (2008–2009) brought Keynesian macroeconomic ideas (see p. 638) back into fashion and put a spotlight on **fiscal stimulus**—the use of fiscal policy to increase production and employment. But whether fiscal policy is truly stimulating, and if so, how stimulating, are questions that generate much discussion and disagreement. You're now going to explore these questions.

Fiscal stimulus can be either *automatic* or *discretionary*. A fiscal policy action that is triggered by the state of the economy with no action by government is called **automatic fiscal policy**. The increase in total unemployment benefits triggered by the rise in the unemployment rate through 2009 is an example of automatic fiscal policy.

A fiscal policy action initiated by an act of Parliament is called **discretionary fiscal policy**. It requires a change in a spending program or in a tax law. A fiscal stimulus act passed by the U.S. government in 2008 (see *Economics in Action* on p. 717) is an example of discretionary fiscal policy.

Whether automatic or discretionary, an increase in government outlays or a decrease in government revenues can stimulate production and jobs. An increase in expenditure on goods and services directly increases aggregate expenditure. And an increase in transfer payments (such as unemployment benefits) or a decrease in tax revenues increases disposable income, which enables people to increase consumption expenditure. Lower taxes also strengthen the incentives to work and invest.

We'll begin by looking at automatic fiscal policy and the interaction between the business cycle and the budget balance.

Automatic Fiscal Policy and Cyclical and Structural Budget Balances

Two items in the government budget change automatically in response to the state of the economy. They are *tax revenues* and *transfer payments*.

Automatic Changes in Tax Revenues The tax laws that Parliament enacts don't legislate the number of tax *dollars* the government will raise. Rather they define the tax rates that people must pay. Tax dollars paid depend on tax rates and incomes. But incomes vary with real GDP, so tax revenues depend on real GDP. When real GDP increases in a business cycle expansion, wages and profits rise, so tax revenues from these incomes rise. When real GDP decreases in a recession, wages and profits fall, so tax revenues fall.

Automatic Changes in Outlays The government creates programs that pay benefits to qualified people and businesses. The spending on these programs results in transfer payments that depend on the economic state of individual citizens and businesses. When the economy expands, unemployment falls and the number of people receiving unemployment benefits decreases, so transfer payments decrease. When the economy is in a recession, unemployment is high and the number of people receiving unemployment benefits increases, so transfer payments increase.

Automatic Stimulus Because government revenues fall and outlays increase in a recession, the budget provides automatic stimulus that helps to shrink the recessionary gap. Similarly, because revenues rise and outlays decrease in a boom, the budget provides automatic restraint to shrink an inflationary gap.

Cyclical and Structural Budget Balances To identify the government budget deficit that arises from the business cycle, we distinguish between the **structural surplus or deficit**, which is the budget balance that would occur if the economy were at full employment, and the **cyclical surplus or deficit**, which is the actual surplus or deficit *minus* the structural surplus or deficit.

Figure 29.8 illustrates these concepts. Outlays *decrease* as real GDP *increases*, so the outlays curve slopes downward; and revenues *increase* as real GDP *increases*, so the revenues curve slopes upward.

In Fig. 29.8(a), potential GDP is $1.7 trillion. If real GDP equals potential GDP, the government has a balanced budget. There is no structural surplus or deficit. But there might be a cyclical surplus or deficit. If real GDP is less than potential GDP at $1.6 trillion, outlays exceed revenues and there is a cyclical deficit. If real GDP is greater than potential GDP at $1.8 trillion, outlays are less than revenues and there is a cyclical surplus.

In Fig. 29.8(b), if potential GDP equals $1.7 trillion (line *B*), the *structural balance is zero*. But if potential GDP is $1.6 trillion (line *A*), the government budget has a *structural deficit*. And if potential GDP is $1.8 trillion (line *C*), the government budget has a structural surplus.

FIGURE 29.8   Cyclical and Structural Surpluses and Deficits

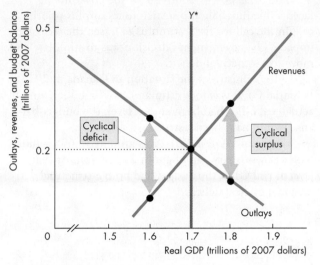

(a) Cyclical deficit and cyclical surplus

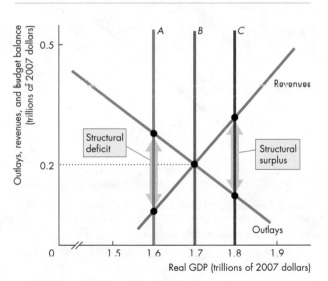

(b) Structural deficit and structural surplus

In part (a), potential GDP is $1.7 trillion. When real GDP is $1.6 trillion, the budget balance is a *cyclical deficit*. When real GDP is $1.8 trillion, the budget balance is a *cyclical surplus*. When real GDP is $1.7 trillion, the government has a *balanced budget*.

In part (b), if potential GDP is $1.6 trillion, the budget balance is a *structural deficit*. If potential GDP is $1.8 trillion, the budget balance is a *structural surplus*. If potential GDP is $1.7 trillion, the *structural balance* is zero.

—— MyEconLab Animation ——

Canadian Structural Budget Balance in 2013 The

Canadian federal budget in 2013 was in deficit at $14 billion and the recessionary gap (the gap between real GDP and potential GDP) was estimated by the Bank of Canada to be less than 1 percent of potential GDP, or about $10 billion. This recessionary gap is small. With a small recessionary gap and a substantial budget deficit, most of the deficit was structural.

We don't now exactly how much of the deficit was structural and how much was cyclical, but *Economics in Action* on the next page provides an illustration and possible breakdown of the deficit into its two parts.

Discretionary Fiscal Stimulus

Most discussion of *discretionary* fiscal stimulus focuses on its effects on aggregate demand. But you've seen (on pp. 710–713) that taxes influence aggregate supply and that the balance of taxes and spending—the government budget deficit—can crowd out investment and slow the pace of economic growth. So discretionary fiscal stimulus has both supply-side and demand-side effects that end up determining its overall effectiveness.

We're going to begin our examination of discretionary fiscal stimulus by looking at its effects on aggregate demand.

Fiscal Stimulus and Aggregate Demand Changes in government expenditure and changes in taxes change aggregate demand by their influence on spending plans, and they also have multiplier effects.

Let's look at the two main fiscal policy multipliers: the government expenditure and tax multipliers.

The **government expenditure multiplier** is the quantitative effect of a change in government expenditure on real GDP. Because government expenditure is a component of aggregate expenditure, an increase in government spending increases aggregate expenditure and real GDP. But does a $1 billion increase in government expenditure increase real GDP by $1 billion, more than $1 billion, or less than $1 billion?

When an increase in government expenditure increases real GDP, incomes rise and the higher incomes bring an increase in consumption expenditure. If this were the only consequence of increased government expenditure, the government expenditure multiplier would be greater than 1.

But an increase in government expenditure increases government borrowing (or decreases government lending if there is a budget surplus) and raises

Economics in Action
Canada's 2013 Budget Deficit

Canada's Conservative government places a high priority on maintaining a federal budget surplus for two reasons. First, it believes that the debt created by the long run of deficits during the 1980s and 1990s remains too large, so it wants to see that debt lowered every year. Second, it believes that aiming for a surplus places a discipline on a Parliament that can always find reasons to spend ever larger amounts on public projects and social programs.

From 2001 to 2004, Canada had a negative output gap, but the budget balance was a structural surplus. In the recession of 2008–2009, the budget moved into a structural deficit, and as the economy expanded in 2010–2013, the budget deficit decreased and remained (see Fig. 1).

In the recession of 2008–2009, the government faced a dilemma. Should it stick to its surplus priority or join the call for fiscal stimulus to lessen the recession's impact? The government's decision was to stimulate and move to a structural deficit.

Figure 2 illustrates the situation in Canada in 2013. Potential GDP was (our estimate) $1,705 billion, and if actual real GDP had been at that level, the budget balance would have been a structural deficit.

Actual real GDP in 2013 was around $1,695 billion, with a recessionary gap of about $10 billion. At that level of real GDP, the budget had both a structural deficit and a cyclical deficit.

Figure 1 The Canadian Business Cycle and Budget Balance

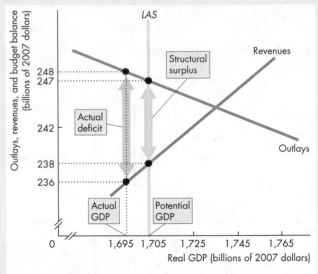

Figure 2 Canada's Structural and Cyclical Deficit

Sources of data: Statistics Canada, CANSIM Tables 380-0080 and 380-0064, and the Bank of Canada's estimate of the output gap.

the real interest rate. With a higher cost of borrowing, investment decreases, which partly offsets the increase in government spending. If this were the only consequence of increased government expenditure, the multiplier would be less than 1.

The actual multiplier depends on which of the above effects is stronger, and the consensus is that the crowding-out effect is strong enough to make the government expenditure multiplier less than 1.

The **tax multiplier** is the quantitative effect of a change in taxes on real GDP. The demand-side effects of a tax cut are likely to be smaller than an equivalent increase in government expenditure. The reason is that a tax cut influences aggregate demand by increasing disposable income, only part of which gets spent. So the initial injection of expenditure from a $1 billion tax cut is less than $1 billion.

A tax cut has similar crowding-out consequences to a spending increase. It increases government borrowing (or decreases government lending), raises the real interest rate, and cuts investment.

The tax multiplier effect on aggregate demand depends on these two opposing effects and is probably quite small.

Graphical Illustration of Fiscal Stimulus Figure 29.9 shows how fiscal stimulus is supposed to work if it is perfectly executed and has its desired effects.

Potential GDP is $1.7 trillion and real GDP is below potential at $1.6 trillion, so the economy has a recessionary gap of $0.1 trillion.

To restore full employment, the government passes a fiscal stimulus package. An increase in government expenditure and a tax cut increase aggregate expenditure by ΔE. If this were the only change in spending plans, the AD curve would shift rightward to become the curve labelled $AD_0 + \Delta E$ in Fig. 29.9. But if fiscal stimulus sets off a multiplier process that increases consumption expenditure and does not crowd out much investment, aggregate demand increases further and the AD curve shifts rightward to AD_1.

With no change in the price level, the economy would move from point A to point B on AD_1. But

FIGURE 29.9   Expansionary Fiscal Policy

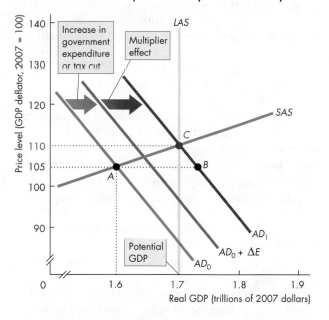

Potential GDP is $1.7 trillion, real GDP is $1.6 trillion, and there is a $0.1 trillion recessionary gap. An increase in government expenditure and a tax cut increase aggregate expenditure by ΔE. The multiplier increases consumption expenditure and the AD curve shifts rightward to AD_1. The price level rises to 110, real GDP increases to $1.7 trillion, and the recessionary gap is eliminated.

— **MyEconLab** Animation —

Economics in Action
Fiscal Stimulus in the United States

As recession fears grew, the Economic Stimulus Act of 2008, a discretionary fiscal policy, aimed to increase aggregate demand.

Tax rebates were the key component of the package, and their effect on aggregate demand depends on the extent to which they are spent and saved.

The last time the U.S. federal government boosted aggregate demand with a tax rebate was in 2001, and a statistical investigation of the effects estimated that 70 percent of the rebates were spent within six months of being received.

The rebates in the 2008 fiscal package were targeted predominantly at low-income individuals and families, so the experience of 2001 would be likely to apply: Most of the rebates would be spent.

The cost of the package in 2008 was about $160 billion, so aggregate demand would be expected to increase by close to this amount and then by a multiplier as the initial spending became someone else's income and so boosted their spending.

The figure illustrates the effects of the package. Before the rebates, aggregate demand was AD_0 and real GDP was $14.8 trillion. The rebates increased aggregate demand to $AD_0 + \Delta E$, and a multiplier increased it to AD_1. Real GDP and the price level increased and the recessionary gap narrowed.

Effects of Fiscal Stimulus

the increase in aggregate demand brings a rise in the price level along the upward-sloping *SAS* curve and the economy moves to point *C*.

At point *C*, the economy returns to full employment and the recessionary gap is eliminated.

When Fiscal Stimulus Is Removed When fiscal stimulus brings a structural budget deficit, government debt grows. Concern about the effect of a deficit on debt often makes the government want to get back to a balanced budget. To do that, government expenditure must be cut and/or taxes must be increased. When these restraining discretionary fiscal policy actions are taken, aggregate demand decreases and a process the reverse of that described and illustrated in Fig. 29.9 kicks in. Care must be taken to try to time this restraint to coincide with an increase in investment and increasing aggregate demand.

Fiscal Stimulus and Aggregate Supply You've seen earlier in this chapter that taxes influence aggregate supply. A tax on labour income (on wages) drives a wedge between the cost of labour and the take-home pay of workers and lowers employment and output (p. 710). A tax on capital income (on interest) drives a wedge between the cost of borrowing and the return to lending and lowers saving and investment (p. 712). With less saving and investment, the real GDP growth rate slows.

These negative effects of taxes on real GDP and its growth rate and on employment mean that a tax *cut* increases real GDP and its growth rate and increases employment.

These supply-side effects of a tax cut occur along with the demand-side effects and are probably much larger than the demand-side effects and make the overall tax multiplier much larger than the government expenditure multiplier—see *Economics in Action*.

An increase in government expenditure financed by borrowing increases the demand for loanable funds and raises the real interest rate, which in turn lowers investment and private saving. This cut in investment is the main reason why the government expenditure multiplier is so small and why a deficit-financed increase in government spending ends up making only a small contribution to job creation. And because government expenditure crowds out investment, it lowers future real GDP.

So a fiscal stimulus package that is heavy on tax cuts and light on government spending works. But an increase in government expenditure alone is not an effective way to stimulate production and create jobs.

The description of the effects of discretionary fiscal stimulus and its graphical illustration in Fig. 29.9 make it look easy: Calculate the recessionary gap and the multipliers, change government expenditure and taxes, and eliminate the gap. In reality, things are not that easy.

Getting the magnitude and the timing right is difficult, and we'll now examine this challenge.

Magnitude of Stimulus Economists have diverging views about the size of the government spending and tax multipliers because there is insufficient empirical evidence on which to pin their size with accuracy. This fact makes it impossible for Parliament to

Economics in Action
How Big Are the Fiscal Stimulus Multipliers?

When a U.S. 2009 fiscal stimulus package cut taxes by $300 billion and increased government spending by almost $500 billion, by how much did aggregate expenditure and real GDP change? How big were the fiscal policy multipliers? Was the government expenditure multiplier larger than the tax multiplier? These questions are about the multiplier effects on *equilibrium real GDP*, not just on aggregate demand.

President Obama's chief economic advisor in 2009, Christina Romer, a University of California, Berkeley, professor, expected the government expenditure multiplier to be about 1.5. So she was expecting the spending increase of $500 billion to go a long way towards closing the $1 trillion output gap by some time in 2010.

Robert Barro, a professor at Harvard University, says this multiplier number is not in line with previous experience. Based on his calculations, an additional $500 billion of government spending would increase aggregate expenditure by only $250 billion because it would lower private spending in a crowding-out effect by $250 billion—the multiplier is 0.5.

Harald Uhlig, a professor at the University of Chicago, says that the government expenditure multiplier on real GDP is even smaller and lies between 0.3 and 0.4, so that a $500 billion increase in government spending increases aggregate expenditure by between $150 billion and $200 billion.

determine the amount of stimulus needed to close a given output gap. Further, the actual output gap is not known and can only be estimated with error. For these two reasons, discretionary fiscal policy is risky.

Time Lags Discretionary fiscal stimulus actions are also seriously hampered by three time lags:

- Recognition lag
- Law-making lag
- Impact lag

Recognition Lag The *recognition lag* is the time it takes to figure out that fiscal policy actions are needed. This process involves assessing the current state of the economy and forecasting its future state.

There is greater agreement about tax multipliers. Because tax cuts strengthen the incentive to work and to invest, they increase aggregate supply as well as aggregate demand.

These multipliers get bigger as more time elapses. Harald Uhlig says that after one year, the tax multiplier is 0.5 so that the $300 billion tax cut would increase real GDP by about $150 billion after 1 year. But with two years of time to respond, real GDP would be $600 billion higher—a multiplier of 2. And after three years, the tax multiplier builds up to more than 6.

The implications of the work of Barro and Uhlig are that tax cuts are a powerful way to stimulate real GDP and employment, but spending increases are not effective.

Christina Romer agrees that the economy didn't perform in line with a multiplier of 1.5 but says other factors deteriorated and without the fiscal stimulus the outcome would have been even worse.

Christina Romer: 1.5

Robert Barro: 0.5

Harald Uhlig: 0.4

Law-Making Lag The *law-making lag* is the time it takes Parliament to pass the laws needed to change taxes or spending. This process takes time because each member of Parliament has a different idea about what is the best tax or spending program to change, so long debates and committee meetings are needed to reconcile conflicting views. The economy might benefit from fiscal stimulation today, but by the time Parliament acts, a different fiscal medicine might be needed.

Impact Lag The *impact lag* is the time it takes from passing a tax or spending change to its effects on real GDP being felt. This lag depends partly on the speed with which government agencies can act and partly on the timing of changes in spending plans by households and businesses. These changes are spread out over a number of quarters and possibly years.

Economic forecasting is steadily improving, but it remains inexact and subject to error. The range of uncertainty about the magnitudes of the spending and tax multipliers make discretionary fiscal stimulus an imprecise tool for boosting production and jobs and the consequences of crowding out raise serious questions about the effects of fiscal stimulus on long-term economic growth.

◆ REVIEW QUIZ

1 What is the distinction between automatic and discretionary fiscal policy?
2 How do taxes and transfer payments programs work as automatic fiscal policy to dampen the business cycle?
3 How do we tell whether a budget deficit needs discretionary action to remove it?
4 How can the federal government use discretionary fiscal policy to stimulate the economy?
5 Why might fiscal stimulus crowd out investment?

Work these questions in Study Plan 29.3 and get instant feedback. Do a Key Terms Quiz.   MyEconLab

◆ You've now seen the effects of fiscal policy, and *Economics in the News* on pp. 720–721 applies what you've learned to examine Japan's extreme situation and the fiscal policy challenge it faces.

A Fiscal Policy Challenge

Japanese Debt: Still Climbing

The Financial Times
March 24, 2014

Last summer Takeshi Fujimaki ran for parliament on a platform of economic Armageddon. Japan's debt was out of control, he told voters, and it was only a matter of time before everyone dumped government bonds, sending yields soaring, and the yen skittering all the way to 1,000 against the dollar. …

Mr. Fujimaki is not a lone crank. Although few share his sense of abject despair, no one disputes that Japan's debt is worryingly high. The International Monetary Fund and OECD both warn that deep cuts to spending must be made, beyond the government's basic pledge to balance its books—excluding debt-servicing costs—by 2020. …

Last … week the Diet [Japan's Parliament] waved through its biggest budget for the fiscal year ahead. Gross debt issuance comes to a record Y182tn ($1.78tn), about the same size as the economy of India. …

Mr. Abe is going all-out for growth because he has to. Barring the type of scenario outlined by Mr Fujimaki, only growth can fix its debt problem. …

State finances have deteriorated partly because of demography. Social security payments to a fast-ageing population have nearly tripled since 1990 to Y31tn—about a third of the total budget—in the fiscal year beginning in April. …

But the real problem is that as the economy languished, Japan collected less and less tax, forcing the state to borrow to plug gaps between income and expenditure. …

Written by Ben McLannahan. Copyright © 2014. Used under licence from *The Financial Times*. All rights reserved.

ESSENCE OF THE STORY

- Since 1990, slow real GDP growth has lowered tax revenues, a fast-aging population has nearly tripled social security payments, and Japan's government debt has soared.

- Only faster real GDP growth or inflation can fix Japan's debt problem.

- The government has pledged to have no deficit—excluding debt interest—by 2020.

- The IMF and OECD say even deeper government spending cuts must be made.

- In March 2014, the Diet (parliament) passed its biggest budget ever, spending 182 trillion yen ($1.78 trillion).

MyEconLab More Economics in the News

ECONOMIC ANALYSIS

- Japan's fiscal policy challenge described in the news article is finding a way to stop and then reverse an ever-rising government debt ratio—government debt as a percentage of GDP.

- Figure 1 shows the scale and upward direction of the problem. Gross debt was 250 percent of GDP in 2014, up from about 70 percent in 1990.

- The news article says that only faster growth or inflation can fix the debt problem. The debt ratio = Debt ÷ GDP. And GDP = PY, where P is the price level and Y is real GDP, so the debt ratio = Debt ÷ PY. Faster growth increases Y faster and inflation increases P faster, either of which lowers the debt ratio.

- There is a third way to fix the debt problem: Cut government spending. And that is the only effective way. The reason is that high government spending crowds out investment, and without an increase in investment real GDP cannot grow faster.

- Figure 2 shows how government spending has crowded out investment. In 1990, investment at 34 percent of GDP was larger than government spending (expenditure on goods and services and transfer payments) at 30 percent. By 2014, investment had shrunk to 20 percent and government spending had increased to 40 percent of GDP.

- The problem with cutting government spending is that in the short run, it decreases aggregate demand and widens the output gap.

- Figure 3 illustrates this short-run consequence of a government spending cut.

- In 2013, Japan's potential GDP was 537 trillion yen, shown by the long-run aggregate supply curve, LAS. The short-run aggregate supply curve was SAS.

- With the 2013 aggregate demand curve AD_0, real GDP was 525 trillion yen and the price level was 91 (91 percent of its 2009 level). Japan was experiencing stagnation and deflation.

- A fiscal policy aimed at cutting government spending and reducing the budget deficit by also increasing taxes would decrease aggregate demand.

- If aggregate demand decreased to AD_1, real GDP would decrease to 500 trillion yen and the recessionary gap would widen.

- Monetary policy might be used alongside fiscal policy to avoid this outcome and prevent real GDP from falling.

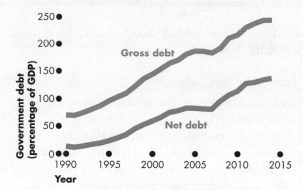

Figure 1 Japan's Government Debt

Figure 2 Crowding Out

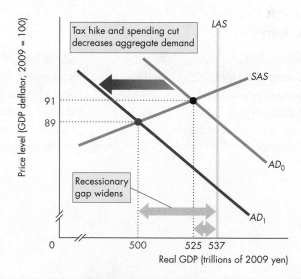

Figure 3 Short-Run Effects of Budget Cuts

- While Japan's fiscal policy problem is much more serious and extreme than that faced by other countries, it provides a valuable experiment from which others, including Canada, can learn.

SUMMARY

Key Points

The Federal Budget (pp. 704–709)

■ The federal budget is used to achieve macroeconomic objectives.

■ Revenues can exceed, equal, or fall short of outlays—the budget can be in surplus, balanced, or in deficit.

■ Budget deficits create government debt.

Working Problem 1 will give you a better understanding of the federal budget.

Supply-Side Effects of Fiscal Policy (pp. 710–713)

■ Fiscal policy has supply-side effects because taxes weaken the incentive to work and decrease employment and potential GDP.

■ The Canadian labour market tax wedge is similar to that in the United States, but smaller than that in France or the United Kingdom.

■ Fiscal policy has supply-side effects because taxes weaken the incentive to save and invest, which lowers the growth rate of real GDP.

■ The Laffer curve shows the relationship between the tax rate and the amount of tax revenue collected.

Working Problems 2 to 4 will give you a better understanding of the supply-side effects of fiscal policy.

Fiscal Stimulus (pp. 714–719)

■ Fiscal policy can be automatic or discretionary.

■ Automatic fiscal policy might moderate the business cycle by stimulating demand in a recession and restraining demand in a boom.

■ Discretionary fiscal stimulus influences aggregate demand *and* aggregate supply.

■ Discretionary changes in government expenditure or taxes have multiplier effects of uncertain magnitude, but the tax multiplier is likely the larger one.

■ Fiscal stimulus policies are hampered by uncertainty about the multipliers and by time lags (lawmaking lags and the difficulty of correctly diagnosing and forecasting the state of the economy).

Working Problems 5 to 11 will give you a better understanding of fiscal stimulus.

Key Terms   MyEconLab Key Terms Quiz

Automatic fiscal policy, 714
Balanced budget, 705
Budget deficit, 705
Budget surplus, 705
Cyclical surplus or deficit, 714
Discretionary fiscal policy, 714

Federal budget, 704
Fiscal policy, 704
Fiscal stimulus, 714
Government debt, 707
Government expenditure
  multiplier, 715

Laffer curve, 713
Structural surplus or deficit, 714
Tax multiplier, 716
Tax wedge, 711

WORKED PROBLEM

MyEconLab   You can work this problem in Chapter 29 Study Plan.

The economy is at full employment, the inflation rate is 2 percent a year, and the government has a budget deficit. The government wants to make real GDP grow faster and is debating whether to spend more on infrastructure or to cut income taxes.

Questions

1. What would be the short-run effects of new infrastructure expenditure?
2. What would be the long-run effects of new infrastructure expenditure?
3. How would lower income taxes change the macroeconomic variables?
4. Which policy would increase the economic growth rate?

Solutions

1. With no change in government receipts, infrastructure expenditure will increase government outlays and the budget deficit. To fund the infrastructure work, the government goes to the loanable funds market. The demand for loanable funds increases and, with no change in the supply of loanable funds, the real interest rate rises. A higher real interest rate increases private saving and decreases private investment. The increased government expenditure crowds out some private investment.

    Aggregate demand increases by an amount equal to the infrastructure expenditure minus the crowded-out private investment plus the induced increase in consumption expenditure. With no change in aggregate supply, real GDP increases to above full employment and creates an inflationary gap.

Key Point: In the short run, a change in government expenditure changes the budget balance, the real interest rate, the quantities of private saving and private investment, aggregate demand, real GDP, and the output gap.

2. Two further things change in the long run.
    (1) An inflationary gap makes the money wage rate rise, and (2) the increase in infrastructure capital increases potential GDP.

    The higher money wage rate decreases short-run aggregate supply and the increase in potential GDP lessens that decrease. The price level rises, and real GDP decreases to its new, higher full-employment level.

Key Point: An output gap brings changes in the labour market and the goods market, and increased capital increases potential GDP. In the long run, real GDP is at a higher full-employment equilibrium.

3. A cut in the tax rate on wage income increases the supply of labour, increases the quantity of labour employed, and increases potential GDP. A cut in the tax rate on interest income increases saving and investment, increases the quantity of capital, and increases potential GDP.

    Lower tax receipts increase the budget deficit, which sends the government to the loanable funds market. The demand for loanable funds increases, which lessens the effect of the cut in the tax on interest income.

    In the short run, the tax cut increases aggregate demand and brings an inflationary gap, which increases the money wage rate and decreases short-run aggregate supply.

    In the long run, the economy returns to full-employment equilibrium, but one in which more people are employed and real GDP is larger.

Key Point: A change in the income tax rate changes the labour market equilibrium and the loanable funds market equilibrium. Employment, private investment, and potential GDP change.

4. A change in the real GDP growth rate is a long-run effect.

    In the long run, an increase in infrastructure capital increases potential GDP and crowds out private investment, which decreases potential GDP. If the crowding out is incomplete, a larger capital stock increases potential GDP. To make real GDP grow faster, capital must keep increasing at a faster pace. A one-shot expenditure on new infrastructure does not have this effect.

    A lower tax rate on interest income increases private investment, the rate of capital accumulation, and the growth rate of real GDP.

Key Point: A one-shot investment in infrastructure increases real GDP but not economic growth. A cut in the tax rate on interest income increases investment, which increases the rate of capital accumulation and the real GDP growth rate.

STUDY PLAN PROBLEMS AND APPLICATIONS

MyEconLab   You can work Problems 1 to 11 in Chapter 29 Study Plan and get instant feedback.

The Federal Budget (Study Plan 29.1)

1. At the end of 2011, China's government debt was ¥4,700 billion (¥ is yuan, the currency of China). In 2012, the government spent ¥6,000 billion and ended the year with a debt of ¥5,300 billion. How much did the government receive in tax revenue in 2012? How can you tell?

Supply-Side Effects of Fiscal Policy (Study Plan 29.2)

2. The government is considering raising the tax rate on labour income and asks you to report on the supply-side effects of such an action. Use appropriate graphs and report *directions* of change, not exact magnitudes. What will happen to:
   a. The supply of labour and why?
   b. The demand for labour and why?
   c. Equilibrium employment and why?
   d. The equilibrium before-tax wage rate and why?
   e. The equilibrium after-tax wage rate and why?
   f. Potential GDP?

3. What fiscal policy action might increase investment and speed economic growth? Explain how the policy action would work.

4. Suppose that instead of taxing *nominal* capital income, the government taxed *real* capital income. Use graphs to explain and illustrate the effect that this change would have on:
   a. The tax rate on capital income.
   b. The supply of and demand for loanable funds.
   c. Investment and the real interest rate.

Fiscal Stimulus (Study Plan 29.3)

5. The economy is in a recession, and the recessionary gap is large.
   a. Describe the discretionary and automatic fiscal policy actions that might occur.
   b. Describe a discretionary fiscal stimulus package that could be used that would not bring an increase in the budget deficit.
   c. Explain the risks of discretionary fiscal policy in this situation.

6. The economy is in a recession, the recessionary gap is large, and there is a budget deficit.
   a. Do we know whether the budget deficit is structural or cyclical? Explain your answer and use a graph to illustrate it.
   b. Do we know whether automatic fiscal policy is increasing or decreasing the output gap? Explain your answer.
   c. If a discretionary increase in government expenditure occurs, what happens to the structural deficit or surplus? Explain.

Use the following news clip to work Problems 7 and 8.

Flaherty Eyes Early Surplus

Jim Flaherty tabled a 2011 budget with a deficit for this year gradually falling to a surplus in 2015. Mr. Flaherty said the budget aims to find that balance between helping Canadian families and businesses and securing economic growth.

Source: *Financial Post*, March 22, 2011

7. What would be the effect of the budget deficit of 2011 on real GDP and jobs?

8. Explain the effect on real GDP and jobs of the government's commitment to cut its budget deficit over the next four years.

Use the following news clip to work Problems 9 to 11.

Recession Threat Demands Immediate Action

The NDP called for immediate action to create jobs by investing in infrastructure and green energy programs to give the economy a kickstart. It needs more than corporate tax cuts, the NDP said.

Source: *CBC News*, September 29, 2011

9. Is the NDP's proposed infrastructure spending a fiscal stimulus? Would such spending be a discretionary or an automatic fiscal policy?

10. Explain whether, and if so how, "investing in infrastructure and green energy programs" would create jobs. Use graphs to illustrate your answer.

11. What would have a larger effect on aggregate demand: corporate tax cuts or an equivalent scale increase in government expenditure on infrastructure and green energy projects?

ADDITIONAL PROBLEMS AND APPLICATIONS

MyEconLab   You can work these problems in MyEconLab if assigned by your instructor.

The Federal Budget

12. **Federal Deficit Narrows to $4.4 billion**

    After the first two months of the current fiscal year, Canada's deficit sits at $4.4 billion, compared with $7.5 billion in the same period of 2009 when the economy was still in recession. The government projects that the budget shortfall of $54 billion it had at the end of the last fiscal year will shrink to just over $49 billion this year.

    Source: *Globe and Mail*, July 29, 2010

    Of the components of government outlays and revenues, which have changed most to contribute to shrinking the deficit during 2009 and 2010?

Supply-Side Effects of Fiscal Policy

Use the following information to work Problems 13 and 14.

Suppose that investment is $160 billion, saving is $140 billion, government expenditure on goods and services is $150 billion, exports are $200 billion, and imports are $250 billion.

13. What is the amount of tax revenue? What is the government budget balance?

14. a. Is the government's budget exerting a positive or negative impact on investment?

    b. What fiscal policy action might increase investment and speed economic growth? Explain how the policy action would work.

15. Suppose that capital income taxes are based (as they are in Canada and most countries) on nominal interest rates. If the inflation rate increases by 5 percent a year, explain and use appropriate graphs to illustrate the effect of the rise in inflation on:

    a. The tax increase on capital income
    b. The supply of loanable funds
    c. The demand for loanable funds
    d. Equilibrium investment
    e. The equilibrium real interest rate

16. **How Did the Global Recession Affect Canada's Economy?**

    Canada weathered the global financial crisis and recession better than many of its peers, principally as a result of the better policies and regulations already in place. Canada was in a much stronger position going into the recession thanks to its low and declining government debt and budget surpluses. The design of government policy and the speed of the policy response can make a huge difference in preventing or mitigating the worst of a recession.

    Source: Conference Board of Canada, March 2011

    a. Explain the potential demand-side effects of "low and declining government debt and budget surpluses."

    b. Explain the potential supply-side effects of "low and declining government debt and budget surpluses."

    c. Draw a graph to illustrate the combined demand-side and supply-side effects of "low and declining government debt and budget surpluses."

Use the following information to work Problems 17 and 18.

Job Creationism

William Watson, an economics professor at McGill University, Montreal, says there's nothing magical, mystical, or personal about job creation. It occurs when someone who wants to sell a product or service contracts with someone else to help them do it. It's not rocket science. To create jobs, the most obvious imperative is "Do no harm." Don't complicate, regulate, or overtax it.

Source: *Financial Post*, October 13, 2011

17. Does William Watson think that job creation is primarily a problem that needs an increase in aggregate demand or aggregate supply?

18. Explain how lowering taxes on employment will create jobs. Use a graph to illustrate your answer.

Fiscal Stimulus

19. The economy is in a boom and the inflationary gap is large.

    a. Describe the discretionary and automatic fiscal policy actions that might occur.

    b. Describe a discretionary fiscal restraint package that could be used that would not produce serious negative supply-side effects.

    c. Explain the risks of discretionary fiscal policy in this situation.

20. The economy is growing slowly, the inflationary gap is large, and there is a budget deficit.

    a. Do we know whether the budget deficit is structural or cyclical? Explain your choice and sketch a graph to illustrate your answer.

    b. Do we know whether automatic fiscal policy is increasing or decreasing aggregate demand? Explain your answer.

    c. If a discretionary decrease in government expenditure occurs, what happens to the structural budget balance? Explain your answer.

Use the following news clip to work Problems 21 to 23.

Is Fiscal Stimulus Necessary?

China's economy is slowing from its normal 9 percent or higher economic growth rate to just below 9 percent. The source of the slowdown is the global economic slowdown that is restricting exports growth and the government's deliberate decision to discourage unproductive investment. The situation now is not like that in 2008 when real GDP growth dropped from 9 percent to 6.8 percent and fiscal stimulus does not appear to be urgently needed.

Source: *China Daily*, June 8, 2012

21. Explain why fiscal stimulus was needed in 2008 but not in 2012.

22. Would you expect automatic fiscal policy to be having an effect in 2012? If so, what effects might it have?

23. Why might stimulus come too late? What are the potential consequences of stimulus coming too late?

Economics in the News

24. After you have studied *Economics in the News* on pp. 720–721, answer the following questions.

    a. What was the state of the Japanese economy in 2013?

    b. Explain the effects of Japan's high level of government spending and debt on the level of employment and potential GDP.

    c. Explain how inflation and faster growth might lower Japan's government debt ratio, and why neither is an attractive option.

    d. Explain how monetary policy might be used to offset a decrease in aggregate demand that a contractionary fiscal policy induced and draw a graph to illustrate your answer.

25. **More Fiscal Stimulus Needed?**

    In *The New York Times* articles and in blogs, economists Paul Krugman and Joseph Stiglitz say that, with slow recovery from recession, there is a need for more fiscal stimulus in both the United States and Europe despite the large federal budget deficit and large deficits in some European countries.

    a. Do you agree with Krugman and Stiglitz? Why?

    b. What are the dangers of not engaging in further fiscal stimulus?

    c. What are the dangers of embarking on further fiscal stimulus when the budget is in deficit?

26. **Cameron Urges Swift Eurozone Debt Action**

    U.K. Prime Minister David Cameron on Monday warned that "time was short" for Eurozone leaders bidding to solve a debt crisis. Cameron called on Germany to accept the "collective responsibility" of the euro project and beef up the zone's 440-billion-euro ($589-billion) bailout fund.

    Source: AFP, October 11, 2011

    a. How does a large budget deficit that brings a large debt-to-GDP ratio create a "debt crisis"?

    b. What are the alternative ways in which a Eurozone nation can address its debt crisis?

    c. What is the dilemma facing a country with a debt crisis and a recession?

30

MONETARY POLICY

After studying this chapter, you will be able to:

◆ Describe Canada's monetary policy objective and the framework for setting and achieving it

◆ Explain how the Bank of Canada makes its interest rate decision and achieves its interest rate target

◆ Explain the transmission channels through which the Bank of Canada influences real GDP, jobs, and inflation

◆ Explain the Bank of Canada's extraordinary policy actions

How does the Bank of Canada make its interest rate decision? How does a change in the Bank's interest rate influence the economy? Can the Bank speed up economic growth and lower unemployment by lowering the interest rate, and can the Bank keep inflation in check by raising the interest rate?

You learned about the functions of the Bank of Canada and its long-run effects on the price level and the inflation rate in Chapter 24. In this chapter, you will learn about the Bank's monetary policy strategy and its influence on the economy. In *Economics in the News* at the end of the chapter, you will see how the Bank of Canada tries to close a recessionary gap and bring the economy to full employment.

◀ Monetary Policy Objectives and Framework

Canada's monetary policy objective and the framework for setting and achieving that objective stem from the relationship between the Bank of Canada and the Government of Canada.

We'll first discuss the objective of monetary policy and then describe the framework and assignment of responsibility for achieving the objective.

Monetary Policy Objective

The objective of monetary policy is ultimately political, and it stems from the mandate of the Bank, which is set out in the Bank of Canada Act.

Bank of Canada Act The objective of monetary policy as set out in the preamble to the Bank of Canada Act of 1935 is as follows:

> To regulate credit and currency in the best interests of the economic life of the nation ... and to mitigate by its influence fluctuations in the general level of production, trade, prices and employment, so far as may be possible within the scope of monetary action ...

In simple language, these words have come to mean that the Bank's job is to control the quantity of money and interest rates in order to avoid inflation and, when possible, prevent excessive swings in real GDP growth and unemployment.

This emphasis on inflation has been made concrete by an agreement between the Bank and the government.

Joint Statement of the Government of Canada and the Bank of Canada In a joint statement (the most recent of which was made in 2011), the Government of Canada and the Bank of Canada agree that:

- The target will continue to be defined in terms of the 12-month rate of change in the total CPI.
- The inflation target will continue to be the 2 percent midpoint of the 1 to 3 percent inflation-control range.
- The agreement will run for another five-year period, ending December 31, 2016.

A monetary policy strategy in which the central bank commits to an explicit inflation target and to explaining how its actions will achieve that target is called **inflation rate targeting**.

Interpretation of the Agreement The inflation-control target uses the Consumer Price Index (or CPI) as the measure of inflation. So the Bank has agreed to keep trend CPI inflation at a target of 2 percent a year.

But the Bank also pays close attention to core inflation (see pp. 502–503), which it calls its operational guide. The Bank believes that the core inflation rate provides a better measure of the underlying inflation trend and better predicts future CPI inflation.

Although the Bank watches the core inflation rate closely, it must take into account the possibility that the eight volatile elements that it excludes have a different trend inflation rate from the remaining items. As it turns out, between 1995 and 2000, the core and overall CPI trends were very similar. Since 2000, the core rate has averaged 0.3 percent per year below the overall CPI inflation rate.

Actual Inflation The performance of Canada's inflation since the mid-1990s, when the current target was initially set, has been close to target. Figure 30.1 shows just how close.

In part (a), you can see the target range of 1 to 3 percent a year. And you can see that the actual inflation rate has only rarely gone outside the target range. You can also see that the inflation rate has been both above target and below target on occasion, so there is no bias or tendency for inflation to be persistently above or below target.

In part (b), you can see the trend of inflation at the 2 percent target midpoint. The CPI was on trend from 1995 through 1998 and again from 2001 through 2007. Between 1999 and 2001, and after 2008, the CPI was below the 2 percent trend line.

The general message of Fig. 30.1 is that the Bank of Canada has done a remarkable job of holding inflation to its 2 percent target with only small and temporary deviations from that goal.

Rationale for an Inflation-Control Target Two main benefits flow from adopting an inflation-control target. The first benefit is that the purpose of the Bank of Canada's policy actions is more clearly understood by financial market traders. A clearer understanding

FIGURE 30.1 Inflation-Control Target and Outcome

(a) Inflation target and outcome

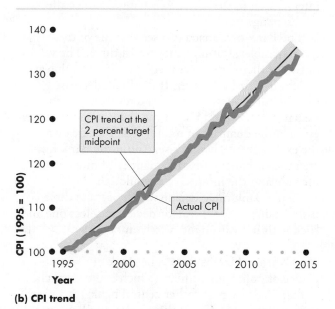

(b) CPI trend

The Bank of Canada and the Government of Canada agree that the inflation-control target range will be 1 percent to 3 percent in part (a) and that policy will aim at keeping the trend of inflation at the 2 percent target midpoint in part (b).

Sources of data: Statistics Canada, CANSIM Table 326-0020, and Bank of Canada, Joint Statement of the Government of Canada and the Bank of Canada on the Renewal of the Inflation-Control Target, November 23, 2006.

———— MyEconLab Animation ————

leads to fewer surprises and mistakes on the part of savers and investors.

The second benefit is that the target provides an anchor for expectations about future inflation. Firmly held expectations of low inflation make the short-run output-inflation (or unemployment-inflation) tradeoff as favourable as possible. (See Chapter 28, pp. 692–693.) Firmly held (and correct) inflation expectations also help to make better economic decisions, which in turn help to achieve a more efficient allocation of resources and more stable economic growth.

Controversy About the Inflation-Control Target Not everyone agrees that the adoption of an inflation-control target brings benefits. Critics argue that by focusing on inflation, the Bank of Canada sometimes permits the unemployment rate to rise or the real GDP growth rate to suffer.

The fear of these critics is that if the inflation rate begins to edge upward towards and perhaps beyond the upper limit of the target range, the Bank of Canada might rein in aggregate demand and push the economy into recession. Related, the Bank might end up permitting the value of the dollar on the foreign exchange market to rise, which will make exports suffer.

One response of supporters of inflation targeting is that by keeping inflation low and stable, monetary policy makes its maximum possible contribution towards achieving full employment and sustained economic growth.

Another response is, "Look at the record." The last time the Bank of Canada created a recession was at the beginning of the 1990s when it was faced with the threat of ongoing double-digit inflation. Since that time, monetary policy has been sensitive to the state of employment while maintaining its focus on achieving its inflation target.

Responsibility for Monetary Policy

The Government of Canada and the Bank of Canada jointly agree on the monetary policy target, but the Bank of Canada Act places responsibility for the conduct of monetary policy on the Bank's Governing Council.

Governing Council of the Bank of Canada The members of the Bank's Governing Council are the Governor, Senior Deputy Governor, and four Deputy

Governors. All the members of the Governing Council are experts in monetary economics and monetary policymaking and, normally, they are people who have been promoted from within the ranks of economists working in the Bank's research and policy departments.

The current Governor (appointed in 2013) is Stephen Poloz, an economist who has had wide experience at the Bank of Canada, in the private sector, at the IMF, and at Export Development Canada.

Bank of Canada Economists The Bank of Canada employs research economists who write papers on monetary policy and the state of the Canadian and international economies. These economists provide the Governing Council with extensive briefings that guide monetary policy.

Consultations with the Government The Bank of Canada Act requires regular consultations on monetary policy between the Governor and the Minister of Finance. The Act also lays out what must happen if the Governor and the Minister disagree in a profound way.

In such an event, the Minister would direct the Bank in writing to follow a specified course and the Bank would be obliged to accept the directive. The Governor would most likely resign in such a situation. While in the past there have been disagreements between the government and the Bank, no formal directive has ever been issued.

You now know the objective of monetary policy and can describe the framework and assignment of responsibility for achieving that objective. Your next task is to see how the Bank of Canada conducts its monetary policy.

REVIEW QUIZ

1 What is the Bank of Canada's monetary policy objective?
2 What are the two parts of the inflation-control target?
3 How does the core inflation rate differ from the overall CPI inflation rate?
4 What is the Bank of Canada's record in achieving its inflation-control target?

Work these questions in Study Plan 30.1 and get instant feedback. Do a Key Terms Quiz.   MyEconLab

◢ The Conduct of Monetary Policy

We're now going to describe how the Bank of Canada conducts its monetary policy. To do so, we're going to answer three questions:

- What is the Bank's monetary policy instrument?
- How does the Bank make its policy decision?
- How does the Bank implement its policy?

The Monetary Policy Instrument

As the sole issuer of Canadian money, the Bank of Canada can decide to control the quantity of money (the monetary base), the price of Canadian money on the foreign exchange market (the exchange rate), or the opportunity cost of holding money (the short-term interest rate). If you need a refresher, check back to Chapter 24, p. 581 to see how the quantity of money affects the interest rate and to Chapter 25, pp. 604–606 to see how the interest rate or direct intervention in the foreign exchange market affects the exchange rate.

The Bank of Canada can set any one of these three variables, but it cannot set all three. The values of two of them are the consequence of the value at which the third one is set. If the Bank decreased the quantity of money, both the interest rate and the exchange rate would rise. If the Bank raised the interest rate, the quantity of money would decrease and the exchange rate would rise. And if the Bank lowered the exchange rate, the quantity of money would increase and the interest rate would fall.

So the Bank must decide which of these three instruments to use. It might decide to select one and stick with it, or it might switch among them.

The Overnight Loans Rate The Bank of Canada's choice of policy instrument (which is the same choice as that made by most other central banks) is a short-term interest rate. Given this choice, the Bank permits the exchange rate and the quantity of money to find their own equilibrium values and has no preset views about what those values should be.

The specific interest rate that the Bank of Canada targets is the **overnight loans rate**, which is the interest rate on overnight loans that the big banks make to each other.

Figure 30.2 shows the overnight loans rate since 1995. The overnight rate was a bit more than 8 percent a year in 1995 and it was twice increased to around 6 percent and once to 4 percent. These

FIGURE 30.2   The Overnight Loans Rate

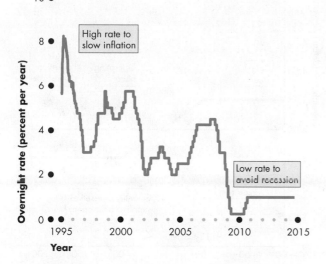

The Bank of Canada sets a target for the overnight loans rate and then takes actions to keep the rate close to its target. When the Bank wants to slow inflation, it raises the overnight loans rate. When inflation is low and the Bank wants to avoid recession, it lowers the overnight loans rate.

Source of data: Statistics Canada, CANSIM Table 176–0048.

————————————————— MyEconLab Animation ————

periods with a high overnight loans rate are ones in which inflation was a concern.

In recent years, the overnight loans rate has been at historically low levels. The reason is that with inflation well anchored inside its target range, the Bank wanted to lean in the direction of avoiding recession.

Since 2000, the Bank has established eight fixed dates on which it announces its overnight loans rate target for the coming period of approximately six weeks. Before 2000, the Bank announced changes in the overnight loans rate whenever it thought a change was required. And even now, the Bank sometimes acts in an emergency between normal announcement dates.

Although the Bank can change the overnight loans rate by any (reasonable) amount that it chooses, it normally changes the rate by only a quarter of a percentage point.[1]

How does the Bank decide the appropriate level for the overnight loans rate?

———————————————

[1] A quarter of a percentage point is also called 25 *basis points*. A basis point is one hundredth of one percentage point.

The Bank's Interest Rate Decision

To make its interest rate decision, the Bank of Canada gathers a large amount of data about the economy, the way it responds to shocks, and the way it responds to policy. It then processes all this data and comes to a judgment about the best level for the overnight loans rate.

The Bank's staff economists use a model of the Canadian economy—a sophisticated version of the aggregate supply–aggregate demand model—to provide the Governor and Governing Council with a baseline forecast. All the available regional, national, and international data on macroeconomic performance, financial markets, and inflation expectations are reviewed, discussed, and weighed in a careful deliberative process that ends with the Governing Council finding a consensus on the interest rate level to set.

After announcing an interest rate decision, the Bank engages in a public communication to explain the reasons for its decision. Twice a year the Bank publishes a highly detailed *Inflation Report* that describes the forces operating on the economy, the outlook for inflation and real GDP growth, and the reasons for the Bank's interest rate decision.

Having made an interest rate decision, how does the Bank ensure that the overnight rate is on target?

Hitting the Overnight Loans Rate Target

Once an interest rate decision is made, the Bank of Canada achieves its target by using two tools: the operating band and open market operations.

The **operating band** is the target overnight loans rate plus or minus 0.25 percentage points. The Bank creates the operating band by setting two other interest rates: *bank rate* and a rate called the *settlement balances rate*.

Bank rate is the interest rate that the Bank of Canada charges big banks on loans. If a bank is short of reserves, it can always obtain reserves from the Bank of Canada, but the bank must pay bank rate on the amount of borrowed reserves.

The Bank of Canada sets bank rate at the target overnight loans rate plus 0.25 percentage points. Because the Bank of Canada is willing to lend funds to banks at this interest rate, bank rate acts as a cap on the overnight loans rate. If a bank can borrow from the Bank of Canada at bank rate, it will not borrow from another bank unless the interest rate is lower than or equal to bank rate.

The Bank of Canada pays banks interest on their reserves at the Bank of Canada—called the **settlement balances rate**—set at the target overnight loans rate minus 0.25 percentage points. Banks won't make overnight loans to other banks unless they earn a higher interest rate than what the Bank is paying.

The alternative to lending in the overnight market is to hold reserves. And the alternative to borrowing in the overnight market is to hold smaller reserves. The demand for reserves is the flip side of lending and borrowing in the overnight market.

Figure 30.3 shows the demand curve for reserves as the curve labelled *RD*. If the entire banking system is borrowing from the Bank of Canada, reserves are negative (on the *x*-axis). If the overnight rate (on the *y*-axis) equals bank rate, banks are indifferent between borrowing reserves and lending reserves. The demand curve is horizontal at bank rate. If the overnight rate equals the settlement balances rate, banks are indifferent between holding reserves and lending reserves. The demand curve is horizontal at the settlement balances rate.

You can see that the overnight loans rate always lies inside the operating band.

The overnight loans rate cannot exceed bank rate because if it did, a bank could earn a profit by borrowing from the Bank of Canada and lending to another bank. But all banks can borrow from the Bank of Canada at bank rate, so no bank is willing to pay more than bank rate to borrow reserves.

The overnight loans rate cannot fall below the settlement balances rate because if it did, a bank could earn a profit by borrowing from another bank and increasing its reserves at the Bank of Canada. But all banks can earn the settlement balances rate at the Bank of Canada, so no bank is willing to lend reserves at a rate below the settlement balances rate.

The Bank of Canada's open market operations determine the actual quantity of reserves in the banking system, and equilibrium in the market for reserves determines the actual overnight loans rate. (We describe how an operation works to change the monetary base in Chapter 24, pp. 572–574.)

If the overnight loans rate is above target, the Bank buys securities to increase reserves, which increases the supply of overnight funds and lowers the overnight rate. If the overnight loans rate is below target, the Bank sells securities to decrease reserves, which decreases the supply of overnight funds and raises the overnight rate. If the overnight loans rate is at the target level, the Bank neither buys nor sells. By using

FIGURE 30.3   The Market for Reserves

The demand curve for reserves is *RD*. If the overnight loans rate equals bank rate, banks are indifferent between borrowing reserves and lending reserves. The demand curve is horizontal at bank rate. If the overnight loans rate equals the settlement balances rate, banks are indifferent between holding reserves and lending reserves. The demand curve is horizontal at the settlement balances rate. Equilibrium, where the quantity of reserves demanded equals the quantity supplied, determines the overnight loans rate.

MyEconLab Animation

open market operations, the Bank of Canada keeps the overnight loan rate on target.

REVIEW QUIZ

1 What is the Bank of Canada's monetary policy instrument?
2 Summarize the Bank of Canada's monetary policy decision-making process.
3 What is the operating band?
4 What happens when the Bank of Canada buys securities in the open market?
5 How is the overnight rate determined in the market for bank reserves?

Work these questions in Study Plan 30.2 and get instant feedback. Do a Key Terms Quiz.   MyEconLab

◢ Monetary Policy Transmission

You've seen that the Bank of Canada's goal is to keep the inflation rate as close as possible to 2 percent a year. And you've seen how the Bank can use its policy tools to keep the overnight loans rate at its desired level.

We're now going to trace the events that follow a change in the overnight loans rate and see how those events lead to the ultimate policy goal—keeping inflation on target.

We'll begin with a quick overview of the transmission process and then look at each step a bit more closely.

Quick Overview

When the Bank of Canada wants to lower the overnight loans rate to a new target, it buys securities in the open market. Other short-term interest rates and the exchange rate also fall. The quantity of money and the supply of loanable funds increase. The long-term real interest rate falls. The lower real interest rate increases consumption expenditure and investment. And the lower exchange rate makes Canadian exports cheaper and imports more costly, so net exports increase. Easier bank loans reinforce the effect of lower interest rates on aggregate expenditure. Aggregate demand increases, which increases real GDP and the price level relative to what they would have been. Real GDP growth and inflation speed up.

When the Bank raises the overnight loans rate, it sells securities in the open market and as the sequence of events that we've just reviewed plays out, the effects are in the opposite directions.

Figure 30.4 provides a schematic summary of these ripple effects for both a cut and a rise in the overnight loans rate.

These ripple effects stretch out over a period of between one and two years. The interest rate and exchange rate effects are immediate. The effects on money and bank loans follow in a few weeks and run for a few months. Real long-term interest rates change quickly and often in anticipation of the short-term interest rate changes. Spending plans change and real GDP growth changes after about one year. The inflation rate changes between one year and two years after the change in the overnight loans rate. But these time lags are not entirely predictable and can be longer or shorter.

We're going to look at each stage in the transmission process, starting with the interest rate effects.

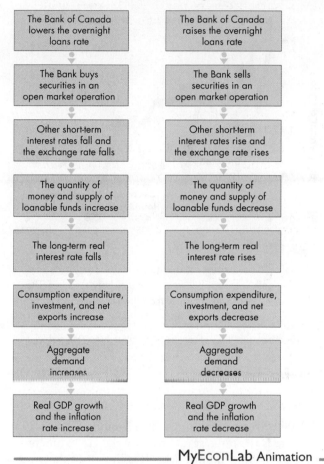

FIGURE 30.4 The Ripple Effects of a Change in the Overnight Loans Rate

The Bank of Canada lowers the overnight loans rate	The Bank of Canada raises the overnight loans rate
The Bank buys securities in an open market operation	The Bank sells securities in an open market operation
Other short-term interest rates fall and the exchange rate falls	Other short-term interest rates rise and the exchange rate rises
The quantity of money and supply of loanable funds increase	The quantity of money and supply of loanable funds decrease
The long-term real interest rate falls	The long-term real interest rate rises
Consumption expenditure, investment, and net exports increase	Consumption expenditure, investment, and net exports decrease
Aggregate demand increases	Aggregate demand decreases
Real GDP growth and the inflation rate increase	Real GDP growth and the inflation rate decrease

MyEconLab Animation

Interest Rate Changes

The first effect of a monetary policy decision by the Bank of Canada is a change in the overnight loans rate. Other interest rates then change. These interest rate effects occur quickly and relatively predictably.

Figure 30.5 shows the fluctuations in three interest rates: the overnight loans rate, the short-term bill rate, and the long-term bond rate.

Overnight Loans Rate As soon as the Bank of Canada announces a new setting for the overnight loans rate, it undertakes the necessary open market operations to hit the target. There is no doubt about where the interest rate changes shown in Fig. 30.5 are generated. They are driven by the Bank of Canada's monetary policy.

FIGURE 30.5   Three Interest Rates

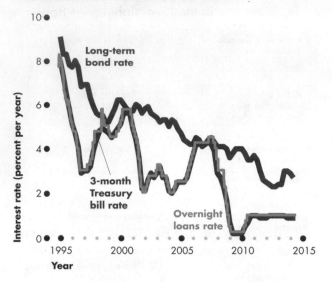

The short-term interest rates—the overnight loans rate and the 3-month Treasury bill rate—move closely together. The long-term bond rate is higher than the short-term rates, and it fluctuates less than the short-term rates.

Source of data: Statistics Canada, CANSIM Tables 176–0043 and 176–0048.

——————————— MyEconLab Animation ———

3-Month Treasury Bill Rate The 3-month Treasury bill rate is the interest rate paid by the Government of Canada on 3-month debt. It is similar to the interest rate paid by Canadian businesses on short-term loans. Notice how closely the 3-month Treasury bill rate follows the overnight loans rate. The two rates are almost identical.

A *powerful substitution effect* keeps these two interest rates close. Chartered banks have a choice about how to hold their short-term liquid assets, and an overnight loan to another bank is a close substitute for short-term securities such as Treasury bills. If the interest rate on Treasury bills is higher than the overnight loans rate, the quantity of overnight loans supplied decreases and the demand for Treasury bills increases. The price of Treasury bills rises and the interest rate falls.

Similarly, if the interest rate on Treasury bills is lower than the overnight loans rate, the quantity of overnight loans supplied increases and the demand for Treasury bills decreases. The price of Treasury bills falls and the interest rate rises.

When the interest rate on Treasury bills is close to the overnight loans rate, there is no incentive for a bank to switch between making an overnight loan and buying Treasury bills. Both the Treasury bill market and the overnight loans market are in equilibrium.

The Long-Term Bond Rate The long-term bond rate is the interest rate paid on bonds issued by large corporations. It is this interest rate that businesses pay on the loans that finance their purchase of new capital and that influences their investment decisions. Two features of the long-term bond rate stand out: It is higher than the short-term rates, and it fluctuates less than the short-term rates.

The long-term interest rate is higher than the two short-term rates because long-term loans are riskier than short-term loans. To provide the incentive that brings forth a supply of long-term loans, lenders must be compensated for the additional risk. Without compensation for the additional risk, only short-term loans would be supplied.

The long-term interest rate fluctuates less than the short-term rates because it is influenced by expectations about future short-term interest rates as well as current short-term interest rates. The alternative to borrowing or lending long term is to borrow or lend using a sequence of short-term securities. If the long-term interest rate exceeds the expected average of future short-term interest rates, people will lend long term and borrow short term. The long-term interest rate will fall. And if the long-term interest rate is below the expected average of future short-term interest rates, people will borrow long term and lend short term. The long-term interest rate will rise.

These market forces keep the long-term interest rate close to the expected average of future short-term interest rates (plus a premium for the extra risk associated with long-term loans). The expected average future short-term interest rate fluctuates less than the current short-term interest rate.

Exchange Rate Fluctuations

The exchange rate responds to changes in the interest rate in Canada relative to the interest rates in other countries—*the Canadian interest rate differential*. We explain this influence in Chapter 25 (see pp. 596–597).

When the Bank of Canada raises the overnight loans rate, the Canadian interest rate differential rises and, other things remaining the same, the Canadian dollar appreciates. And when the Bank lowers the overnight loans rate, the Canadian interest rate differential falls and, other things remaining the same, the Canadian dollar depreciates.

Many factors other than the Canadian interest rate differential influence the exchange rate, so when the Bank changes the overnight loans rate, the exchange rate does not usually change in exactly the way it would with other things remaining the same. So while monetary policy influences the exchange rate, many other factors also make the exchange rate change.

Money and Bank Loans

The quantity of money and bank loans change when the Bank changes the overnight loans rate target. A rise in the overnight loans rate decreases the quantity of money and bank loans, and a fall in the overnight loans rate increases the quantity of money and bank loans. These changes occur for two reasons: The quantity of deposits and loans created by the banking system changes and the quantity of money demanded changes.

You've seen that to change the overnight loans rate, the quantity of bank reserves must change. A change in the quantity of bank reserves changes the monetary base, which in turn changes the quantity of deposits and loans that the banking system can create. A rise in the overnight loans rate decreases reserves and decreases the quantity of deposits and bank loans created; and a fall in the overnight loans rate increases reserves and increases the quantity of deposits and bank loans created.

The quantity of money created by the banking system must be held by households and firms. The change in the interest rate changes the quantity of money demanded. A fall in the interest rate increases the quantity of money demanded; and a rise in the interest rate decreases the quantity of money demanded.

A change in the quantity of money and the supply of bank loans directly affects consumption and investment plans. With more money and easier access to loans, consumers and firms spend more; with less money and loans harder to get, consumers and firms spend less.

The Long-Term Real Interest Rate

Demand and supply in the loanable funds market determine the long-term *real interest rate*, which equals the long-term *nominal* interest rate minus the expected inflation rate. The long-term real interest rate influences expenditure decisions.

In the long run, demand and supply in the loanable funds market depend only on real forces—on saving and investment decisions. But in the short run, when the price level is not fully flexible, the supply of loanable funds is influenced by the supply of bank loans. Changes in the overnight loans rate change the supply of bank loans, which changes the supply of loanable funds and changes the interest rate in the loanable funds market.

A fall in the overnight loans rate that increases the supply of bank loans increases the supply of loanable funds and lowers the equilibrium real interest rate. A rise in the overnight loans rate that decreases the supply of bank loans decreases the supply of loanable funds and raises the equilibrium real interest rate.

These changes in the real interest rate, along with the other factors we've just described, change expenditure plans.

Expenditure Plans

The ripple effects that follow a change in the overnight loans rate change three components of aggregate expenditure:

- Consumption expenditure
- Investment
- Net exports

Consumption Expenditure Other things remaining the same, the lower the real interest rate, the greater is the amount of consumption expenditure and the smaller is the amount of saving.

Investment Other things remaining the same, the lower the real interest rate, the greater is the amount of investment.

Net Exports Other things remaining the same, the lower the interest rate, the lower is the exchange rate and the greater are exports and the smaller are imports.

So eventually, a cut in the overnight loans rate increases aggregate expenditure and a rise in the overnight loans rate curtails aggregate expenditure. These changes in aggregate expenditure plans change aggregate demand, real GDP, and the price level.

Change in Aggregate Demand, Real GDP, and the Price Level

The final link in the transmission chain is a change in aggregate demand and a resulting change in real GDP and the price level. By changing real GDP and the price level relative to what they would have been without a change in the overnight loans rate, the Bank of Canada influences its ultimate goals: the inflation rate and the output gap.

The Bank of Canada Fights Recession

If inflation is low and real GDP is below potential GDP, the Bank acts to restore full employment. Figure 30.6 shows the effects of the Bank's actions, starting in the market for bank reserves and ending in the market for real GDP.

Market for Bank Reserves In Fig. 30.6(a), which shows the market for bank reserves, the Bank lowers the target overnight loans rate from 5 percent to 4 percent a year. To achieve the new target, the Bank

buys securities and increases the supply of reserves of the banking system from RS_0 to RS_1.

Money Market With increased reserves, the banks create deposits by making loans and the supply of money increases. The short-term interest rate falls and the quantity of money demanded increases.

In Fig. 30.6(b), the supply of money increases from MS_0 to MS_1, the interest rate falls from 5 percent to 4 percent a year, and the quantity of money increases from $800 billion to $900 billion. The interest rate in the money market and the overnight loans rate are kept close to each other by the powerful substitution effect described on p. 734.

Loanable Funds Market Banks create money by making loans. In the long run, an increase in the supply of bank loans is matched by a rise in the price level and the quantity of *real* loans is unchanged. But in the short run, with a sticky price level, an increase in the supply of bank loans increases the supply of (real) loanable funds.

FIGURE 30.6   The Bank of Canada Fights Recession

(a) The market for bank reserves

In part (a), the Bank of Canada lowers the overnight loans rate target from 5 percent to 4 percent. The Bank buys securities in an open market operation and increases the supply of reserves from RS_0 to RS_1 to hit the new overnight loans rate target.

(b) Money market

In part (b), the supply of money increases from MS_0 to MS_1, the short-term interest rate falls, and the quantity of money demanded increases. The short-term interest rate and the overnight loans rate change by similar amounts.

In Fig. 30.6(c), the supply of loanable funds curve shifts rightward from SLF_0 to SLF_1. With the demand for loanable funds at DLF, the real interest rate falls from 6 percent to 5.5 percent a year. (We're assuming a zero inflation rate so that the real interest rate equals the nominal interest rate.) The long-term interest rate changes by a smaller amount than the change in the short-term interest rate for the reason explained on p. 734.

The Market for Real GDP Figure 30.6(d) shows aggregate demand and aggregate supply—the demand for and supply of real GDP. Potential GDP is $1.7 trillion, where LAS is located. The short-run aggregate supply curve is SAS, and initially, the aggregate demand curve is AD_0. Real GDP is $1.5 trillion, which is less than potential GDP, so there is a recessionary gap. The Bank of Canada is reacting to this recessionary gap.

The increase in the supply of loans and the decrease in the real interest rate increase aggregate planned expenditure. (Not shown in the figure, a fall

in the interest rate lowers the exchange rate, which increases net exports and aggregate planned expenditure.) The increase in aggregate expenditure, ΔE, increases aggregate demand and shifts the aggregate demand curve rightward to $AD_0 + \Delta E$. A multiplier process begins. The increase in expenditure increases income, which induces an increase in consumption expenditure. Aggregate demand increases further, and the aggregate demand curve eventually shifts rightward to AD_1.

The new equilibrium is at full employment. Real GDP is equal to potential GDP. The price level rises to 110 and then becomes stable at that level. So after a one-time adjustment, there is price stability.

In this example, the Bank of Canada makes a perfect hit, achieving full employment and a stable price level. It is unlikely that the Bank would be able to achieve the precision of this example. If the Bank stimulated demand by too little and too late, the economy would experience a recession. And if the Bank hit the gas pedal too hard, it would push the economy from recession to inflation.

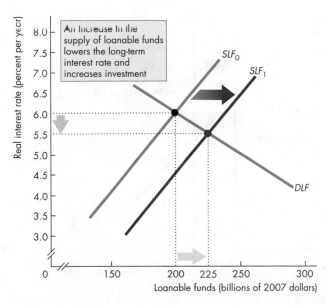

(c) The loanable funds market

In part (c), an increase in the supply of bank loans increases the supply of loanable funds and shifts the supply curve from SLF_0 to SLF_1. The real interest rate falls and investment increases.

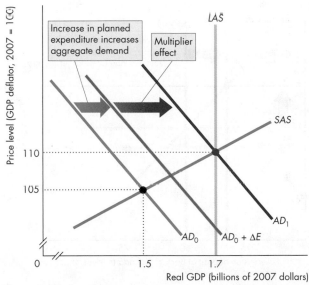

(d) Real GDP and the price level

In part (d), the increase in investment increases aggregate planned expenditure, and the aggregate demand curve shifts from AD_0 to $AD_0 + \Delta E$. Eventually, it shifts rightward to AD_1. Real GDP increases to potential GDP, and the price level rises.

MyEconLab Animation and Draw Graph

The Bank of Canada Fights Inflation

If the inflation rate is too high and real GDP is above potential GDP, the Bank takes actions that are designed to lower the inflation rate and restore price stability. Figure 30.7 shows the effects of the Bank's actions starting in the market for reserves and ending in the market for real GDP.

Market for Bank Reserves In Fig. 30.7(a), which shows the market for bank reserves, the Bank raises the target overnight loans rate from 5 percent to 6 percent a year. To achieve the new target, the Bank sells securities and decreases the supply of reserves of the banking system from RS_0 to RS_1.

Money Market With decreased reserves, the banks shrink deposits by decreasing loans and the supply of money decreases. The short-term interest rate rises and the quantity of money demanded decreases. In Fig. 30.7(b), the supply of money decreases from MS_0 to MS_1, the interest rate rises from 5 percent to

6 percent a year, and the quantity of money decreases from $800 billion to $700 billion.

Loanable Funds Market With a decrease in reserves, banks must decrease the supply of loans. The supply of (real) loanable funds decreases, and the supply of loanable funds curve shifts leftward in Fig. 30.7(c) from SLF_0 to SLF_1. With the demand for loanable funds at DLF, the real interest rate rises from 6 percent to 6.5 percent a year. (Again, we're assuming a zero inflation rate so that the real interest rate equals the nominal interest rate.)

The Market for Real GDP Figure 30.7(d) shows aggregate demand and aggregate supply in the market for real GDP. Potential GDP is $1.7 trillion where LAS is located. The short-run aggregate supply curve is SAS and initially the aggregate demand curve is AD_0. Now, real GDP is $1.8 trillion, which is greater than potential GDP, so there is an inflationary gap. The Bank is reacting to this inflationary gap.

FIGURE 30.7 The Bank of Canada Fights Inflation

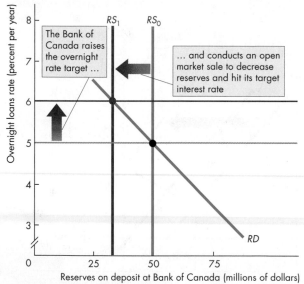

(a) The market for bank reserves

In part (a), the Bank of Canada raises the overnight loans rate from 5 percent to 6 percent. The Bank sells securities in an open market operation to decrease the supply of reserves from RS_0 to RS_1 and hit the new overnight loans rate target.

(b) Money market

In part (b), the supply of money decreases from MS_0 to MS_1, the short-term interest rate rises, and the quantity of money demanded decreases. The short-term interest rate and the overnight loans rate change by similar amounts.

The increase in the short-term interest rate, the decrease in the supply of bank loans, and the increase in the real interest rate decrease aggregate planned expenditure. (Not shown in the figures, a rise in the interest rate raises the exchange rate, which decreases net exports and aggregate planned expenditure.)

The decrease in aggregate expenditure, ΔE, decreases aggregate demand and shifts the aggregate demand curve to $AD_0 - \Delta E$. A multiplier process begins. The decrease in expenditure decreases income, which induces a decrease in consumption expenditure. Aggregate demand decreases further, and the aggregate demand curve eventually shifts leftward to AD_1.

The economy returns to full employment. Real GDP is equal to potential GDP. The price level falls to 110 and then becomes stable at that level. So after a one-time adjustment, there is price stability.

Again, in this example, we have given the Bank a perfect hit at achieving full employment and keeping the price level stable. If the Bank decreased aggregate demand by too little and too late, the economy would have remained with an inflationary gap and the inflation rate would have moved above the rate that is consistent with price stability. And if the Bank hit the brakes too hard, it would push the economy from inflation to recession.

Loose Links and Long and Variable Lags

The ripple effects of monetary policy that we've just analyzed with the precision of an economic model are, in reality, very hard to predict and anticipate.

To achieve price stability and full employment, the Bank needs a combination of good judgment and good luck. Too large an interest rate cut in an under-employed economy can bring inflation, as it did during the 1970s. And too large an interest rate rise in an inflationary economy can create unemployment, as it did in 1981 and 1991. Loose links between the overnight loans rate and the ultimate policy goals make unwanted outcomes inevitable, and long and variable time lags add to the Bank's challenges.

(c) The loanable funds market

In part (c), a decrease in the supply of bank loans decreases the supply of loanable funds and the supply curve shifts from SLF_0 to SLF_1. The real interest rate rises and investment decreases.

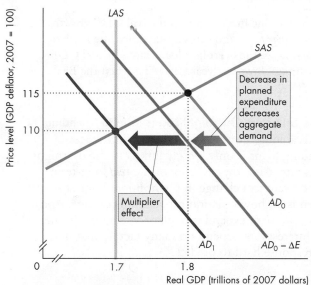

(d) Real GDP and the price level

In part (d), the decrease in investment decreases aggregate planned expenditure and the aggregate demand curve shifts from AD_0 to $AD_0 - \Delta E$. Eventually, it shifts leftward to AD_1. Real GDP decreases to potential GDP and the price level falls.

MyEconLab Animation and Draw Graph

Economics in Action

A View of the Long and Variable Lag

You've studied the theory of monetary policy. Does it really work in the way we've described? It does, and the figure opposite provides some evidence to support this claim.

The blue line in the figure is the overnight loans rate that the Bank of Canada targets *minus* the long-term bond rate. (When the long-term bond rate exceeds the overnight loans rate, this gap is negative.)

We can view the gap between the overnight loans rate and the long-term bond rate as a measure of how hard the Bank is trying to steer a change in the economy's course.

When the Bank is more concerned about recession than inflation and is trying to stimulate real GDP growth, it cuts the overnight loans rate target and the overnight loans rate minus the long-term bond rate falls.

When the Bank is more concerned about inflation than recession and is trying to restrain real GDP growth, it raises the overnight loans rate target and the the overnight loans rate minus the long-term bond rate rises.

The red line in the figure is the real GDP growth rate *one year later*. You can see that when the Bank of Canada raises the overnight loans rate, the real GDP growth rate slows one year later. And when the Bank

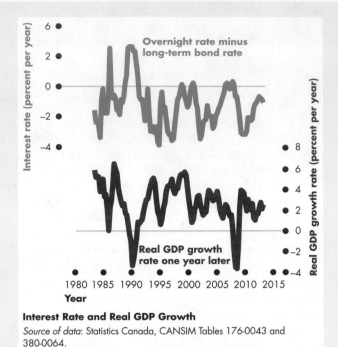

Interest Rate and Real GDP Growth

Source of data: Statistics Canada, CANSIM Tables 176-0043 and 380-0064.

lowers the overnight loans rate, the real GDP growth rate speeds up one year later.

Not shown in the figure, the inflation rate increases and decreases corresponding to the fluctuations in the real GDP growth rate. But the effects on the inflation rate take even longer and are not as strong as the effects on the real GDP growth rate.

Loose Link from Overnight Loans Rate to Spending

The real long-term interest rate that influences spending plans is only loosely linked to the overnight loans rate. Also, the response of the *real* long-term interest rate to a change in the nominal interest rate depends on how inflation expectations change. And the response of expenditure plans to changes in the real interest rate depend on many factors that make the response hard to predict.

Time Lags in the Adjustment Process

The Bank of Canada is especially handicapped by the fact that the monetary policy transmission process is long and drawn out. Also, the economy does not always respond in exactly the same way to a policy change. Further, many factors other than policy are constantly changing and bringing new situations to which policy must respond.

REVIEW QUIZ

1   Describe the channels by which monetary policy ripples through the economy and explain how each channel operates.

2   Do interest rates fluctuate in response to the Bank of Canada's actions?

3   How do the Bank of Canada's actions change the exchange rate?

4   How do the Bank's actions influence real GDP and how long does it take for real GDP to respond to the Bank's policy changes?

5   How do the Bank's actions influence the inflation rate and how long does it take for inflation to respond to the Bank's policy changes?

Work these questions in Study Plan 30.3 and get instant feedback.   MyEconLab

Extraordinary Monetary Stimulus

During the financial crisis and recession of 2008–2009, the Bank of Canada, the U.S. Federal Reserve, and other central banks lowered their overnight loans rate targets to the floor. The overnight rate can't go below zero, so what can a central bank do to stimulate the economy when it can't lower the interest rate?

Central banks answered this question with some extraordinary policy actions, and none more extraordinary than those of the U.S. Federal Reserve (the Fed). To understand those actions, we need to dig a bit into the anatomy of the financial crisis to which central banks responded. That's what we'll now do. We'll look at the key elements in the financial crisis and then look at the U.S. Fed's response and the responses of some other central banks.

The Key Elements of the Crisis

We can describe the crisis by identifying the events that changed the values of the assets and liabilities of banks and other financial institutions. Canada's banks were in better shape to ride the storm than the U.S and European banks, so we focus here on the regions hit hardest.

Figure 30.8 shows the stylized balance sheet of a bank: Deposits plus equity equals reserves plus loans and securities (see Chapter 24, p. 572). Deposits and owners' capital—equity—are the bank's source of funds (other borrowing by banks is ignored here). Deposits are the funds loaned to the bank by households and firms. Equity is the capital provided by the bank's shareholders and includes the bank's undistributed profits (and losses). The bank's reserves are currency and deposits at the central bank. The bank's loans and securities are the loans made by the bank and government bonds, private bonds, asset-backed bonds, and other securities that the bank holds.

Three main events can put a bank under stress:

1. Widespread fall in asset prices
2. A significant currency drain
3. A run on the bank

Figure 30.8 summarizes the problems that each event presents to a bank. A widespread fall in asset prices—a *capital loss*—means a bank must write down the value of its assets so the value of the bank's equity decreases by the same amount as the fall in the value of its assets. If the fall in asset prices is large enough, the bank's equity might fall to zero, in which case the bank is insolvent. It fails.

A significant currency drain means that depositors withdraw funds and the bank loses reserves. This event puts the bank in a liquidity crisis. It is short of cash reserves.

A run on the bank occurs when depositors lose confidence and withdraw their deposits. The bank loses reserves and must call in loans and sell off securities at unfavourable prices. Its equity shrinks.

The red arrows in Fig. 30.8 summarize the effects of these events and the problems they brought in the 2007–2008 financial crisis. A widespread fall in asset prices was triggered by the bursting of a house-price bubble that saw house prices switch from rapidly rising to falling. With falling house prices, sub-prime mortgage defaults occurred and the prices of mortgage-backed securities and derivatives whose values are based on these securities began to fall.

People with money market mutual fund deposits began to withdraw them, which created a fear of a massive withdrawal of these funds analagous to a run on a bank. In the United Kingdom, one bank, Northern Rock, experienced a bank run.

With low reserves and even lower equity, banks turned their attention to securing their balance sheets and called in loans. The loanable funds market and money market dried up.

FIGURE 30.8 The Ingredients of a Financial and Banking Crisis

Event	Deposits	+ Equity	= Reserves	+ Loans and securities	Problem
Widespread fall in asset prices		▼		▼	Solvency
Currency drain	▼		▼		Liquidity
Run on bank	▼	▼	▼	▼	Liquidity and solvency

MyEconLab Animation

Because the loanable funds market is global, the same problems quickly spread to all economies, and foreign exchange markets became highly volatile.

Hard-to-get loans, market volatility, and increased uncertainty transmitted the financial and monetary crisis to real expenditure decisions.

The Policy Actions

Five types of policy action dribbled out over a period of more than a year. They were:

1. Open market operations
2. Extension of deposit insurance
3. Central bank and government swapping government securities for toxic assets
4. Government buying bank shares
5. Fair value accounting

Figure 30.9 summarizes these actions, their effects on a bank's balance sheet (red and blue arrows), and the problem that each action sought to address.

An open market operation is the classic policy (described on pp. 572–574) for providing liquidity and enabling a central bank to hit its overnight rate target. With substantial interest rate cuts, heavy open market operations were used to keep the banks well supplied with reserves. This action lowered bank holdings of securities and increased their reserves.

By extending deposit insurance, people with bank deposits had less incentive to withdraw them. Both deposits and bank reserves increased.

Some central banks bought troubled assets that no one could sell (so-called toxic assets) and sold good-quality government securities in their place. These actions swapped bad loans and securities for good ones and addressed the liquidity problem.

Some governments bought shares in banks. This action boosted bank capital and addressed the insolvency problem.

The final action is not a monetary policy but a change in accounting standards. It relaxed the requirement for institutions to value their assets at current market value—called "mark-to-market"—and permitted them, in rare conditions, to use a model to assess "fair market value."

Taken as a whole, a huge amount of relief was thrown at the financial crisis.

Painfully Slow Recovery

Despite extraordinary monetary (and fiscal) stimulus, at the end of 2011, three years after the first extraordinary stimulus was undertaken, the U.S. economy remained stuck with slow real GDP growth and an unemployment rate greater than 9 percent. Why?

No one knows for sure, but the Fed's critics say that the Fed itself contributed to the problem more than to the solution. That problem is extreme uncertainty about the future that is keeping business investment low. Critics emphasize the need for greater clarity about monetary policy *strategy*. We'll conclude this review of monetary policy by looking at two suggested policy strategies that do bring clarity.

Policy Strategies and Clarity

Unlike the Bank of Canada, with its clear *inflation rate targeting* strategy, the U.S. Fed pursues what is called a *dual mandate*, which is to keep *both* the inflation rate and the unemployment rate low. The pursuit of this dual mandate is a source of confusion and uncertainty about monetary policy. The central problem with the U.S. dual mandate is that it seeks

---

FIGURE 30.9   Policy Actions in a Financial and Banking Crisis

Action	Deposits	+ Equity	= Reserves	+ Loans and securities	Problem addressed
Open market operation			▲	▼	Liquidity
Extension of deposit insurance	▲		▲		Liquidity
Swap government securities for toxic assets			▲	▼	Liquidity
Buy bank shares		▲	▲		Solvency
Fair value accounting		▲		▲	Solvency

MyEconLab Animation

to acheive the impossible. You've seen in Chapter 28 (pp. 684–686) that stabilization policy faces a *tradeoff* between inflation and unemployment in the short run. If policy seeks to lower the inflation rate, the unemployment rate rises in the short run. If policy seeks to lower the unemployment rate, the inflation rate rises in the short run.

In the *long run*, monetary policy influences the inflation rate but has no effect on the unemployment rate, which is determined by the natural unemployment rate.

It is because monetary policy influences only the inflation rate in the long run that inflation rate targeting is an attractive monetary policy strategy. This approach is now used not only by Canada but also by Australia, New Zealand, Sweden, the United Kingdom, and the European Union.

Inflation targeting focuses the public debate on what monetary policy can achieve and the best contribution it can make to attaining full employment and sustained growth. The central fact is that monetary policy is about managing inflation expectations. An explicit inflation target that is taken seriously and towards which policy actions are aimed and explained is a sensible way to manage those expectations.

It is when the going gets tough that inflation targeting has the greatest benefit. It is difficult to imagine a serious inflation-targeting central bank permitting inflation to take off in the way that it did during the 1970s. And it is difficult to imagine deflation and ongoing recession such as Japan has endured for the past 10 years if monetary policy is guided by an explicit inflation target.

One way to pursue an inflation target is to set the policy interest rate (for the Bank of Canada, the overnight loans rate) by using a rule or formula. The most famous and most studied interest rate rule is the *Taylor rule* described in *Economics in Action*.

Supporters of the Taylor rule argue that in computer simulations, the rule works well and limits fluctuations in inflation and output. By using such a rule, monetary policy contributes towards lessening uncertainty—the opposite of current U.S. monetary policy. In financial markets, labour markets, and markets for goods and services, people make long-term commitments. So markets work best when plans are based on correctly anticipated inflation. A well-understood monetary policy helps to create an environment in which inflation is easier to forecast and manage.

The debates on inflation targeting and the Taylor rule will continue!

Economics in Action
The Taylor Rule

The idea of setting the overnight loans rate based on a rule was suggested by Stanford University economist John B. Taylor, and the rule bears his name.

The Taylor rule is a formula for setting the overnight loans rate. Calling the overnight loans rate R, the inflation rate INF, and the output gap GAP (all percentages), the Taylor rule formula is:

$$R = 2 + INF + 0.5(INF - 2) + 0.5GAP.$$

In words, the Taylor rule sets the overnight loans rate at 2 percent plus the inflation rate plus one half of the deviation of inflation from 2 percent, plus one half of the output gap.

If the Bank of Canada had followed the Taylor rule, the overnight loans rate would have been higher on some occasions and lower on others. During 2008, when the overnight loans rate was 1.5 percent, the Taylor Rule would have kept it close to 4 percent.

The Bank believes that because it uses more information than just the current inflation rate and the output gap, it is able to set the overnight loans rate more intelligently than the Taylor rule would set it.

◆ REVIEW QUIZ

1 What are the three ingredients of a financial and banking crisis?
2 What are the policy actions taken by central banks in response to the financial crisis?
3 Why was the U.S. recovery from the 2008–2009 recession so slow?
4 How might inflation targeting improve U.S. monetary policy?
5 How might using the Taylor rule improve the Fed's monetary policy?

Work these questions in Study Plan 30.4 and get instant feedback.   MyEconLab

◆ To complete your study of monetary policy, take a look at *Economics in the News* on pp. 744–745, which examines the Bank of Canada's monetary stimulus in 2014.

The Bank of Canada Stimulus Still Needed in 2014

Canada Is Creating About Half the Jobs It Should Be

Bloomberg News
September 23, 2014

Bank of Canada Senior Deputy Governor Carolyn Wilkins said employment growth that's about half of what's required for recovery is a clear sign that low interest rates will still be needed in world's 11th largest economy. ...

"The average monthly gain in employment is about 6,800, and that's just a little bit over half of what we need," Wilkins said. "There is still excess supply out there, that it's been actually pretty constant for a little while."

Statistics Canada's last labour market report showed a surprise loss of 11,000 jobs, led by a record 111,800 in employees at private companies.

Unemployment remained unchanged at 7.0 percent as 20,800 people left the labour force in August, lowering the participation rate to 66.0 percent, the lowest since November 2001.

Other parts of the labour market also suggest weakness, Wilkins said. "We aren't seeing people finding it really hard to meet new increases in demand," she said. "Wage growth is pretty moderate, particularly when you take into account what has been happening with labour productivity."

Statistics Canada said Sept. 5 that labour productivity rose 1.8 percent in the second quarter, the fastest since the first three months of 1998. The agency also said that average hourly wages of permanent workers rose by 2.3 percent in August from a year earlier, close to the central bank's 2 percent inflation target. ...

Written by Greg Quinn. Copyright © 2014. Used by permission of Bloomberg News. All rights reserved.

ESSENCE OF THE STORY

- Speaking in September 2014, Bank of Canada Senior Deputy Governor Carolyn Wilkins said employment growth was too slow, excess capacity persisted, and wage growth was moderate.

- Statistics Canada's data confirm what Wilkins said.

- The August 2014 unemployment rate was unchanged at 7.0 percent, the labour force participation rate fell to 66 percent, its lowest since November 2001, and wage rates increased by 2.3 percent.

- Second quarter 2014 labour productivity increased 1.8 percent, the fastest since the first quarter of 1998.

- With ongoing slack and modest inflation, low interest rates are still needed to stimulate demand.

MyEconLab More Economics in the News

ECONOMIC ANALYSIS

- In September 2014, the Bank of Canada continued to hold the overnight rate at 1 percent.

- Senior Deputy Governor Wilkins signalled that she believed continued stimulus from a low interest rate was still needed.

- In normal times, with inflation on target and with real GDP equal to potential GDP at full employment, the overnight loans rate would be between 3 percent and 4 percent.

- An overnight loans rate of 1 percent means that the Bank is boosting aggregate demand with monetary stimulus. If the Bank raised the overnight loans rate in stages to 3 percent, it would be withdrawing monetary stimulus and making monetary policy neutral.

- In 2014, the economy was close to full employment and CPI inflation was inside its target range, but real GDP growth and employment growth were slow.

- Figure 1 illustrates the economy in 2014 according to the Bank of Canada's estimate of the output gap (a recessionary gap) and Statistics Canada's GDP data.

- Figure 2 shows an interpretation of what Carolyn Wilkins fears for 2016 in the absence of continued monetary stimulus.

- In Fig. 2, potential GDP grows by 3 percent per year but aggregate demand grows more slowly so that, without monetary stimulus, the output gap would widen and the inflation rate would fall below 2 percent per year.

- Figure 3 shows the outcome in 2016 that the Bank wants to achieve and that it might achieve by maintaing the overnight loans rate at 1 percent, and thereby maintaining substantial monetary stimulus.

- If the Bank gets it right, the price level rises to 116. Inflation at 2 percent per year takes the price level from 112 in 2014 to 116 in 2016, and real GDP increases to equal potential GDP.

- If the Bank gets it wrong by overstimulating aggregate demand, by 2016 the price level will have risen to more than 116—the inflation rate will exceed 2 percent per year—and an inflationary gap will appear.

- If the the Bank gets it wrong by stimulating aggregate demand too little, by 2016 the price level will have risen to less than 116—the inflation rate will be less than 2 percent per year—and a recessionary gap will remain.

Figure 1 The Economy in 2014

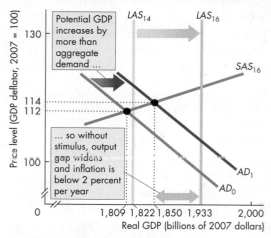

Figure 2 The Economy in 2016 without Monetary Stimulus

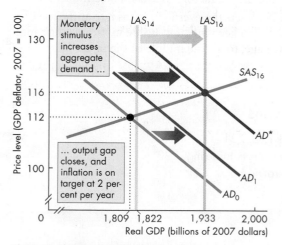

Figure 3 The Economy in 2016 with Monetary Stimulus

SUMMARY

Key Points

Monetary Policy Objectives and Framework
(pp. 728–730)

- The Bank of Canada Act requires the Bank to use monetary policy to avoid inflation and moderate cycles in real GDP and employment.
- The Government of Canada and the Bank of Canada have jointly agreed that the Bank will seek to keep CPI inflation between 1 percent and 3 percent a year and will aim for the 2 percent midpoint.
- The Bank has successfully achieved its inflation-control target.
- The Bank's Governing Council has the responsibility for the conduct of monetary policy, but the Bank and the government must consult regularly.

Working Problems 1 to 3 will give you a better understanding of monetary policy objectives and framework.

The Conduct of Monetary Policy (pp. 730–732)

- The Bank of Canada's monetary policy instrument is the overnight loans rate.
- The Bank sets the overnight loans rate target and announces changes on eight dates each year.
- To decide on the appropriate level of the overnight loans rate target, the Bank monitors the inflation rate and all the factors that influence inflation.
- The Bank sets the overnight loans rate at the level expected to keep inflation inside its target range and, on average, to hit the middle of the target range.

- The Bank achieves its overnight loans rate target by using open market operations.

Working Problems 4 to 8 will give you a better understanding of the conduct of monetary policy.

Monetary Policy Transmission (pp. 733–740)

- A change in the overnight loans rate changes other interest rates, the exchange rate, the quantity of money and loans, aggregate demand, and eventually real GDP and the price level.
- Changes in the overnight loans rate change real GDP about one year later and change the inflation rate with an even longer time lag.

Working Problems 9 to 13 will give you a better understanding of monetary policy transmission.

Extraordinary Monetary Stimulus (pp. 741–743)

- A financial crisis has three ingredients: a widespread fall in asset prices, a currency drain, and a run on banks.
- Central banks responded to financial crisis with classic open market operations and by several other unconventional measures.
- Inflation targeting and the Taylor rule are monetary policy strategies designed to enable the central bank to manage inflation expectations and reduce uncertainty.

Working Problem 14 will give you a better understanding of extraordinary monetary stimulus.

Key Terms

MyEconLab Key Terms Quiz

Bank rate, 731
Inflation rate targeting, 728
Operating band, 731

Overnight loans rate, 730
Settlements balances rate, 732

WORKED PROBLEM

MyEconLab   You can work this problem in Chapter 30 Study Plan.

The economy is at full employment, the inflation rate is 2 percent a year, and the overnight loans rate is at 4 percent a year. But real GDP is growing more slowly than average, so the Bank of Canada decides to lower interest rates.

Questions

1. Which macroeconomic variables change immediately and in which direction?
2. Which macroeconomic variables change over the next few weeks or months and in which direction?
3. Which macroeconomic variables change over the next year or two and in which direction?
4. Does the economic growth rate increase?

Solutions

1. The Bank of Canada lowers its overnight loans rate target and buys securities on the open market. An increase in the monetary base creates excess reserves, and the interest rate at which banks lend and borrow reserves—the overnight loans rate falls.

   The banks buy short-term bills, the price of which rises and the interest rate on which falls. The lower interest rate makes the Canadian dollar depreciate on the foreign exchange market.

Key Point: A change in the overnight loans rate flows immediately into the overnight loans market, the short-term securities market, and the foreign exchange market, changing the short-term interest rate and the Canadian dollar exchange rate.

2. Over the next weeks and months, the banks increase loans. The quantity of money increases and the supply of loans increases. In the loanable funds market, an increase in supply lowers the real interest rate, so saving starts to decrease and investment starts to increase.

   The lower dollar on the foreign exchange market increases exports and decreases imports.

Key Point: A few weeks and months after the Bank changes the interest rate, ripples reach the loanable funds market and a change in the real interest rate starts to change investment.

   Net exports begin to respond to the changed exchange rate.

3. Over the next year, the lower real interest rate increases consumption expenditure and business investment, and the lower dollar continues to increase net exports. With these components of aggregate expenditure increasing, aggregate demand increases and real GDP increases.

   The increase in real GDP is also an increase in income, which induces a further increase in consumption expenditure—an expenditure multiplier process.

   If aggregate demand increases before investment in new capital and new technology changes aggregate supply, the economy moves above full employment and an inflationary gap appears. Businesses face a shortage of labour. As time goes on, wage rates and prices start to rise, and after about two years the inflation rate rises.

Key Point: A change in the real interest rate influences the goods market. Aggregate demand changes and, with no change in aggregate supply, real GDP increases. But the inflation rate changes about two years after the Bank of Canada lowers the interest rate target.

4. The increase in aggregate demand increases real GDP, but will the economic growth rate be higher? With no change in aggregate supply, real GDP will eventually return to its initial level and a short burst of growth will have occurred. But in the long run, the economy will be back to its initial full-employment situation with no faster growth rate and a higher inflation rate.

   For the growth rate to increase, investment in new capital and new technologies must increase the rate of productivity growth to speed the growth rate of aggregate supply. Changing the interest rate will work its way through the economy to increase real GDP in the short term but not create economic growth.

Key Point: When the Bank of Canada changes the interest rate, changes ripple through all markets. The money market, the loanable funds market, the labour market, and the goods market all respond to the interest rate change one after the other, but unless the pace of productivity growth increases, the economic growth will not increase. Monetary policy cannot be used to increase the economic growth rate.

STUDY PLAN PROBLEMS AND APPLICATIONS

MyEconLab   You can work Problems 1 to 14 in Chapter 30 Study Plan and get instant feedback.

Monetary Policy Objectives and Framework

(Study Plan 30.1)

1. "Unemployment is a more serious economic problem than inflation and it should be the focus of the Bank of Canada's monetary policy." Evaluate this statement and explain why the Bank's policy goal is a target inflation rate.

2. "Monetary policy is too important to be left to the Bank of Canada. The government should be responsible for it." How is responsibility for monetary policy allocated between the the Bank of Canada and the government?

3. **Inflation Control Target Renewal**

   The 2011 inflation control target agreement between the Government of Canada and the Bank of Canada runs to the end of 2016.

   > Source: Bank of Canada, November 2011

   a. What role does the inflation control agreement say about the Bank's control of the quantity of money?

   b. Why is it important that the agreement be renewed in 2016 and what might be some obstacles to its renewal?

The Conduct of Monetary Policy (Study Plan 30.2)

4. What are the possible monetary policy instruments and which one does the Bank of Canada use? How has its value behaved since 2000?

5. How does the Bank of Canada hit its overnight loans rate target?

6. What does the Bank of Canada do to determine whether the overnight loans rate should be raised, lowered, or left unchanged?

Use the following news clip to work Problems 7 and 8.

Headwinds May Keep Interest Rates Low

During 2011, Canada is in an environment of substantial headwinds from Europe and the United States, and monetary policy may need to maintain stimulus to achieve the inflation target at full employment.

> Source: Bloomberg, June 24, 2011

7. Explain the situation faced by the Bank of Canada in 2011.

8. a. How would the Bank of Canada "maintain stimulus"?

   b. Why might the Bank of Canada decide to lower the interest rate in the face of "headwinds"?

Monetary Policy Transmission (Study Plan 30.3)

Use the following data to work Problems 9 to 11.

Growth Forecast Through 2016

With low interest rates, business investment and trade are expected to bring growth through 2016.

> Source: TD Economics, September 25, 2014

9. Explain the effects of the Bank of Canada's low interest rates on business investment. Draw a graph to illustrate your explanation.

10. Explain the effects of business investment on aggregate demand. Would you expect it to have a multiplier effect? Why or why not?

11. What actions might the Bank of Canada take to stimulate business investment further?

12. On September 15, 2014, the OECD predicted that global growth would continue at a moderate rate and that Canada's economic growth will strengthen. If the OECD forecasts turn out to be correct, what would most likely happen to the output gap and unemployment in 2015 and 2016?

13. If the Bank of Canada started to raise the overnight loans rate in 2015, explain the process by which this policy action would change real GDP.

Extraordinary Monetary Stimulus (Study Plan 30.4)

14. **Prospects Rise for Fed Easing Policy**

    William Dudley, president of the New York Fed, raised the prospect of the Fed becoming more explicit about its inflation goal to "help anchor inflation expectations at the desired rate."

    > Source: ft.com, October 1, 2010

    a. What monetary policy strategy is William Dudley raising?

    b. How does inflation rate targeting work and why might it "help anchor inflation expectations at the desired rate"?

ADDITIONAL PROBLEMS AND APPLICATIONS

MyEconLab   You can work these problems in MyEconLab if assigned by your instructor.

Monetary Policy Objectives and Framework

Use the following information to work Problems 15 to 17.

The Bank of Canada and the Government of Canada have agreed that the Bank will achieve an inflation rate target.

15. Explain how inflation targeting promotes full employment in the long run.

16. Explain the conflict between inflation targeting and unemployment targeting in the short run.

17. Based on the performance of Canadian inflation and unemployment, has the Bank's inflation targeting been successful?

18. Suppose Parliament decided to strip the Bank of Canada of its monetary policy powers and decided to legislate interest rate changes. How would you expect the policy choices to change? Which arrangement would most likely provide price stability?

Use the following news clip to work Problems 19 to 21.

A World Awash in Government Debt

In the 1980s, it was Argentina, Mexico, and the Philippines that struggled with unsustainable debt loads. In the 1990s, it was Russia and the go-go economies of East Asia. Today, it is the United States, Japan, and Europe.

Source: globalpost.com, August 2, 2011

19. How does a government get funds to cover a budget deficit? How does financing a budget deficit affect the central bank's monetary policy?

20. How was Canada's budget deficit of 2013 influenced by the Bank of Canada's low interest rate policy?

21. a. How would the budget deficit change in 2015 and 2016 if the Bank of Canada moved interest rates up?

    b. How would the budget deficit change in 2015 and 2016 if the Bank of Canada's monetary policy led to a rapid appreciation of the dollar?

22. The U.S. Federal Reserve Act of 2000 instructs the Federal Reserve to pursue its goals by "maintain[ing] long-run growth of the monetary and credit aggregates commensurate with the economy's long-run potential to increase production."

    a. How would following this instruction make the U.S. monetary policy instrument different from Canada's monetary policy instrument?

    b. Why might a central bank increase the quantity of money by more than the increase in potential GDP?

The Conduct of Monetary Policy

23. Looking at the overnight loans rate since 2000, identify periods during which, with the benefit of hindsight, the rate might have been kept too low. Identify periods during which it might have been too high.

Use the following information to work Problems 24 to 28.

At the end of 2009, the unemployment rate was 8.3 percent, the inflation rate was 0.8 percent, and the overnight loans rate target was 0.25 percent. In mid-2014, the unemployment rate was about 7 percent, the inflation rate was 2.1 percent, and the overnight loans rate target was 1 percent.

24. How might the Bank of Canada's decisions that raised the overnight loans rate from 0.25 percent to 1 percent have been influenced by the unemployment rate and the inflation rate?

25. Explain the dilemma that rising inflation and high unemployment poses for the Bank of Canada.

26. Why might the Bank of Canada decide to keep the overnight loans rate at 1 percent in 2014?

27. Why might the Bank of Canada decide to raise the overnight rate in 2015?

28. Why might the Bank of Canada decide to lower the overnight rate in 2015?

Monetary Policy Transmission

Use the following data to work Problems 29 to 31.

From 2007 to 2009, the long-term *real* interest rate paid by the safest corporations increased from 2.3 percent to 3.8 percent. During that same period, the overnight loans rate fell from 4.5 percent to 0.25 percent a year.

29. What role does the long-term real interest rate play in the monetary policy transmission process?

30. How does the overnight loans rate influence the long-term real interest rate?

31. What do you think happened to inflation expectations between 2007 and 2009 and why?

32. **U.S. Dollar Reaches Low Against Yen**

    Traders continued to make bets in favour of the yen, sending the U.S. dollar to a record low against the Japanese currency.

    Source: *The Wall Street Journal*, August 20, 2011

    a. How do "bets in favour of the yen" influence the exchange rate?

    b. How does the U.S. Federal Reserve's monetary policy influence the exchange rate?

Use the following news clip to work Problems 33 and 34.

Top Economist Says America Could Plunge into Recession

Robert Shiller, Professor of Economics at Yale University, predicted that there was a very real possibility that the United States would be plunged into a Japan-style slump, with house prices declining for years.

Source: timesonline.co.uk, December 31, 2007

33. If the U.S. Federal Reserve had agreed with Robert Shiller in December 2007, what actions might it have taken differently from those it did take? How could monetary policy prevent house prices from falling?

34. Describe the time lags in the response of output and inflation to the policy actions you have prescribed.

Extraordinary Monetary Stimulus

35. **U.S. Federal Reserve's Plosser Opposes QE3**

    Federal Reserve Bank of Philadelphia president Charles Plosser does not think that monetary policy can "do much to speed up the slow progress" in the labour market and opposes the Fed's latest round of stimulus, known as QE3, saying he does not think it prudent to risk the Fed's hard-won credibility.

    Source: *Philadelphia Inquirer*, September 25, 2012

    a. Describe the QE3 asset purchases that are causing Charles Plosser concern.

    b. How might asset purchases damage the Fed's credibility?

36. Suppose that the Reserve Bank of New Zealand is following the Taylor rule. In 2009, it sets the official cash rate (its equivalent of the overnight loans rate) at 4 percent a year. If the inflation rate in New Zealand is 2 percent a year, what is its output gap?

Use the following news clip to work Problems 37 and 38.

Bernanke on Inflation Targeting

Inflation targeting promotes well-anchored inflation expectations, which facilitates more effective stabilization of output and employment. Thus inflation targeting can deliver good results with respect to output and employment as well as inflation.

Source: Federal Reserve Board, remarks by Ben Bernanke to the National Association of Business Economists, March 25, 2003

37. What is inflation targeting and how do "well-anchored inflation expectations" help to achieve more stable output as well as low inflation?

38. Explain how inflation targeting as described by Ben Bernanke is consistent with the Fed's dual mandate.

Economics in the News

39. After you have studied *Economics in the News* on pp. 744–745, answer the following questions.

    a. What was the state of the Canadian economy in 2014?

    b. What was Carolyn Wilkin's expectation about future real GDP growth and inflation in September 2014?

    c. How would maintaining the overnight rate at 1 percent influence the market for bank reserves, the loanable funds market, and aggregate demand and aggregate supply?

    d. How would you expect the Canadian dollar exchange rate to feature in the transmission of monetary policy to real GDP and the price level?

31

INTERNATIONAL TRADE POLICY

After studying this chapter, you will be able to:

◆ Explain how markets work with international trade

◆ Identify the gains from international trade and its winners and losers

◆ Explain the effects of international trade barriers

◆ Explain and evaluate arguments used to justify restricting international trade

iPhones, Wii games, and Nike shoes are just three of the items that you might buy that are not produced in Canada. Why don't we produce phones, games, and shoes in Canada? Isn't the globalization of production killing good Canadian jobs?

You will find the answers in this chapter. And you will see why global trade is a win-win deal for buyers and sellers. You will also see why governments restrict trade, and in *Economics in the News* at the end of the chapter, why it is difficult for Canada to reach a free-trade deal with Japan and other Pacific nations.

But first, we study the gains from international trade.

751

How Global Markets Work

Because we trade with people in other countries, the goods and services that we can buy and consume are not limited by what we can produce. The goods and services that we buy from other countries are our **imports**; and the goods and services that we sell to people in other countries are our **exports**.

International Trade Today

Global trade today is enormous. In 2013, global exports and imports were $23 trillion, which is one-third of the value of global production. The United States is the world's largest international trader and accounts for 10 percent of world exports and 12 percent of world imports. Germany and China, which rank 2 and 3 behind the United States, lag by a large margin.

In 2013, total Canadian exports were $566 billion, which is about 27 percent of the value of Canadian production. Total Canadian imports were $486 billion, which is about 32 percent of total expenditure in Canada.

We trade both goods and services. In 2013, exports of services were about 15 percent of total exports and imports of services were about 19 percent of total imports.

What Drives International Trade?

Comparative advantage is the fundamental force that drives international trade. Comparative advantage (see Chapter 2, p. 40) is a situation in which a person can perform an activity or produce a good or service at a lower opportunity cost than anyone else. This same idea applies to nations. We can define *national comparative advantage* as a situation in which a nation can perform an activity or produce a good or service at a lower opportunity cost than any other nation.

The opportunity cost of producing a T-shirt is lower in China than in Canada, so China has a comparative advantage in producing T-shirts. The opportunity cost of producing a regional jet is lower in Canada than in China, so Canada has a comparative advantage in producing regional jets.

You saw in Chapter 2 how Liz and Joe reap gains from trade by specializing in the production of the good at which they have a comparative advantage and then trading with each other. Both are better off.

This same principle applies to trade among nations. Because China has a comparative

Economics in Action
We Trade Metals for Consumer Goods

The figure shows Canada's four largest exports and imports by value. Metals and alloys and machinery and equipment are our biggest exports, and consumer goods and motor vehicle parts are our biggest imports. Trade in automobiles—both exports and imports—has slipped from top spot in earlier years.

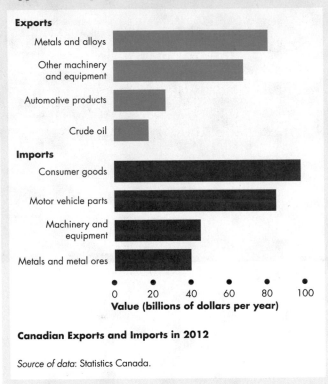

Canadian Exports and Imports in 2012

Source of data: Statistics Canada.

advantage at producing T-shirts and Canada has a comparative advantage at producing regional jets, the people of both countries can gain from specialization and trade. China can buy regional jets from Canada at a lower opportunity cost than that at which Chinese firms can produce them. And Canadians can buy T-shirts from China for a lower opportunity cost than that at which Canadian firms can produce them. Also, through international trade, Chinese producers can get higher prices for their T-shirts and Canadian firms can sell regional jets for a higher price. Both countries gain from international trade.

Let's now illustrate the gains from trade that we've just described by studying demand and supply in the global markets for T-shirts and regional jets.

Why Canada Imports T-Shirts

Canada imports T-shirts because the rest of the world has a comparative advantage in producing T-shirts. Figure 31.1 illustrates how this comparative advantage generates international trade and how trade affects the price of a T-shirt and the quantities produced and bought.

The demand curve D_C and the supply curve S_C show the demand and supply in the Canadian domestic market only. The demand curve tells us the quantity of T-shirts that Canadians are willing to buy at various prices. The supply curve tells us the quantity of T-shirts that Canadian garment makers are willing to sell at various prices—that is, the quantity supplied at each price when all T-shirts sold in Canada are produced in Canada.

Figure 31.1(a) shows what the Canadian T-shirt market would be like with no international trade.

The price of a shirt would be $8 and 4 million shirts a year would be produced by Canadian garment makers and bought by Canadian consumers.

Figure 31.1(b) shows the market for T-shirts with international trade. Now the price of a T-shirt is determined in the world market, not the Canadian domestic market. The world price of a T-shirt is less than $8, which means that the rest of the world has a comparative advantage in producing T-shirts. The world price line shows the world price at $5 a shirt.

The Canadian demand curve, D_C, tells us that at $5 a shirt, Canadians buy 6 million shirts a year. The Canadian supply curve, S_C, tells us that at $5 a shirt, Canadian garment makers produce 2 million T-shirts a year. To buy 6 million T-shirts when only 2 million are produced in Canada, we must import T-shirts from the rest of the world. The quantity of T-shirts imported is 4 million a year.

FIGURE 31.1   A Market with Imports

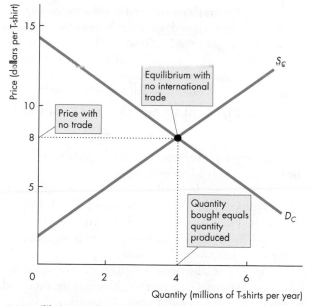

(a) Equilibrium with no international trade

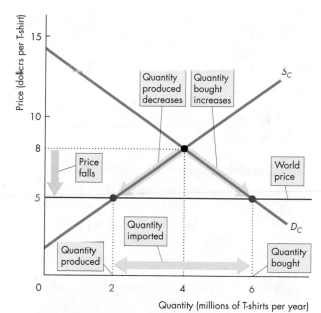

(b) Equilibrium in a market with imports

Part (a) shows the Canadian market for T-shirts with no international trade. The Canadian domestic demand curve D_C and the Canadian domestic supply curve S_C determine the price of a T-shirt at $8 and the quantity of T-shirts produced and bought in Canada at 4 million a year.

Part (b) shows the Canadian market for T-shirts with international trade. World demand for and world supply

of T-shirts determine the world price of a T-shirt, which is $5. The price in the Canadian market falls to $5 a shirt. Canadian purchases of T-shirts increase to 6 million a year, and Canadian production of T-shirts decreases to 2 million a year. Canada imports 4 million T-shirts a year.

FIGURE 31.2 A Market with Exports

(a) Equilibrium without international trade

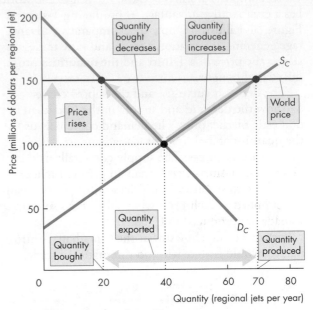

(b) Equilibrium in a market with exports

In part (a), the Canadian market with no international trade, the domestic demand curve D_C and the domestic supply curve S_C determine the price of a regional jet in Canada at $100 million and 40 regional jets are produced and bought each year.

In part (b), the Canadian market with international trade, world demand and world supply determine the world price of a regional jet at $150 million. The price in Canada rises. Canadian production increases to 70 regional jets a year, Canadian purchases decrease to 20 regional jets a year, and Canada exports 50 regional jets a year.

MyEconLab Animation and Draw Graph

Why Canada Exports Regional Jets

Figure 31.2 illustrates international trade in regional jets. The demand curve D_C and the supply curve S_C show the demand and supply in the Canadian domestic market only. The demand curve tells us the quantity of regional jets that Canadian airlines are willing to buy at various prices. The supply curve tells us the quantity of regional jets that Canadian aircraft makers are willing to sell at various prices.

Figure 31.2(a) shows what the Canadian regional jet market would be like with no international trade. The price of a regional jet would be $100 million and 40 airplanes a year would be produced by Bombardier and bought by Canadian airlines.

Figure 31.2(b) shows the Canadian airplane market with international trade. Now the price of a regional jet is determined in the world market, and the world price of a regional jet is higher than $100 million, which means that Canada has a comparative advantage

in producing regional jets. The world price line shows the world price at $150 million.

The Canadian demand curve, D_C, tells us that at $150 million each, Canadian airlines buy 20 regional jets a year. The Canadian supply curve, S_C, tells us that at $150 million each, Bombardier produces 70 regional jets a year. The quantity produced in Canada (70 a year) minus the quantity purchased by Canadian airlines (20 a year) is the quantity exported, which is 50 regional jets a year.

REVIEW QUIZ

1 Describe the situation in the market for a good or service that Canada imports.

2 Describe the situation in the market for a good or service that Canada exports.

Work these questions in Study Plan 31.1 and get instant feedback. Do a Key Terms Quiz. MyEconLab

Winners, Losers, and the Net Gain from Trade

In Chapter 1 (see p. 6), we asked whether globalization is in the self-interest of the low-wage worker in Malaysia who sews your new running shoes and the shoemaker in Toronto—whether it is in the social interest. We're now going to answer these questions. You will learn why producers complain about cheap foreign imports, but consumers of imports never complain.

Gains and Losses from Imports

We measure the gains and losses from imports by examining their effect on the price paid and the quantity consumed by domestic consumers and their effect on the price received and the quantity sold by domestic producers.

Consumers Gain from Imports When a country freely imports something from the rest of the world, it is because the rest of the world has a comparative advantage at producing that item. Compared to a situation with no international trade, the price paid by the consumer falls and the quantity consumed increases. It is clear that the consumer gains. The greater the fall in price and increase in quantity consumed, the greater is the gain to the consumer.

Domestic Producers Lose from Imports Compared to a situation with no international trade, the price received by a domestic producer of an item that is imported falls. Also, the quantity sold by the domestic producer of a good or service that is also imported decreases. Because the domestic producer of an item that is imported sells a smaller quantity and for a lower price, this producer loses from international trade. Import-competing industries shrink in the face of competition from cheaper foreign-produced goods.

The profits of firms that produce import-competing goods and services fall, these firms cut their workforce, unemployment in these industries increases, and wages fall. When these industries have a geographical concentration, such as steel production around Hamilton, Ontario, an entire region can suffer economic decline.

Gains and Losses from Exports

We measure the gains and losses from exports just like we measured those from imports, by their effect on the price paid and the quantity consumed by domestic consumers and their effects on the price received and the quantity sold by domestic producers.

Domestic Consumers Lose from Exports When a country exports something to the rest of the world, it is because the country has a comparative advantage at producing that item. Compared to a situation with no international trade, the price paid by the consumer rises and the quantity consumed in the domestic economy decreases. The domestic consumer loses. The greater the rise in price and decrease in quantity consumed, the greater is the loss to the consumer.

Domestic Producers Gain from Exports Compared to a situation with no international trade, the price received by a domestic producer of an item that is exported rises. Also, the quantity sold by the domestic producer of a good or service that is also exported increases. Because the domestic producer of an item that is exported sells a larger quantity and for a higher price, this producer gains from international trade. Export industries expand in the face of global demand for their product.

The profits of firms that produce exports rise, these firms expand their workforce, unemployment in these industries decreases, and wages rise. When these industries have a geographical concentration, such as oil production in Alberta, an entire region can boom.

Gains for All

You've seen that both imports and exports bring gains. Export producers and import consumers gain, export consumers and import producers lose, but the gains are greater than the losses. In the case of imports, the consumer gains what the producer loses and then gains even more on the cheaper imports. In the case of exports, the producer gains what the consumer loses and then gains even more on the items it exports. So international trade provides a net gain for a country.

◀ REVIEW QUIZ

1 How is the gain from imports distributed between consumers and domestic producers?
2 How is the gain from exports distributed between consumers and domestic producers?
3 Why is the net gain from international trade positive?

Work these questions in Study Plan 31.2 and get instant feedback.   MyEconLab

◆ International Trade Restrictions

Governments use four sets of tools to influence international trade and protect domestic industries from foreign competition. They are:

- Tariffs
- Import quotas
- Other import barriers
- Export subsidies

Tariffs

A **tariff** is a tax on a good that is imposed by the importing country when an imported good crosses its international boundary. For example, the government of India imposes a 100 percent tariff on wine imported from Ontario. So when an Indian imports a $10 bottle of Ontario wine, he pays the Indian government a $10 import duty.

Tariffs raise revenue for governments and serve the self-interest of people who earn their incomes in import-competing industries. But as you will see, restrictions on free international trade decrease the gains from trade and are not in the social interest.

The Effects of a Tariff To see the effects of a tariff, let's return to the example in which Canada imports T-shirts. With free trade, the T-shirts are imported and sold at the world price. Then, under pressure from Canadian garment makers, the Canadian government imposes a tariff on imported T-shirts. Buyers of T-shirts must now pay the world price plus the tariff. Several consequences follow and Fig. 31.3 illustrates them.

Figure 31.3(a) shows the situation with free international trade. Canada produces 2 million T-shirts a year and imports 4 million a year at the world price of $5 a shirt. Figure 31.3(b) shows what happens with a tariff set at $2 per T-shirt.

FIGURE 31.3 The Effects of a Tariff

(a) Free trade

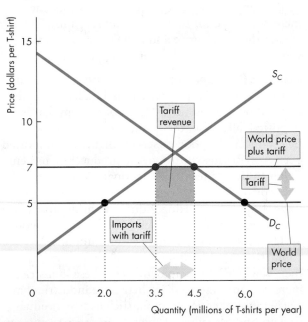

(b) Market with tariff

The world price of a T-shirt is $5. With free trade in part (a), Canadians buy 6 million T-shirts a year. Canadian garment makers produce 2 million T-shirts a year and Canada imports 4 million a year.

With a tariff of $2 per T-shirt in part (b), the price in the Canadian market rises to $7 a T-shirt. Canadian

production increases, Canadian purchases decrease, and the quantity imported decreases. The Canadian government collects a tariff revenue of $2 on each T-shirt imported, which is shown by the purple rectangle.

The following changes occur in the market for T-shirts:

- The price in Canada rises by $2 a T-shirt.
- The quantity of T-shirts bought in Canada decreases.
- The quantity of T-shirts produced in Canada increases.
- The quantity of T-shirts imported into Canada decreases.
- The Canadian government collects a tariff revenue.

Rise in Price of a T-Shirt To buy a T-shirt, Canadians must pay the world price plus the tariff, so the price of a T-shirt rises by the $2 tariff to $7. Figure 31.3(b) shows the new domestic price line, which lies $2 above the world price line.

Decrease in Purchases The higher price of a T-shirt brings a decrease in the quantity demanded along the demand curve. Figure 31.3(b) shows the decrease in the quantity bought from 6 million T-shirts a year at $5 a shirt to 4.5 million a year at $7 a shirt.

Increase in Domestic Production The higher price of a T-shirt stimulates domestic production, and

Canadian garment makers increase the quantity supplied along the supply curve. Figure 31.3(b) shows the increase from 2 million T-shirts at $5 a shirt to 3.5 million a year at $7 a shirt.

Decrease in Imports T-shirt imports decrease by 3 million, from 4 million to 1 million a year. Both the decrease in purchases and the increase in domestic production contribute to this decrease in imports.

Tariff Revenue The government's tariff revenue is $2 million—$2 per shirt on 1 million imported shirts—shown by the purple rectangle.

Winners, Losers, and the Social Loss from a Tariff A tariff on an imported good creates winners and losers and a social loss. When the Canadian government imposes a tariff on an imported good:

- Canadian consumers of the good lose.
- Canadian producers of the good gain.
- Canadian consumers lose more than Canadian producers gain: Society loses.

Canadian Consumers of the Good Lose Because the price of a T-shirt in Canada rises, the quantity of T-shirts demanded decreases. The combination of

Economics in Action
Tariffs Almost Gone

Canadian tariffs were in place before Confederation. They increased sharply in the 1870s and remained high until the 1930s. In 1947, the **General Agreement on Tariffs and Trade (GATT)** was established to reduce international tariffs. Since then, tariffs have fallen in a series of negotiating rounds, the most significant of which are identified in the figure. Tariffs are now as low as they have ever been, but import quotas and other trade barriers persist.

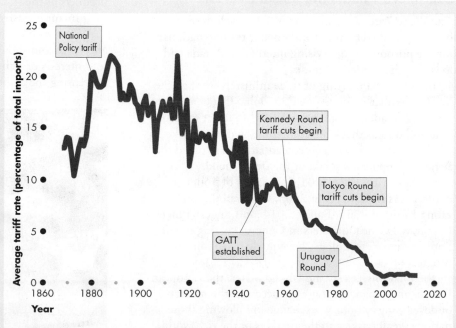

Sources of data: Statistics Canada, *Historical Statistics of Canada*, Catalogue 11-516, July 1999, and CANSIM Tables 380-0002 and 380-0034.

a higher price and smaller quantity bought makes Canadian consumers worse off when a tariff is imposed.

Canadian Producers of the Good Gain Because the price of an imported T-shirt rises by the amount of the tariff, Canadian T-shirt producers are now able to sell their T-shirts for the world price plus the tariff. At the higher price, the quantity of T-shirts supplied by Canadian producers increases. The combination of a higher price and larger quantity produced increases producers' profit. So Canadian producers gain from the tariff.

Canadian Consumers Lose More Than Canadian Producers Gain: Society Loses Consumers lose from the tariff for three reasons:

1. They pay a higher price to domestic producers.
2. They buy a smaller quantity of the good.
3. They pay tariff revenue to the government.

The tariff revenue is a loss to consumers, but it is *not* a social loss. The government can use the tariff revenue to buy public services that consumers value.

But the other two sources of consumer loss include some social loss.

There is a social loss because part of the higher price paid to domestic producers pays the higher cost of domestic production. The increased domestic production could have been obtained at lower cost as an import. There is also a social loss from the decreased quantity of the good bought at the higher price.

Import Quotas

We now look at the second tool for restricting trade: import quotas. An **import quota** is a restriction that limits the quantity of a good that may be imported in a given period.

Most countries impose import quotas on a wide range of items. Canada imposes them on food products such as meat, eggs, honey, and dairy and manufactured goods such as textiles and steel.

Import quotas enable the government to satisfy the self-interest of the people who earn their incomes in the import-competing industries. But you will discover that, like a tariff, an import quota decreases the gains from trade and is not in the social interest.

Economics in Action
Self-Interest Beats the Social Interest

The **World Trade Organization (WTO)** is an international body established by the world's major trading nations for the purpose of supervising international trade and lowering the barriers to trade.

In 2001, at a meeting of trade ministers from all the WTO member-countries held in Doha, Qatar, an agreement was made to begin negotiations to lower tariff barriers and quotas that restrict international trade in farm products and services. These negotiations are called the **Doha Development Agenda** or the **Doha Round**.

In the period since 2001, thousands of hours of conferences in Cancún in 2003, Geneva in 2004, Hong Kong in 2005, Bali in 2014, and ongoing meetings at WTO headquarters in Geneva, costing millions of taxpayers' dollars, have made disappointing progress.

Rich nations, led by the United States, the European Union, and Japan, want greater access to the markets of developing nations in exchange for allowing those nations greater access to the markets of the rich world, especially those for farm products.

Developing nations, led by Brazil, China, India, and South Africa, want access to the markets of farm products of the rich world, but they also want to protect their infant industries.

With two incompatible positions, these negotiations are stalled and show no signs of a breakthrough. The self-interests of rich nations and developing nations are preventing the achievement of the social interest.

The Effects of an Import Quota The effects of an import quota are similar to those of a tariff. The price rises, the quantity bought decreases, and the quantity produced in Canada increases. Figure 31.4 illustrates the effects.

Figure 31.4(a) shows the situation with free international trade. Figure 31.4(b) shows what happens with an import quota of 1 million T-shirts a year. The Canadaian supply curve of T-shirts becomes the domestic supply curve, S_C, plus the quantity that the import quota permits. So the supply curve becomes $S_C + quota$.

The price of a T-shirt rises to $7, the quantity of T-shirts bought in Canada decreases to 4.5 million a year, the quantity of T-shirts produced in Canada increases to 3.5 million a year, and the quantity of T-shirts imported into Canada decreases to the quota quantity of 1 million a year. All the effects of this quota are identical to the effects of a $2 per shirt tariff, as you can check in Fig. 31.3(b).

Winners, Losers, and the Social Loss from an Import Quota An import quota creates winners and losers that are similar to those of a tariff but with an interesting difference.

When the government imposes an import quota:

- Canadian consumers of the good lose.
- Canadian producers of the good gain.
- Importers of the good gain.
- Society loses.

Canadian Consumers of the Good Lose Because the price of a T-shirt in Canada rises, the quantity of T-shirts demanded decreases. The combination of a higher price and smaller quantity bought makes Canadian consumers worse off. So Canadian consumers lose when an import quota is imposed.

Canadian Producers of the Good Gain Because the price of an imported T-shirt rises, Canadian T-shirt producers increase production at the higher domestic price. The combination of a higher price and larger quantity

---

FIGURE 31.4 The Effects of an Import Quota

(a) Free trade

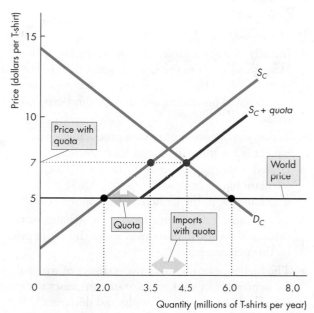

(b) Market with import quota

With free international trade, in part (a), Canadians buy 6 million T-shirts at the world price. Canada produces 2 million T-shirts and imports 4 million a year.

With an import quota of 1 million T-shirts a year, in part (b), the supply of T-shirts in Canada is shown by the

curve $S_C + quota$. The price in Canada rises to $7 a T-shirt. Canadian production increases, Canadian purchases decrease, and the quantity of T-shirts imported decreases.

MyEconLab Animation

◆ ECONOMICS IN THE NEWS

The Changing Market for Coat Hangers

Your Dry Cleaning Bill Is About to Get Worse
The price of wire hangers is a big deal for a dry cleaner, and that price will rise when the Commerce Department puts a 21 percent tariff on hangers made in Vietnam. The tariff is in response to a wire-hanger export subsidy paid to producers in Vietnam.

Source: CNN Money, June 4, 2012

SOME FACTS

Albert J. Parkhouse invented the wire hanger in Jackson, Michigan, in 1903, and for almost 100 years the United States produced and exported wire hangers. During the past 20 years, China and Vietnam have become the major lowest-cost producers.

THE PROBLEM

Explain why the United States has switched from exporting to importing wire hangers. Also explain the effects of the 21 percent tariff. Does Vietnam's export subsidy make the tariff efficient? Illustrate your explanations with a graph.

THE SOLUTION

- Initially, the opportunity cost of producing a wire hanger was lower in the United States than in the rest of the world. The United States had a comparative advantage in producing wire hangers and exported them.

- Today, the opportunity cost of producing a wire hanger is lower in China and Vietnam than in the United States (and other countries). China and Vietnam have a comparative advantage in producing wire hangers, so the United States imports them.

- By imposing a 21 percent tariff on wire hangers, the price in the United States rises above the world price by this percentage.

- The higher price decreases the quantity of wire hangers demanded in the United States, increases the quantity that U.S. producers supply, and decreases U.S. imports of wire hangers.

- The figure illustrates the U.S. market for wire hangers. The demand curve D_{US} and the supply curve S_{US} are assumed not to change. The U.S. price with no international trade is 10 cents per hanger.

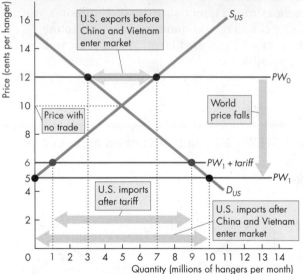

U.S. Market for Wire Hangers

- With a world price PW_0 of 12 cents a hanger, the United States had a comparative advantage in hangers, so it produced 7 million hangers a month, used 3 million, and exported 4 million. The figure shows the quantity of U.S. exports.

- When the world price falls to PW_1 at 5 cents a hanger, the United States stops producing hangers and imports 10 million a month.

- With a 21 percent tariff, the price in the United States rises to $PW_1 + tariff$. U.S. hanger production now becomes 1 million a month, the quantity used decreases to 9 million, and imports decrease to 8 million.

- The fact that the tariff is a response to Vietnam's export subsidy does not make the tariff efficient because marginal benefit exceeds marginal cost by the amount of the tariff.

MyEconLab More Economics in the News

produced increases producers' profit, so Canadian producers gain from the import quota.

Importers of the Good Gain The importer is able to buy the good on the world market at the world market price and sell the good in the domestic market at the domestic price. Because the domestic price exceeds the world price, the importer gains.

Society Loses Society loses because the loss to consumers exceeds the gains of domestic producers and importers. Just like the social losses from a tariff, there is a social loss from the quota because part of the higher price paid to domestic producers pays the higher cost of domestic production. There is a social loss from the decreased quantity of the good consumed at the higher price.

Tariff and Import Quota Compared You've looked at the effects of a tariff and an import quota and can now see the essential differences between them. A tariff brings in revenue for the government while an import quota brings a profit for the importers. All the other effects of an import quota are the same as the effects of a tariff, provided the quota is set at the same quantity of imports that results from the tariff.

Tariffs and import quotas are equivalent ways of restricting imports, benefiting domestic producers, and harming domestic consumers.

Let's now look at some other import barriers.

Other Import Barriers

Two sets of policies that influence imports are:

- Health, safety, and regulation barriers
- Voluntary export restraints

Health, Safety, and Regulation Barriers Thousands of detailed health, safety, and other regulations restrict international trade. For example, Canadian food imports are examined by the Canadian Food Inspection Agency, which is "mandated to safeguard Canada's food supply and the plants and animals upon which safe and high-quality food depends." The discovery of BSE (mad cow disease) in just one cow in 2003 was enough to close down international trade in Canadian beef. The European Union bans imports of many genetically modified foods, such as Canadian-produced soybeans. Although regulations of the type we've just described are not designed to limit international trade, they have that effect.

Voluntary Export Restraints A *voluntary export restraint* is like a quota allocated to a foreign exporter of a good. This type of trade barrier isn't common. It was initially used during the 1980s when Japan voluntarily limited its exports of car parts to the United States.

Export Subsidies

A *subsidy* is a payment by the government to a producer. When the government pays a subsidy, the cost of production falls by the amount of the subsidy so supply increases. An **export subsidy** is a payment by the government to the producer of an exported good so it increases the supply of exports. Export subsidies are illegal under a number of international agreements including the North American Free Trade Agreement (NAFTA) and the rules of the World Trade Organization (WTO).

Although export subsidies are illegal, the subsidies that the Canadian, U.S., and European Union governments pay to farmers end up increasing domestic production, some of which gets exported. These exports of subsidized farm products make it harder for producers in other countries, notably in Africa and Central and South America, to compete in global markets.

Export subsidies bring gains to domestic producers, but they result in inefficient overproduction of some food products in the rich industrial countries, underproduction in the rest of the world, and create a social loss for the world as a whole.

◆ REVIEW QUIZ

1 What are the tools that a country can use to restrict international trade?
2 Explain the effects of a tariff on domestic production, the quantity bought, and the price.
3 Explain who gains and who loses from a tariff and why the losses exceed the gains.
4 Explain the effects of an import quota on domestic production, consumption, and price.
5 Explain who gains and who loses from an import quota and why the losses exceed the gains.

Work these questions in Study Plan 31.3 and get instant feedback. Do a Key Terms Quiz.   MyEconLab

The Case Against Protection

You've just seen that free trade promotes prosperity and protection is inefficient. Yet trade is restricted with tariffs, quotas, and other barriers. Why? Seven arguments for trade restrictions are that protecting domestic industries from foreign competition:

- Helps an infant industry grow.
- Counteracts dumping.
- Saves domestic jobs.
- Allows us to compete with cheap foreign labour.
- Penalizes lax environmental standards.
- Prevents rich countries from exploiting developing countries.
- Reduces offshore outsourcing that sends good Canadian jobs to other countries.

Helps an Infant Industry Grow

Comparative advantages change with on-the-job experience—*learning-by-doing*. When a new industry or a new product is born—an *infant industry*—it is not as productive as it will become with experience. It is argued that such an industry should be protected from international competition until it can stand alone and compete.

It is true that learning-by-doing can change comparative advantage, but this fact doesn't justify protecting an infant industry. Firms anticipate and benefit from learning-by-doing without protection from foreign competition.

When BlackBerry Ltd. started to build smartphones, productivity was at first low. But after a period of learning-by-doing, huge productivity gains followed. BlackBerry Ltd. didn't need a tariff to achieve these productivity gains.

Counteracts Dumping

Dumping occurs when a foreign firm sells its exports at a lower price than its cost of production. Dumping might be used by a firm that wants to gain a global monopoly. In this case, the foreign firm sells its output at a price below its cost to drive domestic firms out of business. When the domestic firms have gone, the foreign firm takes advantage of its monopoly position and charges a higher price for its product. Dumping is illegal under the rules of the World Trade Organization and is usually regarded as a justification for temporary tariffs, which are called *countervailing duties*.

But it is virtually impossible to detect dumping because it is hard to determine a firm's costs. As a result, the test for dumping is whether a firm's export price is below its domestic price. But this test is weak because it is rational for a firm to charge a low price in a market in which the quantity demanded is highly sensitive to price and a higher price in a market in which demand is less price-sensitive.

Saves Domestic Jobs

First, free trade does destroy some jobs, but it also creates other jobs. It brings about a global rationalization of labour and allocates labour resources to their highest-valued activities. International trade in textiles has cost thousands of jobs in Canada as textile mills and other factories closed. But thousands of jobs have been created in other countries as textile mills opened. And thousands of Canadian workers have better-paying jobs than as textile workers because Canadian export industries have expanded and created new jobs. More jobs have been created than destroyed.

Although protection can save particular jobs, it does so at a high cost. For example, until 2005, textile jobs were protected by an international agreement called the Multifibre Arrangement. The U.S. International Trade Commission (ITC) has estimated that because of import quotas, 72,000 jobs existed in the textile industry that would otherwise have disappeared and that the annual clothing expenditure in the United States was $31.9 billion ($160 per family) higher than it would have been with free trade. Equivalently, the ITC estimated that each textile job saved cost $221,000 a year.

Imports don't only destroy jobs. They create jobs for retailers that sell imported goods and for firms that service those goods. Imports also create jobs by creating income in the rest of the world, some of which is spent on Canadian-made goods and services.

Allows Us to Compete with Cheap Foreign Labour

With the removal of tariffs on trade between Canada, the United States, and Mexico, people said we would hear a "giant sucking sound" as jobs rushed to Mexico. That didn't happen. Why?

It didn't happen because low-wage labour is low-productivity labour. If a Canadian or U.S. autoworker earns $30 an hour and produces 15 units of output an hour, the average labour cost of a unit of output is $2. If a Mexican autoworker earns $3 an hour and produces 1 unit of output an hour, the average labour cost of a unit of output is $3. Other things remaining the same, the higher a worker's productivity, the higher is the worker's wage rate. High-wage workers have high productivity; low-wage workers have low productivity.

It is *comparative advantage,* not wage differences, that drive international trade and that enable us to compete with Mexico and Mexico to compete with Canada and the United States.

Penalizes Lax Environmental Standards

Another argument for protection is that it provides an incentive to poor countries to raise their environmental standards—free trade with the richer and "greener" countries is a reward for improved environmental standards.

This argument for protection is weak. First, a poor country cannot afford to be as concerned about its environmental standards as a rich country can. Today, some of the worst pollution of air and water is found in China, Mexico, and the former communist countries of Eastern Europe. But only a few decades ago, London and Los Angeles topped the pollution league chart. The best hope for cleaner air in Beijing and Mexico City is rapid income growth, which free trade promotes. As incomes in developing countries grow, they have the *means* to match their desires to improve their environment. Second, a poor country may have a comparative advantage at doing "dirty" work, which helps it to raise its income and at the same time enables the global economy to achieve higher environmental standards than would otherwise be possible.

Prevents Rich Countries from Exploiting Developing Countries

Another argument for protection is that international trade must be restricted to prevent the people of the rich industrial world from exploiting the poorer people of the developing countries and forcing them to work for slave wages.

Child labour and near-slave labour are serious problems. But by trading with poor countries, we increase the demand for the goods that these countries produce and increase the demand for their labour. When the demand for labour in developing countries increases, the wage rate rises. So, rather than exploiting people in developing countries, trade can improve their opportunities and increase their incomes.

The arguments for protectiuon that we've reviewed leave free trade unscathed. But a new phenomenon is at work in our economy: offshore outsourcing. Surely we need protection from this new source of foreign competition. Let's investigate.

Reduces Offshore Outsourcing that Sends Good Canadian Jobs to Other Countries

Offshore outsourcing—buying goods, components, or services from firms in other countries—brings gains from trade identical to those of any other type of trade. We could easily change the names of the items traded from T-shirts and regional jets (the examples in the previous sections of this chapter) to banking services and call-centre services (or any other pair of services). A Canadian bank might export banking services to Indian firms, and Indians might provide call-centre services to Canadian firms. This type of trade would benefit both Canadians and Indians, provided Canada has a comparative advantage in banking services and India has a comparative advantage in call-centre services.

Despite the gain from specialization and trade that offshore outsourcing brings, many people believe that it also brings costs that eat up the gains. Why?

A major reason is that it seems to send good Canadian jobs to other countries. It is true that some manufacturing and service jobs are going overseas. But others are expanding at home. Canada imports call-centre services, but it exports education, healthcare, legal, financial, and a host of other types of services. The number of jobs in these sectors is expanding and will continue to expand.

The exact number of jobs that have moved to lower-cost offshore locations is not known, and estimates vary. But even the highest estimate is small compared to the normal rate of job creation and labour turnover.

Winners and Losers

Gains from trade do not bring gains for every single person. Canadians, on average, gain from offshore outsourcing, but some people lose. The losers are those who have invested in the human capital to do a specific job that has now gone offshore.

Unemployment benefits provide short-term temporary relief for these displaced workers. But the long-term solution requires retraining and the acquisition of new skills.

Beyond bringing short-term relief through unemployment benefits, government has a larger role to play. By providing education and training, it can enable the labour force of the twenty-first century to engage in the ongoing learning and sometimes rapid retooling that jobs we can't foresee today will demand.

Schools and universities will expand and become better at doing their job of producing a more highly educated and flexible labour force.

AT **ISSUE**

Is Offshore Outsourcing Bad or Good for Canada?

The Royal Bank of Canada, Bell Canada, and Sears Canada engage in offshore outsourcing when they buy finished goods, components, or services from firms in other countries. Buying goods and components has been going on for centuries, but buying *services*, such as customer support call-centre services, is new and is made possible by the development of low-cost telephone and Internet service.

Should this type of offshore outsourcing be discouraged and penalized with taxes and regulations?

Bad	Good

Bad

- Whenever a major company announces job cuts and a decision to send some jobs abroad, there is an outcry from not only the affected workers but also the broader community. It seems clear: Offshore outsourcing is bad for Canadians.

- Surveys of opinion find that around 70 percent of people in advanced economies such as Canada think outsourcing hurts jobs and incomes at home, and only a small minority think it helps.

Good

- Economist N. Gregory Mankiw, speaking about the Canadian situation, but relevant to all countries, said, "I think outsourcing . . . is probably a plus for the economy in the long run."

- Mankiw went on to say that it doesn't matter whether "items produced abroad come on planes, ships, or over fibre-optic cables . . . the economics is basically the same."

- What Greg Mankiw is saying is that the economic analysis of the gains from international trade—exactly the same as what you have studied on pp. 752–755—applies to all types of international trade.

- Offshore outsourcing, like all other forms of international trade, is a source of gains for all.

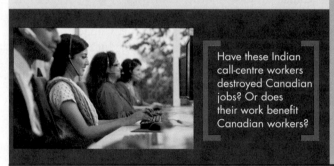

Have these Indian call-centre workers destroyed Canadian jobs? Or does their work benefit Canadian workers?

Avoiding Trade Wars

We have reviewed the arguments commonly heard in favour of protection and the counterarguments against it. But one counterargument to protection that is general and quite overwhelming is that protection invites retaliation and can trigger a trade war. A trade war is a contest in which when one country raises its import tariffs, other countries retaliate with increases of their own, which trigger yet further increases from the first country.

A trade war occurred during the Great Depression of the 1930s when the United States introduced the Smoot-Hawley tariff. Country after country retaliated with its own tariff, and in a short period, world trade had almost disappeared. The costs to all countries were large and led to a renewed international resolve to avoid such self-defeating moves in the future. The costs led to the impetus behind current attempts to liberate trade.

Why Is International Trade Restricted?

Why, despite all the arguments against protection, is trade restricted? There are two key reasons:

- Tariff revenue
- Rent seeking

Tariff Revenue Government revenue is costly to collect. In developed countries such as Canada, a well-organized tax collection system is in place that can generate billions of dollars of income tax and sales tax revenues.

But governments in developing countries have a difficult time collecting taxes from their citizens. Much economic activity takes place in an informal economy with few financial records. The one area in which economic transactions are well recorded is international trade. So tariffs on international trade are a convenient source of revenue in these countries.

Rent Seeking Rent seeking is the major reason why international trade is restricted. **Rent seeking** is lobbying for special treatment by the government to create economic profit or to divert the gains from free trade away from others. Free trade increases consumption possibilities *on average*, but not everyone shares in the gain and some people even lose. Free trade brings benefits to some and imposes costs on others, with total benefits exceeding total costs. The uneven distribution of costs and benefits is the principal obstacle to achieving more liberal international trade.

Returning to the example of trade in T-shirts and regional jets, the benefits from free trade accrue to all the people involved in the production of regional jets and to those producers of T-shirts that do not bear the costs of adjusting to a smaller garment industry. These costs are transition costs, not permanent costs. The costs of moving to free trade are borne by the garment producers and their employees who must become producers of other goods and services in which Canada has a comparative advantage.

The number of winners from free trade is large, but because the gains are spread thinly over a large number of people, the gain per person is small. The winners could organize and become a political force lobbying for free trade. But political activity is costly. It uses time and other scarce resources and the gains per person are too small to make the cost of political activity worth bearing.

In contrast, the number of losers from free trade is small, but the loss per person is large. Because the loss per person is large, the people who lose *are* willing to incur considerable expense to lobby against free trade.

Both the winners and losers weigh benefits and costs. Those who gain from free trade weigh the benefits it brings against the cost of achieving it. Those who lose from free trade and gain from protection weigh the benefit of protection against the cost of maintaining it. The protectionists undertake a larger quantity of political lobbying than the free traders.

Compensating Losers

If, in total, the gains from free international trade exceed the losses, why don't those who gain compensate those who lose so that everyone is in favour of free trade?

Some compensation does take place. When Canada entered the North American Free Trade Agreement (NAFTA) with the United States and Mexico, the United States set up a $56 million fund to support and retrain workers who lost their jobs as a result of the new trade agreement. During NAFTA's first six months, only 5,000 workers applied for benefits under this scheme.

The losers from international trade are also compensated indirectly through the normal unemployment compensation arrangements. But only limited attempts are made to compensate those who lose.

The main reason full compensation is not attempted is that the costs of identifying all the losers and estimating the value of their losses would be enormous. Also, it would never be clear whether a person who has fallen on hard times is suffering because of free trade or for other reasons that might be largely under her or his control. Furthermore, some people who look like losers at one point in time might, in fact, end up gaining. The young autoworker who loses his job in Ontario and gets a job on Alberta's oil patch might resent the loss of work and the need to move. But a year later, looking back on events, he counts himself fortunate.

Because we do not, in general, compensate the losers from free international trade, protectionism is a popular and permanent feature of our national economic and political life.

REVIEW QUIZ

1 What are the infant industry and dumping arguments for protection? Are they correct?
2 Can protection save jobs and the environment and prevent workers in developing countries from being exploited?
3 What is offshore outsourcing? Who benefits from it and who loses?
4 What are the main reasons for imposing a tariff?
5 Why don't the winners from free trade win the political argument?

Work these questions in Study Plan 31.4 and get instant feedback. Do a Key Terms Quiz. MyEconLab

◆ We end this chapter on international trade policy with *Economics in the News* on pp. 766–767, where we apply what you've learned by looking at the benefits of and obstacles to a Canadian free-trade deal with Japan.

Obstacles to Free Trade

Japan May Offer Canada Head Start on Pork Tariffs

Bloomberg
April 23, 2014

Japan, the world's largest pork importer, may accelerate tariff talks with Canada to increase pressure on the United States to ease demands for cuts in agricultural protection, the Asian nation's biggest hog farmers group said.

Canada, the largest pork exporter after the United States and the European Union, has been in talks with Japan on a bilateral trade pact since November 2012. Japan agreed to almost halve its tariff on Australian pork under a deal reached earlier this month between the two governments. The four countries are among 12 nations negotiating the Trans-Pacific Partnership (TPP).

"Canada is eager to boost pork sales to Japan and may seek treatment similar to what Japan gave to Australia," Takashi Koiso, a director at Japan Pork Producers Association, said in an interview in Tokyo. Lawmakers from Prime Minister Shinzo Abe's ruling Liberal Democratic Party said the tariff reduction Japan offered to Australia is a "red line" for the TPP. …

"We cannot accept tariff cuts beyond the level agreed to with Australia, or our industry will be undermined," said Hisao Kuramoto, the pork association's managing director.

Costs to produce pork for Japanese farmers are more than double those in the United States and Canada as the Asian nation imports almost all of its feed grains. Corn and soybean futures in the United States, the largest supplier to Japan, have climbed 19 percent and 13 percent this year respectively. …

Japan imported 738,455 tonnes of pork worth 390 billion yen ($3.8 billion) last year, of which 281,139 tonnes, or 38 percent, was from the United States, according to the agriculture ministry. Canada was the second-biggest supplier with 142,212 tonnes, followed by Denmark with 113,951 tonnes. …

Written by Aya Takada. Copyright © 2014. Used by permission of Bloomberg L.P. All rights reserved.

ESSENCE OF THE STORY

- Japan is the world's largest pork importer and Canada is the world's third-largest pork exporter.

- The cost of producing pork in Japan is more than double the cost in Canada and the United States.

- Japan imported 738,455 tonnes of pork in 2013 of which 142,212 tonnes were from Canada.

- Japan imposes a high tariff on pork imports, but it has done a deal with Australia to almost halve its rate.

- Canada wants Japan to lower its tariff on Canadian pork.

MyEconLab More Economics in the News

ECONOMIC ANALYSIS

- Canada is one of 12 Pacific-rim nations that are attempting to reach a deal that lowers barriers to trade.

- Japan, one of the two largest of the Pacific-rim economies, presents obstacles that stand in the way of a deal.

- The core of the problem is Japan's wish to protect its farmers, who form a strong political lobby.

- Figure 1 shows how Japan is protecting its pork farmers but damaging its consumers' interest.

- The demand curve is D_J and the supply curve is S_J. With a total ban on pork imports (an import quota of zero), the price of pork is $40,000 per tonne and 10 million tonnes are produced and consumed per year.

- If Japan opened up its pork market to free international trade, the price of pork would fall. In Fig. 1, the price falls to the world price (assumed) of $28,000 per tonne, shown by the line PW.

- With free trade, Japan can buy pork at $28,000 per tonne and the price in Japan falls to that level. The quantity of pork demanded increases to 16 million tonnes, the quantity supplied decreases to 6 million tonnes, and 10 million tonnes are imported. (Assumed quantities.)

- With the lower price of pork, Japanese pork producers lose as they cut production and sell less at the lower price. Japanese consumers gain as they increase the quantity of pork they buy and they pay a lower price for it. The gain to consumers exceeds the loss to producers.

- The farm lobby in Japan is strong and the government is unwilling to risk losing votes by permitting free trade in pork. But it has moved in that direction in its deal with Australia, and it is expected to move further in a deal with Canada.

- Figure 2 shows why Canada is interested in this deal. In Canada, the demand curve for pork is D_C and the supply curve is S_C. If there were no international trade in pork, the price in Canada would be $16,000 per tonne and 4 million tonnes would be produced and consumed each year.

- With free trade, Canada can sell pork at the world price of $28,000 per tonne and the price in Canada rises to that level. The quantity of pork demanded by Canadians decreases to 2 million tonnes, the quantity supplied by Canadian pork producers increases to 8 million tonnes, and 6 million tonnes are exported. (Assumed quantities.)

Figure 1 The Market for Pork in Japan

Figure 2 The Market for Pork in Canada

- Canadian consumers buy a smaller quantity of pork and pay a higher price, and Canadian pork producers sell a larger quantity and receive a higher price. The producers' gain exceeds the consumers' loss from free trade in pork. There is a social gain from free trade.

SUMMARY

Key Points

How Global Markets Work (pp. 752–754)

- Comparative advantage drives international trade.
- If the world price of a good is lower than the domestic price, the rest of the world has a comparative advantage in producing that good and the domestic country gains by producing less, consuming more, and importing the good.
- If the world price of a good is higher than the domestic price, the domestic country has a comparative advantage in producing that good and gains by producing more, consuming less, and exporting the good.

Working Problems 1 to 3 will give you a better understanding of how global markets work.

Winners, Losers, and the Net Gain from Trade (p. 755)

- Compared to a no-trade situation, in a market with imports, consumers gain and producers lose but the gains are greater than the losses.
- Compared to a no-trade situation, in a market with exports, producers gain and consumers lose but the gains are greater than the losses.

Working Problem 4 will give you a better understanding of winners, losers, and the net gains from trade.

International Trade Restrictions (pp. 756–761)

- Countries restrict international trade by imposing tariffs, import quotas, and other import barriers.
- Trade restrictions raise the domestic price of imported goods, lower the quantity imported, make consumers worse off, make producers better off, and damage the social interest.

Working Problems 5 to 10 will give you a better understanding of international trade restrictions.

The Case Against Protection (pp. 762–765)

- Arguments that protection helps an infant industry to grow and counteracts dumping are weak.
- Arguments that protection saves jobs, allows us to compete with cheap foreign labour, is needed to penalize lax environmental standards, and prevents exploitation of developing countries are flawed.
- Offshore outsourcing is just a new way of reaping gains from trade and does not justify protection.
- Trade restrictions are popular because protection brings a small loss per person to a large number of people and a large gain per person to a small number of people. Those who gain have a stronger political voice than those who lose and it is too costly to identify and compensate losers.

Working Problem 11 will give you a better understanding of the case against protection.

Key Terms

MyEconLab Key Terms Quiz

Dumping, 762
Exports, 752
Export subsidy, 761

Import quota, 758
Imports, 752
Offshore outsourcing, 763

Rent seeking, 765
Tariff, 756

WORKED PROBLEM

MyEconLab   You can work this problem in Chapter 31 Study Plan.

The table shows the Canadian demand schedule for honey and the supply schedule of honey by Canadian producers. The world price of honey is $8 a jar.

Price (dollars per jar)	Quantity demanded	Quantity supplied
	(millions of jars per year)	
5	10	0
6	8	3
7	6	6
8	4	9
9	2	12
10	0	15

Questions

1. With no international trade, what is the price of honey and the quantity bought and sold in Canada? Does Canada have a comparative advantage in producing honey? With free international trade, does Canada export or import honey?

2. With free international trade, what is the Canadian price of honey, the quantity bought by Canadians, the quantity produced in Canada, and the quantity of honey exported or imported?

3. Do Canadians gain from international trade in honey? Do all Canadians gain? If not, who loses and do the gains exceed the losses?

Solutions

1. With no international trade, the price of honey is that at which the Canadian quantity demanded equals the Canadian quantity supplied. The table shows that this price is $7 a jar at which the equilibrium quantity is 6 million jars a year.

   The price of honey in Canada is less than the world price, which means that the opportunity cost of producing a jar of honey in Canada is *less* than the opportunity cost of producing it in the rest of the world. So Canadian producers have a comparative advantage in producing honey. With free international trade, Canada exports honey.

Key Point: Comparative advantage is determined by comparing the opportunity costs of producing the good in Canada to the world price.

2. With free international trade, the price of honey in Canada rises to the world price of $8 a jar. Canadians cut their consumption of honey to 4 million jars a year while Canadian honey producers expand production to 9 million jars a year. Canada exports 5 million jars a year.

   The figure shows the quantities bought and produced in Canada and the quantity exported.

Key Point: As the domestic price rises to the world price, the quantity demanded decreases and the quantity supplied increases, and the difference is exported.

3. With free international trade in honey, Canada gains from exporting honey.

   The higher price and the larger quantity of honey produced increase the honey producers' profit. Consumers lose because the price of honey rises and they buy a smaller quantity of honey.

   Canada gains because the gain to honey producers exceeds the loss of honey consumers. There is a social gain from free trade.

Key Point: Free trade brings gains to domestic exporters and losses to domestic consumers of the exported good, but the exporting country has a net social gain.

Key Figure

MyEconLab Interactive Graph

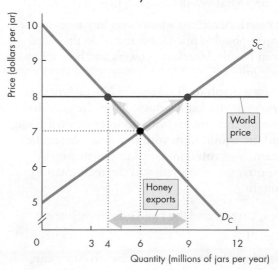

STUDY PLAN PROBLEMS AND APPLICATIONS

MyEconLab   You can work Problems 1 to 11 in Chapter 31 Study Plan and get instant feedback.

How Global Markets Work (Study Plan 31.1)

Use the following data to work Problems 1 to 3. Wholesalers buy and sell roses in containers that hold 120 stems. The table provides data about the wholesale market for roses in North America. The demand schedule is the wholesalers' demand and the supply schedule is the North American rose growers' supply.

Price (dollars per container)	Quantity demanded	Quantity supplied
	(millions of containers per year)	
100	15	0
125	12	2
150	9	4
175	6	6
200	3	8
225	0	10

Wholesalers can buy roses at auction in Aalsmeer, Holland, for $125 per container.

1. a. Without international trade, what would be the price of a container of roses and how many containers of roses a year would be bought and sold in North America?
    b. At the price in your answer to part (a), does North America or the rest of the world have a comparative advantage in producing roses?

2. If North American wholesalers buy roses at the lowest possible price, how many do they buy from North American growers and how many do they import?

3. Draw a graph to illustrate the North American wholesale market for roses. Show the equilibrium in that market with no international trade and the equilibrium with free trade. Mark the quantity of roses produced in North America, the quantity imported, and the total quantity bought.

Winners, Losers, and the Net Gain from Trade
(Study Plan 31.2)

4. Use the information on the North American wholesale market for roses in Problem 1 to:
    a. Explain who gains and who loses from free international trade in roses compared to a situation in which North Americans buy only roses grown locally.
    b. Calculate the value of the roses imported into the United States.

International Trade Restrictions (Study Plan 31.3)

Use the information on the Noth American wholesale market for roses in Problem 1 to work Problems 5 to 10.

5. If a tariff of $25 per container is imposed on imports of roses, explain how the price of roses, the quantity of roses bought, the quantity produced in North America, and the quantity imported change.

6. Who gains and who loses from this tariff?

7. Draw a graph of the North American market for roses to illustrate the effects of the tariff. On the graph, identify the tariff revenue from imported roses.

8. If an import quota of 5 million containers is imposed on roses, what happens to the North American price of roses, the quantity of roses bought, the quantity produced in North America, and the quantity imported?

9. Who gains and who loses from this import quota?

10. Draw a graph to illustrate the effects of the import quota. On the graph, identify the the importers' profit.

The Case Against Protection (Study Plan 31.4)

11. **Chinese Tire Maker Rejects Charge of Defects**
    U.S. regulators ordered the recall of more than 450,000 faulty tires. The Chinese producer of the tires disputed the allegations and hinted that the recall might be an effort to hamper Chinese exports to the United States.
    Source: *International Herald Tribune*,
    June 26, 2007
    a. What does the news clip imply about the comparative advantage of producing tires in the United States and China?
    b. Could product quality be a valid argument against free trade? If it could, explain how.

ADDITIONAL PROBLEMS AND APPLICATIONS

MyEconLab   You can work these problems in MyEconLab if assigned by your instructor.

How Global Markets Work

12. Suppose that the world price of eggs is $1 a dozen, Canada does not trade internationally, and the equilibrium price of eggs in Canada is $3 a dozen. Canada then begins to trade internationally.

    a. How does the price of eggs in Canada change?

    b. Do Canadians buy more or fewer eggs?

    c. Do Canadian egg farmers produce more or fewer eggs?

    d. Does Canada export or import eggs and why?

    e. Would employment in the Canadian egg industry change? If so, how?

13. Suppose that the world price of steel is $100 a tonne, India does not trade internationally, and the equilibrium price of steel in India is $60 a tonne. India then begins to trade internationally.

    a. How does the price of steel in India change?

    b. How does the quantity of steel produced in India change?

    c. How does the quantity of steel bought by India change?

    d. Does India export or import steel and why?

14. A semiconductor is a key component in your laptop, cellphone, and iPod. The table provides information about the market for semiconductors in Canada.

Price (dollars per unit)	Quantity demanded	Quantity supplied
	(billions of units per year)	
10	25	0
12	20	20
14	15	40
16	10	60
18	5	80
20	0	100

Producers of semiconductors can get $18 a unit on the world market.

    a. With no international trade, what would be the price of a semiconductor and how many semiconductors a year would be bought and sold in Canada?

    b. Does Canada have a comparative advantage in producing semiconductors?

15. **Act Now, Eat Later**

    The hunger crisis in poor countries has its roots in Canadian, U.S., and European policies of subsidizing the diversion of food crops to produce biofuels like corn-based ethanol. That is, doling out subsidies to put the world's dinner into the gas tank.

    Source: *Time*, May 5, 2008

    a. What is the effect on the world price of corn of the increased use of corn to produce ethanol in Canada, the United States, and Europe?

    b. How does the change in the world price of corn affect the quantity of corn produced in a poor developing country with a comparative advantage in producing corn, the quantity it consumes, and the quantity that it either exports or imports?

Winners, Losers, and the Net Gain from Trade

16. Draw a graph of the market for corn in the poor developing country in Problem 15(b) to show the changes in the price of corn, the quantity produced, and the quantity consumed by people in that country.

Use the following news clip to work Problems 17 and 18.

South Korea to Resume Canadian Beef Imports

South Korea will reopen its market to most Canadian beef. South Korea banned imports of beef in 2003 amid concerns over a case of mad cow disease. The ban closed what was then the fourth-largest market for Canadian beef, valued at $50 million a year.

Source: Bloomberg, June 28, 2011

17. Explain how South Korea's import ban on Canadian beef affected beef producers and consumers in South Korea. Draw a graph of the beef market in South Korea to show how this ban changed the price of beef, the quantity produced, the quantity consumed, and the quantity imported.

18. Assuming that South Korea is the only importer of Canadian beef, explain how South Korea's import ban on beef affected beef producers and consumers in Canada. Draw a graph of the Canadian beef market to illustrate your answer.

International Trade Restrictions

Use the following information to work Problems 19 to 20.

Before 1995, trade between Canada and Mexico was subject to tariffs. In 1995, Mexico joined NAFTA and all Canadian and Mexican tariffs have gradually been removed.

19. Explain how the price that Canadian consumers pay for goods from Mexico and the quantity of Canadian imports from Mexico have changed. Who are the winners and who are the losers from this free trade?

20. Explain how the quantity of Canadian exports to Mexico and the Canadian government's tariff revenue from trade with Mexico have changed.

21. Suppose that in 2014 tomato growers in Ontario lobby the Canadian government to impose an import quota on Mexican tomatoes. Explain who in Canada would gain and who would lose from such an import quota.

Use the following information to work Problems 22 and 23.

Suppose that in response to huge job losses in the Canadian textile industry, the Canadian government imposes a 100 percent tariff on imports of textiles from China.

22. Explain how the tariff on textiles will change the price that Canadian buyers pay for textiles, the quantity of textiles imported, and the quantity of textiles produced in Canada.

23. Explain how the Canadian and Chinese gains from trade will change. Who in Canada will lose and who will gain?

Use the following information to work Problems 24 and 25.

With free trade between Australia and Canada, Australia would export beef to Canada. But Canada imposes an import quota on Australian beef.

24. Explain how this quota influences the price that Canadian consumers pay for beef, the quantity of beef produced in Canada, and the Canadian and the Australian gains from trade.

25. Explain who in Canada gains from the quota on beef imports and who loses.

The Case Against Protection

26. **Trading Up**
The cost of protecting jobs in uncompetitive sectors through tariffs is high: Saving a job in the sugar industry costs American consumers $826,000 in higher prices a year; saving a dairy industry job costs $685,000 per year; and saving a job in the manufacturing of women's handbags costs $263,000.
Source: *The New York Times*, June 26, 2006
a. What are the arguments for saving the jobs mentioned in this news clip? Explain why these arguments are faulty.
b. Is there any merit to saving these jobs?

Economics in the News

27. After you have studied *Economics in the News* on pp. 766–767, answer the following questions.
a. What is the TPP?
b. Who in Canada would benefit and who would lose from a successful TPP?
c. Illustrate your answer to part (b) with an appropriate graphical analysis assuming that tariffs are not completely eliminated.
d. Who in Japan and other TPP nations would benefit and who would lose from a successful TPP?
e. Illustrate, with an appropriate graphical analysis, who in Japan would benefit and who would lose from a successful TPP, assuming that all Japan's import quotas and tariffs are completely eliminated.

28. **E.U. Agrees to Trade Deal with South Korea**
Italy has dropped its resistance to an E.U. trade agreement with South Korea, which will wipe out $2 billion in annual duties on E.U. exports. Italians argued that the agreement, which eliminates E.U. duties on South Korean cars, would put undue pressure on its own automakers.
Source: *The Financial Times*, September 16, 2010
a. What is a free-trade agreement? What is its aim?
b. Explain how a tariff on E.U. car imports changes E.U. production of cars, purchases of cars, and imports of cars. Illustrate your answer with an appropriate graphical analysis.
c. Explain who gains and who loses from the free-trade deal in cars.
d. Explain why Italian automakers opposed cuts in car import tariffs.

Tradeoffs and Free Lunches

A policy tradeoff arises if, in taking an action to achieve one goal, some other goal must be forgone. The Bank of Canada wants to avoid a rise in the inflation rate and a rise in the unemployment rate. But if the Bank of Canada raises the interest rate to curb inflation, it might lower expenditure and increase unemployment. The Bank of Canada faces a short-run tradeoff between inflation and unemployment.

A policy free-lunch arises if, in taking actions to pursue one goal, some other (intended or unintended) goal is also achieved. The Bank of Canada wants to keep inflation in check and, at the same time, to boost the economic growth rate. If lower inflation brings greater certainty about the future and stimulates saving and investment, the Bank of Canada gets both lower inflation and faster real GDP growth. It enjoys a free lunch.

The first two chapters in this part have described the institutional framework in which fiscal policy (Chapter 29) and monetary policy (Chapter 30) are made, described the instruments of policy, and analyzed the effects of policy. This exploration of economic policy draws on almost everything that you learned in previous chapters.

The final chapter (Chapter 31) explains a free lunch that arises from international trade and the gains that are achieved from *free* trade.

These policy chapters serve as a capstone on your knowledge of macroeconomics and draw together all the strands in your study of the previous chapters.

Milton Friedman, whom you meet below, has profoundly influenced our understanding of macroeconomic policy, especially monetary policy.

Milton Friedman *was born into a poor immigrant family in New York City in 1912. He was an undergraduate at Rutgers and a graduate student at Columbia University during the Great Depression. From 1977 until his death in 2006, Professor Friedman was a Senior Fellow at the Hoover Institution at Stanford University. But his reputation was built between 1946 and 1983, when he was a leading member of the "Chicago School," an approach to economics developed at the University of Chicago and based on the views that free markets allocate resources efficiently and that stable and low money supply growth delivers macroeconomic stability.*

Friedman has advanced our understanding of the forces that determine macroeconomic performance and clarified the effects of the quantity of money. For this work, he was awarded the 1977 Nobel Prize for Economic Science.

By reasoning from basic economic principles, Friedman (along with Edmund S. Phelps, the 2006

> *Inflation is always and everywhere a monetary phenomenon.*
>
> **MILTON FRIEDMAN**
> *The Counter-Revolution in Monetary Theory*

Economics Nobel Laureate) predicted that persistent demand stimulation would not increase output but would cause inflation.

When output growth slowed and inflation broke out in the 1970s, Friedman seemed like a prophet, and for a time, his policy prescription, known as monetarism, was embraced around the world.

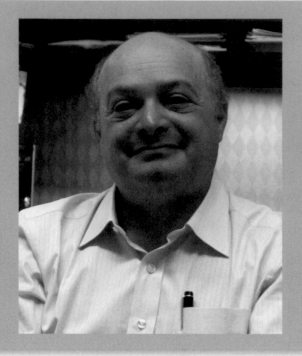

PIERRE SIKLOS is Professor of Economics and Director of the Viessmann European Research Centre at Wilfrid Laurier University in Waterloo, Ontario. He was an undergraduate at McGill University in Montreal, where he was born, and a graduate student at the University of Western Ontario and Carleton University, where he received his PhD in 1981.

Professor Siklos is a macroeconomist who studies inflation, central banks, and financial markets. His work is data driven and he uses statistical methods to uncover the mechanisms at work. His research is published in a variety of international journals.

He has been a visiting scholar at universities around Europe and North America, Australia, and New Zealand. Pierre is a member of the C.D. Howe Institute's Monetary Policy Council.

Michael Parkin and Robin Bade talked with Pierre Siklos about his work and about the problems facing Canada today.

Pierre, why did you become an economist and what attracted you to macroeconomics?

As an undergraduate at McGill University in Montreal I was majoring in mathematics. I was especially interested in statistics and I enrolled in an econometrics course. The econometrics lecturer emphasized how statistical tools could be used to help us understand economic phenomena. I became fascinated by the sheer breadth and scope of the economic phenomena that could be studied with econometric tools. I was particulary impressed by the range of macroeconomic questions that could be studied. After taking that econometrics course, I was hooked and I resolved to take economics in graduate school.

You've specialized in the study of monetary policy: How would you describe the most important principles

> The clear and convincing communication of monetary policy decisions [is] vital.

that you and other economists have discovered for the conduct of monetary policy?

After much research I have come to the conclusion that monetary policy can help smooth business cycle fluctuations in the short to medium term (say around 2–3 years) but not beyond.

Consistently good monetary policy can lead to desirable economic outcomes with low and predictable inflation. Canada's monetary policy during the period of inflation targeting is an example of the achievement of good outcomes with good policy.

Similarly, consistently bad monetary policy can lead to disastrous economic outcomes with hyperinflation, perhaps the single best example of monetary policy that has utterly failed.

The clear and convincing communication of monetary policy decisions plays an important role in the achievement of good policy outcomes, although its vital importance is difficult to demonstrate.

*Read the full interview with Pierre Siklos in MyEconLab

Above full-employment equilibrium A macroeconomic equilibrium in which real GDP exceeds potential GDP. (p. 634)

Absolute advantage A person has an absolute advantage if that person is more productive than another person. (p. 40)

Aggregate demand The relationship between the quantity of real GDP demanded and the price level. (p. 628)

Aggregate planned expenditure The sum of planned consumption expenditure, planned investment, planned government expenditure on goods and services, and planned exports minus planned imports. (p. 648)

Aggregate production function The relationship between real GDP and the quantity of labour when all other influences on production remain the same. (p. 520)

Allocative efficiency A situation in which goods and services are produced at the lowest possible cost and in the quantities that provide the greatest possible benefit. We cannot produce more of any good without giving up some of another good that we *value more highly*. (p. 35)

Arbitrage The practice of seeking to profit by buying in one market and selling for a higher price in another related market. (p. 602)

Automatic fiscal policy A fiscal policy action that is triggered by the state of the economy with no action by the government. (p. 714)

Autonomous expenditure The sum of those components of aggregate planned expenditure that are not influenced by real GDP. Autonomous expenditure equals the sum of investment, government expenditure, exports, and the autonomous parts of consumption expenditure and imports. (p. 652)

Autonomous tax multiplier The change in equilibrium expenditure and real GDP that results from a change in autonomous taxes divided by the change in autonomous taxes. (p. 670)

Balanced budget A government budget in which receipts and outlays are equal. (p. 705)

Balanced budget multiplier The change in equilibrium expenditure and real GDP that results from equal changes in government expenditure and lump-sum taxes divided by the change in government expenditure. (p. 671)

Balance of payments accounts A country's record of international trading, borrowing, and lending. (p. 608)

Bank rate The interest rate that the Bank of Canada charges big banks on loans. (pp. 574, 731)

Below full-employment equilibrium A macroeconomic equilibrium in which potential GDP exceeds real GDP. (p. 635)

Benefit The benefit of something is the gain or pleasure that it brings and is determined by preferences. (p. 9)

Bond A promise to make specified payments on specified dates. (p. 543)

Bond market The market in which bonds issued by firms and governments are traded. (p. 543)

Budget deficit A government's budget balance that is negative—outlays exceed receipts. (p. 705)

Budget surplus A government's budget balance that is positive—receipts exceed outlays. (p. 705)

Business cycle The periodic but irregular up-and-down movement of total production and other measures of economic activity. (p. 473)

Canadian interest rate differential The Canadian interest rate minus the foreign interest rate. (p. 599)

Canadian official reserves The Canadian government's holdings of foreign currency. (p. 608)

Capital The tools, equipment, buildings, and other constructions that businesses use to produce goods and services. (p. 4)

Capital accumulation The growth of capital resources, including *human capital*. (p. 38)

Capital and financial account A record of foreign investment in a country minus its investment abroad. (p. 608)

Central bank A bank's bank and a public authority that regulates the

nation's depository institutions and conducts *monetary policy*, which means it adjusts the quantity of money in circulation and influences interest rates. (p. 571)

Ceteris paribus Other things being equal—all other relevant things remaining the same. (p. 24)

Change in demand A change in buyers' plans that occurs when some influence on those plans other than the price of the good changes. It is illustrated by a shift of the demand curve. (p. 58)

Change in supply A change in sellers' plans that occurs when some influence on those plans other than the price of the good changes. It is illustrated by a shift of the supply curve. (p. 63)

Change in the quantity demanded A change in buyers' plans that occurs when the price of a good changes but all other influences on buyers' plans remain unchanged. It is illustrated by a movement along the demand curve. (p. 61)

Change in the quantity supplied A change in sellers' plans that occurs when the price of a good changes but all other influences on sellers' plans remain unchanged. It is illustrated by a movement along the supply curve. (p. 64)

Chartered bank A private firm, chartered under the Bank Act of 1991 to receive deposits and make loans. (p. 567)

Classical A macroeconomist who believes that the economy is self-regulating and always at full employment. (p. 638)

Classical growth theory A theory of economic growth based on the view that the growth of real GDP per person is temporary and that when it rises above subsistence level, a population explosion eventually brings it back to subsistence level. (p. 529)

Comparative advantage A person or country has a comparative advantage in an activity if that person or country can perform the activity at a lower opportunity cost than anyone else or any other country. (p. 40)

Competitive market A market that has many buyers and many sellers, so no single buyer or seller can influence the price. (p. 56)

Complement A good that is used in conjunction with another good. (p. 59)

Consumer Price Index (CPI) An index that measures the average of the prices paid by urban consumers for a fixed basket of consumer goods and services. (p. 499)

Consumption expenditure The total payment for consumer goods and services. (p. 467)

Consumption function The relationship between consumption expenditure and disposable income, other things remaining the same. (p. 648)

Core inflation rate A measure of the inflation rate that excludes volatile prices in an attempt to reveal the underlying inflation trend. (p. 502)

Cost-push inflation An inflation that results from an initial increase in costs. (p. 685)

Crawling peg An exchange rate that follows a path determined by a decision of the government or the central bank and is achieved in a similar way to a fixed exchange rate. (p. 606)

Creditor nation A country that during its entire history has invested more in the rest of the world than other countries have invested in it. (p. 611)

Crowding-out effect The tendency for a government budget deficit to raise the real interest rate and decrease investment. (p. 555)

Currency The notes and coins held by individuals and businesses. (p. 565)

Currency drain ratio The ratio of currency to deposits. (p. 575)

Current account A record of receipts from exports of goods and services, payments for imports of goods and services, net interest income paid abroad, and net transfers received from abroad. (p. 608)

Cycle The tendency for a variable to alternate between upward and downward movements. (p. 481)

Cyclical surplus or deficit The actual surplus or deficit minus the structural surplus or deficit. (p. 714)

Cyclical unemployment The higher than normal unemployment at a business cycle trough and the lower than normal unemployment at a business cycle peak. (p. 495)

Debtor nation A country that during its entire history has borrowed more from the rest of the world than other countries have lent it. (p. 611)

Default risk The risk that a borrower, also known as a creditor, might not repay a loan. (p. 551)

Deflation A persistently falling price level. (p. 498)

Demand The entire relationship between the price of the good and the quantity demanded of it when all other influences on buyers' plans remain the same. It is illustrated by a demand curve and described by a demand schedule. (p. 57)

Demand curve A curve that shows the relationship between the quantity demanded of a good and its price when all other influences on consumers' planned purchases remain the same. (p. 58)

Demand for loanable funds The relationship between the quantity of loanable funds demanded and the real interest rate when all other influences on borrowing plans remain the same. (p. 549)

Demand for money The relationship between the quantity of real money demanded and the nominal interest rate when all other influences on the amount of money that people wish to hold remain the same. (p. 579)

Demand-pull inflation An inflation that starts because aggregate demand increases. (p. 683)

Depository institution A financial firm that takes deposits from households and firms. (p. 567)

Depreciation The decrease in the value of a firm's capital that results from wear and tear and obsolescence. (p. 468)

Desired reserve ratio The ratio of reserves to deposits that banks *plan* to hold. (p. 575)

Direct relationship A relationship between two variables that move in the same direction. (p. 18)

Discouraged searcher A person who currently is neither working nor looking for work but has indicated that he or she wants a job, is available for work, and has looked for work sometime in the recent past but has stopped looking because of repeated failure. (p. 493)

Discretionary fiscal policy A fiscal action that is initiated by an act of Parliament. (p. 714)

Disposable income Aggregate income minus taxes plus transfer payments. (pp. 630, 648)

Dumping The sale by a foreign firm of exports at a lower price than the cost of production. (p. 762)

Economic growth The expansion of production possibilities. (pp. 38, 514)

Economic model A description of some aspect of the economic world that includes only those features of the world that are needed for the purpose at hand. (p. 11)

Economics The social science that studies the *choices* that individuals, businesses, governments, and entire societies make as they cope with *scarcity* and the *incentives* that influence and reconcile those choices. (p. 2)

Efficient Resource use is efficient if it is *not* possible to make someone better off without making someone else worse off. (p. 5)

Employment-to-population ratio The percentage of people of working age who have jobs. (p. 493)

Entrepreneurship The human resource that organizes the other three factors of production: labour, land, and capital. (p. 4)

Equilibrium expenditure The level of aggregate expenditure that occurs when aggregate *planned* expenditure equals real GDP. (p. 654)

Equilibrium price The price at which the quantity demanded equals the quantity supplied. (p. 66)

Equilibrium quantity The quantity bought and sold at the equilibrium price. (p. 66)

Excess reserves A bank's actual reserves minus its desired reserves. (p. 575)

Exchange rate The price at which one currency exchanges for another in the foreign exchange market. (p. 594)

Expansion A business cycle phase between a trough and a peak—a period in which real GDP increases. (p. 473)

Export subsidy The a payment by the government to the producer of an exported good so it increases the supply of exports. (p. 761)

Exports The goods and services that we sell to people in other countries. (pp. 468, 752)

Factors of production The productive resources used to produce goods and services. (p. 3)

Federal budget The annual statement of the outlays and receipts of the Government of Canada, together with the laws and regulations that approve and support those outlays and taxes. (p. 704)

Final good An item that is bought by its final user during the specified time period. (p. 466)

Financial capital The funds that firms use to buy physical capital and that households use to buy a home or to invest in human capital. (p. 542)

Financial institution A firm that operates on both sides of the market for financial capital. It borrows in one market and lends in another. (p. 544)

Firm An economic unit that hires factors of production and organizes those factors to produce and sell goods and services. (p. 44)

Fiscal policy The use of the federal budget, by setting and changing tax rates, making transfer payments, and purchasing goods and services, to achieve macroeconomic objectives such as full employment, sustained economic growth, and price level stability. (pp. 630, 704)

Fiscal stimulus The use of fiscal policy to increase production and employment. (p. 714)

Fixed exchange rate An exchange rate the value of which is determined by a decision of the government or the central bank and is achieved by central bank intervention in the foreign exchange market to block the unregulated forces of demand and supply. (p. 605)

Flexible exchange rate An exchange rate that is determined by demand and supply in the foreign exchange market with no direct intervention by the central bank. (p. 605)

Foreign currency The money of other countries regardless of whether that money is in the form of notes, coins, or bank deposits. (p. 594)

Foreign exchange market The market in which the currency of one country is exchanged for the currency of another. (p. 594)

Frictional unemployment The unemployment that arises from normal labour turnover—from people entering and leaving the labour force and from the ongoing creation and destruction of jobs. (p. 495)

Full employment A situation in which the unemployment rate equals the natural unemployment rate. At full employment, there is no cyclical unemployment—all unemployment is frictional and structural. (p. 495)

Full-employment equilibrium A macroeconomic equilibrium in which real GDP equals potential GDP. (p. 635)

Goods and services The objects that people value and produce to satisfy human wants. (p. 3)

Government debt The total amount that the government has borrowed. It equals the sum of past budget deficits minus the sum of past budget surpluses. (p. 707)

Government expenditure Goods and services bought by government. (p. 468)

Government expenditure multiplier The quantitative effect of a change in government expenditure on real GDP. It is calculated as the change in real GDP that results from a change in government expenditure divided by the change in government expenditure. (pp. 670, 715)

Government sector balance An amount equal to net taxes minus government expenditure on goods and services. (p. 612)

Gross domestic product (GDP) The market value of all final goods and services produced within a country during a given time period. (p. 466)

Gross investment The total amount spent on purchases of new capital and on replacing depreciated capital. (pp. 468, 542)

Growth rate The annual percentage change of a variable—the change in the level expressed as a percentage of the initial level. (p. 514)

Human capital The knowledge and skill that people obtain from education, on-the-job training, and work experience. (p. 3)

Hyperinflation An inflation rate of 50 percent a month or higher that grinds the economy to a halt and causes a society to collapse. (p. 498)

Import quota A restriction that limits the quantity of a good that may be imported in a given period. (p. 758)

Imports The goods and services that we buy from people in other countries. (pp. 468, 752)

Incentive A reward that encourages an action or a penalty that discourages one. (p. 2)

Induced expenditure The sum of the components of aggregate planned expenditure that vary with real GDP. Induced expenditure equals consumption expenditure minus imports. (p. 652)

Inferior good A good for which demand decreases as income increases. (p. 60)

Inflation A persistently rising price level. (p. 498)

Inflationary gap An output gap in which real GDP exceeds potential GDP. (p. 634)

Inflation rate targeting A monetary policy strategy in which the central bank makes a public commitment to achieve an explicit inflation rate and to explain how its policy actions will achieve that target. (p. 728)

Interest The income that capital earns. (p. 4)

Interest rate parity A situation in which the rates of return on assets in different currencies are equal. (p. 602)

Intermediate good An item that is produced by one firm, bought by another firm, and used as a component of a final good or service. (p. 466)

Inverse relationship A relationship between variables that move in opposite directions. (p. 19)

Investment The purchase of new plant, equipment, and buildings, and additions to inventories. (p. 468)

Keynesian A macroeconomist who believes that left alone, the economy would rarely operate at full employment and that to achieve full employment, active help from fiscal policy and monetary policy is required. (p. 638)

Keynesian cycle theory A theory that fluctuations in investment driven by fluctuations in business confidence—summarized by the phrase "animal spirits"—are the main source of fluctuations in aggregate demand. (p. 679)

Labour The work time and work effort that people devote to producing goods and services. (p. 3)

Labour force The sum of the people who are employed and who are unemployed. (p. 491)

Labour force participation rate The percentage of the working-age population who are members of the labour force. (p. 492)

Labour productivity The quantity of real GDP produced by an hour of labour. (p. 524)

Laffer curve The relationship between the tax rate and the amount of tax revenue collected. (p. 713)

Land The "gifts of nature" that we use to produce goods and services. (p. 3)

Law of demand Other things remaining the same, the higher the price of a good, the smaller is the quantity demanded of it; the lower the price of a good, the larger is the quantity demanded of it. (p. 57)

Law of supply Other things remaining the same, the higher the price of a good, the greater is the quantity supplied of it; the lower the price of a

good, the smaller is the quantity supplied. (p. 62)

Lender of last resort The Bank of Canada is the lender of last resort—depository institutions that are short of reserves can borrow from the Bank of Canada. (p. 571)

Linear relationship A relationship between two variables that is illustrated by a straight line. (p. 18)

Loanable funds market The aggregate of all the individual markets in which households, firms, governments, banks, and other financial institutions borrow and lend. (p. 547)

Long-run aggregate supply The relationship between the quantity of real GDP supplied and the price level when the money wage rate changes in step with the price level to maintain full employment. (p. 624)

Long-run macroeconomic equilibrium A situation that occurs when real GDP equals potential GDP—the economy is on its long-run aggregate supply curve. (p. 632)

Long-run Phillips curve A curve that shows the relationship between inflation and unemployment when the actual inflation rate equals the expected inflation rate. (p. 692)

M1 A measure of money that consists of currency held by individualsd and businesses plus chequable deposits owned by individuals and businesses. (p. 565)

M2 A measure of money that consists of M1 plus all other deposits—non-chequable deposits and fixed term deposits. (p. 565)

Macroeconomics The study of the performance of the national economy and the global economy. (p. 2)

Margin When a choice is made by comparing a little more of something with its cost, the choice is made at the margin. (p. 10)

Marginal benefit The benefit that a person receives from consuming one more unit of a good or service. It is measured as the maximum amount that a person is willing to pay for one more unit of the good or service. (pp. 10, 36)

Marginal benefit curve A curve that shows the relationship between the marginal benefit of a good and the quantity of that good consumed. (p. 36)

Marginal cost The *opportunity cost* of producing *one* more unit of a good or service. It is the best alternative forgone. It is calculated as the increase in total cost divided by the increase in output. (pp. 10, 35)

Marginal propensity to consume The fraction of a *change* in disposable income that is spent on consumption. It is calculated as the *change* in consumption expenditure divided by the *change* in disposable income. (p. 650)

Marginal propensity to import The fraction of an increase in real GDP that is spent on imports. It is calculated as the *change* in imports divided by the *change* in real GDP, other things remaining the same. (p. 651)

Marginal propensity to save The fraction of a *change* in disposable income that is saved. It is calculated as the *change* in saving divided by the *change* in disposable income. (p. 650)

Market Any arrangement that enables buyers and sellers to get information and to do business with each other. (p. 44)

Means of payment A method of settling a debt. (p. 564)

Microeconomics The study of the choices that individuals and businesses make, the way these choices interact in markets, and the influence of governments. (p. 2)

Monetarist A macroeconomist who believes that the economy is self-regulating and that it will normally operate at full employment, provided that monetary policy is not erratic and that the pace of money growth is kept steady. (p. 639)

Monetarist cycle theory A theory that fluctuations in both investment and consumption expenditure, driven by fluctuations in the growth rate of the quantity of money, are the main source of fluctuations in aggregate demand. (p. 679)

Monetary base The sum of Bank of Canada notes, coins, and depository institution deposits at the Bank of Canada. (p. 572)

Monetary policy The Bank of Canada conducts the nation's monetary policy by changing interest rates and adjusting the quantity of money. (p. 630)

Money Any commodity or token that is generally acceptable as a means of payment. (pp. 44, 564)

Money multiplier The ratio of the change in the quantity of money to the change in the monetary base. (p. 576)

Money price The number of dollars that must be given up in exchange for a good or service. (p. 56)

Mortgage A legal contract that gives ownership of a home to the lender in the event that the borrower fails to meet the agreed loan payments (repayments and interest). (p. 543)

Mortgage-backed security A type of bond that entitles its holder to the income from a package of mortgages. (p. 544)

Multiplier The amount by which a change in autonomous expenditure is magnified or multiplied to determine the change in equilibrium expenditure and real GDP. (p. 656)

National saving The sum of private saving (saving by households and businesses) and government saving. (p. 547)

Natural unemployment rate The unemployment rate when the economy is at full employment—natural unemployment as a percentage of the labour force. (p. 495)

Negative externality An externality that arises from either production or consumption and that imposes an external cost. (p. 370)

Neoclassical growth theory A theory of economic growth that proposes that real GDP per person grows because technological change induces an amount of saving and investment that makes capital per hour of labour grow. (p. 529)

Net borrower A country that is borrowing more from the rest of the world than it is lending to it. (p. 610)

Net exports The value of exports of goods and services minus the value of imports of goods and services. (pp. 468, 612)

Net investment The amount by which the value of capital increases—gross investment minus depreciation. (pp. 468, 542)

Net lender A country that is lending more to the rest of the world than it is borrowing from it. (p. 610)

Net taxes Taxes paid to governments minus cash transfers received from governments. (p. 547)

Net worth The market value of what a financial institution has lent minus the market value of what it has borrowed. (p. 546)

New classical A macroeconomist who holds the view that business cycle fluctuations are the efficient responses of a well-functioning market economy bombarded by shocks that arise from the uneven pace of technological change. (p. 638)

New classical cycle theory A rational expectations theory of the business cycle in which the rational expectation of the price level, which is determined by potential GDP and *expected* aggregate demand, determines the money wage rate and the position of the *SAS* curve. (p. 679)

New growth theory A theory of economic growth based on the idea that real GDP per person grows because of the choices that people make in the pursuit of profit and that growth will persist indefinitely. (p. 530)

New Keynesian A macroeconomist who holds the view that not only is the money wage rate sticky but also that the prices of goods and services are sticky. (p. 639)

New Keynesian cycle theory A rational expectations theory of the business cycle that emphasizes the fact that today's money wage rates were negotiated at many past dates, which means that *past* rational expectations of the current price level influence the money wage rate and the position of the *SAS* curve. (p. 679)

Nominal GDP The value of the final goods and services produced in a given year valued at the prices that prevailed in that same year. It is a more precise name for GDP. (p. 471)

Nominal interest rate The number of dollars that a borrower pays and a lender receives in interest in a year expressed as a percentage of the number of dollars borrowed and lent. (p. 548)

Normal good A good for which demand increases as income increases. (p. 60)

Official settlements account A record of the change in official reserves, which are the government's holdings of foreign currency. (p. 608)

Offshore outsourcing A Canadian firm buys finished goods, components, or services from firms in other countries. (p. 763)

Open market operation The purchase or sale of government securities by the Bank of Canada in the loanable funds market. (p. 572)

Operating band The the target overnight loans rate plus or minus 0.25 percentage points: bank rate and the settlement balances rate. (p. 731)

Opportunity cost The highest-valued alternative that we must give up to get something. (pp. 9, 33)

Output gap The gap between real GDP and potential GDP. (pp. 496, 634)

Overnight loans rate The interest rate on overnight loans that the big banks make to each other. (p. 730)

Positive relationship A relationship between two variables that move in the same direction. (p. 18)

Potential GDP The value of production when all the economy's labour, capital, land, and entrepreneurial ability are fully employed; the quantity of real GDP at full employment. (p. 472)

Preferences A description of a person's likes and dislikes and the intensity of those feelings. (pp. 9, 36)

Price level The average level of prices. (p. 498)

Private sector balance An amount equal to saving minus investment. (p. 612)

Production efficiency A situation in which goods and services are produced at the lowest possible cost. (p. 33)

Production possibilities frontier The boundary between those combinations of goods and services that can be produced and those combinations that cannot. (p. 32)

Profit The income earned by entrepreneurship. (p. 4)

Property rights The social arrangements that govern the ownership, use, and disposal of anything that people value. Property rights are enforceable in the courts. (p. 44)

Purchasing power parity A situation in which the prices in two countries are equal when converted at the exchange rate. (p. 602)

Quantity demanded The amount of a good or service that consumers plan to buy during a given time period at a particular price. (p. 57)

Quantity supplied The amount of a good or service that producers plan to sell during a given time period at a particular price. (p. 62)

Quantity theory of money The proposition that in the long run, an increase in the quantity of money brings an equal percentage increase in the price level. (p. 582)

Rational choice A choice that compares costs and benefits and achieves the greatest benefit over cost for the person making the choice. (p. 9)

Rational expectation The best forecast possible, a forecast that uses all the available information. (p. 688)

Real business cycle theory A theory of the business cycle that regards random fluctuations in productivity as the main source of economic fluctuations. (p. 679)

Real exchange rate The relative price of Canadian-produced goods and services to foreign-produced goods and services. (p. 604)

Real GDP The value of final goods and services produced in a given year when valued at the prices of a reference base year. (p. 471)

Real GDP per person Real GDP divided by the population. (pp. 472, 514)

Real interest rate The nominal interest rate adjusted to remove the effects of inflation on the buying power of money. It is approximately equal to the nominal interest rate minus the inflation rate. (p. 548)

Real wage rate The money (or nominal) wage rate divided by the price level. The real wage rate is the quantity of goods and services that an hour of labour earns. (p. 521)

Recession A business cycle phase in which real GDP decreases for at least two successive quarters. (p. 473)

Recessionary gap An output gap in which potential GDP exceeds real GDP. (p. 635)

Relative price The ratio of the price of one good or service to the price of another good or service. A relative price is an opportunity cost. (p. 56)

Rent The income that land earns. (p. 4)

Rent ceiling A regulation that makes it illegal to charge a rent higher than a specified level. (p. 128)

Rent seeking The lobbying for special treatment by the government to create economic profit or to divert consumer surplus or producer surplus away from others. The pursuit of wealth by capturing economic rent. (p. 765)

Reserves A bank's reserves consist of notes and coins in its vaults plus its deposit at the Bank of Canada. (p. 567)

Rule of 70 A rule that states that the number of years it takes for the level of any variable to double is approximately 70 divided by the annual percentage growth rate of the variable. (p. 515)

Saving The amount of income that is not paid in taxes or spent on consumption goods and services. (p. 542)

Saving function The relationship between saving and disposable income, other things remaining the same. (p. 648)

Scarcity Our inability to satisfy all our wants. (p. 2)

Scatter diagram A graph that plots the value of one variable against the value of another variable for a number of different values of each variable. (p. 16)

Self-interest The choices that you think are the best ones available for you are choices made in your self-interest. (p. 5)

Settlements balances rate The interest rate that the Bank of Canada pays on bank reserves held at the Bank of Canada. (p. 732)

Short-run aggregate supply The relationship between the quantity of real GDP supplied and the price level when the money wage rate, the prices of other resources, and potential GDP remain constant. (p. 625)

Short-run macroeconomic equilibrium A situation that occurs when the quantity of real GDP demanded equals the quantity of real GDP supplied—at the point of intersection of the *AD* curve and the *SAS* curve. (p. 632)

Short-run Phillips curve A curve that shows the tradeoff between inflation and unemployment, when the expected inflation rate and the natural unemployment rate are held constant. (p. 692)

Slope The change in the value of the variable measured on the *y*-axis divided by the change in the value of the variable measured on the *x*-axis. (p. 22)

Social interest Choices that are the best ones for society as a whole. (p. 5)

Stagflation The combination of inflation and recession. (pp. 637, 686)

Stock A certificate of ownership and claim to the firm's profits. (p. 544)

Stock market A financial market in which shares of stocks of corporations are traded. (p. 544)

Structural surplus or deficit The budget balance that would occur if the economy were at full employment and real GDP were equal to potential GDP. (p. 714)

Structural unemployment The unemployment that arises when changes in technology or international competition change the skills needed to perform jobs or change the locations of jobs. (p. 495)

Subsidy A payment made by the government to a producer. (p. 140)

Substitute A good that can be used in place of another good. (p. 59)

Supply The entire relationship between the price of a good and the quantity supplied of it when all other influences on producers' planned sales remain the same. It is described by a supply schedule and illustrated by a supply curve. (p. 62)

Supply curve A curve that shows the relationship between the quantity supplied of a good and its price when all other influences on producers' planned sales remain the same. (p. 62)

Supply of loanable funds The relationship between the quantity of loanable funds supplied and the real interest rate when all other influences on lending plans remain the same. (p. 550)

Tariff A tax that is imposed by the importing country when an imported good crosses its international boundary. (p. 756)

Tax multiplier The quantitative effect of a change in taxes on real GDP. It is calculated as the change in real GDP that results from a change in taxes divided by the change in taxes. (p. 716)

Tax wedge The gap between the before-tax and after-tax wage rates. and returns to other factors of production. (p. 711)

Technological change The development of new goods and of better ways of producing goods and services. (p. 38)

Time-series graph A graph that measures time (for example, years, quarters, or months) on the x-axis and the variable or variables in which we are interested on the y-axis. (p. 480)

Tradeoff A constraint that involves giving up one thing to get something else. (p. 9)

Trend The tendency for a variable to move in one general direction. (p. 481)

Unemployment rate The percentage of the people in the labour force who are unemployed. (p. 492)

Velocity of circulation The average number of times a dollar of money is used annually to buy the goods and services that make up GDP. (p. 582)

Wages The income that labour earns. (p. 4)

Wealth The value of all the things that people own—the market value of their assets—at a point in time. (p. 542)

Working-age population The total number of people aged 16 years and over who are not in jail, hospital, or some other form of institutional care. (p. 491)

Note: Key terms and the pages on which they are defined are **bolded.** References to "*f*" denote a figure and "*t*" denote a table.

Chapter 1: University students (p. 1) Fernando Morales/
The Globe and Mail/The Canadian Press Images
Nike factory (p. 6) Adek Berry/AFP/Getty Images
Kiran Mazumdar-Shaw (p. 6) STR New/Reuters
Intel chip (p. 7) Christian Prandl/Imagebroker/Alamy
Smoke stacks (p. 7) Snap Happy/Fotolia
Protest (p. 8) Brendan McDermid/Reuters
Adam Smith (p. 8) Pictorial Press Ltd/Alamy
Children on computer (p. 12) Karelnoppe/Fotolia

Chapter 2: Factory (p. 31) Blackfox Images/Alamy
Adam Smith (p. 53) John Kay/Bettmann/Corbis
Esther Duflo (p. 54) Eric Fougere/VIP Images/Corbis

Chapter 3: Bananas (p. 55) Patti McConville/Alamy
Truffles (p. 69) Poplis, Paul/The food passionates/Corbis
Women having coffee (p. 71) Wavebreak Media Ltd./Corbis
Alfred Marshall (p. 83) Public Domain/Wikipedia
Susan Athey (p. 84) Courtesy of Susan Athey

Chapter 20: Financial analyst (p. 465) Tetra Images/Corbis
McDonald's (U.S.) (p. 474) Jeff Greenberg "0 people
images"/Alamy
McDonald's (China) (p. 474) Andrew Melbourne/Alamy
Chef (p. 475) Tetra Images/Alamy
Mother cooking (p. 475) Denise Hager/Catchlight Visual
Services/Alamy
Joseph Stiglitz (p. 476) Jerome Favre/Bloomberg/Getty Images
Copper mine (p. 476) Friedrich Stark/Alamy

Chapter 21: Job fair (p. 489) Frances Roberts/Alamy
Depression (p. 490) George Grantham Bain Collection/
Library of Congress Prints and Photographs Division
David Hume (p. 511) Library of Congress Prints and
Photographs Division
David Card (p. 512) Courtesy of David Card

Chapter 22: African market (p. 513) AfriPics.com/Alamy
Seamstress (p. 526) Heiner Heine/imageBROKER/Alamy
Steam-powered rail engine (p. 527) Greg Balfour Evans/
Alamy
Robot packing machine (p. 528) Philippe Psaila/Science
Source

Chapter 23: ABN/AMRO trading floor (p. 541) Koen van
Weel/AFP/Getty Images
Fannie Mae (p. 545) Ken Howard/Alamy
Freddie Mac (p. 545) Ken Howard/Alamy

Chapter 24: ATM line (p. 563) Andrew Rubtsov/Alamy
Irving Fisher (p. 569) Dr. Irving Fisher, Economist
(1867–1947)

Mark Carney (p. 569) Pierre Roussel/Alamy
Bank of Canada home page (p. 571) Courtesy of Bank of
Canada
New York Fed (p. 577) Daniel Acker/Bloomberg/Getty
Images

Chapter 25: Currency exchange (p. 593) Roussel Bernard/
Alamy
Joseph Schumpeter (p. 621) INTERFOTO/Personalities/
Alamy
Xavier Sala-i-Martin (p. 622) Courtesy of Xavier Sala-i-
Martin

Chapter 26: Construction workers (p. 623) Tetra Images/
Alamy
Bank of Canada (p. 630) Ruffer/Agencja Fotograficzna
Caro/Alamy
Federal Reserve (p. 630) ICP-UK/Incamerastock/Alamy
European Central Bank (p. 630) Fstockfoto/Shutterstock

Chapter 27: Sheet metal (p. 647) Marjorie Kamys Cotera/
Bob Daemmrich Photography/Alamy

Chapter 28: German unemployment agency (p. 677) SZ
Photo/Eckel, Jochen/DIZ München GmbH/Alamy
John Maynard Keynes (p. 701) ClassicStock.com/
ClassicStock.com/SuperStock
Peter Howitt (p. 702) Courtesy of Peter Howitt

Chapter 29: Joe Oliver news conference (p. 703) Sean
Kilpatrick/The Canadian Press Images
Christina Romer (p. 719) Tom Williams/Roll Call/Getty
Images
Robert Barro (p. 719) Courtesy of Robert J. Barro
Harald Uhlig (p. 719) Courtesy of Harald Uhlig

Chapter 30: Bank of Canada (p. 727) Patrick Doyle/
Bloomberg/Getty Images

Chapter 31: Cargo ship (p. 751) Gerry Rousseau/Alamy
Doha Round (p. 758) Denis Balibouse/Reuters/Corbis
Coat hangers (p. 760) Justin Sullivan/Getty Images News/
Getty Images
Indian office workers (p. 764) Terry Vine/Blend Images/
Alamy
Milton Friedman (p. 773) Marshall Heinrichs/Addison
Wesley/Pearson Education
Pierre Siklos (p. 774) Bill Todd/Pearson Education Canada

NOTES

NOTES

NOTES

NOTES

Economics in the News

Economics in the News boxes show students how to use the economic toolkit to understand the events and issues they are confronted with in the media. An extended Economics in the News at the end of each chapter helps students think like economists by connecting chapter tools and concepts to the world around them.

Economics in Action

Economics in Action boxes apply economic theory to current events to illustrate the importance of economic forces in the world around us.